6/09

Contemporary Theatre, Film and Television

ISSN 0749-064X

Contemporary Theatre, Film and Television

A Biographical Guide Featuring Performers, Directors, Writers, Producers, Designers, Managers, Choreographers, Technicians, Composers, Executives, Dancers, and Critics in the United States, Canada, Great Britain and the World

Thomas Riggs, Editor

Volume 92

GALE
CENGAGE Learning

Detroit • New York • San Francisco • New Haven, Conn • Waterville, Maine • London

Contemporary Theatre, Film & Television, Vol. 92

Editor: Thomas Riggs

CTFT Staff: Erika Fredrickson, Mariko Fujinaka, Annette Petrusso, Susan Risland, Lisa Sherwin, Arlene True, Andrea Votava, Pam Zuber

Project Editor: Michael J. Tyrkus

Editorial Support Services: Ryan Cartmill

Composition and Electronic Capture: Gary Oudersluys

Manufacturing: Drew Kalasky

For product information and technology assistance, contact us at
Gale Customer Support, 1-800-877-4253.
For permission to use material from this text or product,
submit all requests online at **www.cengage.com/permissions.**
Further permissions questions can be emailed to
permissionrequest@cengage.com

Gale
27500 Drake Rd.
Farmington Hills, MI, 48331-3535

LIBRARY OF CONGRESS CATALOG CARD NUMBER 84-649371

ISBN-13: 978-1-4144-3467-4
ISBN-10: 1-4144-3467-7

ISSN: 0749-064X

This title is also available as an e-book.
ISBN 13: 978-1-4144-5712-3
ISBN-10: 1-4144-5712-X
Contact your Gale sales representative for ordering information.

Printed in the United States of America
1 2 3 4 5 6 7 13 12 11 10 09

Contents

Preface

Provides Broad, Single-Source Coverage in the Entertainment Field

Contemporary Theatre, Film and Television (*CTFT*) is a biographical reference series designed to provide students, educators, researchers, librarians, and general readers with information on a wide range of entertainment figures. Unlike single-volume reference works that focus on a limited number of artists or on a specific segment of the entertainment field, *CTFT* is an ongoing publication that includes entries on individuals active in the theatre, film, and television industries. Before the publication of *CTFT*, information-seekers had no choice but to consult several different sources in order to locate the in-depth biographical and credit data that makes *CTFT*'s one-stop coverage the most comprehensive available about the lives and work of performing arts professionals.

Scope

CTFT covers not only performers, directors, writers, and producers, but also behind-the-scenes specialists such as designers, managers, choreographers, technicians, composers, executives, dancers, and critics from the United States, Canada, Great Britain, and the world. With 214 entries in *CTFT 92*, the series now provides biographies on approximately 25,248 people involved in all aspects of theatre, film, and television.

CTFT gives primary emphasis to people who are currently active. New entries are prepared on major stars as well as those who are just beginning to win acclaim for their work. *CTFT* also includes entries on personalities who have died but whose work commands lasting interest.

Compilation Methods

CTFT editors identify candidates for inclusion in the series by consulting biographical dictionaries, industry directories, entertainment annuals, trade and general interest periodicals, newspapers, and online databases. Additionally, the editors of *CTFT* maintain regular contact with industry advisors and professionals who routinely suggest new candidates for inclusion in the series. Entries are compiled from published biographical sources which are believed to be reliable, but have not been verified for this edition by the listee or their agents.

Revised Entries

To ensure *CTFT*'s timeliness and comprehensiveness, entries from previous volumes, as well as from Gale's *Who's Who in the Theatre*, are updated for individuals who have been active enough to require revision of their earlier biographies. Such individuals will merit revised entries as often as there is substantial new information to provide. Obituary notices for deceased entertainment personalities already listed in *CTFT* are also published.

Accessible Format Makes Data Easy to Locate

CTFT entries, modeled after those in Gale's highly regarded *Contemporary Authors* series, are written in a clear, readable style designed to help users focus quickly on specific facts. The following is a summary of the information found in *CTFT* sketches:

- *ENTRY HEADING:* the form of the name by which the listee is best known.

- *PERSONAL:* full or original name; dates and places of birth and death; family data; colleges attended, degrees earned, and professional training; political and religious affiliations when known; avocational interests.

- *ADDRESSES:* home, office, agent, publicist and/or manager addresses.

- *CAREER:* tagline indicating principal areas of entertainment work; resume of career positions and other vocational achievements; military service.

- *MEMBER:* memberships and offices held in professional, union, civic, and social organizations.

- *AWARDS, HONORS:* theatre, film, and television awards and nominations; literary and civic awards; honorary degrees.

- *CREDITS:* comprehensive title-by-title listings of theatre, film, and television appearance and work credits, including roles and production data as well as debut and genre information.

- *RECORDINGS:* album, single song, video, and taped reading releases; recording labels and dates when available.

- *WRITINGS:* title-by-title listing of plays, screenplays, scripts, and musical compositions along with production information; books, including autobiographies, and other publications.

- *ADAPTATIONS:* a list of films, plays, and other media which have been adapted from the listee's work.

- *SIDELIGHTS:* favorite roles; portions of agent-prepared biographies or personal statements from the listee when available.

- *OTHER SOURCES:* books, periodicals, and internet sites where interviews or feature stories can be found.

Access Thousands of Entries Using *CTFT*'s Cumulative Index

Each volume of *CTFT* contains a cumulative index to the entire series. As an added feature, this index also includes references to all seventeen editions of *Who's Who in the Theatre* and to the four-volume compilation *Who Was Who in the Theatre*.

Available in Electronic Format

Online. Recent volumes of *CTFT* are available online as part of the Gale Biographies (GALBIO) database accessible through LEXIS-NEXIS. For more information, contact LEXIS-NEXIS, P.O. Box 933, Dayton, OH 45401-0933; phone (937) 865-6800, toll-free: 800-543-6862.

Suggestions Are Welcome

Contemporary Theatre, Film and Television is intended to serve as a useful reference tool for a wide audience, so comments about any aspect of this work are encouraged. Suggestions of entertainment professionals to include in future volumes are also welcome. Send comments and suggestions to: The Editor, *Contemporary Theatre, Film and Television*, Gale, 27500 Drake Rd., Farmington Hills, MI 48331-3535; or feel free to call toll-free at 1-800-877-GALE.

Contemporary Theatre, Film and Television

ACERNO, John
    See VAN PATTEN, Dick

ACOVONE, Jay 1955–

PERSONAL

Born August 20, 1955, in Mahopac, NY; parents, owners of a dry–cleaning business; married Fonda St. Paul (a talent manager). *Education:* Studied at American Academy of Dramatic Arts and Lee Strasberg Theatre Institute. *Avocational Interests:* Boxing, swimming, skiing (holds instructor's license), motorcycles, auto racing.

Addresses: *Agent*—The Geddes Agency, 8430 Santa Monica Blvd., Suite 200, West Hollywood, CA 90069.

Career: Actor. Worked as a car salesperson, mechanic and filling station attendant, and surveyor.

CREDITS

Film Appearances:
Skip Lee, *Cruising* (also known as *William Friedkin's "Cruising"*), United Artists, 1980.
Plainclothes cop, *Times Square,* AFD, 1980.
Cookie Manero, *Cold Steel,* Cinetel, 1987.
Bobby Arms, *Out for Justice,* Warner Bros., 1991.
Tony Gaudio, *Doctor Mordrid,* Paramount Home Video, 1992.
Cercasi successo disperatamente, 1994.
Opposite Corners, 1995.
Chuck, *Foxfire,* Samuel Goldwyn, 1996.

Schmidt, *Time under Fire* (also known as *Beneath the Bermuda Triangle*), Royal Oaks Entertainment, 1996.
Area 51 guard, *Independence Day* (also known as *ID4*), Twentieth Century–Fox, 1996.
Frank, *Crosscut,* A–pix Entertainment, 1996.
Macelroy, *Snitch,* 1996.
Cop, *The Peacemaker,* DreamWorks, 1997.
Michael Irish, *The Get,* 1998.
Vinny Pallazzo, *Lookin' Italian* (also known as *Showdown*), 1998.
Jack, *Molly,* Metro–Goldwyn–Mayer, 1999.
Peter the pilot, *Cast Away,* Twentieth Century–Fox, 2000.
Eric, *Crocodile Dundee in Los Angeles,* Paramount, 2001.
Melvin Snow, *The Seventh Sense* (short), IFILM, 2001.
Bennie, *Collateral Damage,* Warner Bros., 2002.
Bobby Falcone, *Studio City,* 2003.
Cop on Westside Street, *Terminator 3: Rise of the Machines* (also known as *T3* and *Terminator 3—Rebellion der maschinen*), Warner Bros., 2003.
Lear jet pilot, *S.W.A.T.,* Sony, 2003.
Captain Peters, *Rancid,* Nonstop Sales, 2004.
Jesse, *Traci Townsend,* 2005.
Molina, *Sharkskin 6* (also known as *Crime Guys*), Columbia, 2005.
Jackie, *Mobsters and Mormons,* Halestorm Entertainment, 2005.
John Barrhauser, *Paved with Good Intentions,* 2006.
Donna's male neighbor, *World Trade Center,* Paramount, 2006.
Eerie man, *Shadow People,* 2007.
Wilson, *The Hills Have Eyes II* (also known as *The Hills Have Eyes 2*), Twentieth Century–Fox, 2007.
Gerhard, *InAlienable,* 2008.

Television Appearances; Series:
Brian Emerson, *Search for Tomorrow,* CBS, 1982–84.
Detective Jack Rado, *Hollywood Beat,* ABC, 1985.
Deputy District Attorney Joe Maxwell, *Beauty and the Beast,* CBS, 1987–90.

Del Brakett, *As the World Turns,* CBS, 2003.
Joe Smith, *General Hospital,* ABC, 2008.

Television Appearances; Miniseries:
Quartermaster Maselli (Barracuda), *War and Remembrance,* ABC, 1988.

Television Appearances; Movies:
Leo, *Parole,* CBS, 1982.
Captain Rader, *Women of Valor* (also known as *Women of Valour*), CBS, 1986.
Detective Harris, *Quicksand: No Escape,* USA Network, 1992.
Steve Davis, *Stepfather III* (also known as *Father's Day* and *Stepfather 3: Father's Day*), HBO, 1992.
Detective Falcone, *Conflict of Interest,* HBO, 1992.
Lieutenant Robert Carlino, *A Murderous Affair: The Carolyn Warmus Story* (also known as *Lovers of Deceit: The Carolyn Warmus Story*), ABC, 1992.
Captain Evan Graham, *Nails,* Showtime, 1992.
Richie, *Born to Run,* Fox, 1993.
David Katz, *The Magician,* 1993.
Minelli, *Marked for Murder* (also known as *Hard Time* and *The Sandman*), NBC, 1993.
Bruno Romano, *Columbo: Strange Bedfellows,* ABC, 1995.
Sergeant Wallace, *Crime of the Century,* HBO, 1996.
Murphy, *Crash Dive* (also known as *Crash Dive: The Chase Is On*), HBO, 1997.
Captain Unander, *On the Line,* ABC, 1998.
Lieutenant detective Bob Mankowsky, *Murder, She Wrote: A Story to Die For,* CBS, 2000.
The Dukes of Hazzard: Hazzard in Hollywood, CBS, 2000.
Mr. Moltianni, *The Amati Girls,* Fox, 2000.

Also appeared in *Wolf.*

Television Appearances; Pilots:
Mike Levine, *Locals,* Fox, 1994.

Television Appearances; Specials:
Beyond the Stargate: Secrets Revealed, Sci-Fi Channel, 2005.

Television Appearances; Episodic:
(Television debut) Hospital orderly, *All My Children,* ABC, late 1970s.
Eddie, "Jerry Jumps Right In," *Down and Out in Beverly Hills,* 1987.
Dr. Bruce Jacobs, "The Doctors," *Matlock,* 1987.
Mick, "Running with the Pack," *Werewolf,* 1987.
Matelli, "The Out of Towner," *Hardball,* NBC, 1989.
Detective Sergeant Vinnie Grillo, "O'Malley's Luck," *Murder, She Wrote,* CBS, 1990.

"I'll Dance at Your Wedding," *Jake and the Fatman,* CBS, 1990.
Ray, "S.O.B.," *Silk Stalkings,* USA Network, 1991.
Jake, "Carol's Carnival," *Growing Pains,* 1991.
Detective Rudy Acosta, "Bite the Big Apple," *Murder, She Wrote,* CBS, 1991.
Neil Leeuwen, "Hit the Road Jack," *Civil Wars,* ABC, 1992.
Goucho, "Forbidden Zone," *Red Shoe Diaries,* Showtime, 1992.
Nick Colette, "Family Business," *The Commish,* ABC, 1993.
Tony Fielding, "Crime of Love," *Silk Stalkings,* USA Network, 1993.
Lieutenant Nick Acosta, "Murder on the Thirtieth Floor," *Murder, She Wrote,* CBS, 1994.
Brother Mike, "Carrick O'Quinn," *Renegade,* 1994.
Mr. Ahern, "The Getaway," *Matlock,* ABC, 1995.
Detective Ray Quiller, "The Last Kiss Goodnight," *Silk Stalkings,* USA Network, 1995.
Raymond DiSalvo, "Large Mouth Bass," *NYPD Blue,* ABC, 1995.
Fireman Charlie, "The One with the Candy Hearts," *Friends,* 1995.
Raymond DiSalvo, "Cold Heaters," *NYPD Blue,* ABC, 1995.
"Down South," *High Tide,* 1995.
Gary Hendrickson, "Spare Parts," *The Sentinel,* UPN, 1996.
Dr. Tassler, "Sole Survivors," *Sliders,* Fox, 1996.
Detective Joe Curtis, "Demons," *The X Files,* Fox, 1996.
Victor Rand, "Condor," *Viper,* 1996.
Max Kinkaid, "The Warren Omission," *Dark Skies,* NBC, 1997.
Tommy Annunziato, "Looking for Mr. Goombah," *Total Security,* ABC, 1997.
Burglar, "Sex, Lies, and Activewear," *Renegade,* 1997.
Major Charles Kawalsky, "Children of the Gods," *Stargate SG-1,* Showtime and syndicated, 1997.
Major Charles Kawalsky, "The Enemy Within," *Stargate SG-1,* Showtime and syndicated, 1997.
Joey Pantangelo, "Three Ring Circus," *Silk Stalkings,* USA Network, 1998.
Captain Charles Kawalsky, "The Gamekeeper," *Stargate SG-1,* Showtime and syndicated, 1998.
Clifton Moloney, "Trapped in Paradise," *Diagnosis Murder,* CBS, 1999.
Vincent, "Blind Faith," *Providence,* NBC, 1999.
Vincent, "Taste of Providence," *Providence,* NBC, 1999.
Vincent, "You Bet Your Life," *Providence,* NBC, 1999.
Ben Siegel III, "Way Out West," *Sliders,* Sci-Fi Channel, 1999.
Major Charles Kawalsky, "Point of View," *Stargate SG-1,* Showtime and syndicated, 1999.
Frankie Beans, "Honey, It Takes Two to Mambo," *Honey, I Shrunk the Kids,* 1999.
Johnny Terelli, "True Stories," *Pensacola: Wings of Gold,* syndicated, 1999.
Stu, "Eye of the Storm," *Sliders,* Sci-Fi Channel, 2000.
Detective Stan Brookins, "The Inner Sense: Parts 1 & 2," *The Pretender,* NBC, 2000.

David Haskell/Duffy Haskell, "Per Manum," *The X Files,* Fox, 2001.

O'Ryan, "Money for Nothing: Parts 1 & 2," *The Invisible Man,* Sci–Fi Channel, 2001.

Duffy Haskell, "Essence," *The X Files,* Fox, 2001.

Raymond DiSalvo, "Waking Up Is Hard to Do," *NYPD Blue,* ABC, 2001.

Agent Billingsley, "A Place Called Defiance," *18 Wheels of Justice,* 2001.

Colonel Harry R. Presser, "Dog Robber: Part 2," *JAG* (also known as *JAG: Judge Advocate General*), CBS, 2001.

Keats, "Bite Me," *Charmed,* The WB, 2002.

Aldini, "Left–Overs," *Providence,* NBC, 2002.

Jimmy Gentile, "Quarantine," *Strong Medicine,* Lifetime, 2004.

General Montrose, "What If," *JAG* (also known as *JAG: Judge Advocate General*), CBS, 2004.

Las Vegas, NBC, 2004.

Paul Gionetti, "Tri–Borough," *CSI: NY* (also known as *CSI: New York*), CBS, 2005.

Ray Galardi, "Mr. Monk Gets Stuck in Traffic," *Monk,* USA Network, 2005.

Major Charles Kawalsky, "Moebius: Part 2," *Stargate SG-1* (also known as *La porte des etoiles*), 2005.

Tom Collison in 2005, "Kensington," *Cold Case,* CBS, 2005.

Ray Abazon, "Magic Carpet Fred," *Las Vegas,* NBC, 2005.

Detective Morrison, "Won't Get Fooled Again," *Criminal Minds,* CBS, 2005.

Tom Wagman, "Day 5: 5:00 p.m.–6:00 p.m.," *24,* Fox, 2006.

Stage Appearances:

Larry Mastice, *Marlon Brando Sat Right Here,* Boltax Theatre, New York City, 1980.

Fifi La Belle, *Cap and Bells,* Judith Anderson Theatre, New York City, 1984.

Also appeared as Johnny Del Gatto, *Asphalt;* Artie, *Crooks;* J. J., *On Tina Tuna Walk.*

OTHER SOURCES

Periodicals:
Starlog, March, 1990.

ADAMS, Julie 1926–
(Betty Adams, Julia Adams)

PERSONAL

Original name, Betty May Adams; born October 17, 1926, in Waterloo, IA; daughter of Ralph Eugene (a cotton buyer) and Esther Gertrude Adams; married Ray Danton (an actor, director, and writer), 1954 (divorced, 1981); children: Mitchell, Steven (an assistant director). *Education:* Studied drama at Little Rock Junior College, 1945–46.

Addresses: *Contact*—Twentieth Century, 4605 Lankershim Blvd., Suite 305, North Hollywood, CA 91602.

Career: Actress. Appeared in a television commercial for Tylenol PM pain reliever, 1996. Also worked as a secretary.

Awards, Honors: *Soap Opera Digest* Award nomination, outstanding supporting actress in a daytime serial, 1986, for *Capitol.*

CREDITS

Film Appearances:

(As Betty Adams) Polly Medford, *The Dalton Gang* (also known as *Outlaw Gang*), Lippert Pictures/Screen Guild Productions, 1949.

(As Betty Adams) Starlet, *Red, Hot, and Blue,* Paramount, 1949.

(As Betty Adams) Ann Green, *Hostile Country* (also known as *Outlaw Fury*), Lippert Pictures, 1950.

(As Betty Adams) Ann Green, *Colorado Ranger* (also known as *Guns of Justice*), Lippert Pictures, 1950.

(As Betty Adams) Ann Greene, *West of the Brazos* (also known as *Rangeland Empire*), Lippert Pictures, 1950.

(As Betty Adams) Ann Hayden, *Crooked River* (also known as *Guns of Justice*), Lippert Pictures, 1950.

(As Betty Adams) Ann, *Fast on the Draw* (also known as *Sudden Death*), Lippert Pictures, 1950.

(As Betty Adams) Ann, *Marshal of Heldorado* (also known as *Blazing Guns*), Lippert Pictures, 1950.

(As Julia Adams) Sally Rousseau, *Hollywood Story,* Universal International Pictures, 1951.

Myra Wade, *The Treasure of Lost Canyon,* MCA/Universal, 1951.

(As Julia Adams) Sue Kipps, *Finders Keepers,* Universal International Pictures, 1951.

(As Julia Adams) Chris Paterson, *Bright Victory* (also known as *Lights Out*), Universal International Pictures, 1951.

Laura Baile, *Bend of the River* (also known as *Where the River Bends*), Universal International Pictures, 1952.

Lorna Hardin, *Horizons West,* Universal, 1952.

(As Julia Adams) Rosie, *The Lawless Breed,* Universal, 1952.

Ann Conant, *The Mississippi Gambler,* Universal International Pictures, 1953.

(As Julia Adams) Beth Anders, *The Man from the Alamo,* MCA/Universal, 1953.

Raquel Noriega, *Wings of the Hawk,* Universal International Pictures, 1953.

(As Julia Adams) Valerie Kendrick, *The Stand at Apache River,* Universal, 1953.

(As Julia Adams) Kay Lawrence, *The Creature from the Black Lagoon,* Universal, 1954.

(As Julia Adams) Captain Jane Parker, *Francis Joins the Wacs,* Universal, 1954.

Sheryl Gregory, *The Looters,* Universal International Pictures, 1955.

Judith Watrous, *One Desire,* Universal International Pictures, 1955.

Dr. Kay Lambert, *The Private War of Major Benson,* Universal International Pictures, 1955.

Ellen Gallagher, *Six Bridges to Cross,* Universal International Pictures, 1955.

Nadine MacDougall, *Away All Boats,* Universal International Pictures, 1956.

Kathy Conway, *Four Girls in Town* (also known as *4 Girls in Town*), Universal International Pictures, 1956.

Dee Pauley, *Slaughter on Tenth Avenue,* Universal, 1957.

Clover Doyle, *Slim Carter,* Universal, 1957.

Ruth Nelson Campbell, *Tarawa Beachhead,* Columbia, 1958.

Pauline Howard, *The Gunfight at Dodge City* (also known as *The Bat Masterson Story*), United Artists, 1959.

Helen, *Raymie,* Allied Artists Pictures, 1960.

Dr. Monica Powers, *The Underwater City,* Columbia, 1962.

Gold, Glory, and Custer, Warner Bros., 1962.

Vera Radford, *Tickle Me,* Allied Artists Pictures, 1965.

Mrs. Anderson, *The Last Movie* (also known as *Chinchero*), Universal, 1971.

Elaine Forrester, *McQ,* Warner Bros., 1974.

Hannah McCulloch, *The Wild McCullochs* (also known as *McCullochs*), American International Pictures, 1975.

Dr. Laura Scott, *Psychic Killer* (also known as *The Kirlian Effect, Killer Force,* and *The Kirlian Force*), Avco–Embassy, 1975.

Mother, *The Killer Inside Me,* Warner Bros., 1976.

Goodbye, Franklin High, Cal–Am, 1978.

(In archive footage) *Fade to Black,* American Cinema, 1980.

Nurse Hannelord, *The Fifth Floor,* Film Ventures International, 1980.

Emma Hussey, *Champions,* 1983, Embassy Pictures, 1984.

Mrs. Miller, *Black Roses,* Imperial Video, 1988.

Martha, *Catchfire* (also known as *Backtrack* and *Do It the Hard Way*), Vestron Pictures, 1989.

Herself, *King B: A Life in Movies,* 1993.

Herself, *Back to the Black Lagoon: A Creature Chronicle* (documentary), Universal Studios Home Video, 2000.

Herself, *Creature Feature: 50 Years of the Gill–Man* (documentary), 2004.

Allison's grandmother, *World Trade Center,* Paramount, 2006.

Television Appearances; Series:

Amanda Eaton, *Yancy Derringer,* CBS, 1958–59.

Denise Wilton, *General Hospital,* ABC, 1968.

Martha Howard, *The Jimmy Stewart Show,* NBC, 1971–72.

Ann Rorchek, *Code Red,* ABC, 1981–82.

Paula Denning, *Capitol,* CBS, 1983–87.

Eve Simpson, *Murder, She Wrote,* CBS, 1987–93.

Television Appearances; Miniseries:

Queen, *The Greatest Heroes of the Bible,* 1978.

Television Appearances; Movies:

Joan Simon, *Valley of Mystery* (also known as *Stranded*), 1966.

Dora Paxton, *The Trackers* (also known as *No Trumpets, No Drums*), ABC, 1971.

Dorothy, *Go Ask Alice,* ABC, 1973.

The mother, *Six Characters in Search of an Author* (also known as *Hollywood Television Theatre: Six Characters in Search of an Author*), 1976.

Margaret, *The Conviction of Kitty Dodds* (also known as *Conviction: The Kitty Dodds Story*), CBS, 1993.

Television Appearances; Specials:

Scream Queens: The E! True Hollywood Story, E! Entertainment Television, 2004.

Television Appearances; Pilots:

Ann Rorchek, *Code Red,* ABC, 1981.

Television Appearances; Episodic:

(As Betty Adams) "The Tenor," *Your Show Time,* NBC, 1949.

Dr. Kay Lambert, *The Colgate Comedy Hour* (also known as *Colgate Summer Comedy Hour, Colgate Variety Hour,* and *Michael Todd Revue*), 1955.

"Appointment for Love," *Lux Video Theatre* (also known as *Summer Video Theatre*), 1955.

Anne, "Circle of Guilt," *Studio One* (also known as *Studio One Summer Theatre, Studio One in Hollywood, Summer Theatre, Westinghouse Studio One,* and *Westinghouse Summer Theatre*), CBS, 1956.

"Just Across the Street," *Lux Video Theatre* (also known as *Summer Video Theatre*), 1957.

"Design for November," *Lux Video Theatre* (also known as *Summer Video Theatre*), 1957.

Coleen, "Two Tests for Tuesday," *Climax!* (also known as *Climax Mystery Theatre*), 1957.

Julie Brand, "Man of Fear," *Zane Grey Theater* (also known as *Dick Powell's "Zane Grey Theater"* and *The Westerners*), CBS, 1958.

Janice Ohringer, "The Dungeon," *Playhouse 90,* CBS, 1958.

Carol Longsworth, "Little White Frock," *Alfred Hitchcock Presents,* CBS, 1958.

Amanda Eaton, "Return to New Orleans," *Yancy Derringer,* CBS, 1958.

Amanda Eaton, "Gallatin Street," *Yancy Derringer,* CBS, 1958.

Amanda Eaton, "Loot from Richmond," *Yancy Derringer,* CBS, 1958.

Nora Jepson, "The Tall Shadow," *Zane Grey Theater* (also known as *Dick Powell's "Zane Grey Theater"* and *The Westerners*), CBS, 1958.

Marion Ewell, "Points Beyond," *Goodyear Theatre* (also known as *Award Theatre* and *Golden Years of Television*), 1958.

(As Julia Adams) Paula McGill, "The Hidden One," *Letter to Loretta* (also known as *The Loretta Young Show* and *The Loretta Young Theatre*), 1958.

Milly, "Strange Money," *Letter to Loretta* (also known as *The Loretta Young Show* and *The Loretta Young Theatre*), 1958.

Belle Morgan, "The Brasada Spur," *Maverick,* ABC, 1959.

Helen Archer, "Epilogue," *Alcoa Presents* (also known as *Alcoa Presents: One Step Beyond* and *One Step Beyond*), ABC, 1959.

Amanda Crown, "Project U.F.O.," *Steve Canyon,* 1959.

Julie Brand, "Man of Fear," *Frontier Justice,* 1959.

Linda Webb, "Experiments in Terror," *The Man and the Challenge,* 1959.

Margo Wendice, "The Fifth Stair," *77 Sunset Strip,* ABC, 1959.

Marie La Shelle, "The Canine Caper," *77 Sunset Strip,* ABC, 1959.

Peg Valence, "Dead Weight," *Alfred Hitchcock Presents,* CBS, 1959.

Clara, "Doc Booker," *The Alaskans,* ABC, 1959.

Beatrice Drake, "This Is It, Michael Shayne," *Michael Shayne,* NBC, 1960.

Irene Travers, "Gold, Glory, and Custer—Prelude," *Cheyenne,* ABC, 1960.

Irene Travers, "Gold, Glory, and Custer—Requiem," *Cheyenne,* ABC, 1960.

Wilma White, "The White Widow," *Maverick,* ABC, 1960.

Miriam Galbraith, "Safari," *77 Sunset Strip,* ABC, 1960.

Sarah Crane, "Murder, Anyone?," *Hawaiian Eye,* ABC, 1960.

Nora Sanford, "Nora," *The Rifleman,* ABC, 1960.

Eve Browning, "The Affair with Browning's Woman," *Wrangler,* NBC, 1960.

(As Julia Adams) Mary Hardin, "The Mary Hardin Story," *Tate,* NBC, 1960.

Janet Evans, "Face in the Window," *Checkmate,* CBS, 1960.

Betty Fordham, "Minister Accused," *Alcoa Theatre,* 1960.

"Crash in the Desert," *Markham,* 1960.

Helen Layton, "The Courtship," *Bonanza* (also known as *Ponderosa*), NBC, 1961.

Phyllis Kendall, "Summer Shade," *Alfred Hitchcock Presents,* NBC, 1961.

Merilee Williams, "Facts on the Fire," *Surfside 6,* ABC, 1961.

Julie Owens, "Laugh for the Lady," *Surfside 6,* ABC, 1961.

Gloria Matthews, "Robinson Koyoto," *Hawaiian Eye,* ABC, 1961.

Norma Kellogg, "Open and Close in One," *77 Sunset Strip,* ABC, 1961.

Jill Wilbur, "Return to New March," *Outlaws,* NBC, 1961.

Mary Simpson, "The County Nurse," *The Andy Griffith Show* (also known as *Andy of Mayberry*), CBS, 1962.

Ginny Nelson, "The Horn of Plenty," *Dr. Kildare,* NBC, 1962.

Robin, "330 Independence SW," *The Dick Powell Show* (also known as *The Dick Powell Theatre*), NBC, 1962.

Jean Damion, "The Someday Man," *Checkmate,* 1962.

Captain Meg Thorpe, "A Taste of Peace," *The Gallant Man,* 1963.

Eleanor, "Inquest into a Bleeding Heart," *Arrest and Trial,* 1963.

Valerie Comstock, "The Case of the Lover's Leap," *Perry Mason,* CBS, 1963.

Janice Barton, "The Case of the Deadly Verdict," *Perry Mason,* CBS, 1963.

Anne Kenzie, "Alimony League," *77 Sunset Strip,* ABC, 1964.

Janice Blake, "The Case of the Missing Button," *Perry Mason,* CBS, 1964.

Ellen Yarnell, "The Robrioz Ring," *Kraft Suspense Theatre* (also known as *Crisis* and *Suspense Theatre*), NBC, 1964.

Joanne Clay, "Kill No More," *Kraft Suspense Theatre* (also known as *Crisis* and *Suspense Theatre*), NBC, 1965.

Patricia L. Kean, "The Case of the Fatal Fortune," *Perry Mason,* CBS, 1965.

Lieutenant Betty Russo, "Big Brother," *Twelve O'Clock High,* ABC, 1965.

Carla Cabrial, "Deadlier than the Male," *Burke's Law* (also known as *Amos Burke, Secret Agent*), ABC, 1965.

Leona Mills, "Bitter Harvest," *The Long, Hot Summer,* 1965.

Merian Clay, "No Drums, No Trumpets," *The Virginian* (also known as *The Men from Shiloh*), NBC, 1966.

Edna Wesley, "Target," *The Big Valley,* ABC, 1966.

Liza Carter, "Then the Drink Takes the Man," *Mannix,* CBS, 1967.

"The High and Deadly Affair," *The Girl from U.N.C.L.E.,* 1967.

Janet Masters, "The Emperor of Rice," *The Big Valley,* ABC, 1968.

Norma Howard, "I, the People," *Ironside* (also known as *The Raymond Burr Show*), NBC, 1968.

Laura Carlvic, "One Long–Stemmed American Beauty," *The Outsider,* 1968.

Samantha Semple, "You Can't Tell the Players Without a Programmer," *The Mod Squad,* ABC, 1969.

Claire, "Don't Ignore the Miracles," *Marcus Welby, M.D.* (also known as *Robert Young, Family Doctor*), ABC, 1969.

"Married for a Day," *The Doris Day Show,* CBS, 1969.

Denise Kriton, "Blood Tie," *The F.B.I.,* ABC, 1969.

"Voices," *My Friend Tony,* 1969.

Lynn Craig, "Killer on the Loose," *The Bold Ones: The New Doctors* (also known as *The New Doctors*), 1970.

Lynn Craig, "An Absence of Loneliness," *The Bold Ones: The New Doctors* (also known as *The New Doctors*), 1971.

Patricia Fairley, "Epitaph for a Swinger," *Dan August,* ABC, 1971.

"And the Walls Came Tumbling Down," *The Young Lawyers,* ABC, 1971.

The Mod Squad, ABC, 1972.

Gay Melcor, "The Miracle at Camafeo," *Night Gallery* (also known as *Rod Serling's "Night Gallery"*), NBC, 1972.

Louise Rusk, "The Press Secretary," *The Doris Day Show,* CBS, 1972.

Mrs. Lucas, "Child of Fear," *Cannon,* CBS, 1972.

Edie Reynolds, "Little Girl Lost," *Mannix,* CBS, 1973.

"Scion of Death," *The Mod Squad,* ABC, 1973.

Jeanette Lewis, "The Clayton Lewis Document," *Search,* 1973.

Mrs. Walker, "A Matter of Love," *Lucas Tanner,* NBC, 1974.

Mrs. Avery Walker, "Mr. R.I.N.G.," *Kolchak: The Night Stalker* (also known as *The Night Stalker*), ABC, 1975.

Millicent Bladell, "The Plastic Connection," *Caribe,* ABC, 1975.

Judith, "Labyrinth," *The Streets of San Francisco,* ABC, 1975.

Lee Morgan, "An End and a Beginning," *Marcus Welby, M.D.* (also known as *Robert Young, Family Doctor*), ABC, 1975.

Jennifer Packard, "The Adventure of Veronica's Veils," *Ellery Queen* (also known as *The Adventures of Ellery Queen*), NBC, 1975.

Sylvia Killian, "The Wedding March," *Cannon,* CBS, 1975.

"The Pawn," *Mobile One,* 1975.

Ellie Wilke, "The Stranger," *Medical Center,* CBS, 1976.

Eleanor Simpson, "Murder with Pretty People," *Police Woman,* NBC, 1977.

Dr. Winninger, "Dark Sunrise," *McMillan* (also known as *McMillan & Wife*), NBC, 1977.

"Man in the Middle," *This Is the Life* (also known as *The Fisher Family*), 1977.

Mrs. Daniels, "Main Man," *Quincy* (also known as *Quincy M.E.*), NBC, 1977.

Mother, "Melinda and the Pinball Wizard," *The Runaways* (also known as *Operation Runaway*), NBC, 1978.

Eleanor Simpson, "Murder with Pretty People," *Police Woman,* 1978.

Ellen, "Life and Death," *The Incredible Hulk,* CBS, 1978.

(As Julia Adams) Queen, "Moses: Parts 1 & 2," *Greatest Heroes of the Bible,* 1978.

Laurie Malcolm, "Hot Line," *Trapper John, M.D.,* CBS, 1980.

Sharon Ross, "Honor Thy Elders," *Quincy* (also known as *Quincy M.E.*), NBC, 1980.

Margaret Sorenson, "Murder by Mirrors," *Vega$,* ABC, 1981.

Sylvia Walker, "A Fine Romance," *Too Close for Comfort* (also known as *The Ted Knight Show*), ABC, 1981.

Helen Granger, "Better Than Equal," *Cagney & Lacey,* CBS, 1982.

Dr. Chris Winston, "Science for Sale," *Quincy* (also known as *Quincy M.E.*), NBC, 1982.

Sylvia Walker, "Divorce Chicago Style," *Too Close for Comfort* (also known as *The Ted Knight Show*), syndicated, 1984.

Grandma Beevis, "So Long, Farewell, Auf Wiedersehen, Goodbye," *Beverly Hills, 90210,* Fox, 1993.

Grandma Beevis, "Twenty Years Ago Today," *Beverly Hills, 90210,* Fox, 1993.

Edie Fallon, "Hard–Boiled Murder," *Diagnosis Murder,* CBS, 1997.

Mrs. Damarr, "A Fist Full of Secrets," *Melrose Place,* Fox, 1999.

Old Maggie Beckett, "Roads Taken," *Sliders,* Sci–Fi Channel, 1999.

Bonnie, "Second Chance," *Family Law,* CBS, 2000.

Close to Home, CBS, 2005.

Amelia, "A Tale of Two Cities," *Lost,* ABC, 2006.

Dottie Mills, "Static," *Cold Case,* CBS, 2006.

Betty Willens, "Boo," *CSI: NY* (also known as *CSI: New York*), CBS, 2007.

(Uncredited) Amelia, "The Envelope," *Lost: Missing Pieces,* ABC, 2008.

Also appeared as Anna, "Girl's Best Friend," *King of Diamonds.*

Stage Plays:
(Stage debut) *Dear Sir,* Redding, CA, 1960.

Also appeared in *Father's Day,* Chicago, IL.

OTHER SOURCES

Periodicals:
Starlog, June, 1991.

Electronic:

Julie Adams Website, http://www.julieadams.biz, January 11, 2009.

ALEXANDER, Flex
(Flex, Mark "Flex" Knox)

PERSONAL

Original name, Mark Alexander Knox; born in the Bronx, NY; son of Alethia Knox; married Shanice Wilson (a singer), February 14, 2000; children: Imani Shekinah, Elijah Alexander.

Addresses: *Agent*—Agency for the Performing Arts, 405 South Beverly Dr., Beverly Hills, CA 90212. *Manager*—Principato/Young Management, 9465 Wilshire Blvd., Suite 880, Beverly Hills, CA 90212.

Career: Actor. Performed as standup comedian at clubs, including Uptown Comedy Club, Stand Up New York, the Improv, Laugh Factory, Showtime at the Apollo, and on college campuses. Worked as dancer and choreographer with the rap music group Salt 'n Pepa, and for other recording artists, including Mary J. Blige, Heavy D. and the Boys, Queen Latifah, and Toni Tony Tone.

Member: Phi Beta Sigma.

Awards, Honors: Image Award nominations, outstanding actor in a comedy series, National Association for the Advancement of Colored People (NAACP), 2003, 2004, 2005, BET Comedy Award nominations, outstanding lead actor in a comedy series, Black Entertainment Television, 2004, 2005, all for *One on One;* Image Award nomination, outstanding actor in a television movie, miniseries or dramatic special, 2005, for *Man in the Mirror: The Michael Jackson Story.*

CREDITS

Film Appearances:

(As Mark "Flex" Knox) Contest announcer, *Juice* (also known as *Angel Town 2*), Paramount, 1992.

(As Flex) Hood, *Money Train,* Columbia, 1995.

(As Flex) A Roc, *City of Industry,* Orion, 1997.

(As Flex) *The Sixth Man* (also known as *The 6th Man*), Buena Vista, 1997.

(As Flex) Trigger, *Modern Vampires* (also known as *Revenant* and *Vamps*), Sterling Home Entertainment, 1998.

(As Flex) *Backroom Bodega Boyz,* 1998.

Kadeem, *She's All That,* Miramax, 1999.

Anthony, *Out Cold,* Buena Vista, 2001.

Himself, *Sweet Oranges,* Tri Destined Studios, 2003.

Damien, *Gas,* Twentieth Century–Fox Home Entertainment, 2004.

Marty, *Her Minor Thing,* First Look International, 2005.

(As Flex) Small change Willie, *Shira: The Vampire Samurai,* Hollywood Wizard, 2005.

Three G's, *Snakes on a Plane* (also known as *SoaP*), New Line Cinema, 2006.

Himself, *Snakes on a Set: Behind the Scenes* (documentary short), New Line Cinema, 2006.

Himself, *The Snake Pit: On the Set of "Snakes on a Plane"* (documentary short), New Line Cinema Home Video, 2006.

Himself, *Pure Venom: The Making of "Snakes on a Plane"* (documentary short), New Line Home Video, 2006.

Himself, *Snakes on a Blog* (documentary short), New Line Home Video, 2006.

Himself, *Meet the Reptiles* (documentary short), New Line Home Video, 2006.

Arnold, *Love & Other 4 Letter Words,* Image Entertainment, 2007.

Ossie Paris, *Poor Boy's Game,* THINKFilm, 2007.

Sarge, *The Hills Have Eyes II* (also known as *The Hills Have Eyes 2,* Twentieth Century–Fox, 2007.

Chet, *The List,* Shoreline Entertainment, 2007.

Also appeared in *Ed TV.*

Film Work:

(As Flex) Assistant choreographer, *New Jack City,* Warner Bros., 1991.

Television Appearances; Series:

(As Flex) Various, *Uptown Comedy Club,* 1992.

(As Flex) Reggie Coltrane, *Where I Live,* ABC, 1993.

(As Flex) Tyberius "Ty" Walker, *Homeboys in Outer Space,* UPN, 1996–97.

(As Flex) Neville Watson, *Total Security,* ABC, 1997.

Mark "Flex" Washington, *One on One,* UPN, 2001–2006.

Television Appearances; Movies:

(As Flex) Kelvin, *Ice* (also known as *Eis—Wenn die welt erfriert*), ABC, 1998.

The Apartment Complex, Showtime, 1999.

Pete, *Santa and Pete,* CBS, 1999.

The Force, 1999.

Title role, *Man in the Mirror: The Michael Jackson Story,* VH1, 2004.

Chet, *The List,* ABC Family, 2007.

Deef, *Nice Girls Don't Get the Corner Office,* 2007.

Television Appearances; Pilots:

Nice Girls Don't Get the Corner Office, ABC, 2007.

Television Appearances; Specials:
It's Hot in Here: UPN Fall Preview, UPN, 1996.
Presenter, *The 7th Annual Soul Train Lady of Soul Awards,* syndicated, 2001.
"Source" Hip–Hop Awards Pre–Show, UPN, 2001.
The 4th Annual Soul Train Christmas Starfest, syndicated, 2001.
Presenter, *The 9th Annual Soul Train Lady of Soul Awards,* The WB, 2003.
I Love the '70s, VH1, 2003.
VH1 Big in '04, Vh1, 2004.
The 2nd Annual BET Comedy Awards, Black Entertainment Television, 2005.
Confessional number eight, *Book of Love: The Definitive Reason Why Men Are Dogs,* Black Entertainment Television, 2005.
Made You Look: Top 25 Moments of BET History, Black Entertainment Television, 2005.
An Evening of Stars: Tribute to Patti LaBelle, 2009.

Television Appearances; Episodic:
(As Flex) Himself, *It's Showtime at the Apollo* (also known as *Showtime at the Apollo*), syndicated, 1992.
Cold Dog, "The Concert," *Sister, Sister,* ABC, 1994.
(As Flex) Mecca, "The Friendly Neighborhood Dealer," *New York Undercover* (also known as *Uptown Undercover*), 1994.
(As Flex) Partygoer, "The Medium Is the Message," *The Cosby Mysteries,* NBC, 1995.
(As Flex) Himself, *Def Comedy Jam,* HBO, 1995.
Dread, "Cold Busted," *Moesha,* UPN, 1997.
(As Flex) "McMurder One," *Brooklyn South,* CBS, 1997.
Andy, "J. C. Bowl," *The Parkers,* UPN, 2000.
Darnell Wilkes, "The Remains of the Date," *Girlfriends,* UPN, 2000.
Darnell Wilkes, "Everything Fishy Ain't Fish," *Girlfriends,* UPN, 2000.
Darnell Wilkes, "Never a Bridesmaid," *Girlfriends,* UPN, 2000.
Darnell Wilkes, "Bad Timing," *Girlfriends,* UPN, 2001.
The Sharon Osbourne Show (also known as *Sharon*), syndicated, 2003.
Pyramid (also known as *The $100,000 Pyramid*), syndicated, 2003.
The Wayne Brady Show, syndicated, 2004.
Dennis Miller, CNBC, 2005.
The Tom Joyner Show, 2005.
Flex Washington, "Keeping It Real," *Cuts,* UPN, 2005.
ESPN Hollywood, ESPN, 2006.
Martin Wilson, "Deep Freeze," *CSI: Miami,* CBS, 2007.
American Idol: The Search for a Superstar (also known as *American Idol*), Fox, 2008.

Also appeared in episodes of *Def Comedy Jam* and *New York Undercover,* Fox.

Television Work; Series:
Producer, *One on One,* UPN, 2001–2002.
Co–executive producer, *One on One,* UPN, 2002–2006.
Consultant, *Cuts,* UPN, 2004–2006.

RECORDINGS

Music Videos:
Queen Latifah's "Fly Girl," 1991.

Also appeared in Shanice's "Every Woman Dreams."

WRITINGS

Television Episodes:
(As Flex) *Def Comedy Jam,* 1995.

Television Episode Stories:
One on One, UPN, 2002.

OTHER SOURCES

Periodicals:
St. Petersburg Times, July 22, 2001.

ALEXANDER, Sasha 1973–

PERSONAL

Original name, Suzana S. Drobnjakovic; born May 17, 1973, in Los Angeles, CA; married Luka Pecel (a director and writer), September 18, 1999 (marriage annulled); married Edoardo Ponti (a director and writer), August 11, 2007; children: (second marriage) Lucia Sofia. *Education:* University of Southern California, B.F.A.; trained for the stage in London and with the Royal Shakespeare Company. *Avocational Interests:* Dancing and travel.

Addresses: *Agent*—William Morris Agency, 1 William Morris Pl., Beverly Hills, CA 90212. *Manager*—Steve Dontanville, D/F Management, 8609 East Washington Blvd., Unit 8607, Culver City, CA 90232.

Career: Actress and producer.

Awards, Honors: Festival Award, best actress, San Diego Film Festival, 2008, for *The Last Lullaby.*

CREDITS

Television Appearances; Series:
Jesse Presser, *Wasteland*, ABC, 1999, then Showtime Next, 2001.
Gretchen Witter, *Dawson's Creek*, The WB, 2000–2001.
Caitlin "Kate" Todd, *Navy NCIS: Naval Criminal Investigative Service* (also known as *NCIS* and *NCIS: Naval Criminal Investigative Service*), CBS, 2003–2005.

Television Appearances; Pilots:
Jesse Presser, *Wasteland*, ABC, 1999.
Chloe Jones, *Ball & Chain*, Fox, 2001.
Expert Witness, CBS, 2003.
Emily Atwood, *The Karenskys*, CBS, 2009.

Television Appearances; Movies:
Jazzy, *Supply & Demand* (also known as *Lynda La Plante's "Supply & Demand, Raw Recruit"*), 1997.

Television Appearances; Specials:
Herself, *Who's Your Momma?*, 2004.
Presenter, *The 39th Annual Academy of Country Music Awards*, CBS, 2004.
Presenter, *The 31st Annual People's Choice Awards*, CBS, 2005.

Television Appearances; Episodic:
District Attorney Robin Childs, "Alter Boys," *CSI: Crime Scene Investigation* (also known as *C.S.I.*, *CSI: Las Vegas*, and *Les experts*), CBS, 2001.
The Test, FX Network, 2001.
The interviewer, "The One with Joey's Interview," *Friends*, NBC, 2002.
Laura Carlson, "Surprise!," *Greg the Bunny*, Fox, 2002.
Dr. Jackie Collette, "This Baby's Gonna Fly," *Presidio Med*, CBS, 2002.
Dr. Jackie Collette, "Second Chance," *Presidio Med*, CBS, 2002.
The Wayne Brady Show, syndicated, 2004.
On-Air with Ryan Seacrest, syndicated, 2004.
Allyson Merrill, "War Crimes," *E-Ring*, NBC, 2006.
Juliana, "Outsiders," *The Nine*, ABC, 2006.
Voice of Lori, *I Hate My 30s*, VH1, 2007.

Also appeared in an episode of *The Tracey Ullman Show*.

Film Appearances:
Karen Chambers, *Visceral Matter* (short film), 1997.
Battle of the Sexes (short film), 1997.
Miss America, *Twin Falls Idaho*, Columbia TriStar Home Video, 1999.
Jackie Samantha Gold, *All Over the Guy*, Lions Gate Films, 2001.
Susie, *Lucky 13*, Metro–Goldwyn–Mayer Home Entertainment, 2005.
Melissa, *Mission: Impossible III* (also known as *M:i:III*), Paramount, 2006.
Sarah, *The Last Lullaby*, Chaillot Films/Timbergrove Entertainment, 2008.
Lucy, *Yes Man*, Warner Bros., 2008.
Carolanne, *Play Dead*, Compound B, 2008.
Margaret, *Tenure*, WS Films, 2009.
He's Just Not That Into You, New Line Cinema, 2009.

Film Work:
Coproducer, *Lucky 13*, Metro–Goldwyn–Mayer Home Entertainment, 2005.

Stage Appearances:
Appeared as Katherine in a production of *The Taming of the Shrew*.

WRITINGS

Film:
Coauthor, *Lucky 13*, Metro–Goldwyn–Mayer Home Entertainment, 2005.

AMELL, Stephen 1981–

PERSONAL

Born May 9, 1981, in Toronto, Ontario, Canada.

Addresses: *Manager*—EDB Management, 11301 West Olympic Blvd., Suite 449, Los Angeles, CA 90064.

Career: Actor.

Awards, Honors: Gemini Award nomination (with others), best ensemble performance in a comedy program or series, Academy of Canadian Cinema and Television, 2007, for *Rent-a-Goalie*; Gemini Award, best performance by an actor in a guest role dramatic, 2007, for *ReGenesis*.

CREDITS

Film Appearances:
Detective, *The Tracey Fragments*, THINKFilm, 2007.

Teddy Gordon, *Closing the Ring* (also known as *Richard Attenborough's "Closing the Ring"*), Weinstein Company, 2007.

Guy, *Screams: The Hunting,* Sony Pictures Home Entertainment, 2009.

Television Appearances; Series:

Jason, *Beautiful People,* ABC Family, 2005.

Billy, *Rent–a–Goalie,* 2006–2008.

Nick Harwell, *Heartland,* TNT, 2007–2008.

Television Appearances; Movies:

Buddy Harrelson, *The House Next Door,* Lifetime, 2006.

Television Appearances; Episodic:

Spinning instructor, *Queer as Folk* (also known as *Q.A.F.* and *Queer as Folk USA*), Showtime, 2004.

Doorman, "Ghost in the Machine: Part 2," *Degrassi: The Next Generation* (also known as *Degrassi, nouvelle generation*), CTV and Noggin, 2004.

Ian Harrington, "Paper Anniversary," *1–800–MISSING* (also known as *Missing* and *Porte disparu*), Lifetime, 2005.

Bellboy, "Rivered," *Tilt,* ESPN, 2005.

Adam, "In the Beginning," *Dante's Cove,* Here!, 2005.

Adam, "Then There Was Darkness," *Dante's Cove,* Here!, 2005.

Craig Riddlemeyer, "Let It Burn," *ReGenesis,* TMN, 2006.

Craig Riddlemeyer, "Sleepers," *ReGenesis,* TMN, 2007.

Matthew, "Mouth Open Story Jump Out," *'da Kink in My Hair,* Global, 2007.

Matthew, "Di Heart of Di Matter," *'da Kink in My Hair,* Global, 2008.

AMIEL, Jon 1948–

PERSONAL

Born May 20, 1948, in London, England. *Education:* Cambridge University, degree in English literature.

Addresses: *Manager*—Sleeping Giant Entertainment, 5225 Wilshire Blvd., Suite 524, Los Angeles, CA 90036.

Career: Director and producer. Oxford and Cambridge Shakespeare Company, worked as manager; Hampstead Theatre Club, worked as literary manager; Royal Shakespeare Company, worked as director; British Broadcasting Corporation (BBC), began as story editor, became television director; composer for the stage in London; the 2nd Annual HatcH audiovisual festival, Bozeman, MT, mentor. Also worked on AIDS commercials in England.

Awards, Honors: Samuel Beckett Award, 1984, for *Romance, Romance;* Television Award nomination (with Kenith Trodd and John Harris), best drama series, British Academy of Film and Television Arts, 1987, for *The Singing Detective;* Montreal First Film Prize, Montreal World Film Festival, 1989, and Grand Prix, Paris Film Festival, 1990, both for *Queen of Hearts;* Audience Award and Critics Award, both Deauville Film Festival, 1990, for *Tune in Tomorrow;* Audience Award, Cognac Festival du Film Policier, 1996, for *Copycat.*

CREDITS

Film Director:

Queen of Hearts (also known as *Cappuccino*), Cinecom, 1989.

Tune in Tomorrow (also known as *Aunt Julia and the Scriptwriter*), Cinecom, 1990.

Sommersby, Warner Bros., 1993.

Copycat (also known as *Copykill*), Warner Bros., 1995.

The Man Who Knew Too Little (also known as *Agent Null Null Nix, Agent Null Null Nix—Bill Murray in hirnloser mission,* and *Watch That Man*), Warner Bros., 1997.

Entrapment (also known as *Verlockende Falle*), Twentieth Century–Fox, 1999.

The Core (also known as *Core*), Paramount, 2002.

Creation, 2009.

Film Producer:

Simply Irresistible (also known as *Einfach Unwiderstehlich*), Twentieth Century–Fox, 2000.

Also producer of *Vanilla Fog* (also known as *The Magic Hour*), Twentieth Century–Fox.

Film Appearances:

Director, *To the Core and Back* (documentary short; also known as *To the Core and Back: The Making of "The Core"*), Paramount Home Entertainment, 2003.

Television Work; Series:

Producer, *Tandoori Nights,* Channel 4, 1985.

Producer, *Eyes,* ABC, 2004–2005.

Producer, *Reunion,* Fox, 2005–2006.

Consultant, *Three Moons Over Milford,* ABC Family, 2005–2006.

Executive producer, *The Wedding Bells,* Fox, 2006–2007.

Television Work; Miniseries:

Director, *The Singing Detective* (also known as *Channel Crossings*), BBC, 1986–87, PBS, 1988.

Television Work; Movies:

Director, *Lieve juffrous Rosenberg, waarde Mr. Koonig* (also known as *Dear Janet Rosenberg, Dear Mister Koonig*), 1977.
Director, *Busted,* BBC, 1984.
Director, *Romance, Romance,* 1984.
Director, *The Silent Twins,* BBC, 1985.
Director, *The Last Evensong,* 1985.
Executive producer, *The Wedding Bells* (also known as *For Whom the Bells Toll*), 2007.

Television Work; Specials:

Director, *The Luck Child,* NBC, 1988.

Television Work; Pilots:

Director, *Eyes,* ABC, 2005.

Television Work; Episodic:

Script editor, "Braces High," *Premiere,* 1980.
Director, "Lunch," *BBC2 Playhouse 2,* BBC2, 1982.
Director, "Preview," *BBC2 Playhouse 2,* BBC2, 1982.
Director, "A Sudden Wrench," *Play for Today,* 1982.
Director, "Gates of Gold," *Play for Today,* 1983.
Director, *Tandoori Nights,* Channel 4, 1985.
Director, "The Luck Child," *The Storyteller* (also known as *Jim Henson's "The Storyteller"*), NBC, 1988.
Director, "1986," *Reunion,* Fox, 2005.
Director, "For Whom the Bell Tolls," *The Wedding Bells,* Fox, 2007.
Director, *The Tudors,* Showtime, 2008.

Television Appearances; Specials:

Close Up: Dennis Potter under the Skin (also known as *Dennis Potter: A Television Life*), 1998.
The Fine Art of Separating People from Their Money, Bravo, 1999.
The 50 Greatest Television Dramas (also known as *The 50 Greatest TV Dramas*), 2007.

Television Appearances; Episodic:

"Jodie Foster," *Biography,* Arts and Entertainment, 2005.
"The Singing Detective," *Drama Connections,* 2005.

OTHER SOURCES

Periodicals:

New York Times, September 10, 1989.
Premiere, September, 1990, p. 55.

AMIN, Mark 1950–

PERSONAL

Born February 19, 1950, in Rafsanjan, Iran; immigrated to the United States, 1967; son of Abbas and Nosrat Amin; married Susan, August 8, 1982; children: Soraya, Bijan. *Education:* University of Kansas, B.A., economics, 1972; University of California at Los Angeles, M.B.A., 1975.

Addresses: *Office*—Lionsgate, 2700 Colorado Ave., Suite 200, Santa Monica, CA 90404; Sobini Films, 4553 Glencoe Ave., Suite 230, Marina Del Rey, CA 90292.

Career: Producer and executive. Vidmark Entertainment, co–founder and president, 1984–?; Trimark Pictures, Inc., chairman and chief executive office, 1985–2000; Lions Gate Films, Santa Monica, CA, vice president and member of board of directors, 2000—; Sobini Films, Marina Del Rey, CA, chairman, 2001—.

CREDITS

Film Executive Producer:

Demonwarp, Vidmark Entertainment, 1988.
The Sleeping Car, Triax Entertainment Group, 1989.
Farendj, Trimark Entertainment, 1990.
Servants of the Twilight (also known as *Dean R. Koontz's "The Servants of Twilight"*), Trimark Pictures, 1991.
Whore (also known as *If You're Afraid to Say It … Just See It*), Trimark Pictures, 1991.
Into the Sun, Trimark Pictures, 1992.
Interceptor, Trimark Pictures, 1993.
Leprechaun, Trimark Pictures, 1993.
Deadfall, Trimark Pictures, 1993.
The Philadelphia Experiment (also known as *Philadelphia Experiment 2* and *The Philadelphia Experiment 2*), Trimark Pictures, 1993.
A Million to Juan (also known as *A Million to One*), Samuel Goldwyn Company, 1994.
Dangerous Touch, Trimark Pictures, 1994.
Love and a .45, Trimark Pictures, 1994.
The Stoned Age (also known as *Tack's Chicks*), Vidmark Entertainment, 1994.
Leprechaun 2, Trimark Pictures, 1994.
Two Guys Talkin' About Girls (also known as *… At First Sight*), Vidmark Entertainment, 1995.
The Maddening, Trimark Pictures, 1995.
Leprechaun 3, Trimark Pictures, 1995.
Aurora: Operation Intercept (also known as *Operation Intercept*), Trimark Pictures, 1995.
A Kid in King Arthur's Court, Buena Vista, 1995.
Separate Lives, Trimark Pictures, 1995.

Kicking and Screaming, Trimark Pictures, 1995.

Iron Eagle IV (also known as *Aigle de fer IV*), Trimark Pictures, 1995.

True Crime (also known as *Dangerous Kiss* and *True Detective*), Trimark Home Entertainment, 1996.

Underworld, Legacy Releasing, 1996.

The Dentist, Trimark Pictures, 1996.

Sometimes They Come Back ... Again (also known as *Sometimes They Come Back 2*), Trimark Pictures, 1996.

Never Ever (also known as *The Circle of Passion*), Trimark Pictures, 1996.

Pinocchio's Revenge (also known as *Pinocchio*), Vidmark Entertainment, 1996.

Leprechaun 4: In Space (also known as *Leprechaun 4*), Trimark Pictures, 1997.

Sprung, Trimark Pictures, 1997.

Eve's Bayou, Trimark Pictures, 1997.

Star Kid, Trimark Pictures, 1997.

Standoff, Trimark Pictures, 1998.

Chairman of the Board, Trimark Pictures, 1998.

A Kid in Aladdin's Palace, 1998.

Carnival of Souls (also known as *Wes Craven Presents "Carnival of Souls"*), Trimark Pictures, 1998.

Ground Control (also known as *Jet*), 1998.

King Cobra (also known as *Anaconda 2*), Trimark Pictures, 1999.

Warlock III: The End of Innocence, Trimark Home Video, 1999.

Let the Devil Wear Black, Trimark Pictures, 1999.

Held Up, Trimark Pictures, 1999.

Cord (also known as *Hide and Seek* and *Jeu mortel*), Trimark Home Video, 2000.

Skipped Parts (also known as *The Wonder of Sex*), Trimark Releasing, 2000.

Attraction, Trimark Pictures/Lionsgate, 2000.

Krocodylus (also known as *Blood Surf* and *Crocodile*), Trimark Pictures, 2000.

Frida, Miramax, 2002.

Streets of Legend, Lionsgate, 2003.

Civil Brand, Lionsgate, 2003.

Gardens of the Night, City Lights Media Group, 2008.

The Prince & Me 3: A Royal Honeymoon, First Look International, 2008.

Film Coproducer:

Baywatch: White Thunder at Glacier Bay, Trimark Home Video, 1998.

Film Producer:

Trance (also known as *The Eternal* and *The Eternal: Kiss of the Mummy*), Trimark Pictures, 1998.

The Prince & Me (also known as *The Prince and Me*), Paramount, 2004.

Peaceful Warrior, Universal, 2006.

Burning Bright, 2009.

Television Executive Producer; Movies:

Mob Boss, syndicated, 1990.

Psychic, USA Network, 1992.

Extreme Justice (also known as *S.I.S.—Extreme Justice*), HBO, 1993.

Night of the Running Man, HBO, 1994.

Curse of the Starving Class, Showtime, 1994.

Frank and Jesse, HBO, 1995.

Evolver, Sci–Fi Channel, 1995.

Crossworlds, HBO, 1996.

Trucks, USA Network, 1997.

The Dentist 2 (also known as *The Dentist 2: Brace Yourself* and *The Dentist 2: You Know the Drill*), HBO, 1998.

The Simple Life of Noah Dearborn, CBS, 1999.

Diplomatic Siege, HBO, 1999.

Fear of Flying (also known as *Turbulence II: Fear of Flying* and *Turbulence 2: Fear of Flying*), Cinemax, 1999.

Xchange, HBO, 2000.

The Bogus Witch Party, 2000.

After the Storm, USA Network, 2001.

Framed, TNT, 2002.

WRITINGS

Screenplay Stories:

The Prince & Me (also known as *The Prince and Me*), Paramount, 2004.

Television Movies:

Diplomatic Stage, 1999.

Television Movie Stories:

Diplomatic Stage, 1999.

ANDERS, Andrea 1975–

PERSONAL

Born May 10, 1975, in Madison, WI. *Education:* University of Wisconsin at Stevens Point, B.F.A., 1997; Rutgers University, M.F.A., acting, 2001.

Addresses: *Agent*—Abrams Artists Agency, 9200 Sunset Blvd., Suite 1130, Los Angeles, CA 90069.

Career: Actress.

CREDITS

Film Appearances:

Heather, *The Stepford Wives,* Paramount, 2004.

Brandy, *Sex Drive* (also known as *Sexdrive*), Summit Entertainment LLC, 2008.

Television Appearances; Series:
Elaine, Starr's nanny, *One Life to Live,* ABC, 1998.
Ellie, Olivia's assistant, *The Guiding Light* (also known as *Guiding Light*), CBS, 2001.
Donna Degenhart, *Oz,* HBO, 2003.
Alex Garrett, *Joey,* NBC, 2004–2006.
Nicole Allen, *The Class,* CBS, 2006–2007.
Inda, *Better Off Ted,* ABC, 2008.

Television Appearances; Movies:
Spellbound, 2003.

Television Appearances; Specials:
The 31st Annual People's Choice Awards, CBS, 2005.

Television Appearances; Pilots:
Alex Garrett, *Joey,* NBC, 2004.
Nicole Allen, *The Class,* CBS, 2006.
Linda, *Better Off Ted,* ABC, 2008.

Television Appearances; Episodic:
Emily Hoyt, "The Fire This Time," *Law & Order,* NBC, 2001.
Cathy/Chris Barronson, "Rear Window," *Tru Calling,* Fox, 2004.
Canada A.M. (also known as *Canada A.M. Weekend*), CTV, 2006.
Rena Vining, "Power," *Numb3rs* (also known as *Num3ers*), CBS, 2008.

Stage Appearances:
(Broadway debut) Understudy for Catherine and Claire, *Proof,* Walter Kerr Theatre, New York City, c. 2001.
The assistant desk clerk, and understudy Elaine Robinson, *The Graduate,* Plymouth Theatre, New York City, 2002–2003.

Also appeared in *On the Jump,* Arena Stage, Washington, DC; *New Doors,* Guthrie Theatre, Minneapolis, MN; *Cold/Tender,* New York Stage and Film; *New World Rhapsody,* New York Stage and Film.

ANDERSON, Sam 1945–

PERSONAL

Born May 13, 1945, in Wahpeton, ND; children: two (twins).

Addresses: *Agent*—TalentWorks, 3500 West Olive Ave., Suite 1400, Burbank, CA 91505.

Career: Actor. Appeared in a television commercial for Discover credit card, 1999. Antelope Valley College, Lancaster, CA, drama teacher, c. early 1970s.

Member: Screen Actors Guild.

Awards, Honors: Camie Award (with others), Character and Morality in Entertainment Awards, 2005, for *Secret Santa.*

CREDITS

Film Appearances:
Man in white, *Airplane II: The Sequel* (also known as *Flying High II*), Paramount, 1982.
Duke of Albany, *The Tragedy of King Lear* (also known as *King Lear*), 1982.
Ray Berg, *Movers and Shakers,* United Artists, 1985.
Mr. Ludwig, *La Bamba,* Columbia, 1987.
Mr. Morgan, *Critters 2: The Main Course,* New Line Cinema, 1988.
Warren, *I Come in Peace* (also known as *Dark Angel*), Media Home Entertainment, 1990.
Chairman of the House Committee, *Memoirs of an Invisible Man* (also known as *Les aventures d'un homme invisible*), Warner Bros., 1992.
Culbertson, *Robert A. Heinlein's "The Puppet Masters"* (also known as *The Puppet Masters*), Buena Vista, 1994.
Principal, *Forrest Gump,* Paramount, 1994.
Jimmy Walsh, *After the Game* (also known as *The Last Hand*), 1997.
Dr. Olsen, *Permanent Midnight,* Artisan Entertainment, 1998.
Steven, *Perfect Game,* Up to Bat Productions, 1999.
Alex Holmes, *Sonic Impact,* New City Releasing, 1999.
Ed, *The Independent,* Arrow Entertainment/New City Releasing, 2000.
The man, *The Shangri–la Cafe,* American Film Institute/Nice Girl Films, 2000.
Steven, *Perfect Game,* 2000.
John Harrison, *The Distance,* 2000.
Charles Patton, *Slackers* (also known as *Les complices*), Destination Films/Screen Gems, 2002.
Dr. Robert Roeder Shaw, *The Commission,* 2003.
George, *50 Ways to Leave Your Lover* (also known as *How to Lose Your Lover*), New Line Cinema, 2004.
Bishop, *Dirty Habit,* 2006.

Television Appearances; Series:
Stanley, *Mama Malone,* CBS, 1984.
Principal Willis DeWitt, *Growing Pains,* ABC, 1986–92.
Sam Gorpley, *Perfect Strangers,* ABC, 1987–92.

FBI Agent Morell, *Picket Fences,* CBS, 1992–95.
Dr. Jack Kayson, a recurring role, *ER,* NBC, 1994–2007.
Marvin Seaborne, *Live Shot,* UPN, 1995.
Kevin Davis, *The Cape,* syndicated, 1996.
Voice of Will Hays, *Sex and the Silver Screen,* Showtime, 1996.
President Wesley Butterfield, *Boston Common,* NBC, 1996.
Holland Manners, *Angel,* The WB, 2000–2001.
Dr. Paul Darwell, *Pasadena,* 2002.
Bill Kelly, *Married to the Kellys,* ABC, 2003–2004.
Bernard Nadler, *Lost,* ABC, 2005—.

Television Appearances; Miniseries:
Whitney Horgan, *The Stand* (also known as *Stephen King's "The Stand"*), ABC, 1994.
Innocent Victims, ABC, 1996.
Thomas Paine, *From the Earth to the Moon,* HBO, 1998.
Fox, *NetForce* (also known as *Tom Clancy's "Netforce"*), ABC, 1999.

Television Appearances; Movies:
Joe Dancer: The Big Trade, NBC, 1981.
Druggist, *Policewoman Centerfold,* NBC, 1983.
Paul Iberville, *Murder 1, Dancer 0* (also known as *Joe Dancer III* and *Lights, Camera … Murder*), NBC, 1983.
Judge Thomas S. Kirk, *A Place to Be Loved* (also known as *A Place to Be* and *Shattered Family*), CBS, 1993.
Father Dominic, *Confessions: Two Faces of Evil* (also known as *Mothershed or Berndt?*), NBC, 1994.
Dwight Cooley, *The Man Next Door,* ABC, 1996.
Doctor, *Norma Jean and Marilyn,* 1996.
Roth Lane, *The Sleepwalker Killing* (also known as *Crimes of Passion: "Sleepwalker"* and *From the Files of Unsolved Mysteries: "The Sleepwalker Killing"*), NBC, 1997.
Second congressman, *The Pentagon Wars* (also known as *Situation Normal, All Fed Up* and *SNAFU*), HBO, 1998.
Mr. Gibson, *Secret Santa,* NBC, 2003.
Dr. Reynolds, *Touched,* Lifetime, 2005.

Television Appearances; Specials:
"Growing Pains": The E! True Hollywood Story, E! Entertainment Television, 2001.
The 44th Annual Los Angeles County Holiday Celebration, 2003.

Television Appearances; Pilots:
George Modell, *Rowdies* (also known as *Hack It or Pack It*), ABC, 1986.
Dr. Peters, *The Charmings,* ABC, 1987.
Kevin Davis, *The Cape,* syndicated, 1996.
Mr. Dubois, *K–Ville,* Fox, 2007.

Also appeared in *Conspiracy.*

Television Appearances; Episodic:
Rex Erhardt, "Rumors," *WKRP in Cincinnati,* CBS, 1978.
Mason Nobel, "Johnny Comes Back," *WKRP in Cincinnati,* CBS, 1979.
Mr. Anderson, "The Americanization of Ivan," *WKRP in Cincinnati,* CBS, 1980.
Agent Berwick, "Secrets of Dayton Heights," *WKRP in Cincinnati,* CBS, 1981.
"Dog Day Hospital," *St. Elsewhere,* NBC, 1983.
Mr. Copley, "An Uncredited Woman," *Gloria,* 1983.
Store manager, "Altared Steele," *Remington Steele,* 1983.
Leo Santee, "Death Strip," *T. J. Hooker,* 1984.
Mr. Dobbs, "All's Well That Ends," *E/R* (also known as *Emergency Room*), NBC, 1984.
Benjamin Kelty, "Arms Race," *Blue Thunder,* 1984.
Kenny Sterling, "Last Chance Salon," *Hill Street Blues,* 1984.
Lon Schaeffer, "Fallen Idols," *Hotel* (also known as *Arthur Hailey's "Hotel"*), 1985.
Inspector Frank Howard, "Dead Ends," *Dallas,* CBS, 1985.
Inspector Frank Howard, "Deliverance," *Dallas,* CBS, 1985.
Dr. Synapsis, "Bigalow's Last Smoke," *Tales from the Darkside,* 1985.
Vinny Cochran, "Case X," *Hunter,* 1985.
Larry supporter, "Candidate Larry," *Newhart,* 1985.
Walter Biggs, *Eye to Eye,* 1985.
Ray Jones and John Doe, "Ms. Jones," *Magnum P.I.,* CBS, 1985.
Ellis, "Down–Home Country Blues," *Simon & Simon,* 1985.
Judge, "Life, Liberty and the Pursuit of Traffic Lights," *You Again?,* 1986.
Teddy Peters, "McCormick's Bar and Grill," *Hardcastle and McCormick,* 1986.
Customer, "This Son for Hire," *Valerie* (also known as *The Hogan Family* and *Valerie's Family*), 1986.
Mr. Meyer, "'Twas the Night before Christmas," *The Golden Girls,* CBS, 1986.
Harrison Harper, "Check This," *Perfect Strangers,* ABC, 1986.
Ingraham, "Raj on the Double," *What's Happening Now!,* 1987.
Mike, "Easy Does It," *Cagney & Lacey,* CBS, 1987.
Elias Turner, "Sins of the Father," *Buck James,* 1987.
Dan Finger, "School's Out," *21 Jump Street,* Fox, 1988.
Assistant manager, "The Royale," *Star Trek: The Next Generation* (also known as *Star Trek: TNG*), 1989.
Thomas Edison, "The Game," *Alien Nation,* 1989.
"Dog Day Afternoon, Morning and Night," *Hooperman,* 1989.
Kroger, *Uncle Buck,* 1990, 1991.
"Dances with Sharks," *L.A. Law,* NBC, 1991.
"Something Old, Something Nude," *L.A. Law,* NBC, 1991.
"TV or Not TV," *L.A. Law,* NBC, 1991.
Graphia, *L.A. Law,* NBC, 1991.
Carl Stevens, *Murder, She Wrote,* CBS, 1992.

"Nightmare," *Jake and the Fatman,* 1992.

"Spanky and the Art Gang," *L.A. Law,* NBC, 1993.

Ethan Stevens, "Dead to Rights," *Murder, She Wrote,* CBS, 1993.

Neil Fraser, "Murder at a Discount," *Murder, She Wrote,* CBS, 1993.

Gerry, *Home Free,* ABC, 1993.

Andre the Gourmet, "An Old Friend for Dinner," *Danger Theatre,* Fox, 1993.

Agent Hill, "Cold Turkey," *Melrose Place,* Fox, 1993.

Agent Hill, "Strange Bedfellows," *Melrose Place,* Fox, 1993.

Simon Wolf, "Brooklyn Dodgers," *The Adventures of Brisco County, Jr.* (also known as *Brisco County Jr.*), Fox, 1994.

Drew Ward, "Maybelle's Return," *In the Heat of the Night,* CBS, 1994.

Ernie Pitt, "Many Happy Returns," *Diagnosis: Murder,* CBS, 1994.

Mr. Riley, "Speak No Evil," *Thunder Alley,* ABC, 1994.

Stuart Himes, "Twice Dead," *Murder, She Wrote,* CBS, 1995.

Phil Lettamar, "Trading Up in the Pale Moonlight," *Pointman,* 1995.

The man, "Through a Glass Darkly," *Nowhere Man,* UPN, 1996.

Dan Laughlin, "Murder in Tempo," *Murder, She Wrote,* CBS, 1996.

Agent Jack Pierson, "522666," *Millennium,* Fox, 1996.

Paul Gulliksen, *High Incident,* ABC, 1996.

Narrator, "Will Hays," *Sex and the Silver Screen,* Showtime, 1996.

Leamus, "The Pine Bluff Variant," *The X Files,* Fox, 1997.

Criminal behaviorist, *The Pretender,* NBC, 1997.

"The Devil's Rainbow," *The Visitor,* Fox, 1997.

Larry Peters, "Seize the Day," *Fame L.A.,* 1997.

Howard Sherwood, "Liver, Hold the Mushrooms," *Chicago Hope,* CBS, 1998.

Dr. Ian Copeland, "Sleeper," *Prey* (also known as *Hungry for Survival*), ABC, 1998.

Dr. Ian Copeland, "Collaboration," *Prey* (also known as *Hungry for Survival*), ABC, 1998.

Dr. Harad, "The One Hundredth," *Friends,* NBC, 1998.

Mr. Gable, "Wishboned," *Fantasy Island,* ABC, 1998.

Mark Harrison, "In Dreams," *Ally McBeal,* Fox, 1999.

Ken Harker, "Seduction," *Profiler,* NBC, 1999.

"Say Something," *Any Day Now,* Lifetime, 1999.

Harvey, "Love Shack," *Two Guys, a Girl, and a Pizza Place* (also known as *Two Guys and a Girl*), ABC, 2000.

Dr. Yordsberg, "Out of the Past: Parts 1 & 2," *Diagnosis Murder,* CBS, 2000.

John LaSalle, "Shibboleth," *The West Wing,* NBC, 2000.

Raymond Dart, "Guilt," *JAG* (also known as *JAG: Judge Advocate General*), CBS, 2001.

Judge Flanagan, "One Angry Man," *The Fighting Fitzgeralds,* NBC, 2001.

"Age of Consent," *First Monday,* CBS, 2002.

Dr. Thicketts, "I See Dead Fat People," *The Chronicle* (also known as *News from the Edge*), 2002.

White House Counsel Reinhart, "Life Sentence," *The Court,* ABC, 2002.

Agent Garfield, "Lucky Suit," *Everybody Loves Raymond* (also known as *Raymond*), CBS, 2002.

White House Counsel Reinhart, "Life Sentence," *The Court,* 2002.

Carlisle Tucker, "Admissions," *Family Law,* CBS, 2002.

Arthur Van Halen, "If These Wolves Could Talk," *Wolf Take,* 2002.

Scott Sommer, "Golden Parachutes," *CSI: Miami,* CBS, 2002.

"Pick Your Battles," *Presidio Med,* CBS, 2002.

Girls Club, Fox, 2002.

Gordon Kirby, "The Best Interests of the Child," *Judging Amy,* CBS, 2003.

Congressman Whitehurst, "Kam Li," *Without a Trace* (also known as *W.A.T.*), CBS, 2003.

Scott Dawson, "Monster's Brawl," *Boomtown,* NBC, 2003.

Scott Dawson, "Blackout," *Boomtown,* NBC, 2003.

Cinda's father, "Mother's Daughter," *Miracles,* 2003.

Dr. Mercer, "Ch–Ch–Changes," *CSI: Crime Scene Investigation* (also known as *CSI: Las Vegas, C.S.I.,* and *Les Experts*), CBS, 2004.

Walter Fife, "From Whence We Came," *Boston Legal,* ABC, 2005.

Police commissioner, "Billboard," *Malcolm in the Middle,* Fox, 2005.

Dr. Eliot Peterson, "Time Out of Mind," *Medium,* NBC, 2005.

Ted Holden, "Joseph," *Cold Case,* CBS, 2006.

Dr. Richards, "And Here's to You, Mrs. Azrael," *CSI: NY* (also known as *CSI: New York*), CBS, 2006.

Also appeared as Mike Beiderman, *Married People;* Arnold, "Catch a Falling Star," *The Stockard Channing Show.*

Stage Appearances:

Nick, *The Woods,* Odyssey Theatre Ensemble, Los Angeles, 1986–87.

Kingfish, Los Angeles Theatre Center, Los Angeles, 1988–89.

RECORDINGS

Video Games:

Voice, *Star Wars: X–Wing vs. TIE Fighter,* 1996.

Dr. Journey, *Emergency Room: Code Red,* 2001.

ANTONIO, Lou 1934–
(Louis Antonio, Theo James)

PERSONAL

Full name, Louis Demetrios Antonio; born January 23, 1934, in Oklahoma City, OK; son of James Demetrios (a restaurant owner) and Lucille (a cashier; maiden name, Wright) Antonio; brother of Jim Antonio (an actor); married Lane Bradbury (an actress, writer, and producer; divorced). *Education:* University of Oklahoma, B.A., 1955 (some sources cite 1957); trained for the stage with Lee Strasberg, Lonny Chapman, and Curt Conway. *Avocational Interests:* Softball, basketball, reading, writing.

Addresses: *Agent*—Endeavor Talent Agency, 9601 Wilshire Blvd., 3rd Floor, Beverly Hills, CA 90210.

Career: Actor, director, producer, and writer. Actors' Studio, member, beginning 1958. Also worked as sports reporter, chef, waiter, ranch hand, bricklayer's helper, junk and manure dealer, swimming pool inspector, and "Fuller Brush man."

Member: Actors' Equity Association, Screen Actors Guild, American Federation of Television and Radio Artists, Directors Guild of America, Writers Guild of America.

Awards, Honors: *Theatre World* Award, 1969, for *The Buffalo Skinner;* Humanitas Award, 1977, Emmy Award nomination, outstanding directing in a special program—drama or comedy, 1978, both for *Something for Joey;* Emmy Award nomination, outstanding director, 1979, for *Silent Victory: The Kitty O'Neil Story;* Directors Guild of American Award nomination, outstanding directorial achievement in dramatic series—night, 1994, for *Picket Fences;* Emmy Award nomination, outstanding individual achievement in directing for a drama series, 1995, for "Life Support," *Chicago Hope.*

CREDITS

Stage Appearances:
(Stage debut) David Slater, *The Moon Is Blue,* White Barn Theatre, Terre Haute, IN, 1955.
Sidney Black, *Light Up the Sky,* White Barn Theatre, 1955.
Lord Byron, A. Ratt, Nursie, and the pilot, *Camino Real,* White Barn Theatre, 1955.
Preacher Haggler, *Dark of the Moon,* White Barn Theatre, 1955.
John Goronwyn Jones, *The Corn Is Green,* White Barn Theatre, 1955.
Hotspur, *Richard II,* McCarter Theatre, Princeton, NJ, 1956.
Soldier, *The Secret Concubine,* McCarter Theatre, 1956.
Understudy for Mickey Argent and Tommy Brookman, *The Girls of Summer,* Longacre Theatre, New York City, 1956.
Larrup Rule, *Saddle Tramps,* Cecilwood Theatre, Fishkill, NY, 1957.

Polo, *A Hatful of Rain,* Cecilwood Theatre, 1957.
Will Stockdale, *No Time for Sergeants,* Cecilwood Theatre, 1958.
Sergeant Gregovich, *Teahouse of the August Moon,* Cecilwood Theatre, 1958.
Brick, *Cat on a Hot Tin Roof,* Cecilwood Theatre, 1958.
Cornelius, *The Matchmaker,* Cecilwood Theatre, 1958.
Musician–husband, *Middle of the Night,* Cecilwood Theatre, 1958.
Jake Latta, *Night of the Iguana,* Teatro Caio Melisso, Festival of Two Worlds, Spoleto, Italy, 1959.
Member of ensemble, *Album Leaves* (revue), Teatro Caio Melisso, 1959.
Cliff Lewis, *Look Back in Anger,* Capri Theatre, Atlantic Beach, NY, 1959.
Nikita, *The Power of Darkness,* York Theatre, New York City, 1959.
Lieutenant Ferguson Howard, *The Golden Fleecing,* Cecilwood Theatre, 1960.
Jack, *Amazing Grace,* Cecilwood Theatre, 1960.
Clay, *Cry of the Raindrop,* Cecilwood Theatre, 1960.
Shady one, third patron, and Lecasse, *The Good Soup,* Plymouth Theatre, New York City, 1960.
Clay, *Cry of the Raindrop,* Hedgerow Theatre, Moylan, PA, 1960, then St. Mark's Playhouse, New York City, 1961.
Stavros, *The Garden of Sweets,* American National Theatre and Academy Theatre, New York City, 1961.
Member of ensemble, *Brecht on Brecht* (revue), Theatre De Lys, New York City, 1962, then Playhouse–on–the–Mall, Paramus, NJ, later John Drew Theatre, East Hampton, NY, both 1963.
Sergeant, *Andorra,* Biltmore Theatre, New York City, 1963.
Gaston, *The Lady of the Camellias,* Winter Garden Theatre, New York City, 1963.
Marvin Macy, *The Ballad of the Sad Cafe,* Martin Beck Theatre, New York City, 1963.
Faustus, *Tragical History of Doctor Faustus,* Phoenix Theatre, New York City, 1964.
Jonas, *Ready When You Are, C. B.!,* Brooks Atkinson Theatre, New York City, 1964.
Woody, *The Buffalo Skinner,* Theatre Marquee, New York City, 1969.

Stage Work:
Director, *Missouri Legend,* Cecilwood Theatre, Fishkill, NY, 1960.
Director, *The Chalk Garden,* Elmwood Theatre, Nyack, NY, 1962.
Producer, *Hootsudie,* Actors' Studio West, Merle Oberon Playhouse, Los Angeles, 1972.

Film Appearances:
(Film debut) Cadet, *The Strange One,* Columbia, 1957.
Roustabout, *Splendor in the Grass* (also known as *Splendour in the Grass*), Warner Bros., 1961.

Abdul, *America, America* (also known as *The Anatolian Smile*), Warner Bros., 1963.

Reverend Abraham Hewlett, *Hawaii*, United Artists, 1966.

Koko, *Cool Hand Luke*, Warner Bros., 1967.

Corrigan, *The Phynx*, Warner Bros., 1970.

Himself, *Frankie and Johnny Are Married*, IFC Films, 2003.

Himself, *From the Midst of Pain* (documentary), 2008.

Himself, *A Natural–Born World–Shaker: Making "Cool Hand Luke"* (short), Warner Home Video, 2008.

Film Work:

(As Theo James) Director, *The Gypsy Warriors*, 1978.

Production supervisor, *Private Lives*, 1983.

Executive producer, *Micki + Maud*, Columbia, 1984.

Television Appearances; Series:

Barney, *The Snoop Sisters*, NBC, 1973–74.

Detective Sergeant Jack Ramsey, *Dog and Cat*, ABC, 1977.

Joseph Manucci, *Makin' It*, ABC, 1979.

Television Appearances; Movies:

Donalbain, *Macbeth*, 1961.

Tony, *Sole Survivor*, CBS, 1970.

Barney, *Black Day for Bluebeard*, 1974.

Hugo Jenkins, *Where the Ladies Go*, ABC, 1980.

Movie producer, *Agatha Christie's "Thirteen at Dinner"* (also known as *Thirteen at Dinner*), CBS, 1985.

Dr. Calvin Finch, *Face to Face*, CBS, 1990.

Television Appearances; Specials:

The Power and the Glory, CBS, 1961.

Television Appearances; Pilots:

Road to Reality, ABC, 1960.

Sam Hatch, *Partners in Crime*, NBC, 1973.

Jack Ramsey, *Dog and Cat*, ABC, 1977.

Television Appearances; Episodic:

Love of Life, CBS, 1958.

Tallahassee 7000, CBS, 1959.

My True Story, CBS, 1959.

(Uncredited) Civil service applicant, "The Shield," *Naked City*, ABC, 1959.

Love of Life, CBS, 1960.

Grieve, "The Tender Gun," *Have Gun—Will Travel*, CBS, 1960.

"A Piece of Blue Sky," *Play of the Week*, WNTA, 1960.

"The Wendigo," *Great Ghost Tales*, CBS, 1961.

(As Louis Antonio) "A Hole in the City," *Naked City*, ABC, 1961.

"Portrait of a Painter," *Naked City*, ABC, 1962.

Bo Jackson, "Death Takes the Stand," *The Defenders*, CBS, 1962.

Danny Norton, "The Crowd Pleaser," *The Defenders*, CBS, 1962.

"Color Schemes Like Never Before," *Naked City*, ABC, 1963.

Tony, "And Make Thunder His Tribute," *Route 66*, CBS, 1963.

"The Bull Roarer," *Breaking Point*, ABC, 1963.

Camera Three, CBS, 1963.

Vinnie, "See Hollywood and Die," *The Fugitive*, ABC, 1963.

Captain Wade Ritchie, "The Men and the Boys," *12 O'Clock High*, ABC, 1964.

Captain Pollard, "Target 802," *12 O'Clock High*, ABC, 1965.

Matt Mooney, "A.P.B.," *The Fugitive*, ABC, 1965.

Lupton, "A Competent Witness," *For the People*, CBS, 1965.

Harve Kane, "Outlaw's Woman," *Gunsmoke* (also known as *Gun Law* and *Marshall Dillon*), CBS, 1965.

Niles, "The Inchworm's Got No Wings At All," *The Virginian* (also known as *The Men from Shiloh*), NBC, 1966.

"Liberty Was a Lady," *The Wackiest Ship in the Army*, NBC, 1966.

Don, "Devil's Disciples," *The Fugitive*, ABC, 1966.

Frankie Gellen, "The Shivering Pigeon," *Hawk*, 1966.

"The Eighty–Seven Dollar Bride," *The Road West*, NBC, 1967.

Jud Weskitt, "Hillbilly Honeymoon," *The Monkees*, 1967.

Rich, "Prairie Wolfers," *Gunsmoke* (also known as *Gun Law* and *Marshall Dillon*), CBS, 1967.

Charlie, "Genie, Genie, Who's Got the Genie?: Parts 1 & 2," *I Dream of Jeannie*, 1968.

Curt Tynan, "O'Quillian," *Gunsmoke* (also known as *Gun Law* and *Marshall Dillon*), CBS, 1968.

Stefanoss, "Two For Penny," *The Danny Thomas Hour*, 1968.

Davey, "In Defense of Honor," *Bonanza* (also known as *Ponderosa*), 1968.

Telly Theodakis, "Land Grant," *Here Come the Brides*, 1969.

Smiley, "Gold Town," *Gunsmoke* (also known as *Gun Law* and *Marshall Dillon*), CBS, 1969.

Mace, "The Long Night," *Gunsmoke* (also known as *Gun Law* and *Marshall Dillon*), CBS, 1969.

Harry, "Going Ape," *Bewitched*, 1969.

Kee–Cho, "Mark of the Arrow," *Gentle Ben*, CBS, 1969.

Lokai, "Let That Be Your Last Battlefield," *Star Trek* (also known as *Star Trek: TOS* and *Star Trek: The Original Series*), NBC, 1969.

Telly Theodakis, "To the Victor," *Here Come the Brides*, 1970.

(Uncredited) Stone Mason, "No Tears for Mrs. Thomas," *The Flying Nun*, 1970.

"The Long Road Home," *The Mod Squad*, 1970.

Hal Ingersol, "Murder Off Camera," *Bracken's World*, 1970.

Walter Babson, "Easy To Be Hard," *Storefront Lawyers* (also known as *Men at Law*), 1970.
Robert Siomney, "The Hostage," *Mission: Impossible,* 1970.
Tommy Crawford, "Stone Cold Dead," *Cannon,* 1971.
Arlen parent, "Superstition Rock," *The F.B.I.,* 1971.
Gordon Krager, "Bullet for a Hero," *Dan August,* 1971.
David Harper, "The Burning Ice," *Hawaii Five–O* (also known as *McGarrett*), 1971.
Rudy Blake, "Double Dead," *Mission: Impossible,* 1972.
Frank Cameron, "Inferno," *Cade's County,* 1972.
Jay Warfield, "Tarnished Idol," *The Rookies,* 1973.
Jake, "Death on a Barge," *Night Gallery* (also known as *Rod Serling's "Night Gallery"*), 1973.
Parrish, "Fools Gold," *The F.B.I.,* 1973.
Jack Lembo, "An Ugly Way to Die," *The Rookies,* 1974.
Burglar, "The Theft," *Insight,* 1974.
The director, "Mystery of the Hollywood Phantom: Part 2," *The Hardy Boys/Nancy Drew Mysteries* (also known as *The Nancy Drew Mysteries*), 1977.
Premier Zovostrov, "How Diplomatic of You," *Spy Game,* c. 1997.

Also appeared in *Studio One,* CBS; *Suspicion,* NBC; *United State Steel Hour,* CBS.

Television Producer; Series:
Shell Game, CBS, 1987.

Television Director; Miniseries:
"Chapter I," *Rich Man, Poor Man—Book II,* ABC, 1976.
The Critical List, NBC, 1978.
Breaking Up Is Hard to Do, ABC, 1979.
The Star Maker, NBC, 1981.

Television Producer; Movies:
The Outside Woman, ABC, 1989.

Television Executive Producer; Movies:
Dark Holiday (also known as *Never Pass This Way Again* and *Passport to Terror*), NBC, 1989.

Television Director; Movies:
Love Is Not Forever, 1974.
Sin, American Style, 1974.
Someone I Touched, ABC, 1975.
Something for Joey, CBS, 1977.
The Girl in the Empty Grave (also known as *Abel*), 1977.
A Real American Hero (also known as *Hard Stick*), CBS, 1978.
Silent Victory: The Kitty O'Neil Story, CBS, 1979.
The Chinese Typewriter, 1979.
Something So Right, CBS, 1982.
Between Friends (also known as *Nobody Makes Me Cry*), HBO, 1983.

A Good Sport, CBS, 1984.
Rearview Mirror, NBC, 1984.
Threesome, CBS, 1984.
Agatha Christie's "Thirteen at Dinner" (also known as *Thirteen at Dinner*), CBS, 1985.
One Terrific Guy, CBS, 1986.
Mayflower Madam, CBS, 1987.
Pals, CBS, 1987.
The Outside Woman, ABC, 1989.
Dark Holiday (also known as *Never Pass This Way Again* and *Passport to Terror*), NBC, 1989.
Face to Face, CBS, 1990.
Lies before Kisses, CBS, 1991.
The Rape of Doctor Willis, CBS, 1991.
This Gun for Hire, USA Network, 1991.
The Last Prostitute, Lifetime, 1991.
A Taste for Killing, USA Network, 1992.
Nightmare in the Daylight, CBS, 1992.
The Contender, 1993.

Television Director; Specials:
The Steeler and the Pittsburgh Kid, NBC, 1981.

Television Director; Pilots:
Fools, Females, and Fun: I've Gotta Be Me, NBC, 1974.
Lanigan's Rabbi (also known as *Friday the Rabbi Slept Late*), NBC, 1976.
The Gypsy Warriors, CBS, 1978.
Heaven on Earth, NBC, 1979.
Boston and Kilbride, CBS, 1979.
We're Fighting Back, CBS, 1981.
Gabe and Walker, ABC, 1981.
Shell Game, CBS, 1987.
Sporting Chance, CBS, 1990.

Television Director; Episodic:
Heroic Mission, 1967.
Gentle Ben, CBS, 1967.
"Against a Blank Cold Wall," *Then Came Bronson,* 1969.
"Hector and the Brass Band," *The Flying Nun,* 1969.
"Armando and the Pool Table," *The Flying Nun,* 1970.
"A Gift for El Charro," *The Flying Nun,* 1970.
"The Age of Independence," *The Young Rebels,* 1970.
Getting Together, 1971.
Owen Marshall: Counselor at Law, ABC, 1971.
The Partridge Family, 1971–73.
"To Steal a King," *Banacek,* NBC, 1972.
McCloud, NBC, 1972–75.
"Easy Money," *The Rookies,* 1973.
Griff, ABC, 1973.
Fools, Females, and Fun: Is There a Doctor in the House?, NBC, 1974.
Amy Prentiss, NBC, 1974.
Sons and Daughters, CBS, 1974.
The Rockford Files (also known as *Jim Rockford, Private Investigator*), NBC, 1974–76.
Three for the Road, CBS, 1975.

"Love, Honor and Swindle," *McMillan and Wife* (also known as *McMillan*), NBC, 1975.

"Point of Law," *McMillan and Wife* (also known as *Mc-Millan*), NBC, 1976.

Delvecchio, CBS, 1976.

The Contender, CBS, 1980.

Picket Fences, CBS, 1993–96.

"Many Happy Returns," *Diagnosis Murder,* CBS, 1994.

"Life Support," *Chicago Hope,* CBS, 1995.

"Comic Book Murder," *The Cosby Mysteries,* NBC, 1995.

"Dial 'H' For Murder," *The Cosby Mysteries,* NBC, 1995.

Amazing Grace, NBC, 1995.

"Damned If You Don't," *American Gothic,* CBS, 1995.

Dark Skies, NBC, 1996.

"The Space Flight Episode," *Mr. & Mrs. Smith,* CBS, 1996.

Party of Five, Fox, 1996–2000.

"With Friends Like These," *Spy Game,* ABC, 1997.

"Banshee," *Roar,* Fox, 1997.

Michael Hayes, CBS, 1997.

Vengeance Unlimited (also known as *Mr. Chapel*), ABC, 1998.

"The Dance," *Dawson's Creek,* The WB, 1998.

"Great Expectations," *Wasteland,* 1999.

Get Real, Fox, 1999.

"Hello, I Must Be Going," *Felicity,* The WB, 2000.

The Fugitive, CBS, 2000.

"Friends & Lovers," *C.S.I.: Crime Scene Investigation* (also known as *C.S.I., CSI: Las Vegas,* and *Les Experts*), CBS, 2000.

"Face Lift," *C.S.I.: Crime Scene Investigation* (also known as *C.S.I., CSI: Las Vegas,* and *Les Experts*), CBS, 2000.

The Beast, ABC, 2000.

"Of Fathers and Sons," *UC Undercover,* NBC, 2001.

"To Halve and to Hold," *C.S.I.: Crime Scene Investigation* (also known as *C.S.I., CSI: Las Vegas,* and *Les Experts*), CBS, 2001.

"The Drop In," *The West Wing,* NBC, 2001.

"The Funnies," *The Guardian,* CBS, 2001.

First Monday, CBS, 2002.

Family Affair, The WB, 2002.

"Body of Evidence," *The Handler,* CBS, 2003.

"Uncertainty Principle," *Numb3rs* (also known as *Num3ers*), CBS, 2005.

"Sabotage," *Numb3rs* (also known as *Num3ers*), CBS, 2005.

"1990," *Reunion,* Fox, 2005.

"The Cancer Man Can," *Boston Legal,* ABC, 2006.

"Race Ipsa," *Boston Legal,* ABC, 2006.

"Whose God Is It Anyway?," *Boston Legal,* ABC, 2006.

"Green Christmas," *Boston Legal,* ABC, 2007.

Also directed *Getting Together;* "Stuck in the Blizzard," *To Have & To Hold.*

WRITINGS

Screenplays:
Mission: Batangas, Manson, 1968.

Television Episodes:
"The Framing of Billy the Kid," *Griff,* 1973.

Also wrote episodes of *Gentle Ben,* CBS; *The Young Rebels,* ABC.

ARTERTON, Gemma 1986–

PERSONAL

Born January, 1986, in Gravesfend, Kent, England. *Education:* Graduated from Royal Academy of Dramatic Art, London.

Addresses: *Agent*—Independent Talent Group, Oxford House, 76 Oxford Street, London, UK W1D 1BS.

Career: Actress. Appeared in television commercial for Avon beauty products.

Awards, Honors: National Movie Award nomination, best performance—female, Empire Award nomination, best newcomer, 2008, for *St. Trinian's.*

CREDITS

Film Appearances:
Kelly, *St. Trinian's,* Sony, 2007.

Frankie, *Three and Out* (also known as *A Deal Is a Deal*), World Wide Bonus, 2008.

June, *RocknRolla,* Warner Bros., 2008.

Strawberry Fields, *Quantum of Solace* (also known as *B22, Marc Forster's Quantum of Solace* and *QoS*), Sony, 2008.

Marc Forster–Der weg zu 007, 2008.

Desiree, *The Boat That Rocked,* Universal, 2009.

Television Appearances; Movies:
Liza, *Capturing Mary,* BBC, 2007.

Television Appearances; Episodic:
Film 2008 (also known as *The Film Programme*), BBC, 2008.

Entertainment Tonight (also known as *E.T., ET Weekend, Entertainment This Week* and *This Week in Entertainment*), syndicated, 2008.
Xpose, TV3, 2008.
Elizabeth Bennet, *Lost in Austen,* ITV, 2008.

Television Appearances; Miniseries:
Tess Durbeyfield, *Tess of the D'Urbervilles,* BBC1, 2008.

Television Appearances; Specials:
Empire Movie Awards, ITV, 2008.
Bond on Location (also known as *Bond on Location: The Making of Quantum of Solace, Quantum of Solace: Bond on Location, The Making of Quantum of Solace* and *The Making of Quantum of Solace: Bond on Location*), ITV, 2008.
Quantum of Solace: Royal World Premiere Special, ITV, 2008.

Stage Appearances:
(Debut) Rosaline, *Loves Labour's Lost,* Globe Theatre, London, 2007.

ASHWORTH, Chris 1975–

PERSONAL

Full name, Christopher Michael Ashworth; born March 13, 1975, in Farmville, VA; son of Mike (in law enforcement) and Pat Ashworth. *Education:* Earned two associate's degrees and a bachelor's degree.

Addresses: *Agent*—Pantheon Talent Agency, 1900 Avenue of the Stars, Suite 2840, Los Angeles, CA 90067; Main Title Entertainment, 5225 Wilshire Blvd., Suite 500, Los Angeles, CA 90036–4301.

Career: Actor.

CREDITS

Television Appearances; Series:
Sergei "Serge" Malatov, a recurring role, *The Wire,* HBO, between 2003 and 2008.

Television Appearances; Miniseries:
Second Kreutzfeld guard, *The Lost Room,* Sci–Fi Channel, 2006.

Television Appearances; Movies:
Frank Lipjanic, *Sex and Lies in Sin City: The Ted Binion Scandal,* Lifetime, 2008.

Television Appearances; Episodic:
Dennis Clapp, "Trapped," *Critical Rescue,* The Discovery Channel, 2003.
Phillip Saul, "Alfredo Lopez–Cruz," *America's Most Wanted* (also known as *America's Most Wanted: America Fights Back* and *A.M.W.*), Fox, 2005.
Lieutenant Rick Cheever, "Article 32," *Without a Trace* (also known as *W.A.T.*), CBS, 2008.

Film Appearances:
Gan/Marcus Pavlof, *Aquarius,* Helioglyph Films, 2000.
(Uncredited) News camera man, *Cecil B. DeMented,* Artisan Entertainment, 2000.
(Uncredited) One of the Sentinels players, *The Replacements,* Warner Bros., 2000.
(Uncredited) SWAT team leader, *The Watcher,* MCA/Universal, 2000.
Surfer boy, *Mafioso: The Father, the Son,* American Cinema International, 2004.
Derek, *Hitch* (short film), Tessa Productions, 2004.
Eddie, *Love Lies Bleeding,* Screen Gems, 2007.

Stage Appearances:
Appeared as Alex, *The Best Little Whorehouse in Texas,* Cherry Tree Playhouse; and as Bobby, *The Writer Who Wrote Too Much,* Bobby and Company.

OTHER SOURCES

Periodicals:
Roanoke Times, January 12, 2008.

Electronic:
Chris Ashworth Official Site, http://www.chrisashworth. com, November 29, 2008.

ASPELL, Tom

PERSONAL

Married; children: two sons.

Addresses: *Office*—c/o NBC News, 30 Rockefeller Plaza, New York, NY 10112.

Career: Broadcast journalist, correspondent, and producer. Also worked as scriptwriter and camera operator. Visnews, scriptwriter in London, 1970–71, scriptwriter and camera operator in Hong Kong, beginning 1971, camera operator in Southeast Asia until 1975; freelance camera operator in the Middle East, 1975–78; Columbia Broadcasting System, camera operator for CBS–TV in Beirut, Lebanon, 1978–81; American Broadcasting Companies, television producer in Beirut, 1981–83; NBC News, New York City, producer for Cyprus bureau, beginning 1985, correspondent from Baghdad, Iraq, 1990–92, and Bosnia, beginning 1992.

CREDITS

Television Appearances; Series:
Correspondent, *NBC Nightly News,* NBC, beginning 2001.

Television Appearances; Specials:
Correspondent, *Waging War,* MSNBC, 2001.

Television Appearances; Episodic:
Meet the Press (also known as *Meet the Press with Tim Russert*), NBC, 2006.
Hardball with Chris Matthew, CNBC, 2006.

ASTIN, John 1930–

PERSONAL

Full name, John Allen Astin; born March 30, 1930, in Baltimore, MD; son of Allen Varley (a former director of the National Bureau of Standards) and Margaret Linnie (maiden name, Mackenzie) Astin; married Suzanne Hahn, March 26, 1956 (divorced, 1972); married Anna Marie Duke (an actress; professional name, Patty Duke), August 5, 1972 (divorced, 1985); married Valerie Ann Sandobal, March 19, 1989; children: (first marriage) David, Allen, Thomas (an actor); (second marriage) Sean (an actor), Mackenzie (an actor). *Education:* Attended Washington and Jefferson College, 1948–50; Johns Hopkins University, B.A., 1952; University of Minnesota, graduate study, 1952–53; also attended Washington and Jefferson College. *Religion:* Buddhism.

Addresses: *Agent*—Cunningham, Escott, Slevin and Doherty Talent Agency, 10635 Santa Monica Blvd., Suite 140, Los Angeles, CA 90025.

Career: Actor, director, producer, and writer. Appeared in television commercials, including FedEx, 1997. Johns Hopkins University, visiting professor of acting and directing, 2001—. Leader, with wife, Valerie, of a Buddhist group, Santa Monica, CA.

Member: Writers Guild of America–West (member of board of directors, 1981–85), Actors' Equity Associa-

tion, Screen Actors Guild, American Federation of Television and Radio Artists, Directors Guild of America.

Awards, Honors: Academy Award nomination, best live–action short subject, 1969, for *Prelude;* Daytime Emmy Award nomination, outstanding performer in a children's series, 1993, for *The Addams Family.*

CREDITS

Film Appearances:
The Pusher, 1960.
Glad Hand (social worker), *West Side Story,* United Artists, 1961.
Mr. Everett Beasley, *That Touch of Mink,* Universal, 1962.
(Uncredited) Smoky Anderson, *Period of Adjustment,* 1962.
Clyde Prokey, *Move Over, Darling* (also known as *Something's Gotta Give*), Twentieth Century–Fox, 1963.
Hector Vanson, *The Wheeler Dealers* (also known as *Separate Beds*), Metro–Goldwyn–Mayer, 1963.
Dr. Frieden, *The Spirit Is Willing,* Paramount, 1967.
Mr. Christian/Uncle Jack, *Candy* (also known as *Candy e il suo pazzo mondo*), Cinerama, 1968.
Prelude (short), Excelsior, 1968.
Sergeant Valdez, *Viva Max!,* Commonwealth United, 1969.
Ad, *Bunny O'Hare,* American International Pictures, 1971.
Mr. Turnbull, *Get to Know Your Rabbit,* Warner Bros., 1972.
Vito Garbugli, *Every Little Crook and Nanny,* Metro–Goldwyn–Mayer, 1972.
Pepper and His Wacky Taxi (also known as *Wacky Taxi*), 1972.
Michael O'Toole/Dangerous Ambrose, *The Brothers O'Toole,* CVD, 1973.
Bill Andrews, *Freaky Friday,* Buena Vista, 1977.
Kent Winkdale, *National Lampoon's "European Vacation"* (also known as *European Vacation*), Warner Bros., 1985.
Scotty, *Body Slam,* DeLaurentiis Entertainment Group, 1987.
Dean Dunn, *Teen Wolf Too,* Atlantic, 1987.
Professor Gangreen, *Return of the Killer Tomatoes!* (also known as *Return of the Killer Tomatoes: The Sequel*), New World Pictures, 1988.
Host, *Night Creatures,* 1988.
Verlin Flanders, *Night Life* (also known as *Campus Spirits* and *Grave Misdemeanors*), RCA/Columbia Pictures Home Video, 1989.
Jeronahew/Professor Gangreen, *Killer Tomatoes Strike Back!,* Fox Video, 1990.
Janitor, *Gremlins 2: The New Batch,* Warner Bros., 1990.

Professor Mortimer Gangreen, *Killer Tomatoes Eat France!,* New World Pictures, 1991.

Rollie, *Dreamers,* 1991.

Minister, *Stepmonster,* New Horizons Home Video, 1993.

Zach, *Huck and the King of Hearts,* Prism Entertainment, 1993.

Ranger, *Il silenzio dei prosciutti* (also known as *The Silence of the Hams*), October Films, 1994.

The judge, *Robert Zemeckis Presents: "The Frighteners"* (also known as *The Frighteners*), Universal, 1996.

Himself, *The Making of "The Frighteners"* (documentary), Universal Studios Home Video, 1998.

Title role, *Kid Quick* (short; also known as *The Adventures of Kid Quick*), 2000.

President Sender, *Betaville,* PorchLight Entertainment, 2001.

Father Reilly, *Out of Habit* (short), Hypnotic, 2002.

Voice of Dr. Quantum, *What the Beep!?: Down the Rabbit Hole* (documentary), Samuel Goldwyn Films, 2006.

Professor Peabody, *Starship II: Rendezvous with Ramses,* 2008.

Film Work:

Producer and director, *Prelude,* Excelsior, 1968.

Creative consultant, *Bunny O'Hare,* 1971.

Director, *Pepper and His Wacky Taxi* (also known as *Wacky Taxi*), 1972.

Director, *Night Creatures,* 1988.

Television Appearances; Series:

Harry Dickens, *I'm Dickens—He's Fenster,* ABC, 1962–63.

Gomez Addams, *The Addams Family,* ABC, 1964–66.

Rudy Pruitt, *The Pruitts of Southampton* (also known as *The Phyllis Diller Show*), ABC, 1967.

Various, *Insight,* 1971–78.

Lieutenant Commander Matthew Sherman, *Operation Petticoat* (also known as *Life in the Pink*), ABC, 1977–78.

Buddy Ryan, *Night Court,* NBC, 1984–90.

Ed LaSalle, *Mary,* CBS, 1985–86.

Uncle Charles, *Webster,* 1987–88.

Voice of Dr. Putrid T. Gangreen, *Attack of the Killer Tomatoes* (animated), Fox, 1990–91.

Voice of Bull Gator, *Taz–Mania* (animated), 1992.

Voice of Gomez Addams, *The Addams Family* (animated), 1992.

Radford, *Eerie, Indiana,* NBC, 1992.

Professor Albert Wickwire, *The Adventures of Brisco County, Jr.* (also known as *Brisco County, Jr.*), Fox, 1993–94.

Voice of Terry Duke Tetzloff, "Caller Beware," *Duckman* (animated), USA Network, 1994–97.

Television Appearances; Movies:

Roy Slade, *Sheriff Who,* 1967.

Dr. Stanley Remington, *Two on a Bench,* ABC, 1971.

Dr. Harvey Osterman, *Only with Married Men,* ABC, 1974.

Andrew Tustin, *Skyway to Death,* ABC, 1974.

Manny Wheeler, *The Dream Makers* (also known as *Death of Sammy*), NBC, 1975.

Gomez Addams, *The All–New Addams Family Halloween* (also known as *Halloween with the New Addams Family*), 1977.

Neil Witherspoon, *Mr. Boogedy,* ABC, 1986.

Adventures Beyond Belief (also known as *Neat and Tidy*), syndicated, 1987.

George LaFosse/Max Barret, "The Blue Dulac" (also known as "The Saint" and "The Saint: The Blue Dulac"), *The Mystery Wheel of Adventure,* syndicated, 1989.

First minuteman, *Runaway Daughters* (also known as *Rebel Highway*), Showtime, 1994.

(Uncredited) Golf announcer, *Harrison Bergeron* (also known as *Kurt Vonnegut's "Harrison Bergeron"*), Showtime, 1995.

Stormin' Norman Warner, *School for Life,* ABC Family, 2005.

Television Appearances; Specials:

Gomez Addams, *Halloween with the New Addams Family* (also known as *The All New Addams Family Halloween*), 1977.

ABC's Silver Anniversary Celebration, ABC, 1978.

Mystery Magical Special (also known as *Marc Summers' "Mystery Magical Special"*), 1986.

Harry Anderson's Sideshow, NBC, 1987.

Host, *Night Creatures,* syndicated, 1989.

Presenter, *Soap Opera Digest Awards,* NBC, 1992.

Host, *Haunted Hollywood,* E! Entertainment Television, 1993.

Television Appearances; Pilots:

Title role, *Evil Roy Slade,* NBC, 1972.

Phillip Logan, *Phillip and Barbara,* NBC, 1976.

Lieutenant Commander Matthew Sherman, *Operation Petticoat* (also known as *Life in the Pink* and *Petticoat Affair*), ABC, 1977.

Television Appearances; Episodic:

(Uncredited) Reporter, "The Night America Trembled," *Studio One* (also known as *Studio One Summer Theatre, Studio One in Hollywood, Summer Theatre, Westinghouse Studio One,* and *Westinghouse Summer Theatre*), 1957.

Joe Lambert, "The Town That Wasn't There," *Maverick,* ABC, 1960.

"Wilma's Phantom Lover," *Peter Loves Mary,* 1960.

Harlow, "Strictly Solo," *General Electric Theater* (also known as *G.E. Theater* and *G.E. True Theater*), 1960.

Charlie, "A Hundred Yards over the Rim," *The Twilight Zone* (also known as *The Twilight Zone: The Original Series* and *Twilight Zone*), CBS, 1961.

The coachman, "The Terrible Clockman," *Shirley Temple's Storybook* (also known as *The Shirley Temple Theatre*), 1961.

"Mouse at Play," *The Donna Reed Show*, 1961.

Benson, "Roommates," *Harrigan and Son*, 1961.

Arnold Penn, "The Scott Machine," *The Asphalt Jungle*, 1961.

(Scenes deleted) Hotel clerk, "Remember Pearl Harbor," *Hennesey*, 1961.

Hal Gordon, "The Investment Club," *Hazel*, 1962.

"King's Random," *87th Precinct*, 1962.

"A Quiet Evening," *Dennis the Menace* (also known as *Just Dennis*), 1962.

"Go Read the River," *Route 66*, 1962.

"Preferably, the Less–Used Arm," *Ben Casey*, 1962.

"Dress Rehearsal," *77 Sunset Strip*, 1962.

Gas station attendant, "Journey to Nineveh," *Route 66*, 1962.

"Remember Pearl Harbor," *Hennesey*, 1962.

Tim Poole, "The Yacht–Club Gang," *Checkmate*, 1962.

Dr. Carmichael, "The Bird," *The Gertrude Berg Show* (also known as *Mrs. G Goes to College*), 1962.

Bartley, "An Echo of Faded Velvet," *The Greatest Show on Earth*, 1963.

Joe Hastings, "Bless Our Happy Home," *The Farmer's Daughter*, 1964.

Pete Daley, "The Infernal Triangle," *Destry*, 1964.

Frank Mastin, "I Do, We Don't," *Occasional Wife*, 1966.

Count Sazanov, "The Night of the Tartar," *The Wild, Wild West*, CBS, 1967.

Riddler Number Two, "Batman's Anniversary," *Batman*, ABC, 1967.

Riddler Number Two, "A Riddling Controversy," *Batman*, ABC, 1967.

Title role, "Hard–Luck Henry Haggen," *Gunsmoke* (also known as *Gun Law* and *Marshal Dillon*), CBS, 1967.

Emil Kuchek, "Czech Your Wife, Sir?" *Hey, Landlord*, 1967.

Father Lundigan, "Flight of the Dodo Bird," *The Flying Nun*, 1967.

Dr. Melvin Krillman, "The Coming Out Party," *He & She*, 1967.

Jesse Martin, "The Gold Mine on Main Street," *Death Valley Days* (also known as *Call of the West*, *The Pioneers*, *Trails West*, and *Western Star Theater*), 1968.

Himself, *It Takes Two*, 1969.

"The Experiment," *CBS Playhouse*, CBS, 1969.

Title role, "Abner Willoughby's Return," *Bonanza* (also known as *Ponderosa*), NBC, 1969.

"Love and the Intruder," *Love, American Style*, 1970.

The Andy Williams Show, NBC, 1970.

Millionaire, "Diary of a Mad Millionaire," *The Partridge Family*, ABC, 1970.

Sykes, *McMillan and Wife*, NBC, 1971.

Bo "Buff" Buffingham, "Oscar's New Life," *The Odd Couple*, ABC, 1971.

Jonathan, "Pamela's Voice," *Night Gallery* (also known as *Rod Serling's "Night Gallery"*), NBC, 1971.

Hippie, "Hell's Bells," *Night Gallery* (also known as *Rod Serling's "Night Gallery"*), NBC, 1971.

Keatley, "The Father–Son Weekend," *The Doris Day Show*, 1971.

Slick, "Jump–Up," *The Virginian* (also known as *The Men from Shiloh*), 1971.

Munsch, "The Girl with the Hungry Eyes," *Night Gallery* (also known as *Rod Serling's "Night Gallery"*), NBC, 1972.

Rex Bickers, "Love and the Newscasters," *Love, American Style*, 1972.

Voice of Gomez Addams, "Scooby–Doo Meets the Addams Family," *The New Scooby–Doo Movies* (animated; also known as *Scooby–Doo Meets the Harlem Globetrotters* and *Scooby–Doo's New Comedy Movie Pictures*), 1972.

Charlie Mancini, "Love and the Happy Medium," *Love, American Style*, 1972.

Himself, "Pluto," *The Mouse Factory*, syndicated, 1972.

Himself, "Hunting," *The Mouse Factory*, syndicated, 1972.

Russo, "The Muscle and the Medic," *Temperatures Rising* (also known as *The New Temperatures Rising Show*), 1972.

Sykes, "The Night of the Wizard," *McMillan & Wife* (also known as *McMillan*), 1972.

Sykes, "Cop of the Year," *McMillan & Wife* (also known as *McMillan*), 1972.

Fred Colby, "The Graveyard Shift," *Ghost Story* (also known as *Circle of Fear*), 1973.

Millionaire, "Diary of a Mad Millionaire," *The Partridge Family*, 1973.

The Mike Douglas Show, 1974.

Greenburg, "Hard Day at Blue Nose," *Wide World Mystery*, 1974.

Dr. Irv Kellerman, "Miss Kline, We Love You," *The ABC Afternoon Playbreak* (also known as *ABC Matinee Today*), ABC, 1974.

Quinn, "Our Lady in London," *Get Christie Love!*, 1975.

Donny, "Nothing Left to Lose," *Police Woman*, 1975.

Martin, "The Unindicted Wife," *Marcus Welby, M.D.* (also known as *Robert Young, Family Doctor*), 1975.

Lowen, "A Case of Misdiagnosis," *The Bob Crane Show*, 1975.

Museum curator, "The Museum," *Welcome Back, Kotter*, ABC, 1976.

Dr. Milford, "Firebird," *Police Story*, 1976.

Tattletales, 1976.

"Say It Ain't So, Chief," *Lanigan's Rabbi*, 1977.

Dave the Hermit, "Marooned: Parts 1 & 2," *The Love Boat*, ABC, 1978.

Charles Preston, "Beachcomber/The Last Whodunit," *Fantasy Island*, ABC, 1978.

Password Plus, 1979.

Vito, "Summer of '84," *The Facts of Life*, 1984.

C. W., "A Haunting We Will Go," *Diff'rent Strokes,* 1984.

Ross Hayley, "Hooray for Homicide," *Murder, She Wrote,* CBS, 1984.

Uncle Ray Simon, "Revolution #9 ½," *Simon & Simon,* CBS, 1984.

Super Password, 1984, 1986.

Kenny, "Inside Harry Stone," *Night Court,* NBC, 1985.

Harry Pierce, "Joshua Peabody Died Here, Possibly," *Murder, She Wrote,* CBS, 1985.

Harry Pierce, "A Lady in the Lake," *Murder, She Wrote,* CBS, 1985.

Harry Pierce, "Sticks and Stones," *Murder, She Wrote,* CBS, 1985.

"Baxter and Boz," *Riptide,* 1985.

Akin, "Mansion of the Beast," *Otherworld,* 1985.

"Egyptian Cruise: Parts 1 & 2," *The Love Boat,* ABC, 1986.

Kevin, "Visiting Daze," *St. Elsewhere,* NBC, 1987.

Jack/the Devil, "The Witch Is of Van Oaks," *The Charmings,* 1987.

Uncle Joe, "The Pickle Plot," *Charles in Charge,* 1988.

Win, Lose or Draw, 1988.

Manager of gun club, "The Priest Killer Mystery," *Father Dowling Mysteries* (also known as *Father Dowling Investigates*), 1991.

Nelson Halliwell, "Top Billing," *Tales from the Crypt* (also known as *HBO's "Tales from the Crypt"*), HBO, 1991.

Neville Nessen, "Sex, Lies & UFO's: Part 2," *They Came From Outer Space,* 1991.

"Up All Night," *Mad About You,* NBC, 1994.

Storytime, PBS, 1994.

George Humphries, "The Ice Cream Man Cometh," *Step by Step,* ABC, 1994.

Alexander the Great, "Who Killed Alexander the Great?" *Burke's Law,* CBS, 1994.

Voice of the mole, "Stessed to Kill," *Bonkers* (also known as *Disney's "Bonkers"*), 1994.

Voice of doctor, "Monster Make–Over/Airplane, a Wing and a Scare," *Aaahh!! Real Monsters* (animated), Nickelodeon, 1994.

Storytime, PBS, 1994.

George Humphries, "The Flight before Christmas," *Step by Step,* ABC, 1995.

Fritz Randall, "Film Flam," *Murder, She Wrote,* CBS, 1995.

Dr. Roberts, "Your Feet's Too Big," *The Nanny,* CBS, 1996.

Dr. Roberts, "Tattoo," *The Nanny,* CBS, 1996.

Rhymer, "The Adventures of Ratman and Gerbil or, Holy Homeboys in Outer Space," *Homeboys in Outer Space,* UPN, 1996.

Voice, "The Unusual Suspects," *Quack Pack* (animated), 1996.

Voice, *Johnny Bravo* (animated), Cartoon Network, 1997.

Rhymer, "The Adventures of Ratman and Gerbil, or Holy Homeboys in Outer Space," *Homeboys in Outer Space,* UPN, 1997.

Voice of Superintendent Skinner, "Kids in the Mist," *Recess* (animated; also known as *Disney's "Recess"*: Created by Paul and Joe), 1998.

Voice of Grampapa Addams, "Grandpapa Addams Comes to Visit," *The New Addams Family* (animated), Fox Kids, 1998.

"Storm o' the Century," *The Hughleys,* ABC, 1999.

Voice of Grampapa Addams, "Fester & Granny vs. Grandpapa Addams," *The New Addams Family* (animated), Fox Family, 1999.

Voice of the Great Bangaboo, "The Great Bangaboo," *The Wild Thornberrys* (animated), Nickelodeon, 1999.

Voice of Superintendent Skinner, "The Story of Whomps," *Recess* (animated; also known as *Disney's "Recess"*: Created by Paul and Joe), 1999.

"I Wear My Sunglasses at Night," *The Strip,* UPN, 2000.

Richard Wilson, "All the Rage," *Becker,* CBS, 2000.

Voice of Dave Bishop, "Blizzard Conditions," *As Told by Ginger* (animated), Nickelodeon, 2001.

"Carolyn Jones: Morticia and More," *Biography,* Arts and Entertainment, 2002.

Voice of Santa Claus, "Twinkle's Star," *Higgleytown Heroes* (animated), 2004.

Himself, "There's Something About Mary," *My First Time,* 2006.

Good Morning America, ABC, 2006.

Also appeared in *Hearts Are Wild;* as voice of Sydney, *Aladdin* (animated; also known as *Disney's Aladdin*).

Television Director; Specials:

Night Creatures, syndicated, 1989.

Television Director; Pilots:

Operation Petticoat (also known as *Life in the Pink* and *Petticoat Affair*), ABC, 1977.

Rosetti and Ryan: Men Who Love Women, NBC, 1977.

Ethel Is an Elephant, CBS, 1980.

Getting There, CBS, 1980.

Scared Silly, ABC, 1982.

Two Guys from Muck, NBC, 1982.

Television Director; Episodic:

"The House," *Night Gallery* (also known as *Rod Serling's "Night Gallery"*), NBC, 1970.

"A Fear of Spiders," *Night Gallery* (also known as *Rod Serling's "Night Gallery"*), NBC, 1971.

"The Dark Boy," *Night Gallery* (also known as *Rod Serling's "Night Gallery"*), NBC, 1971.

"Murder by the Barrel," *McMillan and Wife* (also known as *McMillan*), NBC, 1971.

"Death Is a Seven Point Favorite," *McMillan and Wife* (also known as *McMillan*), NBC, 1971.

Holmes and Yoyo (also known as *Holmes and Yo–Yo*), ABC, 1976.

Rosetti and Ryan, NBC, 1977.

Operation Petticoat (also known as *Life in the Pink*), ABC, 1977.

Mr. Merlin, CBS, 1982.

"Meet the New Guy," *CHiPs,* NBC, 1982.

"Rock Devil Rock," *CHiPs,* NBC, 1982.

"Brat Patrol," *CHiPs,* NBC, 1983.

Just Our Luck (also known as *Just My Luck*), ABC, 1983.

"Stage Struck," *Murder, She Wrote,* CBS, 1986.

Television Additional Voices; Episodic:

The Twisted Adventures of Felix the Cat (animated; also known as *The Twisted Tales of Felix the Cat*), 1995.

"While the City Snoozes," *Aladdin* (animated; also known as *Disney's Aladdin*), 1995.

Stage Appearances:

(Stage debut) Readymoney Matt, *The Threepenny Opera,* Theatre de Lys, New York City, 1954.

(Broadway debut) *Major Barbara,* Martin Beck Theatre, 1956.

Morrison, *The Cave Dwellers,* Bijou Theatre, New York City, 1957.

Various, *Ulysses in Nighttown,* Rooftop Theatre, New York City, 1958.

Collins, *The Tall Story,* Belasco Theatre, New York City, 1959.

Also appeared in *Look Homeward, Angel,* Pasadena Playhouse, Pasadena, CA; *A Sleep of Prisoners,* Phoenix Theatre, New York City; as Ebenezer Scrooge, *A Christmas Carol;* Sir Joseph, *H.M.S. Pinafore,* New York City; Henry Saunders, *Lend Me a Tenor;* as Fagin, *Oliver!;* Vladimir, *Waiting for Godot.*

Major Tours:

Edgar Allan Poe: Once Upon a Midnight (solo show), U.S. cities, 1998–99.

Stage Work:

Assistant director, *Ulysses in Nighttown,* Rooftop Theatre, New York City, 1958.

Also worked as coproducer and director of *A Sleep of Prisoners,* Phoenix Theatre, New York City.

WRITINGS

Screenplays:

Prelude, Excelsior, 1968.

(With Coslough Johnson) *All Boxed Up,* 1972.

(With Johnson) *Cummins and Kinneys,* 1973.

AUKIN, David 1942–

PERSONAL

Born February 12, 1942, in Harrow, England; son of Charles and Regina (maiden name, Unger) Aukin; married Nancy Jane Meckler, June 20, 1969; children: Daniel, Jethro. *Education:* St. Edmund Hall, Oxford, B.A.; qualified as a solicitor. *Avocational Interests:* Golf.

Addresses: *Office*—Mentorn International, 43 Whitfield St., London W1T 4HA United Kingdom; DayBreak Pictures, 43 Whitfield St., London W1T 4HA United Kingdom.

Career: Producer. Traverse Theatre, Edinburgh, Scotland, literary advisor, 1970–73; Anvil Productions (some sources cite Oxford Playhouse Company), Oxford, England, administrator and producer, 1974–75; Hampstead Theatre, London, administrator, 1975–78, artistic director, 1978–83; Leicester Haymarket Theatre, director, 1983–86; Royal National Theatre, London, executive director, 1986–90; Channel 4 Television, head of drama department, 1990–97; HAL Films, cofounder, 1998; Act Productions Ltd., partner, 2001; Mentorn International, London, head of drama department; DayBreak Pictures, London, principal and cofounder, 2007—. Oval House Arts Centre, chair, 1970–74; Freehold Company, administrator; cofounder, Joint Stock Company and Foco Novo.

Member: Society of West End Theatre (president, 1988–90), Groucho Club, RAC.

Awards, Honors: *Evening Standard* Drama Award, outstanding achievement, 1978, for work at the Hampstead Theatre; Television Award (with others), best single drama, British Academy of Film and Television Arts, 2006, for *The Government Inspector;* Television Award nomination (with others), best single drama, British Academy of Film and Television Arts, 2008, for *The Trial of Tony Blair;* Television Award (with others), best drama special, British Academy of Film and Television Arts, 2008, for *Britz.*

CREDITS

Stage Work:

Cocreator, *The Young Churchill,* Leicester, England, then Duchess Theatre, London, 1969.

Producer, *The Elephant Man,* Royale Theatre, London, 2002.

Also worked as coproducer, *The Black and White Minstrels,* Traverse Theatre, Edinburgh, Scotland; coproducer, *Caravaggio Buddy,* Traverse Theatre; coproducer,

The Novelist, Traverse Theatre; producer, *Lay By,* Portable Theatre Company; producer, *Bodies,* Hampstead Theatre, London, then West End production; *Clouds,* Hampstead Theatre, then West End production; *Dusa,* Hampstead Theatre, then West End production; *Fish,* Hampstead Theatre, then West End production; *Gloo Joo,* Hampstead Theatre, then West End production; *Outside Edge,* Hampstead Theatre, then West End production; *Stas and Vi,* Hampstead Theatre, then West End production. Also affiliated with *Son of Man,* 1969; *Straight Up,* 1971; *Le Grand Magic Circus in Robinson Crusoe,* 1974; and *From Moses to Mao,* 1974.

Film Executive Producer:
The Break, Castle Hill Productions, 1998.
Elephant Juice, Miramax, 1999.
Mansfield Park, Miramax, 1999.
About Adam, 2000, Miramax, 2001.
Mrs. Henderson Presents, Weinstein Company, 2005.
Endgame, Target Entertainment, 2009.

Film Appearances:
Office worker, *Dresden,* 1999.

Television Executive Producer; Miniseries:
Britz, BBC America, 2008.

Television Executive Producer; Movies:
The Hamburg Cell, HBO, CBC, and France 2, 2004.
The Government Inspector, 2005.
A Very Social Secretary, 2005.
Nostradamus, 2006.
The Trial of Tony Blair, BBC America, 2007.
Confessions of a Diary Secretary, 2007.
Terrorists, 2008.

Television Appearances; Specials:
Himself, *All About "Abigail's Party,"* 2007.

B

BANCROFT, Cameron 1967–
(Cam Bancroft)

PERSONAL

Full name, Cameron M. Bancroft; born May 17, 1967, in Vancouver, British Columbia, Canada (some sources say Winnipeg, Manitoba, Canada); son of Glen (an attorney) and Wendy (a nurse) Bancroft; married, September 1999; children: son, daughter. *Education:* California Institute of the Arts, B.F.A., theater. *Avocational Interests:* Hockey and music.

Addresses: *Agent*—Don Buchwald and Associates, 6500 Wilshire Blvd., Suite 2200, Los Angeles, CA 90048. *Manager*—Kincaid Management, 43 Navy St., Venice, CA 90291.

Career: Actor. National Hockey League's celebrity hockey team, member, 1994—.

Awards, Honors: State Award, California Independent Film Festival, best actor, 2007, for *Simple Things.*

CREDITS

Film Appearances:
(As Cam Bancroft) Joe, *The Boy Who Could Fly,* Twentieth Century–Fox, 1986.
Jack, *Rock 'n Roll High School Forever,* Live Entertainment, 1990.
Bernie, *Love & Human Remains* (also known as *Amour et restes humains*), Sony Pictures Classics, 1993.
Robert Reynolds, *Dream Man,* Republic Pictures Corp., 1995.
Bruce, *Sleeping Together,* Trident Releasing, 1997.

Patterson, *L.A. Without a Map* (also known as *I Love L.A.* and *Los Angeles Without a Map*), United Media, 1998.
Tinker Connolly, *Mystery, Alaska,* Buena Vista, 1999.
Rob Poirer, *MVP 2: Most Vertical Primate* (also known as *MVP: Most Vertical Primate, MVP 2: Most Vertical Primate,* and *Mon primate adore II*), Columbia TriStar Home Video, 2001.
Standard Time, 2001.
Himself, *"MVP 2: Most Vertical Primate"—Behind the Scenes* (documentary short), Warner Home Video, 2001.
Greg Ellenbogen, *Standard Time* (also known as *Anything But Love*), Samuel Goldwyn Films, 2002.
Dr. Evan Gibbs, *Simple Things* (also known as *Country Remedy*), Screen Media Ventures, 2007.

Television Appearances; Series:
Graham, *The Beachcombers,* CBC, 1987–88.
Ray, *General Hospital,* ABC, c. 1989.
Kyle Hansen, *Extreme,* ABC, 1995.
Joe Bradley, *Beverly Hills, 90210,* Fox, 1995–96.
Captain Ezekiel "Zeke" Beaumont, *The Cape,* syndicated, 1996.
Ethaniel, *Code Name: Eternity* (also known as *Code: Eternity*), Sci–Fi Channel, 2000.
Lee Castle, *24,* Fox, 2005.
Joe Seplar, *Beautiful People,* ABC Family, 2005.
Cameron, *Hockeyville* (also known as *Kraft Hockeyville*), 2006.

Television Appearances; Miniseries:
Nicholas, *Zoya* (also known as *Danielle Steel's "Zoya"*), NBC, 1995.
Charles Ingalls, *Little House on the Prairie,* ABC, 2005.
Mike McCormick, *The Path to 9/11,* ABC, 2006.

Television Appearances; Movies:
David Burdock, *83 Hours 'Til Dawn,* CBS, 1990.
Kurtis Stark, *Anything for Love* (also known as *Just One of the Girls*), Fox, 1992.

Eddie, *Moment of Truth: To Walk Again*, NBC, 1994.
Mark, *Moment of Truth: Broken Pledges*, NBC, 1994.
Patrick, *For the Love of Nancy*, ABC, 1994.
Chad Billingsly, *A Family Divided*, NBC, 1995.
Rocket, *She Stood Alone: The Tailhook Scandal*, ABC, 1995.
Jack, *The Other Mother: A Moment of Truth Movie*, Lifetime, 1995.
Roger Lewis, *To Brave Alaska*, ABC, 1996.
Jeff Parker, *Convictions*, Lifetime, 1997.
Jed Benton, *She's No Angel*, Lifetime, 2001.
(As Cam Bancroft) Scott Rivers, *The New Beachcombers*, 2002.
Sterling Brooks, *He Sees You When You're Sleeping* (also known as *Mary Higgins Clark's "He Sees You When You're Sleeping"*), PAX, 2002.
Duffy, *The Crooked E: The Unshredded Truth about Enron*, CBS, 2003.
Scott Shift, *Undercover Christmas* (also known as *L'amour en cadeau* and *Undercover Lover*), CBS, 2003.
Larry, *I Want to Marry Ryan Banks* (also known as *The Reality of Love*), ABC Family, 2004.
Scott Rivers, *A Beachcombers Christmas*, 2004.
Ross, *Don't Cry Now*, Lifetime, 2007.
Bill, *Left Coast*, 2008.
Brian, *The Love of Her Life* (also known as *A Woman's Rage*), Lifetime, 2008.
Beau Canfield, *Mail Order Bride*, Hallmark Channel, 2008.
Daniel Laurens, *Flirting with 40*, 2008.

Television Appearances; Pilots:
Captain Ezekiel Beaumont, *The Cape*, 1996.

Television Appearances; Episodic:
Kemper, "Payback," *Tour of Duty*, CBS, 1990.
Malcolm, "Evie's Three Promises," *Out of This World*, syndicated, 1991.
"Yesterday We Were Playing Football," *The Round Table*, 1992.
Robert, "The Watchers," *Highlander* (also known as *Highlander: The Series*), syndicated, 1993.
David Keogh, "Obsession," *Highlander* (also known as *Highlander: The Series*), syndicated, 1994.
Cryto, "How to Make a Quilt Out of Americans," *Charmed*, The WB, 2000.
Craig Richards, "The Pack," *Special Unit 2* (also known as *SU2*), UPN, 2001.
Ben Wilton, "Dead Man Walking," *Jake 2.0*, 2004.
Terry, "The Campaign Manager," *The Collector*, 2005.
Eric McManus, "1986," *Reunion*, Fox, 2005.
Byron Diller, "Shattered," *CSI: Miami*, CBS, 2005.

Stage Appearances:
Also appeared in *A Lion in Winter*; *The Cherry Orchard*; *A Midsummer Night Dream*.

OTHER SOURCES

Periodicals:
People Weekly, December 23, 1996, p. 60.

BANES, Lisa 1955–

PERSONAL

Born July 9, 1955, in Chagrin Falls, OH. *Education:* Juilliard School, graduated.

Addresses: *Agent*—Tim Angle, Don Buchwald and Associates, 10 East 44th St., New York, NY 10017. *Manager*—David Williams Management, 9614 Olympic Blvd., Suite F, Beverly Hills, CA 90212.

Career: Actress. National Shakespeare Festival, San Diego, CA, member of company, 1981; Acting Company, New York City, past member of company.

Member: Screen Actors Guild.

Awards, Honors: *Theatre World* Award, 1981, for *Look Back in Anger*; Obie Award (with others), best performance, *Village Voice*, 1982, for *My Sister in This House*; Drama Desk Award, outstanding featured actress in a play, 1984, for *Isn't It Romantic?*

CREDITS

Television Appearances; Series:
Doreen Morrison, a recurring role, *The Trials of Rosie O'Neill*, CBS, 1990–92.
Mayor Anita Massengil, *Son of the Beach*, FX Network, 2000–2002.
Eve McBain, *One Life to Live*, ABC, 2004—.

Television Appearances; Movies:
Erica, *One Police Plaza* (also known as *Song for Sara*), CBS, 1986.
Joanna Westrope, *A Killer Among Us*, NBC, 1990.
Diana, *Danger Island* (also known as *The Island* and *The Presence*), NBC, 1992.
Vi Sams, *Revenge on the Highway* (also known as *Overdrive* and *Silent Thunder*), NBC, 1992.
Barbara Forester, *A Family Torn Apart* (also known as *Sudden Fury: A Family Torn Apart*), NBC, 1993.
Marla Tolbert, *Cries from the Heart* (also known as *Touch of Truth*), CBS, 1994.
Rebecca Heaton, *The Avenging Angel*, TNT, 1995.

Jessica Lewisohn, *Mother May I Sleep with Danger?*, NBC, 1996.

Elder, *Last Exit to Earth* (also known *Roger Corman Presents "Last Exit to Earth"*), Showtime, 1996.

Lisa Eubanks, *My Son Is Innocent*, ABC, 1996.

Mayor Walker, *Combustion*, Lifetime, 2004.

Television Appearances; Miniseries:

Anne Kane, *Kane and Abel*, CBS, 1985.

Martha Gellhorn, *Hemingway*, syndicated, 1988.

Barbara Hutton, *Too Rich: The Secret Life of Doris Duke*, CBS, 1999.

Television Appearances; Specials:

Vanessa, *Battle in the Erogenous Zone* (also known as *Combat in the Erogenous Zone* and *War in the Erogenous Zone*), Showtime, 1992.

Television Appearances; Pilots:

Andrea Griffin, *Close Encounters* (also known as *Matchmaker*), CBS, 1990.

Meredith Holt, *Girls Club*, Fox, 2002.

Television Appearances; Episodic:

"No Room at the Inn," *Spenser: For Hire*, 1985.

"Nightscape," *The Equalizer*, 1986.

Cat von Seeger, "How to Survive in Vietnam: Parts 1 & 2," *China Beach*, ABC, 1989.

Kathryn Henning, "Paige's Mom," *Life Goes On* (also known as *Glenbrook*), ABC, 1989.

Liz Chapin, "Don Chapin," *Lifestories*, 1990.

Ms. Mitchell, "Leap of Faith," *L.A. Law*, NBC, 1993.

Barbara Buckley, "The Good Daughter," *Sisters*, NBC, 1993.

Dr. Renhol, "Equilibrium," *Star Trek: Deep Space Nine* (also known as *Deep Space Nine*, *DS9*, and *Star Trek: DS9*), syndicated, 1994.

Mrs. Simms, "White Men Can't Kiss," *Roseanne*, ABC, 1994.

Tippi Von Schlaugger, "The Naked and the Deadline," *High Society*, CBS, 1995.

Lucy Hendrix, "Shooting in Rome," *Murder, She Wrote*, CBS, 1995.

Vivien Barone, "Chapter Ten," *Murder One*, ABC, 1995.

Pamela, "A Lilith Thanksgiving," *Frasier*, NBC, 1996.

Madeline Wyman, "Imagine: Parts 1 & 2," *Michael Hayes*, CBS, 1998.

Georgina Winters, "The Rivals," *Legacy*, UPN, 1999.

Georgina Winters, "Winter's Storm," *Legacy*, UPN, 1999.

Georgina Winters, "A New Beginning," *Legacy*, UPN, 1999.

Georgina Winters, "Where Spirit Lives," *Legacy*, UPN, 1999.

Howard Stern, E! Entertainment Television, 2000.

The Test, FX Network, 2001.

Carolyn Minelli, "Lies of Minelli," *Philly*, ABC, 2002.

Judge Cooke, "Eat and Run," *The Practice*, ABC, 2002.

Meredith Holt, "Book of Virtues," *Girls Club*, Fox, 2002.

Meredith Holt, "Secrets and Lies," *Girls Club*, Fox, 2002.

Meredith Holt, "Hello, Goodbye," *Girls Club*, Fox, 2002.

Viveca, "Ready, Aim, Sing," *It's All Relative*, ABC, 2004.

Georgia Boone, "Dugan Groupie," *The King of Queens*, CBS, 2004.

Georgia Boone, "Entertainment Weekly," *The King of Queens*, CBS, 2004.

Valerie Page, "Harpy Birthday," *Jake in Progress*, ABC, 2005.

Victoria, "Time Flies," *Six Feet Under*, HBO, 2005.

Victoria, "Eat a Peach," *Six Feet Under*, HBO, 2005.

Victoria, "The Silence," *Six Feet Under*, HBO, 2005.

Chef Vivian, "Key Ingredients," *Out of Practice*, CBS, 2005.

Attorney Kimberly Mellon, "Truly, Madly, Deeply," *Boston Legal*, ABC, 2005.

District attorney Margaret Mannheim, "Another Country," *In Justice*, ABC, 2006.

Dr. Rhea Morrison, "SERE," *The Unit*, CBS, 2006.

Dr. Victoria Cole, "Fog," *Saved*, TNT, 2006.

Dr. Victoria Cole, "Family," *Saved*, TNT, 2006.

Vera Keck, "Like It Was," *Desperate Housewives*, ABC, 2006.

Edna Crocker, "Forget Me Not," *Psych*, USA Network, 2007.

Appeared in an episode of *NYPD Blue*, ABC.

Stage Appearances:

Isabella, *The White Devil*, Acting Company, American Place Theatre, New York City, 1980.

The Admirable Crichton, Long Wharf Theatre, New Haven, CT, 1980.

Player Queen Elizabeth, *Elizabeth I*, New York City, 1980.

Alison Porter, *Look Back in Anger*, Roundabout Theatre Company, Stage One, New York City, 1980.

Margaret, *A Call from the East*, Manhattan Theatre Club, New York City, 1981.

Christine, *My Sister in This House*, Second Stage Theatre Company, Park Royal Theatre, New York City, 1981–82.

Title role, *Antigone*, Martinson Hall, Public Theatre, New York City, 1982.

A Doll's House, Yale Repertory Theatre, New Haven, CT, 1982–83.

Olga, *Three Sisters*, Manhattan Theatre Club Stage I, New York City, 1982–83.

Moll, *The Cradle Will Rock*, Douglas Fairbanks Theatre, New York City, 1983.

Harriet Cornwall, *Isn't It Romantic?*, Playwrights Horizons Theatre, New York City, 1983, then Lucille Lortel Theatre, 1984–85.

D. Raleigh Bell, *Fighting International Fat,* Playwrights Horizons Theatre, 1985.

Mrs. Wire, "The Lady of Larkspur Lotion," also Miss Lucretia Collins, Myra, Madame Duvenet, and Flora, *Ten by Tennessee,* Acting Company, Lucille Lortel Theatre, New York City, 1986.

Ronee, *Progress,* Long Wharf Theatre, 1986–87.

Mary, *On the Verge, or, the Geography of Yearning,* John Houseman Theatre, New York City, 1987.

Title role, *Emily,* Manhattan Theatre Club Stage I, 1988.

Cassie Cooper, *Rumors,* Old Globe Theatre, San Diego, CA, then Broadhurst Theatre, New York City, 1988–89.

Portia and Lucilla, *Julius Caesar,* Center Theatre Group, Mark Taper Forum, Los Angeles, 1991.

Vicki, *Money and Friends,* Center Theatre Group, Ahmanson Theatre, Mark Taper Forum, 1992–93.

Lady Croom, *Arcadia,* Vivian Beaumont Theatre, Lincoln Center, New York City, 1995.

Margaret Lord, *High Society* (musical), American Conservatory Theatre, Geary Theatre, San Francisco, CA, 1997, then St. James Theatre, New York City, 1998.

Macbeth, Scottsdale Center for the Arts, Scottsdale, AZ, 2000.

Film Appearances:

Alison Porter, *Look Back in Anger,* 1980.

Mary Berry, *The Hotel New Hampshire,* Orion, 1984.

Toni Greer, *Marie* (also known as *Marie: A True Story*), Metro–Goldwyn–Mayer, 1985.

Mallory, *Young Guns,* Twentieth Century–Fox, 1988.

Bonnie, *Cocktail,* Buena Vista, 1988.

Gynecologist, *Miami Rhapsody,* Buena Vista, 1995.

Woman, *Lieberman in Love,* 1995.

Elfriede Prefontaine, *Without Limits* (also known as *Pre*), Warner Bros., 1998.

Chippy McDuffy, *Pumpkin,* Metro–Goldwyn–Mayer, 2002.

Flora, *Dragonfly* (also known as *Im Zeichen der libelle*), Universal, 2002.

Mom, *A Good Day for Ted Schmetterling,* Pass the Penny Productions, 2005.

Karin Polachek, *Freedom Writers,* Paramount, 2007.

Priscilla, *Brothel,* Mount Parnassus Pictures, 2008.

RECORDINGS

Audio Books; Reader:

Love in Another Town, by Barbara Taylor Bradford, HarperCollins, 1995.

The Final Judgment, by Richard North Patterson, Random AudioBooks, 1995, abridged edition, 1998.

The More Writers in the Garden: A Selection of Garden Writing, edited by Jane Garmey, HighBridge, 1998.

BARKER, Clive 1952–

PERSONAL

Born October 5, 1952, in Liverpool, England; settled in the United States; son of Leonard (a personnel director) and Joan Ruby (a school welfare officer and painter; maiden name, Revill) Barker; companion of David Armstrong (a photographer); stepchildren: Nicole. *Education:* University of Liverpool, B.A.

Addresses: *Office*—Seraphim Films, 1606 Argyle St., Hollywood, CA 90028.

Career: Writer, producer, director, and actor. Also works as illustrator and painter. Dog Factory (theatre group; also known as the Dog Company), London, cofounder, actor, and principal playwright; Seraphim Films, Hollywood, CA, founder and president; Midnight Picture Show, Hollywood, principal. Horror Fall of Fame, member of board of directors. Paintings and drawings represented in shows at Bess Cutler Gallery, New York City, 1993, Laguna Art Museum, South Coast Plaza branch, Costa Mesa, CA, 1995, and elsewhere; exhibitions include "Frontier Tales," 1990, "Los Angeles Art Fare," 1993, "One Flesh," 1997, "The Weird and the Wicked: A Halloween Exhibition of the Erotic and Fantastic," Los Angeles, 1998, and "Visions of Heaven and Hell (and Then Some)," 2005.

Awards, Honors: Two British Fantasy Awards, British Fantasy Society; World Fantasy Award, best anthology or collection, World Fantasy Convention, 1985, for *Clive Barker's Books of Blood;* Critics' Award and International Fantasy Film Award nomination, both Fantasporto, and Fear Section Award, Avoriaz Fantastic Film Festival, all 1988, for *Hellraiser;* Silver Scream Award, Amsterdam Fantastic Film Festival, 1990, Saturn Award nomination, best director, Academy of Science Fiction, Fantasy, and Horror Films, 1991, Critics' Award and International Fantasy Film Award nomination, Fantasporto, 1991, and Special Jury Award, Avoriaz Fantastic Film Festival, 1991, all for *Nightbreed;* Lambda Literary Award, science fiction or fantasy category, 1997, for *Sacrament;* Eyegore Award, Halloween Horror Night, Universal Studios Hollywood, 1998; International Horror Guild Award nomination, c. 2001, for *Coldheart Canyon: A Hollywood Ghost Story;* Bram Stoker Award, Horror Writers Association, 2004, for *Abarat: Days of Magic, Nights of War;* Davidson/Valentini Award, GLAAD Media Awards, Gay and Lesbian Alliance Against Defamation, 2004; best art award, International Horror guild, 2005, for exhibition "Visions of Heaven and Hell (and Then Some)."

CREDITS

Film Director:
Salome (short film), Salvation Films, 1973.
The Forbidden (short film), Salvation Films, 1978.
Hellraiser (also known as *Clive Barker's "Hellraiser"*), New World, 1987.
Nightbreed (also known as *Clive Barker's "Nightbreed"*), Twentieth Century–Fox, 1990.
(And executive producer) *Lord of Illusions* (also known as *Clive Barker's "Lord of Illusions"*), United Artists, 1995.
(And producer) *Tortured Souls: Animae Damnatae* (also known as *Clive Barker's "Tortured Souls: Animae Damnatae"*), 2002, Universal, 2009.

Film Executive Producer:
Hellbound: Hellraiser II (also known as *Hellraiser II*), New World, 1988.
Hellraiser III: Hell on Earth, Dimension Films, 1992.
Candyman (also known as *Clive Barker's "Candyman"*), TriStar, 1992.
Candyman II: Farewell to the Flesh (also known as *Candyman: Farewell to the Flesh*), Gramercy, 1995.
Hellraiser: Bloodline (also known as *Hellraiser IV: Bloodline* and *Hellraiser IV: Bloodlines*), Miramax, 1996.
Gods and Monsters, Lions Gate Films, 1998.

Film Producer:
Mule Skinner Blues, Sundance Channel Home Entertainment, 2001.
The Plague (also known as *Clive Barker's "The Plague"*), Sony Pictures Home Entertainment, 2006.
The Midnight Meat Train (also known as *Clive Barker's "Midnight Meat Train"*), Lions Gate Films, 2008.
Book of Blood, Essential Entertainment, 2008.
Dread, Matador Pictures/Midnight Picture Show/Seraphim Films/Cinema Three, 2009.
Tortured Souls: Animae Damnatae, Universal, 2009.

Film Appearances:
Salome (short film), Salvation Films, 1973.
The Forbidden (short film), Salvation Films, 1978.
Forensic technician, *Sleepwalkers* (also known as *Sleepstalkers* and *Stephen King's "Sleepwalkers"*), Columbia, 1992.
Barn of the Blood Llama, 1997.
Himself, *Clive Barker's Freakz* (short film), Jets Productions/Universal Studios Hollywood, 1998.
The Road to Dracula, Universal, 1999.
She's Alive! Creating the Bride of Frankenstein, 1999.
Ringers: Lord of the Fans (documentary), Sony Pictures Home Entertainment, 2005.
Voice of Edwin Morose, *Teddy Scares* (animated short film), DAVE School Students Productions, 2006.

Demons to Others: The Making of "Hellraiser: The Prophecy" (documentary short film; also known as *Demons to Others*), 2007.
Into the Dark: Exploring the Horror Film (documentary), Blaze Films, 2009.

Television Appearances; Movies:
Anesthesiologist, *Quicksilver Highway* (also known as *The Body Politic* and *Chattery Teeth*), Fox, 1997.

Television Appearances; Miniseries:
Host, *A–Z of Horror* (also known as *Clive Barker's "A–Z of Horror"*), BBC, 1997.
The 100 Scariest Movie Moments, Bravo, 2004.

Television Appearances; Specials:
The Horror Hall of Fame II, syndicated, 1991.
Fear in the Dark, 1991.
The South Bank Show, Bravo, 1995.
Anatomy of Horror, UPN, 1995.
Host, *Lord of Illusions: The Magic of Clive Barker,* Sci–Fi Channel, 1995.
The Making of "Lord of Illusions," Sci–Fi Channel, 1995.
Masters of Fantasy: Clive Barker, Sci–Fi Channel, 1996.
Host, *You Don't Know Jack ... about MonsterFest,* AMC, 2001.

Television Appearances; Episodic:
Late Show with David Letterman (also known as *The Late Show* and *Letterman*), CBS, 1995.
The Big Scary Movie Show, Sci–Fi Channel, 1996.
George Hutchinson, "Don't Dream It's Over," *The Others,* NBC, 2000.
Exposure, NBC, 2000.
Real Time with Bill Maher (also known as *Real Time with Bill Maher: Electile Dysfunction*), HBO, 2003.
The Late Late Show with Craig Ferguson, CBS, 2007.

Television Work:
Producer, *Spirits and Shadows,* Fox, 1997.
Executive producer, *Saint Sinner* (movie; also known as *Clive Barker's "Saint Sinner"*), Sci–Fi Channel, 2002.

Stage Appearances:
Appeared on stage with the Dog Factory.

RECORDINGS

Video Appearances:
The Making of "Psycho," Lions Gate Films Home Entertainment, 1997.

(And executive producer) Narrator, *The World of Gods and Monsters: A Journey with James Whale,* Lions Gate Films Home Entertainment, 1999.

The Road to Dracula, Universal Studios Home Video, 1999.

(And executive producer) *Hellraiser: Resurrection,* Anchor Bay Entertainment, 2000.

(And executive producer) *Hellbound: Hellraiser II—Lost in the Labyrinth,* Anchor Bay Entertainment, 2000.

Voice of Ambrose, *Undying* (video game; also known as *Clive Barker's "Undying"*), Electronic Arts, 2001.

Clive Barker: Raising Hell, Columbia TriStar Home Entertainment, 2004.

Sweets to the Sweet: The Candyman Mythos, Columbia TriStar Home Entertainment, 2004.

Abarat: The Artist's Passion (also known as *Clive Barker's "Abarat": The Artist's Passion*), 2004.

Fangoria: Blood Drive, Fangoria Films/Koch Vision, 2004.

Halloween: 25 Years of Terror, Anchor Bay Entertainment, 2006.

WRITINGS

Screenplays:

Salome (short film), Salvation Films, 1973.

The Forbidden (short film), Salvation Films, 1978.

(With James Caplin) *Underworld* (based on a story by Barker; also known as *Transmutations*), Limehouse Pictures, 1985.

Rawhead Rex (also based on a short story by Barker), Empire, 1987.

Hellraiser (also based on his novella *The Hellbound Heart;* also known as *Clive Barker's "Hellraiser"*), New World, 1987.

Nightbreed (also based on his novella *Cabal;* also known as *Clive Barker's "Nightbreed"*), Twentieth Century–Fox, 1990.

Lord of Illusions (also based on his short story "The Last Illusion"; also known as *Clive Barker's "Lord of Illusions"*), United Artists, 1995.

(With Bernard Rose) *The Thief of Always* (also based on his novel), Universal, 1998.

Tortured Souls: Animae Damnatae (also based on his novella *Tortured Souls;* also known as *Clive Barker's "Tortured Souls: Animae Damnatae"*), 2000, Universal, 2009.

Stage Plays:

Dog, produced by Dog Factory, 1978.

Frankenstein in Love, produced by Dog Factory, c. 1980.

Incarnations: Three Plays by Clive Barker (contains "Colossus," "Frankenstein in Love," and "The History of the Devil"), HarperCollins, 1995.

Forms of Heaven (contains "Crazyface," "Paradise Street," and "Subtle Bodies"), HarperPrism, 1996.

Subtle Bodies, off–Broadway production, 1998.

Author of numerous plays for the Dog Factory, including "The Secret Life of Cartoons;" other plays include "Frankenstein in Love," "The History of the Devil," and "Subtle Bodies."

Television Episodes:

"The Yatterling and Jack," *Tales from the Darkside,* 1987.

Video Games:

Undying (also known as *Clive Barker's "Undying"*), Electronic Arts, 2001.

Demonik, 2006.

Jericho (also known as *Clive Barker's "Jericho"*), Codemasters, 2007.

Short Story Collections:

Clive Barker's Books of Blood, introduction by Ramsey Campbell, three volumes, Sphere, 1984, Berkley Publishing, 1986.

Clive Barker's Books of Blood, Volume Two, Sphere, 1984, Berkley Publishing, 1986.

Clive Barker's Books of Blood, Volume Three, Sphere, 1984, Berkley Publishing, 1986.

Books of Blood, Volumes 1–3, Weidenfeld & Nicolson, 1985, published in one volume, Scream/Press, 1985.

Clive Barker's Books of Blood, Volume Four, Sphere, 1985, published as *The Inhuman Condition: Tales of Terror,* Poseidon, 1986.

Clive Barker's Books of Blood, Volume Five, Sphere, 1985, published as *In the Flesh: Tales of Terror,* Poseidon, 1986.

Clive Barker's Books of Blood, Volume Six, Sphere, 1985.

Books of Blood, Volumes 4–6, Weidenfeld & Nicolson, 1986.

Cabal (includes selections from *Clive Barker's Books of Blood, Volume Six*), Poseidon, 1988.

London, Volume One: Bloodline, Fantaco, 1993.

Books of Blood (six volumes in one), Stealth Press, 2001.

Tapping the Vein, Checker Book, 2002.

(Coeditor) *Clive Barker's Hellraiser: Collected Best II,* Checker Book, 2003.

Work represented in numerous anthologies, including *Cutting Edge* and *I Shudder at Your Touch: Twenty–two Tales of Sex and Horror.*

Novels:

The Damnation Game, Weidenfeld & Nicolson, 1985, Putnam, 1987.

The Hellbound Heart (novella; originally published in *Night Visions 3,* edited by George R. R. Martin, Dark Harvest, 1986, Simon & Schuster, 1988.

Weaveworld, Poseidon, 1987, special self–illustrated edition, Collins, 1987.

The Great and Secret Show: The First Book of the Art, HarperCollins (New York City), 1989.

Imajica, HarperCollins, 1991, published in two volumes as *Imajica I: The Fifth Dominion* and *Imajica II: The Reconstruction,* 1995, published in one volume with new illustrations, 2002.

The Thief of Always: A Fable (self–illustrated juvenile), HarperCollins, 1992.

Everville: The Second Book of the Art (sequel to *The Great and Secret Show*), HarperCollins, 1994.

Sacrament, HarperCollins, 1996.

Galilee, HarperCollins, 1998.

Coldheart Canyon: A Hollywood Ghost Story, Harper-Collins, 2001.

The Abarat Quartet (juvenile), Volume 1: *The First Book of Hours,* Joanna Cotler Books/HarperCollins, 2002.

Abarat: Days of Magic, Nights of War (juvenile), 2004.

Comics:

Saint Sinner, Marvel Comics, 1993–94.

Barker has he has published several book–form comics through Eclipse Books, including *Dread, Life of Death, Rawhead Rex, Revelations, The Son of Celluloid, Tapping the Vein,* and *The Yatterling and Jack;* he has been involved with the publication of numerous other comics, including *Book of the Damned, EctoKid, The Harrowing, Hokum & Hex, Jihad, Pinhead, Razorling,* and *Weaveworld;*

Other:

Theatre Games, Heinemann, 1988.

Clive Barker: Illustrator (illustrations), text by Fred Burke, edited by Steve Niles, Arcane/Ellipse, 1990.

Clive Barker's Nightbreed: The Making of the Film, Fontana, 1990.

Clive Barker's Shadows in Eden (autobiography), edited by Stephen Jones, Underwood/Miller, 1991.

Pandemonium: Further Explorations into the World of Clive Barker, edited by Michael Brown, Eclipse, 1991.

Illustrator II: The Art of Clive Barker, text by Burke, edited by Amacker Bullwinkle, Eclipse, 1993.

Clive Barker's A–Z of Horror (encyclopedia), compiled by Stephen Jones, HarperPrism, 1997.

The Essential Clive Barker, 1999.

Cocreator of the serial novella *Tortured Souls.* Contributor to magazines, including *American Film* and *Omni.*

ADAPTATIONS

The films *Hellbound: Hellraiser II, Hellraiser III: Hell on Earth,* and *Hellraiser VI: Hellseeker* (released by Miramax/Dimension Films in 2002) were all based on characters created by Barker; the film *Hellraiser: Inferno,* released by Destination Films in 2000, was based on Barker's novella *The Hellbound Heart.* The film *Candyman* (also known as *Clive Barker's "Candyman"*) was based on Barker's short story "The Forbidden;" the film *Candyman: Farewell to the Flesh* was also based on a story by Barker; the film *Candyman: Day of the Dead* (also known as *Candyman 3: Day of the Dead*), released by Artisan Entertainment in 1999, was based on characters created by Barker. The 2002 film *Saint Sinner* (also known as *Clive Barker's "Saint Sinner"*) was based on a story by Barker. The 2005 films *Hellraiser: Hellworld* (released by Dimension Home Video) and *Hellraiser: Deader* (released by Miramax and Dimension Films), and the 2006 film *Hellraiser: Prophecy* were all based on characters created by Barker. The film *The Midnight Meat Train* (also known as *Clive Barker's "Midnight Meat Train"*), released by Lions Gate Films in 2008, was based on Barker's short story of the same title. The film *Book of Blood,* released by Essential Entertainment in 2008, was based on Barker's short stories "On Jerusalem Street" and "The Book of Blood." The film *Dread,* developed by Matador Pictures, Midnight Picture Show, Seraphim Films, and Cinema Three for release in 2009, was based on a short story by Barker. The film *Tortured Souls: Animae Damnatae,* released by Universal in 2009, was based on Barker's novella "Tortured Souls." The television movie *Quicksilver Highway,* broadcast by Fox in 1997, was based on his short story "The Body Politic." "Haeckel's Tale" and "Valerie on the Stairs," both 2006 episodes of the Showtime series *Masters of Horror,* were based on Barker's short stories. Many of Barker's works have also been adapted as graphic novels.

OTHER SOURCES

Books:

Authors and Artists for Young Adults, Volume 54, Gale, 2004.

Badley, Linda, *Writing Horror and the Body: The Fiction of Stephen King, Clive Barker, and Anne Rice,* Greenwood Press, 1996.

Barbieri, Suzanne J., *Clive Barker: Mythmaker for the Millennium,* British Fantasy Society, 1994.

Barker, Clive, *Clive Barker's Shadows in Eden,* edited by Stephen Jones, Underwood/Miller, 1991.

Barker, Clive, *Pandemonium: Further Explorations into the World of Clive Barker,* edited by Michael Brown, Eclipse, 1991.

Bestsellers 90, Issue 3, Gale, 1990.

Contemporary Authors, New Revision Series, Volume 133, Gale, 2005.

Contemporary Literary Criticism, Volume 52, Gale, 1989.

Contemporary Popular Writers, St. James Press, 1997.

Hoppenstand, Gary, *Clive Barker's Short Stories: Imagination As Metaphor in the Books of Blood and Other Works,* McFarland and Co., 1994.

Newsmakers, Issue 3, Gale, 2003.
The St. James Encyclopedia of Popular Culture, St. James Press, 2000.
The St. James Guide to Horror, Ghost, and Gothic Writers, St. James Press, 1998.
Winter, Douglas E., *The Dark Fantastic* (biography), 2001.

Periodicals:

Advocate, June 23, 1998, p. 99; January 18, 2000, pp. 105–107; December 4, 2001, pp. 69–70.
Wicked, spring, 2000, pp. 22–26.

Electronic:

Clive Barker Official Site, http://www.clivebarker.com, January 6, 2009.

BARRETT, Chris 1982–

PERSONAL

Born July 24, 1982, in Bryn Mawr, PA. *Education:* Attended Pepperdine University.

Career: Producer, director, and cinematographer. Powerhouse Pictures Entertainment, partner; creator and director of digital short film clips and other film segments that have aired on various television programs, including *Art Fennel Reports, Extra, i–Caught,* and *The Rachel Maddow Show,* as well as the YouTube internet site. Lootz.com (internet marketing company), cofounder and partner, 2003. Known as the first corporate–sponsored college student in America, 2001. Philadelphia Film Festival, member of jury, 2006–08. National Children's Leukemia Foundation, fund–raiser for Teens4aCure.

Awards, Honors: Audience Award, best documentary, Philadelphia Film Festival, 2004, for *The Corporation.*

CREDITS

Film Appearances:

Himself, *Dogma,* 1999.
Hotel guest, *Godless* (short film), 714pictures, 2005.

Documentary Film Appearances:

The Corporation, Zeitgeist Films, 2003.
This Land Is Your Land, Hard Working Movies, 2004.
Maxed Out: Hard Times, Easy Credit, and the Era of Predatory Lenders (also known as *Maxed Out: Our Credit*), Truly Indie/Red Envelope Entertainment, 2006.

Film Associate Producer:

L.A. D.J., Enterprise Entertainment, 2004.
In Justice, 2004.
Fishing for Trauster (short film), 2004.
A Walk in the Park (short film), W47 Films, 2007.

Film Work; Other:

Coproducer, *How to Be: Emo* (short film), Something Directory, 2005.
Producer and director, *After School,* Powerhouse Pictures, 2009.

Television Work; Specials:

Associate producer, *Peoples,* Starz!, 2006.
(And director and cinematographer) *Sundance 2006,* Current TV, 2006.

Television Appearances; Episodic:

Studio Y, 2000.
News 12 New Jersey (also known as *News 12*), 2001.
The Screen Savers, Tech TV, 2001.
MSNBC Live (also known as *MSNBC Dayside* and *MSNBC Right Now*), MSNBC, 2001.
Headline News, Cable News Network, 2001.
I've Got a Secret, Oxygen Network, 2001.
Today (also known as *NBC News Today* and *The Today Show*), NBC, 2001.
Fox and Friends (also known as *Fox and Friends First* and *Fox and Friends Weekend*), Fox News Channel, 2001.
The Early Show, CBS, 2001.
The John Walsh Show, syndicated, 2003.
Inside Edition, syndicated, 2004.
(In archive footage) *Celebrities Uncensored,* E! Entertainment Television, 2004.
Fox News Live, Fox News Channel, 2005.

Television Appearances; Awards Presentations:

The Teen Choice Awards 2001, Fox, 2001.
2005 MTV Movie Awards, MTV, 2005.

Television Appearances; Specials:

MTV Presents: Xbox, the Next Generation Revealed, MTV, 2005.
Sundance 2006, Current TV, 2006.

RECORDINGS

Videos:

Appeared in the music videos "Crawling in the Dark" by Hoobastank, and "Freakin' It" by Will Smith.

WRITINGS

Books:

(With Efren Ramirez) *Direct Your Own Life: How to Be a Star in Any Field You Choose,* Kaplan Publishing, 2008.

OTHER SOURCES

Periodicals:

CosmoGirl!, October, 2003, p. 106.

Entrepreneur, April, 2001, p. 42.

Fortune, September 3, 2001, p. 52.

Los Angeles Times, July 9, 2001, p. E1.

Money, October, 2001, p. 196.

New York Times, July 19, 2001, p. B1.

People Weekly, March 19, 2001, p. 119; December 31, 2001, pp. 126–127.

Philadelphia Inquirer, July 2, 2001, p. B1.

Psychology Today, October, 2003, pp. 72–77.

Teen, June, 2001, p. 98.

USA Today, February 17, 2001, p. D1.

Electronic:

Chris & Luke Web site, http://www.chrisandluke.com, December 9, 2008.

BARROWMAN, John 1967–

PERSONAL

Born March 11, 1967, in Glasgow, Scotland; naturalized U.S. citizen; father, in heavy equipment sales; mother, a singer and record store clerk. *Education:* Attended DePaul University and U.S. International University program in England; also attended University of Iowa.

Addresses: *Agent*—Gavin Barker, Gavin Barker Associates, 2D Wimpole St., London W1G 0EB, England.

Career: Actor and vocalist. Concert performer with Boston Pops, Indianapolis Symphony, London Symphony, and National Symphony orchestras; cabaret performer, beginning at Arci's Place, New York City, 2002, and including appearances throughout Europe; performed at Opryland USA and at Music under the Stars, Faenol Festival, 2008. Duke of Edinburgh Awards Scheme, member of youth support organization; presenter of Dreamers' Workshops for high school students.

Awards, Honors: Laurence Olivier Award nomination, best actor in a musical, Society of West End Theatre, 1998, for *The Fix;* Garland Award, *Backstage West,* c. 1998, for *Putting It Together;* Cymru Award, best Welsh actor, Welsh Division of British Academy of Film and Television Arts, 2007, for "Everything Changes," *Torchwood;* gold record certification, Recording Industry Association of America, 2008, for the album *Another Side.*

CREDITS

Stage Appearances; Musicals:

Billy Crocker, *Anything Goes,* Prince Edward Theatre, London, 1989.

Title role, *Matador,* Queen's Theatre, London, 1991.

Raoul, *Phantom of the Opera,* Her Majesty's Theatre, London, c. 1992.

Claude, *Hair,* Old Vic Theatre, London, 1993.

Chris, *Miss Saigon,* Theatre Royal, Drury Lane Theatre, London, 1993.

Joe Gillis, *Sunset Boulevard,* Adelphi Theatre, London, 1994–95, then (Broadway debut) Minskoff Theatre, c. 1994–1997.

Cal Chandler, *The Fix,* Donmar Warehouse Theatre, London, 1997.

Barry, *Putting It Together* (revue), Mark Taper Forum, Los Angeles, 1998, then Ethel Barrymore Theatre, New York City, 1999–2000.

Beast, *Beauty and the Beast* (musical), Dominion Theatre, London, 1999.

Reflections from Broadway (cabaret performance), Arci's Place, New York City, 2002.

Bobby, *Company,* Sondheim Festival, Eisenhower Theatre, John F. Kennedy Center for the Performing Arts, Washington, DC, 2002.

Billy Crocker, *Anything Goes,* National Theatre, London, 2002.

Appeared as Che, *Evita,* Spektrum Arena Theatre, Oslo, Norway; appeared in the concert performances *Call Me Madam* and *The Magic of the Musicals,* Royal Concert Hall, Glasgow, Scotland.

Stage Appearances; Other:

Wyndham Brandon, *Rope,* Chichester Festival, Minerva Theatre, Chichester, England, 1993.

Prince Charming, *Cinderella* (pantomime), New Wimbledon Theatre, London, c. 2005.

Lieutenant Jack Ross, *A Few Good Men,* Theatre Royal Haymarket, London, 2005.

Jack, *Jack and the Beanstalk* (pantomime), New Theatre Cardiff, Cardiff, Wales, 2006.

Title role, *Aladdin* (pantomime), Hippodrome Theatre, Birmingham, England, 2006–2007.

Title role, *Robin Hood: The Pantomime Adventure,* Hippodrome Theatre, 2008–2009.

Major Tours:

Toured as Alex, *Aspects of Love,* Irish cities; also toured U.S. cities in the cabaret show *Reflections from Broadway.*

Television Appearances; Series:

Presenter of "Electric Circus," *Live and Kicking,* BBC, 1993–94.

Host, *The Movie Game,* BBC, 1994–95.

Peter Fairchild, *Central Park West* (also known as *C.P. W.*), CBS, 1995–96.
Presenter, *5's Company*, Channel 5, 1997.
Peter Williams, *Titans*, NBC, 2000–2001.
Captain Jack Harkness, *Doctor Who*, Sci–Fi Channel, 2005–2008.
Himself, *Doctor Who Confidential* (also known as *Doctor Who Confidential: Cut Down*), BBC, several appearances, beginning 2005.
Captain Jack Harkness, *Torchwood*, BBC America, 2006—.
Himself, *Torchwood Declassified*, BBC3, multiple appearances, beginning 2006.
Judge, *How Do You Solve a Problem like Maria?*, BBC, 2006.
Dancing on Ice, ITV, 2006.
Dancing on Ice: Defrosted, ITV, 2006.
Judge, *Any Dream Will Do*, BBC1, 2007.
Judge, *I'd Do Anything*, BBC1, 2008.
Host, *The Kids Are All Right*, BBC1, 2008.
Judge, *How Do You Solve a Problem Like Maria?*, CBC, 2008.

Television Appearances; Specials:
Ira Gershwin: A Centenary Celebration—Who Could Ask for Anything More?, Arts and Entertainment, 1997.
"Hey, Mr. Producer" (also known as "Hey, Mr. Producer! The Musical World of Cameron Mackintosh"), *Great Performances*, PBS, 1998.
The younger man, *Putting It Together*, Broadway Television Network, 2000.
The 100 Greatest Musicals, Channel 4, 2003.
Host, *Keys to the Castle*, Home and Garden Television, 2006.
Presenter, *The Royal Variety Performance 2006*, BBC, 2006.
The Big Finish, BBC, 2006, 2007.
Audience member, *An Audience with Joan Rivers*, ITV, 2006.
The 50 Greatest Television Dramas (also known as *The 50 Greatest TV Dramas*), Channel 4, 2007.
Eurovision: Making Your Mind Up, BBC, 2007.
Live Earth (also known as *Live Earth Alert, Live Earth 7.7.07, Live Earth: The Concerts for a Climate in Crisis*, and *SOS: The Movement for a Climate in Crisis*), NBC, 2007.
When Joseph Met Maria, BBC, 2007.
The Winner's Story, BBC, 2007.
(In archive footage) *Buzzcocks … Imagine a Mildly Amusing Panel Show*, BBC, 2007.

Television Appearances; Pilots:
Peter Williams, *Titans*, NBC, 2000.

Television Appearances; Episodic:
Surprise Surprise!, ITV, 1994.
To Me, to You!, BBC, 1996.

Children in Need, BBC, 2003, 2007.
The Sound of Musicals, BBC, 2006.
Never Mind the Buzzcocks, BBC, 2006.
8 Out of 10 Cats, Channel 4, 2006.
The Big Questions, BBC, 2007.
"John Barrowman," *A Taste of My Life*, BBC, 2007.
"'Doctor Who' Special," *The Weakest Link* (also known as *Weakest Link Champions' League*), BBC, 2007.
Would I Lie to You?, syndicated, 2007.
Have I Been Here Before?, ITV, 2007.
(In archive footage) *Screenwipe*, BBC4, 2007.
Performer, "Show 6 Results," *Strictly Come Dancing*, BBC, 2007.
"Round Five," *Strictly Come Dancing*, BBC, 2008.
(Uncredited) Audience member, "Round Ten," *Strictly Come Dancing*, BBC, 2008.
"Round Ten Results," *Strictly Come Dancing*, BBC, 2008.
Simon, *Hotel Babylon*, BBC, 2008.
"John Barrowman," *The Making of Me*, BBC, 2008.
Celebrity Ding Dong (also known as *Alan Carr's "Celebrity Ding Dong"*), Channel 4, 2008.

Television Guest Appearances; Episodic:
"John Barrowman," *Lauren Hutton and …*, 1996.
Breakfast, BBC, 2005, 2008.
Loose Women, ITV, multiple appearances, beginning 2005.
GMTV, ITV, 2006.
Richard & Judy, Channel 4, 2006.
The Wright Stuff, Channel 5, 2006.
Something for the Weekend, Channel 4, 2006.
The Heaven and Earth Show (also known as *The Heaven and Earth Show with Gloria Hunniford*), BBC, 2006.
This Morning (also known as *This Morning with Richard and Judy*), ITV, multiple appearances, beginning 2006.
Friday Night with Jonathan Ross, BBC, 2006, 2007, 2008.
The Charlotte Church Show, Channel 4, 2007.
Totally Doctor Who, BBC Wales, 2007.
Guest host, *The Friday Night Project* (also known as *The Sunday Night Project*), Channel 4, 2007.
Happy Hour (also known as *Al Murray's Happy Hour*), ITV, 2007, 2008.
Ready, Steady, Cook, BBC, 2008.
The Xtra Factor, ITV2, 2008.
The Alan Titchmarsh Show, ITV, 2008.
The Paul O'Grady Show (also known as *The New Paul O'Grady Show*), ITV, 2008.

Film Appearances:
Broadway: The Golden Age, by the Legends Who Were There (documentary), Second Act Productions, 2002.
Ben Carpenter, *Shark Attack 3: Megalodon*, Nu Image, 2002.

(Uncredited) Reporter Time Stevens, *Method* (also known as *Dead Even*), DEJ Productions, 2004.
Jack, *De–Lovely,* Metro–Goldwyn–Mayer, 2004.
Lead tenor, *The Producers,* Universal, 2005.
Broadway: The Next Generation (documentary), Second Act Productions, 2009.

Radio Appearances; Specials:
"A Musical Christmas," *Friday Night Is Music Night,* BBC2, 2006.
"Jerry Herman Tribute Concert," *Friday Night Is Music Night,* BBC2, 2007.

Presenter of "Elaine Paige" for *On Sunday,* BBC2, and *The Breakfast Show,* Capital Radio; performed for concert broadcasts of *Call Me Madam; The Magic of Musicals,* BBC, and *National Music Day.*

RECORDINGS

Albums:
Member of ensemble, *Hair: The Musical* (original London cast recording), EMI, 1993.
Member of ensemble, *Godspell* (London studio cast recording), TER, 1993.
Danny Zuko, *Songs from Grease* (London studio recording), TER, 1994.
Member of ensemble, *The Fix* (original London cast recording), 1997.
John Barrowman: Aspects of Lloyd Webber, Jay, 1997.
Reflections from Broadway (solo album), Jay, 2000.
John Barrowman Swings Cole Porter, 2004.
Another Side, 2008.
Music, Music, Music, Sony BMG, 2008.

Contributor to other albums, including *Anything Goes* (original cast recording); *Matador* (studio recording), Sony; *The Music of Andrew Lloyd Webber,* TER; *Phantom of the Opera and Other Broadway Hits,* TER; *Red Red Rose;* and *Songs from Webber's "The Phantom of the Opera, with Bonus Tracks from Sunset Boulevard."* Also recorded the singles "I Was Born to Be Me"/"I'll Dress You in Mourning," 1991; and "What about Us?," 2008.

WRITINGS

Books:
(With sister, Carole E. Barrowman) *Anything Goes* (memoir), Michael O'Mara Books, 2008.

OTHER SOURCES

Books:
Barrowman, John, and Carole E. Barrowman, *Anything Goes,* Michael O'Mara Books, 2008.

Periodicals:
US, October, 1995; April, 1996.
Vanity Fair, November, 1995.

Electronic:
John Barrowman Official Site, http://www.johnbarrowman.com, January 6, 2009.
Playbill Online, http://www.playbill.com, March 12, 1997.

BATES, Jeanne 1918–2007
(Jane Bates, Jeanne R. Bates)

PERSONAL

Born May 21, 1918, in Berkeley, CA; died of breast cancer, November 28, 2007, in Woodland Hills, CA. Actress. Bates began her acting career while still a student at San Mateo Junior College, appearing on radio soap operas in San Francisco. Bates had the lead role, and provided the signature scream, on the radio mystery series *Whodunit.* In 1943 Bates married *Whodunit's* writer Lew X. Landworth, and the pair moved to Hollywood. Bates's film debut also came in 1943, in the Boston Blackie film *The Chance of a Lifetime.* Bates landed the role of Bela Lugosi's first vampire victim in *Return of the Vampire* and had a bit part in the film version of *Death of a Salesman* in 1945. Bates found steady work in television beginning in the 1950s with guest appearances on numerous shows, including *Perry Mason, Lassie, Gunsmoke, The Twilight Zone, The Rockford Files, Wonder Woman, Three's Company, Dallas,* and *That '70s Show.* Bates portrayed Nurse Wills on the television show *Ben Casey* from 1961 to 1966. Bates was also the mother, Mrs. X, in the 1977 David Lynch cult classic *Eraserhead.* Bates passed away at the Motion Picture and Television Country House and Hospital.

PERIODICALS

Los Angeles Times, December 1, 2007.

BEGGS, Kevin L. 1966(?)–
(Kevin Beggs)

PERSONAL

Born c. 1966. *Education:* University of California Santa Cruz, undergraduate degree, politics and theater arts, 1989.

Addresses: *Office*—Lionsgate, 2700 Colorado Ave., Suite 200, Santa Monica, CA 90404.

Career: Producer, executive consultant, production executive, and writer. Lionsgate, Santa Monica, CA, president (television programming and production), 2002—. Hollywood Radio and TV Society, Sherman Oaks, CA, president; National Association of Television Program Executives, cochairman, Los Angeles, CA.

CREDITS

Film Work:
Coproducer, *Thunder in Paradise,* Trimark Pictures, 1993.
Coproducer, *Baywatch: Forbidden Paradise,* Live Home Video, 1995.
Producer, *Baywatch: White Thunder at Glacier Bay,* Trimark Home Video, 1998.
Executive producer, *The Void,* 2001.
(As Kevin Beggs) Executive producer, *Grizzly Man,* Lionsgate, 2005.
(As Kevin Beggs) Executive producer, *Leonard Cohen: I'm Your Man,* Lionsgate, 2005.
(As Kevin Beggs) Executive producer, *The U.S. vs. John Lennon,* Lionsgate, 2006.

Television Work; Series:
Associate to executive producers, *Baywatch,* syndicated, 1992–93.
Producer, *Thunder in Paradise,* syndicated, 1994.
Coproducer, *Baywatch,* syndicated, 1994–96.
Coproducer, *Baywatch Nights* (also known as *Detectives on the Beach*), syndicated, 1995.
Producer, *Baywatch Hawaii,* syndicated, 1999–99.
Executive consultant, *Sheena,* syndicated, 2000.
Executive producer, *Mysterious Ways,* NBC, 2000.
Production executive, *Missing,* Lifetime, 2003–2004.
Executive, *Wildfire,* ABC Family, 2004–2007.
Production executive, *Weeds,* Showtime, 2005–2006.
Production executive, *The Dead Zone,* USA Network, 2005–2006.
Production executive, *Lovespring International,* Lifetime, 2005–2006.
Executive, *I Pity the Fool,* TV Land, 2006.
Studio executive, *Mad Men,* AMC, 2006—.
Executive, *Scream Queens,* VH1, 2008.
Studio executive, *Crash,* Starz, 2008—.

Also worked as legal affairs, *Baywatch,* syndicated.

Television Work; Miniseries:
Production executive, *5ive Days to Midnight,* Sci-Fi Channel, 2004.
Studio executive, *The Lost Room,* Sky One, 2006.

Television Work; Movies:
(As Kevin Beggs) Producer, *Steel Chariots,* Fox, 1997.
Producer, *Assault on Devil's Island* (also known as *Shadow Warriors*), TNT, 1997.
(As Kevin Beggs) Executive consultant, *Shadow Warriors II: Hunt for the Death Merchant* (also known as *Shadow Warriors II* and *Assault on Death Mountain*), TNT, 1999.
Story consultant and executive producer, *Cabin Pressure,* ION, 2001.
Executive, *Infidelity,* Lifetime, 2004.
Production executive, *Brave New Girl,* ABC Family, 2004.
Executive, *Three Wise Guys,* USA Network, 2005.

Television Work; Specials:
Executive, *Dear Santa,* Fox, 2005.

Television Work; Episodic:
(As Kevin Beggs) Production supervisor, "River of No Return: Part 1," *Baywatch,* syndicated, 1992.

Television Appearances; Episodic:
(As Kevin Beggs) Sheriff number six, "X–Cops," *The X–Files,* Fox, 2000.

WRITINGS

Television Movie Stories:
(As Kevin Beggs) *Cabin Pressure* (also known as *Hijack'd*), 2001.

Television Episodes:
"Baywatch at Sea World," *Baywatch,* syndicated, 1992.
Sheena, syndicated, 2000.

OTHER SOURCES

Periodicals:
Variety, October 2, 2004, p. 25; September 29, 2008, p. 16.

BELL, Jim 1967–

PERSONAL

Born July 20, 1967, in Branford, CT; married, wife's name Angelique; children: four sons. *Education:* Harvard University, B.A., 1989.

Addresses: *Office*—c/o NBC News, 30 Rockefeller Plaza, New York, NY 10112.

Career: Broadcast journalist and producer. NBC News, New York City, production associate with Olympic Profiles Unit and producer for network affiliates in host cities, 1991–92, production associate for NBC Olympics, 1992–94, associate director and feature producer, 1994–96, producer, 1996–99, senior coordinating producer (including segments of the 2001 Wimbledon tennis championship matches), 1999–2004, executive producer, 2005—. WNBC–TV, New York City, creator and producer of *Gameday NY* and *Mike'd Up*. Worked as a football coach and English teacher in Barcelona, Spain, c. 1989.

Awards, Honors: Daytime Emmy Award (with others), excellence in morning programming, 2007, for *Today.*

CREDITS

Television Executive Producer; Series:
Today (also known as *NBC News Today* and *The Today Show*), NBC, 2005–2007.
Weekend Today, NBC, 2006–2007.

Television Work Miniseries:
Senior producer and editor, *2002 Olympic Winter Games,* NBC, 2002.
Producer, *Beijing 2008: Games of the XXIX Olympiad,* NBC, 2008.

OTHER SOURCES

Periodicals:
Broadcasting & Cable, November 6, 2006, p. 29.
Crain's New York Business, May 30, 2005, p. 37.
USA Today, April 21, 2005, p. 6D.

BERMAN, David

PERSONAL

Brother of Josh Berman (a producer and writer).

Addresses: *Agent*—Michael Wilson, Agency for the Performing Arts, 405 South Beverly Dr., Beverly Hills, CA 90212.

Career: Actor. CBS–TV, head researcher for the series *CSI: Crime Scene Investigation,* beginning 2000.

CREDITS

Television Appearances; Series:
David Phillips, *CSI: Crime Scene Investigation* (also known as *C.S.I., CSI: Las Vegas,* and *Les experts*), CBS, 2000–2008.
Agent Edward Dockery, *Vanished,* Fox, 2006.

Television Appearances; Pilots:
Agent Edward Dockery, *Vanished,* Fox, 2006.

Television Appearances; Episodic:
Computer technician, "Besieged," *Profiler,* NBC, 2000.
Brian Davis, "Chapter Ten 'Six Months Ago'," *Heroes,* NBC, 2006.

Film Appearances:
Herb Mulligan, *Outside Sales,* Push, 2006.

Internet Appearances; Series:
Lead scientist, *Gemini Division,* NBC.com, 2008.

BERRY, Halle 1968–

PERSONAL

Full name, Halle Maria Berry; born August 14, 1968, in Cleveland, OH; daughter of Jerome Jesse (a hospital attendant) and Judith (a psychiatric nurse; maiden name, Hawkins) Berry; married David Christopher Justice (a professional baseball player), December 31, 1992 (divorced, June 24, 1997); married Eric Benet (a singer), January 19, 2001 (divorced, January 3, 2005); children: (second marriage) India (stepdaughter); (with Gabriel Aubry, a model) Nahla Ariela. *Education:* Attended Cuyahoga Community College, c. 1986.

Addresses: *Agent*—International Creative Management, 10250 Constellation Way, 9th Floor, Los Angeles, CA 90067. *Manager*—Vincent Cirrincione and Associates, 1516 North Fairfax Ave., Los Angeles, CA 90046.

Career: Actress. Appeared in one of Bob Hope's United Services Organization tours; worked as a model; appeared in television commercials for M&Ms candy, Revlon cosmetics, 2000–08, Pepsi Twist soft drinks, and Martin Luther King Memorial Project, 2003; appeared in print ads for Revlon cosmetics, 2000–08, Army Air Force Exchange Service, 2004, and Versace clothing, 2006. Juvenile Diabetes Association, volunteer; Diabetes Award, ambassador, c. 2004.

Awards, Honors: Winner of Miss Teen Ohio beauty pageant; named Miss Teen All–American, 1985; first runner–up for Miss USA pageant, 1986; winner of Miss USA pageant, 1987; Image Award nomination, outstanding lead actress in a motion picture, National Association for the Advancement of Colored People (NAACP), 1992, and MTV Movie Award nominations, best breakthrough performance and most desirable female, 1993, all for *Boomerang;* MTV Movie Award nomination, most desirable female, 1995, for *The Flintstones;* Image Award nomination, outstanding actress in a television movie, 1996, for *Solomon and Sheba;* Image Award nomination, outstanding lead actress in a motion picture, 1996, for *Losing Isaiah;* Blockbuster Entertainment Award, favorite actress in an adventure or drama, 1997, for *Executive Decision;* Career Achievement Award, Acapulco Black Film Festival, 1997; Black Film Award nomination, best actress, Acapulco Black Film Festival, 1998, for *B.A.P.S.;* Distinguished Achievement Award, Miss USA Pageant, 1998; selected one of the "50 most beautiful people," *People Weekly,* 1998; Image Award nominations, outstanding lead actress in a motion picture, 1999, for *Bulworth,* and outstanding lead actress in a television movie, miniseries, or drama special, 1999, for *The Wedding;* Emmy Award, Golden Globe Award, Screen Actors Guild Award, Image Award, and Golden Satellite Award nomination, all best actress in a television miniseries, motion picture, or dramatic special, and Emmy Award nomination (with others), outstanding made–for–television movie, all 2000, for *Introducing Dorothy Dandridge;* Special Image Award, entertainer of the year, NAACP, 2000; MTV Movie Award nomination (with Hugh Jackman, James Marsden, and Anna Paquin), best on–screen team, 2001, for *X-Men;* Academy Award, National Board of Review Award, Screen Actors Guild Award, Silver Berlin Bear, Berlin International Film Festival, Golden Globe Award nomination, Chicago Film Critics Association Award nomination, and Golden Satellite Award nomination, International Press Academy, all best actress in a motion picture drama, and Film Award nomination, female actor of the year—movies, American Film Institute, 2002, Film Award nomination, best performance by an actress in a leading role, British Academy of Film and Television Arts, ALFS Award nomination, actress of the year, London Critics Circle Film Awards, 2003, all for *Monster's Ball;* Image Award, outstanding actress in a motion picture, 2002, for *Swordfish;* BET Award, best actress, Black Entertainment Television, 2002, 2004; Teen Choice Award nomination, choice movie actress—drama/action adventure, 2003, for *X2* and *Die Another Day;* Saturn Award, best supporting actress, Academy of Science Fiction, Fantasy and Horror Films, Black Reel Award nomination, theatrical—best supporting actress, Empire Award nomination, best actress, Image Award, outstanding supporting actress in a motion picture, Blimp Award nominations, favorite female butt kicker and favorite female actress, Kids' Choice Awards, MTV Movie Award nomination, best female performance, 2003, all for *Die Another Day;* ShoWest Award,

female star of the year, 2004; Blimp Award nomination, favorite movie actress, Kids' Choice Awards, 2004, for *X2* and *Gothika;* Black Reel Award nomination, film—best actress, Image Award nomination, outstanding actress in a motion picture, MTV Movie Award nomination, best female performance, Teen Choice Award, choice movie actress—drama/action adventure, 2004, all for *Gothika;* Blimp Award nomination, favorite movie actress, Kids' Choice Awards, 2005, for *Catwoman;* People's Choice Award nomination, favorite female action movie star, 2005, 2007, 2008; Black Movie Award (with others), outstanding television movie, Emmy Award nomination (with others), outstanding made for television movie, 2005, Christopher Award (with others), television and cable, Independent Spirit Award nomination (with others), best first feature, Independent Features Project West, Television Producer of the year Award nomination in Longform (with others), Producers Guild of America, 2006, all for *Lackawanna Blues;* Black Movie Award nomination, outstanding performance by an actress in a leading role, Blimp Award nomination, favorite movie actress, Kids' Choice Awards, Teen Choice Award nomination, movies—choice actress: drama/action adventure, 2006, all for *X-Men: The Last Stand;* Black Reel Award nomination, best actress—television, Emmy Award nomination, outstanding lead actress in a miniseries or a movie, 2005, Golden Globe Award nomination, best performance by an actress in a miniseries or a motion picture made for television, Image Award nomination, outstanding actress in a television movie, miniseries, or dramatic special, 2006, all for *Their Eyes Were Watching God;* Woman of the Year, Hasty Pudding Theatricals, 2006; People's Choice Award, favorite female action star, 2007; Star on the Walk of Fame—motion picture, 2007; Image Award nomination, outstanding actress in a motion picture, 2008, for *Things We Lost in the Fire.*

CREDITS

Film Appearances:
Vivian, *Jungle Fever,* Universal, 1991.
Cory, *The Last Boy Scout,* Warner Bros., 1991.
Natalie, *Strictly Business,* Warner Bros., 1991.
Angela Lewis, *Boomerang,* Paramount, 1992.
Autumn Haley, *The Program,* Buena Vista, 1993.
Kathleen Mercer, *Father Hood* (also known as *Desperado, Honor Among Thieves,* and *Mike Hardy*), Buena Vista, 1993.
Herself, *CB4,* Universal, 1993.
Miss Rosetta Stone, *The Flintstones,* Universal, 1994.
Khaila Richards, *Losing Isaiah,* Paramount, 1995.
Miss Sandra Beecher, *Race the Sun,* TriStar, 1996.
Jean, *Executive Decision* (also known as *Critical Decision*), Warner Bros., 1996.
Josie Potenza, *The Rich Man's Wife,* Buena Vista, 1996.
Herself, *Girl 6,* Twentieth Century–Fox, 1996.

Nisi, *B.A.P.S.* (also known as *B*A*P*S*), New Line Cinema, 1997.

Nina, *Bulworth,* Twentieth Century–Fox, 1998.

Zola Taylor, *Why Do Fools Fall in Love?,* Warner Bros., 1998.

Ringside, 1999.

Welcome to Hollywood, Phaedra Cinema, 2000.

Storm/Ororo Munroe, *X–Men* (also known as *X–Men 1.5*), Twentieth Century–Fox, 2000.

Ginger, *Swordfish,* Warner Bros., 2001.

Leticia Musgrove, *Monster's Ball* (also known as *Le bal du monstre*), Lions Gate Films, 2001.

Jinx, *Die Another Day* (also known as *D.A.D.*), Metro–Goldwyn–Mayer, 2002.

Herself, *"Die Another Day": From Script to Screen,* Sony Pictures Home Entertainment, 2002.

Herself, *Shaken and Stirred on Ice* (documentary short), Metro–Goldwyn–Mayer/United Artists Home Entertainment, 2002.

Storm/Ororo Munroe, *X2* (also known as *X–Men 2, X–2, X–Men 2: X–Men United,* and *X2: X–Men United*), Twentieth Century–Fox, 2003.

Miranda Grey, *Gothika,* Warner Bros., 2003.

Herself, *X–Factor: The Look of "X–Men"* (documentary short), Twentieth Century Fox Home Entertainment, 2003.

Herself, *"X–Men" Production Scrapbook* (documentary), Twentieth Century Fox Home Entertainment, 2003.

Herself, *The Uncanny Suspects* (documentary short), Twentieth Century Fox Home Entertainment), 2003.

Herself, *Inside "Die Another Day"* (documentary short), Metro–Goldwwyn–Mayer Home Entertainment, 2003.

Herself, *Spike Lee's "25th Hour": The Evolution of an American Filmmaker* (documentary short), Touchstone Home Video, 2003.

Patience Phillips/Catwoman, *Catwoman,* Warner Bros., 2004.

(Uncredited) Herself, *The Making of "Catwoman"* (documentary short), 2004.

Voice of Cappy, *Robots* (animated; also known as *Robots: The IMAX Experience*), Twentieth Century–Fox, 2005.

Herself, *The Many Faces of "Catwoman"* (documentary short), Warner Home Video, 2005.

Herself, *The Making of "Robots"* (documentary short), Twentieth Century–Fox, 2005.

Ororo Munroe/Storm, *X–Men: The Last Stand* (also known as *X–Men 3* and *X3*), Twentieth Century–Fox, 2006.

Rowena Price, *Perfect Stranger,* Sony, 2007.

Herself, *Manufacturing Dissent,* Liberation Entertainment, 2007.

Audrey Blake, *Things We Lost in the Fire,* Paramount, 2007.

Herself, *A Discussion About "Things We Lost in the Fire"* (documentary short), DreamWorks Home Entertainment, 2008.

Frankie/Alice, *Frankie and Alice,* 2009.

Film Producer:
Tulia, 2008.
Frankie and Alice, 2009.

Television Appearances; Series:
Emily Franklin, *Living Dolls* (also known as *Planted*), ABC, 1989.
Debbie Porter, *Knots Landing,* CBS, 1991–92.

Television Appearances; Miniseries:
Title role, *Queen* (also known as *Alex Haley's "Queen"*), CBS, 1992.
Shelby Coles, *The Wedding* (also known as *Oprah Winfrey Presents: "The Wedding"*), ABC, 1998.

Television Appearances; Movies:
Nikaule (the Queen of Sheba), *Solomon & Sheba,* Showtime, 1995.
Title role, *Introducing Dorothy Dandridge* (also known as *Face of an Angel*), HBO, 1999.
Janie Starks, *Their Eyes Were Watching God* (also known as *Oprah Winfrey Presents "Their Eyes Were Watching God"*), ABC, 2005.

Television Appearances; Specials:
MTV Video Music Awards, MTV, 1992.
Presenter, *The 25th NAACP Image Awards,* NBC, 1993.
Presenter, *The Essence Awards,* CBS, 1993.
Presenter, *The 19th Annual People's Choice Awards,* CBS, 1993.
A Century of Women (also known as *A Family of Women*), TBS, 1994.
Hollywood Women, ITV, 1994.
Presenter, *The 1st Screen Actors Guild Awards,* NBC, 1995.
The 21st Annual People's Choice Awards, CBS, 1995.
The 27th Annual NAACP Image Awards, Fox, 1996.
Presenter, *The Blockbuster Entertainment Awards,* UPN, 1996.
Cohost, *The 1996 Essence Awards,* Fox, 1996.
Celebrate the Dream: 50 Years of "Ebony," ABC, 1996.
Presenter, *The Blockbuster Entertainment Awards,* UPN, 1997.
Presenter, *The 54th Annual Golden Globe Awards,* NBC, 1997.
Presenter, *The 28th Annual NAACP Image Awards,* Fox, 1997.
Host, *The 1997 World Music Awards,* ABC, 1997.
Host, *The 10th Anniversary Essence Awards* (also known as *The 10th Essence Awards*), Fox, 1997.
Voices of Hope ... Finding the Cures for Breast and Ovarian Cancer, Lifetime, 1997.
Christmas Miracles, ABC, 1997.
Presenter, *The 50th Emmy Awards,* NBC, 1998.
Quincy Jones—The First 50 Years (also known as *Quincy Jones ... A 50-Year Celebration*), ABC, 1998.

Hollywood Glamour Girls, E! Entertainment Television, 1998.

Women of the Net, E! Entertainment Television, 1998.

The 47th Miss USA Pageant, CBS, 1998.

AFI's 100 Years ... 100 Movies, CBS, 1998.

The Blockbuster Entertainment Awards, UPN, 1998.

Intimate Portrait: Halle Berry, Lifetime, 1998.

The 51st Annual Primetime Emmy Awards, Fox, 1999.

The 30th NAACP Image Awards, Fox, 1999.

The Kennedy Center Honors: A Celebration of the Performing Arts, CBS, 1999.

Dorothy Dandridge: Little Girl Lost, Arts and Entertainment, 1999.

"X–Men": Mutant Watch, Fox, 2000.

Presenter, *The VH1/Vogue Fashion Awards,* VH1, 2000.

Presenter, *The 6th Annual Screen Actors Guild Awards,* TNT, 2000.

The 31st NAACP Image Awards, Fox, 2000.

Presenter, *2000 MTV Movie Awards,* MTV, 2000.

The 52nd Annual Primetime Emmy Awards, ABC, 2000.

Presenter, *Lifetime Presents Disney's American Teacher Awards,* Lifetime, 2000.

The 6th Annual Soul Train Lady of Soul Awards, syndicated, 2000.

Great Streets: The Champs Elysees with Halle Barry, PBS, 2001.

The 32nd Annual NAACP Image Awards, Fox, 2001.

Presenter, *The 73rd Annual Academy Awards,* ABC, 2001.

The Concert for New York City, VH1, 2001.

America: A Tribute to Heroes, multiple networks, 2001.

The Making of "Swordfish," 2001.

The 2001 MTV Movie Awards, MTV, 2001.

Presenter, *Nickelodeon's 14th Annual Kids' Choice Awards,* Nickelodeon, 2001.

Presenter, *The 7th Screen Actors Guild Awards,* TNT, 2001.

The 59th Annual Golden Globe Awards, NBC, 2002.

The Orange British Academy Awards, E! Entertainment Television, 2002.

The 74th Annual Academy Awards, ABC, 2002.

The 2002 ABC World Stunt Awards, ABC, 2002.

Essence Awards, Fox, 2002.

The 54th Annual Primetime Emmy Awards, NBC, 2002.

Bond Girls Are Forever, AMC, 2002.

The Bond Girls: The E! True Hollywood Story, E! Entertainment Television, 2002.

Premiere Bond: "Die Another Day," ITV, 2002.

Happy Anniversary Mr. Bond, 2002.

James Bond: A BAFTA Tribute, BBC, 2002.

The Barbara Walters Special, ABC, 2002.

Anatomy of a Scene: "Monster's Ball," Sundance Channel, 2002.

AFI Awards 2001, CBS, 2002.

Women on Top: Hollywood and Power, AMC, 2003.

The Stars' First Time ... On "Entertainment Tonight" With Mary Hart, CBS, 2003.

Presenter, *The 60th Annual Golden Globe Awards,* NBC, 2003.

Hollywood Celebrates Denzel Washington: An American Cinematheque Tribute, AMC, 2003.

The 34th NAACP Image Awards, Fox, 2003.

TV Land Awards: A Celebration of Classic TV (also known as *The 1st Annual TV Land Awards*), TV Land, 2003.

Presenter, *The 75th Annual Academy Awards,* ABC, 2003.

Presenter, *The 9th Annual Screen Actors Guild Awards,* TNT, 2003.

Oscar Countdown 2003, ABC, 2003.

John Travolta: The Inside Story, Channel 5, 2004.

Presenter, *The 2004 MTV Movie Awards,* MTV, 2004.

52 Most Irresistible Women, Spike TV, 2004.

Presenter, *The 2004 Teen Choice Awards,* Fox, 2004.

Ultimate Super Heroes, Ultimate Super Villains, Ultimate Super Vixen, Bravo, 2004.

Tsunami Aid: A Concert of Hope, NBC, 2005.

Presenter, *The 62nd Annual Golden Globe Awards,* NBC, 2005.

Presenter, *The 77th Annual Academy Awards,* ABC, 2005.

Assembling "Robots": The Magic, the Music & the Comedy, Fox, 2005.

Nickelodeon Kids' Choice Awards '05 (also known as *Nickelodeon's 18th Annual Kids' Choice Awards*), Nickelodeon, 2005.

BET Awards 2005, Black Entertainment Television, 2005.

The Teen Choice Awards 2005, Fox, 2005.

Presenter, *The 57th Annual Primetime Emmy Awards,* CBS, 2005.

The WIN Awards, PAX, 2005.

Red Carpet Confidential, CBS, 2005.

(Uncredited) *The 78th Annual Academy Awards,* ABC, 2006.

Legends' Ball (also known as *Oprah Winfrey's "Legends' Ball"*), ABC, 2006.

Bond Girls Are Forever 2006, AMC, 2006.

Forbes Celebrity 100: Who Made Bank?, E! Entertainment Television, 2006.

Just Another Day, 2006.

2006 BAFTA/LA Cunard Britannica Awards, 2006.

Celebrity Debut, ABC, 2006.

Happy Birthday BAFTA, ITV1, 2007.

AFI's 100 Years 100 Greatest Movies: 10th Anniversary Edition, CBS, 2007.

AFI Life Achievement Award: A Tribute to Warren Beatty, USA Network, 2008.

Stand Up to Cancer, NBC, CBS, and ABC, 2008.

The 16th Annual Trumpet Awards, MyNetwork, 2008.

On–camera host, *For Love of Liberty: The Story of America's Black Patriots,* 2009.

Television Appearances; Episodic:

Rene, "Hair Today, Gone Tomorrow," *They Came from Outer Space,* 1991.

Jaclyn, "Love, Hillman–Style," *Amen,* NBC, 1991.

The Tonight Show Starring Johnny Carson, NBC, 1991.

Jaclyn, "Love, Hillman–Style," *A Different World,* NBC, 1991.

The Word, CBS, 1993.

Entertainers with Byron Allen (also known as *Entertainers*), syndicated, 1994.

Late Show with David Letterman (also known as *Letterman* and *The Late Show*), CBS, 1994, 2003, 2004, 2006, 2007.

"Race Issues in America," *Dennis Miller Live,* HBO, 1995.

Herself, "Where the Party At," *Martin,* Fox, 1996.

The Rosie O'Donnell Show, syndicated, 1996, 1997, 2000, 2001.

The Tonight Show with Jay Leno, NBC, 1997, 2001, 2003.

Voice of Betsy, "Room Service," *Frasier,* NBC, 1998.

"Lionel Richie," *Behind the Music* (also known as *VH1's "Behind the Music"*), VH1, 1998.

Host, *Mad TV,* Fox, 1998.

Late Night with Conan O'Brien, NBC, 2000, 2004, 2006.

Mundo VIP, 2001.

"The Making of 'Swordfish,'" *HBO First Look,* HBO, 2001.

Herself, "Handle Your Business," *The Bernie Mac Show,* Fox, 2002.

"Oscars 2002," *Seitenblicke,* 2002.

Leute heute, 2002.

Leticia Musgrove, "Monsters Ball," *Der Kabel 1 Kinotipp,* 2002.

"Halle Barry," *Revealed with Jules Asner,* E! Entertainment Television, 2002.

Mad TV, Fox, 2002.

The Late Late Show with Craig Kilborn (also known as *The Late Late Show*), CBS, 2002.

The Oprah Winfrey Show (also known as *Oprah*), syndicated, 2002, 2004, 2005.

Ant & Dec's Saturday Night Takeaway, 2003.

"Halle Barry," *Style Star,* Style Network, 2003.

Extra (also known as *Extra: The Entertainment Magazine*), syndicated, 2003.

Host, *Saturday Night Live* (also known as *SNL*), NBC, 2003.

"Gothika," *Movie House,* MTV, 2003.

Punk'd, MTV, 2003.

Tinseltown TV, International Channel, 2003.

"X2: X–Men United," *HBO First Look,* HBO, 2003.

"John Travolta," *Biography,* Arts and Entertainment, 2003.

"Peter Boyle," *Biography,* Arts and Entertainment, 2003.

Pulse, Fox, 2004.

Richard & Judy, Channel 4, 2004.

GMTV, ITV, 2004.

T4, Channel 4, 2004.

Rove Live, Ten Network, 2004.

"Parstakerroin voittaa aina," *4Pop,* 2004.

"The Making of 'Catwoman,'" *HBO First Look,* HBO, 2004.

"'Robots,'" *HBO First Look,* HBO, 2005.

Good Day Live, syndicated, 2005.

Good Morning America, ABC, 2005.

Tavis Smiley, PBS, 2005.

Corazon de ..., 2005, 2006.

Live with Regis and Kelly, syndicated, 2005, 2007.

Bl!tz (also known as *Blitz*), 2006.

Le grand journal de Canal+, 2006.

Friday Night with Jonathan Ross, BBC, 2006.

The Insider, syndicated, 2006.

Entertainment Tonight (also known as *E.T.*), syndicated, 2006, 2007, 2008.

Miradas 2, 2007.

Las mananas de Cuatro, 2007.

The Daily Show (also known as *A Daily Show with Jon Stewart, Jon Stewart, The Daily Show with Jon Stewart,* and *The Daily Show with Jon Stewart Global Edition*), Comedy Central, 2007.

iVillage Live, 2007.

The View, ABC, 2007.

Ellen: The Ellen DeGeneres Show, syndicated, 2007.

"Halle Barry," *Inside the Actors Studio* (also known as *The Craft of Theatre and Film*), Bravo, 2007.

"Halle Berry," *Biography,* Arts and Entertainment, 2008.

Television Work; Movies:

Executive producer, *Introducing Dorothy Dandridge* (also known as *Face of an Angel*), HBO, 1999.

Executive producer, *Lackawanna Blues,* HBO, 2005.

RECORDINGS

Video Games:

Voice of Patience Phillips/Catwoman, *Catwoman: The Game,* 2004.

Music Videos:

Limp Bizkit's "Behind Blue Eyes," 2003.

Also appeared in Pras's "Ghetto Superstar (That Is What You Are)."

OTHER SOURCES

Books:

Contemporary Black Biography, Volume 19, Gale, 1998, Volume 57, Thomson Gale, 2007.

Newsmakers 1996, Issue 2, Gale, 1996.

Notable Black American Women, Book 2, Gale, 1996.

Periodicals:

Ebony, February, 1992, p. 36; March, 1997, pp. 22–26.

Empire, Issue 49, 1993, p. 59; February, 1999, p. 64.

Essence, October, 1996, pp. 70–73.

Glamour, August, 1999, pp. 208–11.

Jet, January 20, 1992, p. 34; March 3, 1997, p. 39; April 7, 1997, pp. 22–25.

Just for Black Men, January, 1999, pp. 32–35; September, 1999, pp. 28–30.

Ladies Home Journal, May, 1997, pp. 64–66.

Maxim, June, 2000, pp. 142–45.

Movieline, August, 1999, pp. 58–63, 96; December, 2001, pp. 50–56, 98.

New York Times, March 10, 2002.

Parade, August 22, 1999, pp. 8–9.

People Weekly, May 11, 1998, p. 164.

TV Guide, February 21, 1998, p. 44; August 14, 1999, pp. 22–24; June 10, 2000, pp. 38–42.

US, March 18, 2002, p. 22.

BEST, James 1926–

(James K. Best, Jim Best, Jimmy Best)

PERSONAL

Original name, Jules Guy; born July 26, 1926, in Powderly, KY; raised in Corydon, IN; son of a coal miner; adopted son of Armen and Essa Best; married second wife, Jobee Ayers, 1959 (divorced, 1977); married Dorothy Collier (an actress and producer), August 15, 1986; children: (second marriage) two daughters, including Janeen (a producer, writer, and actress). *Avocational Interests:* Painting (oil and watercolor), songwriting, fishing.

Addresses: *Office*—Best Friend Films, James Best Enterprises, Inc., P.O. Box 5325, Hickory, NC 28603.

Career: Actor, director, writer, and producer. James Best Enterprises, Inc., Hickory, NC, cofounder and principal of Best Friend Films. Mississippi Film Commission, founder; Motion Picture, Television, and Recording Industry of Florida, member of advisory council. University of Mississippi, past artist in residence and acting teacher; also teacher at University of Central Florida, 1987, and in Los Angeles. Artist, with paintings displayed in exhibitions. Formerly worked as a magazine model and metalworker. *Military service:* U.S. Air Force, Military Police, 1945.

Awards, Honors: Crystal Reel Award, best actor in a dramatic series, 1992, for *In the Heat of the Night;* elected to University of Mississippi Hall of Fame.

CREDITS

Film Appearances:

(Uncredited) Police broadcaster in surveillance plane, *I Was a Shoplifter,* Universal, 1950.

Crater, *Winchester '73* (also known as *Montana Winchester*), Universal, 1950.

Frank Addison, *Peggy,* Universal, 1950.

Naval lieutenant, *Mystery Submarine,* Universal, 1950.

Cole Younger, *Kansas Raiders,* Universal, 1950.

Sam, *Comanche Territory,* Universal, 1950.

(Uncredited) Driver, *One Way Street,* Universal, 1950.

Sergeant Ralph Phelps, *Target Unknown,* Universal, 1951.

Bitter Creek Dalton, *The Cimarron Kid,* Universal, 1951.

Bert Keon, *Apache Drums,* Universal, 1951.

Jerry Connell, *Air Cadet* (also known as *Jet Men of the Air*), Universal, 1951.

Joe Rakich (some sources cite Joe McNamara), *Steel Town,* Universal, 1952.

Marvin Johnson, *Ma and Pa Kettle at the Fair* (also known as *Ma and Pa Kettle at the County Fair*), Universal, 1952.

Corporal Ransom, *Francis Goes to West Point,* Universal, 1952.

(Uncredited) Radar operator, *Flat Top* (also known as *Eagles of the Fleet*), Allied Artists, 1952.

Corporal Hassett, *The Battle at Apache Pass,* Universal, 1952.

Corporal Gerard, *Seminole,* Universal, 1953.

Sidney K. Fuller, *Riders to the Stars,* United Artists, 1953.

(Uncredited) Samuel Donaldson, *The President's Lady,* Twentieth Century–Fox, 1953.

Primrose, *Column South,* Universal, 1953.

(Uncredited) Gig Davis, *City of Bad Men,* Twentieth Century–Fox, 1953.

(Uncredited) Charlire, *The Beast from 20,000 Fathoms* (also known as *Monster from Beneath the Sea*), Warner Bros., 1953.

(Uncredited) Lieutenant Friday (some sources cite Lieutenant Finlay), *They Rode West,* Columbia, 1954.

Barr, *Return from the Sea,* Allied Artists, 1954.

(Uncredited) Lieutenant Junior Grade Jorgensen, *The Caine Mutiny,* Columbia, 1954.

Lieutenant Robinson, *The Raid,* Twentieth Century–Fox, 1954.

Private Bliss, *The Yellow Tomahawk,* United Artists, 1954.

Jason Brown, *Seven Angry Men* (also known as *God's Angry Man*), Allied Artists, 1955.

(Uncredited) Man with Jane at youth rally, *A Man Named Peter* (also known as *A Man Called Peter*), Twentieth Century–Fox, 1955.

(Uncredited) Jerry Ames, *When Gangland Strikes,* Republic, 1956.

Jim, *Gaby,* Metro–Goldwyn–Mayer, 1956.

Bill Jackson, *Come Next Spring,* Republic, 1956.

Detective Arnie Arnholf, *Calling Homicide,* Allied Artists, 1956.

(Uncredited) Crew member, *Forbidden Planet,* Metro–Goldwyn–Mayer, 1956.

Millard Chilson Cassidy, *The Rack,* Metro–Goldwyn–Mayer, 1956.

Kermit, *Hot Summer Night,* Metro–Goldwyn–Mayer, 1957.

Ted "Kid" Hamilton, *Last of the Badmen,* Allied Artists, 1957.

Doug Gerhardt, *Man on the Prowl,* United Artists, 1957.

Rhidges, *The Naked and the Dead,* Warner Bros., 1958.

Tom Folliard, *The Left–Handed Gun,* Warner Bros., 1958.

Kit Caswell, *Cole Younger, Gunfighter,* Allied Artists, 1958.

Sergeant David Brent, *Verboten!* (also known as *Forbidden!*), Columbia, 1959.

Billy John, *Ride Lonesome,* Columbia, 1959.

Thorne Sherman, *The Killer Shrews* (also known as *The Attack of the Killer Shrews*), McLendon, 1959.

Sam Mullen, *Cast a Long Shadow,* United Artists, 1959.

Niergaard, *The Mountain Road,* Columbia, 1960.

Jericho Larkin, *Black Gold,* Warner Bros., 1963.

Stuart, *Shock Corridor,* Allied Artists, 1963.

Scotty Grant, *The Quick Gun,* Columbia, 1964.

Sheriff Elkins, *Black Spurs,* Paramount, 1965.

Carter, *Shenandoah,* Universal, 1965.

Dr. Ben Mizer, *Three on a Couch,* Columbia, 1966.

Sergeant Carnavan, *First to Fight,* Warner Bros., 1967.

Drew, *Firecreek,* Warner Bros., 1968.

Sheriff Young, *Sounder,* Twentieth Century–Fox, 1972.

Dewey Barksdale, *Ode to Billy Joe,* Warner Bros., 1976.

Jim, *Nickelodeon,* Columbia, 1976.

Gator, United Artists, 1976.

Texan, *Rolling Thunder,* American International Pictures, 1977.

Reverend Emory Neill, *The Brain Machine* (also known as *The E–Box, Gray Matter, Grey Matter, Mind Warp,* and *Time Warp*), Howco Productions, 1977.

Pacemaker patient, *The End,* United Artists, 1978.

Cully, *Hooper,* Warner Bros., 1978.

(In archive footage) *It Came from Hollywood* (documentary), Paramount, 1982.

(Uncredited) Folliard (in archive footage), *Gunfighters of the Old West,* Simitar Entertainment, 1992.

Wilbur Johnson, *Death Mask,* MTI Home Video, 1998.

John Massey, *Finders Keepers* (short film), 1998.

William Clancy, *House of Forever* (short film), Best Friend Films, 2004.

Hank Larson, *Hot tamale,* Motion Picture Corporation of America, 2006.

The doctor, *Once Not Far From Home* (short film), Stars North, 2006.

Mr. McClancy, *Moondance Alexander,* Fox Faith, 2007.

Some sources cite unconfirmed appearances in other films.

Film Work:
(Uncredited) Director, *Gator,* United Artists, 1976.

Associate producer and (uncredited) director, *The End,* United Artists, 1978.

Television Appearances; Series:
Gotch, *Temple Houston,* NBC, 1963.

Sheriff Rosco P. Coltrane, *The Dukes of Hazzard,* CBS, 1979–85.

Voice of Sheriff Rosco P. Coltrane, *The Dukes* (animated), CBS, 1983.

Television Appearances; Movies:
Skip Taylor, 1953.

Henry Burroughs, *Run, Simon, Run* (also known as *Savage Run* and *The Tradition of Simon Zuniga*), ABC, 1970.

Sheriff Bert Hamilton, *Savages,* ABC, 1974.

Bingo Washington, *The Runaway Barge* (also known as *River Bandits*), NBC, 1975.

Deputy Mayor Pelligrino, *The Savage Bees,* NBC, 1976.

Mr. Parkinson, *Night Train,* ABC, 1990.

Rosco P. Coltrane, *The Dukes of Hazzard: Reunion!* (also known as *Reunion in Hazzard*), CBS, 1997.

Rosco P. Coltrane, *The Dukes of Hazzard: Hazzard in Hollywood,* CBS, 2000.

Television Appearances; Pilots:
Pony Express, NBC, 1957.

Rio, 1961.

Lamarr Skinner, *McLaren's Riders,* CBS, 1977.

Television Appearances; Episodic:
"Night Strike," *Cavalcade of America* (also known as *DuPont Presents the Cavalcade Theatre* and *DuPont Theater*), ABC, 1953.

"McCoy of Abilene," *Hallmark Hall of Fame* (also known as *Hallmark Television Playhouse*), NBC, 1953.

Rick Alston, "Silent Testimony," *Hopalong Cassidy,* NBC, 1954.

Dave Ridley, "Little Britches," *Stories of the Century* (also known as *The Fast Guns*), 1954.

Scott Warren, "Outlaw Mesa," *Annie Oakley,* 1954.

"Annie and the Outlaw's Son," *Annie Oakley,* 1954.

Bank teller, "The Hold–Up," *The Gene Autry Show* (also known as *Melody Ranch*), CBS, 1954.

Ray Saunders, "Hoodoo Canyon," *The Gene Autry Show* (also known as *Melody Ranch*), CBS, 1954.

Henry Jordan, "Frontier Empire," *The Adventures of Kit Carson* (also known as *Kit Carson*), 1954.

"The Phantom Uprising," *The Adventures of Kit Carson* (also known as *Kit Carson*), 1955.

Tiny Stoker, "Million Dollar Wedding," *Death Valley Days* (also known as *Call of the West, The Pioneers, Trails West,* and *Western Star Theater*), 1955.

(As Jimmy Best) Larry Martin, "The Death of Johnny Ringo," *Buffalo Bill Jr.,* 1955.

Jim Blake, "Framed for Murder," *The Lone Ranger*, ABC, 1955.

Paul Kenyon, "The Stone Heart," *The Adventures of Champion* (also known as *Champion the Wonder Horse*), CBS, 1955.

"One Day at a Time," *Cavalcade of America* (also known as *DuPont Presents the Cavalcade Theatre* and *DuPont Theater*), ABC, 1955.

Slate Morley, "Women's Work," *Cavalcade of America* (also known as *DuPont Presents the Cavalcade Theatre* and *DuPont Theater*), ABC, 1956.

Perry Cochran, "Gun Trouble Valley," *Red Ryder*, 1956.

Ben Reed, "The Texicans," *Frontier*, NBC, 1956.

"Andrew and the Deadly Double," *The Adventures of Champion* (also known as *Champion the Wonder Horse*), CBS, 1956.

"Anatol of the Bayous," *Crossroads*, ABC, 1956.

"Gingerbread Man," *Telephone Time*, CBS, 1956.

(As Jim Best) Jason Cartwright, "Out from Texas," *Frontier*, NBC, 1956.

Pyke Dillon, "The Three Graves," *Zane Grey Theater* (also known as *Dick Powell's "Zane Grey Theater"* and *The Westerners*), CBS, 1957.

Mike Norris, "Lynching Party," *Sheriff of Cochise*, 1957.

Jack Milhoan, "Merry–Go–Round Case," *Richard Diamond, Private Detective* (also known as *Call Mr. D.*), CBS, 1957.

Arkansas Trueblood, "Death in an Alley," *Code 3*, 1957.

Rand Marple, "Marple Brothers," *Trackdown*, CBS, 1957.

Andy Fisher, "The Long Night," *Have Gun Will Travel*, CBS, 1957.

William Purdom, "Dragoon Patrol," *West Point* (also known as *The West Point Story*), 1957.

Bob Ahler, "The Mistake," *Trackdown*, CBS, 1958.

Norman Frayne, "Death Sentence," *Alfred Hitchcock Presents*, CBS, 1958.

Stoner, "Sheriff of Red Rock," *Wanted: Dead or Alive*, CBS, 1958.

Matt Porter, "Guilt of a Town," *Tombstone Territory*, ABC, 1958.

Jim Kenyon, "Jebediah Bonner," *The Restless Gun*, NBC, 1958.

Joe Best, "Stampede at Tent City," *Bat Masterson*, NBC, 1958.

Joe Sunday, "Sunday's Child," *Trackdown*, CBS, 1958.

"Guys like O'Malley," *Schlitz Playhouse of Stars* (also known as *Herald Playhouse, The Playhouse,* and *Schlitz Playhouse*), CBS, 1958.

Shag, "The Secret Love of Johnny Spain," *Climax!* (also known as *Climax Mystery Theatre*), CBS, 1958.

"Assassin," *Target*, 1958.

Title role, "The Fred Morgan Story," *The Millionaire* (also known as *If You had a Million*), CBS, 1958.

Webb, "The Enemy on the Flank," *Behind Closed Doors*, NBC, 1958.

Chad Kern, "Trail by Fire," *Rescue 8*, 1959.

Luke Perry, "Six–Up to Bannach," *Wanted: Dead or Alive*, CBS, 1959.

Garth English, "The Andrew Hale Story," *Wagon Train* (also known as *Major Adams, Trail Master*), NBC, 1959.

Dallas, "The Lawbreakers," *Laramie*, NBC, 1959.

Ben Travers, "Client: Nelson," *Black Saddle* (also known as *The Westerners*), NBC, 1959.

Pyke Dillon, "The Three Graves," *Frontier Justice*, CBS, 1959.

Private Boland, "Portrait," *The David Niven Show*, NBC, 1959.

Frank Simms, "Good Deed" (also known as "Gentry's People"), *The David Niven Show*, NBC, 1959.

David Mallory, "Maximum Capacity," *The Man and the Challenge*, NBC, 1959.

Rhodes, "Lonesome as Midnight," *The Lineup* (also known as *San Francisco Beat*), CBS, 1959.

Duke, "Cindy's Fella," *Startime* (also known as *Ford Startime* and *Lincoln–Mercury Startime*), NBC, 1959.

Ben Leach, "Company Man," *Laramie*, NBC, 1960.

"The Story of Julesberg," *Pony Express*, 1960.

Frank Cullen, "Escort Detail," *Overland Trail* (also known as *Overland Stage*), NBC, 1960.

Roy, "The Beau and Arrow Case," *Lock Up*, syndicated, 1960.

Jovan Wilanskov, "Love on Credit," *The DuPont Show with June Allyson* (also known as *The June Allyson Show*), CBS, 1960.

Ted Evans, "Night on a Rainbow," *The Rebel*, ABC, 1960.

Les Hardeen, "High Lonesome," *Stagecoach West*, ABC, 1960.

Bowman Lewis, "The Colonel Harris Story," *Wagon Train* (also known as *Major Adams, Trail Master*), NBC, 1960.

Art Bernard, "The Clayton Tucker Story," *Wagon Train* (also known as *Major Adams, Trail Master*), NBC, 1960.

(As James K. Best) Hennessey, "Cell 227," *Alfred Hitchcock Presents*, CBS, 1960.

Jim Lindsey, "The Guitar Player," *The Andy Griffith Show* (also known as *Andy of Mayberry*), CBS, 1960.

Waares, "Deathwatch," *The Rebel*, ABC, 1960.

Danny Dakota, "Dakota Showdown," *Bat Masterson*, NBC, 1960.

Hardy Couter, "Aftermath" (also known as "The Code of Jonathan West"), *General Electric Theatre* (also known as *G.E. Theatre* and *G.E. True Theatre*), CBS, 1960.

Clay Kirby, "Killer's Road," *The Texan*, CBS, 1960.

Lieutenant John Leonard, "Beyond the Stars," *Men into Space* (also known as *Space Challenge*), CBS, 1960.

Carl Reagan, "The Fugitive," *Bonanza* (also known as *Ponderosa*), 1961.

Jack Craig, "The Arsonist," *Stagecoach West*, ABC, 1961.

Jim Lindsey, "The Guitar Player Returns," *The Andy Griffith Show* (also known as *Andy of Mayberry*), CBS, 1961.

Bish Darby, "Make My Death Bed," *Alfred Hitchcock Presents,* NBC, 1961.

Joe, "The Choice," *The Barbara Stanwyck Show,* NBC, 1961.

Mike Pardee, "The Dead Don't Cry," *Stagecoach West,* ABC, 1961.

Title role, "The Hemp Reeger Case," *Whispering Smith,* NBC, 1961.

Ernie Jordan, "One for the Road," *Surfside 6,* ABC, 1961.

Johnny Rob, "The Grave," *The Twilight Zone* (also known as *The Twilight Zone: The Original Series*), CBS, 1961.

Roy Smith, "Quiet Night in Town: Parts 1 & 2," *Have Gun Will Travel,* CBS, 1961.

Danny, "Strike Out," *Michael Shayne,* NBC, 1961.

Jeff Myrtlebank, "The Last Rites of Jeff Myrtlebank," *The Twilight Zone* (also known as *The Twilight Zone: The Original Series*), CBS, 1962.

Johnny Best, "The Runaway," *Laramie,* NBC, 1962.

Babe Mackie, "The Long Shot Caper," *77 Sunset Strip,* ABC, 1962.

Bob Barrett, "The Day a Town Slept," *The Rifleman,* ABC, 1962.

Banton, "Then the Mountains," *Bronco,* ABC, 1962.

Ernie Riggins, "Satonka," *Cheyenne,* ABC, 1962.

Johnny Olin, "Day in the Sun," *Hawaiian Eye,* ABC, 1962.

"Sweet Sam," *Cheyenne,* ABC, 1962.

Ruel Gridley, "The $275,000 Sack of Flour," *Death Valley Days* (also known as *Call of the West, The Pioneers, Trails West,* and *Western Star Theater*), 1962.

Willy Cain, "Incident at Spider Rock," *Rawhide,* CBS, 1963.

Simon Waller, "Six Impossible Things before Breakfast," *Ben Casey,* ABC, 1963.

Billy–Ben Turner, "Jess–Belle," *The Twilight Zone* (also known as *The Twilight Zone: The Original Series*), CBS, 1963.

Private Hook, "The Warriors," *The Gallant Men,* ABC, 1963.

Martin Potter, "The Case of the Surplus Suitor," *Perry Mason,* CBS, 1963.

Dal Creed, "With a Smile," *Gunsmoke* (also known as *Gun Law* and *Marshal Dillon*), CBS, 1963.

Dan, "Terror at High Point," *The Fugitive,* ABC, 1963.

Les Fay, "Little Angel Blue Eyes," *Redigo,* NBC, 1963.

Brock Quade, "Incident of the Rawhiders," *Rawhide,* CBS, 1963.

Page, "The Legacy," *Bonanza* (also known as *Ponderosa*), 1963.

Ernie Swift, "Open Season," *G.E. True,* CBS, 1963.

Jimmy Burns, "Sixty–Seven Miles of Gold," *Death Valley Days* (also known as *Call of the West, The Pioneers, Trails West,* and *Western Star Theater*), 1964.

Jim Campbell, "Hero of Fort Halleck," *Death Valley Days* (also known as *Call of the West, The Pioneers, Trails West,* and *Western Star Theater*), 1964.

Tom Carmody, "The Jar," *The Alfred Hitchcock Hour,* CBS, 1964.

Sam Beal, "The Glory and the Mud," *Gunsmoke* (also known as *Gun Law* and *Marshal Dillon*), CBS, 1964.

Private Meredith Trenton, "Mail Call," *Combat!,* ABC, 1964.

Curly Beamer, "Go Away, Little Sheba," *Destry,* ABC, 1964.

"Incident at El Toro," *Rawhide,* CBS, 1964.

Jethroe Wyatt, "The Devil's Four," *Daniel Boone,* NBC, 1965.

Vince Zale, "A Matter of Wife and Death," *Honey West,* ABC, 1965.

Tucson (The Cowboy), "Steam Heat," *Burke's Law* (also known as *Amos Burke, Secret Agent*), ABC, 1965.

Curt Westley, "Letter of the Law," *The Virginian* (also known as *The Men from Shiloh*), 1965.

Dr. Joe Sullivan, "A Little Fun to Match the Sorrow," *Ben Casey,* ABC, 1965.

Dr. Peter Kellwin, "The Call of the Dolphin," *Flipper,* NBC, 1965.

Allan Winford, "The Case of the Unwelcome Well," *Perry Mason,* CBS, 1966.

Sam, "Lisa," *I Spy,* NBC, 1966.

Chico, "High Devil," *The Iron Horse,* ABC, 1966.

Arnold Wyatt, "Flame Out," *Felony Squad,* ABC, 1966.

Yale Barton, "Deadline for Death," *The Green Hornet* (also known as *The Kato Show*), ABC, 1966.

Emile, "Blind Man's Bluff," *Hawk,* ABC, 1966.

Rake Hanley, "Meeting at Devil's Fork," *The Guns of Will Sonnett,* ABC, 1967.

The doctor, "Suitable for Framing," *I Spy,* NBC, 1968.

Sheriff Vern Schaler, "The Price of Salt," *Bonanza* (also known as *Ponderosa*), 1968.

George "Lucky" Collins, "The Distant Shore," *Felony Squad,* ABC, 1968.

Frank Lynch, "The Price of Terror," *The Mod Squad,* ABC, 1968.

Title role, "Charlie Noon," *Gunsmoke* (also known as *Gun Law* and *Marshal Dillon*), CBS, 1969.

Harley Bass, "Robber's Roost," *The Guns of Will Sonnett,* ABC, 1969.

Clayt, "Goodbye, Lizzie," *Lancer,* CBS, 1970.

Wiley, "In the Eyes of God," *Dan August,* ABC, 1970.

"Blood Feud," *Hawkins,* CBS, 1973.

Sheriff Gruner, "Luke," *How the West Was Won,* ABC, 1979.

Sheriff Rosco P. Coltrane, "Grits and Greens Strike Again," *Enos,* CBS, 1980.

The Midnight Special, NBC, 1981.

Woody, "Too Many Roscos," *The Dukes of Hazzard,* CBS, 1983.

Mr. Parkinson, "Night Train," *B. L. Stryker* (broadcast as a feature of *The ABC Saturday Mystery*), ABC, 1990.

Nathan Bedford, "Sweet, Sweet Blues," *In the Heat of the Night,* NBC, 1991.
"Dukes of Hazzard," *Inside Fame,* Country Music Television, 2005.
"Crime–fighters," *After They Were Famous,* ITV, 2005.
"Special Edition: The Dukes of Hazzard," *CMT Insider,* Country Music Television, 2006.

Also appeared in *The Big Valley,* ABC, and *Riverboat,* NBC.

Television Appearances; Other:
Hank Garvey, *Centennial* (miniseries), NBC, 1978.
TV Road Trip (special), The Travel Channel, 2002.

Television Director; Episodic:
"Diamonds in the Rough," *The Dukes of Hazzard,* CBS, 1981.
"Cale Yarborough Comes to Hazzard," *The Dukes of Hazzard,* CBS, 1984.
"Dead and Alive," *The Dukes of Hazzard,* CBS, 1984.

Stage Appearances:
Appeared in *Bus Stop* and *Goodbye Charlie,* both Burt Reynolds Dinner Theatre, Jupiter, FL.

Major Tours:
Appeared in *Marinka,* U.S. cities; and *My Sister Eileen,* European cities.

Stage Work:
Directed productions of *The Fantasticks* and *Goodbye Charlie,* both Burt Reynolds Dinner Theatre, Jupiter, FL.

RECORDINGS

Videos:
Voice of Rosco, *The Dukes of Hazzard: Racing for Home* (video game), SouthPeak Interactive, 1999.
The 20th Anniversary Hazzard County BBQ, Warner Home Video, 2004.
Voice of Sheriff Rosco. P. Coltrane, *The Dukes of Hazzard: Return of the General Lee* (video game), Blindlight, 2004.

Appeared in *His Own Words* and *Rosco Remembers.*

WRITINGS

Screenplays:
Gator, United Artists, 1976.
The End, United Artists, 1978.
Hooper, Warner Bros., 1978.
Death Mask, MTI Home Video, 1998.

OTHER SOURCES

Electronic:
James Best Official Site, http://www.jamesbest.com, December 3, 2008.

BEY, John Toles
    See TOLES–BEY, John

BIERKO, Craig 1964–

PERSONAL

Surname is pronounced Bee–er–ko; full name, Craig Philip Bierko; born August 18, 1964 (some sources say July 18, 1965), in Rye (some sources cite Rye Brook), NY; son of Rex (a theatre operator) and Pat (a theatre operator) Bierko. *Education:* Northwestern University, B.S., theater arts, 1986; studied journalism at Boston University.

Addresses: *Agent*—Endeavor, 9601 Wilshire Blvd., 3rd Floor, Beverly Hills, CA 90210. *Manager*—Handprint Entertainment, 1100 Glendon Ave., Suite 1000, Los Angeles, CA 90024. *Publicist*—Baker/Winokur/Ryder, 5700 Wilshire Blvd., Suite 550, Los Angeles, CA 90036.

Career: Actor.

Awards, Honors: *Theatre World* Award, outstanding Broadway debut, Antoinette Perry Award nomination, best actor in a musical, Drama Desk Award nomination, Outer Critics Circle Award nomination, 2000, all for *The Music Man;* Screen Actors Guild Award nomination (with others), outstanding performance by an ensemble in a drama, 2007, for *Boston Legal.*

CREDITS

Film Appearances:
Craig Johnson, *Love Note,* 1987.
Victimless Crimes, 1990.
Timothy, *The Long Kiss Goodnight,* New Line Cinema, 1996.
Christmas radio preacher, *Johns,* Metrodome/First Look Pictures, 1996.
Jon Haas, *'Til There Was You,* Paramount, 1997.
Douglas Hall/John Ferguson/David, *The Thirteenth Floor,* Columbia, 1998.
Richie Maxwell, *Sour Grapes,* Columbia, 1998.

Lacerda, *Fear and Loathing in Las Vegas,* MCA/ Universal, 1998.

Mitch, *The Suburbans,* Columbia TriStar, 1999.

Douglas Hall, John Ferguson, and David, *The Thirteenth Floor* (also known as *Abwarts in die zukunft*), 1999.

The Cherry Picker (short), 2000.

(Uncredited) Boyfriend on test–screened movie, *Kate & Leopold,* Miramax, 2001.

Peter, *I'm With Lucy* (also known as *Autour de Lucy*), Sony, 2002.

George Finney, *Dickie Roberts: Former Child Star* (also known as *Dickie Roberts: (Former) Child Star*), Paramount, 2003.

Voice of Sarge, *Hair High,* Hair High Corp., 2004.

Max Baer, *Cinderella Man,* Universal, 2005.

Tom, *Scary Movie 4,* Weinstein Company, 2006.

Randy Merrick, *Danika,* First Look International, 2006.

Talk show host, *For Your Consideration,* Warner Independent, 2006.

(Uncredited) Sergeant, *Bill* (also known as *Meet Bill*), First Look International, 2007.

Wolverine, *Superhero Movie,* Metro–Goldwyn–Mayer, 2008.

Television Appearances; Series:

Greg, *The Young and the Restless* (also known as *Y&R*), CBS, 1989.

Matt Keating, *Sydney,* CBS, 1990.

Joe Bowman, *The Powers That Be* (also known as *Love Child*), NBC, 1992.

B. J. Cooper, *Madman of the People,* NBC, 1994.

Greg Sherman, *Pride & Joy,* NBC, 1995.

Harlan Brandt, *The Court,* ABC, 2002.

Jeffrey Coho, *Boston Legal,* ABC, 2006–2007.

Jack "Gator" Gately, *Unhitched,* Fox, 2008.

Television Appearances; Movies:

Spencer Hill, *Star* (also known as *Danielle Steel's "Star"*), NBC, 1993.

Terry Hench, *Hench at Home,* 2003.

Television Appearances; Specials:

Carl Warner, "The Day My Kid Went Punk," *ABC Afterschool Specials,* ABC, 1987.

The 54th Annual Tony Awards, CBS, 2000.

The Great American History Quiz: 50 States, History Channel, 2001.

Host, *Reel Comedy: "Dickie Roberts: Former Child Star,"* Comedy Central, 2003.

Evening at Pops: Keith Lockhart's 10th Anniversary Special, PBS, 2004.

Television Appearances; Pilots:

Dave Lister, *Red Dwarf* (also known as *Red Dwarf USA*), NBC, 1992.

The Great Malones, 2006.

Television Appearances; Episodic:

"The Children's Crusade," *Our House,* 1987.

Bellman, "A Slight Case of Murder (2)," *Amen,* 1988.

Waiter, "Don't Change a Hair for Me," *Eisenhower & Lutz,* 1988.

Dirk, "Ramblin' Michael Harris," *Newhart,* 1989.

Dirk, "Malling in Love Again," *Newhart,* 1989.

Johnny Ryan, "Home Again," *Paradise,* 1989.

Johnny Ryan, "Common Good," *Paradise,* 1989.

Johnny Ryan, "The Return of Johnny Ryan," *Paradise,* 1989.

Matt Sargent, "The Puppet Master," *Wings,* NBC, 1990.

Fred, "The Man That Got Away," *Empty Nest,* NBC, 1990.

Alex, "Rootless People," *Murphy Brown,* CBS, 1990.

The Golden Girls, NBC, 1991.

Bill Noonan, "Star Is Newborn," *Baby Talk,* 1991.

Thomas Wilkes, "Trial by Fire," *Bodies of Evidence,* CBS, 1993.

Gardner Malloy, "Weekend in L.A.," *Mad About You,* NBC, 1998.

Late Night with Conan O'Brien, NBC, 1999, 2003, 2004.

Dennis, "In Search of Pygmies," *Ally McBeal,* Fox, 2000.

Ray King, "Defining Moments," *Sex and the City,* HBO, 2001.

Ray King, "What's Sex Got to Do with It?" *Sex and the City,* HBO, 2001.

"Salute to Meredith Willson," *Evening at Pops,* PBS, 2001.

Deputy Marshal Andy Eckerson, "Escape," *Law & Order: Special Victims Unit* (also known as *Law & Order: SVU* and *Special Victims Unit*), NBC, 2003.

The Tony Danza Show, syndicated, 2005.

The Megan Mullally Show, syndicated, 2007.

Bob Easton, "Carly Summers," *Nip/Tuck,* FX Channel, 2007.

The Late Late Show with Craig Ferguson, CBS, 2008.

Jimmy Kimmel Live!, ABC, 2008.

Easy to Assemble, 2008.

Stage Appearances:

(Stage debut) *Gypsy* (musical), Harrison Players, Westchester County, NY, c. 1974.

(Broadway debut) Professor Harold Hill, *The Music Man* (musical), Neil Simon Theatre, 2000–2001.

Laurent LeClaire, *Thou Shalt Not* (musical), Plymouth Theatre, New York City, 2001.

Frank (special video appearance), *Intrigue with Faye,* Acorn Theatre, New York City, 2003.

Ben Jacobson, *Modern Orthodox,* Dodger Stages, New York City, 2004–2005.

Also appeared as Antipholis, *The Boys from Syracuse,* Los Angeles; in *The Boys from Syracuse* (staged workshop), Roundabout Theatre, New York City.

OTHER SOURCES

Periodicals:
Parade, June 24, 2001, p. 18.
People Weekly, November 13, 2000, pp. 94–95; June 1, 2001, p. 32.
Starlog, December, 1995.

BOWEN, Andrea 1990–

PERSONAL

Born March 4, 1990, in Columbus, OH.

Addresses: *Agent*—United Talent Agency, 9560 Wilshire Blvd., Suite 500, Beverly Hills, CA 90212. *Publicist*—McClure and Associates Public Relations, 5225 Wilshire Blvd., Suite 909, Los Angeles, CA 90036.

Career: Actress.

Awards, Honors: Young Artist Award nomination, best performance in a television series—leading young actress, 2005, Screen Actors Guild Awards (with others), outstanding performance by an ensemble in a comedy series, 2005 and 2006, Screen Actors Guild Award nominations, outstanding performance by an ensemble in a comedy series, 2007 and 2008, for *Desperate Housewives;* Prism Award, performance in a television movie or miniseries (tied with Jennie Garth), 2008, for *Girl, Positive.*

CREDITS

Television Appearances; Series:
Zooey Glass, *That Was Then,* ABC, 2002.
Julie Mayer, *Desperate Housewives,* ABC, 2004—.

Television Appearances; Episodic:
Rankin child, "Causa Mortis," *Law & Order,* NBC, 1996.
Bess, "Harvest," *Law & Order,* NBC, 1997.
Sophie Douglas, "Countdown," *Law & Order: Special Victims Unit* (also known as *Law & Order: SVU* and *Special Victims Unit*), NBC, 2001.
Rachel, "Adam 55–3," *Third Watch,* NBC, 2001.
JKX: The Jamie Kennedy Experiment, The WB, 2002.
Ginny, "In with the New," *Arli$$,* HBO, 2002.
Riley Ellis, "Chapter Fifty–Eight," *Boston Public,* 2003.
Riley Ellis, "Chapter Fifty–Nine," *Boston Public,* 2003.
Riley Ellis, "Chapter Sixty–Three," *Boston Public,* 2003.
Stella, "With Arms Outstretched," *One Tree Hill,* The WB, 2003.

Sara Buck, "Seize the Day," *Strong Medicine,* 2003.
The Oprah Winfrey Show (also known as *Oprah*), syndicated, 2005.
The View, ABC, 2005.
Becky Grolnick, "A Day in the Life," *Without A Trace* (also known as *W.A.T*), CBS, 2005.
Voice of teen girl, "The Texas Panhandler," *King of the Hill* (animated), Fox, 2006.
The Tony Danza Show, syndicated, 2006.
The Megan Mullally Show, syndicated, 2006.
Entertainment Tonight (also known as *E.T., ET Weekend, Entertainment This Week* and *This Week in Entertainment*), syndicated, 2007 and 2008.
Voice of teen girl, "Luanne Gets Lucky," *King of the Hill* (animated), Fox, 2007.
Michelle Clark, "Cherry Bomb," *The Closer,* TNT, 2008.

Television Appearances; Movies:
Child, *Un Angelo a New York* (also known as *New York Crossing*), 1996.
Voice of Billie Bartley/Manifest Destiny, *Party Wagon* (animated), Cartoon Network, 2004.
Rachel Sandler, *Girl, Positive* (also known as *Girl Posi+I've*), Lifetime, 2007.

Television Appearances; Specials:
The 31st Annual People's Choice Awards, CBS, 2005.
Emirates Melbourne Cup Day, 2006.
Frosted Pink, 2007.
11th Annual Prism Awards, FX Channel, 2007.
11th Annual Ribbon of Hope Celebration, 2008.
12th Annual Prism Awards, FX Channel, 2008.

Film Appearances:
Witch/fairy, *Highball,* Shoreline, 1997.
Ashley number two, *Red Riding Hood,* Twentieth Century–Fox, 2004.
Patsy, *Luckey Quarter,* 2005.
Voice of girl, *Final Fantasy VII: Advent Children,* Sony, 2005.
Voice of Faline, *Bambi 2* (animated), Buena Vista, 2006.
Candace, *Eye of the Dolphin,* Monterey, 2006.

Also appeared as little girl in *New York Crossing.*

Stage Appearances:
Marta von Trapp, *The Sound of Music,* Martin Beck Theatre, New York City, 1997–98.
Adele, *Jane Eyre,* Brooks Atkinson Theatre, New York City, 2000–2001.

Also performed as young Cosette in *Les Miserables,* Broadway production.

RECORDINGS

Video Games:

Voice of young April/Alatien child, *The Longest Journey* (also known as *Den Lengste reisen*), 1999.

Extreme Skate Adventure (also known as *Disney's Extreme Skate Adventure*), 2003.

Voice of Sally, *The Cat in the Hat* (also known as *Dr. Seuss' "The Cat in the Hat"*), 2003.

Voice of Aerith Gainsborough, *Crisis Core: Final Fantasy VII*, 2007.

Albums:

The Sound of Music, 1998.
Jane Eyre, 2001.

Also recorded *Sugarbeats* and *Broadway Kids.*

BOWEN, Cameron 1988–

PERSONAL

Born September 13, 1988, in Columbus, OH; brother of Andrea Bowen (an actress) and Jillian Bowen (an actress).

Career: Actor.

Awards, Honors: Young Artist Award nomination, best performance in a television series—guest starring young actor, 2005, for *Judging Amy.*

CREDITS

Film Appearances:

Voice of Periwinkle, *Blue's Big Musical Movie* (animated), Paramount Home Video, 2000.

Nick Baxter, *Dynamite* (also known as *Family Under Siege*), PorchLight Entertainment, 2002.

Young Dave Boyle, *Mystic River,* Warner Bros., 2003.

Pollard child, *Seabiscuit,* Universal, 2003.

Big Kostya, *Wristcutters: A Love Story* (also known as *Pizzeria Kamikaze*), Autonomous Films, 2006.

Voice of Nibs, *Tinker Bell* (animated), 2009.

Film Work:

Additional voices, *Kurenai no buta* (animated; also known as *Porco Rosso*), Buena Vista Home Video, 1992.

Automated dialogue replacement (ADR), *Book of Shadows: Blair Witch 2,* Artisan Entertainment, 2000.

ADR, *The Prize Winner of Defiance, Ohio,* Dream-Works, 2005.

Television Appearances; Series:

Bob the Ball, *A Little Curious,* HBO Family, 1998.

Television Appearances; Movies:

Young Charlie, *Flowers for Algernon* (also known as *Charlie*), CBS, 2000.

Television Appearances; Episodic:

7–year–old Rankin son, "Causa Mortis," *Law & Order,* NBC, 1996.

Billy Woodson, "Refuge: Part 1," *Law & Order,* NBC, 1999.

Boy number one, "Journey to the Himalayas," *Third Watch,* NBC, 2000.

Danny Winslow, "Shallow Water: Parts 1 & 2," *Touched by an Angel,* CBS, 2001.

Kevin Sheppard, "Do It Yourself," *The Education of Max Bickford,* CBS, 2001.

Young Frasier, "Deathtrap," *Frasier,* NBC, 2002.

Kevin Nolan, "Pryor Knowledge," *American Dreams* (also known as *Our Generation*), NBC, 2002.

Kevin Nolan, "Solider Boy," *American Dreams* (also known as *Our Generation*), NBC, 2002.

Kevin Nolan, "Heartache," *American Dreams* (also known as *Our Generation*), NBC, 2003.

Martin, "A Saint in the City," *ER,* NBC, 2003.

Kevin, "Coach Tracy," *The Tracy Morgan Show,* NBC, 2004.

Casey Ives, "Sex, Lies and Expedia.com," *Judging Amy,* CBS, 2004.

Leader of quartet, "Oliver & the Otters," *Oliver Beene,* Fox, 2004.

Wayne, "Tiki Lounge," *Malcolm in the Middle,* Fox, 2005.

Ralph Pittino, "Seeds," *Law & Order: Criminal Intent* (also known as *Law & Order: CI*), NBC, 2007.

Television Additional Voices; Episodic:

"The Drill," *Avatar: The Last Airbender* (animated), Nickelodeon, 2006.

Stage Appearances:

Tom Canty, *The Prince and the Pauper,* Fifth Avenue Theatre, Seattle, WA, 2001, and Ordway Theatre, St. Paul, MN.

Also appeared as poor baby, *Whistle Down the Wind,* Broadway production; Jojo, *Seussical the Musical,* Broadway production; Little Jake, *Annie Get Your Gun,*

Lincoln Center; Chip, *Beauty and the Beast,* Broadway production; Gavroche, *Les Miserables,* Broadway production.

RECORDINGS

Video Games:
Morty, *Disney Golf,* Ingram Entertainment, 2002.

BROWN, Campbell 1968–

PERSONAL

Full name, Alma Dale Campbell Brown; born June 14, 1968, in Ferriday, LA (some sources cite Natchez, MS); daughter of James H. (a politician) and Dale Campbell (a painter; maiden name, Fairbanks) Brown; married (according to some sources) Peregrine Roberts (a realtor; marriage ended); married Daniel Samuel Senor (a news analyst), April 2, 2006; children: (with Senor) Eli James. *Education:* Regis College, Denver, CO, B.A. *Religion:* Jewish.

Addresses: *Office*—c/o Cable News Network, 820 First St. N.E., Washington, DC 20002.

Career: Broadcast journalist. KSNT–TV, Topeka, KS, political correspondent, 1993; WWBT–TV, Richmond, VA, reporter, 1993–95; WBAL–TV, Baltimore, MD, reporter, 1995–96; NBC News, New York City, correspondent for news channel, 1996–98, reporter, 1998–2001, White House correspondent, 2001–03, talk show host, 2003–07; Cable News Network, Washington, DC, news anchor, 2007—. WRC–TV, Washington, DC, political reporter, 1995–96. Former English teacher in Prague, Czechoslovakia (now Czech Republic).

CREDITS

Television Appearances; Series:
Correspondent, *MSNBC Live* (also known as *MSNBC Dayside* and *MSNBC Right Now*), MSNBC, 2001.
Correspondent, cohost, and substitute news anchor, *Today* (also known as *NBC News Today* and *The Today Show*), NBC, between 2003 and 2007.
Correspondent, *Dateline NBC* (also known as *Dateline*), NBC, 2004–2006.
Guest hostess, *Hardball with Chris Matthews,* CNBC, between 2004 and 2006.
Anchor, *CNN Election Center* (also known as *Campbell Brown: Election Center* and *Campbell Brown: No Bias, No Bull*), Cable News Network, 2008.

Television Appearances; Specials:
Correspondent, *Katrina's Fury: A Dateline Special,* NBC, 2005.
Host, *Macy's 4th of July Fireworks Spectacular,* NBC, 2006.
CNN Nevada Democratic Party Presidential Primary Debate, Cable News Network, 2007.

Television Appearances; Episodic:
Late Show with David Letterman (also known as *The Late Show, Late Dhow Backstage,* and *Letterman*), CBS, 2005.
Atlanta correspondent, *NBC Nightly News,* NBC, 2005.
Substitute anchor, *NBC Nightly News,* NBC, 2006.
Access Hollywood, syndicated, 2006.
Late Night with Conan O'Brien, NBC, 2006, 2007.
Cohost, *Weekend Today,* NBC, 2006, 2007.
The Tonight Show with Jay Leno, NBC, 2007.
Entertainment Tonight (also known as *Entertainment This Week, E.T., ET Weekend,* and *This Week in Entertainment*), syndicated, 2008.
The Daily Show (also known as *The Daily Show with Jon Stewart, The Daily Show with Jon Stewart Global Edition,* and *Jon Stewart*), Comedy Central, 2008.

Film Appearances:
Last Party (documentary; also known as *The Party's Over*), Film Movement, 2001.
Swing Vote, Buena Vista, 2008.

OTHER SOURCES

Periodicals:
Broadcasting & Cable, June 23, 2008, p. 23.
Cleveland Jewish News, October 25, 2007.
New York Times, April 9, 2006; October 4, 2008, p. B7.
USA Today, July 4, 2007, p. 3D.

Electronic:
CNN Online, http://www.cnn.com, December 6, 2008.
Media Bistro, http://www.mediabistro.com, February 26, 2007.
Washington Post Online, http://www.washingtonpost.com, July 30, 2007.

BROWN, W. Earl 1963–

PERSONAL

Born September 7, 1963, in Murray, KY; married Carrie Pascall; children: one daughter. *Education:* Murray State University, graduated; DePaul University, M.F.A., 1989; studied improvisational theatre with Second City, Chicago, IL.

Addresses: *Agent*—Douglas Lucterhand, Endeavor, 9601 Wilshire Blvd., 3rd Floor, Beverly Hills, CA 90210. *Manager*—Lynn Rawlins, Lynn Rawlins Management, 3933 Patrick Henry Pl., Agoura Hills, CA 91301.

Career: Actor and writer. Sacred Cowboys (band), founding member and performer.

Awards, Honors: Screen Actors Guild Award nomination, outstanding ensemble in a drama series, and Writers Guild Award of America Award nomination, best dramatic series, both (with others), 2007, for *Deadwood.*

CREDITS

Film Appearances:
Paramedic, *Backdraft,* Universal, 1991.
Herb Pennock, *The Babe,* Universal, 1992.
Vinnie DiMarco, *Excessive Force,* New Line Cinema, 1992.
Frick, *Rookie of the Year,* Twentieth Century–Fox, 1993.
Morgue attendant, *New Nightmare* (also known as *A Nightmare on Elm Street 7* and *Wes Craven's "New Nightmare"*), New Line Cinema, 1994.
Thrasher, *Vampire in Brooklyn* (also known as *Wes Craven's "Vampire in Brooklyn"*), Paramount, 1995.
Grace, *Without Evidence,* New Films International, 1995.
Kenneth "Kenny" Jones, *Scream,* Dimension Films, 1996.
Locksmith, *Kiss the Girls,* Paramount, 1997.
Warren Jensen, *There's Something about Mary* (also known as *There's Something More about Mary*), Twentieth Century–Fox, 1998.
(Uncredited) McCloud, *Deep Impact,* Paramount, 1998.
First customer at J. M. Inc., *Being John Malkovich,* USA Films, 1999.
William Kelson, *Lost Souls,* New Line Cinema, 2000.
Bobby, *Dancing at the Blue Iguana,* Lions Gate Films, 2001.
Hank "Terminator" Rogers, *Sugar & Spice,* New Line Cinema, 2001.
Barman, *Vanilla Sky,* Paramount, 2001.
Ronny Roy Pritchett (some sources cite last name as Pritcher), *Dunsmore,* 2001.
Bucky from Kentucky, *Pauly Shore Is Dead* (also known as *You'll Never Wiez in This Town Again*), Dimension Films, 2002.
David Burnet, *The Alamo,* Buena Vista, 2004.
Holister, *Killer Diller* (also known as *Rockin' the House*), 2004, Freestyle Releasing, 2006.
Willie Gratzo, *The Lost Shot,* Buena Vista, 2004.
Jimbo, *The Big White* (also known as *The Big White— Immer aerger mit Raymond* and *Le grand blanc*), Capitol Films, 2005.

Boss McGinn, *Kids in America,* Launchpad Releasing/ Slowhand Cinema Releasing, 2005.
Earl, *Waiting* (short film), Lisa Campbell Filmagic Entertainment, 2007.
Charlie, *A Night at the Zoo* (short film), Travelin' Productions, 2008.
Parson, *Pickin' & Grinnin',* Port Magee Pictures, 2009.
Matthew, *The Last Rites of Ransom Pride,* Horse Thief Pictures/Nomadic Pictures, 2009.

Television Appearances; Series:
Vic, *Sugar Hill,* 1999.
Shadrach, *Push, Nevada,* ABC, 2002.
Dan Dority, *Deadwood,* HBO, 2004–2006.

Television Appearances; Movies:
Pete, *The Woman Who Loved Elvis,* ABC, 1993.
Murder Between Friends, NBC, 1994.
Ken, *Dead Air,* USA Network, 1994.
Sheriff Boyd, *Lily in Winter,* USA Network, 1994.
Dubois, *Wiseguy,* ABC, 1996.
Calloway, *The Cherokee Kid,* HBO, 1996.
Ernie, *Project: ALF* (also known as *Alf—Der Film*), ABC, 1996.
Title role, *Meat Loaf: To Hell and Back,* VH1, 2000.

Television Appearances; Miniseries:
Fatty Malloy, *A Season in Purgatory,* CBS, 1996.
Fredrico Luciano, *Bella Mafia,* CBS, 1997.

Television Appearances; Pilots:
Patrolman, *Angel Street,* CBS, 1992.
Jimmy, *Suspect,* ABC, 2007.
Owen "Buzz" Newitt, *The Minister of Divine,* Fox, 2007.
Sailor, *1%,* HBO, 2008.

Television Appearances; Specials:
Making "Deadwood": The Show Behind the Show, HBO, 2004.

Television Appearances; Episodic:
Hood, "The Ex–Partner," *Bakersfield P.D.,* Fox, 1993.
Al, "The Stand-in," *Seinfeld,* NBC, 1994.
Security guard, "Murder of the Month Club," *Murder, She Wrote,* CBS, 1994.
Brian, "Gladiators," *Ellen* (also known as *These Friends of Mine*), ABC, 1995.
Cabbie, "Neighbors," *The Single Guy,* NBC, 1995.
Roy, "It's Not Such a Wonderful Life," *Nowhere Man,* UPN, 1996.
Floyd Gerber, "Caroline and the Therapist," *Caroline in the City* (also known as *Caroline*), NBC, 1996.
Dusty Wilton, "Murder, Country Style," *Diagnosis Murder,* CBS, 1997.
Sonny, "The Dating Game," *Smart Guy,* The WB, 1997.

Raymond Boudreaux, "The Sum of Her Parts," *Profiler,* NBC, 1998.

Larry Gambozza, "Big Trouble," *Martial Law,* CBS, 1999.

Bruce Rhodes, "Welcome to New York," *NYPD Blue,* ABC, 2000.

Harry Cram, "Cold Hearts," *Chicago Hope,* CBS, 2000.

Falcon, "Subject: Desert Squid! Myth or Legend?" *FreakyLinks,* Fox, 2000.

Menlo, "The Shroud of Rahmon," *Angel* (also known as *Angel: The Series*), The WB, 2000.

Rock & Roll Jeopardy! (game show), VH1, 2000.

Shadow/Warlock, "Pre–Witched," *Charmed,* The WB, 2001.

Thomas Pickens/Roger Peet, "Justice Is Served," *CSI: Crime Scene Investigation* (also known as *C.S.I., CSI: Las Vegas,* and *Les experts*), CBS, 2001.

Bruce Cates, "Excitable Boy," *Wolf Lake,* CBS, 2001.

Victor "Dizzy" Korsky, "The Problem with Corruption," *Dead Last,* The WB, 2001.

Billy Temple, "Brotherly Love," *Philly,* ABC, 2002.

Robert M. Fassl, "Underneath," *The X–Files,* Fox, 2002.

Pete, "It's the Most Wonderful Time of the Year," *Six Feet Under,* HBO, 2002.

Mike Parkhurst and Terry Parkhurst, "22 Skidoo," *NYPD Blue,* ABC, 2003.

Victor "Vic" Lake, "Maternal Instincts," *Cold Case,* CBS, 2004.

Jesse Kramer, "Whacked," *CSI: Miami,* CBS, 2005.

Doug Frohmer, "Man of Steele," *Standoff,* Fox, 2006.

Abner Stone, "Nine Wives," *Numb3rs* (also known as *Num3ers*), CBS, 2007.

Dwayne Tancana, "Bounty Hunters!," *Psych,* USA Network, 2007.

Rulon Farnes, "Redwood," *The Mentalist,* CBS, 2008.

Stage Appearances:

Appeared in a production of *A View from the Bridge,* Steppenwolf Theatre, Chicago, IL.

RECORDINGS

Videos:

The Making of "Dunsmore", Image Entertainment, 2005.

WRITINGS

Television Episodes:

"A Constant Throb," *Deadwood,* HBO, 2006.

BRUNO, Dylan 1972–

PERSONAL

Full name, Dylan A. Bruno; born September 6, 1972, in Milford, CT; son of Scott Bruno (an actor); brother of Chris Bruno (an actor); married Emmeli Hultquist, June 24, 2006; children: Demien Axel. *Education:* Massachusetts Institute of Technology, B.S., 1993. *Avocational Interests:* Skiing.

Addresses: *Agent*—Carlos Gonzalez, Gersh Agency, 232 North Canon Dr., Beverly Hills, CA 90210; (voice work) Danis Panaro Nist, 9201 West Olympic Blvd., Beverly Hills, CA 90212. *Manager*—Principal Entertainment, 1964 Westwood Blvd., Suite 400, Los Angeles, CA 90025.

Career: Actor and producer. Appeared in commercials for Sunny Delight fruit drinks, Chevy cars, and Taco Bell restaurants; voice for Coors beer commercials. Previously worked as a photographer's model.

CREDITS

Television Appearances; Series:

Colby Granger, *Numb3rs* (also known as *Num3ers*), CBS, 2005–2008.

Television Appearances; Movies:

The Colony, ABC, 1995.

Sergeant Talbot, *When Trumpets Fade* (also known as *Hamburger Hill 2*), HBO, 1998.

Fresh Cut Grass, 2000, Showtime, 2004.

Jake, *Going Greek,* 2002, Showtime, 2004.

Blaine Mayhugh, *The Pennsylvania Miners' Story,* ABC, 2002.

Television Appearances; Episodic:

Contestant, *American Gladiators,* syndicated, 1995.

Scott, "Past, Present," *High Sierra Search and Rescue,* NBC, 1995.

Andy Lightner, "The Lady or the Tiger," *High Incident,* ABC, 1996.

Mickey Wallace, "Intolerance," *Promised Land* (also known as *Home of the Brave*), CBS, 1997.

Brad Armitage, "Ripcord," *Nash Bridges* (also known as *Bridges*), CBS, 1997.

Ricky, "Most Likely to Succeed," *Touched by an Angel,* CBS, 2001.

Todd, "Hurricane Anthony," *CSI: Miami,* CBS, 2003.

Detective Rollins, "He Was a Friend of Mine," *Karen Sisco,* ABC, 2004.

Trey Chase, "Secret Service," *North Shore,* Fox, 2004.

Trey Chase, "Burned," *North Shore,* Fox, 2004.

Narrator, "Eleanor," *Rides,* Discovery Channel, 2004.

Billy, "Secrets," *Sex, Love & Secrets,* UPN, 2005.

Billy, "Ambush," *Sex, Love & Secrets,* UPN, 2005.

Felps/Massey, "Independence Day," *The Dead Zone* (also known as *Stephen King's "Dead Zone"*), USA Network, 2006.

Entertainment Tonight (also known as *Entertainment This Week, E.T., ET Weekend,* and *This Week in Entertainment*), syndicated, 2007.

Television Appearances; Other:
Dane Patterson, *The Break* (pilot), Fox, 2003.
Narrator, *Chasing Baja* (special), 2008.

Television Work; Movies:
Producer, *Fresh Cut Grass,* 2000, Showtime, 2004.
Coproducer, *Going Greek,* 2001, Showtime, 2004.

Film Appearances:
Private First Class Alan Toynbe, *Saving Private Ryan,* DreamWorks, 1998.
Mark Bing, *The Rage: Carrie 2,* Metro–Goldwyn–Mayer, 1999.
Willy Jack Pickens, *Where the Heart Is,* Twentieth Century–Fox, 2000.
Billy, *The Simian Line,* Gabriel Film Group, 2001.
Yates, *The One* (also known as *Jet Li's "The One"*), Columbia, 2001.
Johnny Black, *The Anarchist Cookbook,* American World Pictures, 2002.
Jake, *The Fastest Man in the World,* Little Fish Films, 2002.
Traffic cop, *Grand Theft Parsons,* Swipe Films, 2003.
Chet Dickman, *Last of the Romantics,* Gymnopedie Films, 2007.
Scott, *Quid Pro Quo,* Magnolia Pictures, 2008.

RECORDINGS

Video Games:
Voice of barkeeper, *Wing Commander IV: The Price of Freedom,* Electronic Arts, 1995.

BURNS, Edward 1968–
(Ed Burns, Edward J. Burns)

PERSONAL

Some sources cite full name variously as Edward J. Burns, Jr. or Edward F. Burns; born January 29 (some sources cite January 28), 1968, in Woodside, Queens, New York, NY; raised in Long Island, NY; son of Edward J. (a police officer and spokesperson) and Molly (a federal agency manager; maiden name, McKenna) Burns; brother of Brian Burns (a director, producer, and writer); married Christy Turlington (a model and entrepreneur), June 7, 2003; children: Grace, Finn.

Education: Studied film and English at Hunter College, the City University of New York; attended the State University of New York College at Oneonta and the University at Albany, State University of New York. *Avocational Interests:* Cars, sports.

Addresses: *Office*—Wild Ocean Films, 11–17 Beach St., Suite 400, New York, NY 10013 and 1158 26th St., Suite 880, Santa Monica, CA 90403. *Agent*—Creative Artists Agency, 2000 Avenue of the Stars, Los Angeles, CA 90067. *Publicist*—I/D Public Relations, 8409 Santa Monica Blvd., West Hollywood, CA 90069.

Career: Actor, director, producer, and writer. Wild Ocean Films, partner. Irish Twins Productions, co-founder and partner. Affiliated with the production company Marlboro Road Gang Productions. Participated in film festivals and conventions. Worked as a production assistant, at a news outlet, as a van driver and bus person, and mowed lawns. Multiple Sclerosis Society, national ambassador.

Member: Screen Actors Guild, Directors Guild of America, Writers Guild of America, East.

Awards, Honors: Grand Jury Prize, dramatic category, Sundance Film Festival, 1995, Jury Special Prize and nomination for the Grand Special Prize, both Deauville Film Festival, 1995, Independent Spirit Award (with Dick Fisher), best first feature, Independent Feature Project/West, 1996, and Nova Award (with Fisher), most promising producer in theatrical motion pictures, Golden Laurel awards, Producers Guild of America, 1996, all for *The Brothers McMullen;* ShoWest Award, screenwriter of the year, National Association of Theatre Owners, 1996; nomination for the Grand Special Prize, Deauville Film Festival, 1996, for *She's the One;* Online Film Critics Society Award, best ensemble cast performance, and Screen Actors Guild Award nomination, outstanding performance by a cast, both with others, 1999, for *Saving Private Ryan;* Best Feature Award, Savannah Film and Video Festival, 2007, for *Purple Violets;* Teen Choice Award nomination, choice movie actor: horror/thriller, 2008, for *One Missed Call;* as a child, won poetry contests.

CREDITS

Film Appearances:
Barry and Finbar McMullen, *The Brothers McMullen,* Fox Searchlight Pictures, 1995.
Himself, *At Sundance* (documentary), 1995.
Mickey Fitzpatrick, *She's the One,* Twentieth Century–Fox, 1996.
Charlie Ryan, *No Looking Back* (also known as *Long Time, Nothing New*), Gramercy Pictures, 1998.

Private first class Richard Reiben, *Saving Private Ryan,* DreamWorks, 1998.

Francis Sullivan, *Ash Wednesday* (also known as *Hell's Kitchen*), Focus Features/IFC Films, 2001.

Jordy Warsaw, *15 Minutes* (also known as *15 Minuten Ruhm*), New Line Cinema, 2001.

(As Ed Burns) Thomas "Tommy" Riley, *Sidewalks of New York,* Paramount Classics, 2001.

Jake Vig, *Confidence* (also known as *Confidence: After Dark*), Lions Gate Films, 2002.

Store clerk, *Lethargy,* 2002.

(As Ed Burns) Tony Scanlon, *Life or Something Like It* (also known as *Blonde Life*), Twentieth Century–Fox, 2002.

The Last Lane, 2002.

Himself, *The Breakup Artist,* Lantern Lane Entertainment, 2004.

Abel Grey, *The River King,* Alliance Atlantis, 2005.

Dr. Travis Ryer, *A Sound of Thunder,* Warner Bros., 2005.

(As Edward J. Burns) Ethan, *The Holiday* (also known as *Holiday*), Columbia, 2006.

Jack Stanton, *Looking for Kitty,* ThinkFilm, 2006.

(As Edward J. Burns) Paulie, *The Groomsmen,* Bauer Martinez Studios, 2006.

Michael Murphy, *Purple Violets,* One Movie, 2007.

George, *27 Dresses,* Twentieth Century–Fox, 2008.

Jack Andrews, *One Missed Call* (also known as *Don't Pick up the Cell Phone!*), Warner Bros., 2008.

John Reed, *Echelon Conspiracy* (also known as *The Gift*), After Dark Films, 2009.

Film Director:

Brandy (short film), c. 1992.

The Brothers McMullen, Fox Searchlight Pictures, 1995.

She's the One, Twentieth Century–Fox, 1996.

No Looking Back (also known as *Long Time, Nothing New*), Gramercy Pictures, 1998.

Ash Wednesday (also known as *Hell's Kitchen*), Focus Features/IFC Films, 2001.

(As Ed Burns) *Sidewalks of New York,* Paramount Classics, 2001.

The Groomsmen, Bauer Martinez Studios, 2006.

Looking for Kitty, ThinkFilm, 2006.

Purple Violets, One Movie, 2007.

Made other short films, including *Hey Sco* (also known as *Hey Sco!*).

Film Executive Producer:

The Brothers McMullen, Fox Searchlight Pictures, 1995.

Film Producer:

(With Dick Fisher) *The Brothers McMullen,* Fox Searchlight Pictures, 1995.

She's the One, Twentieth Century–Fox, 1996.

No Looking Back (also known as *Long Time, Nothing New*), Gramercy Pictures, 1998.

Ash Wednesday (also known as *Hell's Kitchen*), Focus Features/IFC Films, 2001.

Sidewalks of New York, Paramount Classics, 2001.

The Last Lane, 2002.

The Groomsmen, Bauer Martinez Studios, 2006.

Looking for Kitty, ThinkFilm, 2006.

Purple Violets, One Movie, 2007.

Film Work; Other:

Executive advisor, *She's the One,* Twentieth Century–Fox, 1996.

Television Appearances; Specials:

Himself, *Music in Movies '96,* ABC, 1996.

Himself, *The Beatles Revolution,* ABC, 2000.

Himself, *New York at the Movies,* Arts and Entertainment, 2002.

(As Ed Burns) Himself, *Edge of Outside* (documentary), TCM, 2006.

(As Ed Burns) Himself, *AFI's "100 Years … AFI's '10 Top 10"* (also known as *AFI's "10 Top 10"*), CBS, 2008.

Television Appearances; Episodic:

Himself, *Late Show with David Letterman* (also known as *The Late Show, Late Show Backstage,* and *Letterman*), CBS, 1996.

Himself, "Filmen 'Saving Private Ryan'/Nyheter och vaeder," *Nyhetsmorgon,* 1998.

Himself, "Into the Breach: 'Saving Private Ryan,'" *HBO First Look,* HBO, 1998.

Himself, *Late Night with Conan O'Brien,* NBC, multiple episodes in 1998.

Himself, *The Rosie O'Donnell Show,* syndicated, multiple episodes in 1998.

Himself, "Edward Burns," *Independent Focus,* Independent Film Channel, 2001.

Himself, "Sidewalks of New York," *Anatomy of a Scene,* Sundance Channel, 2001.

(Sometimes credited as Ed Burns) Himself, *The Late Late Show with Craig Kilborn* (also known as *The Late Late Show*), CBS, multiple episodes in 2001.

Himself, *Live Lunch,* 2001.

Himself, *The View,* ABC, 2001.

(As Ed Burns) Himself, *The Daily Show* (also known as *A Daily Show with Jon Stewart, The Daily Show with Jon Stewart, The Daily Show with Jon Stewart Global Edition, Jon Stewart, Ha–Daily Show,* and *I satira tou Jon Stewart*), Comedy Central, 2001, 2006.

Himself, *The Tonight Show with Jay Leno,* NBC, 2002.

Himself, "Confidence," *Anatomy of a Scene,* Sundance Channel, c. 2002.

Himself, *Festival Pass with Chris Gore,* Starz!, c. 2002.

Himself, *The Best Damn Sports Show Period,* Fox Sports Network, 2003.

Himself, *The Caroline Rhea Show,* syndicated, 2003.

Himself, *Live with Regis & Kelly,* syndicated, 2003, 2008.

Guest star, "Anacondas; A Sound of Thunder; The SpongeBob SquarePants Movie; Closer," *Coming Attractions,* E! Entertainment Television, 2004.

Nick, "The Birds and the Bees," *Will & Grace,* NBC, 2005.

Nick, "Dance Cards & Greeting Cards," *Will & Grace,* NBC, 2005.

Nick, "The Fabulous Baker Boy," *Will & Grace,* NBC, 2005.

Himself, "I Wanna Be Sedated," *Entourage,* HBO, 2006.

Himself, "The Release," *Entourage,* HBO, 2006.

Himself, "What about Bob?," *Entourage,* HBO, 2006.

Himself, *Jimmy Kimmel Live!* (also known as *The Jimmy Kimmel Project*), ABC, 2006.

(As Ed Burns) Himself, "Operation: Romanocorp," *The Knights of Prosperity* (also known as *I Want to Rob Jeff Goldblum, Let's Rob Mick Jagger,* and *Untitled Donal Logue Project*) ABC, 2007.

Himself, "The Return of the King," *Entourage,* HBO, 2007.

Himself, *Entertainment Tonight* (also known as *Entertainment This Week, E.T., ET Weekend,* and *This Week in Entertainment*), syndicated, 2007, multiple episodes in 2008.

(In archive footage) Himself, *Cinema tres,* Televisio de Catalunya (TV3, Spain), 2008.

Television Work; Series:

Production assistant and van driver, *Entertainment Tonight* (also known as *Entertainment This Week, E.T., ET Weekend,* and *This Week in Entertainment*), syndicated, until c. 1995.

Creator and executive producer, *The Fighting Fitzgeralds,* NBC, 2001.

Worked on other projects.

Television Director; Specials:

"Lovely Day" segment, *The Concert for New York City,* VH1, 2001.

RECORDINGS

Videos:

Himself, *Making "Saving Private Ryan,"* 2004.

Himself, *"Saving Private Ryan": Boot Camp,* 2004.

Himself, *"Saving Private Ryan": Miller and His Platoon,* 2004.

Himself, *"Saving Private Ryan": Re–Creating Omaha Beach,* 2004.

Music Videos:

Sarah McLachlan, "I Will Remember You," 1995.

Tom Petty and the Heartbreakers, "Walls," 1996.

WRITINGS

Screenplays:

Brandy (short film), c. 1992.

The Brothers McMullen, Fox Searchlight Pictures, 1995, published in *Three Screenplays by Edward Burns,* Hyperion Press, 1998.

She's the One, Twentieth Century–Fox, 1996, published in *Three Screenplays by Edward Burns,* Hyperion Press, 1998.

No Looking Back (also known as *Long Time, Nothing New*), Gramercy Pictures, 1998, published in *Three Screenplays by Edward Burns,* Hyperion Press, 1998.

Ash Wednesday (also known as *Hell's Kitchen*), Focus Features/IFC Films, 2001.

Sidewalks of New York, Paramount Classics, 2001.

Flight of the Phoenix, Twentieth Century–Fox, 2004.

The Groomsmen, Bauer Martinez Studios, 2006.

Looking for Kitty, ThinkFilm, 2006.

Purple Violets, One Movie, 2007.

Made other short films, including *Hey Sco* (also known as *Hey Sco!*).

Collected Screenplays:

Three Screenplays by Edward Burns (contains *The Brothers McMullen, No Looking Back,* and *She's the One*), Hyperion Press, 1998.

Teleplays; Pilots:

(And story) *The Fighting Fitzgeralds,* NBC, 2001.

Author of various pilots.

Comic Books:

(With Jimmy Palmiotti; art and color by Siju Thomas) *Dock Walloper* (also known as *Ed Burns' "Dock Walloper"*), Virgin Comics, beginning 2007.

OTHER SOURCES

Periodicals:

Cosmopolitan, March, 1998, p. 242.

Empire, October, 1998, pp. 100–110, 112, 114.

Entertainment Weekly, November 18, 1996, p. 78.

Glamour, February, 2002, pp. 80–83.

Interview, July, 1996.

Los Angeles Times, March 29, 1998.

Maclean's, April 27, 1998, p. 58; November 19, 2001, p. 114.

Movieline, Volume 7, number 11, 1996, pp. 40–41.

New York Times, January 30, 1995.

Parade, April 14, 2002, pp. 4–5.

People Weekly, September 4, 1995; November 18, 1996, p. 78; November 26, 2001, p. 186.
Playboy, June, 2001, pp. 137–38, 182.
Premiere, April, 1998, pp. 54–55.
Red, October, 2001.
Rolling Stone, August 24, 1995.
US, September, 1996; August, 1998.
USA Today, November 19, 2001.
USA Weekend, March 29, 1998.
U.S. News & World Report, March 30, 1998, p. 8.

Electronic:
Edward Burns, http://www.edwardburns.net, December 8, 2008.

BUTLER, Bill 1921–
(Wilmer Butler, Wilmer C. Butler)

PERSONAL

Born April 7, 1921 (some sources cite 1931), in Cripple Creek, CO; son of Wilmer Herb and Verca Amanda Butler; married Alma H. Smith, November 21, 1943 (divorced, 1983); married, wife's name Iris (an actress), May 28, 1984; children: (first marriage) three; (second marriage) Genevieve (an actress), Chelsea (an actress). *Education:* Attended Iowa Wesleyan College and Iowa State University. *Avocational Interests:* Woodworking.

Addresses: *Agent*—Innovative Artists, 1505 10th St., Santa Monica, CA 90401.

Career: Cinematographer. Also worked as an electronics engineer, lighting consultant, camera operator, photographer, and second unit cinematographer. Worked at a radio station in Gary, IN; WBKB–TV, Chicago, IL; WGN–TV and Radio, Chicago; began in construction as builder of television station, then affiliate of radio station, later member of television station engineering staff and photographer. University of Arizona, Kodak Cinematographer in Residence, 2006. *Military service:* U.S. Army, Signal Corps, served during World War II.

Member: American Society of Cinematographers.

Awards, Honors: Local Emmy Award for electronic camera work in Chicago, IL; Academy Award nomination (with Haskell Wexler), 1976, and Film Award nomination (with Wexler and William A. Fraker), British Academy of Film and Television Arts, 1977, both best cinematography, for *One Flew over the Cuckoo's Nest;* Emmy Award, outstanding cinematography for an entertainment special, 1977, for *Raid on Entebbe;* Emmy Award nomination, outstanding cinematography for a limited series or a special, 1983, for *The Thorn Birds;* Emmy Award, outstanding cinematography for a limited series or a special, 1984, for *A Streetcar Named Desire;* Stockholm Film Festival Award, best cinematography, 1997, for *Deceiver;* lifetime achievement award, American Society of Cinematographers, 2003.

CREDITS

Film Cinematographer:
Fearless Frank (also known as *Frank's Greatest Adventure*), American International Pictures, 1967.
(As Wilmer Butler) *The Rain People,* Warner Bros., 1969.
Adam's Woman (also known as *Return of the Boomerang*), Warner Bros., 1970.
Drive, He Said, Columbia, 1971.
The Return of Count Yorga (also known as *The Abominable Count Yorga* and *Curse of Count Yorga*), American International Pictures, 1971.
(As Wilmer Butler) *Hickey & Boggs,* United Artists, 1972.
(As Wilmer C. Butler) *Melinda,* Metro–Goldwyn–Mayer, 1972.
(As Wilmer C. Butler) *Deathmaster,* American International Pictures, 1972.
(As Wilmer C. Butler) *The Manchu Eagle Murder Caper Mystery,* United Artists, 1973.
The Conversation, Paramount, 1974.
(Uncredited; with Haskell Wexler and William A. Fraker) *One Flew over the Cuckoo's Nest,* United Artists, 1975.
Jaws (also known as *Stillness in the Water*), Universal, 1975.
(With Fraker) *Lipstick,* Paramount, 1976.
The Bingo Long Traveling All–Stars & Motor Kings, Universal, 1976.
Alex & the Gypsy (also known as *Love and Other Crimes*), Twentieth Century–Fox, 1976.
Sunshine, Part II (excerpts from unaired television series; also known as *My Sweet Lady*), 1976.
Demon Seed (also known as *Proteus Generation*), Metro–Goldwyn–Mayer/United Artists, 1977.
Capricorn One, Warner Bros., 1978.
Damien—Omen II (also known as *Omen II* and *Omen II: Damien*), Twentieth Century–Fox, 1978.
Grease, Paramount, 1978.
Uncle Joe Shannon, United Artists, 1978.
Ice Castles, Columbia, 1978.
Rocky II, United Artists, 1979.
Can't Stop the Music (also known as *Discoland*), Associated Film Distribution, 1980.
It's My Turn (also known as *A Perfect Circle*), Columbia, 1980.
(With Fred Batka) *The Night the Lights Went Out in Georgia,* Avco Embassy, 1981.

Stripes, Columbia, 1981.

Rocky III (also known as *Eye of the Tiger*), Metro–Goldwyn–Mayer, 1982.

The Secret of NIMH (also known as *Mrs. Brisby and the Rats of NIMH*), Metro–Goldwyn–Mayer, 1982.

The Sting II, Universal, 1983.

Rocky IV, Metro–Goldwyn–Mayer, 1985.

Beer (also known as *The Selling of America*), Orion, 1986.

Big Trouble, Columbia, 1986.

Wildfire, MCA/Universal Home Video, 1988.

Biloxi Blues (also known as *Neil Simon's "Biloxi Blues"*), Universal, 1988.

Child's Play, Metro–Goldwyn–Mayer, 1988.

Graffiti Bridge (also known as *Purple Rain II*), Warner Bros., 1990.

Hot Shots! (also known as *Hot Shots: An Important Movie!*), Twentieth Century–Fox, 1991.

Cop and a Half, Universal, 1992.

Sniper, TriStar, 1993.

Beethoven's 2nd, Universal, 1993.

(With others) *Mother* (also known as *The Haunted Heart*), Paramount, 1996.

Flipper, Universal, 1996.

Anaconda, Sony Pictures Entertainment, 1997.

Deceiver (also known as *Liar*), Metro–Goldwyn–Mayer, 1998.

Ropewalk (also known as *Hanginaround*), 2000.

Frailty (also known as *Daemonisch* and *Frailty—Nessuno e al sicuro*), Lions Gate Films, 2001.

Berserker (short film), 2005.

Zombie Prom (short film), 2006.

Funny Money, ThinkFilm, 2006.

The Plague (also known as *Clive Barker's "The Plague"*), Sony Pictures Home Entertainment, 2006.

Redline, Chicago Releasing, 2007.

Limousine (also known as *Limo Driver*), Ozumi Films, 2008.

Looking Up Dresses (short film), Lodge Boy Productions, 2008.

Evil Angel, Main Street Movie/Zion Films, 2009.

Documentary Film Appearances:

Visions of Light: The Art of Cinematography (also known as *Visions of Light*), American Film Institute, 1992.

Tell Them Who You Are, 2004.

Cinematographer Style, 2005.

Television Cinematographer; Series:

Ghost Story (also known as *Circle of Fear*), NBC, 1972.

Brooklyn Bridge, CBS, 1991–92.

Dark Skies, NBC, 1996.

Television Cinematographer; Miniseries:

The Thorn Birds, ABC, 1983.

Passing Glory, TNT, 1999.

Joe and Max, Starz!, 2002.

Television Cinematographer; Movies:

Something Evil, CBS, 1972.

I Heard the Owl Call My Name, CBS, 1973.

Deliver Us from Evil (also known as *Running Wild*), ABC, 1973.

The Execution of Private Slovik, NBC, 1974.

Indict and Convict, ABC, 1974.

Fear on Trial, CBS, 1975.

Hustling, ABC, 1975.

Raid on Entebbe, NBC, 1977.

Mary White, ABC, 1977.

Killing at Hell's Gate, CBS, 1981.

Death Ray 2000 (also known as *T. R. Sloane*), NBC, 1981.

A Streetcar Named Desire, ABC, 1984.

When We Were Young (also known as *That Magic Moment*), NBC, 1989.

A Walton Wedding (also known as *John–Boy's Wedding*), CBS, 1995.

Don King: Only in America (also known as *Don King*), HBO, 1997.

Hendrix, Showtime, 2000.

Television Cinematographer; Pilots:

A Clear and Present Danger, NBC, 1970.

Sunshine, CBS, 1973.

Savage (also known as *The Savage File* and *Watch Dog*), NBC, 1973.

The Big Rip–Off (also known as *McCoy*), NBC, 1974.

Target Risk, NBC, 1975.

Bates Motel, NBC, 1987.

Dark Skies, NBC, 1996.

Television Cinematographer; Specials:

The People vs. Paul Crump, 1962.

The Bold Men, NBC, 1965.

Television Cinematographer; Episodic:

"Underworld," *GvsE* (also known as *Good vs Evil*), Sci–Fi Channel, 2000.

Television Appearances:

Hollywood: The Gift of Laughter (miniseries), ABC, 1982.

Jaws: The E! True Hollywood Story (special), E! Entertainment Television, 2002.

RECORDINGS

Videos:

The Making of Steven Spielberg's "Jaws," Universal Home Video, 1995.

The Making of "Frailty," Live Home Video, 2002.

The Shark Is Still Working, Finatic Productions, 2006.

C

CARRINGTON, Debbie Lee 1959–
(Debbi Lee Carrington, Debbie Carrington, Deborah Lee Carrington)

PERSONAL

Full name, Deborah Lee Carrington; born December 14, 1959, in San Jose, CA; father, an insurance manager; mother, a schoolteacher. *Education:* University of California, Davis, graduated, 1982. *Avocational Interests:* Aerobics (certified instructor), sports.

Career: Actress, stunt performer, and stunt double, sometimes credited as Debbie Carrington, Debbi Lee Carrington, or Deborah Lee Carrington.

CREDITS

Film Appearances:
A Munchkin, *Under the Rainbow,* Orion, 1981.
Ewok, *Star Wars: Episode VI—Return of the Jedi* (also known as *Return of the Jedi* and *Star Wars VI: Return of the Jedi*), Twentieth Century–Fox, 1983.
(As Debbie Carrington) Drone, *Invaders from Mars,* Cannon, 1986.
A duck, *Howard the Duck* (also known as *Howard: A New Breed of Hero*), Universal, 1986.
Idee, *Captain Eo* (short film), Buena Vista, 1986.
Little Bigfoot, *Harry and the Hendersons* (also known as *Bigfoot* and *Bigfoot and the Hendersons*), Universal, 1987.
Voice of Valerie Vomit, *The Garbage Pail Kids Movie* (animated), Atlantic Releasing, 1987.
Dr. Ziplock, *Spaced Invaders* (also known as *Martians!!!*), Buena Vista, 1990.
Thumbelina, *Total Recall* (also known as *El vengador del futuro*), TriStar, 1990.

Betty, *Club Fed,* Metro–Goldwyn–Mayer/United Artists Home Entertainment, 1990.
(Uncredited) Crying midget, *The Bonfire of the Vanities,* Warner Bros., 1990.
Emperor Penguin, *Batman Returns,* Warner Bros., 1992.
(As Debbie Carrington) Bwaaa (Fishface), *Mom and Dad Save the World,* Warner Bros., 1992.
Tumbler, *Seedpeople* (also known as *Dark Forest*), Paramount Home Video, 1992.
Cattive ragazze, New Pentax Film, 1992.
Branithar, *The High Crusade* (also known as *High Crusade—Frikassee im weltraum*), Pioneer Entertainment, 1994.
(As Debbie Carrington) Member of gorilla team, *Born to Be Wild* (also known as *Katie*), Warner Bros., 1995.
Alien father, *Men in Black* (also known as *MIB*), Columbia/MCA–Universal, 1997.
A gorilla, *Mighty Joe Young* (also known as *Mighty Joe*), Buena Vista, 1998.
Felicity, *She's All That,* Miramax, 1999.
Surfer girl, *The Independent,* Arrow Releasing, 2001.
Kitty Katz, *Tiptoes* (also known as *Tiny Tiptoes*), Reality Check Productions, 2003.
(Uncredited) Mini Tabitha, *Scary Movie 3* (also known as *Scary Movie 3.5* and *Film de peur 3*), Miramax/Dimension Films, 2003.
Gizzie Blunderbore, *Big Time,* Geofrey Hildrew, 2004.
Elf, *The Polar Express* (also released as *The Polar Express: An IMAX 3D Experience*), Warner Bros., 2004.
Receptionist, *Sunstroke,* 2006.
(As Debbie Carrington) Booing goblin, *Bedtime Stories,* Walt Disney, 2008.
Hot Pocket, *Bitch Slap,* 2009.

Television Appearances; Movies:
Weechee Warrick, *The Ewok Adventure* (also known as *Caravan of Courage* and *Caravan of Courage: An Ewok Adventure*), ABC, 1984.
Weechee Warrick, *Ewoks: The Battle for Endor,* ABC, 1985.

Television Appearances; Pilots:
Zet, *Earthlings,* ABC, 1984.
Sophie, *Special Unit,* Comedy Central, 2006.

Television Appearances; Specials:
The Making of "Captain Eo," 1986.
Gorah, *The Christmas Secret* (also known as *Flight of the Reindeer*), CBS, 2000.

Television Appearances; Episodic:
(As Debbie Carrington) Alien, "Fine Tuning," *Amazing Stories* (also known as *Steven Spielberg's "Amazing Stories"*), NBC, 1985.
Fifth Munchkin, "The Improbable Dream," *What's Happening Now!,* 1985.
(As Debbie Carrington) Troll, "Fools' Gold," *Monsters,* 1989.
Carla Sapper, "Do the Wrong Thing," *WIOU,* 1990.
Alien, "Married ... with Aliens," *Married ... with Children,* Fox, 1990.
Tiny avenger, "The Adventures of Handi–Boy," *In Living Color,* Fox, 1991.
Tiny avenger, "Michael Jackson: Little Timmy's Not My Lover," *In Living Color,* Fox, 1992.
Tiny avenger, "Anton and the Green Card," *In Living Color,* Fox, 1992.
Tammy, "The Stand–in," *Seinfeld,* NBC, 1994.
Debbie, "Silent Night, Baywatch Night: Parts 1 & 2," *Baywatch,* syndicated, 1994.
Title role, "Frankenturkey," *Bone Chillers,* 1996.
First alien, "People's Choice," *Perversions of Science,* HBO, 1997.
Airplane passenger, *Damian Cromwell's Postcards from America,* 1997.
Raquel Gibson, "Loss," *Tracey Takes On ...,* HBO, 1998.
Meetra, "Haunted," *The Journey of Allen Strange,* Nickelodeon, 1998.
Doreen (Mini–Mimi), "Y2K, You're Okay," *The Drew Carey Show,* ABC, 1999.
Doreen (Mini–Mimi), "Drew's Physical," *The Drew Carey Show,* ABC, 1999.
Doreen (Mini–Mimi), "Drew and the Racial Tension Play," *The Drew Carey Show,* ABC, 2000.
Doreen (Mini–Mimi), "Beer Ball," *The Drew Carey Show,* ABC, 2000.
Creature, "Listening to Fear," *Buffy the Vampire Slayer* (also known as *BtVS, Buffy,* and *Buffy, the Vampire Slayer: The Series*), The WB, 2000.
Sadie Muckle, "Madam, I'm Adam," *The Lone Gunmen,* Fox, 2001.
Ginger Jones, "A Simple Twist of Fate," *ER,* NBC, 2002.
Stephanie Renato, "Tall Tales," *Philly,* ABC, 2002.
Alice, "Small Packages," *The District,* CBS, 2002.
Patty, "Loose Lips," *Boston Legal,* ABC, 2004.
Marla, "Flashpants," *Huff,* Showtime, 2004.
Merrily, "Reefer," *Nip/Tuck,* FX Network, 2006.
Patty, "Truth Be Told," *Dexter,* Showtime, 2006.
Karen, "Read between the Minds," *Men in Trees,* ABC, 2008.
Herself, *The Insider,* 2008.

Stage Appearances:
Toured in *Alvin and the Chimpkus Show.*

RECORDINGS

Videos:
Voice of Ewok (in archive footage), *Star Wars: Battlefront* (video game), LucasArts Entertainment, 2004.

Appeared in the music video "Love in an Elevator" by Aerosmith.

OTHER SOURCES

Periodicals:
People Weekly, October 25, 1999, p. 97.

CERVERIS, Michael 1960–

PERSONAL

Born November 6, 1960, in Bethesda, MD; brother of Todd Cerveris (an actor). *Education:* Yale University, graduated, 1983.

Addresses: *Agent*—Innovative Artists, 235 Park Ave. S., 10th Floor, New York, NY 10003. *Publicist*—I/D Public Relations, 150 West 30th St., 19th Floor, New York, NY 10001.

Career: Actor, singer, guitarist, songwriter, and recording artist. Toured German cities with the band Lame, 1995–97; performed with the bands Retriever, c. 2001, and Cerveris, c. 2004; toured with Bob Mould in "The Last Dog and Pony Show," 1998; toured with Pete Townsend. Appeared in commercials, including voice work for Eternity by Calvin Klein.

Member: Actors' Equity Association.

Awards, Honors: *Theatre World* Award and Antoinette Perry Award nomination, best featured actor, both 1993, for *The Who's Tommy;* Grammy Award (with others), best original cast recording, National Academy of Recording Arts and Sciences, 1993, for the cast album from *The Who's Tommy;* Antoinette Perry

Award, best featured actor in a musical, 2004, for *Assassins;* Antoinette Perry Award nomination, best leading actor in a musical, and Drama Desk Award nomination, outstanding actor in a musical, both 2006, for *Sweeney Todd;* Antoinette Perry Award nomination, best leading actor in a musical, and Drama Desk Award nomination, outstanding actor in a musical, both 2007, for *LoveMusik;* Garland Award, *Backstage West,* for Los Angeles performance in *Hedwig and the Angry Inch.*

CREDITS

Stage Appearances:

Moon, off–Broadway production, 1983.

Malcolm, *Macbeth,* Ark Theatre Company, New York City, 1983.

Arthur Rimbaud, *Total Eclipse,* Westside Arts Theatre, New York City, 1984.

Astolfo, *Life Is a Dream,* Ark Theatre Company, 1985.

Levi–Yitskhok, *Green Fields,* American Jewish Theatre, New York City, 1985.

Crow, *The Tooth of Crime,* Hartford Stage Company, Hartford, CT, 1985–86.

Romeo, *Romeo and Juliet,* Indiana Repertory Theatre, Indianapolis, IN, 1985–86.

Frank, *Abingdon Square,* American Place Theatre, New York City, 1987.

Blood Sports, New York Theatre Workshop, Perry Street Theatre, New York City, 1987.

Romeo, *Romeo and Juliet,* Goodman Theatre, Chicago, IL, 1988.

Duke of Aumerle, *Richard II,* Center Theatre Group, Mark Taper Forum, Los Angeles, 1991–92.

Tommy as a young adult, *The Who's Tommy* (musical; also known as *Tommy),* La Jolla Playhouse, La Jolla, CA, 1992–93, then St. James Theatre, New York City, 1993–95.

Thomas Andrews, *Titanic* (musical), Lunt–Fontanne Theatre, New York City, 1997–99.

Hedwig Schmidt/Tommy Gnosis, *Hedwig and the Angry Inch,* Jane Street Theatre, New York City, 1997–2000, then Los Angeles and London, 2000.

Narrator, *Chess* (benefit concerts), Broadway Cares/ Equity Fights AIDS, New York City, 1998.

Joe's dad, *Joe!,* Lamb's Theatre, New York City, 1998.

Tybalt and prince, *Romeo and Juliet* (staged reading), New York City, 1998.

Bursie, *Wild Party,* Manhattan Theatre Company, New York City, 1998.

Kenneth Talley, Jr., *Fifth of July,* Signature Theatre Company, Peter Norton Space, New York City, 2003.

Francois, *Wintertime,* Second Stage Theatre, New York City, then McCarter Theatre, Princeton, NJ, 2004.

John Wilkes Booth, *Assassins* (musical), Roundabout Theatre Company, Studio 54, New York City, 2004.

The Booth Variations, off–Broadway production, 2004.

Giorgio, *Passion* (benefit concert), Ambassador Theatre, New York City, 2004.

Children and Art (benefit concert), Young Playwrights, New York City, 2005.

Title role, *Sweeney Todd* (musical; also known as *Sweeney Todd: The Demon Barber of Fleet Street),* Eugene O'Neill Theatre, New York City, 2005–2006.

Father, *An Oak Tree,* Perry Street Theatre Company, Barrow Street Theatre, New York City, 2006–2007.

Kurt Weill, *LoveMusik* (musical), Manhattan Theatre Club, Biltmore Theatre (now Samuel J. Friedman Theatre), New York City, 2007.

Earl of Kent, *King Lear,* Public Theatre, New York City, 2007.

Posthumus Leonatus, *Cymbeline,* Vivian Beaumont Theatre, Lincoln Center, New York City, 2007–2008.

Wilson Mizner, *Road Show,* Estelle R. Newman Theatre, Public Theatre, New York City, 2008.

Jorgen Tesman, *Hedda Gabler,* Roundabout Theatre Company, American Airlines Theatre, New York City, 2009.

Also appeared as Claudio, *Measure for Measure,* Old Globe Theatre, San Diego, CA; as Bazarov, *Nothing Sacred,* Northlight Theatre, Chicago, IL; and in productions of *Eastern Standard,* Seattle Repertory Theatre, Seattle, WA; *El Dorado,* South Coast Repertory, Costa Mesa, CA; *The Games,* Brooklyn Academy of Music, New York City; *A Little Night Music,* Chicago Shakespeare Theatre, Chicago, IL; *Much Ado about Nothing,* La Jolla, CA; *Passion,* John F. Kennedy Center for the Performing Arts, Washington, DC, and Ravinia Festival, Chicago, IL; *Puck,* Dallas Theatre Center, Dallas, TX; and *The Scottish Play,* Brooklyn, NY; also appeared in productions of *Anyone Can Whistle, Fiddler on the Roof, A Midsummer Night's Dream, My Fair Lady,* and *Sunday in the Park with George.*

Major Tours:

Tommy, *The Who's Tommy* (musical; also known as *Tommy),* German cities, 1995–97.

Film Appearances:

Mike, *Tokyo Pop,* Spectrafilm, 1988.

John Reece, *Strangers,* 1990.

Daniel "Danny" Emerson, *Steel and Lace,* Cinema Home Video, 1991.

Eaglebauer, *Rock 'n' Roll High School Forever,* Live Entertainment, 1991.

Paul, *A Woman, Her Men, and Her Futon,* Republic, 1992.

Himself and Tommy, *The Who's Tommy, the Amazing Journey* (documentary), 1993.

Third restaurant man, *Lulu on the Bridge,* Trimark Pictures, 1998.

Frank, *The Mexican,* DreamWorks, 2001.

Pablo, *Temptation*, 2004.
Himself, *Brief Interviews with Hideous Men*, Salty Features, 2009.
Mr. Destiny, *Cirque du Freak* (also known as *Circus of the Freak*), Universal, 2009.

Television Appearances; Series:
Ian Ware, *Fame*, NBC, 1986–87.
Gary Forbush, *The American Embassy*, Fox, 2002.
(Uncredited) The observer, *Fringe*, Fox, 2008.

Appeared as Ian McLaren in the series *General Hospital*, ABC.

Television Appearances; Specials:
Giorgio, "Passion," *Live from Lincoln Center* (also known as *Great Performances: Live from Lincoln Center*), PBS, 2005.
Broadway under the Stars, CBS, 2005, 2006.
Himself, *Mr. Prince*, Ovation Channel, 2009.

Television Appearances; Pilots:
Gary Forbush, *The American Embassy*, Fox, 2002.
(Uncredited) The observer, *Fringe*, Fox, 2008.

Television Appearances; Miniseries:
Gary Prine, *Doubletake* (also known as *Switch*), CBS, 1985.

Television Appearances; Awards Presentations:
The 51st Annual Tony Awards, CBS, 1997.
The 58th Annual Tony Awards (also known as *The 2004 Tony Awards*), CBS, 2004.
The 60th Annual Tony Awards, 2006.

Television Appearances; Episodic:
Johnny Dark, "The Best Couple I Know," *Leg Work*, 1987.
Nick Kaminsky, "Race Traitors," *The Equalizer*, CBS, 1989.
Ray, "Back to School," *21 Jump Street*, Fox, 1990.
Culp, "To Catch a Con: Part 2," *Gabriel's Fire*, ABC, 1990.
Nick, "Glitter Rock—April 12, 1974," *Quantum Leap*, NBC, 1991.
Bobby Krull, "And Bobby Makes Three," *Dream On*, HBO, 1993.
The Rosie O'Donnell Show, syndicated, 1997.
Syd Booth Goggle, "The Strip Strangler," *CSI: Crime Scene Investigation* (also known as *C.S.I.*, *CSI: Las Vegas*, and *Les experts*), CBS, 2001.
Nick Crowley, "Lust for Life," *Dr. Vegas*, CBS, 2004.
Himself, *Character Studies*, PBS, 2005.
Breakfast with the Arts, Arts and Entertainment, 2006.

Greg Stipe, "Depths," *Law & Order: Criminal Intent* (also known as *Law & Order: CI*), NBC, 2007.
Broadway Beat, 2008.

RECORDINGS

Albums:
(Contributor) *BobMould Band: Live Dog*, 1998.
(With Retriever) *Hinterlands*, 2001.
(With Cerveris) *Dog Eared*, 2004.

Member of ensemble for cast recording of *The Who's Tommy*.

Audio Books:
Narrator of the audio book adaptation of *Catch Me if You Can*, by Frank Abagnale, Jr.

WRITINGS

Albums:
Songwriter, *Dog Eared*, 2004.

OTHER SOURCES

Periodicals:
Back Stage, April 30, 1993, p. 7.
Out, April, 2002, pp. 26, 28.

Electronic:
Cerveris Official Site, http://www.cerveris.com, January 6, 2009.
Michael Cerveris Official Site, http://www.michaelcerveris.com, January 18, 2009.

CHALK, Gary 1953–
(Garry Chalk, Gary Chaulk)

PERSONAL

Born November 13, 1953, in Southampton, England; immigrated to Canada, 1957; married. *Avocational Interests:* Golfing, reading, Russian culture.

Addresses: *Agent*—Characters Talent Agency, 1505 West Second Ave., Suite 200, Vancouver, British Columbia V6H 3Y4, Canada.

Career: Actor and voice artist. Appeared in advertisements. Provided the voice of Slash for the theme park attraction *ReBoot: The Ride* (also known as *Journey into Chaos*), IMAX Corporation. Delivered singing telegrams and telegrams while in costumes.

Awards, Honors: Gemini awards, best performance by an actor in a featured supporting role in a dramatic series, Academy of Canadian Cinema and Television, 2001 and 2002, both for *Cold Squad.*

CREDITS

Film Appearances:

Police officer, *Mr. Patman* (also known as *Crossover*), Film Consortium of Canada, 1980.

Oregon trail mail clerk, *The Grey Fox,* United Artists, 1982.

Chicago worker, *The Journey of Natty Gann,* Buena Vista, 1985.

Police officer, *Certain Fury,* New World Pictures, 1985.

Third deputy, *Fire with Fire* (also known as *Captive Hearts*), Paramount, 1986.

Courthouse reporter, *The Accused* (also known as *Reckless Endangerment, Acusados, Angeklagt, Anklagad, Appel a la justice, Les accuses, Oi katigoroumenoi, Os acusados, Oskarzeni, Oskarzona, Sotto accusa,* and *Syytetty*), Paramount, 1988.

Canadian bartender, *American Boyfriends* (also known as *My American Boyfriend* and *Mes copains americains*), CBS Films, 1989.

Scorby, *The Fly II,* Twentieth Century–Fox, 1989.

Ambulance attendant, *David,* 1993.

(As Garry Chalk) Paramedic, *Intersection,* Paramount, 1994.

Wasser, *Bounty Hunters* (also known as *Outgun*), Dimension Films, 1996.

Voice of Mosely, *Warriors of Virtue* (also known as *Creature Zone* and *Magic warriors*), Metro–Goldwyn–Mayer, 1997.

Wasser, *Hardball* (also known as *Bounty Hunters II* and *Bounty Hunters 2: Hardball*), Dimension Films, 1997.

(Uncredited) Coach, *Disturbing Behavior* (also known as *Disturbing Behaviour*), Columbia/TriStar, 1998.

(As Garry Chalk) Ernie, *Camouflage,* PM Entertainment, 1999.

Puppetman, *Late Night Sessions,* The Asylum, 1999.

Police chief, *The Guilty* (also known as *Coupable ou non–coupable*), Eagle Pictures, 2000.

Dale Dixer, *The Shipment,* Promark Entertainment, 2001.

(As Garry Chalk) Jack Burtrell, *Deadly Little Secrets,* Good Morgan Productions, 2001.

Unleashed, Apollo Media, 2001.

(As Garry Chalk) Agent Bill Chalmers, *Trapped* (also known as *Call, 24 Hours,* and *24 Stunden Angst*), Columbia, 2002.

Sheriff Williams and some sources cite role of J. D., *Freddy vs. Jason* (also known as *Friday the 13th Part XI, FvJ, A Nightmare on Elm Street Part 8,* and *A Nightmare on Friday the 13th*), New Line Cinema, 2003.

(As Garry Chalk) Brunelli, *The Karate Dog,* Screen Media Ventures, 2004.

Police captain, *SuperBabies: Baby Geniuses 2* (also known as *Baby Geniuses 2* and *Baby Geniuses 2: Return of the Super Babies*), Columbia, 2004.

Sergeant, *Caught in the Headlights,* Waterfront Entertainment, 2004.

Dad, *Fishbowl* (short film), 2005.

Bear, *Under the Sycamore Tree,* 2006.

(As Garry Chalk) Boat captain, *Eight Below* (also known as *8 Below*), Buena Vista, 2006.

Mayor, *Breakdown* (short film), Oua Media, 2006.

(As Garry Chalk) Sheriff Dave, *Deck the Halls,* Twentieth Century–Fox, 2006.

Agent Gardenia, *Blonde and Blonder,* Empire Film Group, 2007.

Bert, *Taming Tammy,* 2007.

Himself, *Adventures in Voice Acting* (documentary), 2007.

(As Garry Chalk) McCallum, *Fierce People,* Lionsgate, 2007.

(As Garry Chalk) Chief Faherty, *Battle in Seattle,* 2007, Redwood Palms Pictures, 2008.

Home track announcer, *Free Style,* Samuel Goldwyn, 2008.

Christmas Town, Peace Arch Entertainment Group, 2008.

Carson, *Angel and the Badman,* c. 2008.

E. Herbert Mcinnis, *The Saints of Mt. Christopher,* c. 2008.

Animated Film Appearances:

(English version) Voice of King Gurumes, *Doragon boru: Shenron no densetsu* (anime; also known as *Curse of the Blood Rubies, Dragon Ball: Curse of the Blood Rubies,* and *Dragon Ball: The Legend of Shenron*), originally released in Japan, 1986.

Voice of Captain Dogwood, *The New Adventures of Little Toot,* Starmaker Video, 1992.

Voice, *Cinderella* (also known as *La Cenicienta*), Good-Times Home Video, 1994.

Voice, *Happy, the Littlest Bunny,* GoodTimes Entertainment, 1994.

Voice, *Leo the Lion: King of the Jungle* (also known as *Leo Lion*), 1994.

Voice, *The Nutcracker,* GoodTimes Home Video, 1994.

Voice, *Pocahontas* (also known as *The Adventures of Pocahontas: Indian Princess*), GoodTimes Home Video, 1994.

Voice, *Sleeping Beauty* (also known as *La bella durmiente*), GoodTimes Home Video, 1994.

Voice, *Alice in Wonderland* (also known as *Alicia en el pais de las maravillas*), GoodTimes Home Video, 1995.

Voice, *Black Beauty* (also known as *Hermoso negro*), GoodTimes Home Video, 1995.

Voice, *Curly: The Littlest Puppy,* GoodTimes Home Video, 1995.

Voice, *Heidi,* GoodTimes Entertainment, 1995.

Voice, *Hercules,* GoodTimes Entertainment, 1995.

Voice, *Jungle Book* (also known as *El libro de la selva*), GoodTimes Home Video, 1995.

Voice, *Little Red Riding Hood,* GoodTimes Home Video, 1995.

Voice, *Magic Gift of the Snowman* (also known as *El regalo magico del muneco de nieve*), GoodTimes Home Video, 1995.

Voice, *Snow White* (also known as *Blancanieves*), GoodTimes Entertainment, 1995.

Voice, *The Hunchback of Notre Dame,* GoodTimes Home Video, 1996.

(As Garry Chalk) Voice of Blitzen, *Rudolph the Red–Nosed Reindeer: The Movie,* Legacy Releasing, 1998.

Voice of Tattoo Joe, *The Animated Adventures of Tom Sawyer,* Artisan Entertainment/Family Home Entertainment, 1998.

(As Garry Chalk) Voice of Papa, *Mama, Do You Love Me?* (short animated film), Sony Wonder, 1999.

(English version) Voice of fish waiting for second bus, *Hjaelp, jeg er en fisk* (also known as *A Fish Tale, Help! I'm a Fish,* and *Hilfe! Ich bin ein Fisch*), 2000.

(As Garry Chalk) Voices of Santa Claus and Bumble the abominable snowman, *Rudolph the Red–Nosed Reindeer and the Island of Misfit Toys* (also known as *Rudolph & the Island of Misfit Toys*), Golden Books Family Entertainment, 2001.

Voice of baker, *Barbie of Swan Lake,* Artisan Entertainment, 2003.

Voice of Bluto, *Popeye's Voyage: The Quest for Pappy* (short animated film), Lions Gate Films Home Entertainment, 2004.

(As Garry Chalk) Voice of Herve, *Barbie as the Princess and the Pauper,* Universal, 2004.

(As Garry Chalk) Voices of Gerridommis and Capn' Cragg, *In Search of Santa,* Buena Vista, 2004.

Voice of El Haystack Grande, *The Return of El Malefico* (also known as *Mucha Lucha!: The Return of El Malefico*), Warner Bros., c. 2004.

Voice of Frazer, *Barbie as the Island Princess* (also known as *Island Princess*), Universal Studios Home Entertainment, 2007.

Voice of general, *The Ten Commandments,* Promenade Pictures, 2007.

Voice of the king of the cats, *Tom and Jerry: A Nutcracker Tale,* Warner Bros., 2007.

Voice of Nathan Nelson, *Mosaic* (also known as *Stan Lee Presents "Mosaic"*), Anchor Bay Entertainment, 2007.

Voices of Cavitus and Sol, *I Scream, You Scream!* (part of the *3–2–1 Penguins!* video series), 2007.

Animated Film Additional Voices:

(As Garry Chalk) *Mummies Alive! The Legend Begins* (consists of episodes of the series *Mummies Alive!*), Buena Vista Home Video, 1998.

Television Appearances; Live Action Series:

Silver, *Ninja Turtles: The Next Mutation* (also known as *Hero Turtles: The Next Mutation, NT: TNM, Saban's "Hero Turtles: The Next Mutation,"* and *Saban's "Ninja Turtles: The Next Mutation"*), Fox, 1997–98, also broadcast in other countries on other channels.

(As Garry Chalk) Inspector Andrew Pawlachuk, *Cold Squad* (also known as *Files from the Past, Cold Squad, brigade speciale,* and *Halott uegyek*), CTV (Canada), 1999–2005.

Lieutenant Walter "Mr. Multiples" Eastep, *Dark Angel* (also known as *James Cameron's "Dark Angel"*), Fox, 2000–2002.

(As Garry Chalk) Colonel Chekov, *Stargate SG-1* (also known as *La porte des etoiles* and *Stargaate SG-1*), Showtime and syndicated, 2001–2002, Sci–Fi Channel and syndicated, 2002–2006.

(Sometimes known as Garry Chalk) Papa James Stillson, *The Dead Zone* (also known as *The Dark Half, Dead Zone, Stephen King's "Dead Zone," La morta zona, La zona morta, La zona muerta,* and *Zona smrti*), USA Network, 2002–2005.

Television Appearances; Animated Series:

Voice of Metal–Head, *G.I. Joe* (also known as *Action Force, G.I. Joe: A Great American Hero,* and *Chijo saikyo no Expert Team G.I. Joe*), syndicated, beginning 1984, 1990–92.

Voice of King Hippo, *Captain N: The Game Master* (also known as *Captain N and the Video Game Masters* and *Captain N: Game Master*), NBC, 1989–90.

(English version) Voices of Tiara and village elder, *Dragon Quest—Yuusha Abel Densetsu* (anime; also known as *Dragon Quest, Dragon Quest—Legend of the Hero Abel,* and *Dragon Warrior*), originally broadcast in Japan by Fuji Television, 1989–90, 1991.

Voice, *Camp Candy,* NBC, 1989–91.

Voice of King Hippo, *Captain N & the Adventures of Super Mario Bros. 3,* NBC, 1990–91.

Voices of He–Man, Artilla, President Pell, Alcon, Sergeant Krone, Andros, and Gross, *The New Adventures of He–Man* (also known as *Le nuove avventure di He–Man*), syndicated, 1990–91.

Voice of King Hippo, *Captain N and the New Super Mario World* (also known as *The Super Mario World*), NBC, 1991–92.

Voices of Al Negator, Commander Dogstar, Komplex, and Toadborg, *Bucky O'Hare and the Toad Wars,* syndicated, 1991–92.

(As Garry Chalk; English version) Voices of Sir Brick, Sir Phil, Lord Viper, and Warlord Bash, *Entaku no*

Kishi Monogatari: Moero Arthur (anime; also known as *King Arthur, King Arthur and the Knights of Justice,* and *Round Table Knight's Story: Burn, Arthur*), syndicated, 1992–93, originally broadcast in other countries on various channels.

Voices of Bruno, Madder, and Mayor Maynot, *The Adventures of T-Rex* (also known as *T-Rex*), syndicated, 1992–93.

Voices of Conan's father, Set, and grandfather, *Conan: The Adventurer* (also known as *Conan l'aventurier*), Fox, 1992–93.

Voices of Chopper, Kona, and Wild Willy, *Double Dragon,* syndicated, 1993–94.

Voice of Grounder, *Sonic the Hedgehog* (also known as *The Adventures of Sonic the Hedgehog* and *Sonic*), ABC and syndicated, 1993–95.

Voices of Exotrooper Marsala and Governor general Shiva, *ExoSquad,* syndicated, 1993–95.

Voices of Guts Man and others, *Megaman* (anime; also known as *Mega Man* and *Rockman*), ABC Family Channel and syndicated, c. 1994–95.

Voices of Slash, Turbo, Binome general, and others, *Re-Boot,* ABC, 1994–2001.

Voice of Donovan Bane, *Dark Stalkers* (also known as *Darkstalkers* and *Night Warriors: Darkstalker's Revenge*), UPN, 1995.

Voices of Mike Haggar and Abigail, *Final Fight,* beginning 1995.

Voice of Sarge, *The Littlest Pet Shop,* syndicated, 1995–96.

(As Garry Chalk) Voices of Norris and others, *Action Man,* syndicated (some sources cite Fox), 1995–96.

Voice of Lieutenant Stone, *G.I. Joe Extreme,* syndicated, 1995–97.

Voices of Burke (Colonel Keith Wolfman) and Dhalsim, *Streetfighter: The Animated Series* (also known as *Street Fighter* and *Street Fighter: The Animated Series*), syndicated, 1995–97.

Voices of Optimus Primal, Protohuman, and others, *Beast Wars: Transformers* (also known as *Beast Wars, Beasties, Beasties: Transformers,* and *Transformers: Beast Wars*), syndicated, 1996–99.

Voice of Bad Rap, *Extreme Dinosaurs,* syndicated, 1997.

Voice of Emperor Femur, *Shadow Raiders* (also known as *ShadowRaiders* and *War Planets*), YTV (Canada) and syndicated, 1998–99.

Voice of Sir Nigel, *Pocket Dragon Adventures,* syndicated, beginning 1998, BBC, 1999–2003.

Voice of Optimus Primal, *Beast Machines: Transformers* (also known as *Beast Machines* and *Beast Machines: Battle for the Sparks*), Fox, 1999–2000.

Voice of Uncle Huey, *Weird-Ohs,* YTV (Canada) and syndicated, 1999–2000.

Voice of Dr. Ivo Robotnik, *Sonic Underground* (also known as *Sonic le rebelle*), UPN, BKN, Sci-Fi Channel, and TeleToon (Canada), 1999–2004.

Voice of Mungus the giant, *Dragon Tales,* PBS, 1999–2005.

Voice of Jerry the parrot, *Sitting Ducks,* Cartoon Network, 2001–2004.

Voice of Optimus Prime and (uncredited) voice of Grindor, *Transformers: Armada* (anime; also known as *Super Living–Robot Transformer The Legend of Micron Transformers: Micron Legend, Cho robotto seimeitai transformer micron densetsu,* and *Toransufoma: Arumada*), Cartoon Network, 2002–2003, also broadcast by YTV (Canada), and broadcast by TV Tokyo.

(Sometimes known as Garry Chalk) Voices of Man–at–Arms (Duncan) and Whiplash, *He–Man and the Masters of the Universe* (also known as *He–Man*), Cartoon Network, 2002–2003.

(Sometimes billed as Garry Chalk) Voices of El Haystack Grande and Protozoa, *Mucha Lucha!* (also known as *Mucha Lucha! Gigante!*), The WB and other channels, c. 2002–2005.

(As Garry Chalk) Voice, *Gadget and the Gadgetinis,* syndicated, 2003.

(Sometimes known as Garry Chalk) Voices of Man–at–Arms (Duncan) and Whiplash, *Masters of the Universe vs. the Snake Man* (also known as *He–Man*), Cartoon Network, 2003–2004.

(English version) Voice of PET, *Rockman.exe* (anime; also known as *Megaman, MegaMan NT Warrior, MegaMan NT Warrior Axess,* and *Rockman.exe Axess*), The WB and TeleToon (Canada), 2003–2005, originally broadcast in Japan, beginning 2001.

Voices of Connor Penn and Mortis, *Dragon Booster,* ABC Family Channel, Toon Disney, and CBC, beginning 2004.

Voice of Optimus Prime, *Transformers: Energon* (anime; also known as *Transformer: SuperLink* and *Transformer: Super Link*), Cartoon Network, 2004–2005, also broadcast by other channels, including in Japan by TV Tokyo.

Voice, *Alien Racers,* Fox, beginning 2005, also broadcast on TeleToon (Canada).

Voices of Optimus Prime and Soundwave, *Transformers: Cybertron* (anime; also known as *Transformers Cybertron: Robots in Disguise* and *Transformers: Galaxy Force*), The WB, 2005, Cartoon Network and YTV (Canada), 2005–2006, also broadcast on other channels.

Voices of Hercules (Herry) and Ares, *Class of the Titans,* TeleToon (Canada), beginning 2006.

Narrator, *Eon Kid,* The CW, beginning 2007.

Voice of Captain Pounder, *RollBots,* YTV (Canada), beginning 2009.

Television Appearances; Miniseries:

Second police officer, *Hands of a Stranger,* NBC, 1987.

Boyd Paul Downs, *Small Sacrifices,* ABC, 1989.

Physical education coach, *It* (also known as *Stephen King's "It"*), ABC, 1990.

Sheriff Sine, *Johnson County War,* The Hallmark Channel, 2002.

Television Appearances; Movies:

Gas station attendant, *Into Thin Air,* CBS, 1985.

Police officer on bridge, *Spot Marks the X,* 1986.

A Masterpiece of Murder, NBC, 1986.

Pete, *Stranger in My Bed,* NBC, 1987.

Search team leader, *Deadly Deception,* CBS, 1987.

State trooper, *Sworn to Silence,* ABC, 1987.

Captain Jenkins, *Higher Ground,* CBS, 1988.

Hooter, *The Red Spider,* CBS, 1988.

Carlyle, *I Still Dream of Jeannie,* NBC, 1991.

Goss, *Yes Virginia, There Is a Santa Claus,* ABC, 1991.

(As Garry Chalk) Kiminski, *Blackmail,* USA Network, 1991.

Bryan Cassandro, *Fatal Memories* (also known as *The Eileen Franklin Story*), NBC, 1992.

Ump, *The Comrades of Summer,* HBO, 1992.

Battalion commander, *Woman on the Ledge,* NBC, 1993.

(As Garry Chalk) Chandler (first mate), *The Sea Wolf,* TNT, 1993.

Engineer, *The Odd Couple: Together Again,* CBS, 1993.

(As Garry Chalk) Hard copy reporter, *The Amy Fisher Story* (also known as *Beyond Control*), NBC, 1993.

Jim (Rescue 342 pilot), *Ordeal in the Arctic,* ABC, 1993.

Tom Walton, *Judgment Day: The John List Story,* CBS, 1993.

Woodfield guard, *Without a Kiss Goodbye* (also known as *Falsely Accused* and *The Laurie Samuels Story*), CBS, 1993.

Andy Kaczmarek, *The Disappearance of Vonnie,* CBS, 1994.

Detective Lewis, *Betrayal of Trust* (also known as *Under the Influence*), NBC, 1994.

Lieutenant Bartell, *Beyond Obsession* (also known as *A Daughter's Secret: The Traci di Carlo Story*), ABC, 1994.

Coach Gilbert, *Deceived by Trust: A Moment of Truth Movie,* NBC, 1995.

(As Garry Chalk) Lieutenant colonel Douglas Hart, *Serving in Silence: The Margarethe Cammermeyer Story* (also known as *Serving in Silence* and *Serving in Silence: The Colonel Grethe Cammermeyer Story*), NBC, 1995.

(As Garry Chalk) Maude, *Bye Bye Birdie* (musical), ABC, 1995.

Mike Dombrowski, *Not Our Son,* CBS, 1995.

Mike Kinsey, *Circumstances Unknown,* USA Network, 1995.

Parkinson, *She Stood Alone: The Tailhook Scandal* (also known as *Tailhook*), ABC, 1995.

(As Garry Chalk) Coach Dufecki, *Kidz in the Wood,* NBC, 1996.

Coach Peters, *Stand against Fear* (also known as *Moment of Truth: Stand against Fear, Stand against Fear: A Moment of Truth Movie,* and *Unlikely Suspects*), NBC, 1996.

Detective Gaines, *Generation X,* Fox, 1996.

Detective Larson, *Justice for Annie: A Moment of Truth Movie,* NBC, 1996.

Rasmussen, *Mother Trucker: The Diana Kilmury Story* (also known as *Diana Kilmury Teamster, Teamster,* and *La route d'espoir*), TNT, 1996.

(As Garry Chalk) Sheriff Bill Evans, *Abduction of Innocence* (also known as *Abduction of Innocence: A Moment of Truth Movie*), NBC, 1996.

(As Garry Chalk) Captain Durk, *Five Desperate Hours,* NBC, 1997.

Detective Masters, *Moment of Truth: Into the Arms of Danger* (also known as *Into the Arms of Danger* and *Running Wild*), NBC, 1997.

Coach, *A Champion's Fight* (also known as *A Champion's Fight: A Moment of Truth Movie* and *Shattered Hearts*), NBC, 1998.

Colonel Gardener, *Loyal Opposition: Terror in the White House,* Family Channel, 1998.

Detective Colin, *The Spree,* The Movie Channel, 1998.

Eddie Sullivan, *My Husband's Secret Life,* USA Network, 1998.

Gardner, *Silencing Mary* (also known as *Campus Justice*), NBC, 1998.

(As Garry Chalk) Sergeant Gabe Sawyer, *I Know What You Did* (also known as *Crimes of Passion: I Know What You Did* and *Defense of Murder*), ABC, 1998.

(As Garry Chalk) Timothy Aloysius "Dum–Dum" Dugan, *Nick Fury: Agent of Shield* (also known as *Nick Fury, Nick Fury: Agent of SHIELD,* and *Nick Fury: Agent of S.H.I.E.L.D.*), Fox, 1998.

(As Garry Chalk) White Cloud, *Floating Away,* 1998.

Oklahoma City: A Survivor's Story, Lifetime, 1998.

(As Garry Chalk) Colin Ziff, *Quarantine,* ABC, 1999.

(As Garry Chalk) Edward Mason, *Y2K* (also known as *Countdown to Chaos* and *Y2K: The Movie*), NBC, 1999.

(As Garry Chalk) Herb Kulcheck, *My Mother, the Spy,* Lifetime, 2000.

Milt, *Take Me Home: The John Denver Story,* CBS, 2000.

Walter Bradford, *Shutterspeed,* TNT, 2000.

(As Garry Chalk) District attorney Jerry Jones, *Video Voyeur: The Susan Wilson Story,* Lifetime, 2001.

Sheriff Sam, *Touched by a Killer,* Lifetime, 2001.

Police chief Bud McGee, *Bang Bang You're Dead* (also known as *Bang, Bang, You're Dead*), Showtime, 2002.

(As Garry Chalk) Sheriff Cal, *Lone Hero* (also known as *Heroes solitaire*), HBO, 2002.

(As Garry Chalk) Fred Hodges, *Thanksgiving Family Reunion* (also known as *Holiday Reunion, National Lampoon's "Holiday Reunion," National Lampoon's "Thanksgiving Family Reunion,"* and *National Lampoon's "Thanksgiving Reunion"*), TBS, 2003.

Inspector Ken Dowson, *Cowboys and Indians: The J. J. Harper Story* (also known as *Cowboys and Indians*), CBC, 2003.

Stuart King, *Try to Remember* (also known as *Mary Higgins Clark's "Try to Remember"*), PAX TV, 2004.

Anthony Shepherd, *His and Her Christmas,* Lifetime, 2005.

(Uncredited) Billy Marshall, *Supervolcano* (also known as *Supervulkan*), 2005.

(As Garry Chalk) Steven Draper, *Ladies Night,* USA Network, 2005.

Crouch, *Christmas on Chestnut Street,* Lifetime, 2006.

Jack Lycar (some sources cite role as Jack Lyear), *Truth,* Lifetime, 2006.

Jake, *A Little Thing Called Murder,* Lifetime, 2006.

(As Garry Chalk) Captain Laughlan, *Unthinkable,* Lifetime, 2007.

(As Garry Chalk) Warden Mayfield, *Passion's Web* (also known as *Uncaged Heart*), Lifetime, 2007.

Vice principal Grimes, *Scooby–Doo: In the Beginning,* Cartoon Network, 2009.

Television Appearances; Animated Movies:

Voice of He–Man, *He–Man and the Battle for Primus* (consists of episodes of *The New Adventures of He–Man*), 1990.

(As Garry Chalk) Voice of Grounder, *Sonic Christmas Blast!,* 1996.

Voices of Slash and Turbo, *ReBoot: Daemon Rising* (consists of episodes of *ReBoot*), Cartoon Network and YTV (Canada), 2001.

(As Garry Chalk) Voices of Slash and Turbo, *ReBoot: My Two Bobs* (consists of episodes of *ReBoot;* also known as *ReBoot: The Movie II*), Cartoon Network and YTV (Canada), 2001.

Voice of Warlock, *Sabrina the Teenage Witch in Friends Forever* (also known as *Sabrina: Friends Forever* and *Sabrina the Teenage Witch: Friends Forever*), 2002.

Voices of Harry the Werewolf and Bug–a–Boo, *Scary Godmother Halloween Spooktakular,* Cartoon Network, 2003.

Voices of Harry the Werewolf and Bug–a–Boo, *Scary Godmother: The Revenge of Jimmy,* Cartoon Network, 2005.

Television Appearances; Specials:

Voice, *The Legend of Hiawatha* (animated), CBS, 1983, NBC, 1984.

Ron Roarke, *Secrets of the Unknown,* CBS, 1991.

Television Appearances; Live Action Episodes:

(As Gary Chaulk) Chef, "Out of the Night," *The Hitchhiker* (also known as *Deadly Nightmares* and *Le voyageur*), HBO, 1985.

Hubert, "O.D. Feelin'," *The Hitchhiker* (also known as *Deadly Nightmares* and *Le voyageur*), HBO, 1986.

Murdoch, "Timber," *Danger Bay,* CBC and Disney Channel, 1986.

Phil, "Unlikely Allies," *The Beachcombers* (also known as *Beachcombers*), CBC, 1986.

Burke, "Blackjack," *Airwolf* (also known as *Blackwolf, Lonewolf, Supercopter,* and *Lobo del aire*), USA Network, 1987.

(As Garry Chalk) First Secret Service agent, "Beans for President," *The New Adventures of Beans Baxter,* Fox, 1987.

Hired officer, "My Future's So Bright, I Gotta Wear Shades," *21 Jump Street,* Fox, 1987.

"Flowers of the Mountains," *Airwolf* (also known as *Blackwolf, Lonewolf, Supercopter,* and *Lobo del aire*), USA Network, 1987.

(As Garry Chalk) Bartender, "Dirty Little Wars," *Wiseguy,* CBS, 1988.

Dave, "The Currency We Trade In," *21 Jump Street,* Fox, 1988.

Tony Ellis, "Thin Ice," *MacGyver,* ABC, 1988.

(As Garry Chalk) Harry Dukowski, "Value Judgment," *Danger Bay,* CBC and Disney Channel, 1989.

Major Benteen, "Guardian Spirit," *The New Adventures of Davy Crockett* (also known as *Davy Crockett* and *Davy Crockett: Guardian Spirit*), NBC, 1989.

(As Garry Chalk) Police officer, "Deadly Dreams," *MacGyver,* ABC, 1989.

(As Garry Chalk) Sergeant Harold Gray, "The Ten Percent Solution," *MacGyver,* ABC, 1989.

(Uncredited) Detective Sweeney, "Lesson in Evil," *MacGyver,* ABC, 1990.

Jack Graynor, "Father and Son," *Neon Rider,* CTV (Canada) and syndicated, 1990.

Jeff Chandler, "Just Say No! High," *21 Jump Street,* syndicated, 1990.

(As Garry Chalk) Sergeant Ty Carter, "Chucky," *Broken Badges,* CBS, 1990.

Sheriff, "Who Framed Roger Thornton?," *Booker* (also known as *Booker, P.I.*), Fox, 1990.

"Murder Maybe," *Mom P.I.,* CBC, 1990.

Constable Stuart, "Loyalties," *Neon Rider,* CTV (Canada) and syndicated, 1991.

Lemoyne, "Family Tree," *Highlander* (also known as *Highlander: The Series*), syndicated, 1992.

Lemoyne, "An Innocent Man," *Highlander* (also known as *Highlander: The Series*), syndicated, 1992.

Shaye's father, "A Perfect 10," *Neon Rider,* CTV (Canada) and syndicated, 1992.

Mr. Dubrow, "Stoned," *The Commish,* ABC, 1993.

Cavalry officer Chubb, "O Western Wind: Part 1," *Lonesome Dove: The Series* (series later known as *Lonesome Dove: The Outlaw Years*), CTV (Canada) and syndicated, 1994.

Cavalry officer Chubb, "Down Come Rain: Part 2," *Lonesome Dove: The Series* (series later known as *Lonesome Dove: The Outlaw Years*), CTV (Canada) and syndicated, 1994.

Coach, "Learning Curves," *Madison* (also known as *Working It out at Madison*), CanWest Global Television, 1994.

(As Garry Chalk) Detective Harold Reid, "Faces in the Mask," *M.A.N.T.I.S.,* Fox, 1994.

Coach Vipond, "Family Affairs," *Madison* (also known as *Working It out at Madison*), CanWest Global Television, 1995.

(As Garry Chalk) Detective Barnett, "Caught in the Act," *The Outer Limits* (also known as *The New Outer Limits*), Showtime and syndicated, 1995.

(As Garry Chalk) Detective Harold Reid, "The Delusionist," *M.A.N.T.I.S.*, Fox, 1995.

(As Garry Chalk) Detective Harold Reid, "Spider in the Tower," *M.A.N.T.I.S.*, Fox, 1995.

(As Garry Chalk) Detective Harold Reid, "Switches," *M.A.N.T.I.S.*, Fox, 1995.

Detective Ralph Hoberman, "Brooklyn," *The Commish*, ABC, 1995.

"The Warrior," *Hawkeye*, syndicated, 1995.

(As Garry Chalk) Art Sturges, "Reunion," *The Sentinel* (also known as *Sentinel*), UPN, 1996.

Desk sergeant, "In Sickness and in Wealth," *Strange Luck* (also known as *Drole de chance, Strange Luck—Dem Zufall auf der Spur,* and *Um homem de sorte*), Fox, 1996.

(As Garry Chalk) Lieutenant Graves, "Time Again and World," *Sliders,* Fox, 1996.

Sheriff Hank Parker, "The Inheritance," *Poltergeist: The Legacy* (also known as *Poltergeist, El legado, Poltergeist—Die unheimliche Macht, Poltergeist: El legado,* and *Poltergeist, les aventuriers du surnaturel*), Showtime and syndicated, 1996.

Richard Powell, "A Single Blade of Grass," *Millennium,* Fox, 1997.

Sheriff Kinney, "Forget Me Not," *Two* (also known as *Gejagt—Das zweite Gesicht*), CTV (Canada) and syndicated, 1997.

(As Garry Chalk) General, "Nightmare," *The Outer Limits* (also known as *The New Outer Limits*), Showtime and syndicated, 1998.

Sheldon Lamott, "Second Wave," *First Wave,* Sci–Fi Channel, 1998.

(As Garry Chalk) Sheriff Rice, "The Mesmerizer," *Dead Man's Gun,* Showtime, 1998.

(As Garry Chalk) Harry Lovejoy, "Dead End on Blank Street," *The Sentinel* (also known as *Sentinel*), UPN, 1999.

Lieutenant Mosh, "The Ethel Merman Story," *Beggars and Choosers* (also known as *TV business*), Showtime, 1999.

Lieutenant Mosh, "Once More unto the Breach," *Beggars and Choosers* (also known as *TV business*), Showtime, 1999.

Lieutenant Mosh, "Sex, Drugs & Videotape," *Beggars and Choosers* (also known as *TV business*), Showtime, 1999.

(As Garry Chalk) Quince Toland, "People Like Us," *Viper,* syndicated, 1999.

Riley Cunningham, "Sleepwalker," *Dead Man's Gun,* Showtime, 1999.

(As Garry Chalk) Detective Frank Dayton, "Something about Harry," *The Outer Limits* (also known as *The New Outer Limits*), Showtime and syndicated, 2000.

(As Garry Chalk) Major Vladimir Markovsky, "X–35 Needs Changing," *Seven Days* (also known as *7 Days* and *Seven Days: The Series*), UPN, 2000.

(As Garry Chalk) FBI agent Forsch, "Bad Water," *Breaking News,* Bravo, 2002, series originally produced for TNT.

(As Garry Chalk) "The Last to Know," *Just Cause,* PAX TV, 2002.

Voice of the rod of Lethor, "The Key," *Zixx: Level One* (live action and animated; also known as *Phunkee Zee*), YTV (Canada), 2005.

Voice of the rod of Lethor, "The Rod of Lethor," *Zixx: Level One* (live action and animated; also known as *Phunkee Zee*), YTV (Canada), 2005.

(As Garry Chalk) Bill Bolan, "And the Envelope Please," *The Evidence,* ABC, 2006.

Mr. Polaski, "Paintball," *Alice, I Think,* CTV (Canada), 2006.

(As Garry Chalk) Arnie, "Rocket Club," *Aliens in America,* The CW, 2007.

General, "A Clean Escape," *Masters of Science Fiction,* ABC, 2007.

(As Garry Chalk) Police captain, "Secrets and Lies," *Flash Gordon,* Sci–Fi Channel, 2007.

(As Garry Chalk) Ruben Hennesy, "Higher Court," *Painkiller Jane,* Sci–Fi Channel, 2007.

Sheriff, "Try the Pie," *The 4400* (also known as *4400* and *Los 4400*), USA Network and Sky One, 2007.

(As Garry Chalk) Sheriff Dietrich, "Monster Movie," *Supernatural* (also known as *Sobrenatural*), The CW, 2008.

Some sources cite an appearance in *Mysterious Ways* (also known as *One Clear Moment, Anexegeta phainomena, Les chemins de l'etrange, Mysterious ways—les chemins de l'etrange, Rajatapaus,* and *Senderos misteriosos*), NBC and PAX TV.

Television Appearances; Animated Episodes:

Voice of Pathfinder, "An Officer and a Viperman," *G.I. Joe* (also known as *Action Force, G.I. Joe: A Great American Hero,* and *Chijo saikyo no Expert Team G.I. Joe*), syndicated, 1990.

Voice of Snagg, "The Heart of Rakkir," *Conan: The Adventurer* (also known as *Conan l'aventurier*), Fox, 1992.

Voice of Snagg, "Once and Future Conan," *Conan: The Adventurer* (also known as *Conan l'aventurier*), Fox, 1992.

Voice, *Madeline,* Fox Family Channel, c. 1993.

Voice of Hugh Finster, "20,000 Leaks under the Sea," *Megaman* (anime; also known as *Mega Man* and *Rockman*), ABC Family Channel and syndicated, c. 1995.

Voice of original Megatron, "The Agenda: Part 2," *Beast Wars: Transformers* (also known as *Beast Wars, Beasties, Beasties: Transformers,* and *Transformers: Beast Wars*), syndicated, 1998.

Voice, "When Wishes Come True," *Stories from My Childhood* (also known as *Mikhail Baryshnikov's "Stories from My Childhood"*), PBS, 1998.

Voice, "The Wild Swans," *Stories from My Childhood* (also known as *Mikhail Baryshnikov's "Stories from My Childhood"*), PBS, 1998.

Voice of Mr. Meugniot/the Reverend, "Where Evil Nests," *Spider–Man Unlimited* (also known as *Spiderman Unlimited*), Fox, 1999.

Voice of Mr. Meugniot/the Reverend, "Deadly Choices," *Spider–Man Unlimited* (also known as *Spiderman Unlimited*), Fox, 2000.

Voice of Gangrene, "Green Thoughts," *Action Man: Doom Strikes Back* (also known as *Action Man*), syndicated (some sources cite Fox) and YTV (Canada), 2001.

Voice of Mr. Meugniot/the Reverend, "Matters of the Heart," *Spider–Man Unlimited* (also known as *Spiderman Unlimited*), Fox, 2001.

Voice of Mr. Meugniot/the Reverend, "The Reverend—Sins of the Fathers" (also known as "Sins of the Fathers"), *Spider–Man Unlimited* (also known as *Spiderman Unlimited*), Fox, 2001.

(Sometimes billed as Garry Chalk) Voice of El Kolor De Kurtz, "How Rikochet Got His Move Back/Heart of Lucha," *Mucha Lucha!* (also known as *Mucha Lucha! Gigante!*), The WB and other channels, 2002.

(Sometimes billed as Garry Chalk) Voice of Flea's lungs, "Big Worm/Medico Mayhem," *Mucha Lucha!* (also known as *Mucha Lucha! Gigante!*), The WB and other channels, 2004.

(Sometimes billed as Garry Chalk) Voice of Tibor the Terrible, "Election Daze/Los Pantalones (aka The Brat in the Hat)," *Mucha Lucha!* (also known as *Mucha Lucha! Gigante!*), The WB and other channels, 2004.

(Sometimes billed as Garry Chalk) Voices of General Ignacio Zaragoza and police officer, "Cinco de Pinata (aka Day of the Pinata)/Poocha Lucha," *Mucha Lucha!* (also known as *Mucha Lucha! Gigante!*), The WB and other channels, 2004.

(Sometimes billed as Garry Chalk) Voices of Tibor the Terrible and sentry robot, "The Collector," *Mucha Lucha!* (also known as *Mucha Lucha! Gigante!*), The WB and other channels, 2004.

Voice of the gilded dragon, "All That Glitters," *Dragon Tales*, PBS, 2005.

Voice of a wizard, "To Fly with a New Friend: Parts 1 & 2," *Dragon Tales*, PBS, 2005.

Voice of first villager, "Chaos 102," *Class of the Titans*, TeleToon (Canada), 2006.

Voice of water drain pirate captain, "H2O–NO," *Team Galaxy* (anime), YTV (Canada), 2006.

Television Appearances; Live Action Pilots:

Fred, *Wiseguy*, CBS, 1987.

Security chief, *The Omen*, NBC, 1995.

(As Garry Chalk) Lieutenant Walter "Mr. Multiples" Eastep, *Dark Angel* (also known as *James Cameron's "Dark Angel"*), Fox, 2000.

(As Garry Chalk) Janitor, *Haunted*, UPN, 2002.

Captain Jim Archer, *Tarzan* (also known *Tarzan and Jane* and *Young Tarzan Drama Project*), The WB, 2003.

(As Garry Chalk) Zimmer, *Touching Evil*, USA Network, 2004.

Colonel Briggs, *Eureka* (also known as *EUReKA* and *A Town Called Eureka*), Sci–Fi Channel, 2006.

Television Appearances; Animated Pilots:

Voice, *Barbie and the Rockers*, syndicated, 1987.

Voices of He–Man and Andros, "A New Beginning," *The New Adventures of He–Man* (also known as *Le nuove avventure di He–Man*), syndicated, 1990.

(As Garry Chalk) Voices of Man–at–Arms (Duncan) and Whiplash, "The Beginning," *He–Man and the Masters of the Universe* (also known as *He–Man* and *He–Man and the Masters of the Universe: The Beginning*), Cartoon Network, 2002, series later known as *Masters of the Universe vs. the Snake Man*.

Voice of Hercules (Herry), "Chaos 101," *Class of the Titans*, TeleToon (Canada), 2006.

Television Additional Voices; Animated Series:

(As Garry Chalk) *Mighty Max*, UPN, 1993–94.

Sonic the Hedgehog (also known as *The Adventures of Sonic the Hedgehog* and *Sonic*), ABC and syndicated, 1993–95.

Hurricanes, syndicated, c. 1993–97.

(As Garry Chalk) *Mummies Alive!*, syndicated, 1997.

(As Garry Chalk) *RoboCop: Alpha Commando*, syndicated, 1998–99.

Sabrina the Animated Series (also known as *Sabrina*), ABC, 1999–2000.

Sitting Ducks, Cartoon Network, 2001–2004.

Firehouse Tales, broadcast on the Tickle U programming block on Cartoon Network, beginning 2005.

Team Galaxy (anime), YTV (Canada), beginning c. 2006.

Care Bears: Adventures in Care–a–Lot, CBS, beginning 2007.

Stage Appearances:

Appeared in stage productions, including improvisational productions and children's theatre productions.

RECORDINGS

Videos:

Voice of General Blitz, *G.I. Joe: Sgt. Savage and His Screaming Eagles* (animated; packaged with *G.I. Joe* toys), c. 1995.

Narrator of informative videos.

Video Games:

Voice of Robert Ripley, *Ripley's "Believe It or Not!": The Riddle of Master Lu*, 1995.

(As Garry Chalk) Narrator, *Making History: Louis Riel and the North–West Rebellion of 1885,* 1997.

Voice of Slash, *ReBoot,* 1998.

Voice of Optimus Primal, *Transformer Beast War Metals: Gekitotsu! Gangan Battle,* Bay Area Media, 1999.

(As Garry Chalk) Voice, *Need for Speed: Hot Pursuit 2,* 2002.

Voice of Optimus Prime, *Transformers,* 2004.

(As Garry Chalk) Voice of Devil King, *Devil Kings,* 2005.

(As Garry Chalk) Voice of Al Neri, *The Godfather* (also known as *The Godfather: The Game*), 2006.

Voice of Al Neri, *The Godfather: Blackhand Edition,* 2007.

Voice of Al Neri, *The Godfather: The Don's Edition,* 2007.

CLARK, Ashley Monique 1988–
(Ashley Monique)

PERSONAL

Born December 1, 1988. *Education:* Attended Carter Thor Studio, Los Angeles, CA.

Addresses: *Agent*—JLA Talent, 9151 Sunset Blvd., West Hollywood, CA 90069; Osbrink Agency, 4343 Landershim Blvd., Universal City, CA 91602.

Career: Actress. Appeared in television commercials for Coke products.

CREDITS

Television Appearances; Series:
Sydney Hughley, *The Hughleys,* ABC, 1998–2002.

Television Appearances; Episodic:
Cara Littleton, *Picket Fences,* CBS, 1994.

Little girl, *Chicago Hope,* CBS, 1995.

Blue bird number three, "I, Bowl Buster," *The Fresh Prince of Bel–Air,* NBC, 1996.

Jaleen, a recurring role, *Sunset Beach,* NBC, 1997.

Young Moesha, "My Mom's Not an Ottoman," *Moesha,* UPN, 1997.

Hollywood Squares (also known as *H2* and *H2: Hollywood Squares*), syndicated, 2001.

Kristin, "Still Negotiating," *Still Standing,* CBS, 2003.

Teri, "Laughing Matters," *The Bernie Mac Show,* Fox, 2003.

Kristin, "Still Parading," *Still Standing,* CBS, 2004.

Teri, "Big Brother," *The Bernie Mac Show,* Fox, 2004.

Kristin, "Still Bonding," *Still Standing,* CBS, 2005.

(As Ashley Monique) Karen, "Backpack," *Zoey 101,* Nickelodeon, 2005.

Karen, "Little Beach Party," *Zoey 101,* Nickelodeon, 2005.

Teri, "You Don't Know Squad," *The Bernie Mac Show,* Fox, 2005.

Teri, "The Music Mac," *The Bernie Mac Show,* Fox, 2005.

Teri, "Prison Break," *The Bernie Mac Show,* Fox, 2005.

Keisha, "Believe the Unseen," *ER,* NBC, 2008.

Eviqua Michaels, "Hell Followed," *Sons of Anarchy,* FX Channel, 2008.

Eviqua Michaels, "Capybara," *Sons of Anarchy,* FX Channel, 2008.

Eviqua Michaels, "The Sleep of Babies," *Sons of Anarchy,* FX Channel, 2008.

Eviqua Michaels, "The Revelator," *Sons of Anarchy,* FX Channel, 2008.

Television Appearances; Movies:
Kindergartner, *Encino Woman* (also known as *California Woman*), ABC, 1996.

Television Appearances; Specials:
The 2nd Annual Soul Train Christmas Starfest, syndicated, 1999.

Film Appearances:
Letter to My Mother, 1997.

Child at party and school, *Liar Liar,* Universal, 1997.

Aretha Johnson, *Love Don't Cost a Thing* (also known as *Love Don't Co$t a Thing*), Warner Bros., 2003.

Kee Kee Rodriguez, *Domino,* New Line Cinema, 2005.

CLARK, Duane
(D. B. Clark, Duane B. Clark)

PERSONAL

Son of Richard Wagstaff (a television personality and producer, as Dick Clark) and Loretta (maiden name, Martin) Clark; sister of Cindy Clark (a producer).

Addresses: *Agent*—Andy Elkin, Creative Artists Agency, 2000 Avenue of the Stars, Los Angeles, CA 90067. *Manager*—Andrew Wilson, Evolution Entertainment, 901 North Highland Ave., Los Angeles, CA 90038.

Career: Director, producer, film editor, writer, and songwriter. Proletariat Filmworks, Studio City, CA, worked as director of commercials. Sometimes credited as D. B. Clark or Duane B. Clark.

Awards, Honors: Crystal Heart Award (with Cindy Clark), Heartland Film Festival, Gold Award, best independent theatrical feature film, WorldFest Houston, Audience Award, dramatic category, Sedona International Film Festival, Taos Talking Picture Festival Award, audience favorite, Palm Springs International Film Festival Award, audience favorite, and Best of the Fest Award, drama category, Breckenridge Festival of Film, all 1997, for *Soulmates;* Directors Gold Award, Santa Clarita International Film Festival, and Special Jury Award, best theatrical feature film for family or children, WorldFest Houston, both 2000, for *Family Tree.*

CREDITS

Television Director; Series:
The Practice, ABC, between 2000 and 2003.
CSI: Miami, CBS, between 2004 and 2006.

Television Director; Movies:
Valentine's Day (also known as *Protector*), HBO, 1998.
Kiss My Act, ABC, 2001.
The Gilda Radner Story: It's Always Something, ABC, 2002.

Television Director; Miniseries:
XIII, NBC, 2008.

Television Director; Pilots:
Cape Wrath (also known as *Meadowlands*), Showtime, 2007.

Television Director; Episodic:
"The Wrath of Kali," *Highlander* (also known as *Highlander: The Series*), syndicated, 1995.
"Timeless," *Highlander* (also known as *Highlander: The Series*), syndicated, 1996.
"Looking for Mr. Goombah," *Total Security,* ABC, 1997.
"Who's Poppa?," *Total Security,* ABC, 1997.
"Secrets," *Stargate SG–1* (also known as *La porte des etoiles*), Showtime and syndicated, 1998.
"The Unsinkable Sydney Hansen," *Providence,* NBC, 2000.
"Gobble Gobble," *Providence,* NBC, 2001.
"Rising," *Dark Angel* (also known as *James Cameron's "Dark Angel"*), Fox, 2001.
"Chapter Seventeen," *Boston Public,* Fox, 2001.
"Chapter Twenty–six," *Boston Public,* Fox, 2001.
"Secrets and Lies," *Girls Club,* Fox, 2002.
"Chapter Sixty–three," *Boston Public,* Fox, 2003.
"Ambition," *The Guardian,* CBS, 2003.
"All that You Can't Leave Behind," *One Tree Hill,* The WB, 2003.
"Spirit in the Night," *One Tree Hill,* The WB, 2004.

"Early Rollout," *CSI: Crime Scene Investigation* (also known as *C.S.I., CSI: Las Vegas,* and *Les experts*), CBS, 2004.
"Compulsion," *CSI: Crime Scene Investigation* (also known as *C.S.I., CSI: Las Vegas,* and *Les experts*), CBS, 2005.
"Dog Eat Dog," *CSI: Crime Scene Investigation* (also known as *C.S.I., CSI: Las Vegas,* and *Les experts*), CBS, 2005.
"I Married a Mind Reader," *Medium,* NBC, 2005.
"In the Rough," *Medium,* NBC, 2005.
"What You See Is What You See," *CSI: NY,* CBS, 2005.
"Bad Beat," *CSI: NY,* CBS, 2005.
"Up in Smoke," *CSI: Crime Scene Investigation* (also known as *C.S.I., CSI: Las Vegas,* and *Les experts*), CBS, 2006.
"Federal Response," *Jericho,* CBS, 2006.
"Not What It Looks Like," *CSI: NY,* CBS, 2006.
Snow Day," *CSI: NY,* CBS, 2007.
Cape Wrath (also known as *Meadowlands*), Showtime, 2007.
"Rum," *Crusoe,* NBC, 2008.
"Gunpowder," *Crusoe,* NBC, 2008.
The Philanthropist, NBC, 2009.

Television Appearances; Episodic:
Marva, "The Key of Cee," *Rags to Riches,* NBC, 1987.

Film Director:
Shaking the Tree, 1990, Castle Hill, 1992.
Bitter Harvest, Prism Pictures, 1993.
(And coproducer and film editor) *Soulmates,* Curb Entertainment, 1997.
Family Tree, Independent Artists, 2000.

Film Appearances:
Logger, *Remo Williams: The Adventure Begins* (also known as *Remo: The Adventure Begins, Remo: The First Adventure,* and *Remo: Unarmed and Dangerous*), Orion, 1985.
Radio voice, *Judgement* (short film), AtomFilms, 1995.
Himself, *Scene Smoking: Cigarettes, Cinema & the Myth of Cool* (documentary), 2001.
Real estate man, *Crashing,* Image Entertainment, 2007.

WRITINGS

Screenplays:
Shaking the Tree, 1990, Castle Hill, 1992.
(And songwriter, "Catch Me When I Fall") *Soulmates,* Curb Entertainment, 1997.

Television Episodes:
Writer for *A Brand New Life,* NBC.

COLE, Taylor 1984–

PERSONAL

Full name, Taylor Quinn Cole; born April 29, 1984, in Arlington, TX; daughter of Deborah Quinn; stepdaughter of Shawn Christian (an actor). *Education:* Student at University of Arizona, 2007. *Avocational Interests:* Martial arts, volleyball and other sports.

Addresses: *Manager*—Burstein Co., 15304 Sunset Blvd., Suite 208, Pacific Palisades, CA 90272.

Career: Actress. Worked as a model in Europe and Australia; appeared in commercials for Crest toothpaste, Old Spice deodorant, and other products.

CREDITS

Film Appearances:
Beautiful girl, *That Guy* (short film), Moonlit Images Productions, 2006.
Movin G, Phoenix Entertainment Group, 2007.
Alex, *Loaded,* Allumination Filmworks, 2008.
Desiree Cartier, *April Fool's Day,* Stage 6 Films, 2008.
Jennifer, *An American in China,* Crossroads Pictures, 2008.
Erica Kessen, *12 Rounds,* Fox Atomic, 2009.

Television Appearances; Series:
Erika Spalding, *Summerland,* The WB, 2004–2005.

Television Appearances; Movies:
Kaitlan, *All You've Got* (also known as *Rumble*), MTV, 2006.
Jessie Chase, *Finish Line,* Spike, 2008.

Television Appearances; Episodic:
Brandi, "Double Down," *Numb3rs* (also known as *Num3ers*), CBS, 2006.
Bianca Desmond, "Daddy's Little Girl," *CSI: Crime Scene Investigation* (also known as *C.S.I., CSI: Las Vegas,* and *Les experts*), CBS, 2006.
Sarah Blake, "Provenance," *Supernatural,* The WB, 2006.
Taylor, "Dead Air," *CSI: Miami,* CBS, 2006.
Voice, "Prick Up Your Ears," *Family Guy* (animated; also known as *Padre de familia*), Fox, 2006.
Tasha, "Work Sex," *Do Not Disturb,* Fox, 2008.

Television Appearances; Pilots:
Erika Spalding, *Summerland,* The WB, 2004.

Television Appearances; Awards Presentations:
The 6th Annual Family Television Awards, The WB, 2004.
The Teen Choice Awards 2004, Fox, 2004.

RECORDINGS

Videos:
Appeared in the music videos "Scars" by Papa Roach and "True" by Ryan Cabrera.

COLLIER, Mark 1970–
(Mark C. Collier)

PERSONAL

Born May 27, 1970, in Ocala, FL (some sources say Boynton Beach, FL). *Education:* George Southern University, degree in accounting, 1993; studied acting at the Actors Movement Studio and with William Esper. *Avocational Interests:* The Dallas Cowboys.

Addresses: *Manager*—John Crosby Management, 1310 North Spaulding Ave., Los Angeles, CA 90046.

Career: Actor. Also worked as a bouncer, waiter, and Pilate's instructor. Surfrider Foundation, member; supporter of Free Arts (a children's charity).

Awards, Honors: *Soap Opera Digest* Award nomination, outstanding newcomer, 2003, for *As the World Turns.*

CREDITS

Television Appearances; Series:
Mike Kasnoff, *As the World Turns,* CBS, 2003–2007.

Television Appearances; Specials:
18th Annual "Soap Opera Digest" Awards, SoapNet, 2003.
The 31st Annual Daytime Emmy Awards, NBC, 2004.
The 31st Annual People's Choice Awards, CBS, 2005.
Presenter, *The 32nd Annual Daytime Emmy Awards,* CBS, 2005.

Television Appearances; Episodic:
(Uncredited) David the bartender, *Sunset Beach,* NBC, 1998.

(As Mark C. Collier) Mitch Field, "The Easter Bunny," *Beverly Hills, 90210,* Fox, 2000.

(As Mark C. Collier) Mitch Field, "And Don't Forget to Give Me Back My Black T–shirt," *Beverly Hills 90210,* Fox, 2000.

SoapTalk, SoapNet, 2003, 2006.

"The Girl Whose Lip Puffed Up," *America's Next Top Model* (also known as *ANTM, America's Next Top Model with Tyra Banks,* and *Top Model*), UPN, 2004.

Daniel Nash, "Raging Cannibal," *CSI: Miami,* CBS, 2008.

Stage Appearances:

Appeared in *Lovers and Strangers; Lone Star; Children's Crusade; Six Degrees of Separation; Portrait of a Madonna; David and Lisa.*

RECORDINGS

Music Videos:

Appeared in the Dixie Chicks' "Ready to Run."

OTHER SOURCES

Electronic:

Mark Collier Website, http://www.themarkcollier.com, January 10, 2009.

CONWAY, Gerry 1952–

PERSONAL

Full name, Gerard F. Conway; born September 10, 1952, in New York, NY; married Carla (marriage ended); married Karen Britten, 1992; children: (first marriage) Cara; (second marriage) Rachel.

Addresses: *Agent*—Maggie Field Agency, 12725 Ventura Blvd., Studio City, CA 91604–2437.

Career: Writer, producer, consultant, and actor. Writer for Marvel Comics, including volumes of *Incredible Hulk, The Amazing Spider–Man,* and *Captain Marvel,* 1970–75, 1985–89; created *The Punisher* for Marvel Comics, 1972; writer for DC Comics, c. 1975; writer of syndicated comic strips *Superman* and *Star Trek,* 1984–88.

Awards, Honors: Edgar Award nomination, best television episode teleplay, 2004, 2005, both for *Law & Order: Criminal Intent.*

CREDITS

Television Work; Series:

Producer, *Father Dowling Mysteries* (also known as *Father Dowling Investigates*), ABC, 1991.

Supervising producer and producer, *Under Suspicion,* CBS, 1994–95.

Creative consultant, *Diagnosis Murder,* CBS, 1996–97.

Supervising producer, *Players,* NBC, 1997.

Co–executive producer, *Diagnosis Murders,* CBS, 1997–98.

Co–executive producer, *The Huntress,* USA Network, 2000.

Consulting producer, *Law & Order: Criminal Intent* (also known as *Law & Order: CI*), NBC, 2002–2003.

Supervising producer, *Law & Order: Criminal Intent* (also known as *Law & Order: CI*), NBC, 2003–2004.

Co–executive producer, *Law & Order: Criminal Intent* (also known as *Law & Order: CI*), NBC, 2004–2006.

Television Work; Movies:

Executive consultant, *Perry Mason: The Case of the Skin–Deep Scandal,* NBC, 1993.

Television Work; Episodic:

Executive story editor, "The Royal Mystery," *Father Dowling Mysteries* (also known as *Father Dowling Investigates*), ABC, 1990.

Film Appearances:

Pop group member, *Who Dares Wins,* 1982.

Himself, *Conan: The Making of a Comic Book Legend,* 2002.

Himself, *Army of One: Punisher Origins,* 2004.

WRITINGS

Screenplays:

Fire and Ice, Twentieth Century–Fox, 1983.

Film Stories:

Conan the Destroyer, Universal, 1984.

Television Movies:

Perry Mason: The Case of the Heartbroken Bride, NBC, 1992.

A Twist of the Knife, CBS, 1993.

Perry Mason: The Case of the Killer Kiss, NBC, 1993.

A Perry Mason Mystery: The Case of the Jealous Jokester, NBC, 1995.

Television Episodes:

SuperFriends: The Legendary Super Powers Show (also known as *SuperFriends V*), 1984.

G.I. Joe (also known as *Action Force* and *Chijo saikyo no expert*), 1985–86.

Transformers (also known as *Transformers: 2010, Tatakae! Cho robot seimeitai TRANSFORMERS,* and *The Transformers*), syndicated, 1986.

(With Carla Conway) *The Centurions,* syndicated, 1986.

Matlock, NBC, 1986.

My Little Pony and Friends, 1986–87.

Father Dowling Mysteries, ABC, 1990–91.

Matlock, 1992–93.

"Appointment in Crime Alley," *Batman: The Animated Series* (animated; also known as *The Adventures of Batman & Robin* and *Batman*), Fox, 1992.

"Stormy Weather: Parts 1 & 2," *Jake and the Fatman,* CBS, 1992.

"I Can't Believe I'm Losing You," *Jake and the Fatman,* CBS, 1992.

(And story, with William Read Woodfield) "A Twist of the Knife," *Diagnosis Murder,* CBS, 1993.

"Inheritance of Death," *Diagnosis Murder,* CBS, 1993.

"Murder with Mirrors," *Diagnosis Murder,* CBS, 1994.

"Flashdance with Death," *Diagnosis Murder,* CBS, 1994.

"Lily," *Diagnosis Murder,* CBS, 1994.

"Shaker," *Diagnosis Murder,* CBS, 1994.

"The Plague," *Diagnosis Murder,* CBS, 1994.

"A Very Fatal Funeral," *Diagnosis Murder,* CBS, 1994.

"Second Chance," *Batman: The Animated Series* (animated; also known as *The Adventures of Batman & Robin* and *Batman*), Fox, 1994.

"Night of the Lizard," *Spider–Man,* Fox, 1994.

Under Suspicion, CBS, 1994–95.

Hercules: The Legendary Journeys, 1995.

"Playing for Keeps," *Diagnosis Murder,* CBS, 1995.

Baywatch Nights (also known as *Detectives on the Beach*), 1995.

Pacific Blue, USA Network, 1996.

"Misdiagnosis Murder," *Diagnosis Murder,* CBS, 1996.

"Mind over Murder," *Diagnosis Murder,* CBS, 1996.

(And story, with Steve Hattman) "FMurder," *Diagnosis Murder,* CBS, 1996.

"Black Ops," *Two,* 1996.

"The Servant," *Baywatch Nights* (also known as *Detectives on the Beach*), syndicated, 1997.

(With Joyce Burditt) "In Defense of Murder," *Diagnosis Murder,* CBS, 1997.

"A History of Murder," *Diagnosis Murder,* CBS, 1997.

"Murder, Country Style," *Diagnosis Murder,* CBS, 1997.

(And story, with Lee Goldberg and William Rabkin) "Physician, Murder Thyself," *Diagnosis Murder,* CBS, 1997.

(With Wayne Berwick; and story) "Malibu Fire," *Diagnosis Murder,* CBS, 1997.

Players, NBC, 1997.

"Somewhere over the Rainbow Bridge," *Hercules: The Legendary Journeys,* syndicated, 1998.

(And story, with William N. Fordes) "Hunters," *Law & Order,* NBC, 1999.

(And story, with Fordes) "Justice," *Law & Order,* NBC, 1999.

"Fade Out," *Hercules: The Legendary Journeys,* syndicated, 1999.

"My Best Girl's Wedding," *Hercules: The Legendary Journeys,* syndicated, 1999.

(And story, with Fordes) "Collision," *Law & Order,* NBC, 2000.

(And story, with Fordes) "High & Low," *Law & Order,* NBC, 2000.

Story, with Pamela Norris, "Smartest Guy in the World," *The Huntress,* USA Network, 2001.

"Generations," *The Huntress,* USA Network, 2001.

(With Chris Black) "Ah, Wilderness," *The Huntress,* USA Network, 2001.

"Showdown," *The Huntress,* USA Network, 2001.

(With Black; and story) "With Great Power," *The Huntress,* USA Network, 2001.

Story, with Black, "The Quest: Parts 1 & 2," *The Huntress,* USA Network, 2001.

Law & Order: Criminal Intent (also known as *Law & Order: CI*), NBC, 2003–2006.

CRANSTON, Bryan 1956–
(Lee Stone)

PERSONAL

Full name, Bryan Lee Cranston; born March 7, 1956, in Los Angeles, CA (some sources cite Canoga Park, CA); son of Joe Cranston (an actor) and Peggy Sell; brother of Kyle Cranston (an actor); married Mickey Middleton, November 10, 1077 (divorced April 8, 1982); married Robin Dearden (an actress), 1989; children: (second marriage) Taylor (daughter). *Education:* Attended Valley College. *Avocational Interests:* Baseball.

Addresses: *Agent*—Brett Hansen, United Talent Agency, 9560 Wilshire Blvd., Suite 500, Beverly Hills, CA 90212.

Career: Actor, voice artist, director, producer, and writer. Producer, director, and actor at a local theatre in Daytona Beach, FL; Quintus Productions, cofounder, 1993. Appeared in television commercials for Excedrin pain reliever, 1996, and Honda Accord autos, 2000; appeared in the public service announcement campaign *Express Yourself,* 2001; occasional voice for English versions of Japanese anime cartoons, sometimes credited as Lee Stone.

Awards, Honors: Best of the Fest Award, drama category, Breckenridge Festival of Film, 1999, and

Audience Award, Valleyfest Film Festival, 2000, both for *Last Chance;* Television Critics Association Award nomination, individual achievement in comedy, 2001, Emmy Award nominations, outstanding supporting actor in a comedy series, 2002, 2003, 2004, Golden Globe Award nomination, best supporting actor in a series, miniseries, or movie made for television, 2003, Golden Satellite Award nomination, best actor in a series, comedy, or musical, International Press Academy, 2004, and Young Artist Award nomination (with Jane Kaczmarek), most popular mom and pop in a television series, 2004, all for *Malcolm in the Middle;* Emmy Award, outstanding lead actor in a drama series, 2008, for *Breaking Bad;* DramaLogue Award for *The Steven Weed Show.*

CREDITS

Film Appearances:
First paramedic, "Roast Your Loved One," *Amazon Women on the Moon* (also known as *Cheeseburger Film Sandwich*), Universal, 1987.
The Big Turnaround, Dove Productions, 1988.
Darren, *Corporate Affairs,* Concorde, 1990.
Dr. Frank Darden, *DeadSpace,* Concorde, 1991.
Dr. Robert Stern, "Let's Talk about Love," *Erotique* (also known as *Let's Talk about Sex*), Odyssey Films, 1994.
Club official, *Clean Slate,* Metro–Goldwyn–Mayer, 1994.
(English version) Voice of Matti Tohn, *Oritsu uchugun oneamisu no tsubasa* (animated; also known as *Starquest, Wings of Honneamise,* and *Wings of Honneamise: Royal Space Force*), dubbed version, Tara Releasing, 1995.
Virgil "Gus" Grissom, *That Thing You Do!,* Twentieth Century–Fox, 1996.
Father Brophy, *Street Corner Justice,* New City Releasing, 1996.
Phil Hertzberg, *Strategic Command,* Command Productions, 1997.
War Department colonel, *Saving Private Ryan,* DreamWorks, 1998.
Lance, *Last Chance,* Leo Films, 1999.
Roberto Montalban, *The Big Thing,* K.M. Productions, 2000.
Voice of Ram, *The Prince of Light* (animated; also known as *Warrior Prince*), Showcase Entertainment, 2001.
David, *The Illusion,* Awakened Media, 2004.
Peter, *Seeing Other People,* Lantern Lane Entertainment, 2004.
Voice of Buzz Aldrin, *Magnificent Desolation: Walking on the Moon 3D,* IMAX, 2005.
CSE radio host, *Intellectual Property* (also known as *Dark Mind*), Strategic Film Partners, 2006.
Stan Grossman, *Little Miss Sunshine,* Fox Searchlight, 2006.

Bryce Baxter, *Hard Four,* Foo Dog Productions, 2007.
Himself, *Man of a Thousand Faces,* Television Syndicated Co., 2008.
Love Ranch, Capitol Films, 2009.

Film Work:
Producer and director, *Last Chance,* Leo Films, 1999.

Television Appearances; Series:
Darryl, *Days of Our Lives* (also known as *Days* and *DOOL*), NBC, 1982.
Douglas "Doug" Donovan, *Loving,* ABC, 1983–84.
Dean Stella, *One Life to Live,* ABC, 1985.
Uncle Russell, *Raising Miranda,* CBS, 1988.
Dr. Tim Whatley, a recurring role, *Seinfeld,* NBC, between 1994 and 1997.
Curt Sincic, *The Louie Show,* CBS, 1996.
Voice of Joe Thax, *Eagle Riders* (animated; also known as *La patrouille des aigles*), syndicated, 1996.
Hal, *Malcolm in the Middle,* Fox, 2000–2006.
Walter H. White, *Breaking Bad,* AMC, 2008.

Television Appearances; Miniseries:
Colonel Austin, *North and South II* (also known as *Love and War* and *North and South: Book II*), ABC, 1986.
Officer Dickenson, *I Know My First Name Is Steven* (also known as *The Missing Years*), NBC, 1989.
Astronaut Edwin "Buzz" Aldrin, *From the Earth to the Moon,* HBO, 1998.
The 100 Most Memorable TV Moments, TV Land, 2004.

Television Appearances; Movies:
Dr. Shepherd, *The Return of the Six–Million–Dollar Man and the Bionic Woman,* NBC, 1987.
Professor Harris, *Dead Silence* (also known as *Crash*), Fox, 1991.
Wilson, *The Disappearance of Nora* (also known as *Deadly Recall*), CBS, 1993.
John Sellers, *Prophet of Evil: The Ervil LeBaron Story,* CBS, 1993.
Alan, *The Companion,* USA Network, 1994.
Benny, *Days like This,* 1994.
Special Agent Falsey, *Kissing Miranda,* 1995.
Patrick Dougherty, *The Rockford Files: Punishment and Crime,* CBS, 1996.
Braddock, *Time under Fire* (also known as *Beneath the Bermuda Triangle*), The Movie Channel, 1996.
Ron Gatley, "Bobo," *Terror Tract* (also known as *The House on Terror Tract*), USA Network, 2000.
Nick Wrigley, *'Twas the Night,* The Disney Channel, 2001.
Voice of Santa Claus, *The Santa Claus Brothers* (animated), The Disney Channel, 2001.
Woodrow Snider, *Thanksgiving Family Reunion* (also known as *Holiday Reunion, National Lampoon's*

"Holiday Reunion," National Lampoon's "Thanksgiving Family Reunion," and *National Lampoon's Thanksgiving Reunion*), TBS, 2003.

According to some sources, also appeared in *Love without End* and *Shady Mountain.*

Television Appearances; Pilots:
Ned Landry, *Extreme Blue*, UPN, 1995.
Hal, *Malcolm in the Middle*, Fox, 2000.
Walter H. White, *Breaking Bad*, AMC, 2008.

Television Appearances; Specials:
David, *Men Who Hate Women & the Women Who Love Them* (also known as *Best Sellers: Men Who Hate Women and the Women Who Love Them; The Relationship*), NBC, 1994.
Intimate Portrait: Jane Kaczmarek, Lifetime, 2002.
The Making of "Breaking Bad," AMC, 2007.
Live from the Red Carpet: The 2008 Emmy Awards, E! Entertainment Television, 2008.

Television Appearances; Episodic:
Billy Joe, "Return to Death's Door," *CHiPs* (also known as *CHiPs Patrol*), NBC, 1982.
Frank Lawler/Tommy Maynard, "Who's Trying to Kill Miss Globe?" *Cover Up*, CBS, 1985.
Robert Hollis, "Desperate Monday," *Airwolf* (also known as *Lobo del aire*), CBS, 1986.
Brian East, "Menace, Anyone?" *Murder, She Wrote*, CBS, 1986.
Brian Emerson, "The Gift," *Matlock*, NBC, 1987.
"A Pound of Flesh," *Hill Street Blues*, NBC, 1987.
Martin Randall, "Enquiring Minds," *Falcon Crest*, CBS, 1989.
Tom Logan, "Cruise Ship," *Baywatch*, NBC, 1989.
Jerry Wilber, "Good–Bye Charlie," *Murder, She Wrote*, CBS, 1990.
Lyle Wicks/Miller, "Exactly Like You," *Jake and the Fatman*, CBS, 1990.
Mr. McConnell, *Hull High*, NBC, 1990.
Guest at Billy's bachelor party, "The Difference between Men and Women," *thirtysomething*, ABC, 1991.
Philip "Mark" Moses, "Be My Baby," *The Flash*, CBS, 1991.
Dr. Harding Fletcher (title role), "The Marriage Counselor," *Matlock*, NBC, 1991.
"All about Sleaze," *L.A. Law*, NBC, 1992.
Voice of Snizard, "Foul Play in the Sky," *Mighty Morphin' Power Rangers* (animated; also known as *Mighty Morphin Alien Rangers, Mighty Morph'n Power Rangers*, and *Power Rangers Ninja*), Fox, 1993.
Voice of Twinman, "A Bad Reflection on You," *Mighty Morphin' Power Rangers* (animated; also known as

Mighty Morphin Alien Rangers, Mighty Morph'n Power Rangers, and *Power Rangers Ninja*), Fox, 1993.
Garrett Berlin, "Wheels of Fire," *Viper*, NBC, 1994.
Hank Meese, "Deadly Vision," *Walker, Texas Ranger* (also known as *Walker*), CBS, 1994.
Dr. Tom Bryant, "The Hero," *Touched by an Angel*, CBS, 1995.
Matt McCulla, "Land's End: Parts 1 & 2," *Land's End*, syndicated, 1995.
Sheriff Norman Wade, "The Alpha Strike," *Nowhere Man*, UPN, 1995.
Russell Winslow, "Such a Bargain," *Brotherly Love*, NBC, 1995.
Parker Foreman, "Something Foul in Flappieville," *Murder, She Wrote*, CBS, 1996.
Walter Mason, "Living on the Streets Can Be Murder," *Diagnosis Murder*, CBS, 1996.
"Wet Side Story," *Total Security*, ABC, 1997.
Michael Burroughs, "Clarity Begins at Home," *Moloney*, CBS, 1997.
Ericsson, "The Long Night," *Babylon 5*, syndicated, 1997.
Record executive, "Goode Music," *Goode Behavior*, UPN, 1997.
Witch lawyer, "Troll Bride," *Sabrina, the Teenage Witch* (also known as *Sabrina* and *Sabrina Goes to College*), ABC, 1997.
Robert, "Again with the Pilot," *Alright Already*, The WB, 1997.
Ronny Shea, premiere episode, *Dogs*, ABC, 1997.
Isaac Perlow, "My So–Called Real Life," *Pearl*, CBS, 1997.
Ronald "Cheesy" Meezy, "Honey, I'm the Sorcerer's Apprentice," *Honey, I Shrunk the Kids: The TV Show*, syndicated, 1998.
Internal Affairs Lieutenant Gordon Denton, "Gay Avec," *Brooklyn South*, CBS, 1998.
Internal Affairs Lieutenant Gordon Denton, "Fisticuffs," *Brooklyn South*, CBS, 1998.
Colt Arrow, "Beats Working at a Hot Dog Stand," *V.I.P.* (also known as *V.I.P.—Die Bodyguards*), syndicated, 1998.
Martin Rutgers, "Blood Will Out," *Diagnosis Murder*, CBS, 1998.
Patrick Crump, "Drive," *The X–Files*, Fox, 1998.
Jesus, "Tantric Turkey," *Chicago Hope*, CBS, 1998.
Larry Prince, "The Consultant," *Working*, NBC, 1998.
"Behind the Scenes: Making "From the Earth to the Moon," *HBO First Look*, HBO, 1998.
Tim Sacksky, "Dog Days," *The King of Queens*, CBS, 1999.
Neil Diamond impersonator, "Paranoid Dick," *3rd Rock from the Sun* (also known as *Life as We Know It* and *3rd Rock*), NBC, 1999.
Neil Roberts, "PTB," *The Pretender*, NBC, 1999.
Tim Sacksky, "Time Share," *The King of Queens*, CBS, 1999.
Tim Sacksky, "Soft Touch," *The King of Queens*, CBS, 2000.

Miscellaneous voices, "A Dissertation on the American Justice System by People Who Have Never Been inside a Courtroom, Let Alone Know Anything about the Law, but Have Seen Way Too Many Legal Thrillers," *Clerks* (animated; also known as *Clerks: The Cartoon,* and *Clerks: Uncensored*), ABC, 2000.

Voice, "Leonardo Is Caught in the Grip of an Outbreak of Randal's Imagination and Patrick Swayze Either Does or Doesn't Work in the New Pet Store," *Clerks* (animated; also known as *Clerks: The Cartoon,* and *Clerks: Uncensored*), ABC, 2001.

Voice of helicopter pilot, "Dante and Randal and Jay and Silent Bob and a Bunch of New Characters and Lando Take Part in a Whole Bunch of Movie Parodies ...," *Clerks* (animated; also known as *Clerks: The Cartoon,* and *Clerks: Uncensored*), ABC, 2001.

Tim Sacksky, "Swim Neighbors," *The King of Queens,* CBS, 2001.

Voice of Gary's dad, *Gary & Mike,* UPN, 2001.

Mad TV, Fox, 2002.

Voice of Mr. Jameson, "Nosy: Experiment #199," *Lilo & Stitch: The Series* (animated), The Disney Channel, 2003.

The Bronx Bunny Show, Starz!, 2003.

Voice of publisher, "Star Trek," *American Dad!* (animated), Fox, 2005.

Contestant, *Celebrity Poker Showdown,* Bravo, 2005, 2006.

Hammond Druthers, "Aldrin Justice," *How I Met Your Mother,* CBS, 2006.

Voice, "I Take Thee, Quagmire," *Family Guy* (also known as *Padre de familia*), Fox, 2006.

"Soap Opera Starts," *My First Time,* TV Land, 2006.

Hammond Druthers, "Columns," *How I Met Your Mother,* CBS, 2007.

Lucifer, "The Time of the Redeemer," *Fallen,* ABC Family Channel, 2007.

Lucifer, "Mysterious Ways and All That," *Fallen,* ABC Family Channel, 2007.

The Light Bringer, "Someone Always Has to Die," *Fallen,* ABC Family Channel, 2007.

The Light Bringer, "Il Gran Rifuto," *Fallen,* ABC Family Channel, 2007.

Interviewee, "Finales," *TV Land Confidential* (also known as *TV Land Confidential: The Untold Stories*), TV Land, 2007.

Voice, "Long John Peter," *Family Guy* (animated; also known as *Padre de familia*), Fox, 2008.

Entertainment Tonight (also known as *Entertainment This Week, E.T., ET Weekend,* and *This Week in Entertainment*), syndicated, 2008.

Appeared as a salesman in an episode of *Davis Rules;* also appeared in *Capital News,* ABC.

Television Guest Appearances; Episodic:
The List, VH1, 1999.
To Tell the Truth, syndicated, 2000.

Hollywood Squares (also known as *H2* and *H2: Hollywood Squares*), syndicated, 2000, 2002.

Open Mike with Mike Bullard (also known as *Open Mike* and *The Mike Bullard Show*), Global (Canada), 2003.

Guest host, *Good Day Live,* syndicated, 2003.

The Wayne Brady Show, syndicated, 2003.

The Late Late Show with Craig Kilborn (also known as *The Late Late Show*), CBS, 2004.

ALF's Hit Talk Show, TV Land, 2004.

The Tony Danza Show, syndicated, 2004, 2005, 2006.

SoapTalk, Soap Network, 2004, 2005.

Weekends at the DL, Comedy Central, 2005.

Premiere episode, *Thank God You're Here,* NBC, 2007.

Sunday Morning Shootout (also known as *Hollywood Shootout* and *Shootout*), AMC, 2008.

Talkshow with Spike Ferensten, Fox, 2008.

The Tonight Show with Jay Leno, NBC, 2008.

Television Appearances; Awards Presentations:
The 4th Annual Family Television Awards, ABC, 2002.

Presenter, *The 55th Annual Primetime Emmy Awards,* Fox, 2003.

The 58th Annual Primetime Emmy Awards, NBC, 2006.

2008 Primetime Creative Arts Emmy Awards, E! Entertainment Television, 2008.

The 60th Primetime Emmy Awards, ABC, 2008.

Television Director; Series:
Malcolm in the Middle, Fox, between 2003 and 2005.

Television Director; Pilots:
Special Unit, Comedy Central, 2006.

Television Director; Episodic:
"Stolen Vows," *Big Day,* ABC, 2006.

Stage Appearances:

Appeared in *Eastern Standard, The Steven Weed Show,* and *Wrestlers,* all Los Angeles; appeared in *A Doll's House* and *The Taming of the Shrew,* Santa Cruz Shakespeare Company, Santa Cruz, CA; appeared in Florida productions of *Barefoot in the Park, A Funny Thing Happened on the Way to the Forum, Damn Yankees, Death of a Salesman,* and *Night of the Iguana.*

RECORDINGS

Videos:
Voices of Launch Control Center technician and other characters, *Morudaiba* (animated; also known as *Moldiver*), Pioneer Video, 1993.

Voice of imperial officer for English version, *Chojiku seiki Ogasu 02* (animated; also known as *Super Dimension Century Orguss 02*), Manga Video, 1993.

Voice of Eddie Borrows, *Armitage III,* Pioneer Entertainment, 1994.

(English version; As Lee Stone) Voice of Iasmu Alva Dyson, *Macross Plus,* Manga Video, 1995.

Voice of Eddie Borrows, *Armitage III* (animated; also known as *Armitage III: Polymatrix*), Pioneer Entertainment, 1997.

(English version) Voice of Miles O'Rourke, *Uchu no kishi Tekkaman Buredo* (animated; also known as *Starknight Tekkaman Blade* and *Teknoman*), 2002.

Producer and host, *KidSmartz,* Showtime Entertainment, 2003.

Reflections on "The X–Files," Twentieth Century–Fox Home Entertainment, 2004.

The Bench: Life before "Seinfeld," Columbia TriStar Home Entertainment, 2004.

Running with the Egg: Making a "Seinfeld," Sony Pictures Home Entertainment, 2005.

Appeared in the music video "Boss of Me" by They Might Be Giants, 2001.

WRITINGS

Screenplays:
Last Chance, Leo Films, 1999.

OTHER SOURCES

Periodicals:
People Weekly, October 16, 2000, p. 75.

Electronic:
Bryan Cranston Official Site, http://www.bryancranston.com, January 7, 2009.

CROWLEY, Bob 1952–

PERSONAL

Born 1952, in County Cork, Ireland; brother of John Crowley (a director).

Career: Scenic (set) designer, costume designer, and director. Associate of Royal Shakespeare Company and Royal National Theatre, London.

Awards, Honors: Antoinette Perry Award nominations, best scenic design and best costume design, and Drama Desk Award nominations, outstanding set design and outstanding costume design, all 1987, for *Les liaisons dangereuses;* Laurence Olivier Award, best designer, Society of West End Theatre, 1990, for *Hedda Gabler, Ma Rainey's Black Bottom,* and *The Plantagenets;* Antoinette Perry Award and Drama Desk Award nomination, both best scenic design, 1994, for *Carousel;* London Critics Circle Award, best designer, 1991, for *Murmuring Judges;* Drama Desk Award nomination, outstanding set design, 1995, for *Hapgood;* Antoinette Perry Award nomination, best scenic design, 1998, for *The Capeman;* Antoinette Perry Award nomination and Drama Desk Award nomination, both best scenic design, 1999, for *Twelfth Night; or, What You Will;* Antoinette Perry Award nomination, best scenic design, 1999, for *The Iceman Cometh;* Antoinette Perry Award, best scenic design, and Antoinette Perry Award nomination, best costume design, both 2000, for *Aida;* Antoinette Perry Award nomination and Drama Desk Award, both best scenic design, 2001, for *The Invention of Love;* Laurence Olivier Award, best costume design, 2001, for *Cresside* and *The Witches of Eastwick;* Drama Desk Award nominations, outstanding set design for a musical and outstanding costume design, both 2002, for *Sweet Smell of Success;* London Critics Circle Award, 2003, and Laurence Olivier Award nomination, 2004, both best set design, for *Mourning Becomes Electra;* Antoinette Perry Award, best scenic design, 2006, for *The History Boys;* Antoinette Perry Award and Drama Desk Award, both best scenic design, 2007, for *The Coast of Utopia,* Parts 1–3; Antoinette Perry Award, best scenic design for a musical, Antoinette Perry Award nomination, best costume design for a musical, Drama Desk Award, outstanding set design for a musical, and London *Evening Standard* Award, all 2007, for *Mary Poppins;* Royal Designer to Industry Award.

CREDITS

Stage Work; Set Designer and Costume Designer:
Les liaisons dangereuses, Royal Shakespeare Company, London, then Music Box Theatre, New York City, 1987.

Carousel (musical), Royal National Theatre, Olivier Theatre Upstairs, London, 1993, then Vivian Beaumont Theatre, Lincoln Center, New York City, 1994–95.

Racing Demon, Royal National Theatre, then Vivian Beaumont Theatre, Lincoln Center, 1995.

The Capeman (musical), Marquis Theatre, New York City, 1997–98.

The Judas Kiss, Almeida Theatre, London, then Broadhurst Theatre, New York City, both 1998.

The Iceman Cometh, Almeida Theatre, then Brooks Atkinson Theatre, New York City, 1999.

Amy's View, Royal National Theatre, then Ethel Barrymore Theatre, New York City, 1999.

Putting It Together (musical revue), Ethel Barrymore Theatre, 1999–2000.

Aida (musical), Palace Theatre, New York City, beginning 2000.

Cresside, Albery Theatre, London, 2000.

The Invention of Love, Lyceum Theatre, New York City, 2001.

The Seagull, Delacorte Theatre, Public Theatre, New York City, 2001.

Sweet Smell of Success (musical), Martin Beck Theatre, New York City, 2002.

Mary Poppins (musical), London, then New Amsterdam Theatre, New York City, beginning 2006.

(And director) *Tarzan* (musical), Richard Rodgers Theatre, New York City, 2006–2007.

Stage Work; Set Designer:

Ma Rainey's Black Bottom, West End production, 1989.

The Plantagenets, Royal Shakespeare Company, London, 1989.

Hedda Gabler, Royal National Theatre, London, 1989.

Murmuring Judges, London production, c. 1991.

Richard III, Brooklyn Academy of Music Theatre, New York City, 1992.

The Sea, Lyttelton Theatre, London, 1992.

Hamlet, Royal Shakespeare Company, Barbican Center Theatre, London, 1993.

Hapgood, London, then Mitzi E. Newhouse Theatre, New York City, 1994–95.

Twelfth Night; or, What You Will, Vivian Beaumont Theatre, Lincoln Center, New York City, 1998.

Anastasia (ballet), Royal Ballet, London, then American Ballet Theatre, Metropolitan Opera House, New York City, 1999.

The Witches of Eastwick (musical), Theatre Royal Drury Lane, London, 2000.

Orpheus Descending, Donmar Warehouse Theatre, London, 2000.

Mourning Becomes Electra, Royal National Theatre, Lyttelton Theatre, London, 2003.

The History Boys, Broadhurst Theatre, New York City, 2006.

A Moon for the Misbegotten, Old Vic Theatre, London, 2006, then Brooks Atkinson Theatre, New York City, 2007.

The Coast of Utopia, Part 1: *Voyage,* Vivian Beaumont Theatre, Lincoln Center, 2006–2007.

The Coast of Utopia, Part 2: *Shipwreck,* Vivian Beaumont Theatre, Lincoln Center, 2006–2007.

The Coast of Utopia, Part 3: *Salvage,* Vivian Beaumont Theatre, Lincoln Center, 2007.

The Year of Magical Thinking, Booth Theatre, New York City, 2007.

Set designer for Royal Shakespeare Company productions of *The Crucible, Hamlet, Henry V,* London, *Love's Labour's Lost, Macbeth, Measure for Measure,* and *Othello;* set designer for Royal National Theatre productions of *The Designated Mourner* and *King Lear; The Cryptogram,* London; *The David Hare Trilogy,* London and New York City; *The Importance of Being Earnest,* London; and *When She Danced,* London; set designer (and director, with Stephen Rea) of *The Cure at Troy,* Field Day Company, Ireland; set designer for operas, including *The Cunning Little Vixen,* Chatelet, Paris, *Don Giovanni,* Munich, Germany, *The Magic Flute,* English National Opera, and *La traviata,* Royal Opera House, Theatre at Covent Garden, London.

Television Production Designer; Specials:

Tales from Hollywood, PBS, 1992.

Suddenly Last Summer, PBS, 1993.

La traviata, 1994.

(And costume designer) *The Cunning Little Vixen* (also known as *La petite renarde rusee*), BBC, 1995.

"King Lear," *Performance,* BBC, 1997.

Set designer, *Twelfth Night* (also known as *Twelfth Night; or What You Will* and *William Shakespeare's Twelfth Night;* television broadcast of stage production), PBS, 1998.

(And costume designer) *Putting It Together* (musical revue; television broadcast of stage production), Broadway Television Network, c. 2000.

Television Appearances; Specials:

Broadway '99: Launching the Tony Awards, PBS, 1999.

Film Work:

Costume designer, *The Crucible,* Twentieth Century–Fox, 1996.

Production designer, *The Designated Mourner* (film of live stage production), First Look Pictures Releasing, 1997.

Production designer, *The History Boys* (film of live stage production), Fox Searchlight, 2006.

RECORDINGS

Videos:

Costume designer, *Arena* (also known as *Duran Duran: Arena (An Absurd Notion)*), 1985.

OTHER SOURCES

Periodicals:

Time, August 31, 1998, p. 72.

CRUCHE, Phina
See ORUCHE, Phina

CRUZ, Wilson 1973–

PERSONAL

Born December 27, 1973, in Brooklyn, NY. *Education:* Attended California State University at San Bernardino.

Addresses: *Office*—Latin Hollywood Films, 153 San Vicente Blvd., Suite 2G, Santa Monica, CA 90402. *Manager*—Tammy Rosen, Affirmative Action Entertainment and Productions, 425 North Robertson Dr., Los Angeles, CA 90048.

Career: Actor and voice performer. Young Americans (touring group), performed as singer; Latin Hollywood Films, Santa Monica, CA, producer. Appears at public events and on radio programs as an advocate for gay teenagers.

Awards, Honors: Young Artist Award (with others), best performance by a youth ensemble in a television series, 1995, for *My So–Called Life;* DramaLogue Award, outstanding performance, 1997, and Los Angeles Ovation Award, best featured actor in a musical, 1998, both for *Rent;* ALMA Award, emerging actor in a drama series, American Latin Media Arts Awards, 2000, for *Party of Five;* Visibilidad Award, GLAAD Media Awards, Gay and Lesbian Alliance against Defamation, 2008.

CREDITS

Television Appearances; Series:
Jonathan, a recurring role, *Great Scott!,* Fox, c. 1992.
Enrique "Rickey" Vasquez, *My So–Called Life,* ABC, 1994.
Victor, *Party of Five,* Fox, 1999–2000.
Dr. Junito Vargas, *Noah's Arc,* Logo Network, 2005–2006.
Voice of Evan, *Rick & Steve the Happiest Gay Couple in all the World* (animated), Logo Network, 2007.

Television Appearances; Movies:
Reuben Diaz, *On Seventh Avenue* (also known as *7th Avenue*), NBC, 1996.

Narrator, *MTV True Life: School's Out; The Life of a Gay High School in Texas,* MTV, 2003.

Television Appearances; Pilots:
Enrique "Rickey" Vasquez, *My So–Called Life,* ABC, 1994.
Himself, "The Perfect Pitch," *Brilliant but Cancelled,* Trio, 2002.

Television Appearances; Episodic:
Donahue, 1994.
Bobby, "Double Double Date," *Sister, Sister,* ABC, 1995.
Stephen/Stephanie Grant, "Boy to the World," *Ally McBeal,* Fox, 1997.
Jeffrey Cruz, "Orion in the Sky," *ER,* NBC, 2002.
Jack Sosa, "Access," *The West Wing,* NBC, 2004.
Jack Sosa, "No Exit," *The West Wing,* NBC, 2004.
Man in bar, "Batter Up," *The Closer,* TNT, 2005.
Smoking technician, "Mr. Monk Goes to a Fashion Show," *Monk,* USA Network, 2006.
"Not without My Daughter," *Related,* The WB, 2006.
"Geeks, Freaks, and Sidekicks," *Child Star Confidential,* E! Entertainment Television, 2006.
Todd Ryder, "Cover Story," *Navy NCIS: Naval Criminal Investigative Service* (also known as *NCIS* and *NCIS: Naval Criminal Investigative Service*), CBS, 2007.
Rafael de la Cruz, "Guatemala Gulfstream," *Raising the Bar,* TNT, 2008.
Rafael de la Cruz, "Richie Richer," *Raising the Bar,* TNT, 2008.
Rafael de la Cruz, "Out on the Roof," *Raising the Bar,* TNT, 2008.
Sid Tango, *Pushing Daisies,* ABC, 2008.

Also voice for *American Dad* (animated), Fox.

Television Appearances; Specials:
Totally Gayer, VH1, 2004.
The Evolution Will Be Televised, 2005.
Host, *The Out 100,* Logo Network, 2006.
Fabulous! The Story of Queer Cinema, Independent Film Channel, 2006.
(In archive footage), *100 Greatest Teen Stars,* VH1, 2006.
The Visible Vote '08—A Presidential Forum, MTV, 2007.
11th Annual Ribbon of Hope Celebration, Here!, 2008.

Film Appearances:
Joaquin, *Nixon,* Buena Vista, 1995.
Jesse, *All over Me,* Fine Line, 1996.
Mikey, *Johns,* First Look Pictures, 1997.
James, *Joyride,* Trillion Entertainment, 1997.

Benj Sotomejor, *Supernova,* Metro–Goldwyn–Mayer/ United Artists, 2000.

Angel Melendez, *Party Monster,* Strand Releasing, 2003.

Tony, *Bam Bam and Celeste,* Salty Features/Nuit Blanche Productions/Cho Taussig Productions, 2005.

Kelly, *Coffee Date,* Slowhand Releasing, 2006.

Kyle, *Green Flash,* Metro–Goldwyn–Mayer Home Entertainment, 2008.

Gabriel, *The People I've Slept With,* Margin Films'408 Films, 2008.

Adrian, *The Ode,* Kiran Entertainment/Mega Bolly-wood, 2008.

Nathan, *He's Just Not That into You,* Warner Bros., 2009.

Stage Appearances:

Angel Schunard, *Rent* (musical), Los Angeles produc-tion, 1997, then Nederlander Theatre, New York City, 1997–98.

Appeared in productions of *Becoming Memories, Cradle of Fire, The Roar of the Greasepaint …, Support-ing Cast,* and various Shakespearean productions.

Major Tours:

Michael, *Tick, Tick … Boom!* (musical), U.S. cities, between 2003 ans 2006.

Appeared in a touring production of *Rent.*

RECORDINGS

Videos:

Clik Honors: Elite 25 Awards, Sizzle Miami, 2007.
The Brewing of Coffee Date, TLA Releasing, 2007.

Appeared in the music video "What a Girl Wants" by Christine Aguilera.

OTHER SOURCES

Periodicals:

Advocate, September 28, 1999, pp. 34–36, 38, 40.
New York Times, January 1, 1998, p. E3.

D

DACOSTA, Yaya 1982–

PERSONAL

Birth name, Camara YaYa DeCosta Johnson; born November 15, 1982, in Harlem, NY; father (a scholar) and mother (director and founder of The Central Harlem Montessori School). *Education:* Graduated from Brown University.

Addresses: *Agent*—The Gershwin Agency, 232 N. Canon Dr., Beverly Hills, CA 90210.

Career: Actress.

Awards, Honors: Teen Choice Award nomination, movies—choice breakout, 2006, for *Take the Lead;* Audelco Award, best supporting actress, 2008.

CREDITS

Television Appearances; Series:
America's Next Top Model (also known as *ANTM, America's Next Top Model with Tyra Banks* and *Top Model*), UPN, 2004.
Cassandra Foster, *All My Children* (also known as *AMC*), ABC, 2008—.

Television Appearances; Movies:
Vanessa, *Racing for Time,* Lifetime, 2008.

Television Appearances; Episodic:
Ms. Jenkins, "Prom Night," *Eve,* UPN, 2005.
"America's Next Top Model," *E! True Hollywood Story,* E! Entertainment Television, 2006.

Television Appearances; Specials:
2005 MuchMusic Video Awards, 2005.
The Teen Choice Awards 2006, Fox, 2006.
39th NAACP Image Awards, Fox, 2008.

Film Appearances:
LaRhette, *Take the Lead,* New Line Cinema, 2006.
China Doll, *Honeydripper,* Emerging Pictures, 2007.

RECORDINGS

Music Videos:
"Pullin' Me Back," by Chingy, 2006.
"Beautiful Girls," by Sean Kingston, 2007.

DAVIS, John
(John A. Davis)

PERSONAL

Born in or near Denver, CO; son of Marvin Davis (a studio executive and owner of movie theatres). *Education:* Bowdoin College, graduated, 1977; attended Amherst College; Harvard University, M.B.A., 1981.

Addresses: *Office*—Davis Entertainment, 10201 West Pico Blvd., Building 31, Suite 301, Los Angeles, CA 90035.

Career: Producer. Twentieth Century–Fox, head of low–budget feature films division, 1982–84, vice president for production, 1984; Davis Entertainment, Los Angeles, founder, chair, and producer, 1985—. Also worked as line producer, production supervisor, and production manager. Pasta Pomodoro (restaurant chain), stakeholder.

Awards, Honors: Silver Angel (with others), Excellence in Media Angel Awards, 1994, for *One Christmas;* Film Award (with Merrill H. Karpf), best feature drama film, Santa Clarita International Film Festival, 1998, for *Miracle at Midnight;* ShoWest Award, producer of the year, National Association of Theatre Owners, 2004; Andrew Carnegie Medal (with others), Association for Library Service to Children, 2008, for *Jump In!*

CREDITS

Film Producer:
Predator, Twentieth Century–Fox, 1987.
Coproducer, *Three o'Clock High,* Universal, 1987.
License to Drive, Twentieth Century–Fox, 1988.
(As John A. Davis) *Little Monsters* (also known as *Little Ghost Fighters*), United Artists, 1989.
The Last of the Finest (also known as *Blue Heat* and *Street Legal*), Orion, 1990.
Enid Is Sleeping (also known as *Over Her Dead Body*), Davis Entertainment/Vestron, 1990.
Predator 2, Twentieth Century–Fox, 1990.
Shattered (also known as *Plastic Nightmare*), Metro–Goldwyn–Mayer, 1991.
Fortress, Dimension Films, 1993.
The Firm, Paramount, 1993.
The Thing Called Love, Paramount, 1993.
Grumpy Old Men, Warner Bros., 1993.
Gunmen, Dimension Films, 1994.
Richie Rich, Warner Bros., 1994.
The Hunted, Universal, 1995.
Waterworld, Universal, 1995.
The Grass Harp, Fine Line, 1995.
Grumpier Old Men (also known as *Grumpy Old Men 2*), Warner Bros., 1995.
The Chamber, Universal, 1996.
Courage under Fire, Twentieth Century–Fox, 1996.
Daylight, Universal, 1996.
Out to Sea, Twentieth Century–Fox, 1997.
Digging to China, Legacy Releasing, 1998.
Doctor Dolittle, Twentieth Century–Fox, 1998.
Dudley Do–Right, Universal, 1999.
Coproducer, *Labor Pains,* USA Home Video, 2000.
Heartbreakers, Metro–Goldwyn–Mayer, 2001.
Dr. Dolittle 2 (also known as *DR2* and *DR.2*), Twentieth Century–Fox, 2001.
Behind Enemy Lines, Twentieth Century–Fox, 2001.
Life or Something Like It, Twentieth Century–Fox, 2002.
Daddy Day Care, Columbia, 2003.
Devil's Pond (also known as *Heaven's Pond*), Artisan Entertainment, 2003.
Paycheck, Paramount, 2003.
Garfield (animated; also known as *Garfield: The Movie*), Twentieth Century–Fox, 2004.
I, Robot, Twentieth Century–Fox, 2004.
AVP: Alien vs. Predator (also known as *Alien vs. Predator, AVP,* and *AVP: Alien vs. Predateur*), Twentieth Century–Fox, 2004.

First Daughter, Twentieth Century–Fox, 2004.
Fat Albert, Twentieth Century–Fox, 2004.
Flight of the Phoenix, Twentieth Century–Fox, 2004.
When a Stranger Calls (also known as *Bell Ringer*), Screen Gems, 2006.
Dr. Dolittle 3, Twentieth Century–Fox Home Entertainment, 2006.
Garfield: A Tail of Two Kitties (animated; also known as *Garfield 2*), Twentieth Century–Fox, 2006.
Eragon, Twentieth Century–Fox, 2006.
Norbit, Paramount, 2007.
Garfield Gets Real (animated), Twentieth Century–Fox Home Entertainment, 2007.
AVPR: Aliens vs Predator—Requiem (also known as *Aliens vs. Predator 2, AvPR,* and *AvP2*), Twentieth Century–Fox, 2007.
Dr. Dolittle: A Tinsel Town Tail, Twentieth Century–Fox, 2008.
Dr. Dolittle: Tail to the Chief, Twentieth Century–Fox, 2008.
Garfield's Fun Fest (animated), Twentieth Century–Fox Home Entertainment, 2008.
The Express (also known as *The Express: The Ernie Davis Story*), Universal, 2008.

Film Executive Producer:
Storyville, Twentieth Century–Fox, 1992.
Denise Calls Up, 1995, Sony Pictures Classics, 1996.
Lewis & Clark & George, Davis Entertainment/Dark Matter Productions, 1997.
Bad Manners, Phaedra Cinema, 1997.
Rites of Passage, World International Network, 1999.
29 Palms, Alliance Atlantis Communications, 2002.
Happy Hour, Davis Entertainment–O'Hara/Klein Releasing, 2003.
At Last, Anything for Love, 2005.
Daddy Day Camp, Columbia, 2007.
The Heartbreak Kid, Paramount, 2007.

Television Executive Producer; Movies:
Curiosity Kills, USA Network, 1990.
Silhouette, USA Network, 1990.
Dangerous Passion, ABC, 1990.
Wild Card, USA Network, 1992.
Caught in the Act, USA Network, 1993.
Voyage (also known as *Cruise of Fear*), USA Network, 1993.
This Can't Be Love, CBS, 1994.
Volcano: Fire on the Mountain (also known as *Fire on the Mountain*), ABC, 1997.
Miracle at Midnight, ABC, 1998.
The Jesse Ventura Story, NBC, 1999.
The Settlement, Starz!, 1999.
Little Richard, NBC, 2000.
Bobbie's Girl, Showtime, 2002.
Nadine in Date Land, Oxygen Network, 2005.
Life Is Ruff, The Disney Channel, 2005.
Jump In!, The Disney Channel, 2007.

Television Producer; Movies:

One Christmas (also known as *Truman Capote's "One Christmas"*), NBC, 1994.

Sunk on Christmas Eve, National Geographic Channel, 2001.

Television Executive Producer; Miniseries:

Asteroid (also known as *Asteroid: The Sky Is Falling*), NBC, 1997.

Television Appearances; Specials:

The Making of "Alien vs. Predator," Fox, 2004.

Television Appearances; Episodic:

"The Making of 'Dr. Dolittle 2'," *HBO First Look,* HBO, 2001.

"The Making of 'I, Robot'," *HBO First Look,* HBO, 2004.

"'Alien vs. Predator': Behind the Scenes," *HBO First Look,* HBO, 2004.

RECORDINGS

Videos:

If It Bleeds We Can Kill It: The Making of "Predator," Twentieth Century–Fox Home Entertainment, 2001.

Predator: The Life Inside, Twentieth Century–Fox Home Entertainment, 2001.

Predator: The Unseen Arnold, Twentieth Century–Fox Home Entertainment, 2001.

AVP: The Beginning, Twentieth Century–Fox Home Entertainment, 2004.

AVP: Production, Twentieth Century–Fox Home Entertainment, 2004.

AVP–R: Preparing for War—Development and Production, Twentieth Century–Fox Home Entertainment, 2008.

DAVIS, Palmer

PERSONAL

Education: University of California, Los Angeles, B.A.

Addresses: *Agent*—Brianna Barcus, Clear Talent Group, 10950 Ventura Blvd., Studio City, CA 91604.

Career: Actress. Performer for radio programs, industrial films, music videos, and Internet productions; also voice performer; appeared in commercials for Doritos snack foods, Idaho potatoes, Philadelphia cream cheese, Radio Shack electronics stores, Toyota autos, and other products.

Member: American Federation of Television and Radio Artists, Actors' Equity Association, Screen Actors Guild.

CREDITS

Television Appearances; Series:

Attorney Margaret Finn, a recurring role, *CSI: Crime Scene Investigation* (also known as *C.S.I., CSI: Las Vegas,* and *Les experts*), CBS, between 2001 and 2006.

Angie, *The Rookie: CTU,* Fox, 2007.

Television Appearances; Movies:

Showgirl, *Winchell,* HBO, 1998.

Angela Panati, *The Perfect Husband: The Laci Peterson Story,* USA Network, 2004.

Female cop, *Ordinary Miracles,* Hallmark Channel, 2005.

Television Appearances; Episodic:

Zoner, "The Forbidden Zone," *Red Shoe Diaries,* Showtime, 1996.

Tacts officer, "Class Strike," *Pensacola: Wings of Gold,* syndicated, 1998.

Lucy, "Perfect Frank," *Cover Me: Based on the True Life of an FBI Family* (also known as *Cover Me*), USA Network, 2000.

A dancer, "Won't You Beat My Neighbor?," *Nikki,* The WB, 2000.

Scotty's mother, "The End of the Power Rangers: Part 2," *Power Rangers Wild Force,* ABC, 2002.

Television Appearances; Other:

Also performed as a dancer in scenes of other television programs.

Film Appearances:

A showgirl, *What Women Want,* Paramount, 2000.

Darlene, *Dark Streets,* Samuel Goldwyn Films, 2008.

Susan Forrester, *The Last Blood Line,* 2008.

Also performed as a dancer in scenes of other films.

Stage Appearances:

Appeared as Tess, *Crazy for You,* Sacramento Music Circus, Sacramento, CA; as Gymnasia, *A Funny Thing Happened on the Way to the Forum;* member of ensemble, *Mack n Mable,* regional production; member of ensemble, *Of Thee I Sing;* as Brenda, *Pajama Game,* and as Dorcas, *Seven Brides for Seven Brothers,* both regional productions; in *Suburban Showgirl* (solo show); performed as a Rockette, *Radio City Christmas Spectacular,* Radio City Music Hall, New York City.

Major Tours:
Performed as a Ziegfeld girl in a touring production of *The Will Rogers Follies,* U.S. cities.

OTHER SOURCES

Electronic:
Palmer Davis Official Site, http://www.palmerdavis.com, December 21, 2008.

DAY, Felicia 1979–

PERSONAL

Full name, Kathryn Felicia Day; born June 28, 1979, in Huntsville, AL. *Education:* University of Texas at Austin, B.S., mathematics, B.A., music; studied improvisation at the Empty Stage Theatre and with the Groundlings, Los Angeles, CA. *Avocational Interests:* Professional–level violinist, playing video games, reading (particularly science fiction and fantasy), and writing and performing sketch comedy and improvisational comedy.

Addresses: *Agent*—International Creative Management, 10250 Constellation Way, 9th Floor, Los Angeles, CA 90067. *Manager*—Frontline Management, 5670 Wilshire Blvd., Suite 1370, Los Angeles, CA 90036.

Career: Actress. Appeared in television commercials, including Diet Coke, Carb Countdown Yogurt drink, United States Postal Service, Clearasil Ultra Face Wash, T–Mobile communications, Extra chewing gum, Sears department stores, and Cheetos; appeared in a public service announcement for Parents: The Anti–Drug, 2003; wrote, produced, and appeared as Codex, *The Guild* (an internet series; www.watchtheguild.com), 2007–08; appeared as Penny, "Act I," "Act II," and "Act III," *Dr. Horrible's Sing–Along Blog* (an internet series; www.drhorrible.com), 2008; appeared as fairy, "The Fairy's Obsession" and "The Beginning," *The Legend of Neil* (an internet series, wwww.effinfunny.com/legend–of–neil#); ACME Bravo Sketch Theatre, Travis Oates, member of company.

Member: American Federation of Television and Radio Artists, Screen Actors Guild.

Awards, Honors: YouTube Award, best web series, 2008; Yahoo Video Award, best web series, 2008; SxSW, best web series (On Networks/SXSW Greenlight Award), 2008.

CREDITS

Film Appearances:
Delusional, Artist View Entertainment, 2000.
Strings, 2001.
Maddie, *Backslide* (short), 2003.
Felicia, *Final Sale* (short), 2 Muse Productions, 2004.
Penelope, *Bring It On Again,* 2004.
Tiffany, *The Mortician's Hobby* (short), 2004.
Felicia, *Short Story Time* (short), Creative Fugitives, Inc., 2005.
Trixie, *God's Waiting List,* Codeblack Entertainment, 2006.
Sugar girl, *Splitting Hairs* (short), 2007.
Pipsy, *Dear Me,* 2008.

Also appeared in *Solo; A.W.K.*

Television Appearances; Series:
Vi, *Buffy the Vampire Slayer* (also known as *BtVS, Buffy,* and *Buffy, the Vampire Slayer: The Series*), UPN, 2003.

Also appeared in *Here Comes the Joneses,* The WB.

Television Appearances; Movies:
Call girl, *They Shoot Divas, Don't They?,* VH1, 2002.
June Marie Jacobs, *June,* 2004.
Eloise Hutchinson, *Warm Springs,* HBO, 2005.
Emily, *Mystery Woman: Vision of a Murder,* Hallmark Channel, 2005.
Blue, *Prairie Fever,* Ion, 2008.

Television Appearances; Episodic:
Cherie, "Whose Life Is It Anyway?," *Emeril,* NBC, 2001.
Cookie, "The Crazy–Girl Episode," *Maybe It's Me,* The WB, 2002.
"Of Tombs and Pirates," *Player$,* Tech TV, 2003.
Nicole, "Nexus," *For the People* (also known as *Para la gente*), Lifetime, 2003.
Jesse's friend, "Positive Results," *Strong Medicine,* Lifetime, 2004.
Sarah, "We'll Take Manhattan," *One on One,* UPN, 2004.
Mrs. Heidi Gefsky, "Mr. Monk Gets Drunk," *Monk,* USA Network, 2005.
Campus Ladies, Oxygen Media, 2005.
Natalie, "Hello, Larry," *Love, Inc.,* UPN, 2006.
Danielle, "Changing Partners," *Windfall,* NBC, 2006.
Danielle, "Crash Into You," *Windfall,* NBC, 2006.
Apple, "Not Cancer," *House M.D.* (also known as *House*), Fox, 2008.

Also appeared as Sheila, "God Visits," *Undeclared,* Fox; Alyssa, "The Trash 'N Treasures," *Roommates,* ABC Family; Alyssa, "The Old and the New," *Roommates,*

ABC Family; Alyssa, "The Game Night," *Roommates,* ABC Family; in *Campus Ladies,* Oxygen; *Beyond,* Fox; *Century City,* ABC.

Stage Appearances:
Appeared in *Waterbrains,* Empty Stage Theatre, Los Angeles; *Three,* Empty Stage Theatre; as Luisa, *Fantastiks,* University of Texas at Austin; Cecile, *Les Liasons Dangeureues,* Austin Circle Theatre, Austin, TX.

OTHER SOURCES

Periodicals:
Hollywood Reporter, November 24, 2008.

Electronic:
Felicia Day Website, http://feliciaday.com, January 15, 2009.

---

de ALMEIDA, Joaquim 1957–

PERSONAL

Full name, Joaquim Antonio Portugal Baptista de Almeida; born March 15, 1957, in Lisbon, Portugal; naturalized U.S. citizen, 2005; son of Joao Baptista (a technical director of a pharmaceutical laboratory) and Maria Sora Portugal (a technical director of a pharmaceutical laboratory) de Almeida; married, wife's name Maria Cecilia (a pianist; divorced); married Maria do Carmo Gaivao de Tavares Risques Pereira (divorced); children: (first marriage) two sons, including Lorenzo; (second marriage) Ana Gaivao Risques Baptista.

Addresses: *Agent*—Barry McPherson, Agency for the Performing Arts, 405 South Beverly Dr., Beverly Hills, CA 90212. *Manager*—Estelle Lasher, Principal Entertainment, 1964 Westwood Blvd., Suite 400, Los Angeles, CA 90025.

Career: Actor. Appeared in numerous commercials in Portugal, 1993–99. Xurrascao do Tejo (Portuguese restaurant; also known as O Porcao), founder in the late 1990s. Formerly worked as a gardener at the embassy of Zaire in Austria; also worked as a waiter.

Awards, Honors: Cairo International Film Festival Award, best actor, 1994, for *Retrato de familia;* Globos de Ouro Award (Portuguese Golden Globe Award), best actor, 1995, for *Adao e Eva;* Globos de Ouro Award nomination, best actor, 1997, for *Sostiene Pereira;* Globos de Ouro Award, best actor, 1998, for *Tantacao;*

Globos de Ouro Award nomination, best actor, 2000, for *Inferno;* Globos de Ouro Award and Cinema Brazil Grand Prize nomination, both best actor, 2002, for *O xango de Baker Street;* Screen Actors Guild award nomination (with others), outstanding ensemble in a drama series, 2005, for *24;* Globos de Ouro Award nomination, best actor, 2006, for *Um tiro no escuro;* Avanca Film Festival Award, best actor, 2008, for *Oscar. Una pasion surrealista.*

CREDITS

Film Appearances:
First Soldier's Force member, *The Soldier* (also known as *Codename: The Soldier*), Embassy, 1982.
Leon, *The Honorary Consul* (also known as *Beyond the Limit*), Paramount, 1983.
Himself in "1987," *Cinematon,* 1984.
Andrea Bonnano, *Good Morning, Babylon* (also known as *Good morning Babilonia*), Vestron, 1987.
David Garcia, *The Sun and the Moon* (also known as *The Violins Came with the Americans* and *El sol y la luna*), 1987.
Reinaldo Ferreira, *Reporter X,* 1987.
Tremaine, *Milan noir* (also known as *Black Milan*), 1987.
Mateo, *Terre sacree,* Arion Productions, 1988.
Honore Fragonard, *Les deux Fragonard,* Capital Cinema, 1989.
Love Dream (also known as *Priceless Beauty*), Republic Pictures Home Video, 1989.
Sebastiano Catte, *Disamistade,* Compania Lavoratori del Cinema e del Teatro, 1989.
Luis Barreto, *Segno di fuoco* (also known as *Signe de feu*), 1990.
Title role, *Sandino,* Globo Video, 1990.
Pedro, *A idade maior* (also known as *Alex* and *Am Ende einer kindheit*), Coralie Films International, 1991.
Father Almeida, *El rey pasmado* (also known as *The Dumbfounded King, O rei pasmado,* and *Le roi ebahi*), Golem Distribucion, 1991.
Miguel Montenegro, *Retrato de familia* (also known as *Family Portrait*), Samsa Distributions, 1991.
Pelayo Menendez, *El dia que naci yo,* Ion Films/Laszo Films/Reel Films, 1991.
Francisco Frontaria, *Amor e dedinhos de pe* (also known as *Love and Tiny Toes* and *Amor y deditos del pie*), MGN Filmes, 1991.
Leonardo, *Terra fria* (also known as *Cold Land* and *Tierra fria*), Lusomundo, 1992.
Miguel, *Una estacion de paso* (also known as *A Passing Season* and *Whistle Stop*), 1992.
Luis de Ayala, *El maestro de esgrima* (also known as *The Fencing Master*), Mayfair, 1993.
Jose, *Sombras en una batalla* (also known as *Shadows in a Conflict*), Cayo Largo Films/Sogepaq, 1993.
L'amant, *Amok,* Rezo Films, 1993.

(Uncredited) Voice of Spino, *O fio do horizonte* (also known as *The Line of the Horizon, On the Edge of the Horizon, Le fil de l'horizon,* and *Fluchtpunkt*), K Film, 1993.

El baile de las animas, 1994.

Miguel, *Uma vida normal,* MGN Filmes, 1994.

Colonel Felix Cortez/Roberto Alonzo Landa, *Clear and Present Danger,* Paramount, 1994.

Giovanni, *Only You* (also known as *Him* and *Just in Time*), TriStar, 1994.

Voice of the Cat, *Estoria do gato e da lua* (animated; also known as *Tale about the Cat and the Moon*), Filmografo, 1994.

Francisco, *Adao e Eva* (also known as *Adam and Eve* and *Adan y Eva*), United International Pictures, 1995.

Bucho, *Desperado,* Columbia, 1995.

Manuel, *Sostiene Pereira* (also known as *According to Pereia, Pereira Declares, Afirma Pereira,* and *Pereira pretend*), Mikado/Canal Plus, 1996.

Gigi, *Elles* (also known as *Women* and *Elas*), WinStar Cinema, 1997.

Father Antonio, *Tentacao* (also known as *Temptation*), Lusomundo, 1997.

Emilio, *Corazon loco* (also known as *Crazy Heart*), 1997.

Jose Guerras, *La cucaracha,* Atmosphere Films, 1998.

Ignacio, *On the Run* (also known as *Em fuga*), Phaedra Cinema, 1998.

Reynaldo, *No Vacancy,* No Vacancy LLC, 1999.

Cortina, *One Man's Hero* (also known as *El batallon de San Patricio, Heroes sin patria,* and *Herois sense patria*), Metro–Goldwyn–Mayer, 1999.

Xana, *Inferno,* Lusomundo, 1999.

Sherlock Holmes, *O xango de Baker Street* (also known as *The Xango from Baker Street*), 1999, Columbia TriStar, 2001.

Narrator, *Estoria do gato e da lua,* Cinema Village Features, 1999.

Narrator of Portuguese version, *The Art of Amalia* (also known as *A arte de Amalia*), Avatar, 1999.

Gervasio, *Capitaes de abril* (also known as *April Captains, Captains of April, Capitaines d'avril, Capitanes de abril,* and *Capitani d'aprile*), Wanda Vision, 2000.

Husband, *Agua e Sal* (also known as *Water and Salt*), Atalanta Filmes/Gruppo Pasquino/Gemini Filmes, 2000.

Oliveira, *La voz de su amo* (also known as *His Master's Voice*), Lolafilms Distribucion, 2001.

Admiral Piquet, *Behind Enemy Lines,* Twentieth Century–Fox, 2001.

Fidel Rodrigo, *Stranded: Naufragos* (also known as *The Shelter* and *Stranded*), Sogepaq Distribucion, 2001.

Noh, *Sueurs* (also known as *Sweat*), Metropolitan Filmexport, 2002.

Radman/Constantin, *Entre chiens et loups* (also known as *Break of Dawn*), Moonstone Entertainment, 2002.

Hombres tranquilos (also known as *Quiet Men*), EPC Producciones/Fiction Line/Reaccion Films, 2002.

Narrator, *Demon Island* (also known as *Pinata: Survival Island*), First Look International, 2002.

Roberto Alua, *Imortais, Os,* Samsa Distributors, 2003.

Lolo, *Il fuggiasco* (also known as *The Fugitive*), Istituto Luce, 2003.

Pierre, *Yo puta* (also known as *I, Whore, The Life, The Life: What's Your Pleasure?,* and *Whore*), Screen Media Ventures, 2004.

The president, *Blue Sombrero* (also known as *Blue Balls of Fire*), Ego Check Productions/Insomnia Media Group, 2005.

Rafael, *Um tiro no escuro,* Filmes Lusomundo, 2005.

Yuri, *Moscow,* Valentia Pictures, 2006.

Posdata, Geovision Films, 2006.

Father Sanchez, *The Celestine Prophecy,* RAM Entertainment, 2006.

Max Landa, *Thanks to Gravity* (also known as *Love and Debate*), Voyage Entertainment, 2006.

Hugo, *53 dias de invierno* (also known as *53 Winter Days*), Ovideo, 2006.

Baxter, *El corazon de la tierra* (also known as *The Heart of the Earth*), On Pictures, 2007.

Don Huertero, *The Death and Life of Bobby Z* (also known as *Bobby Z* and *Kill Bobby Z—Ein Deal um leben und tod*), Sony Pictures Home Entertainment, 2007.

Marco Correia, *The Lovebirds,* Lisbon Village Festival, 2007.

Michael, *La cucina,* Chianti Pictures, 2007.

Mouros, *Call Girl,* Filmes Lusomundo, 2007.

President Rene Barrientos, *Che: Part Two,* IFC Films, 2008.

Nick, *The Burning Plain,* 2929 Productions, 2008.

Escobedo, *La conjura de El Escorial* (also known as *The El Escorial Conspiracy*), Sony Pictures, 2008.

Mangini, *Holy Money,* Moviestream, 2008.

Robosapien: Rebooted, CatchPlay, 2009.

Oscar Dominguez, *Oscar. Una pasion surrealista* (also known as *Oscar: The Color of Destiny*), Domain Entertainment, 2009.

Television Appearances; Series:

Caesar Nicoletti, a recurring role, *Falcone,* CBS, 2000.

Ramon Salazar, *24,* Fox, 2003–2004.

Captain Manuel Valenza, *Wanted,* TNT, 2005.

Also appeared in the series *As the World Turns,* CBS.

Television Appearances; Miniseries:

Major Laroche, *Dead Man's Walk* (also known as *Larry McMurtry's "Dead Man's Walk"*), ABC, 1996.

Colonel Sotillo, *Nostromo* (also known as *Joseph Conrad's "Nostromo"* and *Nostromo–Der Schatz in den Bergen*), PBS, 1996.

Gonzalo Leyva, *Camino de Santiago* (also known as *The Road to Santiago*), 1999.
Colombian cocaine kingpin, *Kingpin*, NBC, 2003.

Television Appearances; Movies:
Andrea, *A ilha* (also known as *The Island*), YTV, 1990.
Manuel, *Aqui d'el rei!* (also known as *Lieutenant Lorena* and *El teniente Lorrena*), 1991.
Miguel Carmina, *L'enfant du bout du monde,* 1996.
Avelino de Almeida, *Fatima,* 1997.
Friar Ramon, *Dollar for the Dead* (also known as *Un dolar por los muertos*), TNT, 1998.
Joseph Macheca, *Vendetta,* HBO, 1999.
Salvadoran Archbishop Oscar Romero, *Have No Fear: The Life of Pope John Paul II,* ABC, 2005.

Television Appearances; Pilots:
Captain Manuel Valenza, *Wanted,* TNT, 2005.

Television Appearances; Episodic:
Roberto "Nico" Arroyo, "Bought and Paid For," *Miami Vice,* NBC, 1985.
Carlos Cruz Quarta–Feira, RTP, 1992.
Mundo VIP, SCI, multiple appearances, between 1996 and 2001.
Joaquim Armel, "Psychic Pilgrim," *La Femme Nikita* (also known as *Nikita*), USA Network, 1998.
Noites Marcianas, SIC, 2001.
HermanSIC, SIC, 2001, 2002.
Cartaz, SIC, 2003.
Carlos Carrio, "Slow News Day," *The West Wing,* NBC, 2004.
Voice of Bane, "Traction," *The Batman* (animated), The WB, 2004.
Joseph Trevi, "Man Down," *CSI: Miami,* CBS, 2007.
Exit, Barcelona Television, 2008.
Cartaz cultural, SIC, 2008.
Santos Santana, "Long Pig," *Crusoe,* NBC, 2008.
Santos Santana, "Smoke and Mirrors," *Crusoe,* NBC, 2009.

Television Appearances; Awards Presentations:
Presenter, *VI premios Goya,* Antena 3, 1992.
Globos de Ouro, SIC, 1996, 1998, 1999, 2006.

Stage Appearances:
Blood Wedding, Public Theatre, New York City, 1992.

Appeared in *The Count of Monte Cristo* and in *What Would Jeanne Moreau Do,* Workshop of the Players Art Theatre, New York City.

RECORDINGS

Videos:
Narrator, *Amalia–uma estranha forma de vida,* Arco Films, 1995.

Voices of Mattsson, Silencio, Zuni, and Fateen, *The Chronicles of Riddick: Escape from Butcher Bay* (video game), Tigon Studios, 2004.
Voice of Hector, *Saints Row* (video game), THQ, 2006.

DEMME, Jonathan 1944–
   (Rob Morton)

PERSONAL

Full name, Robert Jonathan Demme; born February 22, 1944, in Baldwin (some sources cite nearby Rockville Centre), NY; son of Robert (a public relations executive and magazine editor) and Dorothy (an actress) Demme; married Evelyn Purcell (a producer and director), 1970 (divorced, 1980); married Joanne Howard (an artist), 1987 (divorced); children: (second marriage) Ramona Castle, Brooklyn James, Josephine. *Education:* Attended University of Florida.

Addresses: *Office*—Clinica Estetico, 521 North Broadway, 2nd Floor, Nyack, NY 10960. *Agent*—Jeff Berg, International Creative Management, 10250 Constellation Way, 9th Floor, Los Angeles, CA 90067.

Career: Director, producer, and writer. Avco Embassy Films, publicist, 1966; Pathe Films, publicist, 1966–67; United Artists, publicist, 1968–69; Clinica Estetico, Nyack, NY, principal. Worked in London as a promoter of American investment in British films and as a producer of commercials for a U.S. company; director of music videos; also worked as camera operator, second unit director, and music coordinator for films. Previously worked as salesman, kennel and animal hospital worker, and usher. *Military service:* U.S. Air Force, 1966.

Member: Directors Guild of America, Writers Guild of America, American Ornithologist's Union.

Awards, Honors: New York Film Critics Circle Award, best director, 1980, for *Melvin and Howard;* National Society of Film Critics Award, best documentary, 1984, and Golden Spur Award, Flanders International Film Festival, 1985, both for *Stop Making Sense;* Grammy Award nomination (with others), best long–form music video, National Academy of Recording Arts and Sciences, 1986, for *Sun City: Artists United against Apartheid;* Critics Award nomination, Deauville Film Festival, 1987, and Independent Spirit Award nomination, best director, Independent Features Project West, 1988, both for *Swimming to Cambodia;* honorary degree, Wesleyan University, Middletown, CT, 1990; National Board of Review Award, New York Film Critics Circle Award, Boston Society of Film Critics Award, Silver Berlin Bear and nomination for Golden Berlin Bear, Berlin International Film Festival, all best director, 1991, Silver Scream Award, Amsterdam Fantastic Film Festival, 1991, Hochi Film Award, best foreign language film, 1991, Academy Award, Saturn Award nomination, Academy of Science Fiction, Fantasy, and Horror Films, Kansas City Film Critics Circle Award, and Chicago Film Critics Association Award, all best director, Directors Guild of America Award (with others) and Golden Globe Award nomination, both best motion picture director, two Film Award nominations, best direction and best film, British Academy of Film and Television Arts, Cesar Award nomination, best foreign film, Academie des Arts et Techniques du Cinema, London Critics Circle Film Award nomination, director of the year, and Blue Ribbon Award, best foreign language film, all 1992, all for *Silence of the Lambs;* Filmmaker Award, Gotham Awards, 1991; nomination for Golden Berlin Bear, 1994, for *Philadelphia;* Pare Lorentz Award (with others), International Documentary Association, 1997, for *Mandela;* nomination for motion picture producer of the year (with others), Producers Guild of America, 2003, for *Adaptation;* Gotham Award and Telluride Mountain Film Award, International Alliance for Mountain Films, both best documentary, 2004, for *The Agronomist;* Billy Wilder Award, National Board of Review, 2006; FIPRESCI Prize, EIUC Award, and Biografilm Award, all Venice Film Festival, 2007, for *Jimmy Carter Man from Plains;* nomination for Golden Lion, Venice Film Festival, 2008, and Independent Spirit Award nominations, best director and best feature film (with others), 2009, all for *Rachel Getting Married.*

CREDITS

Film Producer and Director:
Something Wild, Orion, 1986.
Cousin Bobby (documentary), Cinevista, 1992.
Philadelphia, TriStar, 1993.
Beloved, Buena Vista, 1998.
The Truth about Charlie (also known as *Die wahrheit ueber Charlie*), Universal, 2002.
(And cinematographer) *The Agronomist* (documentary), ThinkFilm/Palisades Pictures, 2003.
The Manchurian Candidate, Paramount, 2004.
Neil Young: Heart of Gold, Paramount, 2006.
Jimmy Carter Man from Plains (documentary), Sony Pictures Classics, 2007.
Rachel Getting Married, Columbia, 2008.
Neil Young Trunk Show (music documentary), Clinica Estetico, 2008.

Film Director:
(Opening sequence) *Secrets of a Door-to-Door Salesman* (also known as *Naughty Wives*), Cannon, 1973.

Caged Heat (also known as *Caged Females* and *Renegade Girls*) New World, 1974.
Crazy Mama, New World, 1975.
Fighting Mad, Twentieth Century–Fox, 1976.
Citizens Band (also known as *The Great American Citizens Band* and *Handle with Care*), Paramount, 1977.
Last Embrace, United Artists, 1979.
Melvin and Howard, Universal, 1980.
Swing Shift, Warner Bros., 1984.
Stop Making Sense (concert film), Island Alive, 1984.
Perfect Kiss (music documentary), 1985.
Swimming to Cambodia (also known as *Spalding Gray's "Swimming to Cambodia"*), Cinecom, 1987.
Married to the Mob, Orion, 1988.
Famous All Over Town, 1988.
The Silence of the Lambs, Orion, 1991.
The Complex Sessions (music documentary), 1994.
Storefront Hitchcock (documentary), Metro–Goldwyn–Mayer, 1998.

Film Producer:
Angels Hard As They Come (also known as *Angels, Angels As Hard As They Come, Angels, Hell on Harleys,* and *Angel Warriors*), New World, 1971.
The Hot Box (also known as *Hell Cats*), New World, 1972.
Miami Blues, Orion, 1990.
One Foot on a Banana Peel, the Other Foot in the Grave: Secrets from the Dolly Madison Room (also known as *Yksi jalka*), Clinica Estetico, 1994.
That Thing You Do!, Twentieth Century–Fox, 1996.
Desolation Angels, McCann and Company Films/Canosa, 1996.
Mandela (also known as *Mandela: Son of Africa, Father of a Nation*), Island, 1996.
Courage and Pain (documentary), Clinica Estetico, 1996.
Into the Rope, Clinica Estetico, 1996.
Ulee's Gold, Orion, 1997.
The Uttmost (documentary), Clinica Estetico, 1998.
Six Ways to Sunday, Stratosphere Entertainment, 1999.
Adaptation, Columbia, 2002.
Beah: A Black Woman Speaks, Women Make Movies, 2003.
I'll Sing for You, First Run Features, 2004.

Film Executive Producer:
(Uncredited) *Amos & Andrew,* Columbia, 1993.
Household Saints, Columbia, 1993.
Roy Cohn/Jack Smith, Strand Releasing, 1994.
Devil in a Blue Dress (also known as *Le diable en robe bleue*), TriStar, 1995.
Shadrach, Columbia, 1998.
Maangamizi: The Ancient One, Gris–Gris, 2000.
The Opportunists, First Look Pictures, 2000.
Crude Independence (documentary), Couple 3 Films, 2009.

Film Appearances:

(Uncredited) Godzilla, *Hollywood Boulevard,* New World, 1976.

Matt Winters, *The Incredible Melting Man,* American International Pictures, 1977.

Roger Corman: Hollywood's Wild Angel, Blackwood Films, 1978.

(Uncredited) Man on train, *Last Embrace,* United Artists, 1979.

Federal agent, *Into the Night,* Universal, 1985.

Himself, *Cousin Bobby* (documentary), Cinevista, 1992.

Narrator, *One Foot on a Banana Peel, the Other Foot in the Grave: Secrets from the Dolly Madison Room* (also known as *Yksi jalka*), Clinica Estetico, 1994.

Dying Is Easy, American Giraffe Productions, 1995.

Major motion picture director, *That Thing You Do!,* Twentieth Century–Fox, 1996.

The Uttmost (documentary), Clinica Estetico, 1998.

Himself, *Pablo,* Kihou Productions, 2008.

Television Work; Movies:

Director, *Columbo: Murder under Glass,* NBC, 1978.

Producer, "Women and Men 2" (also known as "The Art of Seduction," "A Domestic Dilemma," and "Women and Men 2: In Love There Are No Rules"), *HBO Showcase,* HBO, 1991.

Executive producer (and director of "Subway Car from Hell" segment), *Subway Stories: Tales from the Underground* (also known as *Subway*), HBO, 1997.

Television Work; Specials:

Director, "Who Am I This Time," *American Playhouse,* PBS, 1982.

Director, *Alive from Off Center,* PBS, 1984.

Producer and director, *Haiti Dreams of Democracy,* Bravo, 1988.

Segment director, "In the Still of the Night," *Red, Hot & Blue,* ABC, 1990.

Producer, *Haiti: Killing the Dream,* PBS, 1992.

Television Director; Pilots:

Surviving a Family Tree, PBS, 1984, re–broadcast as "A Family Tree," *Trying Times,* PBS, 1987.

Television Director; Episodic:

"Murder in Aspic," *Columbo,* NBC, 1977.

Segment director, "Gidgette Goes to Hell," *Saturday Night Live* (also known as *NBC's Saturday Night, Saturday Night,* and *SNL*), NBC, 1980.

Television Director; Other:

Survival Guide, 1985.

(And producer) *Right to Return: New Home Movies from the Lower 9th Ward* (miniseries), 2007.

Television Appearances; Specials:

Night Times Magazine, PBS, 1988.

Haiti: Killing the Dream, PBS, 1992.

Bruce Springsteen: Blood Brothers, The Disney Channel, 1996.

"Tom Hanks: Hollywood's Golden Boy," *Biography,* Arts and Entertainment, 1997.

Hollywood Salutes Jodie Foster: An American Cinematheque Tribute, TNT, 1999.

Hitchcock: Shadow of a Genius (also known as *Dial H Hitchcock: The Genius Behind the Snowman* and *Dial H for Hitchcock*), Starz!, 1999.

Jonathan Demme and the Making of "The Manchurian Candidate," 2004.

Ultimate Super Heroes, Ultimate Super Villains, Ultimate Super Vixens, Bravo, 2004.

Legends Ball, ABC, 2006.

San Sebastian 2006: Cronica de Carlos Boyero, Canal + Espana, 2006.

9th Annual State of the Black Union: Breaking New Ground, TV–One Lifestyle and Entertainment, 2008.

9th Annual State of the Black Union: Building Blocks for America, TV–One Lifestyle and Entertainment, 2008.

9th Annual State of the Black Union: Memorable Moments, TV–One Lifestyle and Entertainment, 2008.

Ceremonia de inauguracion—56th festival internacional de cine de San Sebastian, TVE, 2008.

Resumen—56th festival internacional de cine de San Sebastian, TVE, 2008.

Ceremonia de clausura—56th festival internacionale de cine de San Sebastian, TVE, 2008.

Television Appearances; Episodic:

"The Films of Roger Corman," *The Directors,* Encore, 1999.

Commercial director, "Gray Matter," *Oz,* HBO, 2000.

Today (also known as *NBC News Today* and *The Today Show*), NBC, 2004.

Film '72 (also known as *Film 2004*), BBC, 2004.

Tavis Smiley, PBS, 2007.

Dias de cine, TVE, 2008.

Cinema tres (also known as *Informatiu cinema*), TV3, 2008.

Also appeared in "The Films of Jonathan Demme," *The Directors,* Encore.

Television Appearances; Miniseries:

Movie Legends in Conversation, 1995.

Television Appearances; Awards Presentations:

The 64th Annual Academy Awards, ABC, 1992.

Presenter, *The 15th Annual Gotham Awards,* NYC, 2005.

Presenter, *Premio Donostia a Meryl Streep,* TVE, 2008.

RECORDINGS

Video Director:

Sun City: Artists United Against Apartheid, Lorimar Home Video, 1986.

"The Perfect Kiss" music video, *New Order: Substance,* Warner Reprise Video, 1989.
"I Got You Babe" music video, *The Pretenders: Greatest Hits,* Warner Music Video, 2000.
Bruce Springsteen: The Complete Video Anthology 1978–2000, Columbia Music Video, 2001.

Director of the music videos "Perfect Kiss" by New Order, 1985; "Murder Incorporated" by Bruce Springsteen, 1995; "If I Should Fall Behind" and "Streets of Philadelphia" by Bruce Springsteen; and "Solitude Standing" by Suzanne Vega; also director of music videos for artists such as Fine Young Cannibals, Chrissie Hynde, and UB40.

Video Appearances:
Sun City: Artists United Against Apartheid, Lorimar Home Video, 1986.
Blood Brothers: Bruce Springsteen and the E Street Band, Columbia Music Video, 2000.
(In archive footage), *Inside the Labyrinth: The Making of "Silence of the Lambs,"* Metro–Goldwyn–Mayer–United Artists, 2001.
People Like Us: Making "Philadelphia," Columbia TriStar Home Video, 2003.
The Truth about "The Truth about Charlie" (also known as *The Making of "The Truth about Charles"*), Universal Studios Home Video, 2003.
Jonathan Demme & Jodie Foster: Making "The Silence of the Lambs," Metro–Goldwyn–Mayer Home Entertainment, 2005.
Jonathan Demme & Jodie Foster: The Beginning, Metro–Goldwyn–Mayer Home Entertainment, 2005.
Jonathan Demme & Jodie Foster: Breaking the Silence, Metro–Goldwyn–Mayer Home Entertainment, 2005.
Narrator, *Heart of Gold: "Rehearsal Diaries,"* Paramount Pictures Home Entertainment, 2006.
Zoom In: Stories behind the Best Independent Films of 2007, NetFlix, 2007.

Albums:
Compiler, *Konbir: Burning Rhythms of Haiti,* A&M Records, 1989.

WRITINGS

Film Scripts:
(With Joe Viola) *Angels Hard As They Come* (also known as *Angels, Angels As Hard As They Come, Angels, Hell on Harleys,* and *Angel Warriors*), New World, 1971.
(With Joe Viola) *The Hot Box* (also known as *Hell Cats*), New World, 1972.
Caged Heat (also known as *Caged Females* and *Renegade Girls*), New World, 1974.

Fighting Mad, Twentieth Century–Fox, 1976.
(As Rob Morton) *Ladies and Gentlemen ... The Fabulous Stains,* Paramount, 1982.
(As Morton) *Swing Shift,* Warner Bros., 1984.
Stop Making Sense (concert film), Island Alive, 1984.
Perfect Kiss (music documentary), 1985.
(Coauthor) *Cousin Bobby* (documentary), Cinevista, 1992.
The Truth about Charlie (also known as *Die Wahrheit ueber Charlie*), Universal, 2002.
(Uncredited) *Intolerable Cruelty,* Universal, 2003.
Jimmy Carter Man from Plains (documentary), Sony Pictures Classics, 2007.

Film Music:
Songwriter, "Stop Making Sense," *An Everlasting Peace,* DreamWorks, 2000.
Composer, *Neil Young Trunk Show* (music documentary), Clinica Estetico, 2008.

Television Movies:
(With others) *Haiti Dreams of Democracy,* Bravo, 1988.

Television Episodes:
Segment "Gidgette Goes to Hell," *Saturday Night Live* (also known as *NBC's Saturday Night, Saturday Night,* and *SNL*), NBC, 1980.

Other:
Contributor of movie reviews to *Film Daily,* 1966–68, and rock music reviews to *Fusion.*

ADAPTATIONS

The film *Black Mama, White Mama* (also known as *Chained Women, Chains of Hate, Hot, Hard, and Mean,* and *Women in Chains*), released by American International Pictures in 1973, was based on a story by Demme.

OTHER SOURCES

Books:
Authors and Artists for Young Adults, Volume 66, Gale, 2005.
Bliss, Michael and Christina Banks, *What Goes Around Comes Around: The Films of Jonathan Demme,* Southern Illinois University Press, 1996.
International Directory of Films and Filmmakers, Volume 2: *Directors,* St. James Press, 1996.
Kael, Pauline, *Pauline Kael on Jonathan Demme: A Selection of Reviews Accompanying the Retrospective Jonathan Demme, an American Director,* Walker Art Center (Minneapolis, MN), 1988.
Newsmakers 1992, Issue Cumulation, Gale, 1992.

Periodicals:
Esquire, September, 1988, p. 207.
Film Comment, January/February, 1991, p. 28.
Interview, February, 1991, p. 16.
New York Times Magazine, March 27, 1988, p. 48.
People Weekly, May 25, 1987, p. 91.
Premiere, September, 1988.
Rolling Stone, May 19, 1988, p. 100; March 24, 1994, p. 60.

DePANDI, Giuliana
    See RANCIC, Giuliana

DICKERSON, Ernest 1951–
    (Ernest R. Dickerson)

PERSONAL

Full name, Ernest Roscoe Dickerson; born June 25, 1951, in Newark, NJ; mother, a librarian; married, wife's name Annette (a college administrator; divorced); married again, wife's name Traci (marriage ended); children: five, including (first marriage) Janet; (second marriage) Ernest III. *Education:* Howard University, B.A.; New York University, M.F.A., 1982.

Addresses: *Agent*—Gersh Agency, 232 North Canon Dr., Beverly Hills, CA 90210. *Manager*—Jennifer Levine, Untitled Entertainment, 1801 Century Park E., Suite 700, Los Angeles, CA 90067.

Career: Director, cinematographer, and writer. Original Film (producers of commercials and public service announcements), founder, 1992. Also works as camera operator and second unit director; work as director or cinematographer includes music videos and commercials for Nike athletic shoes and other products. Howard University, Washington, DC, worked as photographer of surgical procedures at medical school and, later, teacher of film classes. Sometimes credited as Ernest R. Dickerson.

Member: American Society of Cinematographers.

Awards, Honors: Graduate fellow of Academy of Motion Picture Arts and Sciences and Louis B. Mayer Foundation; New York Film Critics Circle Award, best cinematographer, 1989, for *Do the Right Thing;* Below-the-Line Award, Gotham Awards, Independent Features Project, 1991; Mystfest Award nomination, best film, 1993, for *Juice;* Austin Gay and Lesbian International

Film Festival Award, best feature, Grand Jury Award, outstanding American narrative feature, Los Angeles Outfest, and Rosebud Award nomination, best feature, Verzaubert—International Gay and Lesbian Film Festival, all 1999, for *Blind Faith;* Black Reel Award nomination, best network or cable television director, 2000, for *Strange Justice;* Daytime Emmy Award, outstanding single–camera photography, 2003, for *Our America;* Black Reel Award nomination, best television director, 2004, for *Good Fences;* Black Reel Award nomination, best director, 2005, for *Never Die Alone;* Black Reel Award nomination (with others), best television director, 2006, for *Miracle's Boys.*

CREDITS

Film Cinematographer:
Joe's Bed–Stuy Barbershop: We Cut Heads (student film), 1980, First Run Features, 1989.
The Answer, 1980.
Sarah (student film), 1980.
The Brother from Another Planet, Cinecom, 1984.
Desiree, The Movies, 1984.
Krush Groove, Warner Bros., 1985.
Almacita di desolata (also known as *Almacita, Soul of Desolato*), 1985.
She's Gotta Have It, Island Pictures, 1986.
Enemy Territory, Empire Pictures, 1987.
Eddie Murphy Raw (also known as *Raw* and *Raw: The Concert Movie*), Paramount, 1987.
School Daze, Columbia, 1988.
Vampires (also known as *Fright House*), Shooting Star Video Distribution, 1988.
Negatives, 1988.
The Laser Man, Peter Wang/Hong Kong Film Workshop, 1988, Original Cinema, 1990.
Do the Right Thing, Universal, 1989.
Ava & Gabriel: Un historia di amor (also known as *Ava & Gabriel: A Love Story*), 1990.
Def by Temptation, Troma, 1990.
Mo' Better Blues, Universal, 1990.
The Laserman, 1990.
Jungle Fever, Universal, 1991.
Sex, Drugs, Rock and Roll, Avenue Entertainment, 1991.
Cousin Bobby (documentary), Cinevista, 1992.
Malcolm X, Warner Bros., 1992.

Film Director:
Juice (also known as *Angel Town 2*), Paramount, 1992.
Surviving the Game, New Line Cinema, 1994.
Tales from the Crypt Presents: Demon Knight (also known as *Demon Keeper, Demon Knight,* and *Tales from the Crypt: Demon Knight*), Universal, 1995.
Bulletproof, Universal, 1996.
Bones, New Line Cinema, 2001.
Never Die Alone, Fox Searchlight, 2004.

Film Appearances:

Dog 8, *She's Gotta Have It,* Island Pictures, 1986.

Himself, *Visions of Light: The Art of Cinematography* (documentary; also known as *Visions of Light*), American Film Institute, 1992.

Television Work; Series:

Cinematographer, *Law & Order,* NBC, multiple episodes, 1990–91.

Director, *The Wire,* HBO, multiple episodes, between 2003 and 2008.

Television Director; Movies:

Blind Faith, Showtime, 1998.

Ambushed, HBO, 1998.

Futuresport, ABC, 1998.

Strange Justice, Showtime, 1999.

Monday Night Mayhem, TNT, 2002.

(And cinematographer) *Our America,* Showtime, 2002.

Big Shot: Confessions of a Campus Bookie, FX Network, 2002.

Good Fences, Showtime, 2003.

For One Night, Lifetime, 2006.

Television Director; Episodic:

The Untouchables, syndicated, 1993.

"My So Called Life and Death," *Night Visions,* Fox, 2001.

"Still Life," *Night Visions,* Fox, 2001.

"Greatest Detectives in the World," *Third Watch,* NBC, 2004.

"Luminous," *The L Word,* Showtime, 2005.

"Total Recall," *Crossing Jordan,* NBC, 2005.

"L.D.S.K.," *Criminal Minds,* CBS, 2005.

"The Cradle," *Invasion,* ABC, 2005.

"Middleman," *ER,* NBC, 2005.

"You Are Here," *ER,* NBC, 2005.

"Reason to Believe," *ER,* NBC, 2006.

"Silencer," *CSI: Miami,* CBS, 2006.

"And the Envelope Please," *The Evidence,* ABC, 2006.

"Chapter Four: Collision," *Heroes,* NBC, 2006.

"The V Word," *Masters of Horror,* Showtime, 2006.

"The Wrath of Graham," *The 4400* (also known as *Los 4400*), USA Network, 2007.

Tell Me You Love Me, HBO, 2007.

"Release the Hounds," *Weeds,* Showtime, 2007.

"The Dark Time," *Weeds,* Showtime, 2007.

"No Way Back," *Lincoln Heights,* ABC Family Channel, 2007.

"The Day before Tomorrow," *Lincoln Heights,* ABC Family Channel, 2008.

"Truth and Reconciliation," *Burn Notice,* USA Network, 2008.

"Show Me the Mummy," *Eureka* (also known as *A Town Called Eureka*), Sci–Fi Channel, 2008.

"Si se puede," *Dexter,* Showtime, 2008.

Fear Itself, NBC, 2008.

Television Cinematographer; Episodic:

"The Word Processor of the Gods," *Tales from the Darkside,* syndicated, 1984.

H.E.L.P. (also known as *911*), ABC, 1990.

Law & Order, NBC, 1990.

Television Work; Other:

Director, "Spike & Co.: Do It Acappella" (special), *Great Performances,* PBS, 1990.

Cinematographer, "Great Performances 20th Anniversary Special," *Great Performances,* PBS, 1992.

Director, "In the Game of Life" segment, *Miracle's Boys* (miniseries), N Network, 2005.

Television Appearances:

A–Z of Horror (miniseries; also known as *Clive Barker's "A–Z of Horror"*), BBC, 1997.

J. J. Robinson, *Ambushed* (movie), HBO, 1998.

Hitchcocked! (special), Starz!, 2006.

RECORDINGS

Video Appearances:

Urban Gothic (also known as *Urban Gothic: "Bones" and Its Influences*), New Line Home Video, 2002.

Diggin' Up "Bones," New Line Home Video, 2002.

By Any Means Necessary: The Making of "Malcolm X," Warner Home Vide, 2005.

Making a Mark, Columbia TriStar Home Entertainment, 2005.

College Daze, Columbia TriStar Home Entertainment, 2005.

Birth of a Nation: The Making of "School Daze," Columbia TriStar Home Entertainment, 2005.

Ben–Hur: The Epic that Changed Cinema, Warner Home Video, 2005.

The Visions of Stanley Kubrick, Warner Home Video, 2007.

View from the Overlook: Crafting "The Shining," Warner Home Video, 2007.

Standing on the Shoulders of Kubrick: The Legacy of 2001, Warner Home Video, 2007.

Great Bolshy Yarblockos! Making "A Clockwork Orange," Warner Home Video, 2007.

Full Metal Jacket: Between Good and Evil, Warner Home Video, 2007.

Video Work:

Cinematographer, *One Night with Blue Note,* 1985.

Cinematographer, "Born in the U.S.A.," *Bruce Springsteen: Video Anthology 1978–1988,* Columbia Music Video, 1989.

Cinematographer, "Fight the Power," *And Ya Don't Stop: Hip Hop's Greatest Videos, Vol. 1,* Palm Pictures, 2000.

Cinematographer, "Born in the U.S.A.," *Bruce Springsteen: The Complete Video Anthology 1978–2000*, Columbia Music Video, 2001.

Director of music videos, including "Born in the U.S.A." by Bruce Springsteen, "Royal Garden Blues" by Branford Marsalis, "Stir It Up" by Patti LaBelle, and "Tutu" by Miles Davis.

WRITINGS

Screenplays:
(Coauthor) *Juice* (also based on a story by Dickerson; also known as *Angel Town 2*), Paramount, 1992.

OTHER SOURCES

Books:
Contemporary Black Biography, Volume 17, Gale, 1998.

Periodicals:
Entertainment Weekly, September 20, 1996, p. 50.
Premiere, February, 1992, pp. 40, 42; September, 1996, p. 16.
USA Today, September 6, 1996, p. D3.

DICKSON, Ngila 1958–

PERSONAL

First name is pronounced "Nye–luh"; born 1958, in Dunedin, New Zealand; married Hamish Keith.

Addresses: *Agent*—Marsh, Best and Associates, 9150 Wilshire Blvd., Suite 220, Beverly Hills, CA 90212.

Career: Costume designer. Previously worked as a wardrobe supervisor, fashion magazine editor, and rock video stylist.

Awards, Honors: Television Award, best contribution to design, New Zealand Film and Television Awards, 1998, and Cult Television Award, best costumes, both for *Xena: Warrior Princess*; Apex Award, best costume design, fantasy, science fiction, and horror category, Fennecus Award, best costume design for a fantasy, 2001, Sierra Award, Las Vegas Film Critics Society, Academy Award nomination, Film Award nomination, British Academy of Film and Television Arts, Golden

Satellite Award nomination (with Richard Taylor), International Press Academy, Saturn Award nomination (with Taylor), Academy of Science Fiction, Fantasy, and Horror Films, and Phoenix Film Critics Society Award, all best costume design, 2002, for *The Lord of the Rings: The Fellowship of the Ring*; Film Award, British Academy of Film and Television Arts, Saturn Award, Phoenix Film Critics Society Award nomination, Sierra Award, and Online Film Critics Society Award nomination, all best costume design (with Taylor), and Costume Designers Guild Award nomination, excellence in costume design for a period or fantasy film, 2003, all for *The Lord of the Rings: The Two Towers*; Academy Award and Film Award nomination, British Academy of Film and Television Arts, Saturn Award nomination, Golden Satellite Award nomination, Phoenix Film Critics Society Award nomination, and Sierra Award, all best costume design (with Taylor), and Costume Designers Guild Award, excellence in costume design for a period or fantasy film, all 2004, for *The Lord of the Rings: The Return of the King*; Golden Satellite Award, Academy Award nomination, and Phoenix Film Critics Society Award nomination, all best costume design, and Costume Designers Guild Award nomination, excellence in costume design for a period or fantasy film, all 2004, for *The Last Samurai*; Costume Designers Guild Award nomination, excellence in costume design for a period film, 2007, for *The Illusionist*.

CREDITS

Film Costume Designer:
User Friendly, 1990.
My Grandfather Is a Vampire (also known as *Grampire*, *Moonrise*, and *My Grandpa is a Vampire*), Columbia TriStar, 1991.
Crush, Strand Releasing, 1992.
The Rainbow Warrior (also known as *The Sinking of the Rainbow Warrior*), Bonny Dore Productions, 1992.
Jack Be Nimble, Cinevista, 1993.
Heavenly Creatures (also known as *Himmlische Kreaturen*; also released as *Heavenly Creatures: The Uncut Version*), Miramax, 1994.
Peach (short film), Oceania Parker, 1995.
The Lord of the Rings: The Fellowship of the Ring (also known as *The Fellowship of the Ring* and *The Lord of the Rings: The Fellowship of the Ring—the Motion Picture*), New Line Cinema, 2001.
The Lord of the Rings: The Two Towers (also known as *The Two Towers* and *Der Herr der ringe: Die zwei tuerme*), New Line Cinema, 2002.
The Lord of the Rings: The Return of the King (also known as *The Return of the King* and *Der Herr der ringe: Die Rueckkehr des koenigs*), New Line Cinema, 2003.
The Last Samurai (also known as *The Last Samurai: Bushidou*), Warner Bros., 2003.

Without a Paddle, Paramount, 2004.
The Illusionist, Yari Film Group, 2006.
Blood Diamond, Warner Bros., 2006.
Fool's Gold, Warner Bros., 2008.
The International, Columbia, 2009.

Television Costume Designer; Series:
Mysterious Island, Fox Family Channel, 1995.
Xena: Warrior Princess (also known as *Xena*), syndicated, 1995.
Hercules: The Legendary Journeys, syndicated, 1995.

Television Costume Designer; Movies:
Young Hercules, Fox Family Channel, 1998.
Superfire (also known as *Superfire—Inferno in Oregon* and *Firefighter—Inferno in Oregon*), ABC, 2002.
The Extreme Team (also known as *The X–Team*), ABC, 2003.

Television Costume Designer; Miniseries:
The Rainbow Warrior Conspiracy, Seven Network, 1989.

Television Appearances; Specials:
Passage to Middle–Earth: The Making of "The Lord of the Rings," Sci–Fi Channel, 2001.
The 76th Annual Academy Awards, ABC, 2004.

Television Appearances; Episodic:
20/20, ABC, 1996.
"The Last Samurai: An Epic Journey," *HBO First Look,* HBO, 2003.
"'Blood Diamond': Making an African Epic," *HBO First Look,* HBO, 2006.

RECORDINGS

Videos:
The Making of "The Lord of the Rings," 2002.

DISKIN, Ben 1982–

(Benjamin Diskin)

PERSONAL

Full name, Benjamin Isaac Diskin; born August 25, 1982, in Los Angeles county, CA.

Career: Actor and voice artist.

Awards, Honors: Young Artist Award (with others), outstanding young ensemble cast in a motion picture, 1991, for *Kindergarten Cop;* Young Artist Award nomination, best young voice actor in a television program or movie, 1995, for *Problem Child.*

CREDITS

Television Appearances; Animated Series:
Voice of Junior Healy, *Problem Child,* USA Network, 1993–94.
Voices of Numbuh 1 and Numbuh 2, *Codename: Kids Next Door,* Cartoon Network, 2002–2008.
(English version) Voice of Kai, *Blood+,* Cartoon Network, 2007.
Voices of Eddie Brock and Venom, *The Spectacular Spider–Man* (originally broadcast as an Internet series), CW Network, 2008.

Television Appearances; Movies:
Charlie Spiegel, *Just like Dad,* The Disney Channel, 1995.
Voices of Nigel "Numbuh 1" Uno and Hoagie Pennywhistle "Numbuh 2" Gilligan, Jr., *Codename: Kids Next Door—Operation Z.E.R.O.* (animated; also known as *Operation: Z.E.R.O.*), Cartoon Network, 2006.
Voices of Numbuh 1, Numbuh 2, and "delightful children from down the lane," *The Grim Adventures of the Kids Next Door* (animated), Cartoon Network, 2007.

Television Appearances; Specials:
Voices of Numbuh 1 and Numbuh 2, *The Kids Next Door* (animated), Cartoon Network, 2000.

Television Appearances; Episodic:
(As Benjamin Diskin) Young Paul Arnold, "Birthday Boy," *The Wonder Years,* ABC, 1989.
(As Benjamin Diskin) Danny, "Pile of Death," *Get a Life,* Fox, 1990.
Voice of smart slobster, "Smarten Up," *Street Sharks* (animated), ABC and syndicated, 1994.
Young Aaron, "Brain Salad Surgery," *Chicago Hope,* CBS, 1997.
(As Benjamin Diskin) Willie, "Susan's Minor Complication," *Suddenly Susan,* NBC, 1997.
Voice of Eugene Horowitz, "Eugene Goes Bad/What's Opera, Arnold?," *Hey Arnold!* (animated), Nickelodeon, 1997.
Voice of Eugene Horowitz, "The Aptitude Test/Oskar Gets a Job," *Hey Arnold!* (animated), Nickelodeon, 1998.
Marvin, "Personal Trainer," *100 Deeds for Eddie McDowd,* Nickelodeon, 2001.
"Mean Teacher," *Drake & Josh,* Nickelodeon, 2004.

Voice of Hahn, "The Siege of the North: Parts 1 & 2," *Avatar: The Last Airbender* (animated), Nickelodeon, 2005.

Phillip and third geek, "The Ex–Factor," *The O.C.*, Fox, 2005.

Voices of Benji, Travis, and first zombie kid, "E–Scream," *What's New, Scooby–Doo?*, The WB, 2006.

Phillip, "The Avengers," *The O.C.*, Fox, 2006.

According to some sources, also appeared in *Zoey 101*, Nickelodeon.

Television Work; Series:

Additional voices, *The Twisted Adventures of Felix the Cat* (animated; also known as *The Twisted Tales of Felix the Cat*), CBS, 1995.

Film Appearances:

(As Benjamin Diskin) Ben, *Baby Boom*, United Artists, 1987.

Sylvester, *Kindergarten Cop*, Universal, 1990.

Henry, *Out on a Limb*, Universal, 1992.

Stan at age nine, *Mr. Saturday Night*, Columbia, 1992.

Little boy in 1945, *The Pickle* (also known as *The Adventures of the Flying Pickle*), Columbia, 1993.

Voice of second teen, *Fat Albert* (animated), Twentieth Century–Fox, 2004.

Voice of anteater, *Dr. Dolittle: Tail to the Chief*, Twentieth Century–Fox, 2008.

Voice of goblin, *The Spiderwick Chronicles*, Paramount, 2008.

Film Work:

Additional voices, *Recess: School's Out* (animated), Buena Vista, 2001.

RECORDINGS

Video Games:

(As Benjamin Diskin) Voice of fan boy, *Ratchet & Clank: Going Commando* (also known as *Ratchet & Clank: Locked and Loaded* and *Ratchet & Clank 2: Locked and Loaded*), Insomniac Games, 2003.

Voice, *Underground* (also known as *Tony Hawk's Pro Skater 5* and *Tony Hawk's Underground*), Neversoft Entertainment, 2003.

Voice of Ota, *Full Spectrum Warrior*, Pandemic Production, 2004.

Voice of Eric Sparrow, *Underground 2* (also known as *Tony Hawk's Underground 2*), Activision, 2004.

Voices, *The Bard's Tale*, InXile Entertainment, 2004.

Voices of Nigel "Numbuh 1" Uno, Hoagie Pennywhistle "Numbuh 2" Gilligan, Jr., and "delightful children from down the lane," *Codename: Kids Next Door Operation—Video Game*, Cartoon Network Interactive, 2005.

Voice of Jupis Tooki McGanel for English version, *Rogue Galaxy*, Sony Computer Entertainment America, 2005.

(As Benjamin Diskin) Voice, *Tony Hawk's Project 8*, 2006.

Voice of Taejo Tokokahn, *Speed Racer*, Warner Bros. Interactive Entertainment, 2008.

DONIM, Sue
See HARTH, C. Ernst

DORKIN, Cody 1985–
(Cody Lee Dorkin, Cody Lee)

PERSONAL

Full name, Cody Lee Dorkin; born July 6, 1985, in Shingle Springs, CA (some sources say Sacramento, CA).

Career: Actor. Appeared in television commercials, including JCPenny department stores.

CREDITS

Film Appearances:

Lead, *The Taming Power of the Small* (short), 1995.

Robert, *Village of the Damned* (also known as *John Carpenter's "Village of the Damned"*), Universal, 1995.

(As Cody Lee Dorkin) Child number three at toy store, *Nine Months*, Twentieth Century–Fox, 1995.

Randy, *Land of the Free*, New City Releasing, 1998.

Ethan Rourke, *Paper Bullets* (also known as *American Samurai*), MTI Home Video, 2000.

Randy Barrington at age 13, *The Painting* (also known as *Soldier of Change*), Screen Media Ventures, 2001.

Film Work:

Additional voice, *Toy Story* (animated; also known as *Toy Story in 3–D*), Buena Vista, 1995.

Automated dialogue replacement (ADR), *Washington Square*, Buena Vista, 1997.

ADR, *The Proposition*, PolyGram, 1998.

ADR, *Mighty Joe Young* (also known as *Mighty Joe*), Buena Vista, 1998.

ADR, *The Story of Us*, Universal, 1999.

ADR, *The Road to El Dorado* (animated), DreamWorks, 2000.

Television Appearances; Movies:

Andy Knowlton, *The Colony,* USA Network, 1995.

Randy, *Land of the Free,* HBO, 1998.

Brandon Kniffen at age 9, *Just Ask My Children,* 2001.

Television Appearances; Episodic:

Eric Gaines, "Child's Play," *The Client* (also known as *John Grisham's "The Client"*), CBS, 1995.

Eric Gaines, "Sympathy for the Devil," *The Client* (also known as *John Grisham's "The Client"*), CBS, 1996.

Nick Brooks, "Objects Are Closer Than They Appear," *Chicago Hope,* CBS, 1998.

Urkel number two, "Polkapalooza," *Family Matters,* CBS, 1998.

Young Ethan, "BoozeBournes," *Passions,* NBC, 2003.

Patrick, "Guess Who's Coming 'Out' for Dinner," *South of Nowhere,* The N, 2006.

Patrick, "Saturday Night Is for Fighting," *South of Nowhere,* The N, 2007.

Danny, "Quarantine," *Zoey 101,* Nickelodeon, 2007.

Grand theft kid, "News of the Future," *Mind of Mencia,* Comedy Central, 2007.

Also appeared as voice of Jungle Boy, "Super Duped/Bungled in the Jungle/Bearly Enough Time," *Johnny Bravo* (animated), Cartoon Network.

DOTSON, Bob 1946–

PERSONAL

Full name, Robert Charles Dotson; born October 3, 1946, in St. Louis, MO; son of William Henry and Dorothy Mae (maiden name, Bailey) Dotson; married Linda Gay Puckett, July 1, 1972; children: Amy Michelle. *Education:* University of Kansas, B.S., 1968; Syracuse University, M.S., 1969. *Avocational Interests:* History, films.

Addresses: *Office*—c/o NBC News, 30 Rockefeller Plaza, New York, NY 10112.

Career: Broadcast journalist, correspondent, and writer. KMBC–TV, Kansas City, MO, reporter, photographer, and documentary producer, 1967–68; WKY–TV (now KFOR–TV), Oklahoma City, OK, director of special projects, 1969–75; WKYC–TV, Cleveland, OH, correspondent, 1975–77; NBC News, New York City, correspondent for Central America from Dallas bureau, 1977–79, correspondent for national news programs, 1979—, and presenter of the occasional series of special reports "American Story with Bob Dotson."

KANU–FM Radio, Lawrence, KS, news director, 1966–68. University of Oklahoma, visiting professor, 1969–73; Colorado State University, faculty affiliate.

Member: Writers Guild of America, National Academy of Television Arts and Sciences, National Press Photographers Association, Radio and Television News Directors Association, International Platform Association, Explorers Club (New York City), Sigma Delta Chi.

Awards, Honors: More than 100 broadcast journalism awards, including Emmy Award nomination, best community service program, 1972, for the story "Still Got Life to Go"; Emmy Award nomination, best documentary, 1973, for story "Smoke and Steel"; award from Freedoms Foundation of Valley Forge, 1973; Emmy Award, best documentary, Robert F. Kennedy Journalism Award, best program on the problems of the disadvantaged, and Broadcast Media Award, San Francisco State University, all 1974, for story "Through the Looking Glass Darkly"; distinguished journalism citation, Scripps–Howard Foundation, 1974; certificate of recognition for "positive contributions to brotherhood," National Conference of Christians and Jews (now National Conference for Community and Justice), 1974; Alfred I. DuPont–Columbia University Survey of Broadcast Journalism Award and Robert F. Kennedy Journalism Award, outstanding television coverage of the problems of the disadvantaged, both 1975, for story "The Urban Reservation"; silver medal, International Film and Television Festival of New York, 1976, for story "The Cost of Loneliness"; Abe Lincoln Award, exceptional achievement as a broadcaster and citizen, 1976; Epilepsy Foundation of America Award, exceptional investigative reporting, 1977; Emmy Award nomination, outstanding program achievement, 1981, for story "Sunshine Foundation"; Emmy Award nomination, best feature story, 1982, for "The Sunshine Child"; Clarion Award, Women in Communications, 1983, certificate of merit, Gabriel Awards, National Catholic Association of Broadcasters and Allied Communicators, 1984, merit award, Daughters of the American Revolution, 1985, and George Washington Honor Medal, Freedoms Foundation, 1985, all for the television feature " ... In Pursuit of the American Dream"; Gabriel Award and Emmy Award nomination, best news story, both 1987, for "People Who Make a Difference"; Media Access Award, 1987, Emmy Award nomination, best writing, and award from Ohio State University, both 1989, and National Headliners Award, National Headliners Club, 1990, all for "Assignment America"; Sprague Memorial Award, National Press Photographers Association, 1989; Wilbur Award, U.S. Film Festival, CINE Golden Eagle, Council on International Nontheatrical Events, grand prize from Italian Film Festival, and grand prize from Union of Mountain Climbers, all 1990, as well as prizes from Indian, Japanese, and Spanish film festivals, 1991, all for *El Capitan's Courageous Climbers;* Gabriel Award, 1992, for *Bob Dotson's*

America; Electronic Media Grand Prize, National Association for Year Round Education, 1993; Emmy Award, 1994, for story "The River's Edge," *Dateline NBC;* Edward R. Murrow Awards, Radio and Television News Directors Association, best network news writing, 1999, and best reporting, 2001, 2003; Diversity Award, Columbia University, 2001; Emmy Award, best story in a regularly scheduled broadcast, 2003; Daytime Emmy Award (with others), excellence in morning programming, 2007, for *Today.*

CREDITS

Television Appearances; Series:
Host, *Bob Dotson's America,* The Travel Channel, 1996.
Correspondent, *Today* (also known as *NBC News Today* and *The Today Show*), NBC, 1978–85, 2008.
Contributor, *NBC Nightly News,* NBC, beginning 1985.

Also appeared as a correspondent for *Dateline NBC* (also known as *Dateline*), NBC.

WRITINGS

Books:
... *In Pursuit of the American Dream,* Atheneum, 1985.
Make It Memorable: Writing and Packaging TV News with Style, Bonus Books, 2000.

Other:
Author of scripts for the video *El Capitan's Courageous Climbers,* and for stories and reports broadcast by NBC News.

OTHER SOURCES

Electronic:
MSNBC Online, http://www.msnbc.msn.com/, October 20, 2008.

DUFFEY, Todd 1974–
    (Robert Duffey)

PERSONAL

Original name, Robert Gordon Duffey; born April 9, 1974, in Raleigh, NC. *Education:* Attended the University of Houston, the University of Texas at Austin, and the University of Texas at Arlington.

Career: Actor.

Awards, Honors: Bronze Wrangler Award (with others), television feature film, Western Heritage Awards, 1991, for *Across Five Aprils.*

CREDITS

Film Appearances:
Jethro Creighton, *Across Five Aprils* (also known as *Civil War Diary*), 1990.
Young Joseph, *Carried Away* (also known as *Acts of Love*), Fine Line Features, 1996.
Brian, Chotchkie's waiter, *Office Space* (also known as *Cubiculos de la oficina*), Twentieth Century–Fox, 1999.
Kyle, *The Black Rose,* Dreamfactory, 2000.
Harold's boss, *Buttleman* (also known as *Harold Buttleman, Daredevil Stuntman*), 2002.
Male student, *A Whiter Shade of Loud* (short), 2003.
Scooter McNutty, *Barney: Let's Go to the Zoo,* Hit Entertainment, 2003.
Tommy, *Burning Annie,* Warner Home Video, 2004.
Voice of concession guy, *The SpongeBob SquarePants Movie* (animated), Paramount, 2004.
Robert Lewis, *Slaughterhouse of the Rising Sun,* THINK-Film, 2005.
Ken Vincent, *Hollywood Kills,* Shoreline Entertainment, 2006.
Tommy, *Burning Annie,* Armak Productions, 2007.

Television Appearances; Series:
Scooter McNutty, *Barney & Friends* (also known as *Barney*), PBS, 1992.
Murk, *Buffy the Vampire Slayer* (also known as *BtVS, Buffy,* and *Buffy, the Vampire Slayer: The Series*), The WB, 2001.

Television Appearances; Movies:
Davey Coombs, *In the Name of Love: A Texas Tragedy* (also known as *After Laurette*), Fox, 1995.

Television Appearances; Episodic:
Paul Kelly Moore, "Evil in the Night," *Walker, Texas Ranger* (also known as *Walker*), CBS, 1995.
Mitch, "Homecoming," *ER,* NBC, 2000.
Lewis, *Any Day Now,* Lifetime, 2000.
Dee Jay, "Drew's Girl Friday," *The Drew Carey Show,* ABC, 2002.
Voice of teenage boy, "Girl Fight," *George Lopez,* ABC, 2003.
Satyr, "Nymphs Just Wanna Have Fun," *Charmed,* The WB, 2003.
Guy number two, "You Can't Always Get What You Want," *That '70s Show,* Fox, 2004.

Also appeared as beer guy, "Party," *The O'Keefes,* The WB.

RECORDINGS

Video Games:
(As Robert Duffey) Voice, *Tony Hawk's Project 8,* 2006.

DYE, Dale 1944–
(Captain Dale Dye, Captain Dale A. Dye, Dale A. Dye)

PERSONAL

Full name, Dale Adam Dye; born October 8, 1944, in Cape Girardeau, MO; son of Dale Adam and Della Grace (maiden name, Koehler) Dye; some sources cite a marriage to a gunnery sergeant with the surname of Chavez, 1979 (divorced); married Kathryn Gwen Clayton (an actress), September 17, 1983 (divorced); married Julia Dewey Rupkalvis (an actress), February 22, 2006; children: (second marriage) Adrienne Kate (an actress), Christopher (a composer). *Education:* University of Maryland, B.A., English, 1981; attended the Missouri Military Academy; received military training in several disciplines. *Religion:* Roman Catholic.

Addresses: *Contact*—c/o 18208 Herbold St., Northridge, CA 91325. *Agent*—The Kohner Agency, 9300 Wilshire Blvd., Suite 555, Beverly Hills, CA 90212.

Career: Actor, producer, and writer. Warriors, Inc. (technical advisory service), founder and principal, c. 1986, served as a technical and military advisor and military consultant for films and television productions; *Soldier of Fortune* magazine, executive editor, 1984–85; trained troops in Central America in guerilla warfare techniques, beginning c. 1984; affiliated with the Warriors Publishing Group; public speaker at various venues; participant at a variety of events relating to the military. *Military service:* U.S. Marine Corps., 1964–84, participated in thirty–one major combat operations (including duties as a correspondent) in Vietnam and with a multinational peacekeeping force in Beirut, Lebanon; served as a drill instructor and troop handler; served in various locales around the world; served in various ranks, including master sergeant, warrant officer, and first lieutenant, retired as a captain; staff member for the U.S. secretary of defense, the Pentagon; earned the Bronze Star with Valor, the Meritorious Service Medal, two Navy Commendation Medals with Combat D Device, the Navy Achievement Medal with Combat D Device, the Joint Service Commendation Medal, the Combat Action Ribbon, the Vietnamese Cross of Gallantry, the Vietnamese Honor Medal first class, three Purple Hearts, and named a Legionnaire of the Order of Saint Maurice, the Ancient and Honorable Order of Infantrymen.

Member: Screen Actors Guild, Directors Guild of America, Writers Guild of America, East, Marine Corps Combat Correspondents Association, 1st Marine Division Association, Veterans of Foreign Wars (VFW), American Legion.

CREDITS

Film Appearances:
Captain Harris, *Platoon,* Orion, 1986.
Squad leader and dragon gunner, *Invaders from Mars,* Cannon Pictures, 1986.
Captain Hill, *Casualties of War,* Columbia, 1989.
Don (the fire boss), *Always,* MCA/Universal, 1989.
French officer, *The Favorite* (also known as *Intimate Power* and *La nuit du serail*), 1989.
General, *Spontaneous Combustion* (also known as *Fire Syndrome*), Taurus Entertainment Company, 1989.
Infantry colonel, *Born on the Fourth of July,* Universal, 1989.
Radio voice, *84C MoPic* (also known as *84 Charlie Mopic*), New Century Vista Film Company, 1989.
A. K. McNeil, *Fire Birds* (also known as *Wings of the Apache*), Buena Vista, 1990.
Sergeant major, *The Fourth War,* Cannon Films, 1990.
Captain Rivers, *Dead On: Relentless II* (also known as *Dead On, Relentless 2: Dead On, Relentless II: Dead On,* and *Sunset Killer 2*), 1991.
Garvey, *Kid* (also known as *Back for Revenge*), Intercontinental, 1991.
General Y, *JFK,* Warner Bros., 1991, director's cut also released.
Police officer, *The Servants of Twilight* (also known as *Dean R. Koontz's "The Servants of Twilight"*), Trimark Pictures, 1991.
Captain Garza, *Under Siege* (also known as *Piege en haute mer*), Warner Bros., 1992.
Jack, *Cover Story,* 1993.
Larry, *Heaven & Earth* (also known as *Entre ciel et terre*), Warner Bros., 1993.
Senior National Security Council (NSC) officer, *Sniper,* TriStar, 1993.
Brande, *The Puppet Masters* (also known as *Robert A. Heinlein's "The Puppet Masters"*), Buena Vista, 1994.
Charles Ivy, *Guarding Tess,* TriStar, 1994.
Colonel Michael "Mike" Anwalt, *Blue Sky,* Orion, 1994.
Dale Wrigley, *Natural Born Killers,* Warner Bros., 1994, director's cut also released.

Endangered (also known as *The Hunted, The Most Dangerous Predator Is Man,* and *Uncivilized*), New City Releasing, 1994.

Captain Garza, *Under Siege 2: Dark Territory* (also known as *Under Siege 2*), Warner Bros., 1995.

Lieutenant colonel Briggs, *Outbreak* (also known as *A Virus*), Warner Bros., 1995.

First engineer, *Sgt. Bilko* (also known as *Sergeant Bilko*), Universal, 1996.

Frank Barnes, *Mission: Impossible* (also known as *Mission Impossible*), Paramount, 1996.

Dr. German Stone (a psychiatrist), *Trial and Error,* New Line Cinema, 1997.

(As Dale A. Dye) General, *Starship Troopers,* Sony Pictures Entertainment, 1997.

War department colonel, *Saving Private Ryan,* Dream-Works, 1998.

Vernon, *A Table for One* (also known as *Wicked Ways*), A–pix Entertainment, 1999.

General Perry, *Rules of Engagement* (also known as *Les regles d'engagement* and *Rules—Sekunden der Entscheidung*), Paramount, 2000.

Rescue Sequence: Commander Wiley, *Spy Game,* Universal, 2001.

General Temekin, *Missing Brendan* (also known as *Holding out Hope: A Family Crusade*), 2003.

General Kreuger, *The Great Raid,* Miramax, 2005.

Harry, *Naked Run,* A Plus Entertainment, c. 2006.

(As Dale A. Dye) Captain Ruzicka, *Music Within,* Metro–Goldwyn–Mayer, 2007.

Voice of Erik "The Wow Man" Kernan, Sr., *Resurrecting the Champ,* Yari Film Group, 2007.

Film Technical and Military Advisor and Consultant:

Technical advisor, *Invaders from Mars,* Cannon Pictures, 1986.

(As Captain Dale Dye) Technical advisor: military, *Platoon,* Orion, 1986.

(As Captain Dale Dye) Technical advisor, *The Beast of War* (also known as *The Beast*), Columbia, 1988.

Technical advisor, *Casualties of War,* Columbia, 1989.

Technical advisor, *84C MoPic* (also known as *84 Charlie Mopic*), New Century Vista Film Company, 1989.

(As Captain Dale Dye) Technical advisor: military, *Born on the Fourth of July,* Universal, 1989.

(As Captain Dale Dye) Military consultant, *Jacob's Ladder* (also known as *Dante's Inferno*), TriStar, 1990.

Technical advisor, *Cadence* (also known as *Count a Lonely Cadence*), New Line Cinema, 1990.

Technical advisor, *Fire Birds* (also known as *Wings of the Apache*), Buena Vista, 1990.

Technical advisor (military), *The Fourth War,* Cannon Films, 1990.

(As Captain Dale Dye) Military consultant, *Dogfight,* Warner Bros., 1991.

Technical advisor, *JFK,* Warner Bros., 1991, director's cut also released.

(As Captain Dale Dye) Technical advisor: military, *The Last of the Mohicans,* Twentieth Century–Fox, 1992.

(As Captain Dale Dye) Technical advisor: military, *Heaven & Earth* (also known as *Entre ciel et terre*), Warner Bros., 1993.

(As Captain Dale Dye) Technical advisor: military, *Sniper,* TriStar, 1993.

Military advisor, *The War,* Universal, 1994.

(Uncredited) Technical advisor, *Blue Sky,* Orion, 1994.

(As Captain Dale Dye) Technical advisor, *Forrest Gump,* Paramount, 1994.

Technical advisor, *Guarding Tess,* TriStar, 1994.

Technical advisor, *A Low Down Dirty Shame* (also known as *Mister Cool*), Buena Vista, 1994.

(As Captain Dale Dye) Technical advisor, *Natural Born Killers,* Warner Bros., 1994, director's cut also released.

Military technical advisor, *Dead Presidents,* Buena Vista, 1995.

Military technical advisor, *The Walking Dead,* Savoy Pictures, 1995.

(As Captain Dale Dye) Technical advisor: military, *Outbreak* (also known as *A Virus*), Warner Bros., 1995.

(As Captain Dale Dye) Technical advisor: military, *Sgt. Bilko* (also known as *Sergeant Bilko*), Universal, 1996.

(As Dale A. Dye) Technical advisor, *Starship Troopers,* Sony Pictures Entertainment, 1997.

(Uncredited) Technical advisor, *Wag the Dog* (also known as *Bite the Bullet*), New Line Cinema, 1997.

Assistant military advisor, *The Thin Red Line,* Twentieth Century–Fox, 1998.

Military advisor, *Small Soldiers* (live action and animated; also known as *The Commando Elite*), DreamWorks, 1998.

(As Captain Dale Dye) Senior military advisor, *Saving Private Ryan,* DreamWorks, 1998.

(As Captain Dale Dye) Military advisor, *Rules of Engagement* (also known as *Les regles d'engagement* and *Rules—Sekunden der Entscheidung*), Paramount, 2000.

Military advisor, *Tigerland,* Twentieth Century–Fox, 2000.

(As Captain Dale A. Dye) Senior military advisor, *Alexander,* Warner Bros., 2004, another version known as *Alexander: Director's Cut,* another version known as *Alexander Revisited: The Final Cut.*

(As Captain Dale Dye) Senior military technical advisor, *The Great Raid,* Miramax, 2005.

Senior military advisor, *La tigre e la neve* (also known as *The Tiger and the Snow*), 2005, subtitled version released by Strand Releasing, 2006.

(As Captain Dale A. Dye) Military advisor: the Philippines, *Music Within,* Metro–Goldwyn–Mayer, 2007.

Senior military advisor, *Tropic Thunder,* Paramount, 2008.

Some sources state that Dye served as an advisor for other films.

Film Work; Other:
Coproducer, *Fire Birds* (also known as *Wings of the Apache*), Buena Vista, 1990.
Second unit director, *Alexander,* Warner Bros., 2004, another version known as *Alexander: Director's Cut,* another version known as *Alexander Revisited: The Final Cut.*

Television Appearances; Series:
Captain Henry K. "Hank" Madigan (commanding officer), *Supercarrier,* ABC, 1988.

Television Appearances; Miniseries:
Defense attorney, *Billionaire Boys Club* (also known as *Beverly Hills Boys Club*), NBC, 1987.
Chief Bates, *The Neon Empire,* Showtime, 1989.
Colonel Leonard Wood, *Rough Riders* (also known as *Teddy Roosevelt & the Rough Riders*), TNT, 1997.
Colonel Robert F. Sink, *Band of Brothers,* HBO, 2001.
(As Captain Dale Dye) Himself, *The 100 Greatest War Films,* Channel 4 (England), 2005.

Television Appearances; Movies:
Colonel Bates, *The Court–Martial of Jackie Robinson,* TNT, 1990.
Major Green, *Mission of the Shark: The Saga of the U.S.S. Indianapolis* (also known as *Mission of the Shark*), CBS, 1991.
General Hurst, *Within the Rock,* Sci–Fi Channel, 1996.
Captain Halsey Long, *Operation Delta Force II: Mayday,* HBO, 1998.
Mutiny, NBC, 1999.
SWAT lieutenant, *44 Minutes: The North Hollywood Shoot–Out,* FX Network, 2003.

Television Appearances; Specials:
Assistant director, "The Closed Set," *Tales from the Hollywood Hills* (also known as *Tales from the Hollywood Hills: Closed Set* and *Tales from the Hollywood Hills: The Closed Set*), broadcast as part of *Great Performances,* PBS, 1988.
(As Captain Dale Dye) Himself, *The Making of "Band of Brothers,"* 2001.
(As Captain Dale Dye) Himself, *The Price of Freedom: Making The Great Raid,* FX Network, 2005.

Television Appearances; Episodic:
Colonel Paul David Mackay, "Is Someone Crazy in Here or Is It Me," *Raven,* CBS, 1991.
"Rest in Pieces," *L.A. Law,* NBC, 1991.
Master sergeant Hollis, "Desert Son," *JAG* (also known as *JAG: Judge Advocate General*), NBC, 1995.

Major Jack Colquitt, "Who Monitors the Birds?," *Space: Above and Beyond* (also known as *Above and Beyond, Space, Space 2063, Space: 2063, Avaruus 2063, Guerra dos mundos, Gwiezdna eskadra, Rummet aar 2063, Slaget om tellus,* and *Space: guerra estelar*), Fox, 1996.
Colonel Bill Cobb, "Mr. Rabb Goes to Washington," *JAG* (also known as *JAG: Judge Advocate General*), CBS, 1998.
Himself, "Into the Breach: 'Saving Private Ryan,'" *HBO First Look,* HBO, 1998.
General Cole, "Doppelganger: Part 1," *Seven Days* (also known as *7 Days* and *Seven Days: The Series*), UPN, 1998.
Captain Gage, "The Court–Martial of Rio Arnett," *Air America,* syndicated, 1999.
Voice of Lieutenant Tice Ryan, "Happy Luau to You–Au/Rocket Rescue," *Rocket Power* (animated), Nickelodeon, 1999.
Captain Ken Radley, "Souls on Board," *The Others,* NBC, 2000.
Himself, "Charlie Sheen: Born to be Wild," *Biography* (also known as *A&E Biography: Charlie Sheen*), Arts and Entertainment, 2001.
(Sometimes credited as Captain Dale Dye) Firearms instructor, "Good Morning Saigon," *Entourage,* HBO, 2005.
Narrator, "General William Howe: Conqueror of New York," *The Conquerors,* History Channel, 2005.
(Sometimes credited as Captain Dale Dye) Scuba instructor, "Oh, Mandy," *Entourage,* HBO, 2005.
Himself, *Hannity & Colmes* (also known as *Hannity and Liberal to Be Determined*), Fox News Channel, 2005.
General Peter Allyson, "Happy Birthday, Madam President," *Commander in Chief* (also known as *Untitled Geena Davis Project, Welcome Mrs. President, Rouva presidentti,* and *Senora presidenta*), ABC, 2006.
General Peter Allyson, "The Price You Pay," *Commander in Chief* (also known as *Untitled Geena Davis Project, Welcome Mrs. President, Rouva presidentti,* and *Senora presidenta*), ABC, 2006.
General Peter Allyson, "Unfinished Business," *Commander in Chief* (also known as *Untitled Geena Davis Project, Welcome Mrs. President, Rouva presidentti,* and *Senora presidenta*), ABC, 2006.
Sergeant Burn, "And Here's Mike with the Weather," *Las Vegas* (also known as *Casino Eye*), NBC, 2006.
Ralph Somkin, "The Stranger," *The Loop,* Fox, 2007.

Television Appearances; Pilots:
General Stanfield, *Chuck,* NBC, 2007.

Television Work; Series:
Senior military advisor, *Combat Zone,* The Discovery Channel, beginning 2007.

Television Work; Miniseries:
Leader of the Rough Rider Corps, *Rough Riders* (also known as *Teddy Roosevelt & the Rough Riders*), TNT, 1997.
Military advisor, *Band of Brothers,* HBO, 2001.
(As Captain Dale Dye) Unit director and senior military advisor, *The Pacific* (also known as *Untitled World War II Pacific Theater Project*), HBO and Seven Network (Australia), 2009.

Television Advisor; Movies:
Military advisor, *The Court–Martial of Jackie Robinson,* TNT, 1990.
Technical advisor, *Mission of the Shark: The Saga of the U.S.S. Indianapolis* (also known as *Mission of the Shark*), CBS, 1991.
Technical advisor: military, *Within the Rock,* Sci–Fi Channel, 1996.
(As Captain Dale Dye) Military technical advisor, *Mutiny,* NBC, 1999.

Television Work; Episodic:
Military technical advisor, *ER* (also known as *Emergency Room*), NBC, episodes c. 2004–2005.

Television Work; Pilots:
(As Dale A. Dye) Producer, *Semper Fi,* NBC, 2001.

Radio Appearances; Series:
Host and military commentator for a program broadcast by KFI AM 640 (Los Angeles), c. 2003–07.

RECORDINGS

Videos:
Himself, *Return to Normandy* (also known as *The Making of "Saving Private Ryan"*), 1998.
Himself and Captain Harris, *A Tour of the Inferno: Revisiting "Platoon,"* 2001.
Himself, *Death from Above: The Making of "Starship Troopers,"* Columbia/TriStar Home Video, 2002.
(As Captain Dale Dye) Himself, *"Saving Private Ryan": Boot Camp,* 2004.
(As Captain Dale Dye) Himself, *Perfect Is the Enemy of Good,* 2005.
(As Captain Dale Dye) Himself, *Resurrecting "Alexander,"* 2005.
Himself, *The Filthy Thirteen: Real Stories from behind the Lines,* 2006.
Himself, *The Real Heroes of Stalag XVIIB,* 2006.

Video Work:
Training schedules, *A Tour of the Inferno: Revisiting "Platoon,"* 2001.

Video Games:
Narrator in opening film, *Medal of Honor,* Electronic Arts, 1999.
Voice, *Medal of Honor: Allied Assault,* 2002.
(As Captain Dale Dye) Voice of Jack "Gunny" Lauton, *Medal of Honor: Rising Sun,* 2003.
(As Captain Dale Dye) Voice of OSS handler and military police officer narrator, *Medal of Honor: European Assault,* 2005.

Video Game Work; as Captain Dale Dye:
Military advisor, *Medal of Honor,* Electronic Arts, 1999.
Project consultant: military field staff, *Medal of Honor: Underground,* 2000.
Military advisor, *Medal of Honor: Frontline,* 2002.
Military advisor, *Medal of Honor: Rising Sun,* 2003.

WRITINGS

Screenplays:
(Story) *Fire Birds* (also known as *Wings of the Apache*), Buena Vista, 1990.

Novels; as Dale A. Dye:
Run between the Raindrops, Avon Books, 1985.
Platoon (based on the screenplay of the same name by Oliver Stone), Charter Books, 1986.
Outrage, Little, Brown, 1988.
Citadel, Grafton, 1989.
Conduct Unbecoming, Berkeley Books, 1992.
Duty & Dishonor, Jove Books, 1992.
Laos File, Warriors Publishing Group, 2008.

Graphic Novels:
(As Captain Dale Dye; author of introduction) Jason Aaron, *The Other Side,* illustrations and cover art by Cameron Stewart, Vertigo, 2007.

Nonfiction:
Wrote an autobiography; also wrote and posted material on the Internet.

OTHER SOURCES

Periodicals:
Entertainment Weekly, July 24, 1998.
Premiere, January, 1990.

E

EHLE, Jennifer 1969–

PERSONAL

Surname is pronounced EEE–lee; born December 29, 1969, in Winston–Salem, NC; daughter of John Ehle (a writer) and Rosemary Harris (an actress); married Michael Ryan (a writer), November, 2001; children: George. *Education:* Attended the Central School of Speech and Drama, London, England, and the Interlochen Arts Academy, Interlochen, MI.

Addresses: *Agent*—Endeavor, 152 West 57th St., 25th Floor, New York, NY 10019; Independent Talent Group, Oxford House, 76 Oxford St., London W1D 1BS, England.

Career: Actress.

Awards, Honors: Ian Charleson Award, outstanding classical stage performance in Britain by a performer under the age of thirty, 1991, for *Tartuffe;* Radio Times Award, best newcomer, 1992, *The Camomile Lawn;* Television Award, best actress in a television production, British Academy of Film and Television Arts, 1996, for *Pride and Prejudice;* Film Award nomination, best performance by an actress in a supporting role in a film, British Academy of Film and Television Arts, 1998, for *Wilde;* Genie Award nomination, best performance by an actress in a leading role, Academy of Canadian Cinema and Television, 1999, and Golden Satellite Award (with Rosemary Harris), best performance by an actress in a supporting role, drama, International Press Academy, 2001, both for *Sunshine;* Antoinette Perry Award, best lead actress in a play, Variety Club Showbusiness Award, best stage actress, *Theatre World* Award, and Outer Critics Circle Award nomination, outstanding featured actress in a play, all 2000, for *The*

Real Thing; Antoinette Perry Award, best featured actress in a play, and Outer Critics Circle Award nomination, best leading actress in a play, both 2007, for *The Coast of Utopia.*

CREDITS

Television Appearances; Miniseries:
Young Calypso, *The Camomile Lawn,* Channel 4 (England) and Australian Broadcasting Corporation, 1992.
Melissa McKensie (title role), *Melissa,* Channel 4 (England), 1997.
Elizabeth Bennet, *Pride and Prejudice* (also known as *Jane Austen's "Pride and Prejudice"*), BBC, 1995, Arts and Entertainment, 1996, part of *The Complete Jane Austen* broadcast on *Masterpiece Theatre* (also known as *ExxonMobil Masterpiece Theatre* and *Mobil Masterpiece Theatre*), PBS, 2008.

Television Appearances; Movies:
Nadine, *La recreation,* France 2, 1993.
Tasmin, *Micky Love* (also known as *Rik Mayall Presents "Micky Love"* and *Rik Mayall Presents ... "Micky Love"*), Granada Television, 1993.
Emma Desneuves, *Pleasure* (also known as *Alan Bleasdale Presents "Pleasure"*), Channel 4 (England), 1994.
Meryl, *Self Catering* (also known as *Alan Bleasdale Presents "Self Catering"*), Channel 4 (England), 1994.
Penny McAllister, *Beyond Reason* (also known as *A Casual Affair*), Carlton Television, 1994.

Television Appearances; Specials:
Phyllis Maitland, "The Maitlands," *Performance* (also known as *Performance: The Maitlands*), BBC, 1993.
(In archive footage) Constance Lloyd Wilde, *Venice Report,* 1997.

(Uncredited; in archive footage) Elizabeth Bennet, "Pride and Prejudice": The Making of ..., BBC, 1999.

(Uncredited; in archive footage) Elizabeth Bennet, *The Real Jane Austen,* BBC, 2002.

(Uncredited; in archive footage) Elizabeth Bennet, *Pride and Prejudice Revisited,* 2005.

Lorraine Morrisey, "The Russell Girl," *Hallmark Hall of Fame,* CBS, 2008.

Television Appearances; Awards Presentations:
The 54th Annual Tony Awards, CBS and PBS, 2000.
The 61st Annual Tony Awards, CBS, 2007.

Television Appearances; Episodic:
Empress Zita of Austria, "Austria, March 1917," *The Young Indiana Jones Chronicles,* ABC, 1992, later included in *The Adventures of Young Indiana Jones: Adventures in the Secret Service,* 1999.

Herself, *The Rosie O'Donnell Show,* syndicated, 1997.

Herself, *Late Lunch,* Channel 4 (England), 1998.

(In archive footage) Elizabeth Bennet, *Getaway* (also known as *United Travel Getaway*), Nine Network (Australia), 2006.

Herself, "The Coast of Utopia," *Working in the Theatre,* CUNY TV, 2007.

Stage Appearances:
Elmire, *Tartuffe,* Peter Hall Company, Playhouse Theatre, London, 1991.

Amanda, *The Relapse,* Royal Shakespeare Company, Swan Theatre, Stratford–upon–Avon, England, 1995, and Newcastle Playhouse, Newcastle–upon–Tyne, England, 1996.

Lady Anne, *Richard III,* Royal Shakespeare Company, Royal Shakespeare Theatre, Stratford–upon–Avon, England, 1995, and Theatre Royal, Newcastle–upon–Tyne, England, 1996.

Serafina, *The Painter of Dishonour,* Royal Shakespeare Company, The Other Place, Stratford–upon–Avon, England, 1995, and Gulbenkian Studio, Newcastle–upon–Tyne, England, 1996.

Varya Mikhailovna, *Summerfolk,* Royal National Theatre, Olivier Theatre, London, 1999.

Annie, *The Real Thing,* Donmar Warehouse, London, 1999, Albery Theatre, London, 2000, and Ethel Barrymore Theatre, New York City, 2000.

Gilda, *Design for Living,* American Airlines Theatre, New York City, 2001.

Tracy Samantha Lord, *The Philadelphia Story,* Old Vic Theatre, London, 2005.

Lady Macbeth, *Macbeth,* Shakespeare in the Park, Joseph Papp Public Theater, Delacorte Theater, New York City, 2006.

Liubov Bakunin, *The Coast of Utopia: Part 1—Voyage* (also known as *The Coast of Utopia*), Lincoln Center Theater, Vivian Beaumont Theater, New York City, 2006–2007.

Natalie Herzen, *The Coast of Utopia: Part 2—Shipwreck* (also known as *The Coast of Utopia*), Lincoln Center Theater, Vivian Beaumont Theater, 2006–2007.

Malwida von Meysenbug, *The Coast of Utopia: Part 3—Salvage* (also known as *The Coast of Utopia*), Lincoln Center Theater, Vivian Beaumont Theater, 2007.

Appeared in *Laundry and Bourbon* and *1959 Pink Thunderbird,* both at the Edinburgh Festival, Edinburgh, Scotland.

Major Tours:
Pat Green, *Breaking the Code,* Triumph Production tour, 1992.

Film Appearances:
Cynthia Powell, *Backbeat,* Gramercy Pictures, 1994.

Rosemary Leighton–Jones, *Paradise Road,* Twentieth Century–Fox, 1997.

Constance Lloyd Wilde, *Wilde* (also known as *Oscar Wilde*), PolyGram Filmed Entertainment, 1997, Sony Pictures Classics, 1998.

Sally, *Bedrooms and Hallways,* First Run Features, 1998.

Sophie, *This Year's Love,* Entertainment Film Distributors, 1999.

Young Valerie Sonnenschein, *Sunshine* (also known as *The Taste of Sunshine, A Napfeny ize,* and *Sunshine—Ein Hauch von Sonnenschein*), Ascot Elite Entertainment Group, 1999.

A Good Baby, Curb Entertainment, c. 1999.

Christabel LaMotte, *Possession,* USA Films, 2002.

Betsy Chase, *The River King,* Alliance Atlantis Motion Picture Group, 2005.

Alice Ferris, *Alpha Male,* 2006.

Laura Moores, *Before the Rains* (also known as *Kerala* and *Road to the Sky*), Roadside Attractions, 2007.

Abby Tierney, *Pride and Glory,* Warner Bros., 2008.

Some sources cite an appearance in the film *Gothika,* Warner Bros., 2003.

Radio Appearances:
Voice of Amber, *Keystone,* 1992.

Voice of Debra, *Anniversary,* 1992.

Reader, *Something Understood: An Anthology of Spiritual Verse,* 1993.

Voice of Harriet, *Playing the Wife,* 1997.

Voice of Princess Mahjong, *Aladdin,* BBC Radio Four, 1999.

Guest, *Talking Movies,* 2002.

Appeared in other radio productions.

RECORDINGS

Videos:
(In archive footage) Empress Zita of Austria, *The Adventures of Young Indiana Jones: Adventures in the Secret Service* (related to "Austria, March 1917" and "Petrograd, July 1917," both episodes of *The Young Indiana Jones Chronicles*), 1999.

Some sources cite appearances in other recordings.

Audiobooks:
Celia Rees, *Witch Child,* Listening Library, 2001.
William Shakespeare, *The Tempest* (also known as *The Complete Arkangel Shakespeare: The Tempest*), Audio Partners Publishing, 2004.

Some sources cite appearances in other audio recordings.

OTHER SOURCES

Periodicals:
Interview, July, 2000, p. 32.
Newsweek, May 22, 2000, p. 47.

EIDELMAN, Cliff 1964–

PERSONAL

Born December 5, 1964, in Los Angeles, CA; brother of Robin Eidelman (a music editor). *Education:* Studied orchestration and composition at the University of Southern California; attended Santa Monica City College and the Guitar Institute of Technology; also had private music lessons.

Addresses: *Agent*—First Artists Management, 4764 Park Granada, Suite 210, Calabasas, CA 91302. *Publicist*—Chasen & Company, 8899 Beverly Blvd., Suite 405, Los Angeles, CA 90048.

Career: Composer, conductor, music director, and orchestrator.

CREDITS

Film Work:
Music director, *Silent Night,* TAT, 1988, released in the United States as *Magdalene,* Prism Entertainment, 1990.

Music director, *Triumph of the Spirit,* Triumph Releasing, 1989.
Music director, *Crazy People,* Paramount, 1990.
Conductor, *Star Trek VI: The Undiscovered Country,* Paramount, 1991.
Music director, *Delirious,* Metro–Goldwyn–Mayer/Pathe, 1991.
Conductor, *Christopher Columbus: The Discovery* (also known as *Cristobal Colon: el descubrimiento*), Warner Bros., 1992.
Conductor, *Leap of Faith,* Paramount, 1992.
Orchestrator, *Untamed Heart* (also known as *The Baboon Heart* and *Real Love*), Metro–Goldwyn–Mayer, 1993.
Arranger for song "Red Is the Rose," *A Simple Twist of Fate,* Buena Vista, 1994.
Conductor and orchestrator, *Now and Then* (also known as *The Gaslight Addition*), New Line Cinema, 1995.
Conductor, *The Beautician and the Beast,* Paramount, 1997.
Conductor, *Free Willy 3: The Rescue* (also known as *Willy 3*), Warner Bros., 1997.
Conductor and orchestrator, *One True Thing,* MCA/Universal, 1998.
Orchestrator, *Harrison's Flowers* (also known as *Les fleurs d'Harrison*), MCA/Universal, 2000.
Conductor, *An American Rhapsody* (also known as *Amerikai rapszodia*), Paramount Classics, 2001.
Conductor, *The Lizzie McGuire Movie* (also known as *Ciao Lizzie!, Lizzie in Rome, Lizzie McGuire, Lizzie McGuire: Popstar,* and *Lizzie Superstar*), Buena Vista, 2003.
Conductor, *He's Just Not That into You,* New Line Cinema, 2009.

Television Work; Movies:
Orchestrator, *Witness Protection,* HBO, 1999.
Musician (pianist and guitarist), *Sexual Life,* Showtime, 2005.

Stage Work:
Conductor at *Pass the Baton,* a benefit for the Young Musicians Foundation.

WRITINGS

Film Music:
Silent Night, TAT, 1988, released in the United States as *Magdalene,* Prism Entertainment, 1990.
To Die For (also known as *Dracula: The Love Story* and *Dracula: The Love Story to Die For*), Skouras Pictures, 1989.
Triumph of the Spirit, Triumph Releasing, 1989.
Animal Behavior, Cinestar, 1990.
Crazy People, Paramount, 1990.

(And song "Beyond Our Wildest Dreams" with Jim Peterick) *Delirious,* Metro–Goldwyn–Mayer/Pathe, 1991.

Star Trek VI: The Undiscovered Country, Paramount, 1991.

Christopher Columbus: The Discovery (also known as *Cristobal Colon: el descubrimiento*), Warner Bros., 1992.

Leap of Faith, Paramount, 1992.

The Meteor Man, Metro–Goldwyn–Mayer, 1993.

Untamed Heart (also known as *The Baboon Heart* and *Real Love*), Metro–Goldwyn–Mayer, 1993.

My Girl 2, Columbia, 1994.

A Simple Twist of Fate, Buena Vista, 1994.

(Composer of unused score) *Picture Bride,* 1994, Miramax, 1995.

Now and Then (also known as *The Gaslight Addition*), New Line Cinema, 1995.

The Beautician and the Beast, Paramount, 1997.

Free Willy 3: The Rescue (also known as *Willy 3*), Warner Bros., 1997.

Montana (also known as *Killer Games* and *Nothing Personal*), Columbia/TriStar, 1998.

One True Thing, MCA/Universal, 1998.

Harrison's Flowers (also known as *Les fleurs d'Harrison*), MCA/Universal, 2000.

An American Rhapsody (also known as *Amerikai rapszodia*), Paramount Classics, 2001.

Ocean Men: Extreme Dive (also known as *Ocean Men*), nWave, 2001.

The Lizzie McGuire Movie (also known as *Ciao Lizzie!, Lizzie in Rome, Lizzie McGuire, Lizzie McGuire: Popstar,* and *Lizzie Superstar*), Buena Vista, 2003.

The Sisterhood of the Traveling Pants (also known as *The Sisterhood of the Travelling Pants*), Warner Bros., 2005.

Open Window (also known as *Fever*), Image Entertainment, 2006.

He's Just Not That into You, New Line Cinema, 2009.

Also composed music for *Day of the Bird.*

Film Theme Music:

Strike It Rich (also known as *Loser Takes All* and *Money Talks*), Millimeter Films/Miramax, 1990.

Screenplays:

Wrote *Day of the Bird* with Robin Eidelman.

Television Music; Miniseries:

The Final Days, ABC, 1989.

If These Walls Could Talk, HBO, 1996.

Television Music; Movies:

Dead Man Out (also known as *Dead Man Walking*), HBO, 1989.

Judgment, HBO, 1990.

Backfield in Motion, ABC, 1991.

Witness Protection, HBO, 1999.

Sexual Life, Showtime, 2005.

Television Music; Episodic:

"Jacob Have I Loved," *WonderWorks,* PBS, 1989.

"The Reluctant Vampire," *Tales from the Crypt* (also known as *HBO's "Tales from the Crypt"*), HBO, 1991.

Music for the Stage:

Composed the music for a ballet and overture, Santa Monica College.

Video Music:

Music from *Star Trek VI: The Undiscovered Country, Indiana Jed Bloopers, Mess–ups, and More!,* 1992.

OTHER SOURCES

Periodicals:

American Premiere, March/April, 1991, p. 15.

Electronic:

Cliff Eidelman, http://www.cliffeidelman.com, November 9, 2008.

ELFMAN, Bodhi 1969–
(Bodhi Pine Elfman)

PERSONAL

First name is pronounced Boe–dee; born July 19, 1968 (some sources cite 1969), in Los Angeles, CA; son of Richard Elfman (a director and musician) and Marie–Pascale Saboff (an artist and gallery owner; various sources cite first name as Marie or Rhonda); nephew of Danny Elfman (a composer and musician); married Jenna (an actress and producer; original name, Jennifer Mary Butala), February 18, 1995; children: Story Elias. *Education:* Studied acting at the Beverly Hills Playhouse with Milton Katselas. *Religion:* Church of Scientology (some sources cite Elfman as the member of organizations affiliated with the religion).

Addresses: *Agent*—Stone Manners Talent and Literary, 6500 Wilshire Blvd., Suite 550, Los Angeles, CA 90048; Writers and Artists Agency, 8383 Wilshire Blvd., Suite 550, Los Angeles, CA 90211.

Career: Actor. Appeared in advertisements. Appeared in the book *The Hollywood Handbook* (also known as

The Hollywood Handbook: The Insiders' Guide to Success), by Robin Greer, Sarah Reinhardt, and Kevin Dornan, 1997.

CREDITS

Film Appearances:

Centurian Savings and Loan night guard, *Sneakers,* Universal, 1992.

Photo cashier, *Stepmonster,* Concorde Pictures, 1993.

Booger Martin, *Shrunken Heads,* 1994.

Television studio production assistant, *New Nightmare* (also known as *A Nightmare on Elm Street 7* and *Wes Craven's "New Nightmare"*), New Line Cinema, 1994.

(As Bodhi Pine Elfman) Coffee customer, *A Very Brady Sequel,* Paramount, 1996.

Daniel, *Going Home,* 1997.

Sluggo, *The Others,* Cinequanon Pictures International/The Asylum, 1997.

Derek, *Girl,* Kushner–Locke, 1998.

Freddie, *Godzilla,* TriStar, 1998.

(As Bodhi Pine Elfman) Leo Pedranski, *Mercury Rising,* MCA/Universal, 1998.

Math person, *Armageddon,* Buena Vista, 1998.

(As Bodhi Pine Elfman) Tag, *Slappy and the Stinkers* (also known as *Free Slappy* and *Stinkers*), TriStar, 1998.

(As Bodhi Pine Elfman) Van, *Enemy of the State,* Buena Vista, 1998.

Max, *Sand* (also known as *Sandstorm*), Hard Sand Productions, c. 1998.

Arno, *Rituals and Resolutions,* AtomFilms, 1999.

Gilbert "Skinny Freak" O'Reiley, *The Mod Squad,* Metro–Goldwyn–Mayer, 1999.

Alice's manager, *Almost Famous* (also known as *Something Real, Stillwater, The Uncool,* and *Untitled Cameron Crowe Project*), DreamWorks, 2000, director's cut released as *Untitled: Almost Famous the Bootleg Cut.*

Fuzzy Frizzel, *Gone in Sixty Seconds* (also known as *Gone in 60 Seconds*), Buena Vista, 2000.

Howard the Casanova, *Keeping the Faith,* Buena Vista, 2000.

Charley, *The Shrink Is In,* New City Releasing, 2001.

Hugh, *Lost* (short film), 2002.

Hip, Edgy, Sexy, Cool, 2002.

Drummond, *Funky Monkey,* Warner Bros., 2004.

Young professional man, *Collateral,* DreamWorks, 2004.

James, *Love Hollywood Style,* 2006.

Krist Skolnik, *Love Comes to the Executioner,* 2006.

Joel, *Struck* (short film), 2008.

Film Executive Producer:

Struck (short film), 2008.

Television Appearances; Series:

Hiller and Diller, ABC, c. 1997–98.

Sergeant first class Londo Pearl, *Freedom,* UPN, 2000.

Television Appearances; Movies:

Joe, *Doing Time on Maple Drive* (also known as *Faces in the Mirror*), Fox, 1992.

First burglar, *Double Deception,* NBC, 1993.

(As Bodhi Pine Elfman) Gilmore, *Pirates of Silicon Valley,* TNT, 1999.

Odell Redd, *Coyote Waits,* broadcast on *Mystery!* (also known as *An American Mystery! Special*), PBS, 2003, also Granada Television.

Lou, *Fielder's Choice,* The Hallmark Channel, 2005.

Television Appearances; Awards Presentations:

Presenter, *The 2001 IFP/West Independent Spirit Awards,* Independent Film Channel, 2001.

Television Appearances; Episodic:

Mark, "Life after Death," *Life Goes On* (also known as *Glenbrook*), ABC, 1991.

Mark, "Out of the Mainstream," *Life Goes On* (also known as *Glenbrook*), ABC, 1991.

Busboy, "The Best Intentions," *Sisters,* NBC, 1993.

Messenger, "Picture Imperfect," *Melrose Place,* Fox, 1993.

(As Bodhi Pine Elfman) Clerk, "Dial B for Virgin," *Married ... with Children* (also known as *Not the Cosbys*), Fox, 1994.

Garry, "Great Expectations," *Step by Step* (also known as *Eine Starke Familie, Kaos i familien, Notre belle famille, Paso a paso, Steg for Steg,* and *Una bionda per papa*), ABC, 1994.

(As Bodhi Pine Elfman) Garry, "I'll Be Home for Christmas," *Step by Step* (also known as *Eine Starke Familie, Kaos i familien, Notre belle famille, Paso a paso, Steg for Steg,* and *Una bionda per papa*), ABC, 1994.

(As Bodhi Pine Elfman) Garry, "Something Wild," *Step by Step* (also known as *Eine Starke Familie, Kaos i familien, Notre belle famille, Paso a paso, Steg for Steg,* and *Una bionda per papa*), ABC, 1994.

Jan, "Cry Baby Cry," *Dead at 21,* MTV, 1994.

Sean, "Confronting Brandon: The Intervention of an Addict," *Lifestores: Families in Crisis,* HBO, 1994.

Augie Ziff, "The Brain Teaser," *The Faculty,* ABC, 1996.

Bob, "Fake ID–ology," *Hang Time,* NBC, 1996.

Clerk, "My Mother the Alien," *3rd Rock from the Sun* (also known as *Life as We Know It, 3rd Rock,* and *Third Rock from the Sun*), NBC, 1996.

(As Bodhi Pine Elfman) Surfer, "Too Hip for the Room," *Ellen* (also known as *These Friends of Mine*), ABC, 1996.

Bellboy, "The Halloween Show," *George & Leo,* CBS, 1997.

Kevin, "Breaking the Rules," *Ink,* CBS, 1997.

Kevin, "The Debutante," *Ink,* CBS, 1997.

Kevin, "Going to the Dogs," *Ink,* CBS, 1997.
Orderly, "I Brake for Dick," *3rd Rock from the Sun* (also known as *Life as We Know It, 3rd Rock,* and *Third Rock from the Sun*), NBC, 1997.
Ted, "A Closet Full of Hell," *Dharma & Greg,* ABC, 1998.
(As Bodhi Pine Elfman) Trevor Blue, "Genesis," *Sliders,* Sci–Fi Channel, 1998.
(As Bodhi Pine Elfman) "Separation Anxiety," *Party of Five,* Fox, 1998.
Himself, *The Rosie O'Donnell Show,* syndicated, 1999.
Neil, "Veronica Loses Her Olive Again," *Veronica's Closet* (also known as *Veronica, El secreto de Veronica, Les dessous de Veronica, Los secretos de Veronica, Os segredos de Veronica,* and *Veronican salaisuudet*), NBC, 2000.
Neil, "Veronica's Clips," *Veronica's Closet* (also known as *Veronica, El secreto de Veronica, Les dessous de Veronica, Los secretos de Veronica, Os segredos de Veronica,* and *Veronican salaisuudet*), NBC, 2000.
Toby Anders, "The Kid," *The Huntress,* USA Network, 2000.
Andre, "Charity," *Malcolm in the Middle* (also known as *Fighting in Underpants*), Fox, 2001.
Suspicious man, "Falling," *Providence,* NBC, 2001.
Terry, "Home Is Where the Art Is," *Dharma & Greg,* ABC, 2001.
Chris Roland, "No Mas," *Without a Trace* (also known as *Vanished* and *W.A.T*), CBS, 2003.
Fred Finch, "Nobody's Perfect," *Karen Sisco* (also known as *Ofiter Karen*), ABC, 2003.
Kevin O'Malley, "Daddy's Girl," *L.A. Dragnet* (also known as *Dragnet*), ABC, 2003.
Nicky, "Finders Keepers," *ER* (also known as *Emergency Room*), NBC, 2003.
Steven, "Donny, We Hardly Knew Ye," *Las Vegas* (also known as *Casino Eye*), NBC, 2003.
Kyle Donie, "Witch Wars," *Charmed,* The WB, 2004.

Appeared as Will, *Moloney,* CBS; and as Burt, *Phenom,* ABC.

Television Appearances; Pilots:

Ray, *Clerks* (also known as *Clerks.*), 1995.
Trey, *Hollyweird,* Fox, 1998.

RECORDINGS

Videos:

Himself (interviewer), *Farewell: Live from the Universal Amphitheatre Halloween 1995,* 1996.

ELLROY, James 1948–

PERSONAL

Original name, Lee Earle Ellroy; born March 4, 1948, in Los Angeles, CA; son of Armand (an accountant and business manager) and Geneva Odelia (a nurse; maiden name, Hilliker) Ellroy; married Mary Doherty, 1988 (divorced, 1991); married Helen Knode (a writer and journalist), c. 1991 (divorced, 2006). *Avocational Interests:* Reading, classical music.

Addresses: *Agent*—Sobel Weber Associates, Inc., 146 East 19th St., New York, NY 10003; Artists Management Group, 9465 Wilshire Blvd., Suite 212, Beverly Hills, CA 90212. *Manager*—Intellectual Property Group, 9200 Sunset Blvd., Suite 820, Los Angeles, CA 90069

Career: Novelist, screenwriter, and actor. Worked as a caddy at golf courses. Ellroy's papers, including manuscripts and correspondence, are at the Thomas Cooper Library at the University of South Carolina. *Military service:* U.S. Army, 1965.

Awards, Honors: Edgar Award nomination, Mystery Writers of America, 1982, for *Clandestine;* Prix Mystere de la critique, 1990, for *The Big Nowhere;* best book designation, *Time* magazine, 1995, for *American Tabloid;* USC Libraries Scripter Award (with Brian Helgeland and Curtis Hanson), Friends of the USC Libraries, University of Southern California, 1998, for *L.A. Confidential.*

CREDITS

Film Appearances:
Himself, *James Ellroy: Demon Dog of American Crime Fiction* (documentary), First Run Features, 1993.
Himself, *Shotgun Freeway: Drives through Lost L.A.* (documentary), Alpine Releasing, 1995.
Wordfest party guest, *Wonder Boys* (also known as *Die Wonder Boys*), Paramount, 2000.
Right, *Stay Clean* (short film), 2002.
Himself, *Das Bus,* Corticrawl Productions, 2003.
Himself, *Vakvagany,* Corticrawl Productions/Pathfinder Pictures, 2003.
Himself, *Bazaar Bizarre* (documentary; also known as *Bazaar Bizarre: The Strange Case of Serial Killer Bob Berdella*), Corticrawl Productions, 2004.

Film Executive Producer:
Bazaar Bizarre (documentary; also known as *Bazaar Bizarre: The Strange Case of Serial Killer Bob Berdella*), Corticrawl Productions, 2004.

Television Appearances; Documentary Specials:
Himself, *Besuch bei James Ellroy,* [Germany], 2001.
Himself, *Feast of Death* (also known as *James Ellroy's "Feast of Death"*), BBC Two, 2001, Showtime, c. 2003.
Himself, *Just the Facts,* Court TV, c. 2003.
Rankin on the Staircase, BBC Four, 2005.

Television Appearances; Episodic:
Himself, "James Ellroy," *The E! True Hollywood Story* (also known as *James Ellroy: The E! True Hollywood Story* and *THS*), E! Entertainment Television, 1997.
Himself, "Death of a Dream: Karyn Kupcinet" (also known as "Karyn Kupcinet"), *The E! True Hollywood Story* (also known as *Death of a Dream: Karyn Kupcinet: The E! True Hollywood Story, Karyn Kupcinet: The E! True Hollywood Story,* and *THS*), E! Entertainment Television, 1999.
Himself, *Late Night with Conan O'Brien,* 1999, 2004.
Himself, "Jack Webb," *Biography* (also known as *A&E Biography: Jack Webb*), Arts and Entertainment, 2000.
Himself, *The O'Reilly Factor,* Fox News Channel, 2004.
Himself, *The Late Late Show with Craig Ferguson* (also known as *The Late Late Show*), CBS, 2005.
Himself, "Will the US Lose the Terror War?," *The O'Reilly Factor,* Fox News Channel, 2006.
Himself, *Murder by the Book,* Court TV, 2006.
Himself, *Durch die Nacht mit* (also known as *Into the Night with ...* and *Au coeur de la nuit*), 2008.

Appeared in "L.A. Confidences," *Great Writers of the Twentieth Century* (documentary series); subject of the documentary "White Jazz," *The Red Light Zone,* Channel 4 (England).

Film Executive Producer; Pilots:
The Lead Sheet, Arts and Entertainment, 2009.

Ellroy has also worked on other television projects.

RECORDINGS

Videos:
Himself, *L.A. Confidential: Off the Record,* Warner Home Video, 1998.
Himself, *Shadows of Suspense,* Universal Studios Home Video, 2006.
Himself, *Sunlight and Shadow: The Visual Style of "L.A. Confidential,"* Warner Home Video, 2008.
Himself, *Whatever You Desire: Making "L.A. Confidential,"* Warner Home Video, 2008.

WRITINGS

Screenplays:
(Story) *Dark Blue* (also known as *4–29–92* and *The Plague Season*), Metro–Goldwyn–Mayer, 2002.
(With Kurt Wimmer and Jamie Moss; and story) *Street Kings* (also known as *Fake City, Night Watch,* and *The Night Watchman*), Fox Searchlight Pictures, 2008.

Author of various screenplays, including *Destination* (based on his collection *Destination: Morgue!*), *Land of the Living* (based on the novel by Nicci French), *The Man Who Kept Secrets, Mr. Smith, 77,* and *White Heat* (based on the earlier film of the same name). Some sources state that with others, Ellroy wrote *The Jackal* (also known as *The Day of Jackal;* based on the earlier film *The Day of Jackal*), Universal, 1997.

Teleplays; Pilots:
L.A. Sheriff's Homicide (also known as *County 187, LA County 187,* and *L.A. County 187*), NBC, 2000, related pilot UPN, 2003.
The Enforcers, c. 2004.
The Lead Sheet, Arts and Entertainment, 2009.

Novels:
Brown's Requiem, Avon, 1981.
Clandestine, Avon, 1982.
Blood on the Moon, Mysterious Press, 1984, part of the Lloyd Hopkins trilogy, published in *L.A. Noir,* Mysterious Press, 1998.
Because the Night, Mysterious Press, 1985, part of the Lloyd Hopkins trilogy, published in *L.A. Noir,* Mysterious Press, 1998.
Killer on the Road (also known as *Silent Terror*), Mysterious Press, 1986.
Suicide Hill, Mysterious Press, 1986, part of the Lloyd Hopkins trilogy, published in *L.A. Noir,* Mysterious Press, 1998.
The Black Dahlia, Mysterious Press, 1987, part of the L.A. Quartet series.
The Big Nowhere, Mysterious Press, 1988, part of the L.A. Quartet series.
L.A. Confidential, Mysterious Press, 1990, part of the L.A. Quartet series.
(Author of introduction) Jim Thompson, *Heed the Thunder,* Armchair Detective Library, 1991.
White Jazz, Alfred A. Knopf, 1992, part of the L.A. Quartet series.
American Tabloid, Alfred A. Knopf, 1995, part of the American Underworld trilogy.
L.A. Noir (consists of *Blood on the Moon, Because the Night,* and *Suicide Hill*), Mysterious Press, 1998.
The Cold Six Thousand, Alfred A. Knopf, 2001, part of the American Underworld trilogy.
Blood's a Rover, Alfred A. Knopf, c. 2009, part of the American Underworld trilogy.

Author of the manuscript *L.A. Deathtrap* (also known as *L.A. Death Trap*); revised material from this manuscript appeared in other Ellroy novels.

Short Story Collections:
Hollywood Nocturnes, Alfred A. Knopf, 1994, also published as *Dick Contino's Blues and Other Stories,* Arrow, 1994.

(With Otto Penzler) Guest editor and author of introduction, *The Best American Mystery Stories 2002*, Houghton Mifflin, 2002.

Fiction and Nonfiction Collections:

Crime Wave: Reportage and Fiction from the Underside of L.A. (fiction and nonfiction; also known as *Crime Wave*), Vintage Books, 1999.

Breakneck Pace (short stories and essays; originally published on the Internet at http://www.contentville.com), Contentville Press, 2000.

Destination: Morgue! (short stories and essays; also known as *Destination: Morgue! L.A. Tales*), Century, 2004.

Nonfiction:

Murder and Mayhem: An A–Z of the World's Most Notorious Killers, Arrow, 1992.

My Dark Places: An L.A. Crime Memoir (autobiography; also known as *My Dark Places*), Alfred A. Knopf, 1996.

(Author of afterword) Bill O'Reilly, *The No–Spin Zone: Confrontations with the Powerful and Famous in America*, Broadway Books, 2001.

Contributor to periodicals, including the article "My Mother's Killer," published in *GQ*.

ADAPTATIONS

Ellroy's novel *Blood on the Moon* was adapted as the film *Cop*, Atlantic Releasing, 1988; his short story "Since I Don't Have You" formed the basis for an episode of the television series *Fallen Angels* (also known as *Perfect Crimes*, *Crime perfecte*, and *24 horas para a morte*), Showtime, 1993; his novel *L.A. Confidential* was adapted as a film and released by Warner Bros., 1998; his novel *Brown's Requiem* was adapted for film and released in 1998 by Avalanche Releasing; his novel *Killer on the Road* was adapted as the short film *Stay Clean*, 2002; his novel *The Black Dahlia* was adapted as film and released by Universal, 2006; his autobiographical work *My Dark Places: An L.A. Crime Memoir* formed the basis for an installment of *Murder by the Book*, Court TV, 2006; his novel *White Jazz* was adapted as a screenplay; Ellroy's work has served as the source material for various film and television projects.

OTHER SOURCES

Books:

Contemporary Novelists, seventh edition, St. James Press, 2001.

St. James Guide to Crime & Mystery Writers, St. James Press, 1996.

Twentieth–Century Crime and Mystery Writers, third edition, St. James Press, 1991.

Periodicals:

Harper's Bazaar, November, 1996, p. 180.
Interview, December, 1996, p. 70.
Los Angeles Magazine, November, 1996, p. 114.
Los Angeles Times, April 6, 2008, p. E1.
Nation, December 2, 1996, p. 25.
New Statesmen, November 8, 1996, p. 46.
Newsweek, November 11, 1996, p. 79.
New York Times, November 3, 2003, p. E8.
People Weekly, November 25, 1996, p. 93.
Time, April 10, 1995, p. 74.
The Writer, September, 2001, p. 28.
Writer's Digest, July, 1996, p. 26.

EMOND, Linda 1959–

PERSONAL

Born May 22, 1959, in New Brunswick, NJ.

Addresses: *Manager*—Susan Smith Company, 1344 North Wetherly Dr., Beverly Hills, CA 90069.

Career: Actress.

Awards, Honors: Drama Desk Award nomination, outstanding featured actress in a play, 1997, for *Nine Armenians*; Obie Award, best performance, *Village Voice*, 2001–02, Lucille Lortel Award, outstanding actress, Drama Desk Award nomination, outstanding featured actress in a play, 2002, L.A. Drama Critics Award nomination, and L.A. Ovation Award nomination, all for *Homebody/Kabul*; Antoinette Perry Award nomination, best featured actress in a play, 2003, for *Life x 3*; Jeff Award, best actress, Joseph Jefferson Awards, for *Pygmalion*; Jeff Award, best actress, for *The Winter's Tale*; three more Jeff Awards.

CREDITS

Film Appearances:

Gwyneth, *God's Will*, 1989.
Martha Holmes, *Pollock*, Sony Pictures Classics, 2000.
Nina Ellington, *Almost Salinas*, Curb Entertainment, 2001.
Meredith Price, *A Gentleman's Game*, First Look International, 2002.

Margery, *City by the Sea* (also known as *The Suspect*), Warner Bros., 2002.

Dr. Marta Foss, *The Dying Gaul*, Strand Releasing, 2005.

Mediator, *Dark Water*, Buena Vista, 2005.

Leslie Conlin, *North Country*, Warner Bros., 2005.

Herself, *Wrestling with Angels: Playwright Tony Kushner* (documentary; also known as *Wrestling with Angels*), Balcony Releasing, 2006.

Patty Sheridan, *Trade* (also known as *Trade—Willkommen in Amerika*), Roadside Attractions, 2007.

Lucy's mother, *Across the Universe*, Sony, 2007.

Ida King, *Stop–Loss,* Paramount, 2008.

Megan Fullmer, *The Missing Person*, 2009.

Simone Beck, *Julie & Julia,* Columbia, 2009.

Television Appearances; Series:
Kara Richardson, *One Life to Live*, ABC, 1997.

Television Appearances; Movies:
Penny, *I Can Make You Love Me* (also known as *Stalking Laura*), CBS, 1993.

Television Appearances; Specials:
Narrator, *Intimate Portrait: Tippi Hedren*, Lifetime, 2001.

Narrator, *Intimate Portrait: Sela Ward*, Lifetime, 2001.

Narrator, *Intimate Portrait: Rita Moreno*, Lifetime, 2001.

Narrator, *Intimate Portrait: Liz Smith*, Lifetime, 2001.

Narrator, *Intimate Portrait: Laila Ali*, Lifetime, 2001.

Narrator, *Intimate Portrait: Kim Fields*, Lifetime, 2001.

Narrator, *Intimate Portrait: Kelly Ripa*, Lifetime, 2001.

Narrator, *Intimate Portrait: Jasmine Guy*, Lifetime, 2001.

Narrator, *Intimate Portrait: Genie Francis*, Lifetime, 2001.

Narrator, *Intimate Portrait: Calista Flockhart*, Lifetime, 2001.

Narrator, *Intimate Portrait: Betsey Johnson*, Lifetime, 2001.

Narrator, *Intimate Portrait: Paula Zahn*, Lifetime, 2002.

Narrator, *Intimate Portrait: Marion Ross*, Lifetime, 2002.

Narrator, *Intimate Portrait: Lisa Gay Hamilton*, Lifetime, 2002.

Narrator, *Intimate Portrait: Kathy Ireland*, Lifetime, 2002.

Narrator, *Intimate Portrait: Jennie Garth*, Lifetime, 2002.

Narrator, *Intimate Portrait: Jane Kaczmarek*, Lifetime, 2002.

Narrator, *Intimate Portrait: Barbara Eden*, Lifetime, 2002.

The 57th Annual Tony Awards, CBS, 2003.

Narrator, *Intimate Portrait: Vicki Lawrence*, Lifetime, 2003.

Narrator, *Intimate Portrait: Rosanna Arquette*, Lifetime, 2003.

Narrator, *Intimate Portrait: Naomi Judd*, Lifetime, 2003.

Narrator, *Intimate Portrait: Mo'Nique*, Lifetime, 2003.

Narrator, *Intimate Portrait: Linda Lavin*, Lifetime, 2003.

Narrator, *Intimate Portrait: Isabel Sanford*, Lifetime, 2003.

Narrator, *Intimate Portrait: Eve Ensler*, Lifetime, 2003.

Narrator, *Intimate Portrait: Erika Slezak*, Lifetime, 2003.

Narrator, *Intimate Portrait: Bo Derek*, Lifetime, 2003.

Narrator, *Intimate Portrait: Peggy Fleming*, Lifetime, 2003.

Narrator, *Intimate Portrait: Rosie O'Donnell*, Lifetime, 2003.

Narrator, *Intimate Portrait: Stockard Channing*, Lifetime, 2004.

Narrator, *Intimate Portrait: Missy "Misdemeanor" Elliott*, Lifetime, 2004.

Narrator, *Intimate Portrait: Dionne Warwick*, Lifetime, 2004.

Also appeared as narrator, *Intimate Portrait: Penny Marshall*, Lifetime.

Television Appearances; Pilots:
Maureen Bowman, *The Good Life*, NBC, 1994.

Assistant district attorney Strictler, *Wonderland*, ABC, 2000.

Television Appearances; Episodic:
Dr. Emily Connor, "Great Balls Afire," *L.A. Law*, NBC, 1992.

Monica Barker, "Truth of Consequences," *Mann & Machine*, NBC, 1992.

Pamela Reichel, "Legacy," *Reasonable Doubts*, NBC, 1993.

Laura Cochran, "Savior," *Law & Order*, NBC, 1996.

"The War Against Crime," *Feds*, CBS, 1997.

"The Unthinkable," *New York Undercover* (also known as *Uptown Undercover*), Fox, 1997.

Narrator, "Gypsy Rose Lee: Naked Ambition," *Biography*, Arts and Entertainment, 1999.

Dahlia, "Big Girls Don't Cry," *The Sopranos*, HBO, 2000.

Assistant district attorney Strictler, "20/20 Hindsight," *Wonderland*, ABC, 2000.

Carolyn Tyler, "Panic," *Law & Order*, NBC, 2000.

Francine Bradley, "Duty," *Third Watch*, NBC, 2001.

Dr. Christine Fellowes, "Anti–Thesis," *Law & Order: Criminal Intent* (also known as *Law & Order: CI*), NBC, 2002.

Voice, "Emma Goldman," *The American Experience*, PBS, 2004.

Dr. Emily Sopher, "Hate," *Law & Order: Special Victims Unit* (also known as *Law & Order: SVU* and *Special Victims Unit*), NBC, 2004.

Dr. Emily Sopher, "Mean," *Law & Order: Special Victims Unit* (also known as *Law & Order: SVU* and *Special Victims Unit*), NBC, 2004.

Dr. Emily Downey, "Baby Boom," *Law & Order: Trial by Jury*, NBC, 2005.

Rosalie Helton, "Tombstone," *Law & Order*, NBC, 2005.

Abigail Adams, "John & Abigail Adams," *The American Experience,* PBS, 2006.

Headmistress Queller, "School Lies," *Gossip Girl,* The CW, 2008.

Dr. Emily Sopher, "Unorthodox," *Law & Order: Special Victims Unit* (also known as *Law & Order: SVU* and *Special Victims Unit*), NBC, 2008.

Stage Appearances:

(New York debut) Armine and mom, *Nine Armenians,* Manhattan Theatre Club Stage I, 1996–97.

Woman, *Baby Anger,* Playwrights Horizons Theatre, New York City, 1997.

Abigail Adams, *1776,* Roundabout Theatre, New York City, 1997–98.

Elaine, *The Dying Gaul,* Vineyard Theatre, New York City, 1998.

Susannah Fenwick and Ellen, *An Experiment with an Air Pump,* Manhattan Theatre Club Stage I, New York City, 1999.

Maggie Antrobus, *Over and Over,* Signature Theatre, Arlington, VA, 1999.

The homebody, *The Homebody/Kabul,* New York Theatre Workshop, 2001, then the Mark Taper Forum, Los Angeles, and Brooklyn Academy of Music, New York City.

Betty Dulfeet, *The Resistible Rise of Arturo Ui,* National Actors Theatre, Michael Schimmel Center for the Arts, Pace University, New York City, 2002.

Inez, *Life x 3,* Circle in the Square Theatre, New York City, 2003.

Aurelia, *A Spanish Play,* Classic Stage Company, New York City, 2007.

Also appeared in *Pygmalion,* Chicago, IL; *The Winter's Tale,* Chicago, IL; *Far East,* Williamstown, MA; *Ancestral Voices,* Lincoln Center, New York City.

RECORDINGS

Taped Readings:

Good Harbor by Anita Diamant, Simon & Schuster, 2002.

Flirting with Pete by Barbara Delinsky, Simon & Schuster, 2003.

OTHER SOURCES

Electronic:

Linda Emond Website, http://www.lindaemond.com, January 14, 2009.

ENGEL, Georgia 1948–

PERSONAL

Full name, Georgia Bright Engel; born July 28, 1948, in Washington, DC; daughter of Benjamin Franklin (an admiral in the Coast Guard) and Ruth Caroline (maiden name, Hendron) Engel. *Education:* University of Hawaii, B.A., drama, 1969; Academy of the Washington Ballet, graduate. *Religion:* Christian Scientist. *Avocational Interests:* Dancing, reading biographies.

Addresses: *Agent*—Cunningham/Escott/Slevin & Doherty Talent Agency, 10635 Santa Monica Blvd., Suite 140, Los Angeles, CA 90025; Peter Strain & Associates, 5455 Wilshire Blvd., Suite 1812, Los Angeles, CA 90036.

Career: Actress, singer, dancer, and voice artist. Provided voices for advertisements and promotional spots.

Member: Actors' Equity Association, Screen Actors Guild, American Federation of Television and Radio Artists, Museum of Television Broadcasting, Actors Fund of America (life member and honorary member).

Awards, Honors: Film Award nomination, best supporting actress, British Academy of Film and Television Arts, 1972, for *Taking Off;* Emmy Award nominations, outstanding continuing performance by a supporting actress in a comedy series, 1976 and 1977, both for *Mary Tyler Moore;* Emmy Award nominations, outstanding guest actress in a comedy series, 2003, 2004, and 2005, and Prism Award, performance in a television comedy series, 2006, all for *Everybody Loves Raymond.*

CREDITS

Television Appearances; Series:

Georgette Franklin Baxter, *Mary Tyler Moore* (also known as *The Mary Tyler Moore Show* and *Oh Mary*), CBS, 1972–77.

Regular, *The Dean Martin Show* (also known as *Dean Martin Celebrity Roast, The Dean Martin Comedy Hour,* and *Dean Martin's Celebrity Roast*), NBC, 1974.

Mitzi Maloney, *The Betty White Show,* CBS, 1977–78.

Loretta Smoot, *Goodtime Girls* (also known as *The Good Time Girls*), ABC, 1980.

Susan Elliot, *Jennifer Slept Here,* NBC, 1983–84.

Television Appearances; Movies:

Claire Ruth, *A Love Affair: The Eleanor and Lou Gehrig Story,* NBC, 1978.

Kathy Scott, *The Day the Women Got Even,* NBC, 1980.

Voice of Willow Song, *The Special Magic of Herself the Elf* (animated; also known as *The Magic of Herself the Elf*), 1983.

Mama Porter, *Papa Was a Preacher,* 1985.

Television Appearances; Specials:
Dean Martin's California Christmas, NBC, 1975.
Dean's Place, NBC, 1975.
Dean Martin's Red Hot Scandals of 1926, NBC, 1976.
Dean Martin's Red Hot Scandals Part 2, NBC, 1977.
Herself, *The Carpenters: A Christmas Portrait,* ABC, 1978.
Herself, *Night of 100 Stars II* (also known as *Night of One Hundred Stars*), ABC, 1985.
The Thanksgiving Day Parade, Lifetime, 1987.
Herself and Georgette Franklin Baxter, *Mary Tyler Moore: The 20th Anniversary Show,* CBS, 1991.
Herself, *The Mary Tyler Moore Reunion,* CBS, 2002.
Herself, *CBS at 75* (also known as *CBS at 75: A Prime-time Celebration*), CBS, 2003.
Herself, *TV's Greatest Sidekicks,* Lifetime, 2004.

Television Appearances; Awards Presentations:
Presenter, *The 33rd Annual Tony Awards,* CBS, 1979.
The 60th Annual Tony Awards, CBS, 2006.
Presenter, *The 2007 Screen Actors Guild Awards,* TBS and TNT, 2007.
11th Annual Prism Awards, FX Network, 2007.

Television Appearances; Episodic:
Georgette Franklin, "Rhoda's Wedding: Parts 1 & 2," *Rhoda,* CBS, 1974.
Herself, *The Mike Douglas Show,* syndicated, 1975.
Herself, *Tony Orlando and Dawn* (also known as *The Tony Orlando and Dawn Rainbow Hour*), CBS, 1975.
Various characters, *The Captain and Tennille,* ABC, 1976.
Herself, *The Jacksons,* CBS, 1977.
Ambrosia Malspar, "A Bride for Exidor," *Mork & Mindy,* ABC, 1978.
Maxine Bender, "Escape/Cinderella Girls," *Fantasy Island,* ABC, 1978.
Sheila Lawrence, "Taking Sides/A Friendly Little Game/Going by the Book," *The Love Boat,* ABC, 1978.
Yasmine and Brenda Rappaport (some sources cite role as Tracy), "The Sheik/The Homecoming," *Fantasy Island,* ABC, 1978.
Ambrosia Malspar, "The Exidor Affair," *Mork & Mindy,* ABC, 1979.
Ambrosia Malspar, "Exidor's Wedding," *Mork & Mindy,* ABC, 1979.
Cathy Wilton, "The Cheerleaders/Marooned," *Fantasy Island,* ABC, 1979.
Wendy Turner, "A Date with Johnny," *The Associates,* ABC, 1979.
Herself, *The Big Show,* NBC, 1980.
Karen Hughes, "Isaac's Teacher/Seal of Approval/The Successor," *The Love Boat,* ABC, 1981.
Sally Harris, "Romance Times Three/Night of the Tormented Soul," *Fantasy Island,* ABC, 1981.
Voice of Creole (an alligator) in "Creole" segment, "Misunderstood Monsters" (animated stories with live action introductions), *CBS Library,* CBS, 1981.

Kathy, "Burl of My Dreams/Meet the Author/Rhymes, Riddles and Romance," *The Love Boat,* ABC, 1982.
Susan Henderson, "The Devil Stick/Touch and Go," *Fantasy Island,* ABC, 1983.
Herself, "Ted Knight," *This Is Your Life,* syndicated, 1984.
"Love Is Sweet," *The New Love, American Style,* ABC, 1986.
Narrator, "Chickens Aren't the Only Ones," *Reading Rainbow,* PBS, 1987.
Shirley Burleigh, *Coach,* ABC, multiple episodes, 1991–96.
Joan Cosgrove, "The Lying Game," *Working,* NBC, 1998.
Voice of Evelyn (Cassandra's mother), "Hercules and the Big Kiss," *Hercules* (animated; also known as *Disney's "Hercules"* and *Hercules: The Animated Series*), ABC and syndicated, 1998.
Voice of old woman, "Bag of Money/Principal Simmons," *Hey Arnold!* (animated; also known as *Hey, Arnold!*), Nickelodeon, 2000.
Herself, "The Mary Tyler Moore Show," *Inside TV Land,* TV Land, 2001.
Pat MacDougall, *Everybody Loves Raymond* (also known as *Raymond, Alla aelskar Raymond, Alle elsker Raymond, Alle lieben Raymond, Kaikki rakastavat Raymondia, Svi vole Raymonda, Todo el mundo quiere a Raymond, Tothom estima en Raymond, Tout le monde aime Raymond,* and *Tutti amano Raymond*), CBS, multiple episodes, 2003–2005.
Herself, *The View,* ABC, 2006.
Esmeralda, *Passions* (also known as *Harmony's Passions* and *The Passions Storm*), NBC, multiple episodes in 2007.
Herself, *Entertainment Tonight* (also known as *Entertainment This Week, E.T., ET Weekend,* and *This Week in Entertainment*), syndicated, 2008.
Herself, *The Oprah Winfrey Show* (also known as *Oprah*), syndicated, 2008.

Television Appearances; Pilots:
Cleo, *The New Love Boat* (also known as *The Love Boat III*), ABC, 1977.
Mitzi Maloney, "Undercover Woman" (also known as "Undercover Police Woman"), *The Betty White Show,* CBS, 1977.
Loretta Smoot, *Goodtime Girls* (also known as *The Good Time Girls*), ABC, 1980.
Susan Elliot, *Jennifer Slept Here,* NBC, 1983.
Doris, *The Beast,* Fox, 2007.

Stage Appearances:
Lend an Ear (musical revue), Equity Library Theatre, New York City, 1969.
Minnie Fay, *Hello, Dolly!* (musical), St. James Theatre, New York City, 1969–70.

The House of Blue Leaves, Truck and Warehouse Theater, New York City, 1971.

Tip–toes (musical; also known as *Tiptoes*), Goodspeed Opera House, East Haddam, CT, 1978, and Brooklyn Academy of Music, Brooklyn, New York City, 1978–79.

Mickey (a mechanic), *My One and Only* (musical), St. James Theatre, 1984–85.

Herself, *Night of 100 Stars II* (also known as *Night of One Hundred Stars*), Radio City Music Hall, New York City, 1985.

Steel Magnolias, Coconut Grove Playhouse, Miami, FL, 1989–90.

Cut the Ribbons (musical revue), Westside Theatre, New York City, 1992.

Seeress, *The Boys from Syracuse* (musical), American Airlines Theatre, New York City, 2002.

Mrs. Tottendale, *The Drowsy Chaperone* (musical), Marquis Theatre, New York City, 2006–2007.

Major Tours:

Mickey (a mechanic), *My One and Only* (musical), U.S. cities, 1987.

Sister Mary Leo, *Nunsense* (musical), U.S. cities, 1990.

Sister Amnesia and Sister Mary Paul, *Sister Ambrosia's Country Western Nunsense Jamboree* (musical; also known as *Nunsense Jamboree* and *Nunsense 3: The Jamboree*), U.S. cities, c. 1997.

The Odd Couple, U.S. cities, 2001–2002.

Sister Mary Leo, *Nunsense: The 20th Anniversary Tour* (musical), U.S. cities, 2003–2004.

Sister Mary Leo, *Nunsensations: The Nunsense Vegas Revue* (musical; also known as *Nunsensations, Nunsensations!,* and *Nunsensations: The All–New Nunsense Vegas Revue*), U.S. cities, 2005–2006.

Mrs. Tottendale, *The Drowsy Chaperone* (musical), Canadian and U.S. cities, 2007–2008.

Some sources cite an appearance as a nun in *Nuncrackers: The Nunsense Christmas Musical* (also known as *Nuncrackers*).

Film Appearances:

Margot, *Taking Off,* Universal, 1971.

Mrs. Barnes, *Un homme est mort* (also known as *The Outside Man* and *Funerale a Los Angeles*), United Artists, 1973.

Voice of Love–a–Lot Bear, *The Care Bears Movie* (animated), Samuel Goldwyn, 1985.

Betty, *Signs of Life* (also known as *One for Sorrow, Two for Joy*), Avenue Entertainment, 1989.

Voice of giraffe, *Dr. Dolittle 2* (also known as *Doctor Dolittle 2, DR2, DR.2, Docteur Dolittle 2, Elaeintohtori 2,* and *Il Dottor Dolittle 2*), Twentieth Century–Fox, 2001.

Vera, *The Sweetest Thing* (also known as *Untitled Nancy Pimental Project, Allumeuses!, Bonjour l'amour, Edes kis semmiseg, La cosa mas dulce, La cosa piu dolce, Puicute bune, Radalla, Snygg, sexig & singel, Super suess und super sexy,* and *Tudo para ficar com ele*), Columbia/TriStar, 2002.

Voice of Bobbie, *Open Season* (animated), Columbia, 2006.

Sister Mary Leo (some sources cite role as Sister Marie Eugene), *Nunsensations* (musical; also known as *Nunsensations!, Nunsensations: The All–New Nunsense Vegas Revue,* and *Nunsensations: The Nunsense Vegas Revue*), 2007.

RECORDINGS

Videos:

Herself, *Eight Characters in Search of a Sitcom,* Twentieth Century–Fox Home Video, 2003.

Albums:

Various artists, *Ben Bagley's Cole Porter, Volume III,* Painted Smiles Records, 1990.

OTHER SOURCES

Periodicals:

Los Angeles, December, 1990, p. 229.

F

FARINA, Dennis 1944–
(Dennis G. Farina)

PERSONAL

Born February 29, 1944, in Chicago, IL; son of Joseph (a doctor) and Yolanda (a homemaker) Farina; married Patricia, 1970 (divorced, 1980); children: Dennis, Jr., Michael, Joseph (an actor). *Education:* Studied criminal justice at Truman College. *Avocational Interests:* Golf, cigars.

Addresses: *Office*—You're Faded Films, 468 North Camden Dr., Suite 220, Beverly Hills, CA 90210. *Agent*—Endeavor, 9601 Wilshire Blvd., 3rd Floor, Beverly Hills, CA 90210. *Manager*—Gateway Management Company, Inc., 860 Via De La Paz, Suite F10, Pacific Palisades, CA 90272.

Career: Actor. You're Faded Films (a production company), Beverly Hills, CA, partner. Chicago Police Department, police officer, c. 1967–85; also worked at Chicago's South Water Street produce market. Celebrity Chairman of National Law Enforcement Officers Memorial in Washington, D.C. *Military service:* U.S. Army, c. 1962–65.

Awards, Honors: American Comedy Award, best supporting comedy actor, 1996, for *Get Shorty;* Award for Excellence in the Arts, Theatre School of Depaul University, 1997; Joseph Jefferson Award (with others), best ensemble, for *Tracers.*

CREDITS

Film Appearances:
(Film debut) Carl, *Thief* (also known as *Violent Streets*), United Artists, 1981.
Dorato, *Code of Silence,* Orion, 1985.
Freddy, *Jo Jo Dancer, Your Life Is Calling,* Columbia, 1986.
FBI Section Chief Jack Crawford, *Manhunter* (also known as *Red Dragon: The Pursuit of Hannibal Lecter*), DEG, 1986.
Jimmy Serrano, *Midnight Run,* Universal, 1988.
Bankie Como, *Men of Respect,* Columbia, 1991.
Narrator, *The American Gangster* (documentary), 1992.
Mr. Stunder, *Mac,* Samuel Goldwyn, 1992.
Sal, *We're Talkin' Serious Money,* Columbia TriStar Home Video, 1992.
Brian O'Neal, *Street Crimes* (also known as *Dead Even*), PM Entertainment, 1992.
Brian O'Hara, *Another Stakeout* (also known as *Stakeout 2* and *The Lookout*), Buena Vista, 1993.
(Uncredited) Nick Gazzara, *Romeo Is Bleeding,* Gramercy, 1993.
Detective Captain Nick Detillo, *Striking Distance,* Columbia, 1993.
George O'Farrell, *Little Big League,* Columbia, 1994.
Ray "Bones" Barboni, *Get Shorty,* Metro–Goldwyn–Mayer/United Artists, 1995.
Coach Bailey, *Eddie,* Buena Vista, 1996.
Dan De Mora, *That Old Feeling,* Universal, 1997.
Marshall Sisco, *Out of Sight,* MCA/Universal, 1998.
Lieutenant Colonel Anderson, *Saving Private Ryan,* Paramount, 1998.
Captain Adam Greer, *The Mod Squad,* Metro–Goldwyn–Mayer, 1999.
Jack Bangs, *Reindeer Games* (also known as *Deception*), Dimension Films, 2000.
Dick Muller, *Preston Tylk* (also known as *Bad Seed*), New City Releasing, 2000.
Cousin Abraham "Avi" Denovitz, *Snatch* (also known as *Snatch: Pigs and Diamonds*), Sony Pictures Entertainment, 2000.
Carpo, *Sidewalks of New York,* Buena Vista, 2001.
Henry Algott, *Big Trouble,* Buena Vista, 2002.
Planet of the Pitts, Flatline, 2002.
Mr. Warner, *Stealing Harvard,* Columbia, 2002.
Detective Burton, *Paparazzi,* Twentieth Century–Fox, 2004.

Dr. Carlson, *Scrambled Eggs* (short), 2004.

Himself, *This Old Cub* (documentary), Emerging Pictures, 2004.

Himself, *The Making of "Heat"* (documentary), Warner Home Video, 2005.

Edward O'Leary, *You Kill Me,* IFC Films, 2007.

Gilmore3, *Purple Violets,* iTunes, 2007.

L.B.J. Deuce Fairbanks, *The Grand,* Anchor Bay Entertainment, 2007.

Marty Engstrom, *Bag Boy* (also known as *National Lampoon's "Bag Boy"*), National Lampoon, 2007.

Maurice, *Bottle Shock,* Freestyle Releasing, 2008.

Richard Banger, *What Happens in Vegas,* Twentieth Century–Fox, 2008.

Television Appearances; Series:

Lieutenant Mike Torello, *Crime Story,* NBC, 1986–88.

Title role, *Buddy Faro,* CBS, 1998.

Victor Pellet, *In–Laws,* 2002–2003.

Detective Joe Fontana, *Law & Order,* NBC, 2004–2006.

Television Appearances; Miniseries:

Kevin Kelly, *Blind Faith,* NBC, 1990.

Elias Renthal, *People Like Us,* NBC, 1990.

Tom Brereton, *Cruel Doubt,* NBC, 1992.

Mike Cerone, *Drug Wars: The Cocaine Cartel* (also known as *The Drug Wars: Columbia*), NBC, 1992.

Don Roberto Luciano, *Bella Mafia,* CBS, 1997.

Walt Comeau, *Empire Falls,* HBO, 2005.

Television Appearances; Movies:

Patrolman, *Through Naked Eyes,* ABC, 1983.

Hard Knox, NBC, 1984.

The Impostor, ABC, 1984.

Second policeman, *Final Jeopardy,* NBC, 1985.

Veteran cop Ernie, *Triplecross,* 1985.

The Birthday Boy, 1986.

Robert Stroud, Birdman of Alcatraz, *Six Against the Rock,* NBC, 1987.

Pete Carlson, *Open Admissions,* CBS, 1988.

Angelo Buono, *The Case of the Hillside Stranglers* (also known as *The Hillside Stranglers*), NBC, 1989.

Denton, *The Disappearance of Nora* (also known as *Deadly Recall*), CBS, 1993.

Sidney Sheldon *"A Stranger in the Mirror"* (also known as *A Stranger in the Mirror*), 1993.

Detective Harry Lindstrom, *The Corpse Had a Familiar Face,* CBS, 1994.

Craig McKenna, *One Woman's Courage,* NBC, 1994.

Charley Siringo, *Bonanza: Under Attack,* NBC, 1995.

Charlie Ingle, *Out of Annie's Past,* USA Network, 1995.

Television Appearances; Pilots:

Lieutenant Mike Torello, *Crime Story,* NBC, 1986.

William Kazan, *Jack and Mike,* ABC, 1986.

Armand Zaro, "Murder in Triplicate," *Perfect Crimes,* CBS, 1991.

Television Appearances; Specials:

Harry Brennan, *The Killing Floor,* PBS, 1984.

The Italian Passion for Life, PBS, 1999.

The 1999 ALMA Awards, ABC, 1999.

Anatomy of a Scene: "Sidewalks of New York," Sundance Channel, 2001.

The 54th Annual Primetime Emmy Awards, 2002.

NBC's Funniest Out–Takes #2, NBC, 2003.

Narrator, *Wait 'Til Next Year: The Saga of the Chicago Cubs,* HBO, 2006.

And They Came to Chicago: The Italian American Legacy, 2007.

Television Appearances; Episodic:

(As Dennis G. Farina) Albert Lombard, "One Eyed Jack," *Miami Vice,* NBC, 1984.

Ed Coley, "Undercover McCormick," *Hardcastle and McCormick,* 1985.

Vic Terranova, "The Snow Queen: Parts 1 & 2," *Hunter,* 1985.

(As Dennis G. Farina) Albert Lombard, "Lombard," *Miami Vice,* 1985.

Supervisor, "The Killing Floor," *American Playhouse,* 1985.

Cop, "Steele Trying," *Remington Steele,* 1985.

Joe Kaufman, "Sylvie," *Lady Blue,* 1986.

Lieutenant Colonel Edward Edward Vincent, "All About E.E.V.," *China Beach,* ABC, 1988.

Albert Lombard, "World of Trouble," *Miami Vice,* 1989.

Antoine, "Werewolf Concerto," *Tales from the Crypt* (also known as *HBO's "Tales from the Crypt"*), HBO, 1992.

The Tonight Show Starring Johnny Carson, NBC, 1992.

The Rosie O'Donnell Show, syndicated, 1997, 2000, 2002.

"Filmen *Saving Private Ryan*/Nyheter och vader," *Nyhetsmorgon,* 1998.

The Late Late Show with Craig Kilborn, CBS, 2003, 2004.

Dinner for Five, Independent Film Channel, 2004.

Voice of Wildcat, "The Cat and the Canary," *Justice League* (animated; also known as *JL* and *Justice League Unlimited*), Cartoon Network, 2005.

Detective Joe Fontana, "Skeleton," *Law & Order: Trial by Jury,* NBC, 2005.

Unsolved Mysteries, 2008.

Television Work; Series:

Co–executive producer, *Buddy Faro,* CBS, 1998.

Stage Appearances:

The Time of Your Life, Goodman Theatre, Chicago, IL, 1983.

Cokes, *Streamers,* Steppenwolf Theatre, Chicago, then John F. Kennedy Center for the Performing Arts, Washington, DC, 1985.

Also appeared in *Some Men Need Help; A Class C Trial in Yokohama; A Prayer for My Daughter,* Steppenwolf Theatre, Chicago, IL; *Tracers,* Steppenwolf Theatre; *Bleacher Bums,* Organic Theatre, Chicago, IL; *Heat,* Organic Theatre.

OTHER SOURCES

Periodicals:
Chicago Tribune, October 3, 1998, p. 27; August 12, 2005.
Entertainment Weekly, October 27, 1995, p. 65.
People Weekly, September 18, 1995, p. 244.

FAW, Bob

PERSONAL

Native of Salisbury, MD. *Education:* Davidson College, B.A.; London School of Economics and Political Science, London, M.Sc., 1968.

Addresses: *Office*—c/o NBC News, 30 Rockefeller Plaza, New York, NY 10112.

Career: Broadcast journalist and correspondent. KING–TV, Seattle, WA, general assignment reporter and news anchor, 1969–70; WNAC–TV, Boston, MA, general assignment reporter and news producer, 1970–71; WBBM–TV, Chicago, IL, broadcast journalist, 1971–77; CBS News, national reporter based in Chicago, 1977–84, and New York City, 1984–94, including reports that were aired on the program *48 Hours;* NBC News, New York City, national correspondent from Washington, DC, 1994—.

Awards, Honors: Local Emmy Awards, 1973, for a report on fraud in the pet industry, and 1976, for a report on a subway collision; Overseas Press Club Award, 1982, for report on conflict between Israel and Lebanon; Emmy Awards, 1984, for coverage of Jesse Jackson political campaign, 1986, for news series on racism, and 1988, for a report on *48 Hours;* honorary doctorate, Western Maryland College, 1999; Overseas Press Club Award and Emmy Award, both 2000, for news report on Mozambique; also received awards from American Political Science Association, Illinois State Medical Society, Sigma Delta Chi, and other organizations.

CREDITS

Television Appearances; Series:
Correspondent and commentator, *NBC Nightly News,* NBC, 1994—.

Television Appearances; Specials:
Regional correspondent for the Midwest, *Campaign '86: Election Night,* CBS, 1986.
Correspondent, *48 Hours on Crack Street,* CBS, 1986.
Correspondent, *Eye on the Earth,* CBS, 1992.
Correspondent, *Decision '96: The Republican National Convention,* NBC, 1996.
Correspondent, *Decision '96: The Democratic National Convention,* NBC, 1996.

WRITINGS

Books:
(With Nancy Skelton) *Thunder in America: The Improbable Presidential Campaign of Jesse Jackson,* Texas Monthly Press, 1986.

OTHER SOURCES

Electronic:
MSNBC Online, http://www.msnbc.msn.com/, July 26, 2005.

FEDERLINE, Kevin 1978–

PERSONAL

Also known as "K–Fed"; full name, Kevin Earl Federline; born March 21, 1978, in Fresno, CA; son of Mike (a mechanic) and Julie (a bank teller) Federline; married Britney Spears (a singer and recording artist), September 18, 2004 (divorced, 2007); children: (with actress Shar Jackson) Kori Madison, Kaleb Michael; (with Spears) Sean Preston, Jayden James.

Addresses: *Manager*—Dan Dymtrow, DMand Entertainment, 2425 Olympic Blvd., Suite 520E, Santa Monica, CA 90404; (voice work and commercials) Nina Nisenholtz, N2N Entertainment, 1230 Montana Ave., Suite 203, Santa Monica, CA 90403.

Career: Singer, dancer, recording artist, and actor. Toured as a backup dancer with Pink and other performers. Appeared in commercials for Nationwide insurance, Target department stores, and other clients; model for Five Star Vintage clothing. Formerly worked at various odd jobs.

Awards, Honors: Teen Choice Award nomination, choice male television reality or variety star, 2005, for *Britney & Kevin: Chaotic.*

CREDITS

Television Appearances; Miniseries:
Britney & Kevin: Chaotic, UPN, 2005.

Television Appearances; Specials:
InStyle Celebrity Weddings, ABC, 2005.
(In archive footage) *Britney and Kevin: The E! True Hollywood Story,* E! Entertainment Television, 2005.
(Uncredited; in archive footage) *Stars on Trial,* Much-Music, 2005.
WWE Cyber Sunday, 2006.
(In archive footage) *Al TV,* VH1, 2006.
(In archive footage) *Overrated in '06,* MuchMusic, 2006.
(In archive footage) *The Most Annoying People of 2006,* BBC3, 2006.
Britney: Off the Rails, Channel 4, 2007.

Television Appearances; Episodic:
Dirt track dancer, "Home Sweet Homeless," *Nikki,* The WB, 2001.
"Uneasy Rider," *Nikki,* The WB, 2002.
(Uncredited) Party host (in archive footage), *Video on Trial* (also known as *V.O.T.*), MuchMusic, 2005.
(In archive footage) *Exclusiv—Das Star–Magazin,* 2006.
Cole "Pig" Tritt, "Fannysmackin'," *CSI: Crime Scene Investigation* (also known as *C.S.I., CSI: Las Vegas,* and *Les experts*), CBS, 2006.
Himself as mob member, *1 vs. 100,* NBC, 2006.
WWF Raw Is War (also known as *Raw Is War, WWE Monday, WWE Raw,* and *WWF Raw*), USA Network, multiple appearances, 2006–2007.
Entertainment Tonight (also known as *Entertainment This Week, E.T., ET Weekend,* and *This Week in Entertainment*), syndicated, multiple appearances, between 2006 and 2008.
So You Think You Can Dance, Fox, 2007.
Accused, *Video on Trial* (also known as *V.O.T.*), Much-Music, 2007.
Jason, "My Way Home Is Through You," *One Tree Hill,* CW Network, 2008.
Jason, "Its Alright Ma (I'm Only Bleeding)," *One Tree Hill,* CW Network, 2008.
Jason, "In da Club," *One Tree Hill,* CW Network, 2008.
(In archive footage) *The O'Reilly Factor,* Fox News Channel, 2008.
(Uncredited; in archive footage) "Child Stars: Where Are They Now?," *20 to 1,* Nine Network, 2008.

According to some sources, performed voice of Karl Rove for *Lil' Bush: Resident of the United States* (animated), Comedy Central.

Television Guest Appearances; Episodic:
Late Show with David Letterman (also known as *The Late Show, Late Show Backstage,* and *Letterman*), CBS, 2005.

Ellen: The Ellen DeGeneres Show, syndicated, 2005, 2006.
The Tonight Show with Jay Leno, NBC, 2006.
The Tyra Banks Show, UPN, 2006.
CD USA, DirecTV, 2006.
The Megan Mullally Show, syndicated, 2006.

Television Appearances; Awards Presentations:
Presenter, *MTV Video Music Awards,* MTV, 2006.
The Teen Choice Awards 2006, Fox, 2006.

Television Work; Miniseries:
Executive producer (with others) and photographer, *Britney & Kevin: Chaotic,* UPN, 2005.

Film Appearances:
Dancer, *You Got Served,* Screen Gems, 2004.
Dancer, *The Onion Movie* (also known as *News Movie*), Fox Searchlight, 2008.

RECORDINGS

Albums:
Playing with Fire, Reincarnate, 2006.

Singles include "Y'all Ain't Ready," 2005, "Popo Zao," 2006, and "Lose Control," 2006.

Videos:
Groom, "My Prerogative," *Britney Spears: Greatest Hits—My Prerogative,* BMG Distribution, 2004.

Appeared in the music videos "My Prerogative" by Britney Spears and "Port and Beans" by Weezer; dancer in the music video "Let's Get the Party Started" by Pink.

OTHER SOURCES

Periodicals:
Interview, February, 2008, p. 112.
Newsweek, February, 2008, p. 112.
People Weekly, April 18, 2005, p. 21; September 10, 2007, p. 84; January 28, 2008, p. 87.
USA Today, February 10, 2005, p. 3D; July 20, 2006, p. 3D; October 31, 2006, p. 4D.

FERRER, Mel 1917–2008
   (Melchior Gasto Ferrer, Melchior Gaston Ferrer, Melchor Gaston Ferrer)

PERSONAL

Full name, Melchor Gaston Ferrer; born August 25, 1917, in Elberon, NJ; died June 2, 2008, in Santa Barbara, CA. Darkly handsome with stunning features,

Ferrer had a commanding film presence. His most notable cinematic achievements were often intertwined with those of his third wife, acting legend Audrey Hepburn.

The son of a Cuban-born surgeon and a Manhattan socialite, Ferrer began working in summer stock at the age of fifteen and later attended Princeton University, where he won a playwright's award during his sophomore year. Ferrer left Princeton after two years and spent time as a writer and editor. Ferrer made his screen acting debut in *Lost Boundaries* in 1949, portraying a light-skinned African American doctor who is able to pass for being white. A role as a heroic matador torn by inner doubts in *The Brave Bulls* in 1951 made Ferrer a star. Ferrer achieved his greatest critical success as an actor in 1953 with the role of a lame carnival puppeteer in *Lili*.

Ferrer starred opposite Hepburn as Prince Andrei in *War and Peace* in 1956, in the Broadway play *Ondine*, also in 1956, and in the television version of *Mayerling*. Ferrer directed Hepburn in the hit film *Green Mansions* in 1959 and was producer of one of Hepburn's greatest triumphs, *Wait Until Dark*, in 1967. Ferrer and Hepburn were married from 1954 to 1968; Ferrer would ultimately be married four times. Ferrer would also star alongside John Wayne and Richard Attenborough in the 1975 film *Brannigan* and in *Lili Marleen* in 1981, in which Ferrer portrayed a Swiss businessman who helps rescue Jews from Nazis. One of Ferrer's more popular later works was his portrayal of lawyer Phillip Erickson on television's *Falcon Crest* from 1981 until 1984. Ferrer officially retired from acting on his 80th birthday in 1997.

PERIODICALS

Chicago Tribune, June 4, 2008.
Variety, June 9, 2008.
New York Times, June 4, 2008.

FERRETTI, Dante 1943–

PERSONAL

Born February 26, 1943, in Macerata, Macerata, Marche, Italy; married Francesca Lo Schiavo (a production designer and set decorator); children: Edoardo (an assistant director and production assistant). *Education:* Earned a degree in architecture; also studied fine arts.

Addresses: *Manager*—Marsh, Best & Associates, 9150 Wilshire Blvd., Suite 220, Beverly Hills, CA 90212; Casarotto Marsh, Ltd., Waverly House, 7–12 Noel St., London W1F 7GQ, England.

Career: Production designer, art director, set decorator and designer, and costume designer.

Member: Art Directors Guild.

Awards, Honors: Silver Ribbon, best production design (migliore scenografia), Italian National Syndicate of Film Journalists, 1980, for *La citta delle donne;* Premi David di Donatello, best production design (migliore scenografo), Accademia del Cinema Italiano, 1983, for *La nuit de Varennes;* Premi David di Donatello, best production design (migliore scenografo), and Silver Ribbon, best production design (migliore scenografia), both 1984, for *E la nave va;* Silver Ribbon, best production design (migliore scenografia), 1986, for *Ginger e Fred;* Premi David di Donatello, best production design (migliore scenografo), Film Strip in Gold (with Rainer Schaper; also known as Film Award in Gold), outstanding individual achievement: production design, German Film awards, and Silver Ribbon, best production design (migliore scenografia), all 1987, for *The Name of the Rose;* Film Award, best production design, British Academy of Film and Television Arts, Silver Ribbon, best production design (migliore scenografia), and Academy Award nomination (with Francesca Lo Schiavo), best art direction–set decoration, all 1990, for *The Adventures of Baron Munchausen;* Premi David di Donatello, best production design (migliore scenografo), 1990, for *La voce della luna;* Academy Award nomination (with Lo Schiavo), best art direction–set direction, 1991, for *Hamlet;* Silver Ribbon, best production design (migliore scenografia), Academy Award nomination (with Robert J. Franco), best art direction–set direction, and Film Award nomination, best production design, British Academy of Film and Television Arts, all 1994, for *The Age of Innocence;* Film Award, best production design, British Academy of Film and Television Arts, Silver Ribbon, best production design (migliore scenografia), and Academy Award nomination (with Lo Schiavo), best art direction–set decoration, all 1995, for *Interview with the Vampire: The Vampire Chronicles;* Silver Ribbon, best production design (migliore scenografia), 1997, for *Casino;* Academy Award nominations, best art direction–set decoration (with Lo Schiavo), and best costume design, both 1998, for *Kundun;* Cinecitta Award, Premi David di Donatello, 1999; Silver Ribbon, best production design (migliore scenografia), 2000, for *Bringing out the Dead* and *Titus;* Golden Satellite Award nomination, best art direction, production design, International Press Academy, and Excellence in Production Design Award nomination (with others), feature film, Art Directors Guild, both 2000, for *Titus;* Los Angeles Film Critics Association Award, best production design, and Seattle Film Critics Award, best production design, both 2002, Golden Satellite Award, best art direction, Silver Ribbon, best production design (migliore scenografia), Academy Award nomination (with Lo Schiavo), best art direction–set decoration, Film Award nomination, best production design, British Academy of Film and Television Arts, Phoenix Film Critics Society Award nomination, best production design, and Excellence in Production Design Award nomination (with others), feature film—period or fantasy films, Art Directors Guild, all 2003, all for *Gangs of New York;* Outstanding Achievement Award, Los Angeles Italian Film awards, 2003; an exhibition of Ferretti's film design work was featured in the exhibit "Drawing Dreams: Dante Ferretti, Production Designer," at the Academy of Motion Pictures Arts and Sciences, Beverly Hills, CA, and an retrospective of his films was offered at the Los Angeles County Museum of Art, Los Angeles, both 2003; Achievement Award for Production Design, Palm Springs International Film Festival, 2004; Film Award nomination, best production design, British Academy of Film and Television Arts, 2004, for *Cold Mountain;* Los Angeles Film Critics Association Award, San Diego Film Critics Society Award, and Phoenix Film Critics Society Award, all best production design, 2004, Academy Award (with Lo Schiavo), best achievement in art direction, Film Award, best production design, British Academy of Film and Television Arts, Sierra Award, best art direction, Las Vegas Film Critics Society awards, Golden Satellite Award nomination (with Lo Schiavo), best art direction, production design, and Excellence in Production Design Award nomination (with others), feature film—period or fantasy film, Art Directors Guild, all 2005, and Special Silver Ribbon, 2006, all for *The Aviator;* Lifetime Achievement Award, outstanding achievement in production design, Camerimage, 2006; Behind the Camera Award, best production designer, 2006, and Silver Ribbon, best production design (migliore scenografia), 2007, both for *The Black Dahlia;* Hollywood Film Award, production designer of the year, Hollywood Film Festival, 2007; Washington, DC Area Film Critics Association Award, best art direction, San Diego Film Critics Society Award, best production design, and Phoenix Film Critics Society Award, best achievement in production design, all 2007, Academy Award (with Lo Schiavo), best achievement in art direction, 2008, and Excellence in Production Design Award nomination (with others), feature film—period film, Art Directors Guild, 2008, all for *Sweeney Todd: The Demon Barber of Fleet Street;* other awards and honors include multiple UBU awards, a special Leonardo Prize, and a Gold Band.

CREDITS

Film Production Designer:

Assistant production designer, *Il vangelo secondo Matteo* (also known as *The Gospel according to St. Matthew* and *L'evangile selon saint Matthieu*), Arco Films, 1964.
Assistant production designer, *Il campagno Don Camillo* (also known as *Don Camillo in Moscow, Don Camillo en Russie,* and *Genosse Don Camillo*), Francoriz Production/Rizzoli Film, 1965.

Assistant production designer, *Uccellacci e uccellini* (also known as *Hawks and Sparrows* and *The Hawks and the Sparrows*), 1966.
Assistant production designer, *Edipo re* (also known as *Oedipus Rex*), 1967.
Io non vedo, tu non parli, lui non sente, 1971.
La classe operaia va in paradiso (also known as *Lulu the Tool* and *The Working Class Goes to Heaven*), Euro–International Films, 1971.
I racconti di Canterbury (also known as *The Canterbury Tales*), United Artists, 1972.
Sbatti il mostro in prima pagina (also known as *Slap the Monster on Page One* and *Viol en premiere page*), 1973.
Storie scellerate (also known as *Bawdy Tales* and *Roguish Stories*), 1973.
Crime of Love, Documento Film, 1974.
Delitto d'amore (also known as *Somewhere beyond Love*), Documento Film, 1974.
Il fiore della mille e una notte (also known as *Arabian Nights, Flower of the Arabian Nights, A Thousand and One Nights,* and *Les mille et une nuits*), United Artists, 1974.
Mio Dio, come sono caduta in basso! (also known as *How Long Can You Fall?* and *Till Marriage Do Us Part*), 1974.
The Night Porter, Avco–Embassy, 1974.
Salo o le 120 giornate di Sodoma (also known as *Salo, or, the One Hundred Days of Sodom* and *Salo ou les 120 journees de Sodome*), Zebra, 1975.
Todo modo, [Italy], 1976.
Il casotto (also known as *Beach House, The Beach Hut, Casotto,* and *In the Beach House*), [Italy], 1977.
Il mostro, 1977.
La presidentessa, 1977.
Ciao maschio (also known as *Bye Bye Monkey* and *Reve de singe*), Fida, 1978.
Eutanasia di un amore (also known as *Break Up*), [Italy], 1978.
Il gatto (also known as *The Cat* and *Qui a tue le chat?*), Rafran Cinematografica, 1978.
Prova d'orchestra (also known as *Federico Fellini's "Orchestra Rehearsal"* and *Orchestra Rehearsal*), 1978, subtitled version released by New Yorker Films, 1979.
Il minestrone, [Italy], 1980.
La citta delle donne (also known as *City of Women*), 1980, subtitled versions released in 1981.
La pelle (also known as *The Skin* and *La peau*), Triumph Releasing/Columbia, 1981.
Storie di ordinaria follia (also known as *Tales of Ordinary Madness*), 1981, Fred Baker Films, 1983.
Oltre la porta (also known as *Behind the Door, Beyond Obsession, Beyond the Door, Jail Bird,* and *The Secret beyond the Door*), 1982.
La nuit de Varennes (also known as *That Night in Varennes, Il mondo nuovo,* and *La notte di Varennes*), Gaumont, 1982, cut version released by Triumph Releasing, 1983.
Desire (also known as *Desiderio*), Hemisphere, 1983.

E la nave va (also known as *And the Ship Sails On, E la nave va di Federico Fellini,* and *Et vogue le navire*), VIDES, 1983, subtitled version released by Triumph Releasing, 1984.

Il futuro e donna (also known as *The Future Is Woman*), 1984.

Le bon roi Dagobert (also known as *Dagobert*), Filmedis, 1984.

Pianoforte, [Italy], 1984.

Ginger e Fred (also known as *Federcio Fellini's "Ginger & Fred"* and *Ginger and Fred*), Metro–Goldwyn–Mayer/United Artists, 1986.

(With Rainer Schaper) *The Name of the Rose* (also known as *Der Name der Rose, Il nome della rosa,* and *Le nom de la rose*), Twentieth Century–Fox, 1986.

(With Francesca Lo Schiavo) *The Adventures of Baron Munchausen* (also known as *Die Abenteuer des Baron von Muenchhausen*), TriStar, 1989.

La voce della luna (also known as *The Voice of the Moon*), Cecchi Gori, 1989.

(With Lo Schiavo) *Lo zio indegno* (also known as *The Sleazy Uncle*), [Italy], 1989, Quartet Films, 1991.

(With Wolfgang Hundhammer) *Dr. M* (also known as *Club Extinction* and *Docteur M.*), Prism Entertainment, 1990.

Hamlet, Warner Bros., 1990.

(With Robert J. Franco) *The Age of Innocence,* Columbia, 1993.

(With Lo Schiavo) *Interview with the Vampire: The Vampire Chronicles* (also known as *Interview with the Vampire*), Warner Bros., 1994.

Casino, Universal, 1995.

(With Lo Schiavo) *Kundun,* Buena Vista, 1997.

Meet Joe Black (also known as *Death Takes a Vacation*), Universal, 1998.

Bringing out the Dead, Paramount, 1999.

Titus (also known as *Titus Andronicus*), Overseas Film-Group, 1999.

Gangs of New York, Miramax, 2002.

Cold Mountain, Miramax, 2003.

The Aviator (also known as *Aviator*), Miramax, 2004.

The Fine Art of Love: Mine Ha–Ha (also known as *The Grooming, Laughing Water (Mine Ha–Ha),* and *L'educazione fisica delle fanciulle*), 2005.

The Black Dahlia (also known as *Black Dahlia* and *Die Schwarze Dahlie*), Universal, 2006.

Sweeney Todd: The Demon Barber of Fleet Street (musical; also known as *Sweeney Todd*), Warner Bros., 2007.

Shutter Island, Paramount, 2009.

Film Art Director:

Assistant art director, *Lo sbarco di Anzio* (also known as *Anzio* and *The Battle for Anzio*), Columbia, 1968.

Assistant art director, *Meglio vedova* (also known as *Better a Widow*), 1968.

(Uncredited) Assistant art director, *Fellini—Satyricon* (also known as *The Degenerates, Fellini Satyricon, Fellinis Satyricon,* and *Satyricon*), 1969, subtitled version released by United Artists, 1970.

(With Nichola Tamburro) *Medea* (also known as *Medee*), 1969, New Line Cinema, 1971.

Il Decameron (also known as *Decameron, The Decameron, Decamerone,* and *Le Decameron*), United Artists, 1971.

Delitto d'amore (also known as *Somewhere beyond Love*), Documento Film, 1974.

Il fiore della mille e una notte (also known as *Arabian Nights, Flower of the Arabian Nights, A Thousand and One Nights,* and *Les mille et une nuits*), United Artists, 1974.

Mio Dio, come sono caduta in basso! (also known as *How Long Can You Fall?* and *Till Marriage Do Us Part*), 1974.

Salo o le 120 giornate di Sodoma (also known as *Salo, or, the One Hundred Days of Sodom* and *Salo ou les 120 journees de Sodome*), Zebra, 1975.

Storie di ordinaria follia (also known as *Tales of Ordinary Madness*), 1981, Fred Baker Films, 1983.

Oltre la porta (also known as *Behind the Door, Beyond Obsession, Beyond the Door, Jail Bird,* and *The Secret beyond the Door*), 1982.

Desire (also known as *Desiderio*), Hemisphere, 1983.

Film Set Decorator:

Gli imbroglioni (also known as *The Swindlers* and *Los mangantes*), 1963.

"La moglie bionda" segment, *Oggi, domani, dopodomani* (also known as *Kiss the Other Sheik* and *The Man, the Woman and the Money*), 1965.

El Greco, 1966, dubbed version released by Twentieth Century–Fox, 1967.

I bastardi (also known as *The Cats, Sons of Satan, Der Bastard,* and *Le batard*), 1968.

Medea (also known as *Medee*), 1969, New Line Cinema, 1971.

Film Costume Designer:

Mio Dio, come sono caduta in basso! (also known as *How Long Can You Fall?* and *Till Marriage Do Us Part*), 1974.

Kundun, Buena Vista, 1997.

Film Work; Other:

Assistant music arranger, *Il campagno Don Camillo* (also known as *Don Camillo in Moscow, Don Camillo en Russie,* and *Genosse Don Camillo*), Francoriz Production/Rizzoli Film, 1965.

Set designer, *Ginger e Fred* (also known as *Federcio Fellini's "Ginger & Fred"* and *Ginger and Fred*), Metro–Goldwyn–Mayer/United Artists, 1986.

Film Appearances; Documentaries:

(Uncredited) Himself, *Ciao, Federico!,* Carlotta Films/New Line Cinema, c. 1969.

Proprietaire, *Mora,* Tridis, 1982.

Himself, *La rosa dei nomi,* Movie Movie, 1987.

Himself, *A la recherche de Kundun avec Martin Scorsese* (also known as *In Search of Kundun with Martin Scorsese*), 1998, In Pictures, 1999.

Himself (chef decorateur), *Fellini: Je suis un grand menteur* (also known as *Federico Fellini: I'm a Big Liar, Fellini: I'm a Born Liar, I'm a Born Liar, Federico Fellini: Sono un gran bugiardo,* and *Fellini: Sono un gran bugiardo*), 2002.

Television Production Designer; Miniseries:

Il segreto del Sahara (also known as *The Secret of the Sahara*), various channels in various countries, 1987.

Television Production Designer; Specials; Operas:

La traviata, Radiotelevisione Italiana, 1992.
Cavalleria rusticana, Radiotelevisione Italiana, 1996.
Manon Lescaut, Radiotelevisione Italiana, c. 1998.
Un ballo in maschera, Radiotelevisione Italiana, 2001.
Il trovatore, BBC, 2002.

Television Appearances; Awards Presentations:

The 77th Annual Academy Awards, ABC, 2005.
The 80th Annual Academy Awards, ABC, 2008.

Television Appearances; Episodic:

Himself, "Sweeney Todd: The Demon Barber of Fleet Street," *HBO First Look,* HBO, 2008.

Stage Designer; Operas:

La fanciulla del west, Teatro Colon, Buenos Aires, Argentina, 1986.
La traviata, La Scala, Milan, Italy, 1992, 2001.
Cavalleria rusticana, Ravenna Festival, Ravenna, Italy, 1996, and Teatro Comunale di Bologna, Italy.
Manon Lescaut, La Scala, 1998.
Un ballo in maschera, La Scala, 2001.
Il trovatore, Royal Opera House, London, Covent Garden, 2002.
La Boheme, Opera Nationale de Paris, Opera Bastille, Paris, 2005.
Carmen, Macerata Opera Festival, Arena Sferisterio, Macerata, Italy, 2008.
The Fly, LA Opera, Dorothy Chandler Pavilion, Los Angeles, 2008.

Stage designer for the opera *Tosca,* Buenos Aires, Argentina; designer for operas produced at various venues, including productions in Florence, Rome, and Turin, Italy.

RECORDINGS

Videos:

Himself, *Climbing "Cold Mountain,"* 2004.
Himself, *Casino: The Look,* 2005.

Himself, *The Madness and Misadventures of Munchhausen,* 2008.

WRITINGS

Nonfiction:

(Featured in interview in book) Peter Ettedgui, *Production Design & Art Direction,* Screencraft Series, RotoVision, c. 1999.

OTHER SOURCES

Periodicals:

Insight on the News, May 1, 1995, p. 26.
MovieMaker, February 9, 2003.
TCI, February, 1995, pp. 28–31.

FISCHER, Jenna 1974–
(Jenna Fisher)

PERSONAL

Original name, Regina Marie Fischer; born March 7, 1974, in Fort Wayne, IN; daughter of Jim (an engineer) and Anne (an acting teacher) Fischer; married James Gunn (a writer and director), October 7, 2000 (divorced, 2008). *Education:* Truman State University, B.A. *Avocational Interests:* Cartooning.

Addresses: *Agent*—Endeavor, 9601 Wilshire Blvd., 3rd Floor, Beverly Hills, CA 90210. *Manager*—Naomi Odenkirk, Odenkirk Talent Management, 650 North Bronson Ave., Building B145, Los Angeles, CA 90004. *Publicist*—Lewis Kay, Bragman/Nyman/Cafarelli, Pacific Design Center, 8th Floor, 8687 Melrose Ave., Los Angeles, CA 90069.

Career: Actress. Appeared in commercials. Worker as a receptionist and temporary office worker. Volunteer with Kitten Rescue.

Awards, Honors: Emerging Actor Award, Screen Actors Guild, and Tromadance Independent Soul Award, American Film Market, both 2006, for *Lollilove;* Emmy Award nomination, outstanding supporting actress in a comedy series, 2007, and Screen Actors Guild Award (with others), outstanding ensemble in a comedy, 2007, 2008, all for *The Office.*

CREDITS

Television Appearances; Series:

Pam Beesly, *The Office* (also known as *The Office: US Version*), NBC, 2005–2008.

Television Appearances; Pilots:
Rubbing Charlie, CBS, 2003.
Pam Beesly, *The Office* (also known as *The Office: US Version*), NBC, 2005.

Television Appearances; Movies:
Whisper, *Employee of the Month,* Showtime, 2004.

Television Appearances; Specials:
Reel Comedy: Walk Hard, Comedy Central, 2007.
Presenter, *Movies Rock,* CBS, 2007.
Live from the Red Carpet: The ... Screen Actors Guild Awards, E! Entertainment Television, 2007, 2008.
Live from the Red Carpet: The 2008 Emmy Awards, E! Entertainment Television, 2008.

Television Appearances; Episodic:
Waitress, "A Shot in the Dark: Part 2," *Spin City,* ABC, 2001.
Sorority girl, "Prototype," *Undeclared,* Fox, 2001.
Betty, "Sick in the Head," *Undeclared,* Fox, 2001.
Melanie, "The Backup," *Off Centre,* The WB, 2002.
Kim, "Copy That," *What I Like About You,* The WB, 2002.
Camille Freemont, "Maternal Mirrors," *Strong Medicine,* Lifetime, 2003.
Connie, "Kate in Ex–tasy," *Miss Match,* NBC, 2003.
Dottie in 1943, "Factory Girls," *Cold Case,* CBS, 2004.
Stacy Wanamaker, "Don't Lie to Me," *That '70s Show,* Fox, 2005.
Sharon Kinney, "A Coat of White Primer," *Six Feet Under,* HBO, 2005.
Sharon Kinney, "Dancing for Me," *Six Feet Under,* HBO, 2005.
"Tournament 8, Game 4," *Celebrity Poker Showdown,* Bravo, 2006.
"Breaking News," *Studio 60 on the Sunset Strip* (also known as *Studio 60*), NBC, 2007.
(Uncredited) Pam Beesly (in archive footage), "The Office," *Comedy Connections,* BBC, 2007.

Television Guest Appearances; Episodic:
Last Call with Carson Daly, NBC, 2006.
The Tony Danza Show, syndicated, 2006.
Late Night with Conan O'Brien, NBC, 2006.
Late Show with David Letterman (also known as *The Late Show* and *Letterman*), CBS, 2006, 2008.
The Late Late Show with Craig Ferguson, CBS, 2006, 2008.
The Tonight Show with Jay Leno, NBC, multiple appearances, beginning 2006.
Live with Regis and Kelly, syndicated, 2007.
Entertainment Tonight (also known as *Entertainment This Week, E.T., ET Weekend,* and *This Week in Entertainment*), syndicated, 2007, 2008.

Television Appearances; Awards Presentations:
The WIN Awards 2006, Women's Image Network, 2006.
The 58th Annual Primetime Emmy Awards, NBC, 2006.
2008 Primetime Creative Arts Emmy Awards, 2008.

Television Appearances; Miniseries:
30 Even Scarier Movie Moments, Bravo, 2006.

Film Appearances:
Rane, *Channel 493,* 1998.
(As Jenna Fisher) Wendy Miller, *Born Champion,* 1998.
College girl, *The Specials,* Regent Entertainment, 2000.
First dog walker, *Picking Up Chicks with Harland Williams* (short film), IFILM, 2001.
Bitchy French girl, *Les Superficiales* (short film), Open Road Films, 2002.
Hostess, *Melvin Goes to Dinner,* Arrival Pictures, 2003.
Leslie, *The Women* (short film), 2004.
Jenna, *Lollilove,* 2004, Troma Entertainment, 2006.
First sorority girl, *Lucky 13,* Metro–Goldwyn–Mayer Home Entertainment, 2005.
(Uncredited) First woman, *The 40 Year Old Virgin,* Universal, 2005.
Shelby, *Slither* (also known as *Incisions*), Universal, 2006.
Katie Van Waldenberg, *Blades of Glory,* Paramount, 2007.
Michelle, *The Brothers Solomon,* TriStar, 2007.
Darlene Madison, *Walk Hard: The Dewey Cox Story* (also known as *Walk Hard* and *Walk Hard: American Cox, the Unbearably Long, Self–Indulgent Director's Cut*), Columbia, 2007.
Jen Stauber, *The Promotion,* Third Real Releasing, 2008.

Film Director:
Lollilove, 2004, Troma Entertainment, 2006.

RECORDINGS

Video Appearances:
Kelsey, *Doggie Tails, Vol. 1: Lucky's First Sleep–over,* Troma Entertainment, 2003.
Make Your Own Damn Movie!, Troma Entertainment, 2005.
The Making of "Lollilove," Troma Team Video, 2006.
The King of Cult: Lloyd Kaufman's Video Diary (also known as *"Slither"–ing through Hollywood, "Slither"–ing through Hollywood Uncut,* and *"Slither"–ing through Tinseltown*), Troma Team Video, 2006.
Herself and Katie Van Waldenberg, *The Making of "Blades of Glory,"* Paramount Home Video, 2007.

Appeared in the music video "Through Any Window" by Willie Wisely.

Video Work:
(Uncredited) Cinematographer, *The Making of "Lollilove,"* Troma Team Video, 2006.

WRITINGS

Screenplays:
Coauthor, *Lollilove* (also based on a story by Fischer), 2004, Troma Entertainment, 2006.

OTHER SOURCES

Periodicals:
Entertainment Weekly, October 20, 2006, pp. 40–42.
Hollywood Reporter, February 21, 2001, pp. 10, 35.
Interview, April, 2007, p. 84.
Los Angeles Times, August 29, 2003.
Parade, December 9, 2007, p. 26.
People Weekly, March 13, 2006, p. 124.
TV Guide, March 6, 2004, pp. 36–38.

FLEX
    See ALEXANDER, Flex

FRATANGELO, Dawn 1960–

PERSONAL

Full name, Dawn Marie Fratangelo; born June 5, 1960, in Savannah, NY; married second husband, Eric Wishnie (a television news producer), October 11, 1997 (died, 2007); children: (second marriage) three. *Education:* State University of New York College at Plattsburgh, graduated.

Addresses: *Office*—c/o NBC News, 30 Rockefeller Plaza, New York, NY 10112.

Career: Broadcast journalist and news anchor. WPTZ–TV, Plattsburgh, NY, news anchor, 1983–85; KFMB–TV, San Diego, CA, reporter and news anchor, 1986; WCVB–TV, Boston, MA, weekend new anchor; WNBC–TV, New York City, reporter and news anchor, 1991–93; NBC News, New York City, correspondent from Chicago, IL, 1993–96, reporter, 1996, including reports for the cable network MSNBC.

Awards, Honors: Southern California Golden Mike Award, 1986, for reporting on an AeroMexico plane crash in California; Emmy Award, outstanding coverage, 1993, for reporting on flooding in the Midwest; Emmy Award nomination (with others), outstanding instant coverage of a news story, 1999, for reports on shooting at Columbine High School, *Dateline NBC;* Gracie Award, 2001, for reporting on World Trade Center attacks of September 11, 2001; Edward R. Murrow Award; honorary doctorate in journalism, St. Ambrose University.

CREDITS

Television Appearances; Series:
Anchor, *News 4 New York,* 1991–94.
Reporter and substitute anchor, *Today,* NBC, 1991–93.
Substitute anchor, *NBC News at Sunrise,* NBC, 1991–93.
Dateline NBC (also known as *Dateline*), NBC, 1996—.

Also reporter for *NBC Nightly News with Brian Williams,* NBC.

Television Appearances; Episodic:
Hardball with Chris Matthews, CNBC, 2006.

OTHER SOURCES

Electronic:
MSNBC Online, http://www.msnbc.msn.com/, January 2, 2007.

FRIEDMAN, Andrew

PERSONAL

Son of Elliot I. Friedman; married Cara DiPaolo (a writer), 2003.

Addresses: *Manager*—Odenkirk Talent Management, 650 N. Bronson Ave., Building B145, Los Angeles, CA 90004. *Agent*—Greene and Associates, 190 N. Canon Dr., Suite 200, Beverly Hills, CA 90210.

Career: Actor, producer, writer.

CREDITS

Television Appearances; Episodic:
Tuttle friend with glasses, "Grinding the Corn," *Six Feet Under,* HBO, 2004.

Emergency medical technician, "My Last Chance," *Scrubs,* NBC, 2004.

George, "A Fan for All Seasons," *Stacked,* Fox, 2005.

Charlie's uncle, "Charlie Got Molested," *It's Always Sunny in Philadelphia* (also known as *It's Always Sunny*), FX Channel, 2005.

Henry, a recurring role, *Twins,* The WB, 2005.

Captain Spic, *The Underground,* Showtime, 2006.

Photographer, "The World According to Garf," *Big Day,* ABC, 2006.

Photographer, "Skobo and Alice Hooked Up," *Big Day,* ABC, 2006.

Andy, "The New Boss," *10 Items or Less,* TBS, 2006.

Father O'Leary, "Troubled Times: Part 2–Murder & Deception," *Derek and Simon: The Show,* TBS, 2007.

Merl Berger, "The Anonymous Donor," *Curb Your Enthusiasm,* HBO, 2007.

City clerk, "The Game," *Dirty Sexy Money,* ABC, 2007.

Doctor Thompson, "Sonata in Three Parts," *Men in Trees,* ABC, 2008.

Doctor Thompson, "A Tale of Two Kidneys," *Men in Trees,* ABC, 2008.

Andy, "Star Trok," *10 Items or Less,* TBS, 2009.

Andy, "Eye Can See Clearly," *10 Items or Less,* TBS, 2009.

Television Appearances; Pilots:

Desk clerk, *Uncommon Sense,* NBC, 2005.

Alan, *Studio 60 on the Sunset Strip* (also known as *Studio 60*), NBC, 2006.

Television Appearances; Specials:

Killer, *Dinner Date 1,* 2002.

Killer, *Dinner Date 3,* 2002.

Television Appearances; Movies:

Burnout number one, *Since You've Been Gone* (also known as *10 Years Later*), ABC, 1998.

Television Producer; Specials:

Killer, *Dinner Date 1,* 2002.

Killer, *Dinner Date 3,* 2002.

Television Producer; Movies:

Guardians of the Book, 2001.

Film Appearances:

Soup for One, Warner Bros., 1982.

Sarah's Fantasy Player, 1996.

Lionel, *Lionel on a Sunday,* 1997.

Simon, *Guardians of the Book,* 2001.

Lee, *Another Flush,* 2003.

Pablo, *Terry Tate, Office Linebacker: Sensitivity Training,* Hypnotic, 2004.

Frank, *Office Court,* 2005.

Bed, Bath and Beyond shopper, *Bewitched,* Sony, 2005.

Tom, *Closing Escrow,* Magnolia, 2007.

Casper, *Live Free or Die Hard* (also known as *Die Hard 4.0* and *Die Hard 4: Live Free or Die Hard*), Twentieth Century–Fox, 2007.

Nervous dad, *The Brothers Solomon,* Screen Gems, 2007.

Trevor Duncan, *Max Payne,* Twentieth Century–Fox, 2008.

WRITINGS

Television Specials:

Killer, *Dinner Date 1,* 2002.

Killer, *Dinner Date 3,* 2002.

G

GAREL, Saskia 1977–

PERSONAL

Born December 9, 1977, in Kingston, Jamaica.

Career: Actress and singer. Love & Sas (singing duo), performer and recording artist.

Awards, Honors: Two Juno Awards, best rhythm and blues recording, Canadian Academy of Recording Arts and Sciences, both for *Call My Name.*

CREDITS

Television Appearances; Series:
Singer, *Night Man,* syndicated, 1998–99.
Usher, *Spynet,* CBC, 2002.
Danielle, *One on One,* UPN, 2004–2006.

Television Appearances; Movies:
A reporter, *Mistrial,* HBO, 1996.
Judy, *A Tale of Two Bunnies* (also known as *The Price of Beauty*), ABC, 2000.

Television Appearances; Episodic:
Claire, "Deep Sleep," *Earth: Final Conflict* (also known as *EFC, Gene Roddenberry's "Earth: Final Conflict," Invasion planete Terre,* and *Mission Erde: Sie sind unter uns*), syndicated, 2002.
Gina Newcastle, "Eye of the Storm," *Tracker,* syndicated, 2002.
"Loyalty," *Platinum,* UPN, 2003.
Gina Dominic, "Remember When," *She Spies,* syndicated, 2004.

Jamie Rodrigue, "Bound and Gagged, Your Husband Was Snagged," *Wild Card* (also known as *Zoe Busiek: Wild Card*), Lifetime, 2004.

Stage Appearances:
Mimi Marquez, *Rent* (musical), Canadian production, 1998.
Nala as an adult, *The Lion King* (musical), Toronto, Ontario, Canada, 2000.

Appeared as Mercedes in *Up from the Downs,* Watts Village Theatre Company, Los Angeles.

RECORDINGS

Albums; Singer and Songwriter:
Recorded (with Love & Sas) *Call My Name, BMG,* and (solo album) *Movin' On.*

GIUNTOLI, Neil 1959–
(Neil Gray Giuntoli)

PERSONAL

Born December 20, 1959, in Chicago, IL.

Addresses: *Agent*—Mitchell K. Stubbs and Associates, 8675 West Washington Blvd., Suite 203, Culver City, CA 90232.

Career: Actor and writer.

CREDITS

Film Appearances:
Eddie Caputo, *Child's Play,* Metro–Goldwyn–Mayer, 1988.
Shorty, *Next of Kin,* Warner Bros., 1989.

Sergeant Jack Bocci, *Memphis Belle,* Warner Bros., 1990.

Scully, *The Borrower,* Cannon, 1991.

Snyder, *CrissCross* (also known as *Alone Together*), Metro–Goldwyn–Mayer, 1992.

Sammy, *Leather Jackets,* 1992.

Jigger, *The Shawshank Redemption,* Columbia, 1994.

Hellfire gunner, *Waterworld,* Universal, 1995.

Trailer park manager, *Up Close & Personal,* Buena Vista, 1996.

Title role, *Henry: Portrait of a Serial Killer, Part 2* (also known as *Henry: Portrait of a Serial Killer, Part 2—Mask of Sanity*), 1996, Margin Films, 1998.

The Wetonkawa Flash, Indican Pictures, 1999.

Mac, *Palmer's Pick Up,* Winchester Films, 1999.

Midwestern Myth, Players Workshop Productions, 2003.

Harry Grmusa, *Love Comes to the Executioner,* Velocity Home Entertainment, 2006.

Television Appearances; Series:

(As Neil Gray Giuntoli) Donny, a recurring role, *Wiseguy,* CBS, 1990.

Florus Workman, *The Jeff Foxworthy Show* (also known as *Somewhere in America*), NBC, 1996–97.

Television Appearances; Movies:

(As Neil Gray Giuntoli) Dutch Schultz, *The Revenge of Al Capone* (also known as *Capone*), NBC, 1989.

(As Neil Gray Giuntoli) Sam Scoggins, *A Killer Among Us,* NBC, 1990.

Goldstein, *Mission of the Shark: The Saga of the U.S.S. Indianapolis* (also known as *Mission of the Shark*), CBS, 1991.

(As Neil Gray Giuntoli) Jerrod, *Steel Justice,* NBC, 1992.

Ice Box, *Keys* (also known as *Keys to Her Past*), Lifetime, 1994.

The lawyer, *The '70s,* NBC, 2000.

Television Appearances; Pilots:

Officer Kupchek, *The Bakery,* CBS, 1990.

Television Appearances; Episodic:

(As Neil Gray Giuntoli) Walker, "Watchdogs," *Sable,* ABC, 1987.

(As Neil Gray Giuntoli) Mike, "The World: Part 2," *China Beach,* ABC, 1989.

(As Neil Gray Giuntoli) Frank, "Shelter Me," *Baywatch,* NBC, 1989.

Jack, "In Confidence," *Equal Justice,* 1991.

Judd Taylor, "The Assassination: Parts 1 & 2," *Matlock,* NBC, 1992.

(As Neil Gray Giuntoli) Billy Quintaine, "Showdown," *Tales from the Crypt,* HBO, 1992 (some sources cite "Showdown" as a segment of the pilot *Two–Fisted Tales,* Fox, 1991.

Digger Wade, *The Hat Squad,* CBS, 1992.

Private Ryder, "The Leap between the States—September 20, 1862," *Quantum Leap,* NBC, 1993.

Frank Jordan, "Everybody Lies," *Sirens,* ABC, 1993.

Lieutenant Jessup Rienhardt, "The Fear that Follows," *SeaQuest DSV* (also known as *SeaQuest 2032*), NBC, 1994.

Alan, "Luck of the Draw," *ER,* NBC, 1995.

Larry Maldoon, "Hello Goodbye," *Chicago Hope,* CBS, 1995.

Brody, "The Little Kicks," *Seinfeld,* NBC, 1996.

Michael Hayes, CBS, 1997.

Voice of Wheezie, "Texas City Twister," *King of the Hill* (animated), Fox, 1997.

Voice of second closer, "Hilloween," *King of the Hill* (animated), Fox, 1997.

Ross Cheswick, "Seminal Thinking," *NYPD Blue,* ABC, 1998.

Paramedic, "Dude Act like a Lady," *House Rules,* NBC, 1998.

Ralph Witton, "You Never Can Tell," *Ally McBeal,* Fox, 1998.

Detective Ryan, "Moment of Truth," *Sons of Thunder,* CBS, 1999.

Detective Ryan, "Daddy's Girl," *Sons of Thunder,* CBS, 1999.

Detective Ryan, "Underground," *Sons of Thunder,* CBS, 1999.

Detective Ryan, "Thunder by Your Side," *Sons of Thunder,* CBS, 1999.

Joey Boyle, "Philly Folly," *Philly,* ABC, 2001.

Vincent Drake, "Dead Ringer," *CSI: Crime Scene Investigation* (also known as *C.S.I., CSI: Las Vegas,* and *Les experts*), CBS, 2004.

Mark Stutz, "Recycling," *CSI: NY,* CBS, 2005.

First attendant, "Mr. Monk and the Election," *Monk,* USA Network, 2005.

Stage Appearances:

Title role, *Hizzoner,* Prop Theatre, Chicago, IL, 2006.

WRITINGS

Stage:

The Wannabe Wiseguy (workshop performance; also based on a story by Giuntoli and Gordon Clapp), Prop Theatre Group, Chicago, IL, 1999.

(Contributor) *The Farmington Armada,* Farmington, NM, 2002.

Hizzoner, Prop Theatre Group, 2006.

GLEASON, Joanna 1950–

PERSONAL

Original name, Joanna Hall; born June 2, 1950, in Toronto, Ontario, (some sources cite Winnipeg, Manitoba)

Canada; daughter of Monty (a television game show host and producer) and Marilyn Doreen (an actress, writer, and producer; maiden name, Plottel) Hall; sister of Sharon Hall (a writer and director) and Richard Hall (a writer and director); married Paul G. Gleason (an acting coach and director), 1975 (divorced, 1981); married Michael Bennahum (an investment banker and producer), 1984 (divorced, c. 1990); married Chris Sarandon (an actor and producer), 1994; children: (first marriage) Aaron David (a musician and bandleader); (third marriage) three stepchildren. *Education:* Attended University of California, Los Angeles; Occidental College, graduated, 1972.

Addresses: *Agent*—Innovative Artists Talent and Literary Agency, 1505 10th St., Santa Monica, CA 90401. *Manager*—Elin Flack, Elin Flack Management, 435 West 57th St., Suite 3M, New York, NY 10019; Vera Mihailovich, Forward Entertainment, 9255 Sunset Blvd., Suite 805, Los Angeles, CA 90069.

Career: Actress and director. Also teacher of acting classes and workshops.

Member: Actors' Equity Association.

Awards, Honors: *Theatre World* Award, 1977, for *I Love My Wife;* Clarence Derwent Award, Actors' Equity Association, 1985, and Drama Desk Award, outstanding featured actress in a play, both for *A Day in the Death of Joe Egg;* Drama Desk Award, outstanding featured actress in a play, 1986, for *It's Only a Play* and *Social Security;* Outer Critics Circle Award, best actress in a musical, Drama Desk Award, best featured actress in a musical, and Antoinette Perry Award, best featured actress in a musical, all 1988, all for *Into the Woods;* Antoinette Perry Award nomination and Drama Desk Award nomination, both outstanding featured actress in a musical, 2005, for *Dirty Rotten Scoundrels.*

CREDITS

Stage Appearances:
(Stage debut) *Promises, Promises,* Long Beach Opera Company, Long Beach, CA, then San Francisco Light Opera Company, San Francisco, CA, both 1972.
Hamlet, Mark Taper Forum, Los Angeles, 1974.
(Broadway debut) Monica, *I Love My Wife* (musical), Ethel Barrymore Theatre, 1977–79.
Hey, Look Me Over!, Avery Fisher Hall, Lincoln Center, New York City, 1981.
The Real Thing, Plymouth Theatre, New York City, 1983–85.
Jill, *A Hell of a Town,* GeVa Theatre, Rochester, NY, 1984, then Cheryl Crawford Theatre, Westside Arts Center (now Westside Theatre Upstairs), New York City, 1984.

Pam, *A Day in the Death of Joe Egg* (also known as *Joe Egg*), Roundabout Theatre, Haft Theatre, New York City, 1985, then Longacre Theatre, New York City, 1985.
Virginia Noyles, *It's Only a Play,* Manhattan Theatre Club Stage I, New York City, 1985.
Trudy Heyman, *Social Security,* Ethel Barrymore Theatre, 1986.
Baker's wife, *Into the Woods* (musical), Old Globe Theatre, San Diego, CA, 1987, then Martin Beck Theatre, New York City, 1987–88.
Melissa Gardner, *Love Letters,* Long Wharf Theatre, New Haven, CT, 1988, then Promenade Theatre, New York City, 1989.
Artie, *Eleemosynary,* Manhattan Theatre Club Stage II, New York City, 1989.
Nora Charles, *Nick & Nora* (musical), Marquis Theatre, New York City, 1991.
Pigeon sister, *The Odd Couple* (benefit), National Actors Theatre, Belasco Theatre, New York City, 1991.
Baker's wife, *Into the Woods* (benefit performance), Broadway Theatre, New York City, 1997.
Dr. Emma Brookner, *The Normal Heart,* Worth Street Theatre Company, Public Theatre, New York City, 2004.
Muriel Eubanks, *Dirty Rotten Scoundrels* (musical), Old Globe Theatre, then Imperial Theatre, New York City, 2005–2006.
The Cartells, 2006.
Alison, *Something You Did,* Primary Stages Theatre, New York City, 2008.
Happiness, Mitzi E. Newhouse Theatre, New York City, 2009.

Also appeared in a production of *Thorn & Bloom.*

Stage Work; Director:
A Letter from Ethel Kennedy, Manhattan Class Company Theater, New York City, 2002.

Also directed a production of *Call Waiting,* Tiffany Theatre.

Film Appearances:
Diana, *Heartburn,* Paramount, 1986.
Carol, *Hannah and Her Sisters,* Orion, 1987.
Wendy Stern, *Crimes and Misdemeanors,* Orion, 1989.
Assistant District Attorney Liz Kennedy, *FX2: The Deadly Art of Illusion* (also known as *F/X2*), Orion, 1991.
Adult Gertrude, *Mr. Holland's Opus,* Buena Vista, 1995.
Dirk's mother, *Boogie Nights,* New Line Cinema, 1997.
Shirley Dutton, *American Perfekt,* American Perfekt Productions, 1997.
Dr. Rona Harvey, *Let the Devil Wear Black,* Trimark Pictures, 1999.

Mrs. Kitty Donolly, *The Wedding Planner* (also known as *Wedding Planner–verliebt, verlobt, verplant*), Columbia, 2001.

Lois, *The Pleasure of Your Company* (also known as *The Next Girl I See* and *Wedding Daze*), Metro–Goldwyn–Mayer, 2006.

Sarah Graczyk, *The Girl in the Park,* Weinstein Company, 2007.

Therapist, *Sex and the City* (also known as *Sex and the City: The Movie*), Warner Bros., 2008.

Kitty and Aunt Sally, *My Sassy Girl,* Gold Circle Films, 2008.

Barbara Delacorte, *The Women,* Picturehouse, 2008.

Roberta, *The Rebound,* Film Department/Process Productions, 2009.

Broadway: The Next Generation (documentary), Second Act Productions, 2009.

Broadway: Beyond the Golden Age (documentary; also known as *B.G.A. 2* and *Broadway: The Golden Age Two*), Second Act Productions, 2009.

Television Appearances; Series:

Chain Reaction, NBC, 1980.

Nadine Berkus, a recurring role, *Love & War* (also known as *Love Is Hell*), CBS, 1992–95.

Joan Silver, *Temporarily Yours* (also known as *Temp Yours, Temp Mine*), CBS, 1997.

Voices of Maddy Platter and other characters, *King of the Hill* (animated), Fox, between 1997 and 2007.

Connie Randolph, *Bette!,* CBS, 2000–2001.

Attorney Jordan Kendall, a recurring role, *The West Wing,* NBC, 2001–2002.

Also appeared as host of *Personal Side.*

Television Appearances; Movies:

Marie Margulies, *The Boys* (also known as *The Guys*), ABC, 1991.

Irene, *For Richer, For Poorer* (also known as *Father, Son and the Mistress* and *Getting There*), HBO, 1992.

Annemarie, *Born Too Soon,* NBC, 1993.

Shirley, *For the Love of Aaron* (also known as *The Creature, the Kid, and Margaret*), CBS, 1994.

Maude, *Edie & Pen* (also known as *Desert Gamble*), HBO, 1997.

Armacost, *Road Ends* (also known as *Safe House*), Cinemax, 1997.

Silvia, *Fathers and Sons,* Showtime, 2005.

Television Appearances; Specials:

Jinx, "Life under Water," *American Playhouse,* PBS, 1989.

Baker's wife, "Into the Woods," *American Playhouse,* PBS, 1991.

Beverly Hills High, E! Entertainment Television, 1997.

"Monty Hall: Let's Make a Deal," *Biography,* Arts and Entertainment, 1999.

AFI's 100 Years ... 100 Passions, Channel 4, 2002.

Television Appearances; Pilots:

Geri Sanborn, *Why Us?,* NBC, 1981.

Jennifer Simpson, *Great Day,* CBS, 1983.

Kimberly Cleaver, *Still the Beaver* (also known as *The New Leave It to Beaver*), CBS, 1983.

Connie Randolph, *Bette!,* CBS, 2000.

Television Appearances; Miniseries:

Julia, "1974," *If These Walls Could Talk,* HBO, 1996.

Television Appearances; Episodic:

Morgan Winslow, "The New Kid," *Hello, Larry,* NBC, 1979.

Morgan Winslow, "Peer Pressure," *Hello, Larry,* NBC, 1979.

Morgan Winslow, "The Trip: Parts 1 & 2," *Diff'rent Strokes,* 1979.

Morgan Winslow, "Feudin' and Fussin': Parts 1 & 2," *Diff'rent Strokes,* 1979.

Morgan Winslow, "Thanksgiving Crossover: Parts 1 & 2," *Diff'rent Strokes,* 1979.

(Uncredited) Faith Crane, "What Price Glory?," *Bosom Buddies,* ABC, 1981.

Password Plus, NBC, 1981.

"The Activist," *Love, Sidney,* NBC, 1982.

LeAnne the stewardess, "Family," *Tracey Takes On ...,* HBO, 1996.

Leslie, "Inconstant Moon," *The Outer Limits* (also known as *The New Outer Limits*), Showtime and syndicated, 1996.

Iris, "The Match Game," *ER,* NBC, 1996.

Iris, "Fire in the Belly," *ER,* NBC, 1996.

Iris, "Take These Broken Wings," *ER,* NBC, 1996.

Mrs. Rabe, "Anatomy Lesson," *Perversions of Science,* HBO, 1997.

Eileen Borman, *Michael Hayes,* CBS, 1997.

Athena Gillington, "Petty Woman," *Murphy Brown,* CBS, 1997.

Voice of Della, "Generosity," *Adventures from the Book of Virtues* (animated), PBS, 1997.

"The Teacher," *George & Leo,* CBS, 1998.

Katherine Hawkins, "Age," *Tracey Takes On ...,* HBO, 1998.

Kim Clozzi, "The One Where Rachel Smokes," *Friends,* NBC, 1999.

Kim Clozzi, "The One with Ross' Teeth," *Friends,* NBC, 1999.

Charlotte, "What It Should Be and What It Is," *Oh Baby,* Lifetime, 2000.

Defense Attorney Henrietta Lightstone, "Vanished: Parts 1 & 2," *The Practice,* ABC, 2001.

"Every Dog Had His Day," *The Apprentice: Martha Stewart,* NBC, 2005.

Muriel Eubanks (in archive footage), *La mandragora,* TVE, 2005.

Television Appearances; Awards Presentations:
Presenter, *The 56th Annual Tony Awards,* CBS, 2002.
The 59th Annual Tony Awards, 2005.
Presenter, *The 60th Annual Tony Awards,* 2006.

Television Director; Episodic:
"Take Two Donuts and Call Me in the Morning," *The Louie Show,* CBS, 1996.
Oh Baby, Lifetime, 1998.

Also directed an episode of *Love & War* (also known as *Love Is Hell*), CBS.

GLENN, Scott 1941–

PERSONAL

Full name, Theodore Scott Glenn; born January 26, 1941, in Pittsburgh, PA; son of Theodore (a business executive) and Elizabeth (a homemaker) Glenn; married Carol Schwartz (an artist), September 10, 1968; children: Dakota Ann (an actress), Rio Elizabeth (an actress). *Education:* College of William and Mary, B.A., English; trained for the stage at the Actors Studio with Lee Strasberg, 1968. *Religion:* Jewish.

Addresses: *Agent*—International Creative Management, 10250 Constellation Way, 9th Floor, Los Angeles, CA 90067. *Manager*—Parseghian–Planco, 322 Eighth Ave., Suite 601, New York, NY 10001.

Career: Actor. Appeared in productions with La MaMa Experimental Theatre Club and in Seattle stage productions; narrated television commercials for the U.S. Navy, Siebel software, Ruby Tuesday restaurants, and Merrill Lynch investment firms; cohost of video for Universal Studios Hollywood *Backdraft* attraction. Previously worked as a reporter, mountain ranger, and bartender. *Military Service:* U.S. Marine Corps, c. early 1960s.

Member: Actors' Equity Association, Screen Actors Guild, American Federation of Television and Radio Artists, Academy of Motion Picture Arts and Sciences, Actors Studio (lifetime).

Awards, Honors: Drama Desk Award nomination, outstanding actor in a play, 1999, for *Killer Joe.*

CREDITS

Film Appearances:
Tad Jacks, *The Baby Maker,* National General, 1970.
Pursuit of Treasure, 1970.

Long John, *Angels Hard as They Come* (also known as *Angels, Angel Warriors, Angels as Hard as They Come,* and *Angels, Hell on Harleys*), New World, 1971.
Jimbang, *Hex* (also known as *The Shrieking, Charms,* and *Grasslands*), Twentieth Century–Fox, 1972.
Private Glenn Kelly, *Nashville,* Paramount, 1975.
Charlie Hunter, *Fighting Mad,* Twentieth Century–Fox, 1976.
Bill Lester, *She Came to the Valley* (also known as *Texas in Flames*), R.G.V. Pictures, 1977.
Captain Richard Colby, *Apocalypse Now* (also known as *Apocalypse Now Redux*), United Artists, 1979.
Newt, leader of Electric Haze Band, *More American Graffiti* (also known as *Purple Haze*), Universal, 1979.
Wes Hightower, *Urban Cowboy,* Paramount, 1980.
Bill Dalton, *Cattle Annie and Little Britches,* Universal, 1981 Rick Murphy, *The Challenge* (also known as *Equals* and *Swords of the Ninja*), Embassy, 1982.
Terry Tingloff, *Personal Best,* Warner Bros., 1982.
Alan Shepard, *The Right Stuff,* Warner Bros., 1983.
Glasken Trismegestus, *The Keep,* Paramount, 1983.
Joe Wade, *The River,* Universal, 1984.
John Haddad, *Wild Geese II,* Universal, 1985.
Emmett, *Silverado,* Columbia, 1985.
Creasy, *Man on Fire* (also known as *Absinthe* and *Un uomo sotto tiro*), TriStar, 1987.
Colonel Dexter Armstrong, *Off Limits* (also known as *Saigon* and *Saigon: Off Limits*), Twentieth Century–Fox, 1988.
Title role, *Verne Miller* (also known as *The Verne Miller Story* and *Gangland*), Alive, 1988.
Mac Sam, *Miss Firecracker,* Corsair, 1989.
Captain Bart Mancusco, *The Hunt for Red October,* Paramount, 1990.
Jack Crawford, *The Silence of the Lambs,* Orion, 1991.
John "Axe" Adcox, *Backdraft,* Universal, 1991.
H. D. "Shotgun" Dalton, *My Heroes Have Always Been Cowboys,* Samuel Goldwyn Company, 1991.
Himself, *The Player,* Fine Line, 1992.
William B. Rickman, *The Flight of the Dove* (also known as *The Spy Within*), New Horizons Home Video, 1995.
J. P. Stiles, *Tall Tale* (also known as *Tall Tale: The Unbelievable Adventure* and *Tall Tale: The Unbelievable Adventures of Pecos Bill*), Buena Vista, 1995.
Lloyd, *Reckless,* Samuel Goldwyn Company, 1995.
Tony Gartner, *Courage under Fire,* Twentieth Century–Fox, 1996.
Bradley, *Carla's Song* (also known as *La cancion de Carla*), Shadow Distribution, 1996.
Iggy, *Lesser Prophets* (also known as *The Last Bet*), Prophetable Pictures, 1997.
Bill Burton, *Absolute Power,* Sony Pictures Entertainment, 1997.
Senor Grem, *Larga distancia,* Vagabond Films, 1998.
Wynt Perkins, *Firestorm,* Twentieth Century–Fox, 1998.
Cole, *The Last Marshal,* 1999.

Father Moody, *The Virgin Suicides* (also known as *Sophia Coppala's "The Virgin Suicides"*), Paramount Classics, 1999.

Montgomery Wick, *Vertical Limit,* Columbia, 2000.

Roger, *Training Day,* Warner Bros., 2001.

Sergeant Robert Lee, *Buffalo Soldiers* (also known as *Army Go Home!* and *Buffalo Soldiers—Army Go Home!*), Miramax, 2001.

Jack Buggit, *The Shipping News,* Miramax, 2001.

Inside the Labyrinth: The Making of "The Silence of the Lambs" (documentary), Metro–Goldwyn–Mayer/United Artists, 2001.

Clayton Price, *Puerto Vallarta Squeeze,* Showcase Entertainment, 2004.

Voice of Charles Duke, *Magnificent Desolation: Walking on the Moon 3D,* IMAX, 2005.

Sinatra, *Journey to the End of the Night* (also known as *12 Horas ate o amanhecer*), First Look International, 2006.

Himself, *"Backdraft": Bringing Together the Team* (documentary short), Universal Studios, 2006.

Himself, *"Backdraft": The Explosive Stunts* (documentary short), Universal Studios, 2006.

Himself, *"Backdraft": Creating the Villain—The Fire* (documentary short), Universal Studios, 2006.

Steve Gruwell, *Freedom Writers,* Paramount, 2007.

Sheriff Foster, *Camille,* A–Mark Entertainment, 2007.

Ezra Kramer, *The Bourne Ultimatum* (also known as *Das Bourne ultimatum*), Universal, 2007.

Surfer, Dude, Anchor Bay Entertainment, 2008.

Robert Torrelson, *Nights in Rodanthe,* Warner Bros., 2008.

Donald Rumsfeld, *W.,* Lionsgate, 2008.

Also appeared in *Home Town; Two Telegrams.*

Film Work:
Stunts, *Backdraft,* 1991.

Television Appearances; Series:
Calvin Brenner, *The Edge of Night,* CBS, 1969.

Television Appearances; Miniseries:
Martin Darius/Peter Lake, *Gone But Not Forgotten* (also known as *Philip Margolin's "Gone But Not Forgotten"*), Lifetime, 2004.

Television Appearances; Movies:
James Reeger, *Gargoyles,* CBS, 1972.

Michael Boyle, *Countdown to Looking Glass,* HBO, 1984.

Willie Croft, *As Summers Die,* HBO, 1986.

Crawford, *Intrigue,* CBS, 1988.

Jesse Smith, *The Outside Woman,* CBS, 1989.

Henry, *Women and Men 2* (also known as *Women and Men 2: In Love There Are No Rules* and *The Art of Seduction*), HBO, 1991.

John Cain, *Shadowhunter,* Showtime, 1993.

Stephen Broderick, *Slaughter of the Innocents,* HBO, 1993.

Dan Vaughn, *Extreme Justice* (also known as *S.I.S. Extreme Justice*), HBO, 1993.

Gene Ralston, *Past Tense,* Showtime, 1994.

David Eckhart, *Night of the Running Man,* HBO, 1995.

Harry Hawkins, *Edie & Pen* (also known as *Desert Gamble*), HBO, 1996.

Sergeant Muldoon, *Naked City: A Killer Christmas,* Showtime, 1998.

Sergeant Muldoon, *Naked City: Justice with a Bullet,* Showtime, 1998.

Owen Quinn, "The Seventh Stream," *Hallmark Hall of Fame,* CBS, 2001.

Eli "Pappy" Chandler, *A Painted House* (also known as *John Grisham's "A Painted House"*), CBS, 2003.

Joe Johnson, *Homeland Security,* NBC, 2004.

Jack McCain, *Faith of My Fathers,* Arts and Entertainment, 2005.

Coach Earl "Red" Blaik, *Code Breakers,* ESPN, 2005.

Television Appearances; Specials:
Narrator, *Discoveries Underwater,* PBS, 1988.

Presenter, *The 21st Annual People's Choice Awards,* CBS, 1995.

Intimate Portrait: Mariel Hemingway, Lifetime, 1998.

Voice, *Ernest Hemingway: Wrestling with Life,* Arts and Entertainment, 1998.

Intimate Portrait: Connie Chung, Lifetime, 2000.

Narrator, *Extreme Alaska,* Discovery Channel, 2000.

Narrator, *Navy SEALS: Untold Stories,* The Learning Channel, 2000.

Narrator, *Failure Is Not an Option,* History Channel, 2003.

Narrator, *Beyond the Moon: Failure Is Not an Option 2,* 2005.

Hollywood's Greatest Villains, 2005.

Television Appearances; Episodic:
Harry, "The Perfect Hostess," *The Patty Duke Show,* 1965.

Waiter, "Cathy, the Rebel," *The Patty Duke Show,* 1965.

Hal Currin, "Wall of Silence," *Hawk,* 1966.

Nick, "The Outspoken Silence," *The Young Lawyers,* ABC, 1971.

Lonnie Burnett, "Escape," *Ironside* (also known as *The Raymond Burr Show*), 1971.

Mark Hall, "And Scream by the Light of the Moon, the Moon," *The Sixth Sense,* 1972.

(Uncredited) Forklift driver, "Seance," *Emergency!* (also known as *Emergencia* and *Emergency One*), NBC, 1973.

Lenox, "Another Shell Game," *Ironside* (also known as *The Raymond Burr Show*), NBC, 1973.

(Uncredited) "The Big Ripoff," *The Rockford Files* (also known as *Jim Rockford, Private Investigator*), 1974.

"Triad," *Khan!,* 1975.

Dave, "A Bite of the Apple," *Baretta,* 1975.
Narrator, *Discoveries Underwater,* PBS, 1988.
"Firestorm," *HBO First Look,* HBO, 1998.
Voice, *Mobile Suit Gundam* (animated), 1999.
The Howard Stern Radio Show, 1999.
"Surviving *Vertical Limit,*" *HBO First Look,* HBO, 2000.
"The Silence of the Lambs," *Page to Screen,* 2002.
The Daily Show (also known as *A Daily Show with Jon Stewart, Jon Stewart, The Daily Show with Jon Stewart,* and *The Daily Show with Jon Stewart Global Edition*), Comedy Central, 2003.
Narrator, "Seabiscuit," *The American Experience,* PBS, 2003.
Narrator, "Bataan Rescue," *The American Experience,* PBS, 2003.
Tavis Smiley, PBS, 2008.
Sheriff Rollins, "Mr. Monk Is On the Run: Parts 1 & 2," *Monk,* USA Network, 2008.

Also appeared as himself, "The Films of Jonathan Demme," *The Directors.*

Stage Appearances:
The Impossible Years, Playhouse Theatre, New York City, 1965.
Zoo Story, Cherry Lane Theatre, New York City, 1966.
Alice and Wonderland, Actors Studio Theatre, New York City, 1968.
Edmund, *Long Day's Journey into Night,* Actors Studio Theatre, 1968.
Larry, *Angelo's Wedding,* Circle Repertory Company, Circle Repertory Theatre, New York City, 1985.
Pale, *Burn This,* Plymouth Theatre, New York City, 1988.
Ray, *Dark Rapture,* Second Stage Theatre, New York City, 1996.
The Sad Lament of Pecos Bill on the Eve of Killing His Wife's Killer's Head/Action, Signature Theatre, New York City, 1997.
Killer Joe Cooper (title role), *Killer Joe,* Soho Theatre, New York City, 1998–99.
Finishing the Pictures, Goodman Theatre, Chicago, IL, 2004.

Also appeared as the title role, *Jack Street,* Perry Street Theatre, New York City; Smitty, *Fortune in Men's Eyes;* in *Collision Course,* Actors' Playhouse, New York City.

RECORDINGS

Music Videos:
Bob Seger's "American Storm," 1986.

OTHER SOURCES

Periodicals:
Back Stage East, May 31, 1996, p. 48.
Entertainment Weekly, August 11, 1995, p. 62.
Variety, February 2, 1998, p. 37.

GOLOMB, Cazzy

PERSONAL

Born in Honolulu, HI; father, an anthropologist. *Education:* Earned undergraduate degree in biotechnology; studied acting at Playhouse West.

Addresses: *Agent*—Media Artists Group, 6300 Wilshire Blvd., Suite 1470, Los Angeles, CA 90048; Osbrink Talent Agency, 4343 Lankershim Blvd., Suite 100, Universal City, CA 91602; Sports Unlimited, 1911 NW Upshur St., Suite B, Portland, OR 97209. *Manager*—Start Talent Management, 2901 West Coast Highway #200, Newport Beach, CA 92663.

Career: Actress. Previously worked at a biotech company in San Diego, CA.

CREDITS

Film Appearances:
Waitress/make–up artist, *Under the Gun,* 2004.
Elena, *That Game of Chess,* 2005.
Julia, *Spaghetti vs. Noodles* (short), 2005.
Natasha, *Fragments of Daniela,* Omni Media Distribution, 2006.
Tricia, *Agatha* (short), 2006.
Mindy's mother, *Cult,* Gabriel Film Group, 2007.
Angela, *Pastor Jones 4: Sisters in Spirit,* Lightyear Entertainment, 2007.
Avila, *Road Side Assistance,* 2008.
Audrey, *The Vampire's Dance,* 2008.
Deluvina, *The Hunter's Moon,* 2008.

Also appeared in *Jealous.*

Television Appearances; Episodic:
(Uncredited) Ice cream girl, "You're My Best Friend," *That '70s Show,* Fox, 2005.
Girl number two, "The Devil's Lube," *Two and a Half Men,* CBS, 2008.

OTHER SOURCES

Electronic:
Cazzy Golomb Website, http://www.cazzyg.com, January 14, 2009.

GORDON, Joel 1975–

PERSONAL

Born November 15, 1975, in Toronto, Canada.

Career: Actor, director, producer, cinematographer, and writer.

Awards, Honors: Audience Award, Toronto ReelWorld Film Festival, 2002, for *Superbob;* Gemini Award nomination (with Gabriela Schonbach and Michael Chechik), best sports program, Academy of Canadian Cinema and Televison, Leo Award (with Schonbach), best sports program or series, Motion Picture Arts and Sciences foundation of British Columbia, 2005, for "Wrestling with Destiny: The Life and Times of Daniel Igali," *Life and Times;* Leo Award (with Schonbach), best sports program or series, 2005, for *Life and Times;* Gemini Award nomination (with Richard Nielsen), best biography documentary program, 2007, for "Leading Man: The Life and Times of William Hutt," *Life and Times;* Gemini Award nomination, best performing arts program or series, Golden Sheaf Award (with Trey Anthony), documentary—arts/culture, Yorkton Short Film and Video Festival, 2008, for *Embracing Da Kink.*

CREDITS

Television Appearances; Movies:
Machine, *Gang in Blue,* Showtime, 1996.
David Mercer, *Blind Faith,* Showtime, 1998.
Curtis, *My Date with the President's Daughter,* 1998.
Young Terry, *Dangerous Evidence: The Lori Jackson Story,* 1999.
Love Songs, Showtime, 1999.
William, *Vendetta,* 1999.
Mr. Rock 'n' Roll: The Alan Freed Story (also known as *Mr. Rock and Roll* and *The Big Beat Heat*), NBC, 1999.
Hugo, *Changes: An Animorphs Movie,* Nickelodeon, 2000.
Livin' for Love: The Natalie Cole Story (also known as *The Natalie Cole Story*), 2000.
Party guest, *Sanctuary* (also known as *Nora Robert's "Sanctuary"*), 2001.
Petty Officer Third Class Terry Peel, *Danger Beneath the Sea,* 2001.
Shooting victim, *The Day Reagan Was Shot,* 2001.
Circumspect porter, *10,000 Black Men Named George,* 2002.

Television Appearances; Episodic:
"Smokescreen," *Katts and Dogs* (also known as *Rin Tin Tin: K–9 Cop*), CTV and Family Channel, 1990.
Billy, "The Tale of the Dream Machine," *Are You Afraid of the Dark?,* YTV and Nickelodeon, 1993.
Josh, "The Tale of the Long Ago Locket," *Are You Afraid of the Dark?,* YTV and Nickelodeon, 1994.
Marcus, "Flagrant Foul," *The New Ghostwriter Mysteries,* 1997.
Hugo, "Changes: Part 3," *Animorphs* (also known as *AniTV*), Nickelodeon, 2000.

Leap Years, Showtime, 2001.
Darwin, *This Is Wonderland,* CBC, 2004.
Reverend Reese, *The Line,* TMN, 2008.

Television Producer; Episodic:
"Wrestling with Destiny: The Life and Times of Daniel Igali," *Life and Times,* CBC, 2004.
"Leading Man: The Life and Times of William Hutt," *Life and Times,* CBC, 2006.

Television Producer; Specials:
Turning Pages: The Life and Literature of Margaret Atwood, Bravo, 2007.

Television Executive Producer; Specials:
Embracing Da Kink, Global, 2008.

Television Director; Episodic:
"Wrestling with Destiny: The Life and Times of Daniel Igali," *Life and Times,* CBC, 2004.
"Leading Man: The Life and Times of William Hutt," *Life and Times,* CBC, 2006.

Television Director; Specials:
Turning Pages: The Life and Literature of Margaret Atwood, Bravo, 2007.
Embracing Da Kink, Global, 2008.

Television Cinematographer; Special:
Embracing Da Kink, Global, 2008.

Television Cinematographer; Episodic:
"Wrestling with Destiny: The Life and Times of Daniel Igali," *Life and Times,* CBC, 2004.

Film Appearances:
Gameshow, *Jungleground,* Image Entertainment, 1995.
Youth at wall, *Rude,* A–Pix, 1995.
Machine, *Gang in Blue,* Evergreen, 1996.
Reggie, *Night of the Demons III* (also known as *Demon House, Demon Night, Night of the Demons 3* and *La Nuit des demons 3*), Republic, 1997.
David Mercer, *Blind Faith,* Evergreen, 1998.
Brian Winters, *This Is My Father* (also known as *L' Histoire de mon pere*), Sony, 1998.
Jesse in 1865, *Down in the Delta,* Miramax, 1998.
Jock on plane, *Urban Legends: Final Cut* (also known as *Legendes urbaines 2, Legends urbaines: la suite* and *Leyendas urbanas: corte final*), Sony, 2000.
Owen Green, *Max Payne,* Twentieth Century–Fox, 2008.

Film Director:
Red, White & Maple, 2001.
Superbob,.
E–Males, 2008.

Film Producer:
Red, White & Maple, 2001.

Film Executive Producer:
E–Males, 2008.

Stage Appearances:
Derek, *Heaven,* Canadian Stage Company, Toronto, Ontario, Canada, 2000.

WRITINGS

Screenplays:
E–Males, 2008.

Television Specials:
Turning Pages: The Life and Literature of Margaret Atwood, Bravo, 2007.
Embracing Da Kink, Global, 2008.

Television Episodes:
"Leading Man: The Life and Times of William Hutt," *Life and Times,* CBC, 2006.

Television Music; Specials:
Embracing Da Kink, Global, 2008.

GOULET, Robert 1933–2007

PERSONAL

Full name, Robert Gerard Goulet; born November 26, 1933, in Lawrence, MA; died of pulmonary fibrosis, October 30, 2007, in Los Angeles, CA. Actor and singer. Born in Lawrence, MA, the son of French-Canadian parents, Goulet began singing at family gatherings at age five but had a deep fear of singing in public. At age eleven Goulet was forced to sing at a church function. Upon hearing Goulet sing at the church, his father, who would die shortly after, told Goulet that God had given him a voice and he must sing. The family then moved to Edmonton, Alberta, and Goulet won a singing scholarship to attend the Royal Conservatory of Music in Toronto, Ontario. With his velvety baritone voice and matinee-idol looks, Goulet quickly became a television star in Canada while still in his late teens.

During the 1950s Goulet made dozens of appearances on television, radio, and the stage, ultimately becoming host of he CBC production of *General Electric's Showtime.* In 1960 Goulet landed the coveted role of Lancelot in the Broadway musical *Camelot* opposite Richard Burton and Julie Andrews; the role made him a marquee star. Goulet's success led to the recording of more than 60 albums as well as movies, television specials, concerts, and guest performances. He appeared seventeen times on *The Ed Sullivan Show* alone. In 1962 Goulet won a Grammy Award for best new artist and a Tony Award in 1968 for best actor in a musical for his performance in *Happy Time.* Between 1962 and 1970 Goulet had seventeen albums make the popular charts. Goulet's stage credits include *Dreamgirls, Little Women, The Fantastiks, Gentleman Prefer Blondes, The Man of La Mancha,* and *South Pacific.*

In 1970 Goulet gave up recording to concentrate on television, concerts, and, later, Broadway shows. In 1982 Goulet was named Las Vegas entertainer of the year. Goulet's film credits include *Beetlejuice* and *Scrooged* in 1988, *Naked Gun 2 1/2* in 1991, *Mr. Wrong* in 1996, and, as the voice of Wheezy, the Penguin in 1999's *Toy Story 2.* Goulet returned to Broadway to star in *Camelot,* this time as King Arthur, in 1993 and in *La Cage aux Folles* in 2005. During his career Goulet performed at the White House for three presidents and appeared in a command performance for Queen Elizabeth II.

PERIODICALS

USA Today, October 31, 2007.
Variety, November 5, 2007.

H

HAGAN, Sara 1984–

PERSONAL

Full name, Sara Margaret Hagan; born May 24, 1984, in Austin, TX; sister of Katie Hagan (an actress). *Avocational Interests:* Painting and photography.

Addresses: *Agent*—Coast to Coast Talent, Inc., 3350 Barham Blvd., Los Angeles, CA 90068. *Manager*—Evolution Entertainment, 901 North Highland Ave., Los Angeles, CA 90038.

Career: Actress. Appeared in television commercials, including Volkswagen Beetle automobile, AskJeeves website, and Cingular GoPhone.

Awards, Honors: YoungStar Award nomination (with others), best young ensemble cast—television, YoungStar Award nomination, best young actress/performance in a comedy television series, Young Artist Award nomination (with others), best performance in a television series—young ensemble, 2000, all for *Freaks and Geeks.*

CREDITS

Film Appearances:
Faith at age thirteen, *Faith,* American Film Institute, 1997.
Susan the awkward girl, *Architecture of Reassurance* (short), 1999.
Sarah, *Orange County,* Paramount, 2002.
Natalie, *Thunder Geniuses,* 2008.
Truvy, *Spring Breakdown,* Warner Bros., 2009.

Television Appearances; Series:
Millie Kentner, *Freaks and Geeks,* NBC, 1999–2000.

Amanda, *Buffy the Vampire Slayer* (also known as *BtVs, Buffy,* and *Buffy, the Vampire Slayer: The Series*), UPN, 2002–2003.

Television Appearances; Episodic:
Girlfriend number three, "Love's Illusions," *Ally McBeal,* Fox, 1999.
Panelist, *The List,* VH1, 1999.
Jordanna, "Eric Visits Again," *Undeclared,* Fox, 2001.
Melissa, "Chapter Thirty–Five," *Boston Public,* Fox, 2002.
Maggie Parsons, "Christenings," *Judging Amy,* CBS, 2004.
Devo Friedman, "Save Me," *Grey's Anatomy,* ABC, 2005.
Young Suzannah, "Sweet Dreams," *Medium,* NBC, 2005.
Patricia, "Drink the Cup," *Close to Home,* CBS, 2007.
Voice of Lola Ilama, "Save the Drama for Your Llama/ Hornbill & Ted's Bogus Journey," *My Gym Partner's a Monkey,* Cartoon Network, 2007.

HAMILTON, Scott 1958–

PERSONAL

Full name, Scott Scovell Hamilton; born August 28, 1958, in Toledo, OH; raised in Bowling Green, OH; adopted son of Ernest (a professor of biology) and Dorothy (a professor; maiden name, McIntosh) Hamilton; married Tracie Robinson, November 14, 2002; children: Aidan McIntosh, Maxx. *Education:* Attended Metropolitan State College, 1979. *Politics:* Republican.

Addresses: *Agent*—Harry Gold, TalentWorks, 3500 West Olive Ave., Suite 1400, Burbank, CA 91505. *Manager*—Larry Thompson, Larry A. Thompson Organization, 9663 Santa Monica Blvd., Suite 801, Beverly Hills, CA 90210.

Career: Professional ice skater, actor, broadcaster, and producer. Ice Capades National Arena Tour, skater, 1984–86; Scott Hamilton's Amateur Tour, skater, 1986–87; Stars on Ice (touring show; also known as Discover Stars on Ice), cofounder, 1986, performer, c. 1986–2001, producer, 1999–2002; also performed with Broadway on Ice, Festival on Ice, and numerous other groups. Chemocare.com (Internet Web site), founder, 2002; involved with many charitable organizations, including Adult and Pediatric AIDS Research, American Cancer Society, Big Brothers, Make a Wish Foundation, March of Dimes, Special Olympics, and Starlight Foundation.

Awards, Honors: Numerous figure skating awards, including four U.S. figure skating championships, 1981–84, four world figure skating championships, 1981–84, and Olympic gold medal, 1984; March of Dimes Achievement Award, 1984; named professional skater of the year, *American Skating World*, 1986; Jacques Favart Award, International Skating Union, 1988; inducted into World Figure Skating Hall of Fame and U.S. Olympic Hall of Fame, 1990; Spirit of Giving Award, U.S. Ice Skating Association, 1993; Ritter F. Shumway Award, U.S. Figure Skating Association, 1994; Scott Hamilton CARES Initiative was named in his honor by Cancer Alliance for Research, Education, and Survivorship, 1999; Emmy Award nomination (with others), outstanding special class special, 2005, for *An Evening with Scott Hamilton & Friends;* Friends of Scott Hamilton Foundation (to benefit children's hospitals) was named in his honor.

CREDITS

Television Appearances; Miniseries:
Figure skating analyst, *The 1992 Winter Olympics,* CBS, 1992.
Legends Championships, ESPN, 1996.
Commentator, *Olympic Winter Games XVIII* (also known as *Nagano 1998: XVIII Olympic Winter Games*), CBS, 1998.
Figure skating analyst, *2002 Olympic Winter Games* (also known as *Salt Lake City 2002: XIX Olympic Winter Games*), NBC, 2002.
Turin 2006: XX Olympic Winter Games (also known as *Torino 2006: XX Olympic Winter Games*), NBC, 2006.
17th Annual American Century Championship, NBC, 2006.

Television Appearances; Specials:
The 10th Annual Circus of the Stars, CBS, 1985.
Liberty Weekend, ABC, 1986.
The Calgary Olympic Holiday Special, ABC, 1987.
A Very Special Christmas Party, ABC, 1988.
Host, *Salute to Dorothy Hamill,* HBO, 1988.

Judge, *Miss Teen USA* (also known as *The 1988 Miss Teen USA Pageant*), CBS, 1988.
The Ice Capades with Kirk Cameron, ABC, 1988.
Christmas on Ice (also known as *Disney's "Christmas on Ice"*), CBS, 1990.
Cohost, *Vail Figure Skating Festival,* HBO, 1990.
Host, *A Gold Medal Tradition: Lake Placid Figure Skating,* HBO, 1991.
Christmas Fantasy on Ice (also known as *Disney's "Christmas Fantasy on Ice"*), 1992.
Skates of Gold, 1993.
Nancy Kerrigan & Friends, CBS, 1994.
Greatest Hits on Ice (also known as *Disney's "Greatest Hits on Ice"*), CBS, 1994, syndicated, 1995.
Commentator, *Ice Wars: the U.S.A. vs. the World* (also known as *Ice Wars: Four the World*), CBS, 1994, 1995, 1996, 1997, 1999, 2000, 2002.
Holiday Festival on Ice, syndicated, 1994.
The Gold Championship, NBC, 1994.
Host, *The Eighth Annual Genesis Awards,* Discovery Channel, 1994.
... *Stars on Ice* (also known as *The Discover Card Stars on Ice, Discover Stars on Ice,* and *Target Stars on Ice*), CBS, 1994, 1995, 1996, 1997, 1999.
Nancy Kerrigan Special: Dreams on Ice (also known as *Disney's "Nancy Kerrigan Special: Dreams on Ice"*), CBS, 1995.
Ice Stories (also known as *Peggy Fleming's "Ice Stories"*), 1995.
The Houston Symphony Concert on Ice (also known as *The Houston Symphony Concert on Ice Presented by Office Depot*), Arts and Entertainment, 1995.
Halloween on Ice, TNT, 1995.
Host, *Too Hot to Skate,* 1995, CBS, 1997.
Commentator, *Skates X 2: World Team Skating Challenge,* CBS, 1995.
The Planets on Ice, Arts and Entertainment, 1995.
Fox's Rock 'n' Roll Skating Championships, Fox, 1995, 1996, 1997.
Skates of Gold II (also known as *AT&T Skates of Gold II*), NBC, 1995.
Skates of Gold III, ABC, 1995.
Sergei Grinkov: Celebration of a Life, CBS, 1996.
Scott Hamilton: Upside Down (also known as *Disney's "Scott Hamilton: Upside Down"*), ABC, 1996, CBS, 1997.
Host, *Champions on Ice* (also known as *Disney's "Champions on Ice"*), ABC, 1996.
Lumiere, *Beauty and the Beast: A Concert on Ice* (also known as *Disney's "Beauty and the Beast: A Concert on Ice"*), CBS, 1996.
Starlight Skating Championship, Fox, 1996.
The Northwestern Mutual Life World Team Championship, CBS, 1996, 1997.
Cotton Incorporated Ultimate Four (also known as *The Cotton Incorporated Gold Championship*), 1996, NBC, 1997.
America's Choice: The Great Skate Debate (also known as *The Great Skate Debate*), CBS, 1996, 1997.
Scott Hamilton: Back on the Ice, CBS, 1997.

Scootch, *Snowden on Ice,* CBS, 1997.
MCI Presents Three Masters on Ice, TBS, 1997.
The Battle of the Sexes on Ice, 1997, Fox, 1998.
Vail Figure Skating Festival, TBS, 1997.
E! Specials: Ice Skating, E! Entertainment Television, 1998.
Presenter, *The Walt Disney Company Presents the 8th American Teacher Awards,* The Disney Channel, 1998.
Doc, *The Snowden, Raggedy Ann, and Andy Holiday Show,* CBS, 1998.
Oksana Baiul: The E! True Hollywood Story, E! Entertainment Television, 1998.
My Sergei, CBS, 1998.
Nagano: Gateway to Glory, CBS, 1998.
The Great Skate Debate, CBS, 1998.
Battle of the Sexes on Ice II, 1998.
Discover Stars on Ice Presented by Smuckers, TBS, 1998.
Tara Lipinski: From This Moment (also known as *From This Moment*), CBS, 1999.
Intimate Portrait: Oksana Baiul, Lifetime, 1999.
A Home for the Holidays, CBS, 1999.
Christmas in Rockefeller Center, NBC, 1999.
Scott Hamilton: The E! True Hollywood Story, E! Entertainment Television, 2000.
Voice of sideline announcer, *Big Game XXVIII: Road Runner vs. Coyote* (animated), Cartoon Network, 2000.
Target Presents: Scott Hamilton's Farewell to Stars on Ice, CBS, 2000.
Fire on Ice: Champions of American Figure Skating, Arts and Entertainment, 2001.
A Skating Tribute: The Legacy of the 1961 U.S. World Team, ABC, 2001.
Kristi Yamaguchi's Golden Moment, Fox Family Channel, 2001.
Presenter, *A Home for the Holidays with Mariah Carey,* CBS, 2001.
Allstate Presents an All–Star Olympic Salute: Countdown to Salt Lake City, 2002.
OL Salt Lake City, 2002.
Lead figure skating analyst, *XIX Winter Olympics Opening Ceremony,* CBS, 2002.
Intimate Portrait: Kristi Yamaguchi, Lifetime, 2002.
Tai and Randy: The E! True Hollywood Story, E! Entertainment Television, 2002.
Smucker's Stars on Ice, Arts and Entertainment, 2003.
An Evening with Scott Hamilton & Friends, NBC, 2004.
"Katarina Witt," *Biography,* Arts and Entertainment, 2004.
Ice Storm: The Sale and Pelletier Affair, 2006.
Olympic Ice, USA Network, 2006.
Kristi Yamagushi: Friends and Family, NBC, 2006.
Cohost, *Frosted Pink with a Twist,* ABC, 2008.
A Capitol Fourth, PBS, 2008.

Television Appearances; Episodic:
Where in the World Is Carmen Sandiego?, PBS, 1991.
Feed Your Mind!, TBS, 1994.

Himself, "Movie Dinosaurs/Bread Chemistry/Scott Hamilton/Wallaby," *Newton's Apple,* PBS, 1994.
Famous Homes & Hideaways, syndicated, 2000.
Hollywood Squares (also known as *H2* and *H2: Hollywood Squares*), syndicated, between 2000 and 2004.
First guest caller, "Frasier Has Spokane," *Frasier,* NBC, 2002.
Voice of announcer, "Dances with Dogs," *King of the Hill* (animated), Fox, 2002.
Pyramid (also known as *The $100,000 Pyramid*), syndicated, 2002.
"Stars on Ice," *Family Feud,* syndicated, 2004.
Today (also known as *NBC News Today* and *The Today Show*), NBC, 2005, 2007.
Host, "Debut," *Skating with Celebrities,* Fox, 2006.
Celebrity jury member, *Jury Duty,* 2007.
Entertainment Tonight (also known as *Entertainment This Week, E.T., ET Weekend,* and *This Week in Entertainment*), syndicated, 2007, 2008.

Celebrity judge for *Wanna Bet?,* ABC.

Television Producer; Specials:
Sergei Grinkov: Celebration of a Life, CBS, 1996.
Snowden on Ice, CBS, 1997.
The Snowden, Raggedy Ann, and Andy Holiday Show, CBS, 1998.
Discover Stars on Ice Presented by Smuckers, TBS, 1998.

Television Executive Producer; Specials:
Battle of the Sexes on Ice II, Fox, 1998.
Tara Lipinski: From This Moment (also known as *From This Moment*), CBS, 1999.

Film Appearances:
Ricky Medford, *On Edge,* Andora Pictures International, 2001.
Voice of Buzz, *Nine Dog Christmas,* 2001.
Sports anchor, *Blades of Glory,* Paramount, 2007.
Himself, *Pop Star on Ice,* Sundance Channel, 2009.

RECORDINGS

Videos:
1992 Winter Olympics Figure Skating, 1992.
1994 Winter Olympics Figure Skating Competition and Exhibition Highlights, 1994.
1998 Olympic Winter Olympics Figure Skating Competition Highlights, 1998.
The 2002 Olympic Games Figure Skating Competition/ Exhibition, 2002.

WRITINGS

(With Lorenzo Benet) *Landing It: My Life on and off the Ice* (autobiography), Kensington, 1999.

OTHER SOURCES

Books:
Hamilton, Scott, and Lorenzo Benet, *Landing It: My Life on and off the Ice* (autobiography), Kensington, 1999.
Newsmakers 1998, Issue 2, Gale, 1998.
Notable Sports Figures, Gale, 2004.

Periodicals:
People Weekly, April 23, 2001, p. 130.

Other:
Scott Hamilton: The E! True Hollywood Story (television special), E! Entertainment Television, 2000.

HANSEN, Chris 1959–

PERSONAL

Full name, Christopher Edward Hansen; born March 26, 1959, in Lansing, MI; married Mary Joan Gleich; children: two sons. *Education:* Michigan State University, B.A.

Addresses: *Office*—c/o NBC News, 30 Rockefeller Plaza, New York, NY 10112.

Career: Broadcast journalist. Began career as a radio and newspaper reporter in Michigan; worked as a reporter for WILX–TV, Lansing, MI, WFLA–TV, Tampa, FL, and WXYZ–TV, Detroit, MI; WDIV–TV, Detroit, investigative reporter and news anchor, 1988–93; NBC News, New York City, correspondent and hidden–camera investigator, 1993—.

Awards, Honors: Two Emmy Awards, c. 2004, for reporting on the child sex trade in Cambodia; seven Emmy Awards for investigative reporting, coverage of a news story, and coverage of breaking news; Overseas Press Club Award; National Press Club Award; award from International Consortium of Investigative Journalists; journalism awards from Associated Press and United Press International; four Edward R. Murrow Awards; three Clarion Awards; and several National Headliner Awards.

CREDITS

Television Appearances; Series:
Correspondent, *Now with Tom Brokaw and Katie Couric,* NBC, 1993.

Correspondent and investigator, *Dateline NBC* (also known as *Dateline*), NBC, 2005–2008.
Anchor, *Dateline NBC* (also known as *Dateline*), NBC, 2007–2008.

Television Appearances; Specials:
Host and correspondent, *Court TV's Safety Challenge,* Court TV, c. 2003.
Correspondent, *Dateline NBC: Going for Gold,* NBC, c. 2007.

Television Appearances; Episodic:
Himself, "The Break–up," *30 Rock,* NBC, 2006.

Television Guest Appearances; Episodic:
The Tonight Show with Jay Leno, NBC, 2007.
Larry King Live, Cable News Network, 2007.
Late Night with Conan O'Brien, NBC, 2007.
The Daily Show (also known as *The Daily Show with Jon Stewart, The Daily Show with Jon Stewart Global Edition,* and *Jon Stewart*), Comedy Central, 2007.
Jimmy Kimmel Live!, ABC, 2007.
American Gangster, Black Entertainment Television, 2007.
"To Catch a Predator," *Tonight with Trevor McDonald* (also known as *Tonight*), ITV, 2008.

WRITINGS

Books:
To Catch a Predator: Protecting Your Kids from Online Enemies Already in Your Home, Dutton, 2007.

OTHER SOURCES

Electronic:
MSNBC Online, http://www.msnbc.msn.com/, August 7, 2007.

HARTH, C. Ernst 1970–
(Sue Donim, E. Ernst Harth, Ernest Harth, Ernst Harth, Bruno Nicols)

PERSONAL

Full name, Cary Ernst Harth; born February 2, 1970, in Galt, Ontario, Canada; married, wife's name Lea (an actress), June 2, 2002.

Addresses: *Agent*—Audra Jager, Double Agents Talent, 2265 West 41st Ave., Suite 8, Vancouver, British Columbia, Canada V6M 2A3.

Career: Actor, producer, and writer. Also worked as still photographer, casting director, production manager, set builder, and project accountant, sometimes credited as Sue Donim or Bruce Nicols. Appeared in numerous television commercials and print ads in Canada, the United States, and elsewhere, including commercials for Armstrong flooring, 2002, and Sunny Delight fruit juices, 2004. Previously worked as a bouncer at a nightclub and as a professional wrestler under the name "The Bible Thumper."

CREDITS

Film Appearances:

(As Ernst Harth) Trucker, *Strangeview* (short film), Omigod Productions/University of British Columbia, 1993.

Neo–Nazi grocer, *The Scarecrow and the Rainbow Kid* (short film), Black Crow Productions/University of British Columbia, 1993.

Ponech, *Alien IV?* (short film), All Talent Productions/Brown Bag Productions, 1994.

Doorman, *Crash* (also known as *Breach of Trust* and *Dirty Money*), Lions Gate Studios, 1996.

Trucker, *Excess Baggage*, Columbia, 1997.

(As Ernst Harth) Large man, *Henry's Cafe* (short film), Greasy Spoon Films, 1997.

Wayne Newton, *Zacharia Farted*, Jupiter Films/Windowshot Productions, 1998.

Horst Himmelferger, *Saving Grace*, Bradeway Pictures, 1998.

Bedroom ghost, *Best Buds* (also known as *Tommy Chong's "Best Buds"*), filmed, 1998, edited for release, Bong Productions/Coyote Films, 2003.

Shane, *Dudley Do–Right*, Universal, 1999.

Ed, *Noroc*, Versatile Pictures, 1999.

Bearded guy, *Camouflage*, PM Entertainment Group, 1999.

Casino guard, *Little Boy Blues*, Stage 18 Pictures, 1999.

(Uncredited) Streeter, *Dark Water*, Simpatico Pictures, 2001.

(Uncredited) Doorman, *Valentine*, Warner Bros., 2001.

Mr. Campisi, *Say It Isn't So*, Twentieth Century–Fox, 2001.

Harold Shelburne (The Great Child), *Thir13en Ghosts* (also known as *Thirteen Ghosts* and *13 fantomes*), Warner Bros., 2001.

Repair man, *Ignition* (also known as *Mise a feu*), Lions Gate Films, 2001.

"Buffalo" Sedwick, *The Barber* (also known as *Le barbier*), Universal Pictures Canada, 2001, ThinkFilm, 2005.

Dirk, *Stark Raving Mad*, Newmarket Capital Group, 2002.

Barry Neiman, *Dreamcatcher* (also known as *L'attrapeur de reves*), Warner Bros., 2003.

Phil, *Air Bud: Spikes Back* (also known as *Tobby 5: L'as du volley–ball*), Dimension Films, 2003.

John at Cervantes's bar, *Tilt* (short film), Starstruck Pictures, 2003.

Nathaniel Ipswitch, *Art History* (short film), Gold Star Productions, 2003.

Miner 49er, *Scooby Doo 2: Monsters Unleashed*, Warner Bros., 2004.

Ernst, *Are We There Yet?*, Columbia, 2005.

Gang member, *The Long Weekend* (also known as *Un long week–end*), Gold Circle Films, 2005.

Lowell Lee Andrews, *Capote*, Sony Pictures Classics, 2005.

The pedophile, *The Entrance*, Entrance Productions, 2006.

Little Pigeon, *Love and Other Dilemmas*, Maple Pictures, 2006.

Laurie's blind date, *Trick 'r' Treat*, Bad Hat Harry Productions/Legendary Pictures/Little Sam Films/Warner Bros., 2008.

Herbie, *Impulse*, Sony Pictures Home Entertainment, 2008.

Guard, *Space Buddies*, Walt Disney Home Video, 2009.

Film Coproducer:

(Uncredited) *Saving Grace*, Bradeway Pictures, 1998.

Dark Water, Simpatico Pictures, 2001.

Television Appearances; Movies:

(As E. Ernst Harth) Giant, *Green Dolphin Beat* (also known as *Green Dolphin Street*), Fox, 1994.

Luther, *Catch Me if You Can* (also known as *Deadly Game*, *Hide and Seek*, and *Jeu mortel*), Fox Family Channel, 1998.

Esposito, *The Wonder Cabinet*, Fox, 1999.

Club manager, *Blacktop* (also known as *Blacktop: Murder on the Move* and *La route de la peur*), HBO, 2000.

Eightball, *Monster Island*, MTV, 2004.

Earl, *The Muppets' Wizard of Oz*, ABC, 2005.

The janitor, *Scooby Doo: In the Beginning*, Cartoon Network, 2009.

Television Appearances; Pilots:

Mr. Alistair Q. Fink, *The Froome Room*, 1994.

Leon, *Two*, syndicated, 1996.

Patrolman Wenkel, "Rats of Rumfordton," *It's True*, CBS, 1998.

Orderly, *The Heart Department*, CBS, 2001.

Television Appearances; Episodic:

(Uncredited) Ranch kid, "On the Line," *Neon Rider*, syndicated, 1992.

Henry Perez, "Blinded by the Son," *Strange Luck,* Fox, 1996.

Huge man, "The Post–Modern Prometheus," *The X–Files,* Fox, 1997.

Saloon worker, "The Gambler," *Dead Man's Gun,* Showtime, 1998.

Bear, "The Pest House," *Millennium,* Fox, 1998.

Mel Ludwig, "Book of Shadows," *First Wave,* Sci–Fi Channel, 1998.

Large man, "Boo," *So Weird,* The Disney Channel, 1999.

Second Zip Fighter and second Zip Wrangler, "Inga Fossa," *Harsh Realm,* Fox, 1999.

(As C. Ernest Harth) Astrid Troll, "Troll," *So Weird,* The Disney Channel, 2000.

Silverface, "Down to Earth," *The Outer Limits* (also known as *The New Outer Limits*), Showtime and syndicated, 2000.

Jerry Diamond, "On My List," *Hollywood Off–Ramp,* E! Entertainment Television, 2000.

Himself, *Urban Rush,* 2001.

Man on bench, "The Candidate," *The Chris Isaak Show,* Showtime, 2004.

Tiny the Biker, "The Cold Hard Truth," *The Dead Zone* (also known as *Stephen King's "Dead Zone"*), USA Network, 2004.

Himself and Miner 49er, "Inside 'Scooby Doo 2: Monsters Unleashed'," *HBO First Look,* HBO, 2004.

Ronnie, "The Junkie," *The Collector,* 2006.

Teddy, "Fog," *Saved,* TNT, 2006.

Neal Handler, "The Marked," *The 4400* (also known as *Los 4400*), USA Network, 2007.

Security guard, "Psy vs. Psy," *Psych,* USA Network, 2007.

Heavyset man and sloth, "The Magnificent Seven," *Supernatural,* CW Network, 2007.

(Uncredited) Himself, "Vancouver," *Rocky + Drago,* TV6, 2007.

Television Appearances; Other:

Mr. Alistair Q. Fink, *The Froome Room* (series), 1994.

Olaf the Ogre, *Voyage of the Unicorn* (miniseries), Odyssey, 2000.

RECORDINGS

Videos:

(Uncredited) *Thir13en Ghosts Revealed,* Columbia TriStar, 2002.

(Uncredited) Second Zip Fighter (in archive footage), *Inside "Harsh Realm,"* Twentieth Century–Fox Home Entertainment, 2004.

(Uncredited) Lowell Lee Andrews (in archive footage), *Truman Capote: Answered Prayers,* Sony Pictures Home Entertainment, 2006.

Appeared in the music videos "Cyclops" by User; "Justify" by Sound Pressure Manifest; and "Superman's Dead" by Our Lady Peace.

WRITINGS

Television Episodes:
"The Show's a Bomb," *The Froome Room,* 1996.

Film Music:
Songwriter, "Last Train to Trussberg," *Camouflage,* PM Entertainment Group, 1999.

HATCHER, Teri 1964–

PERSONAL

Full name, Teri Lynn Hatcher; born December 8, 1964, in Sunnyvale, CA; daughter of Owen (a nuclear physicist) and Esther (a computer programmer) Hatcher; married Marcus Leithold, June 4, 1988 (divorced, 1989); married Jon Tenney (an actor), May 27, 1994 (divorced, March 5, 2003); children: (second marriage) Emerson Rose. *Education:* Studied mathematics and engineering at Deanza Junior College; studied acting at American Conservatory Theatre. *Avocational Interests:* Playing golf and fishing.

Addresses: *Office*—ISBE Productions, 500 South Buena Vista St., Animation Bldg., Suite 1G–9–11, Burbank, CA 91521. *Agent*—Special Artists Agency, 9465 Wilshire Blvd., Suite 470, Beverly Hills, CA 90212; Paradigm, 360 North Crescent Dr., North Bldg., Beverly Hills, CA 90210.

Career: Actress. ISBE Productions, Burbank, CA, president. Appeared in television commercials, including Bally Total Fitness Clubs, 1995, Discover card, 1997, and Radio Shack, 1999–2000, 2002, and California Travel & Tourism Board, 2006; appeared in print ads for Ray Ban sunglasses, 1995, Repeat Cashmere, 2006, and Clairol's Nice N Easy hair color, 2006–07. Gold Rush, professional cheerleading squad for San Francisco 49ers, cheerleader, 1984; previously worked as a dancer.

Awards, Honors: Golden Apple Award, female discovery of the year, 1996; Saturn Award nomination, best supporting actress, Academy of Science Fiction, Fantasy and Horror Films, 1998, for *Tomorrow Never Dies;* World Actress Award, Women's World Awards, 2005; Emmy Award nomination, outstanding lead actress in a comedy series, Golden Globe Award, best performance by an actress in a television series—musical or comedy, Golden Satellite Award nomination, best actress in a series, comedy or musical, Screen Actors Guild Award, outstanding performance by a female actress in a comedy series, Television Critics Association Award nomination, individual achievement in comedy, 2005, Screen Actors Guild Award (with others), outstanding performance by an ensemble in a comedy series, 2005, 2006, Golden Globe Award nomination, best performance by an actress in a television series—musical or comedy, Teen Choice Award nomination, television—choice actress, 2006, Screen Actors Guild Award nomination (with others), outstanding performance by an ensemble in a comedy series, 2007, 2008, Prism Award nomination, performance in a comedy series, 2008, all for *Desperate Housewives*; People's Choice Award nomination, favorite female television star, 2006.

CREDITS

Film Appearances:

Katherine "Kiki" Tango, *Tango & Cash*, Warner Bros., 1989.

Gretchen, *The Big Picture*, Columbia, 1989.

Ariel Maloney/Dr. Monica Demonico, *Soapdish* (also known as *Sopa de jabon*), Paramount, 1991.

Janice, *Straight Talk*, Buena Vista, 1992.

Dani, *The Cool Surface*, Columbia TriStar Home Video, 1992.

Linda, *All Tied Up* (also known as *Un soltero con mucha cuerda*), Columbia TriStar Home Video, 1992.

Samantha Crain, *Brain Smasher ... A Love Story* (also known as *The Bouncer and the Lady* and *Brainsmasher: A Love Story*), Trimark Pictures, 1993.

Claudette Rocque, *Heaven's Prisoners*, Savoy, 1995.

Becky Foxx, *2 Days in the Valley*, Metro–Goldwyn–Mayer, 1996.

Dead Girl, American International Video Search, 1996.

Paris Carver, *Tomorrow Never Dies* (also known as *TND*), United Artists, 1997.

Herself, *Highly Classified: The World of 007*, 1997.

Charlotte Parker, *Fever*, Lions Gate Films, 1999.

Ms. Gradenko, *Spy Kids*, Miramax, 2001.

Two Girls from Lemoore, Old School, 2001.

Megan Margulius, *The Chester Story*, Velveteen, 2001.

Megan Marguilas, *A Touch of Fate*, PorchLight Entertainment, 2003.

Andrea Flak, *Resurrecting the Champ*, Yari Film Group, 2007.

Voice of Coraline's mother and other mother, *Coraline*, Focus Features, 2009.

Television Appearances; Series:

Amy, Love Boat mermaid, *The Love Boat*, ABC, 1985–86.

Penny Parker, *MacGyver*, 1985–90.

Angelica Clegg, *Capitol*, CBS, 1986–87.

Laura Matthews, *Karen's Song*, Fox, 1987.

T. T. Fagori, *Sunday Dinner*, CBS, 1991.

Lois Lane, *Lois & Clark: The New Adventures of Superman* (also known as *Lois & Clark* and *The New Adventures of Superman*), ABC, 1993–97.

Susan Mayer, *Desperate Housewives*, ABC, 2004—.

Television Appearances; Movies:

Laura Stewart, *Dead in the Water*, USA Network, 1991.

Maria Goldstein, *Since You've Been Gone* (also known as *Ten Years Later*), ABC, 1998.

Shawna Morgan, *Running Mates*, TNT, 2000.

Jane, *Jane Doe* (also known as *Runaway Jane*), USA Network, 2001.

Jordan Ripps, *Momentum* (also known as *Momentum—Wenn gedanken toten konnen* and *Projekt Momentum*), Sci–Fi Channel, 2003.

Television Appearances; Pilots:

Lauri Stevens, "Baby on Board," *CBS Summer Playhouse*, CBS, 1988.

Teresa Gennaro, Salvatore's sister, *The Brotherhood*, ABC, 1991.

Say Uncle, CBS, 2001.

Television Appearances; Specials:

The 45th Annual Primetime Emmy Awards, ABC, 1993.

Presenter, *The 47th Annual Primetime Emmy Awards*, Fox, 1995.

Presenter, *The Walt Disney Company and McDonald's Present the American Teacher Awards*, The Disney Channel, 1996.

Presenter, *The 53rd Annual Golden Globe Awards*, NBC, 1996.

Presenter, *The 54th Annual Golden Globe Awards*, NBC, 1997.

The Secrets of 007: The James Bond Files, CBS, 1997.

James Bond: Shaken and Stirred, ITV, 1997.

Presenter, *Divas Live: An Honors Concert for VH1 Save the Music* (also known as *VH1 Divas Live* and *Celine, Aretha, Gloria, Shania, and Mariah: Divas Live*), VH1, 1998.

(Uncredited) *Saturday Night Live: 25th Anniversary*, NBC, 1999.

Presenter, *The 56th Annual Primetime Emmy Awards*, ABC, 2004.

Presenter, *The 62nd Annual Golden Globe Awards*, NBC, 2005.

The 11th Annual Screen Actors Guild Awards, TNT, 2005.

The 77th Annual Academy Awards—UK, Sky, 2005.

The 3rd Annual TV Land Awards, TV Land, 2005.

Presenter, *The 57th Annual Primetime Emmy Awards*, CBS, 2005.

The Women of "Desperate Housewives": The E! True Hollywood Story, E! Entertainment Television, 2005.

"Barbara Walters' Oscar Night Special," *The Barbara Walters Special,* ABC, 2005.

"The 10 Most Fascinating People of 2005," *The Barbara Walters Special,* ABC, 2005.

The 63rd Annual Golden Globe Awards, NBC, 2006.

Live from the Red Carpet: The 2006 Golden Globe Awards, E! Entertainment Television, 2006.

The 12th Annual Screen Actors Guild Award, TBS, 2006.

Presenter, *The 48th Annual Grammy Awards,* CBS, 2006.

Celebrity Debut, ABC, 2006.

The 17th Annual GLAAD Media Awards, 2006.

The 59th Primetime Emmy Awards, Fox, 2007.

Presenter, *The 2007 Screen Actors Guild Awards,* TNT and TBS, 2007.

Presenter, *Fashion Rocks,* CBS, 2007.

The 6th Annual TV Land Awards (also known as *TV Land Awards 2008),* TV Land, 2008.

Presenter, *The 60th Primetime Emmy Awards,* ABC, 2008.

"TV Guide" Live at the Emmy Awards, 2008.

Television Appearances; Episodic:

Kitty, "Who Was That Mashed Man?" *Night Court,* NBC, 1987.

(Uncredited) Transporter Chief Lieutenant Bronwyn Gail Robinson, "The Outrageous Okona," *Star Trek: The Next Generation,* 1988.

Tracy Shoe, "I'm in the Nude for Love," *L.A. Law,* NBC, 1989.

Donna Eleese, "Star–Crossed–June," *Quantum Leap,* NBC, 1989.

Madeline Stillwell, "Fax or Fiction," *Murphy Brown,* CBS, 1990.

Stacy, "The Thing from the Grave," *Tales from the Crypt* (also known as *HBO's "Tales from the Crypt"),* HBO, 1990.

Marissa, "The Eclipse," *The Exile* (also known as *Paris Steele),* CBS, 1991.

Sidra, "The Implant," *Seinfeld,* NBC, 1993.

Sidra, "The Pilot," *Seinfeld,* NBC, 1993.

Good Morning America, ABC, 1993, 1995, 2005.

Host, "Teri Hatcher/Dave Matthews Band," *Saturday Night Live* (also known as *SNL),* NBC, 1996.

Showbiz Tonight, CNN, 1996.

The Rosie O'Donnell Show, syndicated, 1996, 1998, 1999, 2000.

Late Show with David Letterman (also known as *Letterman* and *The Late Show),* CBS, 1996, 2005, 2007, 2008.

Sidra, "The Finale," *Seinfeld,* NBC, 1998.

Marie, "First Do No Harm," *Frasier,* NBC, 1998.

Late Night with Conan O'Brien, NBC, 1998, 2004.

Hollywood Squares (also known as *H2* and *H2: Hollywood Squares),* syndicated, 2001.

The Tonight Show with Jay Leno, NBC, 2002, 2004, 2005, 2006, 2007.

Howard Stern, 2004.

Liz, "I Remember the Coatroom, I Just Don't Remember You," *Two and a Half Men,* CBS, 2004.

The Tony Danza Show, syndicated, 2004, 2005.

The Oprah Winfrey Show (also known as *Oprah),* syndicated, 2004, 2005, 2006.

Ellen: The Ellen DeGeneres Show, syndicated, 2004, 2006.

The View, ABC, 2004, 2005, 2006, 2007, 2008.

Entertainment Tonight (also known as *E.T.),* syndicated, 2005, 2006, 2007, 2008.

Corazon de ..., 2005, 2006.

Friday Night with Jonathan Ross, BBC, 2005, 2006.

Primetime Live, ABC, 2005.

Caiga quien caiga, 2005.

Access Hollywood, syndicated, 2005.

Extra (also known as *Extra: The Entertainment Magazine),* syndicated, 2005.

Live with Regis and Kelly, syndicated, 2005, 2006, 2007.

Amazon Fishbowl with Bill Maher, 2006.

"Rock the Night Away ...," *In the Mix* (also known as *In the Cutz),* Urban America, 2006.

"A Santana Wins, a Bishop Named Don Juan and Amy's B–Day," *In the Mix* (also known as *In the Cutz),* Urban America, 2006.

"Teri Hatcher," *Inside the Actors Studio* (also known as *Inside the Actors Studio: The Craft of Theatre and Film),* Bravo, 2006.

Jimmy Kimmel Live!, ABC, 2006, 2007.

Rachael Ray, syndicated, 2007.

Wiener Opernball, 2008.

"Idol Gives Back," *American Idol: The Search for a Superstar* (also known as *American Idol),* Fox, 2008.

"Live Results Show: One Contestant Eliminated," *American Idol: The Search for a Superstar* (also known as *American Idol),* Fox, 2008.

"The Top Seven Finalists Perform," *American Idol: The Search for a Superstar* (also known as *American Idol),* Fox, 2008.

"Desperate Housewives," *Infanity,* 2008.

Stage Appearances:

Sally Bowles, *Cabaret,* Pace Theatrical Group, Wilshire Theatre, Los Angeles, 1999.

Also appeared in *The Vagina Monologues,* Westside Theatre (Downstairs), New York City.

Major Tours:

Sarah Bowles, *Cabaret,* U.S. cities, 1999.

RECORDINGS

Music Videos:

Appeared in Michael Bolton's "Missing You Now" and Elton John's "Turn the Lights Out When You Leave."

Taped Readings:
Burnt Toast: And Other Philosophies of Life, Hyperion, 2006.

WRITINGS

Television Episodes:
"It's a Small World After All, *Lois & Clark: The New Adventures of Superman* (also known as *Lois & Clark* and *The New Adventures of Superman*), 1993.

Autobiography:
Burnt Toast: And Other Philosophies of Life, Hyperion, 2006.

OTHER SOURCES

Books:
Newsmakers, Issue 4, Thomson Gale, 2005.

Periodicals:
Cosmopolitan, March, 1994, p. 106.
Esquire, December, 1993, p. 98.

HAWKE, Ethan 1970–
   (E. Hawke)

PERSONAL

Full name, Ethan Green Hawke; born November 6, 1970, in Austin, TX; son of James Steven Hawke (an official) and Leslie Carole Green (an activist and involved in charitable and humanitarian work); married Uma Thurman (an actress), May 1, 1998 (divorced, July 20, 2004); married Ryan Shawhughes, June 18, 2008; children: (first marriage): Maya Ray Thurman–Hawke, Roan Thurman–Hawke (some sources cite name as Levon Roan Thurman–Hawke); (second marriage): Clementine Jane. *Education:* Graduated from the Hun School of Princeton, 1988; studied acting at the McCarter Theatre in Princeton, NJ, and at Carnegie Mellon University; also attended New York University and Harvard University; some sources state that Hawke studied in Great Britain.

Addresses: *Agent*—Creative Artists Agency, 2000 Avenue of the Stars, Los Angeles, CA 90067. *Publicist*—I/D Public Relations, 8409 Santa Monica Blvd., West Hollywood, CA 90069.

Career: Actor, writer, and director. Malaparte Theatre Company (nonprofit theatre company), New York City, cofounder, 1992, and artistic director, 1992–2000. Involved with charities.

Member: Screen Actors Guild, Actors' Equity Association, Directors Guild of America, Writers Guild of America, East.

Awards, Honors: Young Artist Award nomination, best starring performance by a young actor—motion picture, Young Artist Foundation, 1986, for *Explorers;* Young Artist Award nomination, best young actor in a supporting role in a motion picture, 1990, for *Dad;* MTV Movie Award nomination (with Winona Rider), best kiss, 1994, for *Reality Bites;* MTV Movie Award nomination (with Julie Delpy), best kiss, 1995, for *Before Sunrise;* Academy Award nomination, best actor in a supporting role, and Screen Actors Guild Award nomination, outstanding performance by a male actor in a supporting role, both 2002, for *Training Day;* Open Palm Award nomination, Gotham awards, Independent Feature Project, 2002, for *Chelsea Walls;* inducted into the Texas Film Hall of Fame, 2004; Academy Award nomination, best writing, adapted screenplay, Independent Spirit Award nomination, best screenplay, Independent Feature Project/West, Writers Guild of America (WGA) Screen Award nomination, best adapted screenplay, and Online Film Critics Society Award nomination, best screenplay, adapted, all with others, 2005, for *Before Sunset;* Lucille Lortel Award nomination, outstanding lead actor, League of Off–Broadway Theatres and Producers, 2005, for *Hurlyburly;* Boston Society of Film Critics Award and Gotham Award, both best ensemble cast, both with others, 2007, for *Before the Devil Knows You're Dead;* Antoinette Perry Award nomination, best featured actor in a play, 2007, for *The Coast of Utopia.*

CREDITS

Film Appearances:
Ben Crandall, *Explorers,* Paramount, 1985.
Chris, *Lion's Den* (short film), 1988.
Billy Tremont, *Dad,* Universal, 1989.
Todd Anderson, *Dead Poets Society,* Buena Vista, 1989.
Jack, *White Fang,* Buena Vista, 1991.
Tom McHugh, *Mystery Date,* Orion, 1991.
Matthew Price, *Waterland,* Fine Line Features, 1992.
Will Knott, *A Midnight Clear,* InterStar Releasing, 1992.
Nando Parrado, *Alive* (also known as *Alive: The Miracle of the Andes*), Buena Vista, 1993.
Wayne Frobiness, *Rich in Love,* Metro–Goldwyn–Mayer, 1993.
(Uncredited) Don Quixote student, *Quiz Show,* Buena Vista, 1994.
(Uncredited) Jack Conroy, *White Fang 2: Myth of the White Wolf* (also known as *White Fang 2*), Buena Vista, 1994.

Jimmy, *Floundering,* A–pix Entertainment, 1994.

Troy Dyer, *Reality Bites* (also known as *Generation 90*), Universal, 1994.

Himself, *At Sundance* (documentary), 1995.

Jesse, *Before Sunrise,* Columbia, 1995.

Roger, *Search and Destroy* (also known as *The Four Rules*), October Films, 1995.

Vincent Freeman and Jerome, *Gattaca,* Columbia, 1997.

Finnegan "Finn" Bell, *Great Expectations,* Twentieth Century–Fox, 1998.

Jess Newton, *The Newton Boys,* Twentieth Century–Fox, 1998.

Nat, *The Velocity of Gary* (also known as *Gary* and *The Velocity of Gary (Not His Real Name)*), Next Millennium Films, 1998.

Ishmael Chambers, *Snow Falling on Cedars,* MCA/Universal, 1999.

Len Coles, *Joe the King* (also known as *Joe Henry*), Trimark Pictures, 1999.

Title role, *Hamlet,* Miramax, 2000.

Tell Me, 2000.

Officer Jake Hoyt, *Training Day,* Warner Bros., 2001.

Vince, *Tape,* Lions Gate Films, 2001.

Voice of Jesse, *Waking Life* (animated), Twentieth Century–Fox, 2001.

(Uncredited) Voice of Sam, *Chelsea Walls* (also known as *Chelsea Hotel, Hotel Chelsea,* and *Last Word on Paradise*), Lions Gate Films, 2001.

Himself, *All the Love You Cannes!* (documentary), Troma Entertainment, 2002.

Ray, *The Jimmy Show,* First Look Pictures Releasing, 2002.

Himself, *PollyDAYS* (also known as *Pollydays*), 2003.

James Costa, *Taking Lives,* Warner Bros., 2004.

Jesse, *Before Sunset,* Warner Independent Pictures, 2004.

Jack Valentine, *Lord of War,* Lions Gate Films, 2005.

Sergeant Jake Roenick, *Assault on Precinct 13* (also known as *Assaut sur le central 13*), Focus Features, 2005.

(Uncredited) Earl Jamieson, *One Last Thing …,* 2005, Magnolia Pictures, 2006.

Pete, *Fast Food Nation,* Fox Searchlight Pictures, 2006.

Vince, *The Hottest State,* THINKFilm, 2006.

Hank Hanson, *Before the Devil Knows You're Dead,* THINKFilm, 2007.

Himself, *Chelsea on the Rocks* (documentary; also known as *Chelsea Hotel*), 2008.

Lefty, *Tonight at Noon,* 2008.

Paulie, *What Doesn't Kill You,* Yari Film Group, 2008.

Staten Island, EuropaCorp., 2008, 2009.

Himself, *Corso: The Last Beat* (documentary), Arkwright Ventures, 2009.

Sal, *Brooklyn's Finest,* Warner Bros., 2009.

Researcher, *Daybreakers,* Lions Gate Films, c. 2009.

New York, I Love You (also known as *New York, je t'aime*), Palm Pictures, c. 2009.

Appeared in other projects.

Film Director:

Straight to One (short film), 1993.

Chelsea Walls (also known as *Chelsea Hotel, Hotel Chelsea,* and *Last Word on Paradise*), Lions Gate Films, 2001.

The Hottest State, THINKFilm, 2006.

Film Work; Other:

Editor, *Straight to One* (short film), 1993.

(As E. Hawke) Pixelography worker, *Hamlet,* Miramax, 2000.

Executive producer of other projects.

Television Appearances; Specials:

Himself, *Poetry, Passion, the Postman: The Poetic Return of Pablo Neruda,* 1996.

Himself, "Sam Shepard: Stalking Himself," *Great Performances,* PBS, 1998.

Himself, *Spotlight on Location: Snow Falling on Cedars,* 2000.

Himself, *Willie Nelson & Friends: Live and Kickin',* USA Network, 2003.

(In archive footage) Himself, *"Pulp Fiction" on a Dime: A 10th Anniversary Retrospect,* 2004.

Himself, *Fashion Week Diaries,* 2005.

(Uncredited; in archive footage) Jake, *Boffo! Tinseltown's Bombs and Blockbusters,* HBO, 2006.

Some sources cite appearances in other programs.

Television Appearances; Awards Presentations:

(In archive footage) Todd Anderson, *The 62nd Annual Academy Awards,* ABC, 1990.

Presenter, *The 72nd Annual Academy Awards,* ABC, 2000.

The 2000 MTV Movie Awards, MTV, 2000.

Presenter, *17th Annual IFP/West Independent Spirit Awards,* Independent Film Channel, 2002.

Presenter, *The 74th Annual Academy Awards,* ABC, 2002.

Hollywood Celebrates Denzel Washington: An American Cinematheque Tribute, American Movie Classics, 2003.

Presenter, *The 58th Annual Tony Awards* (also known as *The 2004 Tony Awards*), CBS, 2004.

Presenter, *50th Annual Drama Desk Awards,* 2005.

Presenter, *The 59th Annual Tony Awards,* CBS, 2005.

The 61st Annual Tony Awards, CBS, 2007.

Television Appearances; Episodic:

Himself, *The Rosie O'Donnell Show,* syndicated, 1997, 2002.

Himself, *The Tonight Show with Jay Leno,* NBC, 1997, 2002.

Himself, *Late Night with Conan O'Brien,* NBC, 1997, 2000, multiple episodes in 2004, multiple episodes in 2005, 2006, 2007, 2008.

Himself, *Late Show with David Letterman* (also known as *The Late Show, Late Show Backstage,* and *Letterman*), CBS, 1998, 2001, 2004, 2005.

Himself, "Training Day: Crossing the Line," *HBO First Look,* HBO, 2001.

The Early Show, CBS, 2001.

Freeride with Greta Gaines, Oxygen, 2001.

Today (also known as *NBC News Today* and *The Today Show*), NBC, 2001.

Himself, *Bo' Selecta!,* Channel 4 (England), 2002.

Himself, *Breakfast,* BBC, 2002.

Himself, *Inside the Actors Studio* (also known as *Inside the Actors Studio: The Craft of Theatre and Film*), Bravo, 2002.

Himself, *The View,* ABC, 2002, multiple episodes in 2004, 2005, 2007.

CIA agent James L. Lennox, "Double Agent," *Alias,* ABC, 2003.

(In archive footage) Himself, *Celebrities Uncensored,* E! Entertainment Television, 2003.

Himself, *Extra* (also known as *Extra: The Entertainment Magazine*), syndicated, 2003.

Himself, "Kurja muodonmuutos," *4Pop,* 2004.

Guest star, "The Chronicles of Riddick; I, Robot; Before Sunset; The Village," *Coming Attractions,* E! Entertainment Television, 2004.

Guest star, "Secret Window; Taking Lives; Harry Potter 3; Scooby-Doo 2," *Coming Attractions,* E! Entertainment Television, 2004.

Presenter, "America: The Book," *Book TV,* C-SPAN, 2004.

Himself, *The Daily Show* (also known as *A Daily Show with Jon Stewart, The Daily Show with Jon Stewart, The Daily Show with Jon Stewart Global Edition, Jon Stewart, Ha-Daily Show,* and *I satira tou Jon Stewart*), Comedy Central, 2004.

Himself, *On-Air with Ryan Seacrest,* syndicated, 2004.

Himself, *T4,* Channel 4, 2004.

Himself, *20/20* (also known as *ABC News 20/20*), ABC, 2004.

Himself, "Assault on Precinct 13: Caught in the Crosshairs," *HBO First Look,* HBO, 2005.

Himself, *The Charlie Rose Show* (also known as *Charlie Rose*), PBS, 2005.

Himself, *Live with Regis & Kelly,* syndicated, 2005, 2007.

Himself, "The Coast of Utopia," *Working in the Theatre,* CUNY TV, 2007.

Himself, "Ethan Hawke," *Sunday Morning Shootout* (also known as *Hollywood Shootout* and *Shootout*), American Movie Classics, 2007.

Voice of Jason, "Squaw Bury Shortcake," *Robot Chicken* (animated), Cartoon Network, 2007.

Himself, *Entertainment Tonight* (also known as *Entertainment This Week, E.T., ET Weekend,* and *This Week in Entertainment*), syndicated, 2007.

Himself, *Jimmy Kimmel Live!* (also known as *The Jimmy Kimmel Project*), ABC, 2007.

(In archive footage) Troy Dyer, "La Nova Canco i el karaoke," *60/90,* 2008.

Himself, *Eigo de shabera–night,* 2008.

Himself, *TMZ on TV,* syndicated, multiple episodes in 2008.

Appeared as himself in "The Films of Richard Linklater," *The Directors,* Encore.

Television Work:
Worked on projects for television.

Stage Appearances:
Saint Joan, McCarter Theatre, Princeton, NJ, 1983.

Young Casanova, *Casanova,* New York Shakespeare Festival, Joseph Papp Public Theater, Martinson Hall, New York City, 1991.

Memo, *A Joke,* Malaparte Theatre Company, New York City, 1992.

Konstantin Treplev, *The Seagull,* National Actors Theatre, Lyceum Theatre, New York City, 1992–93.

Xavier "Ex" Reynolds, *Sophistry,* Playwrights Horizons, New York City, 1993.

Max, *Sons and Fathers,* Malaparte Theatre Company, 1994.

Vince, *Buried Child,* Steppenwolf Theatre, Chicago, IL, 1995.

Homer Wells, *The Cider House Rules,* Seattle Repertory Theatre, Seattle, WA, 1996.

Kilroy, *Camino Real,* Williamstown Theatre Festival, Main Stage, Williamstown, MA, 1999.

Ray Moss, *The Late Henry Moss,* Signature Theatre Company, New York City, 2001.

The Late Henry Moss (reading), Americana: Play Reading Season, Peacock Theatre, Dublin, Ireland, 2003.

Henry Percy (Hotspur), *Henry IV,* Lincoln Center, Vivian Beaumont Theater, New York City, 2003–2004.

Eddie, *Hurlyburly,* New Group, Acorn Theatre on Theatre Row and 37 Arts Theatre, both New York City, 2005.

Michael Bakunin, *The Coast of Utopia: Part 1—Voyage* (also known as *The Coast of Utopia*), Lincoln Center Theater, Vivian Beaumont Theater, 2006–2007.

Michael Bakunin, *The Coast of Utopia: Part 2—Shipwreck* (also known as *The Coast of Utopia*), Lincoln Center Theater, Vivian Beaumont Theater, 2006–2007.

Michael Bakunin, *The Coast of Utopia: Part 3—Salvage* (also known as *The Coast of Utopia*), Lincoln Center Theater, Vivian Beaumont Theater, 2007.

Peter Trofimov, *The Cherry Orchard,* The Bridge Project, Brooklyn Academy of Music, Harvey Theater, Brooklyn, New York City, 2009.

Appeared in other productions.

Stage Director:
Wild Dogs, Malaparte Theatre Company, New York City, 1994.
Things We Want, New Group, Acorn Theatre on Theatre Row, New York City, 2007.

RECORDINGS

Videos:
Himself and Jesse, *On the Set of "Before Sunset,"* 2004.
Himself, *Dead Poets: A Look Back,* 2006.
Himself, *The Making of "Lord of War,"* 2006.
Himself, *The Manufacturing of "Fast Food Nation,"* 2007.
Himself, *Directed by Sidney Lumet: How the Devil Was Made,* 2008.
Do Not Alter, Paramount Home Entertainment, 2008.
Welcome to Gattaca, Paramount Home Entertainment, 2008.

Music Video Director:
Lisa Loeb & Nine Stories, "Stay" (also known as "Stay (I Missed You)"), 1994.

Soundtrack Albums; with Others:
Performer of "I'm Nuttin'" and reader of "Marriage," *Reality Bites,* RCA, 1994.
Reader of "Fable of the Mermaid and the Drunks," *Il postino,* Hollywood Records, 1995.

Audiobooks:
Robert Stone, *Damascus Gate,* Publishing Mills, 2000.
Scott Lasser, *Battle Creek,* Publishing Mills, 2001.
Jack London, *The Call of the Wild,* Ultimate Classics, New Millennium Audio, 2002.
Kurt Vonnegut, *Slaughterhouse–Five,* Caedmon, 2003.

WRITINGS

Screenplays:
Straight to One (short film), 1993.
(With Richard Linklater and Julie Delpy; based on a story by Linklater and Kim Krizan) *Before Sunset,* Warner Independent Pictures, 2004, published with *Before Sunrise* in *Before Sunrise & Before Sunset: Two Screenplays,* Vintage Books, 2005.
The Hottest State (based on his novel), THINKFilm, 2006.

Novels:
The Hottest State, Little, Brown, 1996.
Ash Wednesday, Alfred A. Knopf, 2002.
Manhattan Story, Fayard, 2003.

Author of the unpublished novel *Eleven Waverly Place,* a novel rewritten as *The Hottest State.*

OTHER SOURCES

Books:
International Dictionary of Films and Filmmakers, Volume 3: *Actors and Actresses,* fourth edition, St. James Press, 2000.
Newsmakers, issue 4, Gale, 1995.
The Writers Directory, twenty–fourth edition, St. James Press, 2008.

Periodicals:
Chaplin, Volume 37, number 2, 1995.
Details, January, 1998, pp. 79–83, 120–21.
Detour, November, 1997.
Empire, April, 1998.
Entertainment Weekly, December 27, 1996, p. 143.
Interview, April, 1998.
Newsweek, September 30, 1996, p. 80.
Premiere, March, 1998; October 2, 2002; July/August, 2004.
Rolling Stone, March 9, 1995, p. 44.
Sun–Times (Chicago), January 3, 2000.
Time Out New York, October 16, 1997.
US, January, 1998; October 29, 2002.

HEADLEY, Heather 1974–

PERSONAL

Born February 8, 1974, in Barataria, Trinidad and Tobago; immigrated to the United States; daughter of Iric (a minister) and Hannah (a minister) Headley; married Brian Musso (a consultant and former professional football player), September 6, 2003. *Education:* Studied musical theatre and communications at Northwestern University; also studied the piano.

Addresses: *Agent*—Paradigm Talent Agency, 10100 Santa Monica Blvd., Suite 2500, Los Angeles, CA 90067.

Career: Actress, singer, and songwriter. Involved in the "I Want My 9 Months" campaign, the March of Dimes; also affiliated with other charities.

Awards, Honors: Won second place in a radio talent show for children, Trinidad, 1970s; Grammy Award (with others), best musical show album, National Academy of Recording Arts and Sciences, 1998, for *The Lion King*; Antoinette Perry Award, best actress in a musical, Drama Desk Award, outstanding actress in a musical, Drama League Award, Jeff Award, best actress in a principal role in a nonresident production, Joseph Jefferson awards Committee, and Sarah Siddons Award, all 2000, for *Aida*; named one of thirty women to watch, *Essence* magazine, 2000; *Soul Train* Award nomination, best R&B/soul or rap new artist—solo, 2002, *Soul Train* Lady of Soul Award, best R&B/soul or rap new artist—solo, 2003, and *Soul Train* Lady of Soul Award nomination, best R&B/soul single—solo, 2003, all for "He Is"; Grammy Award nomination, best R&B vocal performance, 2003, for "I Wish I Wasn't"; Grammy Award nomination, best new artist, 2003; Image Award nominations, outstanding female artist and outstanding new artist, both National Association for the Advancement of Colored People (NAACP), 2003; *Billboard* Music Award nomination, R&B/hip–hop new artist of the year, 2003; *Soul Train* Lady of Soul Award nomination, best R&B/soul album—solo, 2003, for *This Is Who I Am*; *This Is Who I Am* received a gold certification from the Recording Industry Association of America; Cool Like That Award, BET J (Black Entertainment Television jazz channel), 2006.

CREDITS

Stage Appearances:

The World Goes Round (musical revue), Marriott Lincolnshire Theatre, Lincolnshire, IL, c. 1990.

Member of the chorus and understudy for the role of Sarah, *Ragtime* (musical), Marriott Lincolnshire Theatre, 1996, and Ford Centre for the Performing Arts, Toronto, Ontario, Canada, 1996–97.

Nala, *The Lion King* (musical), New Amsterdam Theatre, New York City, beginning 1997.

Aida, *Elaborate Lives: The Legend of Aida* (musical), Alliance Theatre Company, Atlanta, GA, 1998, produced as *Aida* (musical), Cadillac Palace Theatre, Chicago, IL, beginning 1999, and Palace Theatre, New York City, 2000–2004.

Tilda Mullen, *Do Re Mi* (concert production of musical), *City Center Encores!* (also known as *Encores!* and *Encores! Great American Musicals in Concert*), City Center Theatre, New York City, 1999.

Lorrell Robinson, *Dreamgirls* (benefit concert production of musical), Ford Center for the Performing Arts, New York City, 2001.

Herself, *We Are One: The Obama Inaugural Celebration at the Lincoln Memorial*, Washington, DC, 2009.

Appeared in other productions.

Film Appearances:

Herself, *Breakin' All the Rules* (also known as *The Break Up Handbook*, *The Sexpert*, and *Untitled Jamie Foxx Comedy*), Screen Gems, 2004.

Rosa Negra singer, *Dirty Dancing: Havana Nights* (also known as *Dancing Havana*, *Dirty Dancing 2*, *Dirty Dancing 2: Havana Nights*, and *Havana Nights: Dirty Dancing 2*), Lions Gate Films, 2004.

Film Work:

(With Kenny Lattimore) Performer of song "Love Will Find a Way," *The Lion King 2: Simba's Pride* (animated musical; also known as *The Lion King II: Simba's Pride* and *Simba's Pride*), Buena Vista Home Video, 1998.

Performer of song "He Is," *Breakin' All the Rules* (also known as *The Break Up Handbook*, *The Sexpert*, and *Untitled Jamie Foxx Comedy*), Screen Gems, 2004.

Performer of songs "Represent Cuba" and "Represent—Havana Nights," *Dirty Dancing: Havana Nights* (also known as *Dancing Havana*, *Dirty Dancing 2*, *Dirty Dancing 2: Havana Nights*, and *Havana Nights: Dirty Dancing 2*), Lions Gate Films, 2004.

Performer of song "Ain't It Funny," *Diary of a Mad Black Woman* (also known as *Tyler Perry's "Diary of a Mad Black Woman"* and *Tyler Perry's "Diary of a Mad Black Woman: The Movie"*), Lions Gate Films, 2005.

Television Appearances; Specials:

Herself, "My Favorite Broadway: The Love Songs," *Great Performances*, PBS, 2001.

Herself, *Walt Disney World Christmas Day Parade*, ABC, 2002.

Performer, *The 2003 Essence Music Festival*, UPN, 2003.

Herself, "Andrea Bocelli: Amore under the Desert Sky," *Great Performances*, PBS, 2006.

Herself, *An American Celebration at Ford's Theatre*, ABC, 2006.

Herself, "Vivere: Andrea Bocelli Live in Tuscany," *Great Performances*, PBS, 2007.

Herself, *Christmas in Washington*, TNT, 2007.

Herself, *We Are One: The Obama Inaugural Celebration at the Lincoln Memorial*, HBO, 2009.

Television Appearances; Awards Presentations:

Presenter, *The 55th Annual Tony Awards*, CBS, 2001.

The First Ten Awards: Tony 2001, PBS, 2001.

Cohost, *Ninth Annual Soul Train Lady of Soul Awards*, The WB, 2003.

Presenter, *17th Annual Soul Train Music Awards*, The WB, 2003.

An Evening of Stars: Tribute to Stevie Wonder, 2006.

The Mark Twain Prize: Neil Simon (also known as *The Kennedy Center Presents: The 2006 Mark Twain Prize*), PBS, 2006.

Television Appearances; Episodic:
Herself, *The Rosie O'Donnell Show,* syndicated, multiple episodes in 2000.
Herself, *Soul Train,* syndicated, 2002, 2006.
Herself, "Heather Headley," *Sidewalks Entertainment* (also known as *Sidewalks* and *Sidewalks Entertainment Hour*), syndicated, 2003.
Herself, *The Tonight Show with Jay Leno,* NBC, 2003, 2006.
Herself, *Ellen: The Ellen DeGeneres Show* (also known as *Ellen* and *The Ellen DeGeneres Show*), syndicated, 2006.
Herself, *It's Showtime at the Apollo* (also known as *Showtime at the Apollo*), syndicated, 2006.
Herself, *Martha,* syndicated, 2006.
Herself, *Tavis Smiley,* PBS, 2006.
Herself, *Today* (also known as *NBC News Today* and *The Today Show*), NBC, 2006.

Appeared in other programs, including *Good Morning America* (also known as *GMA*), ABC; *Late Show with David Letterman* (also known as *The Late Show, Late Show Backstage,* and *Letterman*), CBS; *Live with Regis & Kelly,* syndicated; and *The View,* ABC.

Radio Appearances:
Radio appearances include performing in a talent show for children, Trinidad, 1970s.

RECORDINGS

Solo Albums:
This Is Who I Am, RCA, 2002.
In My Mind, RCA, 2006.
Audience of One, EMI Gospel, 2009.

Albums; with Others:
Ragtime (Toronto cast recording), RCA, 1996.
The Lion King (original Broadway cast recording), Walt Disney Records, 1998.
The Lion King 2: Simba's Pride (soundtrack recording; also known as *The Lion King II: Simba's Pride*), Walt Disney Records, 1998.
(With Kenny Lattimore) "Love Will Find a Way," *From the Soul of a Man* (album by Lattimore), Columbia, 1998.
(With Lattimore) "Love Will Find a Way," *Return to Pride Rock: Songs Inspired by "The Lion King 2: Simba's Pride"* (also known as *Return to Pride Rock: Songs Inspired by "The Lion King II: Simba's Pride"*), Walt Disney Records, 1998.
Do Re Mi (New York cast recording; also known as *Do Re Mi: 1999 Original Cast Recording*), DRG, 1999.
"Elaborate Lives," *Aida* (concept recording; also known as *Elton John and Tim Rice's "Aida"*), Rocket Records, 1999.

Aida (original Broadway cast recording), Walt Disney Records, 2000.
My Favorite Broadway: The Love Songs, Hybrid/Sire, 2001.
Disney on Broadway, Walt Disney Records, 2002.
Dreamgirls in Concert: The First Complete Recording, Nonesuch, 2002.

Performer of "I Know the Lord Will Make a Way," *Oh Happy Day,* EMI Gospel/Vector.

Singles:
"He Is," 2002.
"I Wish I Wasn't," 2003.
"In My Mind," 2006.
"Me Time," 2006.

Videos:
Pocket Queen, *Elmo's Magic Cookbook,* Sesame Workshop, 2001.
Herself, *Smokie Norful: Live in Memphis,* EMI CMG Distribution, 2009.

Music Videos:
"He Is," 2002.
"I Wish I Wasn't," 2003.
"In My Mind," 2006.
"Me Time," 2006.

WRITINGS

Albums; Songs with Others:
This Is Who I Am, RCA, 2002.
In My Mind, RCA, 2006.
Audience of One, EMI Gospel, 2009.

Singles:
"He Is," 2002.
"I Wish I Wasn't," 2003.
"In My Mind," 2006.
"Me Time," 2006.

OTHER SOURCES

Books:
Who's Who among African Americans, twenty–second edition, Gale, 2008.

Periodicals:
Essence, January, 2002, p. 45.
Newsweek, April 3, 2000, p. 76.
New York Times, April 6, 2000.
Parade, January 25, 2004, p. 18.

Electronic:
Heather Headley, http://www.heatherheadley.com, January 15, 2009.

HECTOR, Jamie 1975–

PERSONAL

Born October 7, 1975, in Brooklyn, NY.

Addresses: *Agent*—Don Buchwald and Associates, 6500 Wilshire Blvd., Suite 2200, Los Angeles, CA 90048. *Manager*—Roberson's Artist Management, 630 9th Avenue, New York, NY 10036.

Career: Actor. Opened a store for his line of clothing "Royal Addiction" in Brooklyn, NY.

CREDITS

Film Appearances:
"I Love You" Leech, *He Got Game,* Buena Vista, 1998.
Gangsta in red, *Ghost Dog: The Way of the Samurai* (also known as *Ghost Dog, Ghost Dog–Der weg des Samurai* and *Ghost Dog, la voie du samourai*), Lions Gate, 1999.
T. K., *Prison Song,* New Line Cinema, 2001.
Jogger number two, *Central Park Jog,* 2002.
Dunn, *Paid in Full,* Miramax, 2002.
Danny, *The Fast Life,* 2003.
Banny, *Five Deep Breaths,* 2003.
Dante, *MVP,* Xenon, 2003.
Devon, *Everyday People,* HBO, 2004.
Courtland, *Brooklyn Bound,* Image, 2004.
Lincoln DeNeuf, *Max Payne,* Twentieth Century–Fox, 2008.
Damien "D–Rock" Butler, *Notorious,* Fox Searchlight, 2009.

Film Work:
Automated dialogue replacement (ADR), *Slow Burn,* Lionsgate, 2007.

Television Appearances; Series:
Marlo Stanfield, *The Wire,* HBO, 2006—.

Television Appearances; Episodic:
Rasta, "They Say It's Your Birthday," *The Beat,* UPN, 2000.
Jean Marchier, "Burn, Baby, Burn," *Law & Order,* NBC, 2000.
Legros, " ... And Zeus Wept," *Third Watch,* 2001.

Doc, "Justice," *Law & Order: Special Victims Unit* (also known as *Law & Order: SVU* and *Special Victims Unit*), NBC, 2002.
Quite Frankly with Stephen A. Smith, ESPN, 2006.
Carnell, *The Game,* UPN, 2007.
"On a Heroic Scale," *Heroes Unmasked,* BBC, 2008.
"Shock of the Old," *Heroes Unmasked,* BBC, 2008.
Corporal Adams, "Patriots and Tyrants," *Jericho,* CBS, 2008.
Benjamin "Knox" Washington, a recurring role, *Heroes,* NBC, 2008.

Television Appearances; Movies:
Devon, *Everyday People,* HBO, 2004.
Rasheed, *Blackout,* Black Entertainment Television, 2007.

Television Appearances; Specials:
The Wire: It's All Connected, HBO, 2006.
The Wire Odyssey, HBO, 2007.

RECORDINGS

Video Games:
The Warriors, 2005.
Pedestrian, *Grand Theft Auto: Liberty City Stories* (also known as *GTA: Liberty City Stories*), 2005.

Videos:
How We Live: The Reality of "Brooklyn Bound", Image, 2005.
Narrator, *Life After Death: The Movie* (also known as *Life After Death: The Movie–Ten Years Later*), Fontana, 2007.

Music Videos:
"A Dozen Roses," Monica, 2006.

HEIMANN, Betsy
(Betsy Faith Heimann)

PERSONAL

Born in Chicago, IL; daughter of Herman Heimann and Florence D. (maiden name, Petacque)) Stern. *Avocational Interests:* Playing fiddle.

Addresses: *Agent*—United Talent Agency, 9560 Wilshire Blvd., Suite 500, Beverly Hills, CA 90212.

Career: Costume designer. Los Angeles County Museum, member of costume council, 1989.

Awards, Honors: Sierra Award nomination, best costume design, Las Vegas Film Critic Society Award nomination, 2000, Costume Designers Guild Award nomination, excellence in costume design for film—period/fantasy, 2001, both for *Almost Famous.*

CREDITS

Film Costume Designer:
Skatetown, U.S.A., Sony, 1979.
High Road to China, Warner Bros., 1983.
Sky Bandits (also known as *Gunbus*), Galaxy International Releasing, 1986.
Surrender, Warner Bros., 1987.
Elvira, Mistress of the Dark (also known as *Elvira*), New World Pictures, 1988.
Medium Rare, 1989.
Tune in Tomorrow … (also known as *Aunt Julia and the Scriptwriter*), Cinecom International Films, 1990.
Welcome Home, Roxy Carmichael, Paramount, 1990.
One Good Cop (also known as *One Man's Justice*), Buena Vista, 1991.
Reservoir Dogs, Miramax, 1992.
(As Betsy Faith Heimann) *The Adventures of Huck Finn* (also known as *The Adventures of Huckleberry Finn*), Buena Vista, 1993.
Gunmen, Dimension Films, 1994.
Pulp Fiction, Miramax, 1994.
Renaissance Man (also known as *Army Intelligence* and *By the Book*), Buena Vista, 1994.
The Tie That Binds, Buena Vista, 1995.
Get Shorty, Metro–Goldwyn–Mayer, 1995.
2 Days in the Valley, Metro–Goldwyn–Mayer, 1996.
Jerry Maguire, TriStar, 1996.
Switchback, Paramount, 1997.
Going West in America, Paramount, 1997.
Mercury Rising, Universal, 1998.
Out of Sight, Universal, 1998.
Simon Birch (also known as *Angels and Armadillos*), Buena Vista, 1998.
Anywhere But Here, Twentieth Century–Fox, 1999.
Almost Famous, DreamWorks, 2000.
The Family Man, Universal, 2000.
Vanilla Sky, Paramount, 2001.
Stealing Harvard, Sony, 2002.
Red Dragon (also known as *Roter Drache*), Universal, 2002.
Man of the House, Sony, 2005.
Be Cool, Metro–Goldwyn–Mayer, 2005.
Art School Confidential, Sony, 2006.
Lady in the Water, Warner Bros., 2006.
Rush Hour 3, New Line Cinema, 2007.
The Happening, Twentieth Century–Fox, 2008.

Film Costumer: Women:
Tom Horn, Warner Bros., 1980.
The Competition, Sony, 1980.
UFOria, Universal, 1985.

Film Assistant Costumer:
Homework (also known as *Growing Pains* and *Short People*), Jensen Farley Pictures, 1982.

Film Appearances:
Herself, *A Director's Journey: The Making of "Red Dragon"* (documentary short), Universal Home Video, 2003.

Television Costume Designer; Series:
Karen Sisco, ABC, 2003.

Television Costume Designer; Movies:
This Girl for Hire, CBS, 1983.
The Dirty Dozen: The Next Mission, NBC, 1985.
Stranger on My Land, ABC, 1988.
One Against the Wind, CBS, 1991.

Television Work; Movies:
Costumes, *The Girl, the Gold Watch & Dynamite,* syndicated, 1981.
Costumes for Richard Dreyfus and Elijah Wood, *Oliver Twist,* ABC, 1997.

Television Costume Designer; Pilots:
Prison Break (also known as *Prison Break: On the Run*), Fox, 2005.

Television Work; Specials:
Production coordinator and costume designer, *The Pee–wee Herman Show,* 1981.

HEINDL, Scott

PERSONAL

Addresses: *Agent*—Kirk Talent Agencies, Inc., 134 Abbott St., Suite 402, Vancouver, British Columbia V6B 2K4 Canada.

Career: Actor.

CREDITS

Film Appearances:
Ron, *The Falling* (also known as *Faithless*), 1998.

Floyd the Fisherman, *Along Came a Spider* (also known as *Im Netz der spinne* and *Le masque de l'araignee*), Paramount, 2001.
Second man in restaurant, *Freddy Got Fingered,* Twentieth Century–Fox, 2001.
Snownook guy, *Out Cold,* Buena Vista, 2001.
Steve Spizak, *The Stickup,* Twentieth Century Fox Home Entertainment, 2001.
Papa, *Blue Boy and Girl in Pink,* 2002.
NS5 robot, *I, Robot,* Twentieth Century–Fox, 2004.
Gedge, *Blade: Trinity,* New Line Cinema, 2004.
Zack, "The Girl with Golden Breasts," *Trapped Ashes,* Lionsgate, 2006.
James Doyle, *You Kill Me,* IFC Films, 2007.
Chase, *The Betrayed,* Metro–Goldwyn–Mayer, 2008.
Jake, *Dancing Trees,* 2008.
Graham, *The Art of War II: Betrayal,* Stage 6 Films, 2008.

Television Appearances; Series:
Bob, *Viper,* syndicated, 1996.
Goth guy, *Big Sound,* Global, 2000.
Kyle Mackenzie, *Falcon Beach,* Global Television Network, 2006.
Wraith, *Stargate: Atlantis* (also known as *La porte d'Atlantis*), Sci–Fi Channel, 2006–2008.

Television Appearances; Miniseries:
Drug enforcement agency supervisor number two, *Traffic* (also known as *Traffic: The Miniseries*), USA Network, 2004.
Thomas Lebeck, *Into the West,* TNT, 2005.

Television Appearances; Movies:
Carl, *Survival on the Mountain,* NBC, 1997.
Messenger, *Jitters,* Lifetime, 1997.
Werner Von Stucker, *Nick Fury: Agent of S.H.I.E.L.D.* (also known as *Nick Fury* and *Nick Fury: Agent of Shield*), Fox, 1998.
Bar patron, *Shutterspeed,* TNT, 2000.
Mine worker, *Blacktop* (also known as *Blacktop: Murder on the Move* and *La route de la peur*), HBO, 2000.
Bobby Satchel, *Alaska,* 2003.
Jed Kaplan, *Before I Say Goodbye* (also known as *Mary Higgins Clark's "Before I Say Goodbye"* and *Mary Higgins Clark: Avant de te dire adieu*), Court TV, 2003.
Lieutenant Hutton, *The Colt,* Hallmark Channel, 2005.
Kyle Mackenzie, *Falcon Beach,* 2005.
Ray Oakum, *Safe Harbor,* Lifetime, 2006.
Jesse Carne, *Montana Sky* (also known as *Nora Robert's "Montana Sky"*), Lifetime, 2007.

Television Appearances; Pilots:
Thug number two, *Dark Angel* (also known as *James Cameron's "Dark Angel"*), Fox, 2000.
Harvey Rockwell, *Wolf Lake,* CBS, 2001.

Television Appearances; Episodic:
Billy, "Unruhe," *The X Files,* Fox, 1996.
Jacob Tyler, "The Thin White Line," *Millennium,* Fox, 1997.
Damon, "Like It's 1999," *The Crow: Stairway to Heaven,* syndicated, 1998.
Jimmy, "Fallen Angel," *Poltergeist: The Legacy,* Showtime, Sci–Fi Channel, and syndicated, 1998.
Long–haired man, "A Room with No View," *Millennium,* Fox, 1998.
Danny, "The Judgment of Joe Bean Bonner," *Dead Man's Gun,* 1998.
George, "Lunatic Fringe," *The Net,* USA Network, 1999.
The long–haired man, "Antipas," *Millennium,* Fox, 1999.
"Red Flag," *First Wave,* Sci–Fi Channel, 1999.
Lance Rivet, "Deadbeat Walking," *Cold Squad,* CTV, 1999.
Dorian, "The Demons of the Night: Part 1," *The Immortal,* syndicated, 2000.
Dorian, "The Hunted," *The Immortal,* syndicated, 2000.
Lance Rivet, "Death by Intent: Parts 1 & 2," *Cold Squad,* CTV, 2000.
Jack, "Gill Girl," *Dark Angel* (also known as *James Cameron's "Dark Angel"*), Fox, 2001.
Goth guy, "Dire Straits," *Big Sound,* 2001.
Eddie Wolcott, "Here There Be Monsters," *The Dead Zone* (also known as *Stephen King's "Dead Zone"*), USA Network, 2002.
The Kreetor, "Hunted," *The Twilight Zone,* UPN, 2002.
Tommy, "At First It Was Funny," *Da Vinci's Inquest* (also known as *Coroner Da Vinci*), 2002.
Tommy, "Doing the Chicken Stratch," *Da Vinci's Inquest* (also known as *Coroner Da Vinci*), 2003.
Tommy, "For Just Bein' Indian," *Da Vinci's Inquest* (also known as *Coroner Da Vinci*), 2003.
Bruce Tobek, "Reasonable Doubts," *Just Cause,* Court TV, 2003.
Trent, "Deux Ex Machina," *Jeremiah,* Showtime, 2003.
Father Neil Ennison, "The Exorcist," *The Collector,* 2006.
The White Prince, "Hunters," *Blade: The Series,* Spike TV, 2006.
Guard number one, "Combat," *Smallville* (also known as *Smallville: Beginnings* and *Smallville: Superman the Early Years*), The CW, 2007.
Harry Beeman, "Ghost in the Machine," *Painkiller Jane,* Sci–Fi Channel, 2007.

HENNAH, Dan

PERSONAL

Born in Hastings, New Zealand; married Chris (an art department coordinator), March 17, 1973. *Education:* Studied architecture at the Wellington Polytechnic School of Architecture.

Career: Production designer, art director, and set decorator.

Awards, Honors: National Board of Review Award (with others), best production design/art direction, 2001, Academy Award nomination (with Grant Major), best art direction–set decoration, Golden Satellite Award nomination (with Major), Excellence in Production Design Award nomination (with others), feature film—period or fantasy films, Art Directors Guild, 2002, all for *The Lord of the Rings: The Fellowship of the Ring;* Excellence in Production Design Award (with others), feature film—period or fantasy films, Art Directors Guild, Academy Award nomination (with Major and Alan Lee), best art direction—set decoration, 2003, both for *The Lord of the Rings: The Two Towers;* Academy Award (with Major and Lee), best art direction—set decoration, Excellence in Production Design Award (with others), feature film—period or fantasy film, Art Directors Guild, Golden Satellite Award (with others), best art direction, International Press Academy, 2004, all for *The Lord of the Rings: The Return of the King;* Sierra Award (with Simon Bright), best art direction, Las Vegas Film Critics Society, 2005, Academy Award nomination (with Major and Bright), best achievement in art direction, Excellence in Production Design Award nomination (with others), feature film—period or fantasy film, Art Directors Guild, 2006, all for *King Kong.*

CREDITS

Film Work:

Art director, *Nate and Hayes* (also known as *Savage Islands*), Paramount, 1983.

Location manager, *Second Time Lucky,* 1984.

Production designer, *Mesmerized* (also known as *Shocked* and *My Letter to George*), Vestron Video, 1986.

Art director: white water unit, *White Water Summer* (also known as *The Rites of Summer*), 1987.

Supervising art director, *The Rescue,* Buena Vista, 1988.

Production assistant, *Huo shao dao* (also known as *The Burning Island, Island of Fire, Island on Fire, The Prisoner,* and *When Dragons Meet*), New City Releasing, 1990.

Art director, *The Rainbow Warrior* (also known as *The Sinking of the Rainbow Warrior*), 1992.

Production designer, *Cumulus 9* (also known as *C–9, Cloud 9,* and *Cumulus 9*), AML Productions, 1992.

Art director, *The Frighteners* (also known as *Robert Zemeckis Presents: "The Frighteners"*), MCA/Universal, 1996.

Supervising art director and set decorator, *The Lord of the Rings: The Fellowship of the Ring* (also known

as *The Fellowship of the Ring* and *The Lord of the Rings: The Fellowship of the Ring: The Motion Picture*), New Line Cinema, 2001.

Supervising art director and set decorator, *The Lord of the Rings: The Two Towers* (also known as *The Two Towers* and *Der Herr der ringe: die zwei turme*), New Line Cinema, 2002.

Supervising art director and set decorator, *The Lord of the Rings: The Return of the King* (also known as *The Return of the King* and *Der Herr der ringe: die ruckkehr des konigs*), New Line Cinema, 2003.

Assistant art director, *The Long and Short of It* (short), 2003.

Supervising art director, set decorator, and vehicle assistant, *King Kong* (also known as *Kong: The Eighth Wonder of the World* and *Peter Jackson's "King Kong"*), Universal, 2005.

Supervising art director and set decorator, *The Water Horse* (also known as *The Water Horse: Legend of the Deep*), Sony, 2007.

Production designer, *Underworld: Rise of the Lycans,* Sony, 2009.

Production designer, *The Laundry Warrior,* 2009.

Production designer, *Dante's Inferno: Documentary* (also known as *Dante's Inferno*), 2009.

Also worked as dressing prop, *Mutiny on the Bounty.*

Film Appearances:

(Uncredited) Man of Rohan, *The Lord of the Rings: The Two Towers* (also known as *Der Herr der ringe: Die zwei turme* and *The Two Towers*), 2002.

Himself, *The Making of "The Lord of the Rings"* (documentary), 2002.

Himself, *Kong's New York, 1933* (documentary short), Universal, 2006.

Himself, *Skull Island: A Natural History* (documentary short), Universal, 2006.

Himself, *Recreating the Eighth Wonder: The Making of "King Kong"* (documentary short), Universal, 2006.

Television Production Designer; Series:

A Twist in the Tale (also known as *William Shatner's "A Twist in the Tale"*), 1998.

The Legend of William Tell, 1998.

The Tribe, Channel 5, 1999.

Treasure Island, 1999.

Television Work; Movies:

Production designer, *Adrift,* CBS and CTV, 1993.

Associate designer, *99–1,* 1994.

Production designer, *Return to Treasure Island* (also known as *Jim Hawkins–Ruckkehr nach Treasure Island* and *Die Ruckkehr zur schatzinsel*), 1996.

Television Work; Miniseries:

Art director, *Heart of the Country,* 1986.

Television Appearances; Specials:

Passage to Middle–Earth: The Making of "The Lord of the Kings," Sci–Fi Channel, 2001.

The Lord of the Rings: The Two Towers, Return to Middle Earth, The WB, 2002.

The 76th Annual Academy Awards, ABC, 2004.

HENSON, Elden 1977–

(Elden Ratliff, Elden Ryan Ratliff)

PERSONAL

Original name, Elden Ryan Ratliff; born August 30, 1977, in Rockville, MD; mother, a professional photographer; brother of Garette Ratliff Henson (an actor) and Erick Ratliff (an actor). *Education:* Attended Emerson College, 1996–97.

Addresses: *Agent*—Sheree Cohen, Kohner Agency, 9300 Wilshire Blvd., Suite 555, Beverly Hills, CA 90212.

Career: Actor. Roulette Entertainment (production company), cofounder. Began working as a model at age two, including work for the Ford Agency, New York City; appeared in numerous commercials.

Awards, Honors: Young Artist Award nomination (with others), outstanding young ensemble cast in a motion picture, 1993, for *The Mighty Ducks.*

CREDITS

Film Appearances:

(Film debut; uncredited) Ring bearer, *A Little Sex,* Universal, 1982.

(Uncredited) *The Verdict,* Twentieth Century–Fox, 1982.

(Uncredited) *Daniel,* Paramount, 1983.

(As Elden Ratliff) Eric Boyett, *Turner & Hooch,* Buena Vista, 1989.

(As Elden Ratliff) Steve Mills, *Marilyn Hotchkiss' Ballroom Dancing and Charm School* (short film), Carousel Films and Video, 1990.

(As Elden Ratliff) Third fisher friend, *Radio Flyer,* Columbia TriStar, 1992.

(As Elden Ratliff) Fulton Reed, *The Mighty Ducks* (also known as *Champions* and *The Mighty Ducks Are the Champions*), Buena Vista, 1992.

(As Elden Ryan Ratliff) Fulton Reed, *D2: The Mighty Ducks* (also known as *The Mighty Ducks 2*), Buena Vista, 1994.

(As Elden Ratliff) Bobby, *Foxfire,* Samuel Goldwyn Films, 1996.

(As Elden Ryan Ratliff) Fulton Reed, *D3: The Mighty Ducks,* Buena Vista, 1996.

Narrator and Maxwell "Max" Kane, *The Mighty,* Miramax, 1998.

Jesse Jackson, *She's All That,* Miramax, 1999.

Pnub, *Idle Hands,* Columbia, 1999.

Elden Madden, *Cast Away,* Twentieth Century–Fox, 2000.

Michael "Mike", *Manic,* IFC Films, 2001.

Roger Rodriguez, *O* (also known as *The One*), Lions Gate Films, 2001.

Sammy, *Cheaters* (also known as *Chea+ers*), Destination Films/New Line Cinema, 2002.

Ron, *Evil Alien Conquerors,* First Look International, 2002.

Sheep, *Pack of Dogs* (short film), 2002.

Turk, *Dumb and Dumberer: When Harry Met Lloyd,* New Line Cinema, 2003.

Bart Bowland, *The Battle of Shaker Heights,* Miramax, 2003.

Author, *Under the Tuscan Sun* (also known as *Sotto il sole della Toscana*), Buena Vista, 2003.

Lenny, *The Butterfly Effect,* New Line Cinema, 2004.

Samson and (in archive footage) Steve Mills, *Marilyn Hotchkiss' Ballroom Dancing and Charm School* (feature film), Samuel Goldwyn Films, 2005.

Salesman, *The Moguls* (also known as *The Amateurs* and *Dirty Movie*), Newmarket Films, 2005.

Billy Z, *Lords of Dogtown* (also known as *American Knights* and *Dogtown Boys*), Columbia, 2005.

Gunnars, *Deja Vu,* Buena Vista, 2006.

Taylor, *Rise* (also known as *Rise: Blood Hunter*), Samuel Goldwyn Films, 2007.

Fudge, *Not Since You,* Wonder Entertainment, 2008.

Plastic, Plastic Films, 2009.

Some sources cite an appearance in *Radioactive Dreams,* 1985.

Film Work:

(As Elden Ratliff) Additional voices, *Jaws: The Revenge,* Universal, 1987.

Television Appearances; Episodic:

(As Elden Ratliff) Freckle–faced boy, "Mummy Daddy," *Amazing Stories* (also known as *Steven Spielberg's "Amazing Stories"*), NBC, 1985.

(As Elden Ratliff) Matthew, "All I Want for Christmas," *Fame,* syndicated, 1986.

Alan Bailey, "I Was a Middle Aged Werewolf," *Highway to Heaven,* NBC, 1987.

(Uncredited) Cub Scout, "A Few Good Scouts," *The Ben Stiller Show,* Fox, 1993.

"Breaking Bread," *Touched by an Angel,* CBS, 1998.

Will Caray, "Brotherhood," *Law & Order: Special Victims Unit* (also known as *Law & Order: SVU* and *Special Victims Unit*), NBC, 2004.

Matthew Marley, "Four," *Smith,* CBS, 2007.

Matthew Marley, "Five," *Smith,* CBS, 2007.

(Uncredited) Matthew Marley, "Six," *Smith,* CBS, 2007.

Matthew Marley, "Seven," *Smith,* CBS, 2007.

Fingerless guy, "The War Comes Home," *ER,* NBC, 2007.

Damon, "In Which Sam Gets Taken for a Ride," *Private Practice,* ABC, 2007.

Also appeared in *Project Greenlight,* HBO.

Television Appearances; Other:

As the World Turns (series), CBS, c. 1983.

(As Elden Ratliff) Don Beaulieu at age ten, *Elvis and Me* (miniseries), ABC, 1988.

Daniel Huffman, *A Gift of Love: The Daniel Huffman Story* (movie), Showtime, 1999.

RECORDINGS

Videos:

The Making of "The Mighty," Buena Vista Home Entertainment, 1999.

Audio Books:

Narrator of *Freak the Mighty.*

OTHER SOURCES

Periodicals:

San Francisco Chronicle, October 11, 1998.

HILDRETH, Mark 1978–

PERSONAL

Born January 24, 1978, in Vancouver, British Columbia, Canada. *Education:* National Theatre School of Canada, graduated.

Addresses: *Agent*—Characters Talent Agency, 150 Carlton St., Toronto, Ontario, Canada M5A 2K1; Russ Mortensen, Pacific Artists Management, 1285 West Broadway, Suite 685, Vancouver, British Columbia, Canada V6H 3X8.

Career: Actor and voice artist. Savage God (resident performance ensemble), member of company.

Awards, Honors: Young Artist Award nomination (with others), best young acting ensemble in a television comedy, drama series, or special, 1989, for *After the Promise;* Jessie Richardson Theatre Award, best leading actor in a leading theatre, Vancouver Professional Theatre Alliance, 2001, for *Candida;* Leo Award nomination, best actor in a feature–length drama, Motion Picture Arts and Sciences Foundation of British Columbia, 2005, for *Everyone;* Leo Award nomination, best supporting actor in a feature–length drama, 2005, for *Earthsea;* Leo Award nomination, best supporting actor in a dramatic series, 2006, for "DaVinci's Notebook," *Young Blades.*

CREDITS

Television Appearances; Series:

Voice of Beany, *Beany and Cecil,* ABC, 1988.

Voice of Caz, *The New Adventures of He–Man* (animated; also known as *Le nuove avventure di He–Man*), syndicated, 1990.

Finger, *The Odyssey,* CBS, 1992–94.

Voice of Ziv "ZZ" Zulander, *The Bots Master* (animated; also known as *The Botz Master, ZZ Bots,* and *Le maitre des bots*), syndicated, 1993.

Voice of Ingred, *Hurricanes* (animated), 1993.

Cody, *Final Fight,* 1995.

Voice of Dr. Briefs, *Dragon Ball Z* (animated; also known as *DBZ*), Cartoon Network, 1996–97.

Voice of Vega, *Streetfighter: The Animated Series* (animated), USA Network, 1997.

Voice of Heero Yuy, *Mobile Suit Gundam Wing* (animated; also known as *Gundam Wing*), Cartoon Network, 2000.

Stanton, *Call of the Wild* (also known as *Jack London's "Call of the Wild"*), CBS, 2000.

Voice of Alex Mann, *Action Man* (animated), Fox, 2000–2001.

(English version) Voice of Adams, *Ultimate Muscle: The Kinnikuman Legacy* (animated), Fox, 2002.

Voice of R. J. Harrison, *Stargate: Infinity* (animated), Fox, 2002.

Voice, *Gadget and the Gadgetinis* (animated), 2003.

Siroc, *Young Blades,* I Network, 2005.

River Sorenon, *This Space for Rent,* CBC, 2006.

Also voice for *Kido senshi Gandamu* (animated; also known as *Mobile Suit Gundam*).

Television Appearances; Miniseries:

Lieutenant on air base, *Taken* (also known as *Steven Spielberg Presents "Taken"*), Sci–Fi Channel, 2002.

Jasper, *Earthsea* (also known as *Legend of Earthsea*), Sci–Fi Channel, 2004.

Television Appearances; Movies:

Bradley Ryder, "Love Is Never Silent," *Hallmark Hall of Fame* (also known as *Hallmark Television Playhouse*), NBC, 1985.

Raymond at age ten, *After the Promise*, CBS, 1987.

Johnny at age twelve, *My Son Johnny* (also known as *Bad Seed*), CBS, 1991.

Voice of Terry Bogard, *Fatal Fury: Legend of the Hungry Wolf* (animated), 1992.

Jeremy, *Relentless: Mind of a Killer*, NBC, 1993.

Craig Grant, *Shock Treatment*, 1995.

Joe Saeba, *City Hunter: Secret Service* (also known as *City Hunter* and *Secret Police*), 1996.

Rusty Walker, *Past Perfect*, HBO, 1998.

Second young soldier, *Y2K* (also known as *Countdown to Chaos* and *Y2K: The Movie*), NBC, 1999.

Voice of Heero Yuy, *Mobile Suit Gundam Wing: The Movie–Endless Waltz* (animated; also known as *Endless Waltz* and *Gundam Wing: The Movie–Endless Waltz*), Cartoon Network, 2000.

Voices of Dasher and Dancer, *Donner* (animated), ABC Family Channel, 2001.

James Gilman, *No Night Is Too Long*, BBC, 2002.

Voice of Hightech, *G.I. Joe: Spy Troops the Movie* (animated), 2003.

Voice of Sutton, *Jammin' in Jamaica* (animated), Nickelodeon, 2004.

Voice of Prince Dev, *Dragons: Fire & Ice* (animated; also known as *Dragon—Feu et glace*), Teletoon, 2004.

Voice of Prince Dev, *Dragons II: The Metal Ages* (animated), YTV, 2005.

Television Appearances; Episodic:

Camp Candy, NBC, 1989.

Allan, "Playing Solitaire," *Madison*, 1994.

Allan, "Junior Partner," *Madison*, 1994.

Mick, "Time Bomb," *The Odyssey*, CBS, 1994.

Gabriel, "Hester," *Hawkeye*, 1995.

Voice, "The Wild Swans," *Stories from My Childhood* (animated; also known as *Mikhail Baryshnikov's "Stories from My Childhood"*), 1998.

Jack McKenna, "Honey, It's Quarkzilla," *Honey, I Shrunk the Kids: The TV Show*, syndicated, 1998.

Jack McKenna, "Honey, You're Driving Me like Crazy," *Honey, I Shrunk the Kids: The TV Show*, syndicated, 1999.

Mark, "Each Tub Must Stand on Its Own Bottom," *Hope Island*, PAX, 1999.

Jack McKenna, "Honey, I Shrink, Therefore I Am," *Honey, I Shrunk the Kids: The TV Show*, syndicated, 2000.

Raymo, "Digital Babylon," *Level 9*, UPN, 2000.

Tim, "Rest Stop," *Night Visions*, Fox, 2001.

Danny, "Zero Option," *UC: Undercover*, NBC, 2001.

Voice, *Alienators: Evolution Continues*, Fox, 2001.

Voice of Angel/Warren Worthington III, "On Angel's Wings," *X–Men: Evolution* (animated), The WB, 2001.

Voice of Angel/Warren Worthington III, "Under Lock and Key," *X–Men: Evolution* (animated), The WB, 2002.

Brendan Lahey, "Bunker Hill," *Andromeda* (also known as *Gene Roddenberry's "Andromeda"*), syndicated, 2002.

Malcolm, "Enemy Mind," *The Dead Zone* (also known as *Stephen King's "Dead Zone"*), USA Network, 2002.

Ted Kasselbaum, "Lies, Speculation & Deception," *Just Cause*, PAX, 2003.

Voice of Angel/Warren Worthington III, "Ascension: Parts 1 & 2," *X–Men: Evolution* (animated), The WB, 2003.

Sickert, "The Ripper," *The Collector*, 2005.

Chuck, "Phased and Confused," *Eureka* (also known as *A Town Called Eureka*), Sci–Fi Channel, 2008.

Voice of Quicksilver, "Hindsight: Part 2," *Wolverine and the X–Men* (animated), 2008.

Voice of Quicksilver, "Time Bomb," *Wolverine and the X–Men* (animated), 2008.

Voices of Quicksilver and Pietro Maximoff, "Past Discretions," *Wolverine and the X–Men* (animated), 2008.

Also appeared in episodes of *Birdland*, ABC; and *Falcon Beach*, Global.

Television Appearances; Specials:

The Making of "Eighteen," 2006.

Television Additional Voices; Animated Series:

Conan and the Young Warriors, CBS, 1994.

Action Man, Fox, 1995.

Sabrina's Secret Life, 2003–2004.

Krypto the Superdog, 2005.

Film Appearances:

Troy, *They* (also known as *Wes Craven Presents "They"*), Miramax/Dimension Films, 2002.

Grant, *Everyone*, TLA Releasing, 2005.

Macauley, *Eighteen*, TLA Releasing, 2005.

Cryer, *Pirates of the Caribbean: At World's End* (also known as *Pirates 3* and *P.O.T.C. 3*), Buena Vista, 2007.

Stage Appearances:

Eugene, *Candida,* Vancouver Playhouse, Vancouver, British Columbia, Canada, 2001.

Christopher Marlowe, *Dead Reckoning,* Performance Works at Granville Island, Vancouver, British Columbia, Canada, 2002.

Also appeared as Silvio, *Carlo Goldonis: The Servant of Two Masters;* Cale Blackwell, *Fire;* Macduff, *Macbeth;* and Richard of Gloucester, *Richard III.*

RECORDINGS

Animated Videos:

Voices of Sir Gallop, Sir Zeke, and Sir Trunk, *King Arthur and the Knights of Justice* (originally an animated television series), 1992.

Voice of Jack, *Kishin Heidan* (also known as *Alien Defender Geo–Armor: Kishin Corps, Kishin Corps,* and *Machine God Corps*), Pioneer, 1993.

(English version) Voice of Terry Bogard, *Fatal Fury 2: The New Battle,* 1993.

Voice of Terry Bogard, *Garou densetsu* (also known as *Fatal Fury: The Motion Picture*), 1994.

Voice of Terry Bogard, *Fatal Fury 1,* 1995.

Voice of Issei Nishikiyori, *Please Save My Earth,* Viz Video, 1996.

Voice of Terry Bogard, *Fatal Fury 2,* 1996.

Voice of Terry Bogard, *Fatal Fury 3,* 1998.

Voice of Stefan, *Barbie as Rapunzel,* Artisan Entertainment, 2002.

Voice of Prince Daniel, *Barbie of Swan Lake,* Artisan Entertainment, 2003.

Voice of Hi–Tech, *G.I. Joe: Valor vs. Venom,* Paramount Home Video, 2004.

Voice of Dominic, *Barbie as the Princess and the Pauper,* Lions Gate Films Home Entertainment, 2004.

Voice of Sutton, *My Scene Goes Hollywood,* Buena Vista Home Video, 2005.

Voice of Aiden, *Barbie and the Magic of Pegasus 3–D,* Lions Gate Films Home Entertainment, 2005.

Also voice of Eric for English version of *The Humanoid,* Central Park Media.

Video Games:

(Uncredited) Voice of Heero Yuy, *Gundam: Battle Assault 2,* Bandai Games, 2002.

Voice, *SSX 3,* Electronic Arts, 2003.

(Uncredited) Voice of Heero Yuy, *Battle Assault 3 Featuring Gundam Seed,* Bandai Games, 2004.

Voice of Roy Jones, *Company of Heroes: Opposing Fronts,* THQ, 2007.

Voices of soldiers, *Metal Gear Solid 4: Guns of the Patriots* (also known as *Metal Gear Solid 4* and *MGS4*), Konami Digital Entertainment, 2008.

OTHER SOURCES

Electronic:

Mark Hildreth Official Site, http://www.mark-hildreth.com, January 24, 2009.

HILTON, Tyler 1983–

PERSONAL

Full name, Tyler James Hilton; born November 22, 1983, in Palm Springs, CA. *Education:* Attended high school in La Quinta, CA.

Addresses: *Agent*—Jim Ornstein, William Morris Agency, 1 William Morris Pl., Beverly Hills, CA 90212. *Manager*—Victoria Blake, Victoria Blake Management, 23622 Calabasas Rd., Suite 230, Calabasas, CA 91302.

Career: Actor, singer, guitarist, songwriter, and recording artist. Performer at clubs and on concert tours.

Awards, Honors: Teen Choice Award nomination, choice crossover artist, 2005; Teen Choice Award nomination, choice male television breakout performance, 2005, for *One Tree Hill.*

CREDITS

Television Appearances; Series:

Chris Keller, *One Tree Hill,* The WB, 2004–2006, then CW Network, 2006–2007.

Television Appearances; Specials:

The Teen Choice Awards, Fox, 2004, 2005.

Himself as Elvis Presley, *Celebrating the Man in Black: The Making of "Walk the Line,"* 2005.

New Year's Eve Live!, Fox, 2005.

Host, *Where Music Meets Film,* Fuse, 2008.

Television Appearances; Episodic:

Folk singer, "Old Enough to Fight," *American Dreams* (also known as *Our Generation*), NBC, 2004.

Television Guest Appearances; Episodic:
The Tony Danza Show, syndicated, 2005.
The Tonight Show with Jay Leno, NBC, 2005.
All That, Nickelodeon, 2005.
Total Request Live (also known as *Total Request with Carson Daly, TRL,* and *TRL Weekend*), MTV, 2005, 2006.
The Bonnie Hunt Show, CBS, 2008.

Film Appearances:
Elvis Presley, *Walk the Line,* Twentieth Century–Fox, 2005.
Murphey Bivens, *Charlie Bartlett,* Metro–Goldwyn–Mayer, 2007.

RECORDINGS

Albums:
Tyler Hilton, 2001.
The Tracks of Tyler Hilton, Maverick Records, 2004.
One Tree Hill: Music from the WB Television Series, 2005.
One Tree Hill, Volume 2: Friends with Benefit, 2006.

Singles include "How Love Should Be," 2005.

Videos:
Appeared as Drew in the music video "Teardrops on My Guitar" by Taylor Swift, 2006.

WRITINGS

Songwriter:
Songs include "Glad" and "When the Stars Go Blue."

HODGES, Tom 1965–
(Thom Hodges, Thomas E. Hodges)

PERSONAL

Born July 1, 1965, in Chicago, IL.

Addresses: *Manager*—Verve Entertainment, 6140 West Washington Blvd., Culver City, CA 90232.

Career: Actor, producer, director, and writer. Sometimes credited as Thom Hodges.

Awards, Honors: Lumiere Award, New Orleans Film Festival, and Special Festival Award, Stony Brook Film Festival, both 2000, for *Last Request;* Audience Award, best short film, Deep Ellum Film Festival, and Bob Award, Crested Butte Reel Fest, both 2003, for *Stunt Cocks.*

CREDITS

Film Appearances:
(As Thomas E. Hodges) Bruno, *Lucas,* Twentieth Century–Fox, 1986.
Tiny, *Revenge of the Nerds II: Nerds in Paradise,* Twentieth Century–Fox, 1987.
Wesley, *Critters 2: The Main Course,* New Line Cinema, 1988.
Louis "Louie" Jones, *Steel Magnolias,* TriStar, 1989.
Aunt Sparkle and Butler, *Tales of Two Sisters,* Vista Street Entertainment, 1989.
Bob and Schecky's mother, *Going Overboard* (also known as *Babes Ahoy*), 1989.
Marjorie Zipp, *The Dark Backward* (also known as *The Man with Three Arms*), Strand Releasing, 1991.
Don Curran, *Frame Up,* Poor Robert Productions, 1991.
Dylan, *Excessive Force,* New Line Cinema, 1992.
Les Parker, *The Baby Doll Murders,* Republic, 1993.
Lars, *Heavyweights,* Buena Vista, 1995.
The Killers Within, 1995.
Groom, *Michael,* New Line Cinema, 1996.
Shoot the Moon, Sugardaddy Productions, 1996.
Third "asshole," *I Love You, Don't Touch Me!,* Metro–Goldwyn–Mayer/United Artists, 1998.
Emergency room nurse, *Stigmata,* Metro–Goldwyn–Mayer, 1999.
Bork, *Homo Erectus* (also known as *National Lampoon's "The Stoned Age"*), National Lampoon, 2007.
Tim "Tiny" Wonders, *The Grand,* Anchor Bay Entertainment, 2007.
Stuart, *Look,* Liberated Artists, 2007.
Eric, *Overnight,* Red Eye Productions/Fusion Film Group, 2009.

Film Producer:
(And director) *Shoot the Moon,* Sugardaddy Productions, 1996.
(And director) *Last Request,* Kismet Productions, 1999.
Humanoid, Johnny Plastic Productions, 2003.
(And director) *Stunt Cocks,* Broken Glass Pictures/Legacy Group Productions, 2004.
Fly Like Mercury, Johnny Plastic Productions, 2008.

Television Appearances; Movies:
Rob, *Night of Courage,* ABC, 1987.
Ray Jacobs, *In the Best Interest of the Children,* NBC, 1992.
Mark Schwartz, *It's Nothing Personal,* NBC, 1993.

Condo manager, *The Disappearance of Christina,* USA Network, 1993.

Jim Schoenfeld, *They've Taken Our Children: The Chowchilla Kidnapping* (also known as *Vanished without a Trace*), ABC, 1993.

Second soldier, *Blind Justice* (also known as *Canaan's Way*), HBO, 1994.

Pat Prince, *Since You've Been Gone* (also known as *Ten Years Later*), ABC, 1998.

Jake, *Judas Kiss,* Cinemax, 1998.

Passenger cop, *Late Last Night,* Starz!, 1999.

Television Appearances; Series:

Rich, a recurring role, *Valerie* (also known as *The Hogan Family, The Hogans,* and *Valerie's Family*), NBC, between 1986 and 1989.

Bob, *Damian Cromwell's Postcards from America,* 1997.

Voice of computer, *Titans of Justice* (animated), 2006.

Television Appearances; Specials:

Tom, "A Family Again," *ABC Afterschool Specials,* ABC, 1988.

Matt, *Another Round,* 1992.

Title role, *The Great O'Grady,* Showtime, 1993.

Karl, *Seed: A Love Story,* Lifetime, 1998.

Television Appearances; Miniseries:

Jeff, *Nutcracker: Money, Madness & Murder,* NBC, 1987.

Television Appearances; Episodic:

Hal, "Where Have All the Children Gone?" *Airwolf* (also known as *Lobo del aire*), CBS, 1985.

Tiny, "No Day at the Beach," *Amazing Stories* (also known as *Steven Spielberg's "Amazing Stories"*), NBC, 1986.

Not Kuzak, "Gibbon Take," *L.A. Law,* 1986.

Ernie, "A Winter's Tale," *The Facts of Life,* NBC, 1987.

Cole, "Papa Simon," *The Wizard,* CBS, 1987.

Mike Parker, "In with the 'In' Crowd," *Highway to Heaven,* NBC, 1987.

"Dusk to Dawn," *Vietnam War Story,* HBO, 1988.

Corporal Nichols, "Who's Happy Now?" *China Beach,* ABC, 1989.

Alexander Duckworth, "Vietnam Rag," *Tour of Duty,* CBS, 1990.

Mark, "Start of the Fire," *Equal Justice,* 1990.

Carl Slotkin, "Julie Gets Validated," *Nurses,* NBC, 1992.

Carl Slotkin, "Love and Death," *Nurses,* NBC, 1993.

Billy Clancy, "Crime Wave Dave," *Walker, Texas Ranger* (also known as *Walker*), CBS, 1993.

Lieutenant Hogan, "High Ground," *JAG* (also known as *JAG: Judge Advocate General*), NBC, 1996.

Pechetti, "Empok Nor," *Star Trek: Deep Space Nine* (also known as *Deep Space Nine, DS9,* and *Star Trek: DS9*), syndicated, 1997.

Third pool player, "On the Road," *Mad About You,* NBC, 1997.

Mr. Copely, "Civil Wars," *Dr. Quinn, Medicine Woman,* CBS, 1997.

Jasper, "An Angel on the Roof," *Touched by an Angel,* CBS, 1998.

Also appeared in an episode of *Eddie Dodd,* ABC.

Television Work; Series:

Producer and director, *Titans of Justice* (animated), 2006.

Stage Appearances:

Keith, *D Girl,* Century City Playhouse, Los Angeles, 1997.

WRITINGS

Screenplays:

Shoot the Moon, Sugardaddy Productions, 1996.

ADAPTATIONS

"The Best of Friends, Worst of Times," an episode of the television series *Valerie* (also known as *The Hogan Family, The Hogans,* and *Valerie's Family*), broadcast by NBC in 1990, was based on a story by Hodges.

HOPKINS, Anthony 1937–
(Sir Anthony Hopkins)

PERSONAL

Given name is pronounced An–tony; full name, Philip Anthony Hopkins; born December 31, 1937, in Port Talbot, South Wales, England; son of Richard Arthur (a baker) and Muriel Annie (maiden name, Yeates) Hopkins; immigrated to the United States, naturalized citizen, April 12, 2000; married Petronella Barker, 1967 (divorced, 1972); married Jennifer Lynton (a production secretary), January 13, 1973 (divorced, 2002); married Stella Arroyave (an antiques dealer), March 1, 2003; children: (first marriage) Abigail. *Education:* Graduated from Cardiff College of Music and Drama, 1957; graduated from the Royal Academy of Dramatic Art, 1963. *Avocational Interests:* Piano, reading, painting.

Addresses: *Agent*—Independent Talent Group, Oxford House, 76 Oxford St., London W1D 1BS United Kingdom; Endeavor, 9601 Wilshire Blvd., 3rd Floor,

Beverly Hills, CA 90210. *Publicist*—Rogers and Cowan Public Relations, 8687 Melrose Ave., Pacific Design Center, 7th Floor, Los Angeles, CA 90069.

Career: Actor and director. Appeared in repertory with Nottingham Repertory Company, Nottingham, England; Phoenix Theatre, Leicester, England; Liverpool Playhouse, Liverpool, England; and Hornchurch Repertory Company, Hornchurch, England; Royal Shakespeare Company, member; National Theater ensemble, member; appeared in television commercials for Agilent Technologies, 1999, and Barclays Bank, 2000. Library Theatre, Manchester, England, assistant stage manager, 1960; Ruskins School of Acting, Santa Monica, CA, volunteer instructor. Also worked at a steel factory near Port Talbot, Wales. *Military service:* British Army, bombardier in Royal Artillery, 1958–60.

Member: Academy of Motion Picture Arts and Sciences, American Film Institute, British Academy of Film and Television Arts.

Awards, Honors: Film Award nomination, best supporting actor, British Academy of Film and Television Arts, 1969, for *The Lion in Winter;* Plays and Players London Theatre Critics Award, most promising newcomer, 1971, for work with the National Theatre; Television Award, best actor, British Academy of Film and Television Arts, 1972, for *War and Peace;* New York Drama Desk Award, outstanding actor in a play, American Authors and Celebrity Forum Award, and Outer Critics Circle Award, distinguished performance, all 1975, for *Equus;* Emmy Award, outstanding lead actor in a drama special, and Outer Critics Circle Award, both 1976, for *The Lindbergh Kidnapping Case;* Los Angeles Drama Critics Award, best actor, 1977, for *Equus;* Saturn Award, best actor—horror, Academy of Science Fiction, Fantasy and Horror Films, 1978, for *Audrey Rose;* Golden Globe Award nomination, best motion picture actor, and Film Award nomination, best actor, British Academy of Film and Television Arts, both 1979, for *Magic;* Emmy Award, outstanding lead actor in a limited series or special, 1981, for *The Bunker;* Emmy Award nomination, outstanding lead actor in a limited series or special, 1982, for *The Hunchback of Notre Dame;* Film Actor Award, Variety Club, 1984, for *The Bounty;* British Theatre Association Award, best actor, Laurence Olivier Award, Society of West End Theatre, Plays and Players London Theatre Critics Award, best actor, and Stage Actor Award, Variety Club, all 1985, for *Pravda;* CableACE Award, best actor in a movie or miniseries, 1986, for *Mussolini;* Best Actor Award, Moscow Film Festival, 1987, for *84 Charing Cross Road;* Commander, Order of the British Empire, 1987; honorary D.Litt., University of Wales, 1988; Golden Globe Award nomination, best performance by an actor

in a miniseries or motion picture made for television, 1989, for *The Tenth Man;* Academy Award, best actor, National Board of Review Award, best supporting actor, New York Film Critics Circle Award, best actor, Film Award, best actor, British Academy of Film and Television Arts, Boston Society of Film Critics Award, best supporting actor, 1991, Golden Globe Award nomination, best performance by an actor in a motion picture, ALFS Award nomination, actor of the year, London Film Critics Circle, and Saturn Award, best actor, Academy of Science Fiction, Fantasy and Horror Films, 1992, all for *The Silence of the Lambs;* Knighted, 1993; Los Angeles Film Critics Association Award, best actor, National Board of Review Award, best actor, 1993, and Film Award, best leading actor, British Academy of Film and Television Arts, 1994, all for *Shadowlands;* Los Angeles Film Critics Association Award, best actor, 1993, ALFS Award, actor of the year, London Film Critics Circle, Academy Award nomination, best actor in a leading role, Golden Globe Award nomination, best performance by an actor in a motion picture—drama, Southeastern Film Critics Association Award, best actor, David di Donatello Award, best foreign actor, Film Award nomination, best leading actor, British Academy of Film and Television Arts, 1994, all for *The Remains of the Day;* Bronze Wrangler Award (with others), theatrical motion picture, Western Heritage Awards, 1995, for *Legends of the Fall;* Screen Actors Guild Award nomination, outstanding performance by a male actor in a leading role, Golden Globe Award nomination, best performance by an actor in a motion picture—drama, and Academy Award nomination, best actor in a leading role, all 1996, for *Nixon;* Commander, Order of Arts & Letters, France, 1996; ShoWest Award, actor of the year, 1998; Donostia Lifetime Achievement Award, San Sebastian International Film Festival, 1998; Screen Actors Guild Award nomination, outstanding performance by a male actor in a supporting role, Online Film Critics Society Award nomination, best supporting actor, Golden Globe Award nomination, best performance by an actor in a supporting role, Broadcast Film Critics Association Award, best supporting actor, and Academy Award nomination, best supporting actor, 1998, for *Amistad;* Saturn Award nomination, best actor, Academy of Science Fiction, Fantasy and Horror Films, 1999, for *Meet Joe Black;* Virginia Film Award, Virginia Film Festival, 2000; Man of the Year Award, Hasty Pudding Theatricals, Harvard University, 2001; ALFS Award nomination, British actor of the year, London Film Critics Circle, 2001, for *Titus;* MTV Movie Award nominations, best kiss (with Julianne Moore) and best villain, 2001, Saturn Award nomination, best actor, Academy of Science Fiction, Fantasy and Horror Films, 2002, for *Hannibal;* People's Choice Award nomination, favorite motion picture star in a drama, 2002; Master Screen Artist Tribute, USA Film Festival, 2002; Star on Hollywood Walk of Fame, 2003; Hollywood Film Award, outstanding achievement in acting—male performer, 2003; Hollywood Film Award (with others), ensemble of the year, 2006, Screen Actors Guild Award nomination (with others), outstanding performance by a cast in a motion picture, 2007, both for *Bobby;* New Zealand Screen Award, best performance by an actor in a leading role, 2006, for *The World's Fastest Indian;* Cecil B. DeMille Award, Golden Globe Awards, 2006, for lifetime achievement; Youth Jury Award and Golden Leopard Award nomination, Locarno International Film Festival, 2007, both for *Slipstream;* Academy Fellowship, British Academy of Film and Television Arts, 2008.

CREDITS

Film Appearances:

Voice of Marcus Crassus, *Spartacus* (restored version), Universal, 1960.

Brechtian, *The White Bus* (also known as *Red, White and Zero*), 1967.

Prince Richard the Lionhearted, *The Lion in Winter*, Avco–Embassy, 1968.

Claudius, *Hamlet* (also known as *Shakespeare's "Hamlet"*), Columbia, 1969.

John Avery, *The Looking Glass War*, Columbia, 1970.

Philip Calvert, *When Eight Bells Toll* (also known as *Alistair Maclean's "When Eight Bells Toll"*), Cinerama, 1971.

David Lloyd George, *Young Winston*, Columbia, 1972.

Torvald Helmer, *A Doll's House*, Paramount, 1973.

Kostya, *The Girl from Petrovka*, Universal, 1974.

Superintendent John McCleod, *Juggernaut* (also known as *Terror on the Britannic*), United Artists, 1974.

Elliot Hoover, *Audrey Rose*, United Artists, 1977.

Lieutenant Colonel John Frost, *A Bridge Too Far*, United Artists, 1977.

Captain Johnson, *International Velvet*, Metro–Goldwyn–Mayer/United Artists, 1978.

Corky/voice of Fats the dummy, *Magic*, Twentieth Century–Fox, 1978.

Adam Evans, *A Change of Seasons*, Twentieth Century–Fox, 1980.

Dr. Frederick Treves, *The Elephant Man*, Paramount, 1980.

Lieutenant William Bligh, *The Bounty*, Orion, 1984.

Bill Hooper, *The Good Father*, Skouras, 1986.

Frank Doel, *84 Charing Cross Road*, Columbia, 1987.

Dafydd Llewellyn, *A Chorus of Disapproval*, Southgate Entertainment, 1987.

Major Angus Barry ("Cassius"), *The Dawning*, TVS Entertainment/Vista, 1988.

Tim Cornell, *Desperate Hours*, Metro–Goldwyn–Mayer/United Artists, 1990.

Errol Wallace, *The Efficiency Expert* (also known as *Spotswood*), Miramax, 1991.

Dr. Hannibal Lecter, *The Silence of the Lambs*, Orion, 1991.

Professor Abraham Van Helsing/Ships captain/Cesare, *Bram Stoker's "Dracula"* (also known as *Dracula*), Columbia, 1992.

McCandless, *Freejack*, Warner Bros., 1992.

Henry Wilcox, *Howards End*, Sony Pictures Classics, 1992.

George Hayden, *Chaplin* (also known as *Charlot*), TriStar, 1992.

Voice of reader, *Earth and the American Dream*, 1992.

Priest, *The Trial*, Angelika Films, 1993.

James Stevens, butler of Darlington House, *The Remains of the Day*, Columbia, 1993.

C. S. "Jack" Lewis, *Shadowlands*, Savoy Pictures, 1993.

Bob Glass, *The Innocent* (also known as *Und der Himmel steht still*), 1993.

Dr. John Harvey Kellogg, *The Road to Wellville*, Columbia, 1994.

Colonel William Ludlow, *Legends of the Fall*, TriStar, 1994.

Himself, *A Century of Cinema*, 1994.

(As Sir Anthony Hopkins) Actor, *In Ismail's Custody*, 1994.

Richard M. Nixon, *Nixon*, Buena Vista, 1995.

Ieuan Davies, *August*, Samuel Goldwyn, 1996.

Pablo Picasso, *Surviving Picasso*, Warner Bros., 1996.

John Quincy Adams, *Amistad*, Dreamworks SKG, 1997.

Bookworm, Fox Film, 1997.

Charles Morse, *The Edge*, Twentieth Century–Fox, 1997.

Narrator, *The Lost Children of Berlin*, 1997.

Don Diego de la Vega/Older Zorro, *Mark of Zorro* (also known as *The Mask of Zorro*), Columbia, 1998.

William Parrish, *Meet Joe Black*, MCA/Universal, 1998.

Himself, *Junket Whore*, 1998.

Himself, *The Uttmost*, 1998.

Ethan Powell, *Instinct*, Buena Vista, 1999.

Narrator, *Siegfried & Roy: The Magic Box* (also known as *The Magic Box*), IMAX, 1999.

Titus Andronicus, *Titus*, 1999.

Himself, *The Making of "Amistad,"* 1999.

(Uncredited) Mission Commander Swanbeck, *Mission: Impossible* (also known as *M: I–2*), Paramount, 2000.

Narrator, *How the Grinch Stole Christmas* (also known as *Dr. Seuss' "How the Grinch Stole Christmas,"* *Der Grinch*, and *The Grinch*), MCA/Universal, 2000.

Conversations with Jon Turteltaub (also known as *Spotlight on John Turteltaub*), Buena Vista, 2000.

(Uncredited) Himself, *The Making of "Titus,"* 2000.

Hannibal Lecter, *Hannibal*, MCA/Universal, 2001.

Ted Brautigan, *Hearts in Atlantis*, Warner Bros., 2001.

Himself, *Blind Loyalty, Hollow Honor: England's Fatal Flaw* (documentary short), Columbia TriStar Home Entertainment, 2001.

Himself, *Behind the Scenes: "Hannibal"* (documentary), 2001.

Himself, *Inside the Labyrinth: The Making of "The Silence of the Lambs"* (documentary), Metro–Goldwyn–Mayer/United Artists Home Entertainment, 2001.

Himself, *"The Remains of the Day": The Filmmaker's Journey* (documentary short), Columbia TriStar Home Entertainment, 2001.

Himself, *Breaking the Silence: The Making of "Hannibal"* (documentary), Metro–Goldwyn–Mayer Home Entertainment, 2001.

Gaylord Oakes, *Bad Company* (also known as *Ceska spojka*), Buena Vista, 2002.

Dr. Hannibal Lecter, *Red Dragon* (also known as *Roter Drache*), MCA/Universal, 2002.

Coleman Silk, *The Human Stain* (also known as *La couleur du mensonge* and *Der Menschliche Makel*), Miramax, 2003.

Himself, *Noin,* 2003.

Himself, *A Director's Journey: The Making of "Red Dragon"* (documentary short), Universal Home Video, 2003.

Daniel Webster, *The Devil and Daniel Webster* (also known as *Shortcut to Happiness*), Yari Film Group Releasing, 2004.

Old Ptolemy, *Alexander* (also known as *Alexander Revisited: The Final Cut, Alexander: Director's Cut,* and *Alexandre*), Warner Bros., 2004.

Himself, *On the Set of "Alexander"* (documentary short), Warner Home Video, 2004.

I–J

IRWIN, John
   See VAN PATTEN, Dick

JACKSON, Shar 1976–
   (Sharisse Jackson)

PERSONAL

Original name, Sharisse Jackson; born August 31, 1976, in Boston, MA; children: (with Kevin Federline, an actor and singer) Kori, Kaleb; Donnie, Cassie. *Education:* Studied acting with the Al Fann Theatrical Ensemble and Bob Feldman; earned bachelor's degree in psychology and master's degree in forensic science.

Addresses: *Agent*—Sovereign Talent Group, 10474 Santa Monica Blvd., Suite 301, Los Angeles, CA 90025. *Publicist*—It Girl Public Relations, 5301 Beethoven St., Suite 220, Los Angeles, CA 90066.

Career: Actress. Previously worked as a model; appeared in television commercials, including the Jack LaLanne Power Juicer.

CREDITS

Film Appearances:
(As Sharisse Jackson) Tamika, *CB4,* Universal, 1993.
Monique, *Good Burger,* Paramount, 1997.
Felicia, *Love & Basketball* (also known as *Love and Basketball*), New Line Cinema, 2000.
Family Reunion: The Movie, Artisan Entertainment, 2003.
Alexa, *The House That Jack Built,* FourTwoFive Films, 2008.

Daphne, *Toxic,* Weinstein Company, 2008.
Beautiful girl, *The Fish,* 2009.
Uwamma Layne, *Steppin: The Movie,* Weinstein Company, 2009.

Television Appearances; Series:
Niecy Jackson, *Moesha,* UPN, 1996–2000.
Celebrity Rap Superstar, MTV, 2007.
Herself, *Ex Wives Club,* ABC, 2007.

Television Appearances; Movies:
Carlene, *Grand Avenue,* HBO, 1996.

Television Appearances; Specials:
It's Hot in Here: UPN Fall Preview, UPN, 1996.
The 67th Annual Hollywood Christmas Parade, UPN, 1998.
VH1 Big in '04, VH1, 2004.
Wendy Williams is on Fire on the Red Carpet, VH1, 2005.
50 Shocking Celebrity Confessions, E! Entertainment Television, 2006.

Television Appearances; Pilots:
Tammy, *Minor Adjustments,* NBC, 1995.

Television Appearances; Episodic:
Rhonda, "Up in the Attic," *Roc,* Fox, 1993.
Monica, "Boyz in the Woodz," *Hangin' With Mr. Cooper,* ABC, 1993.
Charlayne, "Get the Jet," *Tall Hopes,* CBS, 1993.
Juanita, "In the Driver's Seat," *Getting By,* NBC, 1994.
Janelle, "Dad," *South Central,* Fox, 1994.
Janelle, "Dog," *South Central,* Fox, 1994.
Crystal, "Guns and Gossip," *My So–Called Life,* ABC, 1994.
Crystal, "Father Figures," *My So–Called Life,* ABC, 1994.
Sara Louise, *On Our Own,* ABC, 1994.

Teen girl, *Me and the Boys,* ABC, 1994.
Cicely, *Me and the Boys,* ABC, 1994.
Tammy, *Minor Adjustments,* 1995.
Lynette, *The Parent 'Hood,* The WB, 1995.
Carol, *Hangin' With Mr. Cooper,* ABC, 1995.
Angel, "That's My Mama," *The Steve Harvey Show,* The WB, 1996.
Desire, "Young at Heart," *Sister, Sister,* The WB, 1998.
Stacey, "Achy Breaky Heart," *Smart Guy,* The WB, 1998.
Niecy, "Prom Misses, Prom Misses," *Clueless,* UPN, 1999.
Niecy Jackson, "Kimberlae," *The Parkers,* UPN, 1999.
Niecy Jackson, "Scary Kim," *The Parkers,* UPN, 2000.
Celebrity contestant, "Mazatlan, Mexico (I)," *Search Party,* E! Entertainment Television, 2000.
Celebrity contestant, "Mazatlan, Mexico (II)," *Search Party,* E! Entertainment Television, 2000.
Niecy Jackson, "Old Dog," *Girlfriends,* UPN, 2001.
Voice of Bethany, "Hip–Hop Helicopter," *The Proud Family* (animated), The Disney Channel, 2002.
Valerie, "Spinning Wheels," *The Bernie Mac Show,* Fox, 2006.
"Painful Celebrity Breakups," *The Dr. Keith Ablow Show,* The WB, 2006.
Entertainment Television (also known as *E.T.*), syndicated, 2007.
"Top 25 Heartaches," *BET's Top 25 Countdown,* Black Entertainment Television, 2008.
"The Package Deal: Dating Someone with Kids," *Baisen After Dark,* 2008.
Alyson, "Everybody Hates Ex–Cons," *Everybody Hates Chris,* The CW, 2008.

RECORDINGS

Music Videos:
Appeared in Missy Eliot's "One Minute Man."

OTHER SOURCES

Periodicals:
Essence, January, 2005, p. 158.
USA Today, May 25, 2007, p. 2E.

JAEGER, Sam 1977–

PERSONAL

Full name, Samuel Heath Jaeger; born January 29, 1977, in Perrysburg, OH; son of Charles and LeAnne Jaeger; married Amber Marie Mellott, August 25, 2007. *Education:* Otterbein College, B.F.A., 1999.

Addresses: *Agent*—Greene and Associates, 190 North Canon Dr., Suite 200, Beverly Hills, CA 90210.

Career: Actor.

CREDITS

Film Appearances:
Red Crown operator number one, *Behind Enemy Lines,* Twentieth Century–Fox, 2001.
Captain R. G. Sisk, *Hart's War,* Metro–Goldwyn–Mayer, 2002.
Deputy, *Blood Work,* Warner Bros., 2002.
Colt Skyler, *Advantage Hart,* 2003.
Jerry's best friend, *Sexual Life,* Sexual Life, Inc., 2005.
Nick Fisher, *Lucky Number Slevin* (also known as *Lucky # Slevin, Lucky Number S7evin,* and *The Wrong Man*), Metro–Goldwyn–Mayer, 2006.
The filmmaker, *S.C.R.E.W.E.D.* (short), Nurick Films, 2006.
Dennis, *Catch and Release,* Sony, 2006.
Max, *Breaking Down Carla* (short), 2007.
Nathan Weiss, *Within,* 2008.
Thom, *Take Me Home,* 2009.

Film Work:
Producer, *Advantage Hart* (short), 2003.
Director and producer, *Take Me Home,* 2009.

Also worked as coproducer, *Quiz Bowl* (short); director, *Untold* (short).

Television Appearances; Series:
Kevin O'Neil, *Girls Club,* Fox, 2002.
Matt Dowd, *Eli Stone,* ABC, 2008–2009.

Television Appearances; Pilots:
Kevin O'Neil, *Girls Club,* Fox, 2002.
Tom, *More, Patience,* Fox, 2006.
Matt Dowd, *Eli Stone,* ABC, 2008.

Television Appearances; Movies:
Double Platinum, ABC, 1999.
Dave Reichert, *The Riverman,* Arts and Entertainment, 2004.

Television Appearances; Episodic:
Bill Conway, "Admissions," *Law & Order,* NBC, 1999.
Bill Kelley, "In This White House," *The West Wing,* NBC, 2000.
Andy Paulsen, "Something Battered, Something Blue," *That's Life,* CBS, 2001.
"Quo Vadis?," *ER,* NBC, 2001.
Steve Larkin, "My Philosophy," *Scrubs,* NBC, 2003.

Kevin the Bellman, "Lucky Strike," *CSI: Crime Scene Investigation* (also known as *C.S.I., CSI: Las Vegas,* and *Les Experts*), CBS, 2003.
Kamal "Tim Garrity" Muhammad, "Passing the Stone," *NYPD Blue,* ABC, 2004.
Vince's partner, "Ties That Bind," *Commander in Chief,* ABC, 2006.
Tom, "Heather's Visit," *Notes from the Underbelly,* ABC, 2007.
Current TV, 2007.

RECORDINGS

Video Games:
Greg Tikara, *Code Blue,* 2000.

WRITINGS

Screenplays:
Advantage Hart (short), 2003.
Take Me Home, 2009.

Also cowrote *Quiz Bowl* (short).

JAMES, Theo
See ANTONIO, Lou

JENNEY, Lucinda 1954–
(Lucinda Jenny)

PERSONAL

Born April 23, 1954, in Long Island City, NY; children: Marion Moseley (an actress).

Addresses: *Agent*—Domain, 9229 Sunset Blvd., Suite 415, Los Angeles, CA 90069. *Manager*—J. B. Roberts, Thruline Entertainment, 9250 Wilshire Blvd., Suite 100, Beverly Hills, CA 90212.

Career: Actress.

Awards, Honors: Independent Spirit Award nomination, best supporting actress, Independent Features Project West, 1994, for *American Heart.*

CREDITS

Film Appearances:
Imposters, International Film Circuit, 1979.

Hearts and Diamonds (also known as *Ocean City*), East 7th Street Productions, 1984.
Olivia, *The Whoopee Boys,* Paramount, 1986.
Rosalie Testa, *Peggy Sue Got Married,* TriStar, 1986.
Bobby, *The Verne Miller Story* (also known as *Gangland* and *Verne Miller*), Manson International, 1987.
Iris, *Rain Man,* Metro–Goldwyn–Mayer/United Artists, 1988.
Judy Jacklin Belushi, *Wired,* Taurus Entertainment, 1989.
Second passerby at Democratic Convention, *Born on the Fourth of July,* Universal, 1989.
Lena, *Thelma & Louise,* Metro–Goldwyn–Mayer, 1991.
Charlotte, *American Heart,* Triton Pictures, 1992.
Anne Loomis, *Matinee,* Universal, 1993.
Christine, *Mr. Jones,* TriStar, 1993.
Weird woman, *Leaving Las Vegas,* United Artists, 1995.
Marion, *Grace of My Heart,* Gramercy, 1996.
Heidi Halleck, *Thinner* (also known as *Stephen King's "Thinner"*), Paramount, 1996.
Rosie Trickle, *The Last Time I Committed Suicide,* Kushner–Locke, 1997.
Lieutenant Blondell, *G.I. Jane,* Buena Vista, 1997.
Jenny Baily, *Mad City,* Warner Bros., 1997.
Kate Amerson, *Loved,* Imperial Entertainment, 1997.
Caroline Baxter, *Desert Blue,* Samuel Goldwyn Company, 1998.
Mrs. Jacobs, *What Dreams May Come,* PolyGram Filmed Entertainment, 1998.
Sara as an adult, *Practical Magic,* Warner Bros., 1998.
(As Lucinda Jenny) Actress at Alison Ander's house, *Welcome to Hollywood,* Phaedra Cinema, 1998.
Kate, *Sugar Town,* October Films, 1999.
Laurie, *The Deep End of the Ocean,* Sony Pictures Entertainment, 1999.
Vincent's mom, *Crime and Punishment in Suburbia,* Metro–Goldwyn–Mayer/United Artists, 2000.
Trina Walsh, *How to Kill Your Neighbor's Dog* (also known as *Mad Dogs and Englishmen*), Artistic License, 2000.
Arleen Yoast, *Remember the Titans,* Buena Vista, 2000.
(Uncredited) Helen O'Donnell, *Thirteen Days,* New Line Cinema, 2000.
Courtney Oakley, *Crazy/Beautiful,* Buena Vista, 2001.
Denise Smallwood, *The Mothman Prophecies,* Sony Pictures Entertainment, 2002.
Kathy, *S.W.A.T.,* Columbia, 2003.
Betty, *Hide & Seek,* DaDoo Productions, 2006.
Sheryl "Chic" Van Scoyoc, *The Final Season,* Yari Film Group, 2007.
At the Beach, 2007.

Television Appearances; Movies:
Wanda, *The Kid from Nowhere,* NBC, 1982.
Mary, *Out of the Darkness,* CBS, 1985.
Carolyn, *First Steps,* CBS, 1985.
Neighbor lady, *The Thanksgiving Promise,* ABC, 1986.
Beth, *Shoot First: A Cop's Vengeance* (also known as *Vigilante Cop*), NBC, 1991.

Gross's secretary, *The Water Engine,* TNT, 1992.

Bernice Dayton, *The Habitation of Dragons,* TNT, 1992.

Marci Benedetti, *Next Door,* Showtime, 1994.

Elizabeth "Liz" Knowlton, *Eye of the Stalker* (also known as *Moment of Truth: Eye of the Stalker*), NBC, 1995.

Jeanine, *A Stranger in Town,* CBS, 1995.

Debbie Vickers, *The Late Shift,* HBO, 1996.

Sharon, *First–Time Felon,* HBO, 1997.

Molly, *Scattering Dad,* CBS, 1998.

Ella's mother, "2000" segment, *If These Walls Could Talk 2,* HBO, 2000.

Cindy Thomas, *The Pennsylvania Miners' Story,* ABC, 2002.

Television Appearances; Series:

Lanie Kellis, a recurring role, *The Shield,* FX Network, 2003.

Television Appearances; Specials:

Diane, *Two Over Easy,* Showtime, 1994.

"Patricia Heaton," *Biography,* Arts and Entertainment, 2003.

Television Appearances; Pilots:

Lucy, "Microcops," *CBS Summer Playhouse,* CBS, 1989.

Officer Anne Bonner, *High Incident,* ABC, 1996.

Nadine Walden, *The Visitor,* Fox, 1997.

Television Appearances; Episodic:

"Hell Hath No Fury," *Spenser: For Hire,* ABC, 1986.

Annie Pierce, "Vote of Confidence," *Miami Vice,* NBC, 1988.

Pamela Wilgis, JMJ Wilgis, Isbella Wilgis, and Sister Mary Maude, "Extreme Unction," *Homicide: Life on the Street* (also known as *Homicide*), NBC, 1994.

Ginny, "The Black Bargain," *Fallen Angels,* Showtime, 1995.

Officer Anne Bonner, "Till Death Do Us Part," *High Incident,* ABC, 1996.

Officer Anne Bonner, "Coroner's Day Off," *High Incident,* ABC, 1996.

Officer Anne Bonner, "Sometimes a Vague Notion," *High Incident,* ABC, 1996.

Mrs. Dog Face, "Every Dog Has Its Day," *EZ Streets,* CBS, 1997.

Nadine Walden, "Fear of Flying," *The Visitor,* Fox, 1997.

Rose Carlton, "Hammer Time," *NYPD Blue,* ABC, 1998.

Rosalind, "A Prayer for the Lying," *L.A. Doctors* (also known as *L.A. Docs*), CBS, 1998.

Linda Palmer, "First Love: Parts 1 & 2," *Cracker* (also known as *Cracker: Mind over Murder*), Arts and Entertainment, 1999.

Angela Jamison, "Summary Judgments," *The Practice,* ABC, 2000.

Angela Jamison, "Germ Warfare," *The Practice,* ABC, 2000.

Teddy Green, "The Race," *Gideon's Crossing,* ABC, 2001.

Allison Cossey, "Not Stumbling, but Dancing," *Judging Amy,* CBS, 2002.

Karen Kroft, "Swiss Diplomacy," *The West Wing,* NBC, 2002.

Flora Hawkins, "Milfay," *Carnivale* (also known as *La feria ambulante*), HBO, 2003.

Helen Singer, "Day 3: 1:00 p.m.–2:00 p.m.," *24,* Fox, 2003.

Helen Singer, "Day 3: 2:00 p.m.–3:00 p.m.," *24,* Fox, 2003.

Helen Singer, "Day 3: 3:00 p.m.–4:00 p.m.," *24,* Fox, 2003.

Helen Singer, "Day 3: 6:00 p.m.–7:00 p.m.," *24,* Fox, 2003.

Renee Bishop, "Married with Children," *Law & Order,* NBC, 2004.

Judy Strand, "Missing Pieces," *Crossing Jordan,* NBC, 2004.

Kenneth's ex–wife, "Untitled," *Six Feet Under,* HBO, 2004.

Sister Mary Eucharist, "Damned if You Do," *House M.D.* (also known as *House*), Fox, 2004.

Elise Garrett, "In the Wee Small Hours: Parts 1 & 2," *Law & Order: Criminal Intent* (also known as *Law & Order: CI*), NBC, 2005.

Sheriff Beth McGuire, "Leaving Las Vegas," *CSI: Crime Scene Investigation* (also known as *C.S.I., CSI: Las Vegas,* and *Les experts*), CBS, 2007.

Shirley Reed, "8:03 AM," *Cold Case,* CBS, 2007.

Carolanne Adama, "A Day in the Life," *Battlestar Galactica* (also known as *BSG*), Sci–Fi Channel, 2007.

Allison, "Sea Change," *ER,* NBC, 2007.

Zena Davis, "Mr. Monk Is Up All Night," *Monk,* USA Network, 2007.

Also appeared in *All My Children,* ABC; and *As the World Turns.*

Stage Appearances:

Gemini, Little Theatre, New York City, 1977–81.

Cinderella, *Cinders,* New York Shakespeare Festival, LuEsther Hall, Public Theatre, New York City, 1984.

The woman, "True to Life," and Tanya, "The Ground Zero Club," *Young Playwrights Festival,* Playwrights Horizons Theatre, New York City, 1985.

Ann, *Aven'u Boys,* John Houseman Theatre, New York City, 1993.

Title role, *Miss Julie,* Williamstown Theatre Festival, Williamstown, MA, 1996.

Also appeared in *Rosemary with Ginger,* Met Theatre.

JENSEN, Todd

PERSONAL

Education: San Diego State University, B.A., finance, 1985; University of Capetown, M.B.A., international business, 1994; studied with the Groundlings, at the Joanne Baron Studio, and at the William Esper Studio.

Addresses: *Contact*—5058 Wilshire Blvd., Suite 205, Los Angeles, CA 90036.

Career: Actor. Appeared in industrial films and worked as a voice artist.

Member: Screen Actors Guild, American Federation of Television and Radio Artists, Actors' Equity Association.

CREDITS

Film Appearances:
Dune Surfer, Moviworld, 1988.
Forced Alliance, Trident Releasing, 1989.
Jason, *Night of the Cyclone* (also known as *Perfume of the Cyclone*), 1990.
Simon Rush, *Prey for the Hunter,* Power Pictures, 1993.
Wendell Huston, *Woman of Desire,* Nu Image Films, 1993.
Joe Hutton, *Project Shadowchaser II* (also known as *Armed and Deadly, Night Scenes: Project Shadowchaser II, Night Siege,* and *Shadowchaser II*), Nu Image Films, 1994.
Michael Edelander and Throne, *Armageddon: The Final Challenge,* 1994.
Miguel Rodriguez, *Trigger Fast* (also known as *Guns of Honor: Trigger Fast*), Trimark Pictures, 1994.
Phillip Ryan, *Cyborg Cop* (also known as *Cyborg Ninja*), Trimark Pictures, 1994.
Rick, *Freefall* (also known as *Firefall*), Nu World/October Films, 1994.
Second detective, *Fleshtone,* 1994.
Roger Martin, *The Mangler,* New Line Cinema, 1995.
Roper, *Never Say Die,* Nu Image Films, 1995.
Michael Cavanaugh, *Orion's Key* (also known as *Alien Chaser, Project Shadowchaser 4,* and *Shadowchaser: The Gates of Time*), Nu Image Films/Unapix Films, 1996.
Tomas "Tom" Lansdale, *Warhead,* Trimark Pictures, 1996.
Ashley, *Breeders* (also known as *Deadly Instincts*), 1998.
Bob Johnson, *Operation Delta Force 5: Random Fire* (also known as *Operation Delta Force 5* and *Operation Python*), Martien Holdings, 1999.

Joshua Carter, *The Meeksville Ghost,* 2001.
Nick Carlton, *Target of Opportunity,* Nu Image Films, 2004.
Ben Stiles, *Raging Sharks* (also known as *Shark Invasion*), Nu Image Films, 2005.
Harry Prince, *Zodiac Killer* (also known as *Curse of the Zodiac* and *Ulli Lommel's "Zodiac Killer"*), 2005.
Parks, *The Cutter,* Nu Image Films, 2005.
Agent Smith, *End Game,* Millennium Films, 2006.
Dream City, Concorde/New Horizons, 2006.
Captain Sandman, *Finding Rin Tin Tin,* Nu Image Films, 2007.
Security chief Valentine, *Nightmare City 2035,* 2007.
Coach Harris, *Train* (also known as *Terror Train*), Lionsgate, 2008.
Detective Wallace MacTee, *Hero Wanted,* Nu Image Films, 2008.
John Polonius, *The Prince & Me 3: A Royal Honeymoon,* First Look Pictures Releasing, 2008.
Wray, *The Shepherd: Border Patrol* (also known as *The Shepherd*), Stage 6, 2008.
It's Alive, Millennium Films, 2008.
Thick as Thieves (also known as *The Code*), Millennium Films, 2008.
Agent Fletcher, *Echelon Conspiracy* (also known as *The Gift*), After Dark Films, 2009.
Detective Traxler, *Ninja,* Nu Image Films, 2009.
U.S. marshal, *Wrong Turn 3,* Twentieth Century–Fox Home Entertainment, 2009.

Television Appearances; Series:
John Hammond, *Rhodes,* BBC, CBC, and South African Broadcasting Corporation, 1996, broadcast on *Masterpiece Theatre* (also known as *ExxonMobil Masterpiece Theatre* and *Mobil Masterpiece Theatre*), PBS, 1998.

Television Appearances; Miniseries:
Lon Ysabel also known as Ysabel Kid and Miguel Rodriguez, *Guns of Honor* (also known as *Guns of Honour: Rebel Rousers*), 1994.

Television Appearances; Movies:
Hutch, *Operation Delta Force* (also known as *Great Soldiers*), HBO, 1997.
William, *Bridge of Time,* ABC, 1997.
Lombardi, *Operation Delta Force II: Mayday* (also known as *Operation Delta Force 2: Mayday*), HBO, 1998.
Sean, *Sabretooth,* Sci-Fi Channel, 2002.
Big Bo, *Mega Snake* (also known as *Megasnake* and *MegaSnake*), Sci-Fi Channel, 2007.
Colonel, *Bats: Human Harvest* (also known as *Bats 2*), Sci-Fi Channel, 2007.
Sheriff Mercer, *Copperhead,* Sci-Fi Channel, 2008.
Monster Ark (also known as *Genesis Code*), Sci-Fi Channel, 2008.
Hudson, *Termination Shock,* Sci-Fi Channel, 2009.

Television Appearances; Episodic:

Scott Hewlett, "Chapter Four, Year Two," *Murder One,* ABC, 1996.

Second reporter, "Part VI," *The Practice,* ABC, 1997.

First FBI agent, "Back to Business," *CI5: The New Professionals,* Sky, 1999.

Stage Appearances:

Appeared in stage productions.

RECORDINGS

Music Videos:

Appeared in music videos.

JOACHIM, Suzy

PERSONAL

Career: Actress.

Awards, Honors: Leo Award nomination, best performance by a female in a motion picture, Motion Picture Arts & Sciences Foundation of British Columbia, 2000, for *A Twist of Faith.*

CREDITS

Film Appearances:

Catherine Sienna, *Impolite,* 1992.

Vicky, *Ultimate Desires* (also known as *Beyond the Silhouette*), 1992.

Dorothy Raynor, *Time Runner* (also known as *In Exile*), North American Releasing, 1993.

Caroline, *Crackerjack,* 1994.

Sales clerk, *Flinch,* 1994.

Dr. Kari Dovell, *Hideaway,* TriStar, 1995.

Sheila Wills, *Unforgettable,* Metro–Goldwyn–Mayer, 1996.

Trish, *Barbecue: A Love Story* (also known as *Barbecue ... A Love Story*), Prophecy Entertainment, 1997.

Doctor, *Disturbing Behavior,* Metro–Goldwyn–Mayer, 1998.

Tina, *Rupert's Land,* 1998.

Monica Storks (some sources cite role as Monica Stoeks), *A Twist of Faith* (also known as *Beyond Redemption* and *Crack in the Mirror*), 1999.

Allana, *How to Kill Your Neighbor's Dog* (also known as *Mad Dogs and Englishmen*), Artistic License Films, 2000.

Elaine Vandergeld, *White Chicks,* Columbia, 2004.

Lisa (Jeff's date at the barbeque), *Martian Child,* New Line Cinema, 2007.

Television Appearances; Series:

Meaghan Lee Rose, a recurring role, *Jeremiah* (also known as *Jeremiah—Krieger des Donners*), Showtime, 2002–2003.

Television Appearances; Miniseries:

Autumn Robber, *Snow Queen,* The Hallmark Channel, 2002.

Television Appearances; Movies:

Cord's secretary, *Diagnosis of Murder* (also known as *A Diagnosis of Murder*), CBS, 1992.

Woman at bar, *Born to Run,* Fox, 1993.

Mary Simpson, *Guitarman,* [Canada], 1994.

Carmen, *Circumstances Unknown,* USA Network, 1995.

Florence Bisaillon, *Falling from the Sky: Flight 174* (also known as *Freefall: Flight 174*), ABC, 1995.

Jennifer, *A Family Divided,* NBC, 1995.

Detective Sandy Unger, *Mother, May I Sleep with Danger?,* NBC, 1996.

Linda Collings, *Maternal Instincts,* USA Network, 1996.

Kathy Hewitt, *The Alibi,* ABC, 1997.

Television Appearances; Episodic:

Diana, "The Twelfth Step," *Neon Rider,* CTV (Canada), 1991.

Inez Valens, "Loyalties," *Street Justice,* syndicated, 1991.

Gracie, "Dog Days," *The Commish,* ABC, 1994.

Connie Martel, "Brooklyn," *The Commish,* ABC, 1995.

Jennifer, "2Shy," *The X–Files,* Fox, 1995.

Graphologist, *The Marshal,* ABC, 1995.

Dr. Manson, "Leap of Faith," *Two* (also known as *Gejagt—Das zweite Gesicht*), CTV (Canada) and syndicated, 1997.

Merylee DeCesare, "Go Like You Know," *The Net,* USA Network, 1998.

Virgin Mary holograph, "Our Lady of the Machine," *Welcome to Paradox* (also known as *Betaville*), Sci–Fi Channel, 1998.

Female Gua agent, "All about Eddie," *First Wave,* Sci–Fi Channel, 1999.

Putrescence, "Keeping up with the Joneses," *The New Addams Family,* Fox Family Channel and YTV (Canada), 1999.

Adele Pearson, "Crystal Clear," *Mysterious Ways* (also known as *One Clear Moment, Anexegeta phainomena, Les chemins de l'etrange, Mysterious ways— les chemins de l'etrange, Rajatapaus,* and *Senderos misteriosos*), NBC and PAX TV, 2000.

Catherine Walsh, "Decompression," *The Outer Limits* (also known as *The New Outer Limits*), Showtime, Sci–Fi Channel, and syndicated, 2000.

Juliette's mother, "Daised and Confused," *Higher Ground,* Fox Family Channel, 2000.

Juliette's mother, "Mended Fences," *Higher Ground,* Fox Family Channel, 2000.

Juliette's mother, "What Remains," *Higher Ground,* Fox Family Channel, 2000.

"Death by Gossip," *Hollywood Off–Ramp,* E! Entertainment Television, 2000.

Diana Murphy, "Of Father and Sons," *UC: Undercover* (also known as *Undercover*), NBC, 2001.

Dr. Mary Matisse, "The Brink," *Seven Days* (also known as *7 Days* and *Seven Days: The Series*), UPN, 2001.

Dominique Cullen, "The Box," *Cold Squad* (also known as *Files from the Past, Cold Squad, brigade speciale,* and *Halott uegyek*), CTV (Canada), 2001.

FBI agent Rebecca Goldstein Whitney, "The Wives of Christmas Past," *Just Cause,* PAX TV, 2002.

Lorraine Hansen, "Azoth the Avenger Is a Friend of Mine," *The Twilight Zone,* UPN, 2002.

Casting director, "Criminal Favors," *The Chris Isaak Show,* Showtime, 2004.

Doctor professor Kor–Kavo, "Machinery of the Mind," *Andromeda* (also known as *Gene Roddenberry's "Andromeda"*), syndicated, 2004.

Television Appearances; Pilots:

Waitress, *Party of Five,* Fox, 1994.

FBI agent Rebecca Goldstein Whitney, *Just Cause,* PAX TV, 2002.

Appeared as Hannah in the unaired pilot for *Wolf Lake,* CBS.

RECORDINGS

Video Games:

Voice of Robin Morales, *The 11th Hour,* Virgin Interactive Entertainment, 1995.

JOHNSON, Shane 1976–
(Shane Mikael Johnson)

PERSONAL

Born in 1976; married Keili Lefkovitz (an actress); children: one. *Education:* Graduated from Whitman College, 1998.

Addresses: *Agent*—The Geddes Agency, 8430 Santa Monica Blvd., Suite 200, West Hollywood, CA 90069. *Manager*—Joan Sittenfield Management, 8350 Santa Monica Blvd., Suite 108, West Hollywood, CA 90069.

Career: Actor. Very Busy Productions (a production company), cofounder; appeared in television commercials, including Ford automobiles, 2006.

CREDITS

Film Appearances:

Soldier on the beach, *Saving Private Ryan,* Dream-Works, 1998.

Barry, *Love, Lust & Joy,* 2000.

(As Shane Mikael Johnson) Red crown operator number two, *Behind Enemy Lines,* Twentieth Century–Fox, 2001.

Jeremy, *Pumpkin,* Metro–Goldwyn–Mayer, 2002.

Scott, *Black Cadillac,* First Look International, 2003.

Runyan, *Take,* Liberation Entertainment, 2007.

Las Vegas producer, *The Great Buck Howard,* Magnolia Pictures, 2008.

Television Appearances; Movies:

(As Shane Mikael Johnson) Timothy Wilkison, *The Big Time,* TNT, 2002.

Television Appearances; Pilots:

Strong Medicine, Lifetime, 2000.

Television Appearances; Episodic:

Arli$$, HBO, 1996.

Good–looking guy, "Kim Kelly Is My Friend," *Freaks and Geeks,* NBC, 2000.

(As Shane Mikael Johnson) Necrotic fasciotomy patient, "A Hopeless Wound," *ER,* NBC, 2002.

(As Shane Mikael Johnson) Colin, "Primal Scream," *Birds of Prey* (also known as *BOP*), The WB, 2002.

Kyle Richardson, "Mother and Child in the Bay," *Bones,* Fox, 2006.

Liam Griffin, "Love Run Cold," *CSI: NY* (also known as *CSI: New York*), CBS, 2006.

Sean "Coop" Cooper, "Forever Blue," *Cold Case,* CBS, 2006.

Bones, Fox, 2006.

T. J. Pratt, "To Kill a Predator," *CSI: Miami,* CBS, 2008.

Will Cooper, "I Will, I'm Will," *Raising the Bar,* TNT, 2008.

Will Cooper, "Richie Richer," *Raising the Bar,* TNT, 2008.

RECORDINGS

Video Games:

(English version) Voice of Megumi Kitanji, *Sabarashiki kono sekai* (also known as *The World Ends With You*), Square Enix, 2007.

K

KAELIN, Kato 1959–
   (Brian "Kato" Kaelin)

PERSONAL

Original name, Brian Kaelin; born March 9, 1959, in Milwaukee, WI; married Cynthia Coulter, July 9, 1983 (divorced, 1989); children: one daughter.

Career: Actor, television show host, and extras casting. KLSX–FM, Los Angeles, CA, disc jockey, 1995; appeared in television commercials, including Trivial Pursuit 90s edition, and AskJeeves.com website; appeared in an episode of the internet series *Tom Green Live!*, www.tomgreen.com. Conducted *The 16th Minute* (a lecture tour), 1998.

CREDITS

Film Appearances:
(As Brian "Kato" Kaelin) Chat Frederick IV, *Beach Fever,* 1987.

Dean Lesher, *Night Shadow,* Quest Entertainment, 1989.

Regalia, *Prototype* (also known as *Prototype X29A*), Vidmark Entertainment, 1992.

Bond trader number one and police officer, *Save Me,* 1993.

(Uncredited) Party guest, *Hail Caesar,* Turner Home Video, 1994.

Surf, Sand and Sex (also known as *Sex on the Beach*), 1994.

Beggar, *Cyborg 3: The Recycler* (also known as *Cyborg 3* and *Cyborg 3: The Creation*), Warner Home Video, 1994.

(Uncredited) Extra, *Inner Sanctum II* (also known as *Inner Sanctum 2*), MDP Worldwide, 1994.

Soul of the Avenger, 1997.

Roommate, *Right Hand Woman,* 1998.

Driveway announcer, *BASEketball,* MCA/Universal, 1998.

(Uncredited) Kree, *The Decade,* Coyote Arm Films, 1999.

Himself, *Perfect Fit,* Atmosphere Films, 1999.

Himself, *Pauly Shore Is Dead,* CKrush Entertainment, 2003.

Himself, *Mayor of the Sunset Strip,* Samuel Goldwyn Films, 2003.

Himself (segments), *Strip Poker* (also known as *Girls of National Lampoon's "Strip Poker"*), National Lampoon Productions, 2005.

Himself, *Hookers Inc.,* Cinema Epoch, 2006.

Celebrity judge number three, *Dorm Daze 2* (also known as *Dorm Daze 2: College @ Sea* and *National Lampoon's "Dorm Daze 2: College @ Sea"*), Hill & Brand Productions, 2006.

Jonathan, *Revamped,* Millennium Concepts, 2007.

Photographer, *The Still Life,* Warner Home Video, 2007.

Living "The Still Life" (documentary short), Polychrome Pictures, 2007.

Himself, *Stuntmen,* Shoreline Entertainment, 2008.

Film Work:
Extras wrangler, *Save Me,* 1993.

Extras casting, *Possessed by the Night,* Sony Pictures Home Entertainment, 1994.

Extras casting, *Red Sun Rising,* Imperial Entertainment Corporation, 1994.

Extras casting, *Bad Blood* (also known as *Viper*), Live Home Video, 1994.

Extras casting, *Inner Sanctum II* (also known as *Inner Sanctum 2*), MDP Worldwide, 1994.

Television Appearances; Series:
Host, *Talk Soup,* E! Entertainment Television, 1994.
Host, *Eye for an Eye,* syndicated, 2004–2005.

Television Appearances; Specials:
A Night to Die For, 1995.

Corey Feldman: The E! True Hollywood Story, E! Entertainment Television, 1998.

People v. Simpson: Unfinished Business, Court TV, 1999.

Cohost, *Celebrity Homes,* E! Entertainment Television, 1999.

Houseguest, FX Channel, 2002.

Celebrity Boot Camp, Fox, 2002.

Jonathan, *Fatal Kiss,* 2002.

Gossip: Tabloid Tales, Arts and Entertainment, 2002.

I Love the '90s, VH1, 2004.

Burn, 2007.

The Fantastic Two, 2007.

Television Appearances; Episodic:

Mad TV, Fox, 1995.

"We Regret to Inform You," *Mr. Show with Bob and David* (also known as *Mr. Show*), HBO, 1995.

Joseph Weston, *The Watcher,* UPN, 1995.

Politically Incorrect, 1995, 1999.

Howard Stern, E! Entertainment Television, 1997.

Pictionary, 1998.

Happy Bender, game show host, "Smart and Stupid," *Unhappily Ever After* (also known as *Unhappily ...*), The WB, 1998.

Smoking teacher, "Tiffany Tutors the Teachers," *Unhappily Ever After* (also known as *Unhappily ...*), The WB, 1999.

Himself, "The Getaway," *It's Like, You Know ...,* ABC, 1999.

Himself, "Always Leave' Em Laughing," *Beggars and Choosers,* Showtime, 1999.

"Newsmakers Edition," *Weakest Link* (also known as *The Weakest Link USA*), NBC, 2001.

Rick, "Norm vs. Homelessness," *The Norm Show* (also known as *Norm*), ABC, 2001.

The Test, FX Channel, 2001.

"Surviving the Glare," *20/20* (also known as *ABC News 20/20*), ABC, 2002.

Dog Eat Dog, NBC, 2002.

Instructor, "Present Perfect," *Sabrina, the Teenage Witch* (also known as *Sabrina* and *Sabrina Goes to College*), The WB, 2003.

House of Clues, Court TV, 2004.

SoapTalk, SoapNet, 2004, 2005.

Mind of Mencia, Comedy Central, 2005.

Rita Cosby Live & Direct, MSNBC, 2005.

The Big Idea with Donny Deutsch, CNBC, 2005.

"Olly's Follies," *Sunset Tan,* E! Entertainment Television, 2007.

"The Reveal," *Sunset Tan,* E! Entertainment Television, 2007.

"Hunting with the Stars," *Reality Bites Back,* Comedy Central, 2007.

Gimme My Reality Show!, Fox Reality, 2008.

Television Work; Movies:

Assistant to the executive producer, *Savate* (also known as *The Fighter*), HBO, 1995.

RECORDINGS

Music Videos:

Appeared in Moby's "We Are All Made of Stars," 2002.

WRITINGS

Nonfiction:

Wrote articles for *Details,* 1996, 1999; *POV,* 1998.

OTHER SOURCES

Periodicals:

Esquire, June, 2002, p. 102.

People Weekly, March 13, 1995, p. 39; December 25, 1995, p. 148.

.

KARNES, Jay 1963–

PERSONAL

Born June 27, 1963, in Omaha, NE; married Julia Campbell; children: twin girls. *Education:* Graduated from University of Kansas, 1989.

Addresses: *Agent*—Innovative Artists, 1505 10th St., Santa Monica, CA 90401. *Lawyer*—Lichter, Grossman, Nichols, Adler and Feldman, Inc., 9200 Sunset Blvd., Suite 1200, Los Angeles, CA 90069. *Manager*—Framework Entertainment, 9057 Nemo St., Suite C, W. Hollywood, CA 90069.

Career: Actor.

CREDITS

Television Appearances; Series:

Detective Holland "Dutch" Wagenbach, *The Shield,* FX Channel, 2002–2008.

Television Appearances; Episodic:

Brad Anderson, "Collateral Damage," *The Pretender,* NBC, 1998.

David Ross, "Physician, Heal Thyself," *Chicago Hope,* CBS, 1998.

Lieutenant Ducane, "Relativity," *Star Trek: Voyager* (also known as *Voyager*), UPN, 1999.

Jonah Stoddard, "Tattoo," *Pensacola: Wings of Gold,* syndicated, 1999.

Jerome Parker, "Even Better Than the Real Thing," *The Strip*, UPN, 1999.

Dr. Mcgrath, "Short Calendar," *Judging Amy*, CBS, 1999.

Simon Prune, "Boy Next Door," *Ally McBeal*, Fox, 2000.

Mark Torry, "Hard Cell," *Nash Bridges* (also known as *Bridges*), CBS, 2000.

Don Russell, "Dog Days," *Judging Amy*, CBS, 2000.

Corporate guy, "Bully for Martin," *Frasier*, NBC, 2001.

Artie Russo, "It's Raining Men," *Cold Case*, 2004.

Assistant State Attorney Ron Russell, "Dream a Little Dream," *Judging Amy*, CBS, 2005.

Martin Rausch, "Bettor or Worse," *Numb3rs* (also known as *Num3ers*), CBS, 2005.

"Sins of Omission," *Burn Notice*, USA Network, 2008.

Internal Affairs officer Wagenbach, "For Gedda," *CSI: Criminal Scene Investigation* (also known as *C.S.I., CSI: Las Vegas* and *Les Experts*), CBS, 2008.

Agent Scott Kohn, a recurring role, *Sons of Anarchy*, FX Channel, 2008.

Television Appearances; Miniseries:

Investigator, *From the Earth to the Moon*, HBO, 1998.

Film Appearances:

Donald Trout, *The Joyriders*, Porchlight, 1999.

Kevin's lawyer, *The Next Best Thing*, Paramount, 2000.

Holland "Dutch" Wagenbach, *Under the Skin* (video), Twentieth Century–Fox Home Video, 2005.

Michael Levy, *Broken Angel*, Warner Bros., 2008.

Adult Roger, *Chasing 3000*, 2008.

RECORDINGS

Video Games:

Voice of Detective Dutch Wagenbach, *The Shield*, 2007.

KASCH, Cody 1987–

PERSONAL

Born August 21, 1987, in Camarillo, CA; son of Taylor (cofounder of Flying H Theater Company) and Jodi (cofounder of Flying H Theater Company).

Addresses: *Agent*—Talentworks, 3500 W. Olive Ave., Suite 1400, Burbank, CA 91505.

Career: Actor. Part of a band called "The Flying H."

Awards, Honors: Screen Actors Guild Award (with others), outstanding performance by an ensemble in a comedy series, Young Artist Awards nomination, 2005, for *Desperate Housewives*.

CREDITS

Television Appearances; Series:

Robert "Robbie" Miller, *Normal Ohio*, Fox, 2000.

Tom Butler, *Out There*, 2004.

Zach Young, *Desperate Housewives*, ABC, 2004–2007.

Television Appearances; Episodic:

Kid, *Martial Law*, CBS, 1999.

Jason Bender, "Family Matters," *ER*, NBC, 2000.

Wounded boy, "Luciferous," *The Others*, 2000.

"Heist," *Nash Bridges* (also known as *Bridges*), CBS, 2000.

Scott Simpson Jr., "Death Penalties," *The Practice*, ABC, 2000.

Brian, "Love Is Love," *Any Day Now*, Lifetime, 2000.

Austin Cooper, "Chapter Thirty–Five," *Boston Public*, Fox, 2002.

Josh Stover, "Better Laid Than Never: Part 1," *NYPD Blue*, ABC, 2002.

Devin, "Miss Turnstiles," *Family Affair*, The WB, 2003.

Trevor "T. J." Jankowski Jr., "Haystack," *Boomtown*, NBC 2003.

Troy, "Future Jock," *Phil of the Future*, The Disney Channel, 2004.

The Oprah Winfrey Show (also known as *Oprah*), syndicated, 2005.

Kyle Ackerman, "Raw," *Law & Order: Special Victims Unit* (also known as *Law & Order: SVU* and *Special Victims Unit*), NBC, 2005.

Max Kalen, "Early Bird Catches the Word," *Side Order of Life*, Lifetime, 2007.

Owen Savage, "Elephant's Memory," *Criminal Minds*, CBS, 2008.

Television Appearances; Specials:

The 31st Annual People's Choice Awards, CBS, 2005.

Film Appearances:

Jake, *Homefront*, Bull Creek, 2005.

String, *Asylum*, Twentieth Century–Fox, 2008.

Neil Conners, *Chain Letter*, 2008.

Doofus, *The 2 Bobs*, 2009.

KASSAR, Mario 1951–
   (Mario F. Kassar)

PERSONAL

Full name, Mario F. Kassar; born October 10, 1951, in Beirut, Lebanon; married Dina.

Addresses: *Office*—Magnetik Media, 2308 Broadway, Santa Monica, CA 90404.

Career: Producer. Kassar Films International (foreign distribution company), founder, c. 1969; Carolco Pictures, cofounder, 1976, partner (with Andrew Vajna), cochair, 1976–89, chair, 1989–95; MK Productions, Santa Monica, CA, founder, c. 1995, producer, c. 1995–?; C–2 Pictures, co–president, 2002—; Columbia/TriStar, executive, 2003—; Mangetik Media, Santa Monica, CA, president.

CREDITS

Film Executive Producer:
The Silent Partner, EMC Film Corp., 1978.
The Changeling, Associated Film Distribution, 1980.
The Amateur, Twentieth Century–Fox, 1981.
Victory (also known as *Escape to Victory*), Paramount, 1981.
First Blood (also known as *Rambo: First Blood* and *Rambo*), Orion, 1982.
Superstition (also known as *The Witch*), Almi Pictures, 1982.
Rambo: First Blood, Part II, TriStar, 1985.
Extreme Prejudice, TriStar, 1987.
Angel Heart (also known as *Aux portes de l'enfer*), TriStar, 1987.
Red Heat, TriStar, 1988.
Iron Eagle II, TriStar, 1988.
Rambo III (also known as *Rambo: First Blood Part III*), TriStar, 1988.
Johnny Handsome, TriStar, 1989.
DeepStar Six, TriStar, 1989.
Total Recall (also known as *El vengador del futuro*), TriStar, 1990.
Narrow Margin, TriStar, 1990.
Mountains of the Moon, TriStar, 1990.
Jacob's Ladder (also known as *Dante's Inferno*), TriStar, 1990.
Air America, TriStar, 1990.
(With Gale Ann Hurd) *Terminator 2: Judgment Day* (also known as *T2, El Exterminator 2,* and *T2—Terminator 2: Judgment Day*), TriStar, 1991.
(With Steve Martin) *L.A. Story,* TriStar, 1991.
(With Nicholas Clainos and Brian Grazer) *The Doors,* TriStar, 1991.
Rambling Rose, Seven Arts, 1991.
Light Sleeper, Fine Line, 1991.
Basic Instinct (also known as *Ice Cold Desire*), TriStar, 1992.
Aces: Iron Eagle III, New Line Cinema, 1992.
Universal Soldier, TriStar, 1992.
Cliffhanger (also known as *Cliffhanger—l'ultima sfida* and *Cliffhanger, traque au sommet*), TriStar, 1993.
Heaven & Earth (also known as *Entre ciel et terre*), Warner Bros., 1993.
Stargate (also known as *Stargate, la porte des etoiles*), Metro–Goldwyn–Mayer, 1994.
Cutthroat Island (also known as *Corsari, L'ile aux pirates,* and *Die Piratenbraut*), Metro–Goldwyn–Mayer, 1995.
Last of the Dogmen, Savoy Pictures, 1995.
Showgirls, Metro–Goldwyn–Mayer, 1995.

Film Producer:
(With Richard Attenborough and Terence Clegg) *Chaplin* (also known as *Charlot*), TriStar, 1992.
Lolita, Samuel Goldwyn Company, 1997.
I Spy (also known as *I–Spy*), Columbia, 2002.
(As Mario F. Kassar) *Terminator 3: Rise of the Machines* (also known as *T3* and *Terminator 3—Rebellion der maschinen*), Warner Bros., 2003.
(As Mario F. Kassar) *Basic Instinct 2* (also known as *Basic Instinct—Neues Spiel fur Catherine Tramell* and *Instinto basico 2—adiccion al riesgo*), Sony, 2006.

Film Appearances:
Your Ticket Is No Longer Valid (also known as *Finishing Touch, A Slow Descent into Hell,* and *L'ultime passion*), 1979.
Himself, *Guts and Glory* (short; also known as *Guts & Glory*), Artisan Entertainment, 2002.
Himself, *We Get to Win This Time* (documentary short), Artisan Entertainment, 2002.
Himself, *Drawing First Blood* (documentary short; also known as *Drawing First Blood: 20 Years Later* and *Making of "First Blood"*), Artisan Entertainment, 2002.
Himself, *East Meets West: "Red Heat" and the Kings of Carolco* (documentary short), Lions Gate Films, 2004.

Television Work; Series:
(As Mario F. Kassar) Executive producer, *Terminator: The Sarah Connor Chronicles,* Fox, 2008—.

Television Work; Movies:
Executive producer, *Robin Hood,* 1991.

Television Work; Pilots:
(As Mario F. Kassar) Executive producer, *Terminator: The Sarah Connor Chronicles,* Fox, 2008.

Television Appearances; Specials:
(As Mario F. Kassar) Himself, *Inside "Terminator 3: Rise of the Machines,"* 2003.

Television Appearances; Episodic:
Himself, "Inside *Terminator 3: Rise of the Machines,*" *HBO First Look,* HBO, 2003.
Breakfast, 2003.

OTHER SOURCES

Electronic:

Mario Kassar Website, http://www.mariokassar.com, December 5, 2008.

KENIN, Dylan

PERSONAL

Education: Graduated from the University of Southern California School of Theatre.

Career: Actor. Evidence Room Theatre company, member; spent four summers in repertoire at Theatre at the Edinburgh Fringe Festival in Scotland and at the Espace Pierre Cardin in Paris.

CREDITS

Film Appearances:
Becky's husband, *Buttleman* (also known as *Harold Buttleman, Daredevil Stuntman*), 2002.
Jump Rope MC, *The Ropes* (short), 2005.
Department of motor vehicles photo subject, *Validation* (short), 2007.
Leader, *Carriers,* Paramount Vantage, 2007.
Bitten man, *The Flock,* Genius Products, 2007.
Josh, *Linda, as in Beautiful* (short), 2007.
Hendricks, *Love Lies Bleeding,* Screen Gems, 2008.
Davis office man, *The Phone Book* (short), 2008.
Boyfriend, *Tennessee,* Vivendi Entertainment, 2008.
Masked Warrior, *The War of Game* (short), Tough Guppy Productions, 2008.
Gestapo officer, *Brother's War,* Artist View Entertainment, 2009.
Train guard, *Game,* Lionsgate, 2009.

Television Appearances; Series:
Victor, *24,* Fox, 2007.

Television Appearances; Miniseries:
Captain Fetterman, *Into the West,* TNT, 2005.
Matt, "The Key and the Clock," *The Lost Room,* Sky One, 2006.
Denton Fogg, *Comanche Moon,* CBS, 2008.

Television Appearances; Movies:
Sergeant Teegarden, *Living Hell* (also known as *Organizm*), Sci-Fi Channel, 2008.

Television Appearances; Episodic:
Fuzzy, *The Young and the Restless* (also known as *Y&R*), CBS, 2004, 2005.

Sentry, "Kill Billie: Vol. 1," *Charmed,* The WB, 2005.
Roger Holstein, "Soft Target," *Numb3rs* (also known as *Num3ers*), CBS, 2005.
Louie, "Ames v. Kovac," *ER,* NBC, 2006.
White guard, "Chasing Ghosts," *The Shield,* FX Channel, 2007.
Amped up guy, "Grin and Bear It," *Ugly Betty,* ABC, 2007.
Gang member, "Oversight," *Jericho,* CBS, 2008.
Detective Garrity, "Good Cop, Dead Cop," *In Plain Sight,* USA Network, 2008.
Clozza, "Eagles and Angels," *Prison Break* (also known as *Prison Break: On the Run*), Fox, 2008.
Chad, "Love/Hate," *General Hospital: Night Shift,* Soap-Net, 2008.

Stage Appearances:
Appeared as Bradley, *Buried Child;* Kip, *Raised in Captivity;* Darth Vadar and Chewbacca, *Star Wars Trilogy in Thirty Minutes.*

KNIGHT, Tiffany
See LYNDALL-KNIGHT, Tiffany

KNOX, Mark "Flex"
See ALEXANDER, Flex

KOTB, Hoda 1964–

PERSONAL

Surname is pronounced "Kot-bee"; born August 9, 1964, in Norman, OK; married Burzis Kanga, December 3, 2005 (divorced, 2007). *Education:* Virginia Polytechnic Institute and State University, B.A., 1986.

Addresses: *Office*—c/o NBC News, 30 Rockefeller Plaza, New York, NY 10112.

Career: Broadcast journalist and news anchor. CBS News, news assistant in Cairo, Egypt, 1986; WXVT-TV, Greenville, MS, news anchor, between 1986 and 1989; WQAD-TV, Moline, IL, general assignment reporter and morning news anchor, between 1986 and 1989; WINK-TV, Fort Myers, FL, reporter and weekend news anchor, 1989–91; WWL-TV, New Orleans, LA, reporter and news anchor, 1992–98; NBC News, New York City, reporter and correspondent, including reports for the cable channel MSNBC, 1999—.

Awards, Honors: Journalism awards include Edward R. Murrow Award, Radio and Television News Directors Association, 2002; Gracie Allen Award, Foundation of American Women in Radio and Television, 2003; National Headliner Award, 2004; George Peabody Foster Broadcasting Award, Henry W. Grady School of Journalism and Mass Communications, University of Georgia, 2006, for a report "The Education of Ms. Groves," *Dateline NBC;* Alfred I. duPont–Columbia University Award, 2008; also received at least four Emmy Award nominations.

CREDITS

Television Appearances; Series:
Correspondent, *Dateline NBC* (also known as *Dateline*), NBC, beginning 1998.
Host, *Your Total Health,* syndicated, beginning 2004.
Correspondent and substitute news anchor, *Today* (also known as *NBC News Today* and *The Today Show*), NBC, beginning 2007.

Television Appearances; Specials:
Correspondent, *Katrina's Fury: A Dateline Special,* NBC, 2005.
Host, *The Quill Awards 2007,* NBC, 2007.
Correspondent, *Dateline NBC: Going for Gold,* NBC, 2008.
Host, "The Baby Borrowers: Lessons Learned," *The Baby Borrowers* (also known as *The Baby Borrowers Town Hall Special*), NBC, 2008.

Television Appearances; Episodic:
Entertainment Tonight (also known as *Entertainment This Week, E.T., ET Weekend,* and *This Week in Entertainment*), syndicated, 2008.

OTHER SOURCES

Periodicals:
Broadcasting & Cable, August 13, 2007, p. 3; August 20, 2007, p. 3.
People Weekly, August 4, 2008, p. 97.

Electronic:
MSNBC Online, http://www.msnbc.msn.com/, February 6, 2008.

KRENZ, Joyce

PERSONAL

Born in Winnipeg, Manitoba, Canada; married Victor, August 26, 1977; children: two.

Career: Actress.

Awards, Honors: Blizzard Award, best performance by a Manitoban actress, Manitoba Motion Picture Industry Association (MMPIA) 2001, for *Milgaard.*

CREDITS

Film Appearances:
Teacher, *The Crown Prince* (short; also known as *Le prince heritier*), National Film Board of Canada, 1988.
First woman, *The Hands of Ida* (short), 1995.
Landlady, *Heater,* The Asylum, 1999.
Mrs. Cohen, *Nostradamus,* Regent Entertainment, 2000.
Woman in tub, *Bad Girls from Valley High,* Universal Home Entertainment, 2005.
Housekeeper, *Catch and Release,* Sony, 2006.
Mrs. Logue, *Blue State,* Metro–Goldwyn–Mayer Home Entertainment, 2007.
Auntie Doll, *The Stone Angel,* Vivendi Entertainment, 2007.
Auntie, *My Winnipeg,* IFC Films, 2007.

Television Appearances; Movies:
Personnel woman, *Nights Below Station Street,* Lifetime, 1998.
Landlady, *Life in a Day,* UPN, 1999.
Evelyn Culver, *Milgaard* (also known as *Erreur judiciaire: l'histoire de David Milgaard* and *Hard Time: The David Milgaard Story*), Lifetime, 1999.
Mrs. Taweel, *Naughty or Nice,* ABC, 2004.

Television Appearances; Episodic:
Clerk, "The Case of the Liberated Beasts," *The Adventures of Shirley Holmes,* YTV, 1997.
Cat owner, "The Case of the Doggone Cats," *The Adventures of Shirley Holmes,* YTV, 1998.
Cal, "This Shit Is Evil," *Da Vinci's Inquest* (also known as *Coroner Da Vinci*), CBC, 2000.
Jay's mom, "One Night at Mercy," *The Twilight Zone,* UPN, 2002.
Nadia, "Doing the Chicken Scratch," *Da Vinci's Inquest* (also known as *Coroner Da Vinci*), CBC, 2003.
(Uncredited) Old lady, "Chemical Reactions," *Men in Trees,* ABC, 2007.

Also appeared as loud woman, "The Fugitive," *My Life as a Dog.*

Stage Appearances:
Mrs. Schumacher, *Dirty Dancing,* Toronto, Ontario, Canada, 2007–2008.

KURYLENKO, Olga 1979–

PERSONAL

Born November 14, 1979, in Berdyansk, Ukraine; daughter of Kostyantyn and Marina; married Cedric Van Mol, 2000 (divorced, 2004); married Damian Gabrielle, 2006 (divorced, 2007).

Addresses: *Contact*—Creative Artists Agency, 2000 Avenue of the Stars, Los Angeles, CA 90067.

Career: Actress.

Awards, Honors: Certificate of Excellence, best actress, Brooklyn International Film Festival, 2006, for *L' Annulaire*.

CREDITS

Film Appearances:
Iris, *L' Annulaire* (also known as *The Ring Finger*), 2005.
Sofia, *Le Serpent* (also known as *The Serpent* and *The Snake*), 2006.
The vampire, *Paris Je t'ame* (also known as *Paris I Love You*), First Look, 2007.
Nika Boronina, *Hitman*, Twentieth Century–Fox, 2007.
Natasha, *Max Payne*, Twentieth Century–Fox, 2008.
Marc Forster–Der weg zu 007, 2008.
Camille, *Quantum of Solace* (also known as *B22, Marc Forster's "Quantum of Solace"* and *QoS*), Sony, 2008.
Galia, *Kirot* (also known as *Murs*), 2009.

Television Appearances; Series:
Mina Harud, *Tyranny*, 2008.

Television Appearances; Episodic:
Tout le monde en parle, 2005.
La Matinale, 2005.

Entertainment Tonight (also known as *E.T., ET Weekend, Entertainment This Week* and *This Week in Entertainment*), syndicated, 2008.
"The South Bank Show: Bond," *The South Bank Show*, ITV, 2008.
"Bond Girl Special," *Made*, 2008.
Xpose, 2008.
"Roger Moore," *Vivement dimanche*, 2008.
Cartelera, 2008.
Quelli che ... il calcio, 2008.
Jimmy Kimmel Live!, ABC, 2008.
Cinema tres (also known as *Informatiu cinema*), 2008.
Dias de cine, 2008.

Television Appearances; Movies:
Sophia, *Le Porte–bonheur*, 2006.

Television Appearances; Specials:
Bond on Location (also known as *Bond on Location: The Making of Quantum of Solace, Quantum of Solace: Bond on Location, The Making of Quantum of Solace* and *The Making of Quantum of Solace: Bond on Location*), ITV, 2008.
Quantum of Solace: Royal World Premiere Special, 2008.
Bond Girl Diaries, 2008.

Television Appearances; Miniseries:
Eva Pires, *Suspectes* (also known as *Secrets*), 2007.

RECORDINGS

Video Games:
Voice of Camille, *Quantum of Solace* (also known as *007: Quantum of Solace, James Bond: Quantum of Solace, QOS, Quantum of Solace: The Game* and *Quantum of Solace: The Video Game*), 2008.

WRITINGS

Television Series:
Tyranny, 2008.

L

LANSING, Sherry 1944–

PERSONAL

Full name, Sherry Lee Lansing; born July 31, 1944, in Chicago, IL; daughter of David Duehl (in real estate; some sources cite surname as Heimann) and Margo Lansing (in real estate and business); stepdaughter of Norton L. Lansing (in sales and business); married Michael Brownstein, 1960s (divorced); married William Friedkin (a director, producer, and writer), July 6, 1991; stepchildren: Josh. *Education:* University of Chicago Lab School, graduated, 1962; Northwestern University, B.S. (cum laude), speech and theatre, 1966.

Addresses: *Office*—The Sherry Lansing Foundation, 2121 Avenue of the Stars, Suite 2020, Los Angeles, CA 90067. *Agent*—Creative Artists Agency, 2000 Avenue of the Stars, Los Angeles, CA 90067 (personal appearances); Jankow & Nesbit Associates, 445 Park Ave., New York, NY 10022 (literary agent).

Career: Executive, producer, and actress. Los Angeles Public Schools, teacher, 1966–69; model and affiliated with the Max Factor Company, 1969–70, and the Alberto–Culver Company, 1969–70; worked as a script reader; Wagner International, executive story editor, 1970–73; Heyday Productions, Universal City, CA, vice president of production, 1973–75; Metro–Goldwyn–Mayer (MGM) Studios, Culver City, CA, executive story editor, later vice president of creative affairs, 1975–77; Columbia Pictures, Burbank, CA, senior vice president of production, 1977–80; Twentieth Century–Fox Productions, Beverly Hills, CA, president of production, 1980–83; Jaffe–Lansing Productions, founder, 1983, president, 1983–92; Paramount Pictures, chairperson of motion pictures group, 1992–2005; The Sherry Lansing Foundation (fund–raising and informational organization), Los Angeles, founder, 2005,

chairperson, beginning 2005, cofounder of Stand Up to Cancer (SU2C) and affiliated with PrimeTime LAUSD (a group placing retirees to work with the Los Angeles Unified School District, the LAUSD). Cofounder of Stop Cancer, a philanthropic organization; cofounder of the Big Sisters of Los Angeles Future Fund. Member of the board of trustees for the American Film Institute, Teach for America, the University of Chicago, QUALCOMM, and the American Association for Cancer Research; member of the executive committee of the board of directors of the Friends of Cancer Research; board member of the Albert and Mary Lasker Foundation and The Carter Center; affiliated with the American Red Cross Board of Governors and Civic Ventures. Regent for the University of California, beginning 1999, and chairperson and vice chairperson of various committees. California Institute for Regenerative Medicine (CRIM), member of the independent citizens' oversight committee, beginning 2004, and chairperson, cochairperson, and patient advocate for various groups within the committee. Member of the California governor's advisory committee on educational excellence and affiliated with other groups relating to education; member of the advisory committee for Donors Choose and RAND Health.

Awards, Honors: Economic Equity Award, Women's Equity Action League, 1980; Crystal Award, Women in Film Crystal awards, 1981; Distinguished Community Service Award, Brandeis University, 1982; Academy Award nomination (with Stanley R. Jaffe), best picture, 1988, for *Fatal Attraction;* Alfred P. Sloan Memorial Award, 1989; Simon Wiesenthal Center Distinguished Service Award for the Performing Arts, 1992; Pioneer of the Year, Foundation of the Motion Picture Pioneers, 1996; received a star on the Hollywood Walk of Fame, 1996; Overcoming Obstacles Achievement Award for Business, 1996; Silver Achievement Award, Young Women's Christian Association (YWCA), 1996; named one of the fifty most powerful women in entertainment, *Hollywood Reporter,* 1999; Milestone Award, Producers Guild of America, 2000; named one of the thirty most powerful women in America, *Ladies' Home Jour-*

nal, 2001; President's Award, Academy of Science Fiction, Fantasy & Horror Films, 2002; honorary doctorate in fine arts, American Film Institute (AFI), 2003; All–America Advertising Award, *Parade* magazine, 2003; Woodrow Wilson Award for Corporate Citizenship, 2003; named one of the one hundred most powerful women in entertainment, *Hollywood Reporter,* 2003 and 2004; Horatio Alger Humanitarian Award, 2004; Legacy Award, Big Brothers Big Sisters (Los Angeles), 2005; Exemplary Leadership in Management (ELM) Award, Anderson School of Management, University of California, Los Angeles, 2005; handprints and footprints at Grauman's Chinese Theatre, beginning 2005; Cancer Research Public Service Award, American Association of Cancer Research, 2006; Jean H. Hersholt Humanitarian Award, Academy awards, Academy of Motion Pictures Arts and Sciences, 2007; named one the fifty most powerful women in business, *Fortune* magazine, 2007; Paltrow Mentorship Award, Women in Film, 2008.

CREDITS

Film Executive Producer:
Firstborn (also known as *First Born* and *Moving In*), Paramount, 1984.
Racing with the Moon, Paramount, 1984.

Film Producer:
Fatal Attraction, Paramount, 1987.
The Accused (also known as *Reckless Endangerment, Acusados, Angeklagt, Anklagad, Appel a la justice, Les accuses, Oi katigoroumenoi, Os acusados, Oskarzeni, Oskarzona, Sotto accusa,* and *Syytetty*), Paramount, 1988.
Black Rain, Paramount, 1989.
School Ties, Paramount, 1992.
Indecent Proposal, Paramount, 1993.

As a studio executive, worked on other projects.

Film Appearances:
Amelita, *Rio Lobo* (also known as *San Timoteo*), Paramount, 1970.
Susan, *Loving,* Columbia, 1970.

Film Appearances as Herself; Documentaries:
Calling the Shots, World Artists, 1988.
Coming Attractions: The History of the Movie Trailer, The Andrew J. Kuehn Foundation, 2006.
The Brothers Warner, 2008.

Television Executive Producer; Movies:
Mistress, CBS, 1987.
When the Time Comes, ABC, 1987.

Television Coproducer; Specials:
Stand Up to Cancer, CBS, 2008.

Television Appearances as Herself; Documentary Miniseries:
Hollywood Women, Independent Television, 1994.
The Jewish Americans, PBS, 2008.

Television Appearances as Herself; Documentary Specials:
A Father ... a Son ... Once upon a Time in Hollywood, HBO, 2005.
Boffo! Tinseltown's Bombs and Blockbusters, HBO, 2006.

Television Appearances; Awards Presentations:
The 79th Annual Academy Awards, ABC, 2007.

Television Appearances; Episodic:
Bridget, *The Good Guys,* CBS, 1968.
Jennifer Britain, "The Titan," *Dan August,* ABC, 1971.
Marcia Yeager, "A Killing at the Track," *Ironside* (also known as *The Raymond Burr Show*), NBC, 1971.
Guest, *At Rona's,* NBC, 1989.
Voice of Angela, "The Focus Group," *Frasier* (also known as *Dr. Frasier Crane*), NBC, 1996.
Voice of Angela, "You Can Go Home Again," *Frasier* (also known as *Dr. Frasier Crane*), NBC, 1996.
Herself, "Dawn Steel," *The E! True Hollywood Story* (also known as *Dawn Steel: The E! True Hollywood Story* and *THS*), E! Entertainment Television, 1998.
Herself, "Kurt Russell: Hollywood's Heavy Hitter," *Biography* (also known as *A&E Biography: Kurt Russell*), Arts and Entertainment, 1999.
Herself, *The Hollywood Fashion Machine,* American Movie Classics, 1999.
Herself, "The Films of Adrian Lyne," *The Directors,* Encore, 2003.
Herself, *Sunday Morning Shootout* (also known as *Hollywood Shootout* and *Shootout*), American Movie Classics, 2004.
Herself, "Fatal Attraction," *Movies That Shook the World,* American Movie Classics, 2005.
Herself, *Entertainment Tonight* (also known as *Entertainment This Week, E.T., ET Weekend,* and *This Week in Entertainment*), syndicated, 2008.

Appeared as Doris (a temporary secretary), in *Banyon,* NBC.

RECORDINGS

Videos:
Herself, *Black Rain: Making the Film—Part 1,* Paramount, 2006.

Herself, *Black Rain: Making the Film—Part 2,* Paramount, 2006.

Herself, *Black Rain: Post–Production,* Paramount, 2006.

Herself, *Black Rain: The Script, the Cast,* Paramount, 2006.

OTHER SOURCES

Periodicals:

Chicago Tribune, July 15, 2002.

Films in Review, November, 1984.

Harper's Bazaar, April, 2005, pp. 121–22.

Hollywood Reporter, December, 1999, pp. 11–50.

Newsweek, January 24, 2005, p. 60.

New York Times, March 23, 1984.

Variety, April 13, 1977; July 15, 2002, pp. S8–S9.

Electronic:

The Sherry Lansing Foundation, http://www.sherrylansingfoundation.org, September 12, 2008.

LARSON, Brie 1989–

PERSONAL

Full name, Brianne Sidonie Desaulniers; born October 1, 1989, in Sacramento, CA. *Education:* Trained as a child at American Conservatory Theatre.

Addresses: *Agent*—Chris Fioto, Gersh Agency, 232 North Canon Dr., Beverly Hills, CA 90210. *Manager*—Anne Woodward, Station 3, 8522 National Blvd., Suite 108, Culver City, CA 90232.

Career: Actress, voice performer, singer, and songwriter. Performs as a singer on concert tours.

Awards, Honors: Young Artist Award nomination, best leading young actress in a television comedy series, 2002, for *Raising Dad;* Young Artist Award nomination (with others), best young ensemble cast in a feature film, 2005, for *Sleepover;* Young Artist Award nomination, best leading young actress in a feature film, 2007, for *Hoot.*

CREDITS

Film Appearances:

Little Angel, *Special Delivery,* Calling Productions, 1999.

Second racing girl, *Madison,* Metro–Goldwyn–Mayer, 2001.

One of the Six Chicks, *13 Going on 30* (also known as *Suddenly 30*), Columbia, 2004.

Liz, *Sleepover,* Metro–Goldwyn–Mayer, 2004.

Beatrice Leep, *Hoot,* New Line Cinema, 2006.

Voice of a penguin, *Farce of the Penguins,* ThinkFilm, 2006.

Angie, *The Beautiful Ordinary* (also known as *Remember the Daze*), First Look International, 2007.

Allison, *The Babysitter* (short film), Atom Films, 2008.

Kate, *Tanner Hall,* Two Prong Lesson, 2008.

Suzy Decker, *House Broken,* Echelon Entertainment, 2008.

Emily, *Just Peck,* Jerry Leider Productions, 2009.

Film Work:

Additional voices, *Dudley Do–Right,* Universal, 1999.

Also worked on other films as post–production voice performer in automated dialogue replacement loop groups.

Television Appearances; Series:

Emily Stewart, *Raising Dad,* The WB, 2001–2002.

Kate Gregor, *The United States of Tara,* Showtime, 2008–2009.

Television Appearances; Pilots:

Samantha, *Schimmel,* Fox, 2000.

Emily Stewart, *Raising Dad,* The WB, 2001.

Kate Gregor, *The United States of Tara,* Showtime, 2008.

Television Appearances; Movies:

Courtney Enders, *Right on Track,* The Disney Channel, 2003.

Television Appearances; Specials:

The Teen Choice Awards 2004, Fox, 2004.

79th Annual Macy's Thanksgiving Day Parade, NBC, 2005.

Television Appearances; Episodic:

Girl scout, *The Tonight Show with Jay Leno,* NBC, 1998.

Lily Quinn, "Right My Fire," *To Have & to Hold,* CBS, 1998.

Lily Quinn, "The Kids Are All Right?" *To Have & to Hold,* CBS, 1998.

Rachel, "Into the Fire," *Touched by an Angel,* CBS, 1999.

Robin Robin, "Fall on Your Knees," *Popular,* The WB, 1999.

Hollywood Squares (also known as *H2* and *H2: Hollywood Squares*), syndicated, 2001.

Judge, *Pet Star,* Animal Planet, 2005.

Krista Eisenberg, "Slam (aka Slambook)," *Ghost Whisperer,* CBS, 2008.

Television Work; Movies:

Song performer, "She Said," *Go Figure,* The Disney Channel, 2005.

RECORDINGS

Albums:

Finally Out of P.E., Casablanca, 2005.

Singles include "Life after You" and "She Said," both Casablanca, 2005.

Videos:

Appeared in the music video "She Said," Casablanca, 2005.

WRITINGS

Songwriter:

"Coming Around," *Hoot,* New Line Cinema, 2006.

LaSARDO, Robert 1963–
(Robert La Sardo, Robert A. LaSardo, Robert Lasardo)

PERSONAL

Born September 20, 1963, in Brooklyn, New York, NY. *Education:* Studied acting at the Stella Adler Conservatory and the Actors Studio; graduated with honors from the Fiorello H. LaGuardia High School of Music & Art and Performing Arts, New York City; studied acting with Anthony Abeson.

Addresses: *Agent*—Silver Massetti & Szatmary, 8730 West Sunset Blvd., Suite 440, West Hollywood, CA 90069. *Manager*—Kass & Stokes Management, 9229 Sunset Blvd., Suite 504, Los Angeles, CA 90069.

Career: Actor. Worked at a video store, c. 1980s. *Military service:* U.S. Navy, served c. 1981–85.

CREDITS

Film Appearances:

Carlo Forza, *China Girl,* Great American Films Limited Partnership/Street Lite/Vestron Pictures, 1987.

Tony, *Ich und Er* (also known as *Me and Him*), Columbia, 1987.

Perry, *Moving,* Warner Bros., 1988.

Spooky, *Short Circuit 2,* TriStar, 1988.

Blade, *Rooftops,* New Visions Entertainment Corporation, 1989.

First mugger, *Penn & Teller Get Killed* (also known as *Dead Funny*), Warner Bros., 1989.

(As Robert Lasardo) Luis, *True Blood* (also known as *Edge of Darkness*), Fries Entertainment/Movie House, 1989.

Skinhead, *Renegades,* Universal, 1989.

(As Robert Lasardo) Italian guard, *King of New York,* Seven Arts, 1990.

Punk, *Hard to Kill* (also known as *Seven Year Storm*), Warner Bros., 1990.

(As Robert Lasardo) Bochi, *Out for Justice,* Warner Bros., 1991.

ATM robber, *Jimmy Hollywood,* Paramount, 1994.

Deputy Dog, *Drop Zone,* Paramount, 1994.

(As Robert Lasardo) First client, *Leon* (also known as *The Cleaner, Leon: The Professional,* and *The Professional*), Columbia, 1994.

Smitty, *Waterworld,* MCA/Universal, 1995.

(As Robert La Sardo) Tattoo artist, *One Tough Bastard* (also known as *North's War* and *One Man's Justice*), Live Entertainment, 1995.

Paulo, *Tiger Heart,* PM Entertainment Group, 1996.

Angelo Castillo, *Under Oath* (also known as *Blood Money* and *Urban Justice*), 1997.

Eric, *Livers Ain't Cheap* (also known as *The Real Thing*), Trimark Pictures, 1997.

Sarkasian, *Gang Related,* Orion, 1997.

(As Robert A. LaSardo) Candyman, *Carnival of Souls* (also known as *Wes Craven Presents "Carnival of Souls"*), Trimark Pictures, 1998.

Diesel, *Love Kills,* Trident Releasing, 1998.

Leo, *Crossfire,* Scorpio Production, 1998.

Manuel, *Running Woman,* Concorde Pictures, 1998.

Matt Myers, *Strangeland* (also known as *Dee Snider's "StrangeLand"*), Raucous Releasing, 1998.

Pub thug, *Nightwatch,* Dimension Films/Miramax, 1998.

Felipe Batista, *In Too Deep,* Dimension Films/Miramax, 1999.

Nervous suspect, *Blue Streak,* Columbia, 1999.

Tony, *Four Faces of God,* 17 Productions/Four Face Films/Galilay Entertainment, 1999.

T. J., *Mercy Streets,* Providence Entertainment, 2000.

Thin biker, *Bubble Boy,* Buena Vista, 2001.

Rico, *Pandemonium,* LKH Films/Resilient Films, 2002.

(As Robert Lasardo) Usup, *In Hell* (also known as *The Savage* and *The S.H.U.*), Nu Image Films, 2003.

Paco, *Latin Dragon* (also known as *La justicia del dragon*), Screen Media, 2004.

Roland, *Dirty,* Silver Nitrate Entertainment, 2005.

Rico, *Never Down,* Vanguard, 2007.

Rivera, *Half Past Dead 2* (also known as *Justified*), Sony Pictures Home Entertainment, 2007.

Hector Grimm, *Death Race,* Universal, 2008.

Mo, *Tortured,* Sony Pictures Entertainment, 2008.
Scott, *Autopsy,* Seven Arts, 2008.
Maurice Keenan, *Uncle Bob,* 2009.
Bobby Boy, *Double Tap* (also known as *Clean Sweep*), Ginepri Pictures Releasing, c. 2009.

Film Executive Producer:
Never Down, Vanguard, 2007.

Television Appearances; Series:
Corporal Jesus "Answer Man" Zappara, a recurring role, *China Beach,* ABC, 1989–90.
Escobar Gallardo, *Nip/Tuck,* FX Network, 2003–2007.
Manuel "Manny" Ruiz, *General Hospital* (also known as *Hopital central* and *Hospital general*), ABC, 2005–2006.
Father Mateo Ruiz, *General Hospital* (also known as *Hopital central* and *Hospital general*), ABC, beginning 2007.

Television Appearances; Miniseries:
Osvaldo Cesarus, *Murder One: Diary of a Serial Killer,* ABC, 1997.

Television Appearances; Movies:
Spike, *Blood Run* (also known as *Outside the Law*), 1994.
Second robber, "Anger" segment, *Favorite Deadly Sins* (also known as *National Lampoon's "Favorite Deadly Sins"*), Showtime, 1995.
Kazz, *Last Man Standing,* HBO, 1996.
Agent Rodriguez, *Double Tap,* HBO, 1997.
Gries, *Wishmaster 2: Evil Never Dies,* HBO, 1999.

Television Appearances; Episodic:
Garage attendant, "Renunciation," *Law & Order* (also known as *Law & Order Prime*), NBC, 1991.
Luis Hernandez, "Tempest in a C–Cup," *NYPD Blue,* ABC, 1993.
Sol, "Them Bones," *Harry and the Hendersons,* syndicated, 1993.
(As Robert Lasardo) Tattoo artist, "Portrait by the Artist on the Young Man," *Dream On,* HBO, 1993, also broadcast on Fox.
Felipe, "Most Wanted," *Renegade,* USA Network and syndicated, 1995.
Baby Boy Doe, "Skirt Chasers," *Nash Bridges* (also known as *Bridges*), CBS, 1996.
Jake, "Code Name: Scorpion," *High Tide,* syndicated, 1996.
Chaz (muscle person), "Blind Man's Bluff," *The Sentinel* (also known as *Sentinel*), UPN, 1997.
Jesus, "Imagine: Part 1," *Michael Hayes,* CBS, 1997.
Osvaldo Cesarus, "Chapter Fourteen, Year Two," *Murder One,* ABC, 1997.
Osvaldo Cesarus, "Chapter Eighteen, Year Two," *Murder One,* ABC, 1997.

Torres, "Fear of Flying," *L.A. Doctors* (also known as *L.A. Docs, Kliniken, Kohtaloni Los Angeles,* and *Medicos de Los Angeles*), CBS, 1998.
Crowe, "Valma and Louise," *V.I.P.* (also known as *V.I.P.—Die Bodyguards*), syndicated, 1999.
Freddie Ascencion, "Show & Tell," *NYPD Blue,* ABC, 1999.
Hector Flores, "End Game," *Martial Law* (also known as *Le flic de Shanghai, Ley marcial,* and *Piu forte ragazzi*), CBS, 1999.
Hector Flores, "Requiem," *Martial Law* (also known as *Le flic de Shanghai, Ley marcial,* and *Piu forte ragazzi*), CBS, 1999.
Adam Beckwith, "Kidnapped," *Pacific Blue,* USA Network, 2000.
Cissy Alvarez, "The Amazing Maleeni," *The X–Files,* Fox, 2000.
Doyle, "Jackpot: Part 1," *Nash Bridges* (also known as *Bridges*), CBS, 2000.
New World Order leader, "V.I.P., R.I.P.," *V.I.P.* (also known as *V.I.P.—Die Bodyguards*), syndicated, 2000.
Ray Murphy, "Road to Hell," *18 Wheels of Justice* (also known as *Highway to Hell—18 Rader aus Stahl, La loi du fugitif,* and *Oikeutta tien paeaell*), The National Network, 2000.
Anzuelo, "The Siege," *UC: Undercover* (also known as *Undercover*), NBC, 2001.
Diego Flores, "Fork You Very Much," *Philly,* ABC, 2001.
Hector "Kiki" Acevedo, "Johnny Got His Gold," *NYPD Blue,* ABC, 2001.
Lowry, "Maximum Byers," *The Lone Gunmen* (also known as *Lone Gunmen, Au coeur du complot,* and *Die Einsamen Schutzen*), Fox, 2001.
Sanchez Ramirez, "The Problem with Corruption," *Dead Last,* The WB, 2001.
Jojo Rizal, "Two Days of Blood," *The Shield* (also known as *The Barn* and *Rampart*), FX Network, 2002.
Owen "Shadow" Little, "Things Done Changed," *Fastlane,* Fox, 2002.
"True Val Story," *V.I.P.* (also known as *V.I.P.—Die Bodyguards*), syndicated, 2002.
Hector "Kiki" Acevedo, "Shear Stupidity," *NYPD Blue,* ABC, 2003.
Lionel, "As It Is in Heaven," *Touched by an Angel,* CBS, 2003.
Pope, "Execution," *Boomtown,* NBC, 2003.
Jesus Torres, "Hubris," *Cold Case* (also known as *Anexihniastes ypothesis, Caso abierto, Cold case—affaires classees, Cold Case—Kein Opfer ist je vergessen, Doegloett aktak, Kalla spaar, Todistettavasti syyllinen,* and *Victimes du passe*), CBS, 2004.
Arturo, "Ambush," *Sex, Love & Secrets* (also known as *Sex, Lies & Secrets* and *Wildlife*), UPN, 2005.
Arturo, "Secrets," *Sex, Love & Secrets* (also known as *Sex, Lies & Secrets* and *Wildlife*), UPN, 2005.
Gary Helms, "Happy Borthday," *Judging Amy,* CBS, 2005.
Johnny Currea, "Doggone," *Blind Justice,* ABC, 2005.

Julian Borgia (tattooed man and crash victim), "Hope and Mercy," *Ghost Whisperer,* CBS, 2005.

Julian Borgia, "On the Wings of a Dove," *Ghost Whisperer,* CBS, 2005.

Santo, "Shots," *Eyes,* ABC, 2005.

Memmo Fierro, "One of Our Own," *CSI: Miami* (also known as *CSI Miami*), CBS, 2006.

Memmo Fierro, "Rampage," *CSI: Miami* (also known as *CSI Miami*), CBS, 2006.

Miguel Villeda, "The Woman in the Garden," *Bones* (also known as *Brennan, Bones—Die Knochenjaegerin, Dr. Csont,* and *Kondid*), Fox, 2006.

Paulie, "The Serranos," *Mind of Mencia,* Comedy Central, 2006.

Himself, *Soap Talk,* SOAPnet, 2006.

Busando Maldito, "Let Her Go," *Life,* NBC, 2007.

(As Robert Lasardo) Hector Hernandez, "For Whom the Skel Rolls," *Shark,* CBS, 2007.

Emilio Alvarado, "Grissom's Divine Comedy," *CSI: Crime Scene Investigation* (also known as *C.S.I., CSI, CSI: Las Vegas, CSI: Weekends,* and *Les experts*), CBS, 2008.

Jack, "Here Comes the Boom," *The Cleaner,* Arts and Entertainment, 2008.

Television Appearances; Pilots:

Adam Beckwith, *Pacific Blue,* USA Network, 1996.

Escobar Gallardo, "Pilot–McNamara/Troy," *Nip/Tuck,* FX Network, 2003.

Silvio Machado, *Wanted,* TNT, 2005.

RECORDINGS

Videos:

Himself, *The Making of "Mercy Streets,"* 2001.

Video Games:

Voice, *Scarface: The World Is Yours,* Vivendi Universal Games, 2006.

OTHER SOURCES

Periodicals:

Venice, March, 2006; September, 2008.

Electronic:

Robert LaSardo, http://www.robertlasardo.com, January 16, 2008.

LAURIE, Darcy 1966–
    (Darcie Laurie, Darcie Lawrey)

PERSONAL

Born March 28, 1966, in Montreal, Quebec, Canada. *Avocational Interests:* Writing, collecting box films and memorabilia.

Career: Actor.

CREDITS

Film Appearances:

Banger number one, *Highlander III: The Sorcerer* (also known as *Highlander III, Highlander 3: The Final Conflict, Highlander 3: The Sorcerer,* and *Highlander: The Final Dimension*), Dimension Films, 1994.

Buster Powell, *Underworld,* Legacy Releasing, 1996.

Perierra, *See Spot Run,* Warner Bros., 2001.

Tony Franco, *Out of Line,* Curb Entertainment, 2001.

Drunk guy, *Liberty Stands Still* (also known as *Liberty Stands Still—Im visier des morders*), Lions Gate Films Home Entertainment, 2002.

Man in elevator, *Final Destination 2,* New Line Cinema, 2003.

Brian, *The Lost Angel,* Franchise Pictures, 2004.

Smitty, *Walking Tall,* Metro–Goldwyn–Mayer, 2004.

Convict, *The Chronicles of Riddick* (also known as *The Chronicles of Riddick: The Director's Cut*), Universal, 2004.

(As Darcy Lawrey) Biker, *Chaos* (also known as *Hit & Blast*), Lionsgate, 2005.

Timothy Laurents, *Hollow Man II,* Sony Pictures Home Entertainment, 2006.

Spoonie, *Vice,* 2008.

Television Appearances; Series:

Gideon, *SK8* (also known as *Skate*), NBC, 2001.

Dix, *Dark Angel* (also known as *James Cameron's "Dark Angel"*), Fox, 2001–2002.

Bob Tremblay, *Intelligence,* CBC, 2006–2007.

Television Appearances; Miniseries:

Simonelli driver, *Vendetta II: The New Mafia* (also known as *Bride of Violence 2* and *Donna d'onore 2*), syndicated, 1993.

The prisoner, *Atomic Train,* NBC, 1999.

Lucien Auguste, *Into the West,* TNT, 2005.

Television Appearances; Movies:

Omar/Chris, *Meltdown* (also known as *Angst uber Amerika*), FX Channel, 2004.

Second guy, *The Wool Cap,* TNT, 2004.

Bob Tremblay, *Intelligence,* CBC, 2005.

Lawrence Malishak, *A Job to Kill For,* Lifetime, 2006.

Television Appearances; Pilots:

Biker guy, *The Chronicle* (also known as *News from the Edge*), Sci–Fi Channel, 2001.

Television Appearances; Episodic:

(Uncredited) Engineer number two, "Piper Maru," *The X–Files,* Fox, 1996.

Harry Kant, "Something Wicked," *Highlander* (also known as *Highlander: The Series*), syndicated, 1996.

Bum, "Dark Priest," *Poltergeist: The Legacy,* Showtime, 1996.

Bartender, "A.D.," *Two,* syndicated, 1996.

Cave dweller, "The First Commandment," *Stargate SG–1* (also known as *La porte des etoiles*), Showtime, 1997.

Tony Grant, "His Brother's Keeper," *The Sentinel,* UPN, 1997.

Trini, "Forget Me Not," *Viper,* syndicated, 1997.

E. Jacob Woodcock, "The Pest House," *Millennium,* Fox, 1998.

Tin–Tin/Mike Tremayne, "The Soul Can't Rest," *The Crow: Stairway to Heaven,* syndicated, 1998.

Tin–Tin/Mike Tremayne, "It's a Wonderful Death," *The Crow: Stairway to Heaven,* syndicated, 1999.

Mick Meloni, "Safe House," *Viper,* syndicated, 1999.

Narc, "This Shit Is Evil," *Da Vinci's Inquest* (also known as *Coroner Da Vinci*), CBC, 2000.

Hoppy, "Loyalties," *Cold Squad,* CTV, 2000.

Tasker, *Call of the Wild,* Animal Planet, 2000.

Garth, "Life on the Wire," *UC: Undercover,* NBC, 2001.

Meyers, "The Straw," *Special Unit 2* (also known as *SU2*), UPN, 2002.

"Sayid," "The Story Vanishes," *Breaking News,* Bravo, 2002.

Santos, "Tagged," *The Twilight Zone,* UPN, 2003.

Officer Marques, "Doe or Die," *John Doe,* Fox, 2003.

Norad guy, "Letters from the Other Side: Part 2," *Jeremiah,* Showtime, 2003.

Andrew Chennery, "Y Me," *Touching Evil,* USA Network, 2004.

Murph, "Mr. Ellis Himself Would Been Proud," *Da Vinci's Inquest* (also known as *Coroner Da Vinci*), CBC, 2004.

Murph, "That's Why They Call it a Conspiracy," *Da Vinci's Inquest* (also known as *Coroner Da Vinci*), CBC, 2004.

Mortician, "Borders," *Cold Squad,* CTV, 2005.

Ivan, "The Superhero," *The Collector,* City TV, 2005.

Tass'an, "Babylon," *Stargate SG–1* (also known as *La porte des etoiles*), Sci–Fi Channel, 2005.

Paul Marshall, "Down for the Count," *The Evidence,* ABC, 2006.

(As Darcie Laurie) Jakob, "Delivery," *Blade: The Series,* Spike TV, 2006.

Jimmy Stryon, "Vortex," *The Dead Zone* (also known as *Stephen King's "Dead Zone"*), USA Network, 2006.

Rusty, "No Man Is an Island," *Men in Trees,* ABC, 2007.

Pawnshop owner, "Come to Your Senses," *Kyle XY,* ABC Family, 2007.

Also appeared as Reyas, "The Grand Alliance," *Tom Stone* (also known as *Stone Undercover*), CBC.

LEE, Cody Benjamin 1997–
(Cody Lee)

PERSONAL

Born July 18, 1997, in CA; twin brother of Brody Nicholas Lee (an actor)

Addresses: *Agent*—Hervey, Grimes Talent Agency, 10561 Missouri Ave., Suite 2, Los Angeles, CA 90025.

Career: Actor.

Awards, Honors: Young Artist Award nomination, best supporting young actor in a television movie, miniseries, or special, 2008, for *The Last Day of Summer.*

CREDITS

Television Appearances; Series:
One of the fifth–graders, *Are You Smarter than a 5th Grader?,* Fox, 2007.

Television Appearances; Movies:
Travis, *The Last Day of Summer,* Nickelodeon, 2007.

Television Appearances; Episodic:
Nicholas, "The Truth about Cats and Dogs," *For Your Love,* The WB, 2000.

Nicholas, "The Replacements," *For Your Love,* The WB, 2001.

Logan, "The Son Also Rises," *Invasion,* ABC, 2006.

(As Cody Lee) Danny Tavez, "No Man's Land," *CSI: Miami,* CBS, 2007.

Journeyman, NBC, 2007.

Yo on E!, E! Entertainment Television, 2007.

Dancer, "Boogie Toasties," *Just Jordan,* Nickelodeon, 2008.

First boy, "Happy Birthday Nate," *Eli Stone,* ABC, 2008.

Entertainment Tonight (also known as *Entertainment This Week, E.T., ET Weekend,* and *This Week in Entertainment*), syndicated, 2008.

Guest on talk shows.

Film Appearances:
(As Cody Lee) *De las Calles* (short film), 2006.

Mateus, *Amarelinha* (short film), Shorts International, 2007.

(As Cody Lee) Indian boy, *The Shiftling,* Digital Shadow Films, 2008.

Daniel, *The Human Contract,* 100% Womon/ Overbrook Entertainment/Tycoon Entertainment, 2008.

Brian, *Broken Windows,* Meherio Productions/Sightline Entertainment, 2008.

(As Cody Lee) Jared, *Blood and Bone,* Remarkable Films/Michael Mailer Films, 2008.

Young Alexander, *Sutures,* Sutures LLC, 2008.

(As Cody Lee) First twin, *Wreck the Halls,* Ouat Media, 2009.

Stage Appearances:

Appeared in a lead role, *The Cinderella Story,* Madrid Theatre; as a member of ensemble, *Kids of the Kingdom;* and as a singer and dancer, *LA Hip Kids.*

LeGROS, James 1962–
(James Le Gros, James Legros)

PERSONAL

Born April 27, 1962, in Minneapolis, MN; raised in Redlands, CA; father, a real estate broker; mother, a teacher; son–in–law of Robert Loggia (an actor); married Kristina Loggia (an actress and photographer), 1992; children: two sons. *Education:* Attended the University of California, Irvine.

Addresses: *Agent*—David Lillard, IFA Talent Agency, 8730 Sunset Blvd., Suite 490, Los Angeles, CA 90069. *Manager*—Louise Spinner Ward, Talent Entertainment Group, 9111 Wilshire Blvd., Beverly Hills, CA 90210. *Publicist*—Matt Labov, Baker Winokur Ryder, 9100 Wilshire Blvd., Sixth Floor West, Beverly Hills, CA 90212.

Career: Actor. South Coast Repertory Theatre, apprentice.

Member: Screen Actors Guild.

Awards, Honors: Independent Spirit Award nomination, best supporting actor, Independent Feature Project/ West, 1996, for *Living in Oblivion;* Screen Actors Guild Award nomination (with others), outstanding performance by an ensemble in a comedy series, 2001, for *Ally McBeal;* Gotham Award nomination (with others), best ensemble cast, Independent Feature Project, 2007, for *The Last Winter.*

CREDITS

Film Appearances:

Jewe, *The Ladies Club* (also known as *The Sisterhood* and *The Violated*), New Line Cinema, 1986.

(As James Le Gros) Metron, *Solarbabies* (also known as *Solar Warriors*), Metro–Goldwyn–Mayer, 1986.

Buddy MacGruder, *Real Men,* United Artists, 1987.

Second tough person, **batteries not included,* Universal, 1987.

Teenage cowboy, *Near Dark,* De Laurentiis Entertainment Group, 1987.

(As James Le Gros) Zack Jaeger, *Fatal Beauty,* Metro– Goldwyn–Mayer, 1987.

Mike Pearson, *Phantasm II* (also known as *Phantasm II: The Never Dead Part Two*), Universal, 1988.

Member of Vietnam platoon, *Born on the Fourth of July,* Universal, 1989.

(As James Le Gros) Rick, *Drugstore Cowboy,* Avenue Pictures, 1989.

Carl, *Hollywood Heartbreak,* 1990.

Lance, *Blood and Concrete* (also known as *Blood and Concrete, a Love Story*), IRS Media, 1991.

Roach, *Point Break,* Twentieth Century–Fox, 1991.

Tommy, *The Rapture,* Fine Line Features, 1991.

Andy, *Singles,* Warner Bros., 1992.

Carl, *Leather Jackets,* 1992.

Crasher, *Where the Day Takes You,* New Line Cinema, 1992.

Rusty, *Nervous Ticks,* IRS Media, 1992.

Skippy, *My New Gun,* IRS Media, 1992.

Deems Taylor, *Mrs. Parker and the Vicious Circle* (also known as *Mrs. Parker and the Round Table*), Fine Line Features, 1994.

Dodger, *Don't Do It,* Triboro Entertainment Group, 1994.

John Boyz, *Floundering,* Strand Releasing, 1994.

William Tucker, *Bad Girls,* Twentieth Century–Fox, 1994.

Mike, Jr., *The Low Life,* 1994, Cinepix Film Properties/ Cabin Fever Entertainment, 1996.

Avakian, *Panther,* Gramercy Pictures, 1995.

Chad Palomino, *Living in Oblivion,* Sony Pictures Classics, 1995.

Chris, *Safe,* Sony Pictures Classics, 1995.

Thoreau, *Destiny Turns on the Radio* (also known as *Johnny Destiny* and *Mister Destiny*), Savoy Pictures, 1995.

John, *Just Looking,* Black Crow Productions, 1995, Sony Pictures Classics, 1997.

Fenton Ray, *Boys,* Buena Vista, 1996.

Grill, *The Destiny of Marty Fine,* Castle Hill Productions, 1996.

John Wheeler, *Infinity,* First Look Pictures Releasing, 1996.

Lieutenant Michael Killip, *Countdown* (also known as *Serial Bomber, Two—One—Zero,* and *Kurisumasu mokushi–roku*), 1996.

Cezanne, *The Myth of Fingerprints,* Sony Pictures Classics, 1997.

Max, *Wishful Thinking,* Miramax, 1997.

(As James Le Gros) Billy Hill, *Thursday,* Legacy Releasing/Volcanic Films, 1998.

Charlie (the car dealer), *Psycho,* MCA/Universal, 1998.

D. J., *There's No Fish Food in Heaven* (also known as *Life in the Fast Lane*), Lionsgate/Storm Entertainment, 1998.

Hunter, *The Pass* (also known as *Highway Hitcher*), York Entertainment, 1998.

Jerry Miller, *Enemy of the State*, Buena Vista, 1998.

(As James Le Gros) Takowsky, *L.A. without a Map* (also known as *I Love L.A.* and *Los Angeles without a Map*), United Media, 1998.

Bicker, *Jump*, Arrow Releasing, 1999.

Peter Barnes, *Drop Back Ten*, Outrider Pictures/E Films, 1999.

Jack, *If You Only Knew* (also known as *Ein Apartment zum Verlieben*), Eternity Pictures, 2000.

Jack, *World Traveler*, ThinkFilm, 2001.

Joe "Mac" McBeth, *Scotland, PA*, 2001, Lot 47 Films, 2002.

(As James Le Gros) Paul, *Lovely & Amazing*, 2001, Lionsgate/Good Machine, 2002.

(As James Le Gros) Ferrell, *Catch That Kid* (also known as *Mission without Permission* and *Mission: Possible—Diese Kids sind nicht zu fassen!*), Twentieth Century–Fox, 2004.

(As James Le Gros) Hugh, *November*, Sony Pictures Classics, 2004.

Soldier, *Straight into Darkness*, Screen Media, 2004.

(As James Le Gros) Dante, *Trust the Man*, Fox Searchlight Pictures, 2005.

James Hoffman, *The Last Winter* (also known as *Sioasti veturinn*), Antidote Films, 2006, IFC First Take, 2007.

(As James Le Gros) Officer George Bawart, *Zodiac* (also known as *Chronicles*), Paramount, 2007.

Paul Dewey, *Cough Drop*, 2007.

Julieen, *Visioneers*, 2008.

Palmer, *Sherman's Way*, 2008.

Stil, *Dry Rain*, 2008.

Ted Heinkin, *Vantage Point*, Columbia, 2008.

Dan, *Winged Creatures*, Peace Arch Entertainment/Columbia, c. 2008.

Clive Burkham, *Skateland*, 2009.

Revis, *Welcome to Academia*, 2009.

Rupert, *Thicker*, 2009.

Television Appearances; Series:

Mark Albert, *Ally McBeal*, Fox, 2000–2001.

Special agent Raymond "Ray" Fuller, *Sleeper Cell* (also known as *Sleeper Cell: American Terror*), Showtime, 2005.

Television Appearances; Movies:

Car attendant, *The Ratings Game* (also known as *The Mogul*), The Movie Channel, 1984.

First boy, *Kicks* (also known as *Destination Alcatraz*), ABC, 1985.

Howard Hickock, *Guncrazy*, Showtime, 1992.

Cougar, *Marshal Law*, Showtime, 1996.

(As James Legros) Raylan Givens, *Pronto*, Showtime, 1997.

Dan McIvers, *Border Line*, NBC, 1999.

Hunter, *The Pass*, Showtime, 1999.

Amos, "Andy & Amos" segment, *Common Ground*, CBS, 2000.

Doug Peeno, *Damaged Care*, Showtime, 2002.

Troy, *Big Shot: Confessions of a Campus Bookie*, FX Network, 2002.

Matthew Paradise, *Paradise*, Showtime, 2004.

Josh, *Sexual Life*, Showtime, 2005.

Television Appearances; Specials:

Freddie Cruz, "Ace Hits the Big Time," *CBS Schoolbreak Special*, CBS, 1985.

Himself, *Sleeper Cell: Know Your Enemy*, Showtime, 2005.

Television Appearances; Episodic:

Trasher, "The Rotten Apples," *Knight Rider*, NBC, 1984.

(As James Le Gros) Blade, "Fenster Hall: Parts 1 & 2," *Punky Brewster*, NBC, 1985.

Punk boy, "Slither," *Simon & Simon*, CBS, 1985.

Lucas Miller, "When Whitney Met Linda," *Class of '96*, Fox, 1993.

Mr. Schlosser, "Springtime for David," *Roseanne*, ABC, 1996.

Lieutenant Ben Conklin, "Dead Man's Switch," *The Outer Limits* (also known as *The New Outer Limits*), Showtime, Sci–Fi Channel, and syndicated, 1997.

Dr. Max Rocher, "A Hole in the Heart," *ER* (also known as *Emergency Room*), NBC, 1998.

Dr. Max Rocher, "Of Past Regret and Future Fear," *ER* (also known as *Emergency Room*), NBC, 1998.

Dr. Max Rocher, "Suffer the Little Children," *ER* (also known as *Emergency Room*), NBC, 1998.

Dwight Anthony, "Under the Radar," *L.A. Doctors* (also known as *L.A. Docs, Kliniken, Kohtaloni Los Angeles*, and *Medicos de Los Angeles*), CBS, 1998.

Jim, "The One with the Tea Leaves," *Friends* (also known as *Across the Hall, Friends Like Us, Insomnia Cafe*, and *Six of One*), NBC, 2002.

Himself, *Intimate Portrait: Diane Lane* (also known as "Diane Lane," *Intimate Portrait*), Lifetime, 2002.

(As James Le Gros) Dwight Jacobs, "Red Ball," *Law & Order* (also known as *Law & Order Prime*), NBC, 2005.

Television Appearances; Pilots:

Jackie Frye, *The 900 Lives of Jackie Frye* (second pilot), ABC, c. 1997.

Barry, *The Street Lawyer*, ABC, 2003.

Rabbi, *1%*, HBO, 2009.

RECORDINGS

Videos:

Himself, "*Psycho*" *Path*, Universal Studios Home Video, 1999.

OTHER SOURCES

Periodicals:
Entertainment Weekly, May 19, 2000, p. 55.
Premiere, February, 2002, p. 25.

LEMMONS, Kasi 1961–

PERSONAL

Original name, Karen Lemmons; born February 24, 1961, in St. Louis, MO (some sources cite Boston, MA); father, a biology teacher; mother, a poet and psychotherapist; married Vondie Curtis–Hall (an actor, writer, and director), 1995; children: Henry Hunter, Zora. *Education:* Attended New York University, University of California, Los Angeles, and New School for Social Research; trained for the stage at Lee Strasberg Theatre Institute, New York School of Ballet; Circle in the Square Professional Theatre School; and Alvin Ailey American Dance Center; studied mime with Marcel Marceau.

Addresses: *Agent*—Frank Wuliger, Gersh Agency, 232 North Canon Dr., Beverly Hills, CA 90210. *Manager*—Stephanie Davis, 3 Arts Entertainment, 9460 Wilshire Blvd., 7th Floor, Beverly Hills, CA 90212.

Career: Actress, producer, director, film editor, and writer. Boston Children's Theatre, Boston, MA, former child actress; Film Independent, Los Angeles, secretary and member of executive committee.

Awards, Honors: National Board of Review Award, outstanding directorial debut, 1997, Independent Spirit Award (with others), best first feature, Independent Features Project West, and Black Film Award, best director, Acapulco Black Film Festival, 1998, all for *Eve's Bayou;* Image Award, outstanding directing in a motion picture, National Association for the Advancement of Colored People (NAACP), 2008, for *Talk to Me.*

CREDITS

Film Appearances:
Perry, *School Daze,* Columbia, 1988.
Jackie, *Vampire's Kiss,* Hemdale Releasing, 1989.
Cookie, *The Five Heartbeats,* Twentieth Century–Fox, 1991.
Special Agent Ardelia Mapp, *The Silence of the Lambs,* Orion, 1991.

Bernadette "Bernie" Walsh, *Candyman* (also known as *Clive Barker's "Candyman"*), TriStar, 1992.
Nina Blackburn, *Fear of a Black Hat,* Samuel Goldwyn, 1993.
Marie Mitchell, *Hard Target,* Universal, 1993.
June Vanderpool, *DROP Squad,* Gramercy, 1994.
Madonna, *Gridlock'd,* Gramercy, 1997.
Angenelle, *'Til There Was You,* Paramount, 1997.
Teresa, *Liar's Dice,* 1998.
Herself, *Sisters in Cinema,* Our Film Works, 2003.
Angry black woman, *Waist Deep,* Focus Features, 2006.

Film Director:
(And cinematographer, film editor, and sound editor) *Fall from Grace,* 1987.
Eve's Bayou, Trimark Pictures, 1997.
The Caveman's Valentine (also known as *The Sign of the Killer*), Universal, 2001.
Talk to Me, Focus Features, 2007.

Television Appearances; Series:
Nella Franklin, *As the World Turns,* CBS, 1986–89.
Tess Parker, *Another World* (also known as *Another World: Bay City*), NBC, 1989–90.

Television Appearances; Movies:
Hostage, *11th Victim* (also known as *The Lakeside Killer*), CBS, 1979.
Rachel Isum Robinson, *The Court–Martial of Jackie Robinson,* TNT, 1990.
Carol North, *Afterburn* (also known as *The Janet Harduval Story*), HBO, 1992.
Grace, *Zooman* (also known as *Zooman and the Sign*), Showtime, 1995.

Television Appearances; Specials:
Subaya, "The Gift of Amazing Grace," *ABC Afterschool Specials,* ABC, 1986.
Host, *Puzzle Weekend,* syndicated, 1987.
Lifetime Women's Film Festival, Lifetime, 1998.
Clerk, "Override," *Directed By,* Showtime, 1994.
In the Company of Women, Independent Film Channel, 2004.

Television Appearances; Episodic:
"Resurrection," *Spenser: For Hire,* ABC, 1985.
Miss McKegney, "The Birth: Parts 1 & 2," *The Cosby Show,* NBC, 1988.
Zandili, "The Day of the Covenant," *The Equalizer,* CBS, 1988.
Lois, "Life after Death," *A Man Called Hawk,* 1989.
Alex Robbins, "Spy Games," *Under Cover,* ABC, 1991.
Alex Robbins, "Before the Storm," *Under Cover,* ABC, 1991.
Alex Robbins, "Sacrifice," *Under Cover,* ABC, 1991.

Paula Raynor, "The Survivor," *Murder, She Wrote,* CBS, 1993.
Diane Warren, "Night of the Gladiator," *Walker, Texas Ranger* (also known as *Walker*), CBS, 1993.
Chemotherapy technician, "It's All in Your Head," *ER,* NBC, 2002.
"The Silence of the Lambs," *Page to Screen,* Bravo Canada, 2002.

Television Appearances; Awards Presentations:

Presenter, *The 2001 IFP/West Independent Spirit Awards,* Independent Film Channel, 2001.
The 17th Annual Gotham Awards, 2007.

Television Appearances; Other:

Marcy Potts, *Adam's Apple* (pilot), CBS, 1986.
Melanie Bryant, *The Big One: The Great Los Angeles Earthquake* (miniseries; also known as *Earthquake Los Angeles: The Big One* and *The Great Los Angeles Earthquake*), NBC, 1990.

Television Director; Specials:

Dr. Hugo, Lifetime, 1994.

Stage Appearances:

Shakespeare's Sonnets, Globe Playhouse, Los Angeles, 1980.
Balm in Gilead, off–Broadway production, 1984.

Also appeared in a Los Angeles production of *Romeo and Juliet.*

RECORDINGS

Videos:

Bernadette Walsh (in archive footage), *Boogeymen: The Killer Compilation,* Paramount, 2001.
Sweets to the Sweet: The Candyman Mythos, Columbia TriStar Home Entertainment, 2004.

WRITINGS

Screenplays:

Author of narrative text, *Fall from Grace,* 1987.
Eve's Bayou, Trimark Pictures, 1997.

Television Specials:

Dr. Hugo, Lifetime, 1994.

Television Episodes:

According to some sources, writer for episodes of *The Cosby Show,* NBC.

OTHER SOURCES

Books:

Contemporary Black Biography, Volume 20, Gale Group, 1998.

Periodicals:

Los Angeles Times, November 6, 1997, p. 12.

LOWE, John B.
(John Lowe)

PERSONAL

Addresses: *Agent*—Characters Talent Agency, 1505 West 2nd Ave., Suite 200, Vancouver, British Columbia V6H 3Y4 Canada.

Career: Actor. Formerly the artistic director of St. Albert Children's Theatre; Broccolo Creative (a film development company). Acting teacher, 1989—; Stage One Theatre School, Western Canada Theatre, lead instructor.

CREDITS

Film Appearances:

Train conductor, *Heart of the Sun,* 1998.
Conductor, *MVP: Most Valuable Primate,* Keystone Family Pictures, 2000.
Delaney, *The Operative,* Studio Home Entertainment, 2000.
Executive, *Slap Shot 2: Breaking the Ice,* Universal Home Entertainment, 2002.
Professor Carter, *The Butterfly Effect,* New Line Cinema, 2004.
Priest, *Fido,* Lionsgate, 2006.
Pappa, *Night Travellers* (short), 2008.
Rueben Markel, *The Hessen Affair,* 2009.
Mr. Sinclair, *The Haunting in Connecticut,* Lionsgate, 2009.

Film Work:

Director and producer, *Windows of White* (short), 1999.

Also worked as director and producer, *Broccoli* (short); director and producer, *With AB* (short).

Television Appearances; Series:

Rupert Mowat, *Nothing Too Good of a Cowboy,* CBC, 1998–2000.
Arthur Kirkland, *Less Than Kind,* 2008.

Television Appearances; Miniseries:

Small Sacrifices, ABC, 1989.

The priest, *Atomic Train,* NBC, 1999.

David Ziff, *Living with the Dead* (also known as *Talking to Heaven*), CBS, 2002.

Dr. Findlay, "Maintenance," *Taken* (also known as *Steven Spielberg Presents "Taken"*), Sci–Fi Channel, 2002.

Television Appearances; Movies:

(Uncredited) Jumpmaster, *Ordeal in the Arctic,* ABC, 1993.

Dr. Lawrence Andruss, *Voyage of Terror* (also known as *Die Schreckensfahrt der Orion Star* and *The Fourth Horseman*), Fox Family, 1998.

Golden Ridge official, *Golf Punks* (also known as *National Lampoon's "Golf Punks"*), Fox Family, 1998.

British vice counsel, *The Linda McCartney Story* (also known as *L'histoire de Linda McCartney*), CBS, 2000.

Santa Claus, *The Ultimate Christmas Present,* The Disney Channel, 2000.

Harry Maculwain, *Trapped,* USA Network, 2001.

Mr. Brand, *Shadow Realm,* Sci–Fi Channel, 2002.

Professor Miller, *Critical Assembly* (also known as *Ground Zero*), NBC, 2003.

Man in audience, *The Goodbye Girl* (also known as *Neil Simon's "The Goodbye Girl"*), TNT, 2004.

Dr. Aldaron, *Absolute Zero,* Sci–Fi Channel, 2005.

Gary, *The Secrets of Comfort House* (also known as *Sombres Secrets*), Lifetime, 2006.

Television Appearances; Episodic:

Reverend Sam Hanes, "Anamnesis," *Millennium,* Fox, 1998.

Dr. Leavitt, "The Pine Bluff Variant," *The X–Files,* Fox, 1998.

Judge Hargrove, "Hangman," *Dead Man's Gun,* Showtime, 1998.

Steven Deville, "Lights, Camera, Addams!," *The New Addams Family,* Fox Family, 1999.

Engineer, "Sacrifice," *Poltergeist: The Legacy,* Sci–Fi Channel, 1999.

Priest, "Mabus," *First Wave,* Sci–Fi Channel, 2000.

Drunk, "Wicked Wicked West," *The Immortal,* syndicated, 2000.

Dr. Ernie Haas, "The Long Goodbye," *Beggars and Choosers,* Showtime, 2001.

Mr. Brand, "Patterns," *Night Visions,* Fox, 2002.

Ian Northby, "True Believers: Part 1," *Cold Squad,* CTV, 2003.

Husband, "The Candidate," *The Chris Isaak Show,* Showtime, 2004.

Nelson, "A Shock to the System," *Saved,* TNT, 2006.

Also appeared as Rich, "The Tux," *The Sausage Factory* (also known as *MTV's "Now What?,"* *Much Ado About Whatever,* and *Special Ed*), MTV.

Stage Appearances:

Appeared in *Here on the Flight Path,* Sunshine Theatre, Kelowna, British Columbia, Canada; *An Inspector Calls,* Chemainus Theatre Festival, Chemanius, British Columbia, Canada; *Measure for Measure,* Citadel Theatre, Edmonton, Alberta, Canada; *For the Pleasures of Seeing Her Again,* Sunshine Theatre; *The Drawer Boy,* Sunshine Theatre; *Dear Santa,* Western Canada Theatre, Kamloops, British Columbia, Canada, and the Gateway; *Over the River and Through the Woods,* Western Canada Theatre and the Gateway; *Greater Tuna; Giant Ants!*

WRITINGS

Screenplays:

Windows of White (short), 1999.

Also wrote *Broccoli* (short); *With AB* (short).

LUHRMANN, Baz 1962–

PERSONAL

Original name, Mark Anthony Luhrmann; born September 17, 1962, in Sydney, New South Wales, Australia; son of Leonard (a farmer, filling station owner, and operator of local movie theatre) Luhrmann; mother, a dress shop owner and ballroom dance teacher; married Catherine Martin (a production designer, costume designer, and producer), January 26, 1997; children: Lillian Amanda, William Alexander. *Education:* Attended National Institute of Dramatic Arts, Sydney, Australia, 1985.

Addresses: *Office*—Bazmark Films, 10201 West Pico Blvd., Los Angeles, CA 90035. *Agent*—Endeavor, 9601 Wilshire Blvd., 3rd Floor, Beverly Hills, CA 90210.

Career: Director, writer, producer, production designer, and actor. Six Years Old Company (theatre group), founder and artistic director, beginning c. 1985; Bazmark Films, Los Angeles, cofounder and president, 1997—. Director of commercials, including a long ad for Chanel No. 5 perfume featuring Nicole Kidman and Rodrigo Santoro, 2004. Bazmark Music, owner of record label; BazMark.Inq., founder, 1996. Named ambassador of Australian Theatre for Young People, 2005. Former political campaign manager for Australian Prime Minister Paul Keating.

Awards, Honors: World Youth Theater Festival Awards, best production and best director, 1986, for *Strictly Ballroom;* Mo Award, operatic performance of the year,

1990, for *La Boheme;* Victorian Green Room Award, best director, c. 1990, for *Lake Lost;* Prix de Jeuness (youth award), Cannes Film Festival, Audience Prize, Sydney Film Festival, Audience Prize, Melbourne Film Festival, Calsberg People's Choice Award from Toronto International Film Festival, Australian Film Institute Awards, best director and best screenplay (with Craig Pearce), and Vancouver International Film Festival Award, most popular film, all 1992, Robert Festival Award, best foreign film, Film Award nominations, best adapted screenplay (with Craig Pearce) and best film (with Tristram Miall), British Academy of Film and Television Arts, London Critics Circle Film Award, newcomer of the year, and Golden Aphrodite, Love Is Folly International Film Festival of Bulgaria, all 1993, and Golden Precolumbian Circle nomination, best film, Bogota Film Festival, 1994, all for *Strictly Ballroom;* Critic's Prize, Edinburgh Festival, 1994, for *A Midsummer Night's Dream;* Film Awards, best adapted screenplay (with Pearce) and David Lean Award for Direction, British Academy of Film and Television Arts, Alfred Bauer Award and nomination for Golden Berlin Bear, Berlin International Film Festival, Screen International Award nomination from European Film Awards, Australian Film Institute Award nomination (with Gabriella Martinelli), best foreign film, 1997, London Film Critics Circle Award nomination, director of the year, 1998, all for *Romeo + Juliet;* Byron Kennedy Award, Australian Film Institute, 1999; World Soundtrack Award (with others), most creative use of existing material on a soundtrack, Screen International Award, nomination for Golden Palm, Cannes Film Festival, Australian Film Institute Award nominations, best direction and best film (with others), IF Award nominations, best direction and best feature film (with others), and Hollywood Film Festival Award, Hollywood movie of the year, all 2001, Golden Laurel Award (with others), motion picture producer of the year, Producers Guild of America, Robert Festival Award, best non–American film, Screen Award nomination (with Pearce), best screenplay written directly for the screen, Writers Guild of America, Golden Satellite Award, best director, International Press Academy, and Golden Satellite Award nomination (with Pearce), best original screenplay, Film Critics Circle of Australia Award, best director, Film Critics of Australia Award nomination (with Pearce), best original screenplay, Empire Award, best director, Critics Choice Award, best director, Broadcast Film Critics Association, Academy Award nomination (with others), best picture, David Lean Award for Direction nomination, and Film Award nominations, best film (with others) and best original screenplay (with Pearce), British Academy of Film and Television Arts, Golden Globe Award nomination, best director of a motion picture, Directors Guild of America Award nomination, outstanding directorial achievement in a motion picture, Cesar Award nomination, best foreign film, Academie des Arts et Techniques du Cinema, Chicago Film Critics Association Award nomination, Phoenix Film Critics Society Award nomination, Vancouver Film Critics Circle Award, and Online Film Critics Society Award nomination, all best director, Bodil Award nomination, best non–American film, Film Award nomination (with others), American Film Institute, nomination for Silver Ribbon, best director of a foreign film, Italian National Syndicate of Film Journalists, 2002, all for *Moulin Rouge!;* Antoinette Perry Award nomination, 2001, for *La Boheme;* Auteur Award, Golden Satellite Awards, and Golden Satellite Award nomination, best original screenplay (with others), 2008, for *Australia;* Golden Satellite Award nomination, best original song (with others), 2008, for "By the Boab Tree," *Australia.*

CREDITS

Film Director:
Strictly Ballroom (short film), 1986.
Strictly Ballroom (feature film), Miramax, 1992.
(And producer) *Romeo + Juliet* (also known as *Romeo and Juliet* and *William Shakespeare's "Romeo + Juliet"*), Twentieth Century–Fox, 1996.
(And film producer and song producer) *Moulin Rouge!,* Twentieth Century–Fox, 2001.
(And producer) *Australia,* Twentieth Century–Fox, 2008.

Film Appearances:
Pete, *Winter of Our Dreams,* Enterprises/Satori, 1981.
First student, *The Dark Room,* 1982.
Able Seaman A. W. Huston, *The Highest Honor—A True Story* (also known as *Minami Jujisei* and *Southern Cross*), Nelson Entertainment, 1982.
William Shakespeare (documentary), Films for the Humanities and Sciences, 2000.
Himself, *Oh My God* (documentary), Rodger Pictures, 2008.

Television Appearances; Specials:
20th Century Fox: The Blockbuster Years, AMC, 2000.
The Night Club of Your Dreams: The Making of "Moulin Rouge," HBO, 2001.
Baz Luhrmann: The Show Must Go On, 2001.
Spinning Around: The Kylie Minogue Story, Channel 5, 2002.
Bollywood for Beginners, 2002.
Nicole Kidman: An American Cinematheque Tribute (also known as *The 18th Annual American Cinematheque Award*), AMC, 2003.
The 100 Greatest Musicals, Channel 4, 2003.
AFI's 100 Years ... 100 Songs, CBS, 2004.
My Shakespeare, 2004.
"The World of Nat King Cole," *American Masters,* PBS, 2006.
(In archive footage) *Boffo! Tinseltown's Bombs and Blockbusters,* HBO, 2006.
Nicole Kidman: The E! True Hollywood Story, E! Entertainment Television, 2007.

Television Appearances; Episodic:
Jerry Percival, "The Itinerants: Parts 1 & 2," *A Country Practice,* Seven Network, 1981.

Jerry Percival, "Pig in a Poke: Parts 1 & 2," *A Country Practice,* Seven Network, 1982.

Jerry Percival, "Come Blow Your Horn: Parts 1 & 2," *A Country Practice,* Seven Network, 1982.

"The Night Club of Your Dreams: The Making of 'Moulin Rouge!'," *HBO First Look,* HBO, 2001.

Pop–komissio, 2001.

Havoc's Luxury Suites and Conference Facility, 2001.

Rove Live, Ten Network, 2001.

Tinseltown TV, International Channel, 2003.

"Michael Powell," *Artworks Scotland,* 2005.

Jimmy Kimmel Live!, ABC, 2008.

Entertainment Tonight (also known as *Entertainment This Week, E.T., ET Weekend,* and *This Week in Entertainment*), syndicated, multiple appearances, 2008.

Le grand journal de Canal+, 2008.

Dias de cine, 2008.

"Baz Luhrmann Special," *The Culture Show,* BBC, 2008.

Cinema tres (also known as *Informatiu cinema*), 2008.

Cartelera, 2008.

Television Appearances; Awards Presentations:
AFI Awards 2001, CBS, 2002.
The 74th Annual Academy Awards, ABC, 2002.
The 57th Annual Tony Awards, CBS, 2003.

Television Appearances; Other:
Kids of the Cross (movie), 1983.
(In archive footage) *Long Way Round* (miniseries), Sky, 2004.

Television Director:
Kids of the Cross (movie), 1983.
"La Boheme" (special; broadcast of 1993 stage production), *Great Performances,* PBS, 1994.

Stage Director:
Crocodile Creek, New Moon Theatre Company, Australia, 1987.
Dance Hall, Sydney Festival, Sydney, 1989.
(And production designer) *La Boheme,* Australian Opera, Melbourne, Australia, 1990, revived, 1993.
Lake Lost (opera), Australian production, 1990.
A Midsummer Night's Dream, Australian Opera, then Edinburgh Festival, Edinburgh, Scotland, 1994.
La Boheme, Broadway Theatre, New York City, 2001.

Major Tours:
Director, *Strictly Ballroom,* National Institute of Dramatic Arts, Sydney, Australia, then World Youth Theatre Festival, Czechoslovakia, c. 1986, later Wharf Theatre, Sydney, and World Expo, Brisbane, Australia.

RECORDINGS

Album Producer:
Baz Luhrmann Presents … Something for Everybody, EMD/Capitol, c. 1999.

Also producer of the single, "Everybody's Free to Wear Sunscreen," 1999.

Videos:
Leonardo DiCaprio: A Life in Progress, Twentieth Century–Fox, 1998.

Director of music videos, including "Beat Me Daddy" by Ignatius Jones, "Come What May" by Ewan McGregor and Nicole Kidman, and "Love in the Air" by John Paul Young.

WRITINGS

Screenplays:
Strictly Ballroom (short film; based on previous stage play), 1986.
(With Craig Pearce; and lyricist, "Rumba de Burros") *Strictly Ballroom* (feature film; based on short film), Miramax, 1992.
(With Pearce) *Romeo + Juliet* (also known as *Romeo and Juliet* and *William Shakespeare's "Romeo + Juliet"*), Twentieth Century–Fox, 1996.
(With Pearce; and songwriter) *Moulin Rouge!,* Twentieth Century–Fox, 2001.
(And songwriter) *Australia* (also based on story by Luhrmann), Twentieth Century–Fox, 2008.

Songs have also been featured in other films.

Stage Plays:
(With Craig Pearce and Andrew Bovell) *Strictly Ballroom,* produced at National Institute of Dramatic Arts, Sydney, Australia, then World Youth Theatre Festival, Czechoslovakia, c. 1986, later Wharf Theatre, Sydney, and World Expo, Brisbane, Australia.

Also cocreator of the opera *The Pure Merino Fandango.*

Other:
(With Miro Bilbrough and Sue Adler) *Moulin Rouge: The Splendid Illustrated Book that Charts the Journey of Baz Luhrmann's Motion Picture,* Newmarket Press, 2001.

Guest editor of the first issue of the periodical *Australian Vogue.*

OTHER SOURCES

Books:
Authors and Artists for Young Adults, Volume 74, Gale, 2007.
Cook, Pam, *Baz Luhrmann,* BFI Publishing, 2006.
Luhrmann, Baz, Miro Bilbrough, and Sue Adler, *Moulin Rouge: The Splendid Illustrated Book that Charts the Journey of Baz Luhrmann's Motion Picture,* Newmarket Press, 2001.
Newsmakers, Issue 3, Gale, 2002.

Periodicals:
Billboard, April 10, 1999, p. 11.
Newsweek, May 28, 2001, p. 58.
Variety, April 2, 2001, p. 35; April 16, 2001, p. 7.

LUX, Danny
(Danny Scott Lux)

PERSONAL

Raised in CA. *Education:* Graduated from Granada Hills High School.

Addresses: *Manager*—International Creative Management, 10250 Constellation Way, Ninth Floor, Los Angeles, CA 90067.

Career: Composer and musician. Worked for the composer Mike Post.

Awards, Honors: Broadcast Music, Inc. (BMI) awards (with Mike Post), 1995 and 1996, both for *NYPD Blue;* Emmy Award nomination, outstanding main title theme music, 1997, for the pilot of *Crisis Center;* BMI TV Award, 1999, for *Ally McBeal;* Emmy Award nomination, outstanding main title theme music, 1999, for *Profiler.*

CREDITS

Television Work; Series:
Song engineer, *Cop Rock* (musical), ABC, 1990.
Music editor, *Sabrina, the Teenage Witch* (also known as *Sabrina* and *Sabrina Goes to College*), ABC, 1997–98.

Film Work:
Score mixer and score producer, *Halloween: Resurrection* (also known as *Hall8ween, Halloween 8, Hal-* loween: Evil Never Dies, Halloween: Homecoming, Halloween: The Homecoming, Halloween H2K, Halloween H2K: Evil Never Dies, and Halloween: MichaelMyers.com), Miramax/Dimension Films, 2002.
Performer and producer of song "If We Build It," *The Benchwarmers,* Columbia, 2006.

WRITINGS

Television Music; Series:
Silk Stalkings, CBS and USA Network, 1992–93.
L.A. Law, NBC, 1993–94.
NYPD Blue, ABC, 1994–96.
The Jeff Foxworthy Show (also known as *Somewhere in America*), ABC, 1995–96, NBC, 1996–97.
NewsRadio (also known as *News Radio, The Station, Dias de radio,* and *Dies de radio*), NBC, 1995–97.
Party of Five, Fox, 1996–97.
Sliders, Fox, 1996–97, Sci–Fi Channel, 1998–2000.
Profiler, NBC, 1996–2001.
Crisis Center (also known as *The Center*), NBC, 1997.
Ally McBeal, Fox, 1997–2002.
Sabrina, the Teenage Witch (also known as *Sabrina* and *Sabrina Goes to College*), ABC, 1997–2000, The WB, 2000–2003.
Significant Others, Fox, 1998.
Dawson's Creek, The WB, 1998–99.
Profiler, NBC, 1998–2000.
Ally (edited from the series *Ally McBeal*), Fox, 1999.
Young Americans (also known as *Monkey Writer from Goonies*), The WB, 2000.
Million Dollar Mysteries, Fox, 2000–2001.
Boston Public, Fox, 2000–2004.
Robotica, The Learning Channel, 2001–2002.
State of Grace, ABC Family Channel, 2001–2002.
The American Embassy (also known as *Emma Brody*), Fox, 2002.
John Doe (also known as *Der Fall John Doe!* and *Mies vailla nimeae*), Fox, 2002–2003.
The Bachelor (later season known as *The Bachelor: London Calling*), ABC, 2002—.
Strong Medicine, Lifetime, 2003.
Karen Sisco (also known as *Ofiter Karen*), ABC, 2003, USA Network, 2004.
Century City, CBS, 2003–2004.
The Bachelorette, ABC, 2003—.
Medical Investigation (also known as *The Cure*), NBC, 2004–2005.
Boston Legal (also known as *Fleet Street, The Practice: Fleet Street,* and *The Untitled Practice*), ABC, 2004–2008.
The Law Firm, NBC and Bravo, 2005.
Grey's Anatomy (also known as *Complications, Procedure, Surgeons, Under the Knife,* and *Grey's Anatomy—Die jungen Aerzte*), ABC, 2005—.

My Name Is Earl (also known as *Earl*), NBC, 2005—.
Pepper Dennis, The WB, 2006.
The Wedding Bells (also known as *The Wedding Planners* and *The Wedding Store*), Fox, 2007.
Canterbury's Law, Fox, 2008.

Television Themes; Series:
Spellbinder, Nine Network (Australia), 1995, Disney Channel, beginning 1996.
Sliders, Fox, 1996–97, Sci–Fi Channel, 1998–2000.
Profiler, NBC, 1996–2001.
Crisis Center (also known as *The Center*), NBC, 1997.
Sabrina, the Teenage Witch (also known as *Sabrina* and *Sabrina Goes to College*), The WB, 2000–2003.
Strong Medicine, Lifetime, 2002–2006.
Medical Investigation (also known as *The Cure*), NBC, 2004–2005.
Boston Legal (also known as *Fleet Street, The Practice: Fleet Street,* and *The Untitled Practice*), ABC, 2005–2006.

Television Main Title Music; Series:
Million Dollar Mysteries, Fox, 2000–2001.

Television Additional Music; Series:
Pointman, syndicated, 1995.

Television Music; Miniseries:
Trista & Ryan's Wedding, ABC, 2003.

Television Music; Movies:
Sabrina Goes to Rome, ABC, 1998.
Lucky 7 (also known as *Lucky Seven*), ABC Family Channel, 2003.
I Do (but I Don't), Lifetime, 2004.
Infidelity, Lifetime, 2004.
Campus Confidential, ABC Family Channel, 2005.
Spring Break Shark Attack (also known as *Dangerous Waters: Shark Attack*), CBS, 2005.
Widow on the Hill, Lifetime, 2005.
Read It and Weep, Disney Channel, 2006.
Relative Chaos, ABC Family Channel, 2006.
Holiday in Handcuffs, ABC Family Channel, 2007.
The Circuit, ABC Family Channel, 2008.

Television Additional Music; Movies:
Camp Rock (musical; also known as *Rock Camp Rules*), Disney Channel, 2008.

Television Music; Specials:
Cop Files, UPN, 1995, 1996.
Breaking the Magician's Code: Magic's Biggest Secrets Finally Revealed, Fox, 1997.

Breaking the Magician's Code 2: Magic's Biggest Secrets Finally Revealed, Fox, 1998.
Magic's Biggest Secrets Finally Revealed 3 (also known as *Breaking the Magician's Code: Magic's Biggest Secrets Finally Revealed 3*), Fox, 1998.
Breaking the Magician's Code: Magic's Biggest Secrets Finally Revealed 4—Unmasking the Magician: The Final Reveal), Fox, 1998.
World's Worst Drivers Caught on Tape (also known as *World's Worst Drivers*), Fox, 1998.
World's Worst Drivers Caught on Tape 2 (also known as *World's Worst Drivers*), Fox, 1998.
Exposed! Pro Wrestling's Greatest Secrets, NBC, 1999.
Cheating Spouses: Caught on Tape, 2000.
Sexiest Bachelor in America Pageant (also known as *The Sexiest Bachelor in America*), Fox, 2000.
Surprise Wedding, Fox, 2000.
Unauthorized Brady Bunch: The Final Days (also known as *Unauthorized: Brady Bunch—The Final Days*), Fox, 2000.
Who Wants to Marry a Multi–Millionaire?, Fox, 2000.
Cheating Spouses: Caught on Tape 2, 2001.
Surprise Wedding II, Fox, 2001.
Who Wants to Be a Princess?, Fox, 2001.
World's Worst Drivers Caught on Tape 3 (also known as *World's Worst Drivers*), Fox, 2001.
The Bachelor: The Women Tell All, ABC, 2002, 2005, 2006, 2007.
The Bachelor: Aaron and Helene Tell All, ABC, 2003.
The Bachelor: After the Rose, ABC, 2003.
Psychic Secrets Revealed, NBC, 2003.
The Bachelorette: The Men Tell All, ABC, 2003, 2005.
The Bachelor: Where Are They Now?, ABC, 2003, 2008.
The Bachelorette: After the Final Rose, ABC, 2004.
Countdown to the Emmys, ABC, 2004.
The Bachelor: After the Final Rose, ABC, 2004, 2007.
The Bachelor: The Final Rose Live, ABC, 2005.
The Bachelor: Paris The Women Tell All, ABC, 2006.
Getting into Grey's Anatomy, ABC, 2006.
(As Danny Scott Lux) *Grey's Anatomy: Complications of the Heart,* ABC, 2006.
(As Danny Scott Lux) *Grey's Anatomy: Every Moment Counts,* ABC, 2006.
(As Danny Scott Lux) *Grey's Anatomy: Straight to the Heart,* ABC, 2006.
(As Danny Scott Lux) *Grey's Anatomy: Under Pressure,* ABC, 2006.
(As Danny Scott Lux) *Come Rain or Come Shine: From Grey's Anatomy to Private Practice,* ABC, 2007.
Magic's Biggest Secrets Revealed, MyNetworkTV, 2008.

Television Main Title Music; Specials:
The Bachelor: After the Final Rose, ABC, 2004.
The Bachelorette: After the Final Rose, ABC, 2005.

Television Music; Episodic:
"How Am I Driving?," *L.A. Law,* NBC, 1994.
"Gun of a Son," *10–8: Officers on Duty* (also known as *10–8* and *10–8: Police Patrol*), ABC, 2004.

Television Music; Pilots:
Sabrina the Teenage Witch (also known as *Sabrina* and *Sabrina Goes to College*), Showtime, 1996.
Ally McBeal, Fox, 1997.
Crisis Center (also known as *The Center*), NBC, 1997.
Hack, CBS, 2002.
My Name Is Earl (also known as *Earl*), NBC, 2005.
Canterbury's Law, Fox, 2008.

Film Music:
Score with Chicks, 1994.
Has–Been, 1998.
Halloween: Resurrection (also known as *Hall8ween, Halloween 8, Halloween: Evil Never Dies, Halloween: Homecoming, Halloween: The Homecoming, Halloween H2K, Halloween H2K: Evil Never Dies,* and *Halloween: MichaelMyers.com*), Miramax/Dimension Films, 2002.
Stolen Summer, Miramax, 2002.
Song "If We Build It," *The Benchwarmers,* Columbia, 2006.
Nine Dead, Hartbreak Films/Louisiana Media Productions, 2008.
Verboten (short film), 2008.

Lux's songs and music has appeared in various films and television programs.

LYNDALL–KNIGHT, Tiffany
(Tiffany Knight, Tiffany Lyndall Knight)

PERSONAL

Born in Toronto, Ontario, Canada; children: two. *Education:* Graduated from George Brown Theatre School, Toronto, Ontario, Canada; studied journalism at an Australian university.

Career: Actress. Spent a season at Bard on the Beach (a Shakespeare festival), Vancouver, British Columbia, Canada.

Awards, Honors: Gemini Award nomination (with others), best performance in a performing arts program or series, Academy of Canadian Cinema and Television, 2003, for *Year of the Lion;* four Jessie Theater Richard Award nominations.

CREDITS

Film Appearances:
(As Tiffany Knight) Mob woman, *I, Robot,* Twentieth Century–Fox, 2004.
(Uncredited) Gloria Guiness, *Capote,* Sony Pictures Classics, 2005.
Miss Mills, *Fido,* Lionsgate, 2006.
Humongous, U.S.A. (short), 2007.
Actor number two in play, *Elegy,* Samuel Goldwyn Films, 2008.
Kate, *Mothers & Daughters,* 2008.
(As Tiffany Knight) Darla the teacher, *Case 39,* Paramount, 2009.

Television Appearances; Series:
Billie Simms, *Da Vinci's City Hall* (also known as *Le maire Da Vinci*), CBC, 2005–2006.
The Hybrid, *Battlestar Galactica* (also known as *BSG*), Sci–Fi Channel, 2006–2008.

Television Appearances; Movies:
(As Tiffany Knight) Sally McDonald, *Y2K* (also known as *Countdown to Chaos* and *Y2K: The Movie*), NBC, 1999.
(As Tiffany Knight) Journalist, *A Little Thing Called Murder,* Lifetime, 2006.

Television Appearances; Episodic:
(As Tiffany Knight) La Moore, "Touchstone," *Stargate SG–1* (also known as *La porte des etoiles*), Sci–Fi Channel, 1998.
(As Tiffany Knight) Hargo, "Second Chances," *Mercy Point,* UPN, 1999.
(As Tiffany Knight) Gua technician, "Target 117," *First Wave,* Sci–Fi Channel, 1999.
(As Tiffany Knight) Technician, "Zig Zag," *The Outer Limits* (also known as *The New Outer Limits*), Showtime, 2000.
(As Tiffany Knight) Television commercial lady, "Brainiac," *Dark Angel* (also known as *James Cameron's "Dark Angel"*), Fox, 2002.
(As Tiffany Knight) Nurse, "Reaper," *Smallville* (also known as *Smallville: Superman the Early Years*), The WB, 2002.
(As Tiffany Knight) Samantha, "Sensuous Cindy," *The Twilight Zone,* UPN, 2002.
(As Tiffany Knight) Evalla, "Revisions," *Stargate SG–1* (also known as *La porte des etoiles*), Sci–Fi Channel, 2003.
Lucy Sondheim, "Send in the Clown," *Dead Like Me,* Showtime, 2004.
(As Tiffany Lyndall Knight) Lenore Jarvis, "Day 1,370: Part 2," *The Days,* ABC, 2004.

Legal aid number one, "O Brother, Where Art Thou," *Killer Instinct,* Fox, 2005.

Sirenelle, "Guardian of the Golden Gate," *Zixx: Level Two,* YTV, 2005.

Doctor, "Faith," *Supernatural,* The WB, 2006.

Caroyla, *Beautiful People,* ABC Family, 2006.

Female lab tech, "Descent," *Blade: The Series,* Spike TV, 2006.

Jessica Ellis, "Angels & Demons," *Blade: The Series,* Spike TV, 2006.

Verden mother, "Pride," *Flash Gordon,* Sci–Fi Channel, 2007.

Stage Appearances:

Appeared as Maria, *Twelfth Night,* Bard on the Beach, Vancouver, British Columbia, Canada; Regan, *King Lear,* Bard on the Beach.

WRITINGS

Stage Plays:

Cowrote *Turning the Tempest,* Curtain Call Company.

M

MACCARONE, Sam 1975–

PERSONAL

Born March 14, 1975, in San Jose, CA.

Addresses: *Lawyer*—Morris, Yorn, Barnes, and Levine, 2000 Avenue of the Stars, 3rd Floor, N. Tower, Los Angeles, CA 90067.

Career: Actor, director, editor, producer, writer.

CREDITS

Film Appearances:
Baggy skater, *Clueless,* Paramount, 1995.
Stu, *High School High,* TriStar, 1996.
Eddie Spender, *Kung Fu Corleon & the Video Bandits* (video), 1999.
Kip, *Gung Fu: The New Dragon,* 2000.
Mr. Freaky, *Tales from the Crapper* (video), Troma Team Video, 2004.
Tucker, *Pledge This!* (also known as *National Lampoon's "Pledge This!"*), 2006.
TV: The Movie (also known as *National Lampoon's "TV: The Movie"*), Xenon, 2006.
Billy Bob the bartender, *Electric Apricot* (also known as *National Lampoon Presents "Electric Apricot: Quest for Festeroo"*), National Lampoon, 2006.
Scott, *Gangsta Rap: The Glockumentary,* THINKFilm, 2007.
Stevens, *Waylaid,* Unified, 2007.
Phillip Fellini, *The Life of Lucky Cucumber,* 2008.
Tony, *Tom Cool,* Shoreline, 2009.

Film Executive Producer:
Kung Fu Corleon & the Video Bandits (video), 1999.

Film Director:
Kung Fu Corleon & the Video Bandits (video), 1999.
TV: The Movie (also known as *National Lampoon's "TV: The Movie"*), Xenon, 2006.
The Life of Lucky Cucumber, 2008.

Film Editor:
TV: The Movie (also known as *National Lampoon's "TV: The Movie"*), Xenon, 2006.
Ziggy Marley: Love Is My Religion Live (video), Tuff Gong, 2008.
The Life of Lucky Cucumber, 2008.

Television Appearances; Series:
Brad T, *Saved by the Bell: The New Class,* NBC, 1993.
Mall Jerk, *Hang Time,* NBC, 1995.
Captain Jackson, *Captain Jackson,* 1999.
Writer, *I Really Wanna Direct,* E! Entertainment Television, 2007.
The Preston Lacy Show, MTV, 2008.

Television Appearances; Specials:
MC Amish, *The Hot Show,* 2002.
Celebrities Uncensored, E! Entertainment Television, 2003.
The Teen Choice Awards 2006, Fox, 2006.
Jason Smith in Geiko insurance spoof, *The 2006 Billboard Music Awards,* Fox, 2006.
Customer, *Arby's Action Sports Awards,* 2006.

Television Appearances; Episodic:
"Prey Nightclub," *Home James,* VH1, 2005.
Reality Mix, 2006.
Extra (also known as *Extra: The Entertainment Magazine*), syndicated, 2006.
KTLA Morning News (also known as *KTLA Morning Show*), KTLA, 2006.
"Best of 01/08–01/11, 2007," *Howard Stern on Demand* (also known as *Howard TV on Demand*), 2007.

"Steve–O," *Howard Stern on Demand* (also known as *Howard TV on Demand*), 2007.

Television Producer; Series:
Captain Jackson, 1999.

Television Producer; Specials:
Disco Masters, MTV, 1999.

Television Director; Series:
Captain Jackson, 1999.
The Preston Lacy Show, MTV, 2008.

Television Director; Specials:
Disco Masters, MTV, 1999.

Television Editor; Series:
Captain Jackson, 1999.

WRITINGS

Screenplays:
TV: The Movie (also known as *National Lampoon's TV: The Movie*), Xenon, 2006.
The Life of Lucky Cucumber, 2008.

Television Series:
Captain Jackson, 1999.
The Preston Lacy Show, MTV, 2008.

Television Specials:
Disco Masters, MTV, 1999.
The 2006 Billboard Music Awards, Fox, 2006.
Arby's Action Sports Awards, 2006.
Nickelodeon Kids Choice Awards '08, Nickelodeon, 2008.

MacDONALD, James
(James G. MacDonald, James G. Macdonald, James McDonald)

PERSONAL

Born in Oconomowoc, WI.

Career: Actor. Appeared as Agent C, *Gemini Division* (an internet series), NBC.com.

CREDITS

Film Appearances:
(As James G. Macdonald) Hardy's friend, *Some Kind of Wonderful,* Paramount, 1987.

(As James G. MacDonald) Luke, "The Black Cat," *Due occhi diabolici* (also known as *Two Evil Eyes*), Taurus Entertainment Company, 1990.
Funeral director, *Riff–Raff,* Fine Line, 1991.
Lieutenant, *Malcolm X* (also known as *X*), Warner Bros., 1992.
(As James G. MacDonald) Park ranger baker, *Broken Arrow,* Twentieth Century–Fox, 1996.
(As James G. MacDonald) Sick Sean's dad, *The Fan,* TriStar, 1996.
First Officer Ted Kary, *Turbulence,* Metro–Goldwyn–Mayer, 1997.
(As James G. MacDonald) Terry Jasper, *Volcano,* Twentieth Century–Fox, 1997.
SWAT team leader Francis, *Mercury Rising,* Universal, 1998.
Detective Frehil, *Sour Grapes,* Sony, 1998.
Capcom, *Space Cowboys,* Warner Bros., 2000.
(As James McDonald) Staff Sergeant Thomas, *Tigerland,* Twentieth Century–Fox, 2000.
Local in Nebraska bar, *Joy Ride* (also known as *Road Kill*), Twentieth Century–Fox, 2001.
Negotiator, *Phone Booth,* Twentieth Century–Fox, 2002.
SWAT team commander, *Hostage* (short; also known as *The Hire: Hostage*), BMW Films, 2002.
Danny Broome, *Hollywood Homicide,* Sony, 2003.
Ray, *Home of the Brave,* Metro–Goldwyn–Mayer, 2006.
Paul Grunning, *Fissure,* 2008.
Henrick, *Montana Amazon,* 2009.

Television Appearances; Movies:
N.Y.P.D. Mounted (also known as *N.Y. Mounted*), CBS, 1991.
Class of '61, ABC, 1993.
Charles Stanton, *One More Mountain,* ABC, 1994.
(As James G. MacDonald) Area 51 officer, *Roswell* (also known as *Incident at Roswell* and *Roswell: The U.F.O. Cover–Up*), Showtime, 1994.
Gerry, Eclectic cafe, *Eye of the Stalker* (also known as *Moment of Truth: Eye of the Stalker*), NBC, 1995.
The businessman, *The Ultimate Lie,* NBC, 1996.
Mechanic, *Blackout,* HBO, 1996.
(As James G. MacDonald) *Vanishing Point,* Fox, 1997.
Charlie Orr, *Rose Hill,* CBS, 1997.
Detective Mark Beckner, *Perfect Murder, Perfect Town: JonBenet and the City of Boulder,* CBS, 2000.

Television Appearances; Specials:
Vince Tabor, "Soldier Boys," *CBS Schoolbreak Special,* CBS, 1987.
Earl, *Seed: A Love Story,* Lifetime, 1998.

Television Appearances; Pilots:
Jim Patterson, "B Men," *CBS Summer Playhouse,* CBS, 1989.
Detective Joe Franklin, *Justice,* Fox, 2006.

Television Appearances; Episodic:
Vance, *Sweet Justice*, NBC, 1994.
(As James G. MacDonald) Gerald O'Brien, "Order on the Court," *Courthouse*, CBS, 1995.
(As James G. MacDonald) Wainwright, "Little Green Men," *Star Trek: Deep Space Nine* (also known as *DS9, Deep Space Nine,* and *Star Trek: DS9*), syndicated, 1995.
Officer Pratt, *Moloney*, CBS, 1996.
(As James G. MacDonald) Detective Stein, "Ted," *Buffy the Vampire Slayer* (also known as *BtVS, Buffy,* and *Buffy, the Vampire Slayer: The Series*), The WB, 1997.
Walt Rockwell, "Against All Enemies," *JAG* (also known as *JAG: Judge Advocate General*), CBS, 1997.
(As James G. MacDonald) Detective Stein, "Becoming: Part 2," *Buffy the Vampire Slayer* (also known as *BtVS, Buffy,* and *Buffy, the Vampire Slayer: The Series*), The WB, 1998.
"Fools Russian," *Brooklyn South*, CBS, 1998.
Rex Raskin, "Superfriends," *Fantasy Island*, ABC, 1998.
Eitner, "Heat in the Hole," *Pacific Blue*, USA Network, 1998.
(As James G. MacDonald) Detective Stein, "Consequences," *Buffy the Vampire Slayer* (also known as *BtVS, Buffy,* and *Buffy, the Vampire Slayer: The Series*), The WB, 1999.
(As James G. MacDonald) Will Richmond, "Wagon Train: Parts 1 & 2," *The Magnificent Seven*, CBS, 1999.
Garth, "Escape from New York," *Sex and the City*, HBO, 2000.
Lenny, *Nash Bridges*, CBS, 2000.
Bartender, "The Dry Spell," *Three Sisters*, NBC, 2001.
Gary McGregor, "The Birthday Present," *Touched by an Angel*, CBS, 2001.
Officer number one, "3:00 a.m.–4 a.m.," *24*, Fox, 2001.
Mike Bigelow, "Baby Love," *NYPD Blue*, ABC, 2001.
Staff Sergeant Wakefield, "Guilt," *JAG* (also known as *JAG: Judge Advocate General*), CBS, 2001.
Caleb Pierce, *Family Law*, CBS, 2001.
John Ruark, "Blood Lust," *CSI: Crime Scene Investigation* (also known as *C.S.I., CSI: Las Vegas,* and *Les Experts*), CBS, 2002.
Bob Jenkins, "Cold Comfort," *The Division* (also known as *Heart of the City*), Lifetime, 2003.
Caleb McGinty, "29 Seconds," *Peacemakers*, USA Network, 2003.
"Street Boss," *The Handler*, CBS, 2003.
Captain Faul, "Hung Out to Dry," *Navy NCIS: Naval Criminal Investigative Service* (also known as *NCIS* and *NCIS: Naval Criminal Investigative Service*), CBS, 2003.
Detective Leclaire, "Grief," *Touching Evil*, USA Network, 2004.
Staff Sergeant Timothy Mallory, "This Just In from Baghdad," *JAG* (also known as *JAG: Judge Advocate General*), CBS, 2004.
Officer Gary McWayne, "Shot in the Dark," *ER*, NBC, 2004.

Richard, "Wishing," *Cold Case*, CBS, 2005.
FBI Incident Commander Hall, "Delta Does Detroit," *E-Ring*, NBC, 2005.
Kevin, "Odds or Evens," *Without a Trace* (also known as *W.A.T.*), CBS, 2006.
(As James MacDonald) Willis Meeks, "Morale, Welfare, and Recreation," *The Unit*, CBS, 2006.
Agent Bennett, "The Elephant in the Room," *Commander in Chief*, ABC, 2006.
Man chasing Sara, "The Velocity of Sara," *Vanished*, Fox, 2006.
Man chasing Sara, "Warm Springs," *Vanished*, Fox, 2006.
Detective Dennison, "Profiler, Profiled," *Criminal Minds*, CBS, 2006.
(As James MacDonald) Gunnery Sergeant Hill, "Semper Fidelis," *Jericho*, CBS, 2007.
Lionel Struthers, "No Strings," *Standoff*, Fox, 2007.
Second cop, "Go," *Weeds*, Showtime, 2007.
Peter O'Dell, "Don of the Dead," *In Plain Sight*, USA Network, 2008.
Dan Becks, "Cheating Death," *CSI: Miami*, CBS, 2008.

Stage Appearances:
Chris Boxer, Mark, Ray, Television attendant, and waiter, *The Heidi Chronicles*, Plymouth Theatre, New York City, c. 1989–90.
Skyler, "A Man At His Best," *Young Playwrights Festival (1991)*, Playwrights Horizons Theatre, New York City, 1991.

Stage Director:
A Number, New York Theatre Workshop, New York City, 2004.

MACHT, Gabriel 1972–
(Gabriel Swann)

PERSONAL

Full name, Gabriel S. Macht; born January 22, 1972, in the Bronx, New York, NY; son of Stephen (an actor, director, and instructor) and Suzanne Victoria Pulier (an archivist and museum curator) Macht; married Jacinda Barrett (an actress), December 29, 2004; children: Satine Anais Geraldine. *Education:* Carnegie Mellon University, B.F.A., drama. *Avocational Interests:* Watching films, spending time with family members, billiards, whitewater rafting, snowboarding, traveling, rooting for the New York Yankees.

Addresses: *Agent*—International Creative Management, 10250 Constellation Way, Ninth Floor, Los Angeles, CA 90067 and 825 Eighth Ave., New York, NY 10019;

United Talent Agency, 9560 Wilshire Blvd., Fifth Floor, Beverly Hills, CA 90212. *Manager*—Management 360, 9111 Wilshire Blvd., Beverly Hills, CA 90210; 3 Arts Entertainment, 9460 Wilshire Blvd., Seventh Floor, Beverly Hills, CA 90212. *Publicist*—PMK/HBH Public Relations, 700 San Vicente Blvd., Suite G910, West Hollywood, CA 90069 (some sources cite 8500 Wilshire Blvd., Suite 700, Beverly Hills, CA 90211).

Career: Actor. Mad Dog Theatre Company, New York City, member. Appeared at conventions.

Awards, Honors: Young Artist Award nomination, best young motion picture actor, Young Artist Foundation, 1982, for *Why Would I Lie?*

CREDITS

Film Appearances:
(As Gabriel Swann) Jorge, *Why Would I Lie?*, Metro–Goldwyn–Mayer, 1980.
Steve Castillo, *The Object of My Affection*, Twentieth Century–Fox, 1998.
Troy, *The Adventures of Sebastian Cole*, Paramount Classics, 1998.
Charlie, *Simply Irresistible* (also known as *The Magic Hour, Vanilla Fog,* and *Einfach unwiderstehlich*), Twentieth Century–Fox, 1999.
Mickey, *The Bookie's Lament* (also known as *Not for Nothin'*), 1999.
Dirk, *101 Ways (The Things a Girl Will Do to Keep Her Volvo)*, The Asylum, 2000.
Frank James, *American Outlaws*, Warner Bros., 2001.
Stackhouse, *Behind Enemy Lines*, Twentieth Century–Fox, 2001.
Officer Seale, *Bad Company* (also known as *Black Sheep, Czech Mate, The Double,* and *9 Days*), Buena Vista, 2002.
Gram Parsons, *Grand Theft Parsons*, Swipe Films, 2003.
Zack, *The Recruit*, Buena Vista, 2003.
Lawson Pines, *A Love Song for Bobby Long*, Lionsgate, 2004.
John Russell, Jr., *The Good Shepherd*, Universal, 2006.
Johnny, *Because I Said So*, Universal, 2007.
The Spirit/Denny Colt (title role), *The Spirit* (also known as *Will Eisner's "The Spirit"*), Lionsgate, 2008.
Bo Durant, *One Way to Valhalla*, 2009.
Buck Dolby, *Middle Men*, 2009.
United Nations operative, *Whiteout*, Warner Bros., 2009.

Film Producer:
The Bookie's Lament (also known as *Not for Nothin'*), 1999.

Television Appearances; Series:
Dr. Mark Gabriel, *The Others*, NBC, 2000.

Television Appearances; Movies:
Spooky Hallstead, *Guilty until Proven Innocent*, NBC, 1991.
Johnny Draper, *Follow the River*, ABC, 1995.
William Holden, *The Audrey Hepburn Story* (also known as *Audrey Hepburn* and *Untitled Audrey Hepburn Bio*), ABC, 2000.
R. J. O'Brian, *Archangel*, BBC, 2005.

Television Appearances; Episodic:
Tal Weaver, "Leading from the Heart," *Beverly Hills 90210*, Fox, 1991.
Naked man, "Snowbound," *Spin City* (also known as *Spin*), ABC, 1997.
Barkley, "Models and Mortals," *Sex and the City* (also known as *Sex & the City, Sex and the Big City, O sexo e a cidade, Seks i grad, Sex og singelliv, Sexo en la ciudad, Sexo en Nueva York, Sinkkuelae-maeae,* and *Szex es New York*), HBO, 1998.
Luke, "Best Laid Plans," *Wasteland* (also known as *wasteLAnd*), ABC, 1999.
Himself, *eTalk Daily* (also known as *eTalk* and *e–Talk Daily*), CTV (Canada), 2007.
Himself, *Entertainment Tonight* (also known as *Entertainment This Week, E.T., ET Weekend,* and *This Week in Entertainment*), syndicated, 2008.
Himself, *Jimmy Kimmel Live!* (also known as *The Jimmy Kimmel Project*), ABC, 2008.

Television Appearances; Pilots:
Dr. Mark Gabriel, *The Others*, NBC, 2000.

Appeared as Don Emrick in the unaired pilot for *Numb3rs* (also known as *Numbers* and *Num3ers*), CBS.

Stage Appearances:
What the Butler Saw, Arena Stage, Kreeger Theater, Washington, DC, 1994–95.
The visitor (Elvis), *Picasso at the Lapin Agile*, Promenade Theatre, New York City, 1995–96, and Theatre in the Square, San Francisco, CA, 1996.
to whom it may concern, Mad Dog Theatre Company, Williamstown Theatre Festival, Williamstown, MA, 1996, produced in an office building in Manhattan, New York City, beginning 1996, and at the BITEF (Belgrade International Theatre Festival), Belgrade, Serbia, 1997.
The soldier, *La Ronde*, Williamstown Theatre Festival, The Other Stage, Williamstown, MA, 1997.
Christian, *Cyrano de Bergerac*, Roundabout Theatre Company, Laura Pels Theatre, New York City, 1997–98.

Appeared in other productions, including *Molly's Dream* and *Twelfth Night* (also known as *Twelfth Night, or What You Will*), some sources state that both were produced at the Williamstown Theatre Festival.

MANKIEWICZ, Josh

PERSONAL

Son of Frank Mankiewicz (a politician).

Career: Correspondent.

CREDITS

Television Appearances; Series:
Correspondent, *Front Page,* Fox, 1993.
Correspondent, *Dateline NBC,* NBC, 2004–2008.

Television Appearances; Episodic:
Correspondent, "Cold Water Survivors," *Living Dangerously,* 2003.

Television Appearances; Specials:
Anchor, *Values and America: An MSNBC Town Hall Meeting,* MSNBC, 1998.
Correspondent, *Michael Jackson Unmasked,* NBC, 2003.
Correspondent, *Katrina's Fury: A Dateline Special,* NBC, 2005.
Correspondent, *Dateline NBC: Going for Gold,* NBC, 2007.

MARTELLA, Vincent 1992–

PERSONAL

Born October 15, 1992, in Rochester, NY.

Addresses: *Agent*—UTA, 9560 Wilshire Blvd., Suite 500, Beverly Hills, CA 90212. *Manager*—A Management, 500 S. Buena Vista St., Production Bldg., Suite 357, Burbank, CA 91521.

Career: Actor. Appeared in many television commercials.

Awards, Honors: Young Artist Award nomination, best performance in a television series, 2006, 2008, Teen Choice Award nomination, choice sidekick, 2006, for *Everybody Hates Chris.*

CREDITS

Television Appearances; Series:
Greg, *Everybody Hates Chris,* 2005—.

Phineas, *Phineas & Ferb,* The Disney Channel, 2007–2008.

Television Appearances; Episodic:
Scoop, "Sick Days & Spelling Bee," *Ned's Declassified School Survival Guide* (also known as *Neds ultimativer schulwahnsinn*), 2004.
Scoop, "Rumors & Photo Day," *Ned's Declassified School Survival Guide* (also known as *Neds ultimativer Schulwahnsinn*), 2004.
Scoop, "School Websites and Valentine's Day," *Ned's Declassified School Survival Guide* (also known as *Neds ultimativer Schulwahnsinn*), 2006.

Also appeared as Robin Reveta, "The Bully," *Cracking Up,* Fox.

Television Appearances; Pilots:
Stacked, Fox, 2005.

Television Appearances; Movies:
Scott, *Bait Shop,* USA Network, 2008.

Television Appearances; Specials:
The 31st Annual People's Choice Awards, CBS, 2005.
36th NAACP Image Awards, Fox, 2005.
2005 BET Comedy Awards, Black Entertainment Television, 2005.
The 7th Annual Family Television Awards, The WB, 2005.
The 32nd Annual People's Choice Awards, CBS, 2006.
The 37th NAACP Image Awards, Fox, 2006.
The Teen Choice Awards 2006, Fox, 2006.
8th Annual Family Friendly Awards, CW 2006.
38th NAACP Image Awards, Fox, 2007.
The 59th Primetime Emmy Awards, Fox, 2007.
39th NAACP Image Awards, Fox, 2008.
The 60th Primetime Emmy Awards, ABC, 2008.

Film Appearances:
Billy, *Duece Bigalow: European Gigolo,* Sony, 2005.
Scott, *Bait Shop,* Lionsgate, 2008.
Artonius, *Role Models,* Universal, 2008.

MASON, Sarah
See WRIGHT, Sarah

McCULLOUCH, Gerald 1967–
(Gerald McCullough)

PERSONAL

Born March 30, 1967, in Los Angeles, CA. *Education:* Studied musical theatre at Florida State University.

Addresses: *Agent*—Stone Manners Talent and Literary, 6500 Wilshire Blvd., Suite 550, Los Angeles, CA 90048.

Career: Actor. Sang in the country western revue at Six Flags Over Georgia amusement park; appeared in television commercials, including UPS delivery service, Tylenol pain reliever, Payless Shoes stores, Dunkin' Donuts, AOL internet service provider, and Saab autos; appeared in numerous print ad campaigns.

Awards, Honors: Special Interest Programming Award, best short film, Rhode Island International Film Festival, 2002, for *The Moment After*.

CREDITS

Film Appearances:
Reporter, *Smut*, 1999.
Medium cop, *Home the Horror Story*, 2000.
Mr. Lark, *Auggie Rose* (also known as *Beyond Suspicion*), 2000.
Tracey, *The Moment After* (short), 2002.
Rhys O'Connor, *Locked*, 2006.
Himself, *The Making of Michael Lucas' "Dangerous Liaisons,"* 2006.

Film Work:
Director, *The Moment After* (short), 2002.

Television Appearances; Series:
Dan McGrath, *Beverly Hills, 90210,* Fox, 1995.
Bobby Dawson, *CSI: Crime Scene Investigation* (also known as *CSI: Las Vegas, C.S.I.,* and *Les Experts*), CBS, 2000—.

Also appeared as guest host, *FYE!,* E! Entertainment Television.

Television Appearances; Movies:
Rod Brock, *Pirates of Silicon Valley,* TNT, 1999.

Television Appearances; Pilots:
(As Gerald McCullough) Technician number two, *Chicago Hope,* CBS, 1994.

Television Appearances; Episodic:
Tom, "Home Is Where the Heart Is," *In the Heat of the Night,* NBC, 1990.
John Gorman, " ... And a Nice Chianti," *7th Heaven* (also known as *Seventh Heaven*), The WB, 1998.
Frank, "Suddenly Sperm," *Melrose Place,* Fox, 1998.
Frank, "Unpleasantville," *Melrose Place,* Fox, 1999.

FBI agent, "Yankee White," *Navy NCIS: Naval Criminal Investigative Service* (also known as *NCIS* and *NCIS: Naval Criminal Investigative Service*), CBS, 2003.
Kevin Quinn, "Amends," *Law & Order: Criminal Intent* (also known as *Law & Order: CI*), NBC, 2007.

Also appeared as contestant, *The Price Is Right.*

Stage Appearances:
Jesus, *Jesus Christ Superstar,* European cities.

WRITINGS

Screenplays:
The Moment After (short), 2002.

MENDOZA, Natalie 1978–
(Natalie Jackson Mendoza)

PERSONAL

Born August 12, 1978, in Hong Kong; sister of Rebecca Jackson Mendoza (an actress and singer); married Eliot Kennedy, April, 2006. *Education:* Studied acting at the Bristol Old Vic Theatre, 2003.

Addresses: *Agent*—RGM Associates, 64–76 Kippax St., Level 2, Surrey Hills, New South Wales 2010 Australia.

Career: Actress. Jackson Mendoza (a pop group), former member; sang with the Melbourne Symphony Orchestra. Appeared as the face of Voodoo Dolls surf/ ski apparel clothing line.

CREDITS

Film Appearances:
Tran, *Muggers,* REP Distribution, 2000.
(As Natalie Mendoza) China Doll, *Moulin Rouge,* Twentieth Century–Fox, 2001.
(As Natalie Mendoza) Jade, *Horseplay,* 2003.
(As Natalie Mendoza) Sphinx receptionist, *Code 46,* United Artists, 2003.
(As Natalie Mendoza) Juno, *The Descent,* Lionsgate, 2005.
(As Natalie Mendoza) Mina, *The Great Raid,* Miramax, 2005.
Cecilia "Chill" Reyes, *Surviving Evil,* Fries Film Group, 2008.
Juno, *The Descent: Part 2,* 2009.

Television Appearances; Series:
Kyra, *BeastMaster,* 1999–2000.
Jackie Clunes, *Hotel Babylon,* BBC American and
   BBC1, 2006–2008.

Television Appearances; Miniseries:
Appeared in *Dancin' Daze,* ABC [Australia].

Television Appearances; Movies:
Jade, *Fearlesss,* syndicated and pay per view, 1999.
(As Natalie Mendoza) Liat, *South Pacific* (also known
   as *Rodgers & Hammerstein's "South Pacific"*), ABC,
   2001.

Television Appearances; Specials:
The Music of Andrew Lloyd Webber (also known as *The
   Music of Andrew Lloyd Webber starring Sarah
   Brightman and Anthony Warlow*), 1995.

Television Appearances; Pilots:
Ellie, *Hard Knox,* syndicated, 2001.

Television Appearances; Episodic:
(As Natalie Mendoza) Sim, *Wildside,* ABC [Australia],
   1998.
(As Natalie Mendoza) Lishala, "Jeremiah Crichton," *Far-
   scape,* Sci–Fi Channel, 1999.

Stage Appearances:
Cats, Australian production, 1993.
Miss Saigon, Sydney, Australia, 1995.
Les Miserables, Sydney, Australia, 1998.

Also appeared in *Sweet Charity,* Australian production.

MENOUNOS, Maria 1978–

PERSONAL

Born June 8, 1978, in Medford, MA. *Education:* Graduated from Emerson College, Boston.

Addresses: *Agent*—CAA, 2000 Avenue of the Stars, Los
Angeles, CA 90067; Special Artists Agency, 9465
Wilshire Blvd., Suite 470, Beverly Hills, CA 90212.

Career: Correspondent, actress. Miss Massachusetts
Teen USA, 1996. Appeared in television commercials
for Pantene hair care products.

Awards, Honors: Teen Choice Awards nomination,
choice personality, 2006, for *Access Hollywood.*

CREDITS

Television Appearances; Series:
Host, *Channel One News,* 1990.
Correspondent, *Today* (also known as *NBC News Today*
   and *The Today Show*), NBC, 2005—.
Access Hollywood, syndicated, 2005—.
Host, *Clash of the Choirs,* NBC, 2007.
Host, *Hollywood Green with Maria Menounos,* NBC,
   2008.

Television Appearances; Episodic:
Reporter, "Free Sabrina," *Sabrina, the Teenage Witch*
   (also known as *Sabrina* and *Sabrina Goes to Col-
   lege*), The WB, 2002.
Correspondent, *Entertainment Tonight* (also known as
   E.T., ET Weekend, Entertainment This Week and
   This Week in Entertainment), syndicated,
   2002–2005.
The Late Late Show with Craig Kilborn (also known as
   The Late Late Show), CBS, 2003.
Chris Sanders, "Trip Box," *Without a Trace* (also known
   as *W.A.T*), CBS, 2003.
Judge, *Pet Star,* Animal Planet, 2003.
Punk'd, MTV, 2003.
Jimmy Kimmel Live!, ABC, 2003.
The View, ABC, 2003.
Glinda, "We'll Take Manhattan," *One on One,* UPN,
   2004.
Jules, a recurring role, *One Tree Hill,* The WB,
   2004–2005.
Jimmy Kimmel Live!, ABC, 2004.
Howard Stern, E! Entertainment Television, 2004.
The Tony Danza Show, syndicated, 2004 and 2005.
Last Call with Carson Daly, NBC, 2004.
Jimmy Kimmel Live!, ABC, 2005.
"Aquamom," *Entourage,* 2006.
Tamara, "My Extra Mile," *Scrubs,* ABC, 2006.
"Day 1: Behind the Scenes," *Howard Stern on Demand*
   (also known as *Howard TV on Demand*), 2006.
"Debut Press Conference," *Howard Stern on Demand*
   (also known as *Howard TV on Demand*), 2006.
"Beer League Special," *Howard Stern on Demand* (also
   known as *Howard TV on Demand*), 2006.
Jimmy Kimmel Live!, ABC, 2007.
The Morning Show with Mike & Juliet, Fox, 2007.
The View, ABC, 2007.
Last Call with Carson Daly, NBC, 2007, 2008.

Television Appearances; Specials:
VH1 Goes Inside the Miss America Pageant, VH1,
   2003.
John Ritter Remembered, VH1, 2003.
Host, *Countdown to the Emmys 2003,* Fox, 2003.

Presenter, *17th Annual Soul Train Music Awards,* The WB, 2003.
Host, *Countdown to the Oscars,* ABC, 2004.
The Teen Choice Awards 2004, Fox, 2004.
The 5th Annual Latin Grammy Awards, CBS, 2004.
The 76th Annual Academy Awards, ABC, 2004.
Maxim Hot 100, VH1, 2004.
Host, *Countdown to the Emmys,* ABC, 2004.
Video Game Awards 2005, Spike TV, 2005.
Presenter, *VH1 Big in '05 Awards,* VH1, 2005.
Host, *The Eurovision Song Contest Semi Final,* 2006.
Host, *The Eurovision Song Contest,* 2006.
AFI Life Achievement Award: A Tribute to Sean Connery, 2006.
Correspondent, *The 2006 Emmy Red Carpet Special,* NBC, 2006.
Spike TV's Video Game Awards 2006, Spike TV, 2006.
Lucky Shops, CBS, 2007.
Presenter, *The 34th Annual People's Choice Awards,* 2008.
Starz Inside: Fashion in Film, Starz, 2008.
Host, *New Kids on the Block Live from Boston,* VH1, 2008.

Film Appearances:
Sexy nurse, *Fantastic Four,* Twentieth Century–Fox, 2005.
Gladys, *Fweinds.com,* 2006.
Jennifer, *Kickin It Old Skool,* Yari, 2007.
Voice of Risandra, *In the Land of Merry Misfits,* 2007.
Tropic Thunder, Paramount, 2008.

Film Executive Producer:
Longtime Listener, 2006.
Fwiends.com, 2006.
In the Land of Merry Misfits, 2007.
Operation Shock and Awe ... some, 2008.

Film Producer:
Longtime Listener, 2006.
Fwiends.com, 2006.
In the Land of Merry Misfits, 2007.
Operation Shock and Awe ... some, 2008.

Film Director:
Longtime Listener, 2006.

RECORDINGS

Video Games:
Voice of Eva Adara, *James Bond 007: From Russia with Love* (also known as *From Russia with Love, From Russia with Love 007, From Russia with Love: The Video Game* and *From Russia with Love: The Game*), 2005.

Music Videos:
Appeared in Jessica Simpson's video "A Public Affair."

OTHER SOURCES

Publications:
Fitness, October, 2008, pp. 54–58.

MIKLASWESKI, Jim 1949–

PERSONAL

Born in 1949.

Career: Correspondent.

CREDITS

Television Appearances; Series:
Correspondent, *NBC Nightly News,* NBC, 1998–2006.
Hardball with Chris Matthews, CNBC, 2006–2007.
Chief Pentagon correspondent, *Today,* NBC, 2008.

Television Appearances; Episodic:
Countdown w/ Keith Olbermann, MSNBC, 2006.
MSNBC Live (also known as *MSNBC Dayside* and *MSNBC Right Now*), MSNBC, 2006.

Television Appearances; Specials:
Inside Television, PBS, 1988.
Reporter, *Presidential Inauguration,* NBC, 1989.
Correspondent, *Decision '96: The Democratic National Convention,* PBS, 1996.
Correspondent, *Waging War,* MSNBC, 2001.

MIROJNICK, Ellen 1949–

PERSONAL

Born July 7, 1949, in New York, NY; daughter of Abe (a garment industry executive) and Sunny (maiden name, Schneider); married Barry (marriage ended, c. 1987); children: Lili. *Education:* Attended the Manhattan High School of Music and Art; attended the School of Visual Arts, New York City, 1967–68; studied fashion design at the Parsons School of Design, 1968–70. *Avocational Interests:* Painting.

Career: Costume designer and actress. Happy Legs, Inc., New York City, head designer, 1970–76.

Member: International Alliance of Theatrical and Stage Employees, Costume Designers Guild.

Awards, Honors: Cutty Sark Men's Wear Award, 1988; Film Award nomination (with John Mollo), best costume design, British Academy of Film and Television Arts, 1993, for *Chaplin;* Saturn Award, best costume design, Academy of Science Fiction, Horror, and Fantasy Films, 1997, for *Starship Troopers;* Emmy Award nomination, outstanding costume design for a variety or music program, 1997, for *Rodgers and Hammerstein's "Cinderella";* Costume Designers Guild Award nomination, excellence in costume design for film—contemporary, 2003, for *Unfaithful.*

CREDITS

Film Costume Designer:
French Quarter, Crown, 1978.
The Flamingo Kid, Twentieth Century–Fox, 1984.
Reckless, Metro–Goldwyn–Mayer/United Artists, 1984.
Remo Williams: The Adventure Begins (also known as *Remo: Unarmed and Dangerous, Remo Williams: The Adventures Begins* and *Remo: The First Adventure*), Orion, 1985.
Nobody's Fool, Island, 1986.
Fatal Attraction (also known as *Diversion*), Paramount, 1987.
Wall Street, Twentieth Century–Fox, 1987.
Talk Radio, Universal, 1988.
Cocktail, Buena Vista, 1988.
Always, Universal, 1989.
Black Rain, Paramount, 1989.
Jacob's Ladder (also known as *Dante's Inferno*), TriStar, 1990.
Narrow Margin, TriStar, 1990.
Mobsters (also known as *The Evil Empire*), Universal, 1991.
Switch (also known as *Blake Edwards' "Switch"*), Warner Bros., 1991.
Basic Instinct (also known as *Ice Cold Desire*), TriStar, 1992.
(With John Molla) *Chaplin* (also known as *Charlot*), TriStar, 1992.
Cliffhanger (also known as *Cliffhanger–l'ultima sfida* and *Cliffhanger, traque au sommet*), TriStar, 1993.
Speed, Twentieth Century–Fox, 1994.
Intersection, Paramount, 1994.
Exit to Eden, Savoy Pictures, 1994.
Strange Days, Twentieth Century–Fox, 1995.
Showgirls, Metro–Goldwyn–Mayer, 1995.
Twister, Warner Bros./Universal, 1996.
Mulholland Falls, Metro–Goldwyn–Mayer, 1996.
The Ghost and the Darkness, Paramount, 1996.

Starship Troopers, Sony Pictures Entertainment, 1997.
Face/Off (also known as *Face Off*), Paramount, 1997.
A Perfect Murder (also known as *Dial M for Murder*), Warner Bros., 1998.
Mickey Blue Eyes, Warner Bros., 1998.
The Haunting (also known as *La maldicion*), Dream-Works Distribution LLC, 1999.
Hollow Man (also known as *Hollow Man—Unsichtbare Gefahr*), Sony Pictures Entertainment, 2000.
What Women Want, Paramount, 2000.
One Night at McCool, USA Films, 2001.
America's Sweethearts, Sony Pictures Entertainment, 2001.
Rat Race (also known as *Course folle*), Paramount, 2001.
Don't Say a Word, Twentieth Century–Fox, 2001.
Unfaithful (also known as *Infidele* and *Untreu*), Twentieth Century–Fox, 2002.
It Runs in the Family (also known as *Family Business*), 2003.
Twisted (also known as *Twisted—Der erste verdacht*), Paramount, 2004.
The Chronicle of Riddick (also known as *The Chronicles of Riddick: The Director's Cut*), Universal, 2004.
Failure to Launch, Paramount, 2006.
The Sentinel, Twentieth Century–Fox, 2006.
Deja Vu, Buena Vista, 2006.
King of California, First Look Pictures, 2007.
Cloverfield (also known as *1–18–08* and *Monstrous*), Paramount, 2008.
Mirrors (also known as *Oglinzi malefice*), Twentieth Century–Fox, 2008.
G–Force, Buena Vista, 2009.
G.I. Joe: Rise of the Cobra, Paramount, 2009.

Film Assistant Costume Designer:
Fame, Metro–Goldwyn–Mayer/United Artists, 1980.
Endless Love, Universal, 1981.

Film Costume Consultant:
Agent Cody Banks (also known as *L'Agent Cody Banks*), Metro–Goldwyn–Mayer, 2003.

Film Appearances:
Physics teacher, *Reckless,* Metro–Goldwyn–Mayer/United Artists, 1984.
Herself, *"Black Rain": The Script, the Cast,* 2006.
Herself, *"Black Rain": Making the Film—Part 1,* 2006.

Television Work; Movies:
Costume designer, *Rivkin: Bounty Hunter,* CBS, 1981.
Wardrobe, *Brass,* CBS, 1985.
Costume designer, *Rodgers and Hammerstein's "Cinderella"* (also known as *Cinderella*), ABC, 1997.

Television Costume Designer; Episodic:
"Metamorphosis," Fame, 1982.

Television Appearances; Specials:
Hollywood Fashion Machine Special: The Costume Designer, 2000.

Television Appearances; Episodic:
"Costume Design," *The Hollywood Fashion Machine,* AMC, 1999.
Movies That Shook the World, AMC, 2005.

OTHER SOURCES

Periodicals:
American Film, June, 1989, p. 46.
Theatre Crafts, January, 1984, p. 57.

MONAGHAN, Dominic 1976–

PERSONAL

Full name, Dominic Benard Patrick Luke Monaghan; born December 8, 1976, in Berlin, Germany; immigrated to England, 1989; son of Austin (a teacher) and Aureen (a nurse) Monaghan. *Education:* Attended Sixth Form College and Aquinas College, 1994–95. *Religion:* Roman Catholic. *Avocational Interests:* Writing, music, fashion, soccer, video games, and surfing.

Addresses: *Agent*—Special Artists Agency, 9465 Wilshire Blvd., Suite 470, Beverly Hills, CA 90212; Agency for the Performing Arts, 405 South Beverly Dr., Beverly Hills, CA 90212; United Agents, 12–26 Lexington St., London W1F 0LE United Kingdom. *Publicist*—PMK/HBH Public Relations, 700 San Vicente Blvd., Suite G910, West Hollywood, CA 90069.

Career: Actor. Worked in youth theatres in Manchester, England, 1995. Previously worked as a mail sorter at the post office, in British Home Stories, and as a saute chef at Quincey's, Didsbury, Manchester, England.

Awards, Honors: Empire Award nomination (with Billy Boyd), best debut, Screen Actors Guild Award nomination (with others), outstanding performance by the cast of a theatrical motion picture, Phoenix Film Critics Society Award (with others), best acting ensemble, 2002, all for *The Lord of the Rings: The Fellowship of the Ring;* Screen Actors Guild Award nomination (with others), outstanding performance by the cast of a theatrical motion picture, Phoenix Film Critics Society Award (with others), best acting ensemble, Online Film Critics Society Award (with others), best ensemble, DVDX Award nomination (with others), best audio

commentary (new for DVD), 2003, all for *The Lord of the Rings: The Two Towers;* National Board of Review Award (with others), best acting in an ensemble, 2003, Screen Actors Guild Award (with others), outstanding performance by a cast in a motion picture, Phoenix Film Critics Society Award nomination (with others), best acting ensemble, Critics Choice Award (with others), Broadcast Film Critics Association, best acting ensemble, 2004, all for *The Lord of the Rings: The Return of the King;* Saturn Award nomination, best supporting actor on television, Academy of Science Fiction, Fantasy and Horror Films, Prism Award nomination, performance in a drama series storyline, 2005, Screen Actors Guild Award (with others), outstanding performance by an ensemble in a drama series, 2006, all for *Lost.*

CREDITS

Film Appearances:
Etienne, *Monsignor Renard,* 1999.
Meriadoc "Merry" Brandybuck, *The Lord of the Rings: The Fellowship of the Ring* (also known as *The Fellowship of the Ring* and *The Lord of the Rings: The Fellowship of the Ring: The Motion Picture*), New Line Cinema, 2001.
Meriadoc "Merry" Brandybuck, *The Lord of the Rings: The Two Towers* (also known as *The Two Towers*), New Line Cinema, 2002.
Himself and Meriadoc "Merry" Brandybuck, *The Making of "The Lord of the Rings,"* (documentary), 2002.
Himself, *A Day in the Life of a Hobbit* (documentary short), New Line Home Video, 2002.
Jack, *An Insomniacs Nightmare* (short), Jagged Edge Films, 2003.
Himself, *J.R.R. Tolkien: Origins of Middle–Earth* (documentary short), New Line Home Video, 2003.
Meriadoc "Merry" Brandybuck, *The Lord of the Rings: The Return of the King* (also known as *The Return of the King*), New Line Cinema, 2003.
Goat, *Spivs,* Image Entertainment, 2004.
Sol, *The Purifiers,* New Line Home Video, 2004.
Owen Scott, *Shooting Livien,* TLA Releasing, 2005.
Narrator and himself, *Ringers: Lord of the Fans* (documentary), Sony Pictures Home Entertainment, 2005.
Himself, *Du kommst nicht vorbei–fans im bann des ringes* (short), Traumflieger, 2005.
Himself, *The Ring Comes Full Circle* (documentary short), Sony Pictures Home Entertainment, 2005.
Himself, *Before They Were Lost: Personal Stories and Audition Tapes* (documentary short), Buena Vista Home Entertainment, 2005.
Himself, *Welcome to Oahu: The Making of the Pilot* (documentary short), Buena Vista Home Entertainment, 2005.

Himself, *Rock & Ringers* (documentary short), Sony Pictures Home Entertainment, 2005.

Himself and Charlie Pace, *Fire + Water: Anatomy of an Episode* (documentary short), Buena Vista Home Entertainment, 2006.

Arthur Blake, *I Sell the Dead,* 2008.

Barnell Bohusk and Beak, *X–Men Origins: Wolverine,* Twentieth Century–Fox, 2009.

Seth, *Pet,* Metro–Goldwyn–Mayer, 2009.

Television Appearances; Series:

Geoffrey Shawcross, *Hetty Wainthropp Investigates,* BBC1, 1996–98, then PBS, 1997, 1999, 2000.

Charlie Pace, *Lost,* ABC, 2004—.

Television Appearances; Miniseries:

Jimmy Furey, *This Is Personal: The Hunt for the Yorkshire Ripper,* 2000.

Television Appearances; Movies:

Sasha, *Hostile Waters* (also known as *Im Fahrwasser des todes* and *Peril en mer*), HBO, 1997.

Television Appearances; Specials:

Etienne Pierre Rollinger, *Monsignor Renard,* PBS, 2000.

Himself and Meriadoc "Merry" Brandybuck, *Quest for the Ring,* Fox, 2001.

Himself and Meriadoc "Merry" Brandybuck, *National Geographic: Beyond the Movie—"The Lord of the Rings,"* 2001.

Passage to Middle–Earth: The Making of "The Lord of the Rings," Sci–Fi Channel, 2001.

The Lord of the Rings: The Two Towers, Return to Middle Earth, The WB, 2002.

Making the Movie (also known as *Making the Movie: "The Lord of the Rings"*), MTV, 2002.

G–Phoria, G4, 2003.

"The Lord of the Rings": The Quest Fulfilled, 2003.

The 2004 MTV Movie Awards, MTV, 2004.

I Love the '90s, VH1, 2004.

VH1 Big in '04, VH1, 2004.

Journey to Middle Earth: The Lord of the Rings: The Return of the King, Arts and Entertainment, 2004.

I Love the '90s: Part Deux, VH1, 2005.

The 57th Annual Primetime Emmy Awards, CBS, 2005.

The 32nd Annual People's Choice Awards, CBS, 2006.

Presenter, *VH1 Big in '06 Awards,* VH1, 2006.

(Uncredited) *The 64th Annual Golden Globe Awards,* NBC, 2007.

"Steven and Liv Tyler": The E! True Hollywood Story, E! Entertainment Television, 2007.

AFI's 10 Top 10 (also known as *AFI's 100 Years … AFI's 10 Top 10*), CBS, 2008.

Television Appearances; Pilots:

Host, *CQC,* 2008.

Television Appearances; Episodic:

SM:TV Live, ITV1, 2001.

Richard and Judy, Channel 4, 2001.

"Troldspejlet special: Ringenes herre–Eventyret om ringen," *Troldspejlet,* 2001.

Total Request Live (also known as *TRL, TRL Weekend,* and *Total Request with Carson Daly*), MTV, 2001, 2003.

"Voodoo That You Do … with Hobbits!," *Player$,* Tech TV, 2003.

"Grind," *Player$,* Tech TV, 2003.

Punk'd, MTV, 2003.

The Sharon Osbourne Show (also known as *Sharon*), syndicated, 2003.

"Filmland Special–Ringenes Herre: Kongen vender tilbage," *Filmland,* 2003.

"Kuninkaan paluu—tarun paatos," *4Pop,* 2003.

Tinseltown TV, International Channel, 2003.

(Uncredited) "New Orleans, Mardi Gras Orpheus Parade," *Get Out,* 2004.

Film 2004 (also known as *The Film Programme*), BBC, 2004.

Jimmy Kimmel Live!, ABC, 2004, 2005, 2006, 2007, 2008.

On–Air with Ryan Seacrest, syndicated, 2004.

Good Day Live, syndicated, 2004.

Entertainment Tonight (also known as *E.T.*), syndicated, 2005.

Ellen: The Ellen DeGeneres Show, syndicated, 2005, 2006, 2007.

The Late Late Show with Craig Ferguson, CBS, 2005, 2006.

The Tonight Show with Jay Leno, NBC, 2005, 2006, 2007, 2008.

Mad TV, Fox, 2005, 2008.

Corazon de …, 2006.

Friday Night with Jonathan Ross, BBC, 2006.

Live with Regis and Kelly, syndicated, 2006.

Rachael Ray, syndicated, 2006.

Late Night with Conan O'Brien, NBC, 2006, 2007.

The View, ABC, 2007.

Tyler Martin, *Chuck,* NBC, 2008.

Stage Appearances:

Appeared as Harry, *The Resurrectionists,* Bolton Octagon/Croyden Warehouse; Chuck, *Annie and Fanny from Bolton to Rome,* Bolton Octagon; in *Whale,* UK production.

Radio Appearances:

Narrator, *Stockton,* BBC Radio 4, 1999.

RECORDINGS

Video Games:

Voice of Meriadoc Brandybuck, *Lord of the Rings: Battle for Middle Earth II—Rise of the Witch King,* Electronic Arts, 2006.

MONIQUE, Ashley
    See CLARK, Ashley Monique

MONK, Debra 1949–
    (Deborah Monk)

PERSONAL

Born February 27, 1949, in Middletown, OH; married John Miller (a music coordinator; divorced). *Education:* Graduate of Frostburg State College and Southern Methodist University. *Religion:* Southern Baptist.

Addresses: *Agent*—Gage Group, 14724 Ventura Blvd., Suite 505, Sherman Oaks, CA 91403. *Manager*—Principal Entertainment, 1964 Westwood Blvd., Suite 400, Los Angeles, CA 90025.

Career: Actress, director, and writer. Colonnades Theatre Laboratory, member of company, 1978–79; Arena Stage, Washington, DC, member of company, 1979–80; Actors Theatre of Louisville, Louisville, KY, guest artist, 1983–86; appeared with Seattle Repertory Company and Bay Street Theatre. Previously worked as a waitress, secretary, and rockabilly singer.

Awards, Honors: Drama Desk Award (with others), best ensemble, 1988, for *Oil City Symphony;* Antoinette Perry Award, best featured actress in a play, 1993, for *Redwood Curtain;* Helen Hayes Award, leading actress, 1994, for *Three Hotels;* Antoinette Perry Award nomination, best supporting or featured dramatic actress, 1994, for *Picnic;* Antoinette Perry Award nomination, best featured actress in a musical, 1997, for *Steel Pier;* Emmy Award, outstanding guest actress in a drama series, 1999, for "Hearts and Souls," *NYPD Blue;* Obie Award, *Village Voice,* 2000, for *The Time of the Cuckoo;* Antoinette Perry Award nomination, best leading actress in a musical, Drama Desk Award, outstanding featured actress in a musical, 2007, both for *Curtains;* four Drama Desk Award nominations, c. 1981–82.

CREDITS

Stage Appearances:
Moliere in Spite of Himself, Hartman Theatre Company, Stamford, CT, 1981.
Prudie Cupp, *Pump Boys and Dinettes,* Westside Arts Theatre, New York City, then Colonnades Theatre, later Princess Theatre, New York City, 1981–82.

'84 Shorts, Actors Theatre of Louisville, Louisville, KY, 1984–85.
Astronauts, Actors Theatre of Louisville, 1985–86.
Oil City Symphony, Circle in the Square, New York City, 1987–88.
Mother, *And the Air Didn't Answer,* Young Playwrights Festival, Playwrights Horizons Theatre, New York City, 1988.
The Beach, Yale Repertory Theatre, New Haven, CT, 1988–89.
Mrs. Boyle, *Prelude to a Kiss,* Helen Hayes Theatre, New York City, 1990.
Sara Jane Moore, *Assassins,* Playwrights Horizons Theatre, 1990–91.
Lily Connors, *Nick and Nora,* Marquis Theatre, New York City, 1991.
Jan Kirkland, *Man in His Underwear,* Playwrights Horizons Theatre, 1992.
Mame, *The Innocent's Crusade,* Manhattan Theatre Club, New York City, 1992.
Geneva Simonson, *Redwood Curtain,* Old Globe Theatre, San Diego, CA, 1992–93, then Brooks Atkinson Theatre, New York City, 1993.
Barbara Hoyle, *Three Hotels,* Circle Repertory Company, New York City, 1993.
A Cheever Evening, Playwrights Horizons Theatre, 1993.
Rosemary Sydney, *Picnic,* Center Stage Right, Criterion Theatre, New York City, 1994.
Easter Bonnet Competition: Back to Basics, Palace Theatre, New York City, 1995.
Phyllis, "Central Park West," *Death Defying Acts,* Variety Arts Theatre, New York City, 1995–96.
Joanne, *Company,* Center Stage Right, Criterion Theatre, 1995.
Shelby Stevens, *Steel Pier,* Richard Rodgers Theatre, New York City, 1997.
Essie Miller, *Ah, Wilderness!,* Vivian Beaumont Theatre, New York City, 1997.
Leona Samish, *The Time of the Cuckoo,* Mitzi E. Newhouse Theatre, New York City, 2000.
Madame Raquin, *Thou Shalt Not,* Plymouth Theatre, New York City, 2001.
Polina Andreyevna, *The Seagull,* Delacorte Theatre, New York City, 2001.
Doctor, *Reckless,* Biltmore Theatre, New York City, 2004.
Matron Mama Morton, *Chicago,* Ambassador Theatre, New York City, 2006.
Marnie, *Show People,* Second Stage Theatre, New York City, 2006.
Carmen Bernstein, *Curtains,* Al Hirschfield Theatre, New York City, 2007.

Also appeared in *A Narrow Bed,* off–Broadway production.

Stage Director:
Pump Boys and Dinettes, Pennsylvania State Company, Allentown, PA, 1985–86.

Film Appearances:
Aunt Dorothy, *Prelude to a Kiss,* Twentieth Century–Fox, 1992.

Mrs. Wegman, *For Love or Money* (also known as *The Concierge*), Universal, 1993.

Alison, *Fearless* (also known as *Joyride*), Warner Bros., 1993.

Kintner's secretary, *Quiz Show,* Buena Vista, 1994.

Skeptical therapist, *Reckless,* Samuel Goldwyn, 1995.

Madge, *The Bridges of Madison County,* Warner Bros., 1995.

Mom, *Jeffrey,* Orion, 1995.

Lewis's mom, *Bed of Roses* (also known as *Amelia and the King of Plants*), New Line Cinema, 1996.

Martha Hackett, *The Substance of Fire,* Miramax, 1996.

Lieutenant Ambrose, *Mrs. Winterbourne,* TriStar, 1996.

Jilted lover, *The First Wives Club,* Paramount, 1996.

Dr. Judith Gruszynski, *Extreme Measures,* Columbia, 1996.

Pam Garrety, *The Devil's Advocate* (also known as *Devil's Advocate* and *Im Auftrag des teufels*), Warner Bros., 1997.

Mrs. Lester, *In and Out,* Paramount, 1997.

Helen, *Bulworth,* Twentieth Century–Fox, 1998.

Nancy Cummings, *Center Stage* (also known as *Centre Stage*), Sony Pictures Entertainment, 2000.

Edna Burroughs, *Milwaukee, Minnesota,* Tartan Films (US), 2001.

Officer Avon, *Briar Patch* (also known as *Plain Dirty*), 2002.

Mama Sunshine, *Palindromes,* Wellspring Home Entertainment, 2004.

Young Dahlia's teacher, *Dark Water,* Buena Vista, 2005.

Lick Me–Bite Me, *The Producers,* Universal, 2005.

Nancy Lachman, *The Savages,* Fox Searchlight, 2007.

Film Work:
Executive producer, *Landlocked,* 2007.

Television Appearances; Series:
Sandra Thorpe, *Loving,* ABC, 1994.

Katie Sipowicz, *NYPD Blue,* ABC, 1996–2001.

Various, *A Nero Wolfe Mystery* (also known as *Nero Wolfe*), Arts and Entertainment, 2001–2002.

Louise O'Malley, *Grey's Anatomy,* ABC, 2006–2008.

Television Appearances; Movies:
Geneva Simonson, "Redwood Curtain," *Hallmark Hall of Fame,* ABC, 1995.

Nadine, *Ellen Foster,* CBS, 1997.

Mrs. Paroo, *The Music Man,* ABC, 2003.

Maggie, *Eloise at the Plaza,* ABC, 2003.

Maggie, *Eloise at Christmastime,* ABC, 2003.

Television Appearances; Specials:
Psychiatrist, "Women and Wallace," *American Playhouse,* PBS, 1990.

"Public Law 106: The Becky Bell Story," *Lifestories: Families in Crisis,* HBO, 1992.

The 47th Annual Tony Awards, CBS, 1993.

"A Tribute to Stephen Sondheim," *A&E Stage,* Arts and Entertainment, 1995.

The 51st Annual Tony Awards, CBS, 1997.

The 51st Annual Primetime Emmy Awards, Fox, 1999.

The 61st Annual Tony Awards, CBS, 2007.

Television Appearances; Pilots:
Prudie Cupp, *Pumpboys and Dinettes on Television,* NBC, 1983.

Television Appearances; Episodic:
Kathleen "Kate" O'Brien, "Coma," *Law & Order,* NBC, 1994.

Katie Sipowicz, "A Death in the Family," *NYPD Blue,* ABC, 1996.

Madison Harcourt, *Dellaventura,* CBS, 1997.

The Rosie O'Donnell Show, syndicated, 1997, 2000.

"Breaking In, Breaking Out, Breaking Up, Breaking Down," *Trinity,* NBC, 1999.

"My Favorite Broadway: The Leading Ladies," *Great Performances,* PBS, 1999.

Jeannie Yancey, "The Mother," *Kristin,* NBC, 2001.

Dr. Madelyn Stahl, "Born Again," *Law & Order,* NBC, 2002.

Nurse Karen, "No Sex Please, We're Skittish," *Frasier,* NBC, 2003.

Judge, "In God We Trust," *Law & Order,* NBC, 2005.

Marcella, "Children and Art," *Desperate Housewives,* ABC, 2006.

Andrew's mom, "Mother's Milk," *Notes from the Underbelly,* ABC, 2007.

Deniece Parsons, "A Regular Earl Anthony," *Damages,* FX Channel, 2007.

Deniece Parsons, "Blame the Victim," *Damages,* FX Channel, 2007.

Warden Pellis, "Untethered," *Law & Order: Criminal Intent* (also known as *Law & Order: CI*), NBC, 2007.

Also appeared in "Yankee Glory," *New York News;* as Clare Cunningham, "Requiem for a Horse," *LateLine.*

RECORDINGS

Taped Readings:
Low Country by Mark Pumphrey, HarperAudio, 1998.

WRITINGS

Plays:
(With others) *Pump Boys and Dinettes,* produced at Westside Arts Theatre, 1981, then Colonnades Theatre, later Princess Theatre, all New York City, 1982.

(With others) *Oil City Symphony,* produced at Circle in the Square, New York City, 1987–88.

Television Pilots:

Pumpboys and Dinettes on Television, NBC, 1983.

MONROE, Meredith 1968–
    (Meridith Monroe, Meredith Munroe)

PERSONAL

Full name, Meredith Leigh Monroe; born December 30, 1968 (some sources say 1969), in Houston, TX; married Steven Kavovit (a massage therapist), August, 1999.

Addresses: *Agent*—Agency for the Performing Arts, 405 South Beverly Dr., Beverly Hills, CA 90212. *Manager*—Thruline Entertainment, 9250 Wilshire Blvd., Suite 100, Beverly Hills, CA 90212.

Career: Actress and producer. Appeared in television commercials, including the Illinois Lottery, Tide detergents, Walt Disney World, Tylenol sinus medications, Dove personal care products, Route 66 Clothing, L'Oreal personal care products, Ford Explorer sport utility vehicle, Mentos breath mints, and 7–Up beverages; appeared on five book covers in the Nancy Drew/Hardy Boys series; appeared on packaging for such products as the Conair hair crimper.

Member: Alpha Chi Omega.

Awards, Honors: Teen Choice Award nomination, Television—breakout performance, 1999, for *Dawson's Creek.*

CREDITS

Film Appearances:

(Uncredited) Finale trumpet player, *Il silenzio dei prosciutti* (also known as *The Silence of the Hams*), October Films, 1994.
Weather girl, *Strong Island Boys,* 1997.
Trudy Kockenlocker, *Norville and Trudy,* 1997.
Karissa, *Fallen Arches,* A Plus Entertainment, 1998.
Amy, *Full Ride,* PorchLight Entertainment, 2001.
Judy Woods, *The Year That Trembled,* Novel City Pictures, 2002.
Hadley Weston, *New Best Friend,* TriStar, 2002.
"The Girl" Jesse, *G–S.P.O.T.* (also known as *The Girl, the Swank, the Poet, the Old Man & the Thespian*), 2002.

Pre–crime public service announcer, *Minority Report,* DreamWorks, 2002.
Amy Lear, *Full Ride,* Allumination Filmworks, 2002.
Ms. McKenna, *Shadow Man* (short), 2004.
Amanda, *Vampires: The Turning,* Sony Pictures Home Entertainment, 2005.
Suzy Beacon, *bgFATLdy,* 2008.
Phaedra, *Wake,* 2009.
Sara Crane, *Nowhere to Hide,* 2009.

Film Work:

Coproducer, *G–S.P.O.T.* (also known as *The Girl, the Swank, the Poet, the Old Man & the Thespian*), 2002.

Television Appearances; Series:

Tracy Daiken, *Dangerous Minds,* ABC, 1996–97.
Andrea "Andie" McPhee, *Dawson's Creek,* The WB, 1998–2001.
Haley Hotchner, *Criminal Minds,* CBS, 2005–2007.

Television Appearances; Movies:

Laura Elizabeth Ingalls Wilder, *Beyond the Prairie: The True Story of Laura Ingalls Wilder,* CBS, 2000.
Laura Elizabeth Ingalls Wilder, *Beyond the Prairie, Part 2: The True Story of Laura Ingalls Wilder,* CBS, 2001.
Leah Karniegian, *111 Gramercy Park,* 2003.
Gail Hollander, *The One,* ABC Family, 2003.
Clare, *Manhood,* Showtime, 2003.
Young Nora, *Fathers and Sons,* Showtime, 2005.
Alison Morgan, *Not My Life,* Lifetime, 2006.

Television Appearances; Specials:

The 1999 Teen Choice Awards, Fox, 1999.
Andie McPhee and herself, *Dawson's Creek: Behind the Scenes,* The WB, 1999.
Presenter, *The 2nd Annual TV Guide Awards,* Fox, 2000.
(As Meredith Munroe) Jenny, *2000 MTV Movie Awards,* MTV, 2000.

Television Appearances; Episodic:

Tracy Daiken, "Everybody Wants It," *Dangerous Minds,* ABC, 1997.
Jill, "Kristy's Other Mother," *Hang Time,* NBC, 1997.
Brianna, "A Girl's Gotta Pierce," *Jenny,* NBC, 1997.
Meredith Bix, "Brushed," *Promised Land* (also known as *Home of the Brave*), CBS, 1997.
Rachel, *Sunset Beach,* NBC, 1998.
"You Are Too Beautiful," *Night Man* (also known as *NightMan*), The Disney Channel and syndicated, 1998.
Claire Mosley, "Manhunt," *The Magnificent Seven,* CBS, 1998.
Sarah Nolan, "Con–undrum," *Players,* NBC, 1998.

Devon Booker, "Faustian Fitz," *Cracker* (also known as *Cracker: Mind Over Murder*), ABC, 1999.

RoveLive, Ten Network, 2000.

Andrea "Andie" McPhee, "The Graduate," *Dawson's Creek,* The WB, 2001.

Jeanette/Carol Manning, "Illusions," *The Division* (also known as *Heart of the City*), 2002.

Olivia Haynes, "Statewide Swing," *Mister Sterling,* 2003.

Michelle Turner, "Double Dutch," *Joan of Arcadia,* CBS, 2004.

Claudia Sanders, "Under the Influence," *CSI: Miami,* CBS, 2004.

Kate Ross, "Snack Daddy," *Kevin Hill,* UPN, 2004.

Lola, "Sports Medicine," *House M.D.* (also known as *House*), Fox, 2005.

Lilly, "Broken Hearts," *Strong Medicine,* Lifetime, 2005.

Cindy Mulvaney in 1965, "A Perfect Day," *Cold Case,* CBS, 2005.

Beth, "Masquerading with Fran," *Living with Fran,* The WB, 2006.

Sister Bridget, "Double Cross," *CSI: Crime Scene Investigation* (also known as *CSI: Las Vegas, C.S.I.,* and *Les Experts*), CBS, 2006.

Celia Fuller, "Family," *Masters of Horror,* Showtime, 2006.

(As Meridith Monroe) Clarissa Bancroft, "The Man in the Mansion," *Bones,* Fox, 2007.

Rebecca, "Fall from Grace," *Crossing Jordan,* NBC, 2007.

"The Fantasy," *The Wedding Bells,* Fox, 2007.

Nina Weber, "In Abstentia," *Shark,* CBS, 2007.

Cynthia, "The Mortal Cure," *Moonlight,* CBS, 2008.

Chloe Metz, "Vaginatown," *Californication,* Showtime, 2008.

Leah, "Know When to Fold," *Private Practice,* ABC, 2008.

Also appeared in *Cracker,* Arts and Entertainment.

RECORDINGS

Video Games:

Voice of Virginia "Pepper" Potts, *Iron Man,* Sega of America, 2008.

OTHER SOURCES

Periodicals:

People Weekly, May 21, 1999, p. 58.

MORALES, Natalie 1972–

PERSONAL

Full name, Natalie Leticia Morales; born June 6, 1972, in Taipei, Taiwan; daughter of Mario, Jr. (an American air force career officer) and Penelope Morales; married Joe Rhodes, August 22, 1998; children: Joseph "Josh" Steven, Luke Hudson. *Education:* Rutgers University, B.A. (summa cum laude), 1994.

Addresses: *Office*—c/o NBC News, 30 Rockefeller Plaza, New York, NY 10112. *Agent*—Rick Ramage, N. S. Bienstock, 1740 Broadway, 24th Floor, New York, NY 10019.

Career: Broadcast journalist, correspondent, and news anchor. Court TV (now truTV), marketing and public relations assistant, 1997–98; News 12—The Bronx, Bronx, NY, news reporter, producer, photographer, and editor, 1998–99; WVIT–TV, Hartford, CT, correspondent and coanchor of morning news, c. 1999–2002; NBC News, New York City, anchor and correspondent for the MSNBC channel, 2002–06, national correspondent, 2006—. WNBC–TV, New York City, reporter and cohost for the documentary campaign *Save Our Sound.* Chemical Bank, worked as member of management training program, 1994–96.

Awards, Honors: Daytime Emmy Award (with others), excellence in morning programming, 2007, for *Today.*

CREDITS

Television Appearances; Series:

Anchor, *MSNBC Live* (also known as *MSNBC Dayside* and *MSNBC Right Now*), MSNBC, 2002.

Correspondent and substitute news anchor, *Today* (also known as *NBC News Today* and *The Today Show*), NBC, 2003–2008.

Host, *Early Today,* NBC, 2004.

Cohost, *Today* (also known as *NBC News Today* and *The Today Show*), NBC, 2007—.

Television Appearances; Specials:

Host, *Quest for Atlantis: Startling New Secrets,* Sci–Fi Channel, 2006.

The Red Dress Collection 2007 Fashion Show, 2007.

Host, *Macy's 4th of July Fireworks Spectacular,* NBC, 2007, 2008.

Television Appearances; Episodic:

Correspondent, *Countdown w/Keith Olbermann,* MSNBC, 2006.

The Tonight Show with Jay Leno, NBC, 2006.

News anchor, *Weekend Today,* NBC, 2006.

Correspondent, "Going for the Gold," *Dateline NBC* (also known as *Dateline*), NBC, 2007.

Late Night with Conan O'Brien, NBC, 2007.

Substitute anchor, *NBC Nightly News,* NBC, 2008.

OTHER SOURCES

Periodicals:
Broadcasting & Cable, August 13, 2007, p. 3; November 19, 2007.
TV Guide, February 27, 2006, p. 10; December 24, 2007, p. 70.

Electronic:
MSNBC Online, http://www.msnbc.msn.com, June 8, 2006.

MORRISON, Keith 1934–

PERSONAL

Born in 1934, in Lloydminster, Saskatchewan, Canada; married Suzanne Perry; children: six.

Career: Correspondent, actor.

CREDITS

Television Appearances; Series:
CTV National News, CTV, 1961.
Canada A.M. (also known as *Canada A.M. Weekend*), CTV, 1972.
Correspondent, *Real Life with Jane Pauley,* NBC, 1990.
Mr. Balinikoff, *Good Advice,* CBS, 1992–93.
Blossom, NBC, 1992–93.
Journalist, *Dateline NBC* (also known as *Dateline*), NBC, 2006.

Television Appearances; Episodic:
Keith Morrison, a newscaster, "The Trip: Part 1 & 2," *Seinfeld,* NBC, 1992.

Television Appearances; Specials:
Correspondent, *The Renewal at Easter,* NBC, 1988.
Reporter, *Treasure at the South Pole,* NBC, 1990.
Correspondent, *Voyage of Mystery,* NBC, 1992.
African–American Artists: Affirmation Today, PBS, 1996.
Correspondent, *ER 200: A Dateline Special,* NBC, 2003.

Television Appearances; Miniseries:
America's Top Sleuths, The Sleuth Channel, 2006.

WRITINGS

Television Specials:
Real Life with Jane Pauley, NBC, 1990.

MORTON, Rob
See DEMME, Jonathan

MOSES, Mark 1958–

PERSONAL

Full name, Mark W. Moses; born February 24, 1958, in New York, NY; father, in advertising sales; brother of Burke Moses (an actor and singer); married Annie La Russa (an actress); children: Walker. *Education:* Attended Ithaca College; New York University, B.F.A., drama; studied acting with Olympia Dukakis.

Addresses: *Agent*—Innovative Artists, 1505 10th St., Santa Monica, CA 90401.

Career: Actor. Also worked as a house painter.

Member: Screen Actors Guild.

Awards, Honors: Screen Actors Guild awards (with others), outstanding performance by an ensemble in a comedy series, 2005 and 2006, both for *Desperate Housewives;* Screen Actors Guild awards (with others), outstanding performance by an ensemble in a drama series, 2009, for *Mad Men.*

CREDITS

Television Appearances; Series:
Richard Peyton, *Grand,* NBC, 1990.
Matt Parker, *The Single Guy,* NBC, 1995–96.
Paul Young, *Desperate Housewives* (also known as *Beautes desespereees, Desperate housewives—I segreti di Wisteria Lane, Desupareto na tsuma tachi, Esposas desesperadas, Frustrerte fruer, Gotowe na wszystko, Kucanice, Meeleheitel koduperenaised, Mujeres desesperadas, Noikokyres se apognosi, Szueletett felesegek,* and *Taeydelliset naiset*), ABC, 2004–2006.
Herman "Duck" Phillips, *Mad Men,* American Movie Classics, beginning 2007.

Appeared in recurring roles in the series *Guiding Light* (also known as *The Guiding Light*), CBS; and *One Life to Live* (also known as *Between Heaven and Hell* and *One Life to Live: The Summer of Seduction*), ABC.

Television Appearances; Miniseries:
General Ulysses S. Grant, *North and South* (also known as *Fackeln im Sturm, Jaettu maa, Nord et sud, Nord och syd, Nord og syd, Nord si sud, Nord y sur, Pohi ja louna,* and *Polnoc poludnie*), ABC, 1985.

Sergeant Owen, *Gettysburg* (also known as *The Killer Angels*), TNT, 1994, originally released as a feature film by New Line Cinema, 1993, director's cut also released and broadcast.

Woodbury Kane, *Rough Riders* (also known as *Teddy Roosevelt & the Rough Riders*), TNT, 1997.

Voice, *The Roman Empire in the First Century* (documentary; also known as *Empires: The Roman Empire in the First Century*), PBS, 2001.

Television Appearances; Movies:

Tom Adams, *The Tracker* (also known as *Dead or Alive*), HBO, 1988.

Alan, *Battle in the Erogenous Zone,* Showtime, 1992.

Joel McKelvey, *Perry Mason: The Case of the Fatal Framing* (also known as *Perry Mason: The Case of the Posthumous Painter*), NBC, 1992.

Michael Turner, *A Kiss Goodnight,* 1994.

Dick Clayton, *James Dean* (also known as *James Dean: An Invented Life* and *The James Dean Story*), TNT, 2001.

Saving Jessica Lynch (also known as *Saving Jessica Lynch: The Rescue of an American Soldier*), NBC, 2003.

Charlie, *Ice Twisters,* Sci–Fi Channel, 2009.

Television Appearances; Specials:

Ira Martin, "The Silence at Bethany," *American Playhouse,* PBS, 1988.

Paul Young, "Special: The Juiciest Bites" (also known as "The Juiciest Bites"), *Desperate Housewives* (also known as *Beautes desespereees, Desperate housewives—I segreti di Wisteria Lane, Desupareto na tsuma tachi, Esposas desesperadas, Frustrerte fruer, Gotowe na wszystko, Kucanice, Meeleheitel koduperenaised, Mujeres desesperadas, Noikokyres se apognosi, Szueletett felesegek,* and *Taeydelliset naiset*), ABC, 2007.

Television Appearances; Episodic:

Rich Albert, "Teacher's Pet," *Family Ties,* NBC, 1986.

David, "An Illegitimate Concern," *The Golden Girls* (also known as *Golden Girls, Miami Nice, Bnot Zahav, Cuori senza eta, Las chicas de oro, Les craquantes, Los anos dorados, Oereglanyok, Pantertanter,* and *Tyttoekullat*), NBC, 1990.

Donald Ware, "The Cookie Monster," *Matlock,* NBC, 1990.

"The Movie Mystery," *Father Dowling Mysteries* (also known as *Father Dowling Investigates*), ABC, 1990.

Brad, "George Looks down the Wrong End of a Thirty–Eight," *The George Carlin Show,* Fox, 1994.

Paul Dyer, "Love Bandit," *Silk Stalkings,* USA Network, 1994.

Robin Westlin, "The Restless Remains," *Diagnosis Murder,* CBS, 1994.

Stuart Walsh, "The Letter of the Law," *The Commish,* ABC, 1994.

Mark, *Winnetka Road,* NBC, 1994.

Ben Atkins, "It's Not Easy Being Green," *Party of Five,* Fox, 1995.

Reverend Charles Buchanan, "Becoming a Buchanan," *The Five Mrs. Buchanans* (also known as *The 5 Mrs. Buchanans*), CBS, 1995.

Reverend Charles Buchanan, "The Heart of the Matter," *The Five Mrs. Buchanans* (also known as *The 5 Mrs. Buchanans*), CBS, 1995.

Stuart Tyler, "How to Murder Your Lawyer," *Diagnosis Murder,* CBS, 1995.

Jack Hunter, "Al Anonymous," *LateLine,* NBC, 1998.

Ron Greenfield, "Wag the Doc," *Chicago Hope,* CBS, 1998.

Agent Margolis, "Rules of Engagement," *Pensacola: Wings of Gold* (also known as *Pensacola*), syndicated, 1999.

Fred Swedlowe, "Hollywood Shuffle," *It's Like, You Know ...,* ABC, 1999.

Gary Moses, "Damages," *Family Law,* CBS, 1999.

Naroq, "Riddles," *Star Trek: Voyager* (also known as *Voyager*), UPN, 1999.

Seth, "The Last Day of the Rest of Your Life," *Touched by an Angel,* CBS, 1999.

Deke Carson and Earl Ticktin, "Real Deal SEAL," *JAG* (also known as *JAG: Judge Advocate General*), CBS, 2000.

Frank (mystery book writer), "The Wailing," *Beyond Belief: Fact or Fiction* (also known as *Beyond Belief* and *Strange Truth: Fact or Fiction*), Fox, 2000.

Mark Pruitt, "Shaken, Not Stirred," *Judging Amy,* CBS, 2000.

Scott Shelton, "Sex, Lies and Larvae," *CSI: Crime Scene Investigation* (also known as *C.S.I., CSI, CSI: Las Vegas, CSI: Weekends,* and *Les experts*), CBS, 2000.

Assistant district attorney, "Hats Off to Larry," *Ally McBeal,* Fox, 2001.

Don Schneider, "Coyote," *Boomtown,* NBC, 2002.

Nathan, "Once upon a Family," *Presidio Med,* CBS, 2002.

Nathan, "Secrets," *Presidio Med,* CBS, 2002.

Opposing lawyer, "Woman," *Ally McBeal,* Fox, 2002.

"It's Raining Men," *Providence,* NBC, 2002.

Dan Harris, "Gimme Shelter," *10–8: Officers on Duty* (also known as *10–8* and *10–8: Police Patrol*), ABC, 2003.

Dr. Rosenfeld, "Life's Illusions," *American Dreams* (also known as *Bandstand, Miss American Pie,* and *Our Generation*), NBC, 2003.

Donald Richter, "Abu el Banat," *The West Wing* (also known as *West Wing* and *El ala oeste de la Casablanca*), NBC, 2003.

Henry Winslow, "Character Evidence," *The Practice,* ABC, 2003.

Mr. Marks, "When Night Meets Day," *ER* (also known as *Emergency Room*), NBC, 2003.

Mr. Smith, "Long Bad Summer: Part 1," *7th Heaven* (also known as *Seventh Heaven* and *7th Heaven: Beginnings*), The WB, 2003.

Andrew Moss, "Who's Your Daddy?," *NYPD Blue,* ABC, 2004.

Dr. Miles Marks, "Things That Go Jump in the Night," *Las Vegas* (also known as *Casino Eye*), 2004.

Richard, "The Block Party," *Malcolm in the Middle* (also known as *Fighting in Underpants*), Fox, 2004.

Richard Lowe, "Party Favors," *The District* (also known as *Washington Police, The District—Einsatz in Washington, Mannions distrikt,* and *Poliisipaeaellikkoe Mannion*), CBS, 2004.

"Catskills," *Oliver Beene,* Fox, 2004.

Contestant, "Tournament 7, Game 1," *Celebrity Poker Showdown,* Bravo, 2005.

Himself, *Good Morning America* (also known as *GMA*), ABC, 2005.

Himself, *The Oprah Winfrey Show* (also known as *Oprah*), syndicated, 2005.

Himself, *The View,* ABC, 2005, 2006.

Attorney George McDougal, "Hope and Glory," *Boston Legal* (also known as *Fleet Street, The Practice: Fleet Street,* and *The Untitled Practice*), ABC, 2007.

Rob Darcy, "Without You," *Without a Trace* (also known as *Vanished* and *W.A.T.*), CBS, 2007.

Himself, *Jimmy Kimmel Live!* (also known as *The Jimmy Kimmel Project*), ABC, 2007.

Paul Young, *Desperate Housewives* (also known as *Beautes desesperees, Desperate housewives—I segreti di Wisteria Lane, Desupareto na tsuma tachi, Esposas desesperadas, Frustrerte fruer, Gotowe na wszystko, Kucanice, Meeleheitel koduperenaised, Mujeres desesperadas, Noikokyres se apognosi, Szueletett felesegek,* and *Taeydelliset naiset*), ABC, multiple episodes, beginning 2007.

Attorney George McDougal, "Roe," *Boston Legal* (also known as *Fleet Street, The Practice: Fleet Street,* and *The Untitled Practice*), ABC, 2008.

James Grall, "Inconceivable," *Law & Order: Special Victims Unit* (also known as *Law & Order's Sex Crimes, Law & Order: SVU,* and *Special Victims Unit*), NBC, 2008.

Appeared as a teacher, *Davis Rules,* ABC and CBS; some sources cite an appearance in *As the World Turns,* CBS.

Television Appearances; Pilots:

Man, *Big Shots in America,* NBC, 1985.

Richard Peyton, "A Tale of One City," *Grand,* NBC, 1990.

Empire City (also known as *Deadly Instinct*), CBS, 1991.

Jake, "Revised 'Old' Pilot (aka Invitation to a Wedding)," *The Crew* (also known as *Cabin Pressure*), Fox, 1995.

Matt Parker, *The Single Guy,* NBC, 1995.

World on a String, Fox, 1997.

Henry Archer, "Broken Bow: Parts 1 & 2," *Enterprise* (also known as *Enterprise: Broken Bow, Star Trek:* *Enterprise, Star Trek: Series V,* and *Star Trek: Untitled Fifth Series*), UPN, 2001.

Teacher at the Learning Annex, *What's Up, Peter Fuddy?,* Fox, 2001.

Albert McCullough, *In My Life,* The WB, 2002.

Paul Young, *Desperate Housewives* (also known as *Beautes desesperees, Desperate housewives—I segreti di Wisteria Lane, Desupareto na tsuma tachi, Esposas desesperadas, Frustrerte fruer, Gotowe na wszystko, Kucanice, Meeleheitel koduperenaised, Mujeres desesperadas, Noikokyres se apognosi, Szueletett felesegek,* and *Taeydelliset naiset*), ABC, 2004.

Senator Trent Rogers, *The Hill,* ABC, 2007.

Made an uncredited appearance as Paul Young in the unaired pilot for *Desperate Housewives,* ABC.

Film Appearances:

Lieutenant Wolfe, *Platoon,* Orion, 1986.

Win Hockings, *Someone to Watch over Me,* Columbia, 1987.

Optimistic doctor at veterans hospital, *Born on the Fourth of July,* Universal, 1989.

Jordan, *Dead Men Don't Die,* Academy Entertainment, 1990.

Randy Derringer and Abbey, *Hollywood Heartbreak,* 1990.

Jac Holzman, *The Doors,* TriStar, 1991.

Sergeant Owen, *Gettysburg* (also known as *The Killer Angels*), New Line Cinema, 1993, director's cut also released and broadcast, broadcast as a television miniseries, TNT, 1994.

Michael Bedford, *Just in Time,* Leucadia Film Corporation, 1997.

Tim Urbanski, *Deep Impact,* Paramount, 1998.

Colonel Benton Lacy, *One Man's Hero* (also known as *Heroes sin patria*), Metro–Goldwyn–Mayer/Orion, 1999.

Rick Taylor, *Treehouse Hostage,* Trimark Pictures, 1999.

Alan Shepard, *Race to Space,* Lionsgate, 2000.

Father in video, *Red Dragon* (also known as *Roter Drache*), Universal, 2002.

Jonathan Clifton, *The Remembering Movies,* Hypnotic, 2002.

Dr. Norris, *A One Time Thing,* 2004.

FBI agent, *After the Sunset,* New Line Cinema, 2004.

Coffee shop customer, *Monster–in–Law* (also known as *Das Schwiegermonster*), New Line Cinema, 2005.

Narrator, *Forgotten China* (documentary), Pretty Dangerous Films, 2005.

American officer, *Letters from Iwo Jima,* Paramount, 2006.

Football dad, *Two Tickets to Paradise* (also known as *Life's a Trip*), First Look Pictures Releasing, 2006.

Tom Fuller, *Big Momma's House 2,* Twentieth Century–Fox, 2006.

Attorney General Wyatt, *Swing Vote,* Buena Vista, 2008.

Film Work:
Director of the film *Asphalt Cowboys.*

Stage Appearances:
Barclay, *Another Country,* Long Wharf Theatre, New Haven, CT, 1983.

Understudy for the role of Paul, *The Lady and the Clarinet,* Lucille Lortel Theatre, New York City, 1983.

Slab Boys, Playhouse Theatre, New York City, 1983.

King of Navarre, *Love's Labour's Lost,* New York Shakespeare Festival, Joseph Papp Public Theater, New York City, 1989.

Our Country's Good, Center Theatre Group, Mark Taper Forum, Los Angeles, 1989.

Peter, *The Pavilion,* Old Globe, Cassius Carter Center Stage, San Diego, CA, 2001.

Title role, *Burleigh Grimes* (also known as *Burleigh Grime$*), New World Stages Stage III, New York City, 2006.

Appeared in summer stock and regional productions.

WRITINGS

Screenplays:
Author of the screenplays *Chuckles, The Last Order,* and *Playable Lies.*

MUNROE, Meredith
See MONROE, Meredith

MURPHY, Dennis

PERSONAL

Married Marilyn. *Education:* Graduated from Williams College, Williamstown, MA.

Career: Correspondent.

Awards, Honors: Emmy Award nomination (with others), outstanding instant coverage of a news story, News and Documentary Emmy Awards, 1999, for *Dateline NBC.*

CREDITS

Television Appearances; Series:
Correspondent, *Now with Tom Brokaw and Katie Couric,* NBC, 1994.
Correspondent, *Dateline NBC,* (also known as *Dateline*), NBC, 2004—.

Television Appearances; Specials:
Reporter, *Decision '88,* NBC, 1988.
Correspondent, *Katrina's Fury: A Dateline Special,* NBC, 2005.
Correspondent, *Remembering Tim Russert,* NBC, 2008.

N

NELLIGAN, Kate 1950–

PERSONAL

Original name, Patricia Colleen Nelligan; born March 16, 1951 (some source say 1950), in London, Ontario, Canada; daughter of Patrick Joseph (a municipal employee in charge of ice rinks and recreational parks) and Josephine Alice (a schoolteacher; maiden name, Dier) Nelligan; married Robert Reale (a pianist and songwriter), February 19, 1989 (divorced); children: Gabriel Joseph. *Education:* Attended York University, Downsview, Ontario; trained for the stage at Central School of Speech and Drama, London. *Avocational Interests:* Reading, cooking.

Addresses: *Agent*—Great North Artists Management, 350 Duponte, Toronto M5R 1V9 Canada.

Career: Actress. Previously a competitive amateur tennis player.

Awards, Honors: Plays and Players London Theatre Critics Award, most promising actress, 1978, for *Knuckle;* Evening Standard Award, best actress, 1978, London Critics Award, best actress, Laurence Olivier Award, best actress, Society of West End Theatre and Antoinette Perry Award nomination, best actress in a play, 1983, all for *Plenty;* Distinguished Performance Award, Drama League of New York, 1983; Antoinette Perry Award nomination, best actress in a play, 1984, for *A Moon for the Misbegotten;* Antoinette Perry Award nomination, best actress in a featured role, 1988, for *Serious Money;* Antoinette Perry Award nomination, best actress in a play, 1989, for *Spoils of War;* Academy Award nomination, best supporting actress, 1992, for *The Prince of Tides;* Film Award, best supporting actress, British Academy of Film and Television Arts, D.

W. Griffith Award, and National Board of Review Award, best supporting actress, 1991, all for *Frankie and Johnny;* Genie Award nomination, best performance by an actress in a leading role, Academy of Canadian Cinema and Television, 1991, for *White Room;* Emmy Award nomination, outstanding lead actress in a drama series, 1992, and Gemini Award, best guest performance in a series, Academy of Canadian Cinema and Television, 1993, for *Road to Avonlea;* Genie Award, best performance by an actress in a supporting role, 1996, for *Margaret's Museum;* Gemini Award nomination, best supporting actress in a drama, 1996, for *Million Dollar Babies;* Screen Actors Guild Award nomination (with others), outstanding performance by a cast, 2000, for *The Cider House Rules;* Gemini Award nomination, best performance by an actress in a leading role in a dramatic program or miniseries, 2001, for *Blessed Stranger: After Flight 111;* Gemini Award nomination, best performance by an actress in a leading role in a dramatic program or miniseries, 2004, for *Human Cargo.*

CREDITS

Film Appearances:

Isabel, *The Romantic Englishwoman* (also known as *Une anglaise romantique*), New World, 1975.

Anna Seaton, *Licking Hitler,* British Film Institute, 1977.

Lucy Seward, *Dracula,* Universal, 1979.

Peabody, *Mr. Patman* (also known as *Crossover*), Film Consortium of Canada, 1980.

Agent, 1980.

Vivien Lanyon, *Forgive Our Foolish Ways,* 1980.

Lucy, *Eye of the Needle,* United Artists, 1981.

Susan Selky, *Without a Trace,* Twentieth Century–Fox, 1983.

Eleni Gatzoyiannis (title role), *Eleni,* Warner Bros., 1985.

The Mystery of Henry Moore (documentary), TV Arts, 1985.

Sarah Howell, *Il giorno prima* (also known as *The Day Before, Controle, Mind Control,* and *Control*), Columbia, 1987.

Jane, *The White Room,* 1990.

Lila Wingo Newbury, *The Prince of Tides,* Columbia, 1991.

Cora, *Frankie and Johnny* (also known as *Frankie & Johnny*), Paramount, 1991.

Eve, *Shadows and Fog,* Orion, 1992.

Lana Ravine, *Fatal Instinct,* Metro–Goldwyn–Mayer, 1993.

Narrator, *Into the Deep,* Sony Picture Classics, 1994.

Charlotte Russell, *Wolf,* Columbia, 1994.

Narrator, *By Woman's Hand,* 1994.

Constance Saunders, *How to Make an American Quilt,* Universal, 1995.

Catherine MacNeil, *Margaret's Museum* (also known as *Le musee de Margaret*), Cinepix, 1995.

Joanna Kennelly, *Up Close & Personal,* Buena Vista, 1996.

Narrator, *Stolen Moments,* National Film Board of Canada, 1997.

Narrator, *Rape: A Crime of War,* 1997.

U.S. Marshal Catherine Walsh, *U.S. Marshals,* Warner Bros., 1998.

Mrs. Jones, *Boy Meets Girl,* ARTO–Pelli, 1998.

Olivia, *The Cider House Rules,* Miramax, 1999.

Joanne, *Premonition,* Sony, 2007.

Television Appearances; Series:

Leonora Biddulph, *The Onedin Line,* syndicated, 1973–74.

Television Appearances; Miniseries:

Title role, "Therese Raquin," *Masterpiece Theatre,* PBS, 1981.

JoAnn Thatcher, *Love and Hate: A Marriage Made in Hell* (also known as *Love and Hate: The Story of Colin and JoAnn Thatcher*), NBC, 1990.

Anne Balfour, *Golden Fiddles,* 1990.

Helena Reid, *Million Dollar Babies* (also known as *Les jumelles Dionne*), CBS, 1994.

Mrs. Which, *A Wrinkle in Time* (also known as *Un raccourci dans le temps*), ABC, 2003.

Nina Wade, *Human Cargo,* 2004.

Television Appearances; Movies:

The Four Beauties, 1973.

Mercedes, *The Count of Monte Cristo* (also known as *Il conte di Montecristo*), NBC, 1975.

Bethune, 1977.

Isabella, *Measure for Measure* (also known as *The Complete Dramatic Works of William Shakespeare: "Measure for Measure"*), 1979.

Ruth Hession, *Victims* (also known as *In Our Hands*), NBC, 1982.

Kitty Keeler, *Kojak: The Price of Justice,* CBS, 1987.

Kay, *Terror Stalks the Class Reunion* (also known as *For Better and for Worse, For Better ... and for Worse,* and *Mary Higgins Clark: Pour le meilleur et pour le pire*), syndicated, 1992.

Holly Plum, *The Diamond Fleece,* USA Network, 1992.

Stephanie Chadford, *Shattered Trust: The Shari Karney Story* (also known as *Conspiracy of Silence: The Shari Karney Story*), NBC, 1993.

Susan Miori, *Liar, Liar* (also known as *Liar, Liar: Between Father and Daughter*), CBS, 1993.

Kate, *Old Times,* syndicated, 1993.

Elise, *Spoils of War* (also known as *In Spite of Love*), ABC, 1994.

Sheila Walker, *A Mother's Prayer,* USA Network, 1995.

Elizabeth Mink, *Captive Heart: The James Mink Story,* CBS, 1995.

Margaret Pfeiffer, *Calm at Sunset* (also known as *Calm at Sunset, Calm at Dawn*), CBS, 1996.

Kathryn McClain, *Love Is Strange,* Lifetime, 1998.

Justice Sara Marie Brandwynne, *Swing Vote* (also known as *The Ninth Justice*), ABC, 1999.

Kate O'Rourke, *Blessed Stranger: After Flight 111,* 2000.

Elizabeth, *Walter and Henry,* Showtime, 2001.

Vera Miller, *In from the Night,* CBS, 2006.

Television Appearances; Specials:

Laura, *The Arcata Promise,* PBS, 1974.

Marguerite, *The Lady of the Camellias,* 1976.

Backstage at Masterpiece Theatre: A 20th Anniversary Special (also known as *Backstage at Masterpiece Theatre*), PBS, 1991.

The 49th Annual Golden Globe Awards, TBS, 1992.

The 64th Annual Academy Awards, 1992.

Narrator, *Marcel Proust: A Writer's Life,* PBS, 1993.

Also appeared in *Dreams of Leaving.*

Television Appearances; Episodic:

Alice Keppel, "Daisy," *The Edwardians,* 1973.

Christine, "The Four Beauties," *Country Matters,* 1973.

Laura, "The Arcata Promise," *Great Performances,* PBS, 1977.

Hilary, "Do As I Say," *Play for Today,* 1977.

Anna Seaton, "Licking Hitler," *Play for Today,* 1978.

Caroline, "Dreams of Leaving," *Play for Today,* 1980.

Barbara Hoyle, "Three Hotels," *American Playhouse,* PBS, 1991.

Sidney Carver, "After the Honeymoon," *Road to Avonlea* (also known as *Avonlea* and *Tales from Avonlea*), 1992.

The Rosie O'Donnell Show, syndicated, 1997.

Emily Murphy, "Emily Murphy," *Heritage Minute,* 1998.

Gepetto, "Resurrection," *Eleventh Hour,* CBS, 2008.

Stage Appearances:

(Stage debut) Corrie Bratter, *Barefoot in the Park,* Little Theatre, Bristol, England, 1972.

Hypatia, *Misalliance,* Bristol Old Vic Company, Bristol, England, 1972–73.

Stella Kowalski, *A Streetcar Named Desire,* Bristol Old Vic Company, 1972–73.

Pegeen Mike, *The Playboy of the Western World,* Bristol Old Vic Company, 1972–73.

Grace Harkaway, *London Assurance,* Bristol Old Vic Company, 1972–73.

Title role, *Lulu,* Bristol Old Vic Company, 1972–73.

Sybil Chase, *Private Lives,* Bristol Old Vic Company, 1972–73.

(London debut) Jenny, *Knuckle,* Comedy Theatre, 1974.

Ellie Dunn, *Heartbreak House,* National Theatre Company, Old Vic Theatre, London, 1975.

Marianne, *Tales from the Vienna Woods,* National Theatre Company, Olivier Theatre, London, 1977.

Rosalind, *As You Like It,* Royal Shakespeare Company, Royal Shakespeare Theatre, Stratford–upon–Avon, England, 1977.

Susan Traherne, *Plenty,* National Theatre Company, Lyttelton Theatre, London, 1978.

(Broadway debut) Susan Traherne, *Plenty,* New York Shakespeare Festival, Public Theatre, 1982, later Plymouth Theatre, New York City, 1983.

Josie Hogan, *A Moon for the Misbegotten,* American Repertory Theatre, Cambridge, MA, then Cort Theatre, New York City, both 1984.

Virginia Woolf (title role), *Virginia,* New York Shakespeare Festival, Public Theatre, 1985.

Marylou Baines/Mrs. Etherington/Dolcie Starr, *Serious Money,* Royale Theatre, New York City, 1988.

Elise, *Spoils of War,* Promenade Theatre, then Second Stage Theatre, later Music Box Theatre, all New York City, 1988.

Melissa Gardner, *Love Letters,* Edison Theatre, New York City, 1989.

Ruth Benson, *Bad Habits,* Manhattan Theatre Club, New York City, 1990.

Pigeon sisters, *The Odd Couple,* Belasco Theatre, New York City, 1991.

Lyssa Dent Hughes, *An American Daughter,* Cort Theatre, 1997.

OTHER SOURCES

Books:

International Dictionary of Films and Filmmakers, Volume 3: *Actors and Actresses,* St. James Press, 1996.

Periodicals:

People, January 27, 1992, p. 57.

NEVILLE, John 1925–

PERSONAL

Born May 2, 1925, in London, England; immigrated to Canada, 1972; naturalized Canadian citizen; son of Reginald Daniel (a truck driver) and Mabel Lillian (maiden name, Fry) Neville; married Caroline Hooper (an actress), December 9, 1949; children: three sons, three daughters. *Education:* Trained for the stage at the Royal Academy of Dramatic Arts. *Avocational Interests:* Music and opera.

Addresses: *Contact*—24 Wellesley St. W #511, Toronto, Ontario M4Y 2X6 Canada.

Career: Actor and director. Lowestoft Repertory Company, England, member, 1948; Birmingham Repertory Company, England, member, 1949–50; Bristol Old Vic Company, England, member, 1950–58; joined Nottingham Playhouse Company, England, 1961, director, 1963–68; Citadel Theatre, Edmonton, Alberta, Canada, artistic director, 1973–78; Neptune Theatre, Halifax, Nova Scotia, Canada, artistic director, 1978–83; Stratford Shakespearean Festival, Ontario, Canada, artistic director, 1984–90; directed productions for the Stratford Shakespearean Festival, 1987–90. Nottingham University, honorary professor of drama, 1967—; Howard and Wyndham, Ltd., drama advisor. *Military service:* Served in the Royal Navy for two years during World War II.

Member: British Actors' Equity Association, Royal Academy of Dramatic Arts (associate membership).

Awards, Honors: Order of the British Empire, 1965; honorary doctorates of fine arts, Lethbridge University, Alberta, Canada, 1979, and Nova Scotia College of Art and Design, 1981; Gemini Award nomination, best performance by an actor in a continuing leading dramatic role, Academy of Canadian Cinema and Television, 1999, for *Emily of New Moon;* Member of the Order of Canada, 2006.

CREDITS

Stage Appearances:

(Stage debut) Walk–on, *Richard III,* New Theatre, London, 1947.

Lysander, *A Midsummer Night's Dream,* Open Air Theatre, London, 1948.

Chatillon, *King John,* Open Air Theatre, 1948.

Gregers Werle, *The Wild Duck,* Bristol Old Vic Theatre Company, Old Vic Theatre, Bristol, England, 1950–53.

Marlow, *She Stoops to Conquer,* Bristol Old Vic Theatre Company, Old Vic Theatre, 1950–53.

Richard, *The Lady's Not for Burning,* Bristol Old Vic Theatre Company, Old Vic Theatre, 1950–53.

Dunois, *Saint Joan,* Bristol Old Vic Theatre Company, Old Vic Theatre, 1950–53.

Edgar, *Venus Observed,* Bristol Old Vic Theatre Company, Old Vic Theatre, 1950–53.

Valentine, *Two Gentlemen of Verona,* Bristol Old Vic Theatre Company, Old Vic Theatre, then London, 1950–53.

The Duke, *Measure for Measure,* Bristol Old Vic Theatre Company, Old Vic Theatre, 1950–53.

Title role, *Henry V,* Bristol Old Vic Theatre Company, Old Vic Theatre, 1950–53.

Fortinbras, *Hamlet,* Old Vic Theatre Company, London, 1953–54.

Bertram, *All's Well That Ends Well,* Old Vic Theatre Company, 1953–54.

Ferdinand, *The Tempest,* Old Vic Theatre Company, 1953–54.

Macduff, *Macbeth,* Old Vic Theatre Company, 1954–55.

Title role, *Richard II,* Old Vic Theatre Company, 1954–55, revived, 1955–56.

Berowne, *Love's Labour's Lost,* Old Vic Theatre Company, 1954–55.

Orlando, *As You Like It,* Old Vic Theatre Company, 1954–55.

Henry Percy, *Henry IV, Part I,* Old Vic Theatre Company, 1954–55.

Marc Antony, *Julius Caesar,* Old Vic Theatre Company, 1955–56.

Autolycus, *The Winter's Tale,* Old Vic Theatre Company, 1955–56.

Alternated as Othello and Iago, *Othello,* Old Vic Theatre Company, 1955–56.

Troilus, *Troilus and Cressida,* Old Vic Theatre Company, 1955–56.

Romeo, *Romeo and Juliet,* Old Vic Theatre Company, 1955–56.

Title role, *Richard II,* Old Vic Theatre Company, 1955–56.

Macduff, *Macbeth,* Old Vic Theatre Company, 1956.

(Broadway debut) Romeo, *Romeo and Juliet,* Winter Garden Theatre, New York City, 1956.

Thersites, *Troilus and Cressida,* Old Vic Theatre Company, London, then Winter Garden Theatre, 1956.

Title role, *Hamlet,* Old Vic Theatre Company, 1957–58.

Angelo, *Measure for Measure,* Old Vic Theatre Company, 1957–58.

Sir Andrew Aguecheek, *Twelfth Night,* Old Vic Theatre Company, 1957–58.

Victor Fabian, *Once More with Feeling,* New Theatre, London, 1959.

Nestor, *Irma La Douce,* Lyric Theatre, London, 1959.

Jacko, *The Naked Island,* Arts Theatre, London, 1960.

Title role, *Macbeth,* Nottingham Playhouse Company, England, 1961.

Sir Thomas More, *A Man for All Seasons,* Nottingham Playhouse Company, 1961.

The Stranger, *The Lady from the Sea,* Queen's Theatre, London, 1961.

The Evangelist, *The Substitute,* Palace Theatre, London, 1961.

Don Frederick, *The Chances,* Chichester Festival, Chichester, England, 1962.

Orgilus, *The Broken Heart,* Chichester Festival, 1962.

Petruchio, *The Taming of the Shrew,* Nottingham Playhouse Company, 1962.

D'Artagnan, *The Three Musketeers,* Nottingham Playhouse Company, 1962.

Joseph Surface, *The School for Scandal,* Nottingham Playhouse Company, then Haymarket Theatre, London, 1962.

Title role, *Coriolanus,* Nottingham Playhouse Company, 1963.

John Worthing, *The Importance of Being Earnest,* Nottingham Playhouse Company, 1963.

Title role, *Alfie,* Mermaid Theatre, then Duchess Theatre, both London, 1963.

Bernard Shaw, *The Bashful Genius,* Nottingham Playhouse Company, 1964.

Moricet, *The Birdwatcher,* Nottingham Playhouse Company, 1964.

Title role, *Oedipus the King,* Nottingham Playhouse Company, 1964.

Title role, *Richard II,* Nottingham Playhouse Company, 1965.

Corvino, *Volpone,* Nottingham Playhouse Company, 1965.

Barry Field, *The Spies Are Singing,* Nottingham Playhouse Company, 1966.

Title role, *Doctor Faustus,* Nottingham Playhouse Company, 1966.

Willy Loman, *Death of a Salesman,* Nottingham Playhouse Company, 1967.

Iago, *Othello,* Nottingham Playhouse Company, 1967.

Kolpakov and others, *Beware of the Dog,* Nottingham Playhouse Company, then St. Martin's Theatre, London, 1967.

Henry Gow, "Mr.", and Alec Harvey, "Mrs.", in *Mr. and Mrs.* (double bill), Palace Theatre, 1968.

King Magnus, *The Apple Cart,* Mermaid Theatre, 1970.

Garrick, *Boswell's Life of Johnson,* Edinburgh Festival, Scotland, 1970.

Benedick, *Much Ado about Nothing,* Edinburgh Festival, 1970.

Macheath, *The Beggars' Opera,* Chichester Festival, 1972.

Sir Colenso Ridgeon, *The Doctor's Dilemma,* Chichester Festival, 1972.

Prospero, *The Tempest,* National Arts Centre Theatre, Ottawa, Canada, 1972.

Judge Brack, *Hedda Gabler,* Manitoba Theatre Centre, Winnipeg, Canada, 1972.

Oh, Coward, Citadel Theatre, Edmonton, Alberta, Canada, 1972.

Bethune, Citadel Theatre, 1972.

Pygmalion, Citadel Theatre, 1972.

Sherlock Holmes, Broadway production, 1975.

Willy, *Happy Days,* Citadel Theatre, then National Theatre, London, 1977.

Othello, Neptune Theatre, Halifax, Nova Scotia, Canada, 1978.

Staircase, Neptune Theatre, Halifax, 1978.

Pastor Manders, *Ghosts,* New York and Washington, DC, 1982.

Don Armado, *Love's Labour's Lost,* Stratford Shakespearean Festival, Ontario, Canada, 1983.

Dear Antoine, Grand Theatre, London, Ontario, Canada, 1983.

Arsenic and Old Lace, Grand Theatre, 1983.

Shylock, *The Merchant of Venice,* Stratford Shakespearean Festival, 1984.

Anton Chekhov, *Intimate Admiration,* Stratford Shakespearean Festival, 1987.

Henry Higgins, *My Fair Lady,* Stratford Shakespearean Festival, 1988.

Sir Peter Teazle, *The School for Scandal,* Royal National Theatre, London, 1990.

The Winter's Tale, Barbican Theatre, London, 1993.

Richard de Beauchamp, Earl of Warwick, *Saint Joan,* Lyceum Theatre, New York City, 1993.

Major Tours:

Romeo, *Romeo and Juliet,* U.S. cities, 1956.

Title role, *Richard II,* U.S. cities, 1956.

Macduff, *Macbeth,* U.S. cities, 1956.

Thersites, *Troilus and Cressida,* U.S. cities, 1956.

Title role, *Hamlet,* Old Vic Theatre Company, U.S. cities, 1958–59.

Sir Andrew Aguecheek, *Twelfth Night,* Old Vic Theatre Company, U.S. cities, 1958–59.

Title role, *Macbeth,* Maltese cities, 1961.

Thomas More, *A Man for All Seasons,* Maltese cities, 1961.

Title role, *Macbeth,* Nottingham Playhouse Company, West African cities, 1963.

Humbert Humbert, *Lolita,* U.S. cities, 1970.

Stage Director:

Henry V, Old Vic Theatre, London, 1960.

Twelfth Night, Nottingham Playhouse, England, 1962.

A Subject of Scandal, Nottingham Playhouse, 1962.

Concern, Nottingham Playhouse, 1962.

The Importance of Being Earnest, Nottingham Playhouse, 1963.

Memento Mori, Nottingham Playhouse, 1964.

The Mayor of Zalamea, Nottingham Playhouse, 1964.

Listen to the Knocking Bird, Nottingham Playhouse, 1964.

Richard II, Nottingham Playhouse, 1965.

Collapse of Stout Party, Nottingham Playhouse, 1965.

Measure for Measure, Nottingham Playhouse, 1965.

Saint Joan, Nottingham Playhouse, 1966.

Moll Flanders, Nottingham Playhouse, 1966.

Antony and Cleopatra, Nottingham Playhouse, 1966.

Jack and the Beanstalk, Nottingham Playhouse, 1966.

Death of a Salesman, Nottingham Playhouse, 1967.

Honour and Offer, Fortune Theatre, London, 1969.

The Rivals, National Arts Centre Theatre, Ottawa, Canada, 1972.

Romeo and Juliet, Citadel Theatre, Edmonton, Alberta, Canada, 1972.

Les Canadiens, Neptune Theatre, Halifax, Nova Scotia, Canada, 1978.

The Seagull, Neptune Theatre, 1978.

Hamlet, Grand Theatre, London, Ontario, Canada, 1983.

Mother Courage, Stratford Shakespearean Festival, Ontario, Canada, 1987.

Othello, Stratford Shakespearean Festival, 1987.

The Three Sisters, Stratford Shakespearean Festival, 1989.

Also directed the opera *Don Giovanni,* Festival Theatre of Canada.

Film Appearances:

Lord Alfred Douglas, *Oscar Wilde* (also known as *Forbidden Passion* and *Oscar Wilde: The Movie*), FAW, 1960.

Roger, *Mr. Topaze* (also known as *I Like Money*), 1961.

Julian Ratcliffe, second lieutenant, *Billy Budd,* Allied Artists, 1962.

Dr. Mark Davidson, *Unearthly Stranger* (also known as *Beyond the Stars*), American International, 1964.

Sherlock Holmes, *A Study in Terror* (also known as *Fog*), Columbia, 1966.

Wellington, *The Adventures of Gerard* (also known as *Adventures of Brigadier Gerard*), 1970.

General Wolseley, *Riel,* 1979.

Baron Karl Friedrich Hieronymous Munchausen, *The Adventures of Baron Munchausen* (also known as *Die Abenteuer des Baron von Muenchhausen*), Columbia, 1989.

Mr. Andrews, the butler, *Baby's Day Out,* Twentieth Century–Fox, 1994.

Mr. Laurence, *Little Women,* Columbia, 1994.

Mr. Endymion Hart–Jones, *The Road to Wellville,* Columbia, 1994.

Waiter, *Dangerous Minds,* Buena Vista, 1995.

Cruzzi, *Swann,* Norstar, 1996.

Thaddeus, *High School High,* Columbia, 1996.

Follenfant, *Sabotage,* New City Releasing, 1996.

General Staedert, *The Fifth Element* (also known as *Le cinquieme element*), Columbia, 1997.

Dr. Yealland, *Regeneration* (also known as *Behind the Lines*), Alliance, 1997.

Shopkeeper, *Shadow Zone: My Teacher Ate My Homework,* Catalyst, 1997.

The well–manicured man, *The X–Files: The Unopened File* (also known as *Aux frontieres du reel*), Twentieth Century–Fox, 1998.

Dean Adams, *Urban Legend* (also known as *Mixed Culture*), TriStar, 1998.

Bradley, *Goodbye Lover,* Warner Bros., 1999.

Gustave Sors, *Sunshine* (also known as *A napfeny ize* and *Sunshine–Ein Hauch von Sonnenschein*), Paramount, 1999.

Duke of Dingwall, *The Duke* (also known as *Hubert* and *Hubert, son altesse canine*), Buena Vista Home Video, 1999.

Jock Beale, *Water Damage*, Critical Mass Releasing, 1999.

Uncle Henrick, *Dinner at Fred's*, Imperial, 1999.

Bishop George Bell, *Bonhoeffer: Agent of Grace* (also known as *Bonhoeffer–Die letzte stufe*), Norflicks, 2000.

Judge H. Chadwick, *Custody of the Heart*, 2000.

Marmeladov, *Crime and Punishment*, Metro–Goldwyn–Mayer, 2000.

Dr. Reese, *Harvard Man*, Lions Gate Films, 2001.

Spider, Odeon, 2002.

Preacher, *Time of the Wolf* (also known as *L'enfant et le loup* and *L'heure du loup*), Third Millennium, 2002.

Terrence, *Spider*, Sony Pictures Classics, 2002.

Narrator, *Sea and Stars* (animated short), National Film Board of Canada, 2002.

Orson Stewart, *Between Strangers* (also known as *Coeurs inconnus* and *Cuori estranei*), Equinox, 2002.

Henry Neville, *Hollywood North*, Franchise Pictures, 2003.

Malcolm Woodward, *Moving Malcolm*, Mongrel Media, 2003.

Old man, *The Statement* (also known as *Crimes contre l'humanite*), Sony Pictures Classics, 2003.

Narrator, *White Knuckles*, Tulchin Entertainment, 2004.

Lord Rawston, *Separate Lies*, Fox Searchlight, 2005.

Voice of Donkey, *The Tragic Story of Nling* (animated short), 2006.

Himself, *Hamlet (Solo)* (documentary), 2007.

Himself, *The Madness and Misadventures of Munchhausen* (documentary), Sony Pictures Home Entertainment, 2008.

Television Appearances; Series:

The Company of Five, 1968.

Desmond, *Grand*, NBC, 1990.

The well–manicured man, a recurring role, *The X–Files*, Fox, 1995–98.

Uncle Malcolm, *Emily of New Moon*, CBC, 1998.

Voice of Eternity, *The Silver Surfer*, Fox, 1998.

First Elder Cole, *Amazon* (also known as *Amazonas–Gefangene de Dschungels* and *Peter Benchley's "Amazon"*), syndicated, 1999–2000.

Voice of Sparky, *Rockabye Bubble*, 2000.

Deaton Hill, *The Eleventh Hour*, 2002.

Television Appearances; Miniseries:

John Churchill, "The First Churchills," *Masterpiece Theatre*, PBS, 1971.

Professor Billby, *By Way of the Stars* (also known as *Der Lange weg des Lukas B.*), 1992.

Dwight Sanderson, *Chercheurs d'or* (also known as *Adventures of Smoke Bellew* and *Jack London's "Wilderness Tales"*), 1996.

British High Commissioner, *Trudeau*, 2002.

Television Appearances; Movies:

Henry V, *The Life of Henry V*, BBC, 1957.

Robert Browning, *The Barretts of Wimpole Street*, 1961.

Wilkie, *Shaggy Dog* (also known as *The Company of Five: Shaggy Dog*), 1968.

General Wolseley, *Riel*, 1979.

Voice of Viktor, *Johann Gift to Christmas*, 1991.

Dr. Cecil Chambers, *Journey to the Center of the Earth*, NBC, 1993.

Lord de Quincy, *Stark* (also known as *Ben Elton's "Stark"*), 1993.

General Sir Alan Brooke, *Dieppe*, 1993.

Frilo, the magnificent, *The Song Spinner*, Showtime, 1995.

Judge Mulhauser, *Time to Say Goodbye?*, Lifetime, 1997.

Bosch, *Johnny 2.0*, Sci–Fi Channel, 1998.

Judge H. Chadwick, *Custody of the Heart*, Lifetime, 2000.

Voice, *Gahan Wilson's "The Kid,"* Showtime, 2001.

Mr. Cunningham, *The Stork Derby* (also known as *Course a la cigogne* and *La course aux enfant*), Lifetime, 2002.

George's father, *Escape from the Newsroom*, 2002.

Director, *Control Factor* (also known as *Cortex controle*), Sci–Fi Channel, 2003.

Television Appearances; Specials:

Romeo, *Romeo and Juliet*, NBC, 1955.

Hillsborough, *The Rebel*, CBS, 1975.

The World's a Stage with John Neville, 2007.

Television Appearances; Episodic:

Peter, "The Bachelor," *BBC Sunday–Night Theatre*, 1951.

Paul Gardiner, "A Question of Fact," *ITV Television Playhouse*, ITV, 1955.

Romeo, "Romeo and Juliet," *Producers' Showcase*, 1957.

Ejlert Lovborg, "Hedda Gabler," *ITV Play of the Week* (also known as *Play of the Week*), ITV, 1957.

Title role, "Hamlet," *DuPont Show of the Month*, CBS, 1959.

Maxime/Saint–Just, "Poor Bitos," *Theatre 625*, 1965.

Inspector Franz Mittermayer, "The Order," *The Wednesday Play*, 1967.

The man, "George's Room," *Half Hour Story*, 1967.

Wilkie, "Shaggy Dog," *The Company of Five*, 1968.

Pickering, "The Death Watcher," *Shadows of Fear*, 1971.

Dr. Thorndyke, "A Message from the Deep Sea," *The Rivals of Sherlock Holmes*, 1971.

Andrew, "Third Party," *Love Story*, 1972.

Sir Everard, "Knightmare," *Shirley's World*, 1972.

"Triple Cross," *The Protectors*, 1972.

"Richard Burton: In from the Cold," *Great Performances,* PBS, 1989.

"Acid Test," *E.N.G.,* 1992.

Percy Methley, "A Dark and Stormy Night," *Road to Avonlea* (also known as *Avonlea* and *Tales from Avonlea*), 1992.

Professor Hilton, "The Accused," *Class of '96,* 1993.

Isaac Newton, "Descent: Part 1," *Star Trek: The Next Generation* (also known as *Star Trek: TNG*), 1993.

Leonard Price, "Thief of Hearts," *Viper,* NBC, 1994.

Sir David Browning, "Message for Posterity," *Performance,* 1994.

Oscar Hammond, "F/X: The Illusion," *F/X: The Series,* syndicated, 1996.

Arthur Jameson, "Past, Present, Future," *The Education of Max Bickford,* 2002.

The seeker, *Odyssey 5,* Showtime, 2002.

Mr. Wiley, *Queer as Folk* (also known as *Q.A.F.* and *Queer as Folk USA*), Showtime, 2002.

OTHER SOURCES

Books:

Gaines, Robert A., *John Neville Takes Command: The Story of the Stratford Shakespearean Festival in Production,* William Street Press (Stratford, Ontario, Canada), 1987.

International Dictionary of Theatre, Volume 3: *Actors, Directors, and Designers,* St. James Press, 1996.

Trewin, J. C., *John Neville,* 1961.

Periodicals:

Theatre Week, July 31, 1989, p. 26.

NEWMAN, Barry 1938–

PERSONAL

Full name, Barry Foster Newman; born November 7, 1938, in Boston, MA; son of Carl Henry and Sarah (maiden name, Ostrovsky) Newman. *Education:* Brandeis University, B.A., anthropology. *Avocational Interests:* Jazz saxophone, golf, tennis.

Addresses: *Agent*—The Gersh Agency, 130 West 42nd St., Suite 1804, New York, NY 10036; Greene and Associates, 8899 Beverly Blvd., Suite 705, Los Angeles, CA 90048-2428. *Manager*—N2N Entertainment, 1230 Montana Ave., Suite 203, Santa Monica, CA 90403.

Career: Actor.

Awards, Honors: Emmy Award nomination, outstanding lead actor in a drama series, 1975, and Golden Globe Award nomination, best television actor—drama, 1976, both for *Petrocelli.*

CREDITS

Film Appearances:

Al Riccardo, *Pretty Boy Floyd,* Continental Distributing, 1960.

The Moving Finger, Moyer Productions, 1963.

Anthony J. "Tony" Petrocelli (title role), *The Lawyer,* Paramount, 1969.

Kowalski, *Vanishing Point,* Twentieth Century–Fox, 1971.

William "Bill" Mathison, *The Salzburg Connection* (also known as *Top Secret*), Twentieth Century–Fox, 1972.

John Talbot, *Fear Is the Key,* Paramount, 1973.

Dr. Frank Whitman, *City on Fire,* Avco–Embassy Pictures, 1979.

Dr. Ben Corcoran, *Amy* (also known as *Amy on the Lips*), Buena Vista, 1981.

Norman Bassett, *Daylight,* Universal, 1996.

Jack Skolnick, *Brown's Requiem,* Avalanche Releasing, 1998.

Senator Lassetter, *Goodbye Lover,* Warner Bros., 1998.

Dr. Chamberlain, *Fugitive Mind,* Royal Oaks Communications/Flashstar, 1999.

Hal (Kit's agent), *Bowfinger* (also known as *Big Movie* and *Bowfinger's Big Thing*), Universal, 1999.

Jim Avery, *The Limey,* Artisan Entertainment, 1999.

Greydon Lake, *G–Men from Hell,* Government Action, 2000.

Monty, *True Blue,* Columbia/TriStar, 2001.

Simon, *Jack the Dog,* Jung N Restless Productions, 2001.

Walter Sullivan, *40 Days and 40 Nights* (also known as *40 jours et 40 nuits*), Miramax, 2002.

Boris, *Grilled,* New Line Cinema, 2006.

Frank, *What the #$*! Do We (K)now?* (also known as *What the Bleep Do We Know!?*), Samuel Goldwyn, 2006.

Television Appearances; Series:

John Barnes, *The Edge of Night* (also known as *Edge of Night*), CBS, 1964–65.

Anthony J. "Tony" Petrocelli, *Petrocelli,* NBC, 1974–76.

Dr. Garrett Braden, *Nightingales,* NBC, 1989.

Television Appearances; Movies:

Alan Fitch, *Sex and the Married Woman,* NBC, 1977.

Johnny Campana, *King Crab,* ABC, 1980.

Barney Duncan, *... Deadline ...,* Nine Network (Australia) and CBS, 1982.

Detective Flynn, *Fantasies* (also known as *The Studio Murders*), ABC, 1982.

Peter Baylin, *Having It All,* ABC, 1982.

Bernie Segal, *Fatal Vision,* NBC, 1984.

Richard Chapman, *Second Sight: A Love Story* (also known as *Emma and I*), CBS, 1984.

Ben Taylor, *My Two Loves,* ABC, 1986.

Jason Rudd, *Miss Marple: The Mirror Crack'd from Side to Side* (also known as *Miss Marple*), BBC, 1992, broadcast as *Miss Marple: The Mirror Crack'd,* Arts and Entertainment, 1993, also broadcast on Seven Network (Australia).

Axel Trank, *Der Blaue Diamant* (also known as *Hunt for the Blue Diamond*), 1993.

Andy Capasso, *MacShayne: Winner Takes All,* NBC, 1994.

Donald Simpson, *Good Advice,* HBO, 2001.

Simon, *Manhood,* Showtime, 2003.

Television Appearances; Specials:

Night of 100 Stars III (also known as *Night of One Hundred Stars*), NBC, 1990.

Himself, *Movies' Greatest Cars,* Sky, 2005.

Himself, *'Tis Autumn: The Search for Jackie Paris,* 2006.

Kowalski, *Wanderlust,* Independent Film Channel, 2006.

Television Appearances; Episodic:

Police officer, "Hush–Hush," *Way Out,* CBS, 1961.

"Secret Document X256" (also known as "Secret Document"), *The Armstrong Circle Theater* (also known as *Armstrong Circle Theater* and *Circle Theater*), NBC, 1963.

Assistant guru, "The Groovy Guru," *Get Smart* (also known as *Superagent 86*), NBC, 1968.

Himself, *Film Night,* BBC, 1973.

Himself, *The Tonight Show Starring Johnny Carson* (also known as *The Best of Carson*), NBC, 1973, multiple episodes in 1975.

Himself, *The Irv Kupcinet Show,* syndicated, 1975.

Himself, *The Mike Douglas Show,* syndicated, 1975.

Himself, *Dinah!* (also known as *Dinah* and *Dinah and Friends*), syndicated, multiple episodes in 1975, 1976, 1977.

Himself, *The Peter Marshall Variety Show,* syndicated, 1976.

Cohost, *The Mike Douglas Show,* syndicated, 1976.

Himself, *Celebrity Sweepstakes,* NBC, 1977.

Himself, *The Alan Thicke Show* (also known as *Prime Cuts;* recut version known as *Fast Company*), 1980.

Dr. Gabe McCracken, "The Cutting Edge," *Quincy M.E.* (also known as *Quincy*), NBC, 1983.

Himself, "Private Eyes," *The Fall Guy,* ABC, 1984.

Former police lieutenant Ed McMasters, "Snow White, Blood Red," *Murder, She Wrote,* CBS, 1988.

Lieutenant Amos "Jake" Ballinger, "Class Act," *Murder, She Wrote,* CBS, 1989.

Guest, *The New Hollywood Squares* (also known as *The Hollywood Squares*), syndicated, 1989.

Frank Askoff, "How Am I Driving?," *L.A. Law,* NBC, 1994.

Frank Askoff, "Whistle Stop," *L.A. Law,* NBC, 1994.

Jimmy Wexler, "A Sudden Fish," *NYPD Blue,* ABC, 1994.

Andrew Bascombe, "Game, Set, Murder," *Murder, She Wrote,* CBS, 1995.

Mark Radner, "Top Gum," *NYPD Blue,* ABC, 1998.

Bill Allen (Claire's father), "Grand Delusions," *Cupid,* ABC, 1999.

Professor Max Bloom, "The Accomplice," *The O.C.* (also known as *California Teens, Newport Beach, O.C., O.C., California, Orange County, A Narancsvidek, O.C.—Um estranho no paraiso,* and *Zycie na fali*), Fox, 2005.

Professor Max Bloom, "The Lonely Hearts Club," *The O.C.* (also known as *California Teens, Newport Beach, O.C., O.C., California, Orange County, A Narancsvidek, O.C.—Um estranho no paraiso,* and *Zycie na fali*), Fox, 2005.

Professor Max Bloom, "The Second Chance," *The O.C.* (also known as *California Teens, Newport Beach, O.C., O.C., California, Orange County, A Narancsvidek, O.C.—Um estranho no paraiso,* and *Zycie na fali*), Fox, 2005.

Television Appearances; Pilots:

Anthony J. "Tony" Petrocelli, *Night Games* (pilot for the series *Petrocelli*), NBC, 1974.

Dr. Garrett Braden, *Nightingales,* NBC, 1989.

Appeared as George, *Wilder Days,* ABC.

Television Work:

Producer, *Everybody Happy,* 1991.

Worked on various projects.

Stage Appearances:

The musician, *Nature's Way,* Coronet Theatre, New York City, 1957.

Larry, *Maybe Tuesday,* Playhouse Theatre, New York City, 1958.

Detective sergeant Trotter, *The Mousetrap,* Maidman Playhouse, New York City, 1960–61.

Young man and understudy for the role of Sonny, *Night Life,* Brooks Atkinson Theatre, New York City, 1962.

Sheik Orsini, *What Makes Sammy Run?,* 54th Street Theatre, New York City, 1964–65.

Night of 100 Stars III (also known as *Night of One Hundred Stars*), Radio City Music Hall, New York City, 1990.

NICKALLS, Grant

PERSONAL

Born in Huntsville, Ontario, Canada.

Career: Actor.

CREDITS

Film Appearances:
Scott, *Speciman,* Ardustry Home Entertainment, 1996.
Jason, *Dirty Work* (also known as *Sale boulot*), Metro–Goldwyn–Mayer, 1998.
Joe, *Angel Eyes* (also known as *Ojos de angel*), Warner Bros., 2001.
Jack Bridges, *Glitter,* Twentieth Century–Fox, 2001.
Helicopter pilot, *The Incredible Hulk,* Universal, 2008.

Television Appearances; Series:
David Silverman, *Paradise Falls,* Showcase, 2001.
Matt and lawyer, *Doc,* PAX, 2002–2003.
Constable Ian Faraday, *This Is Wonderland,* CBC, 2005.

Television Appearances; Miniseries:
Jed, *Seasons of Love* (also known as *Love on the Land*), CBS, 1999.

Television Appearances; Movies:
Marty, *A Husband, a Wife and a Lover* (also known as *A Strange Affair*), CBS, 1996.
Steve Ellinger, *My Date with the President's Daughter,* ABC, 1998.
Paul Jarvis, *Hangman,* TMC, 2001.
Billy Campbell, *Power and Beauty,* Showtime, 2002.
Richard Devries, *Comfort and Joy,* Lifetime, 2003.
Simon Castillo, *Obituary,* Lifetime, 2006.
David Foster, *Celine,* CBC, 2008.

Television Appearances; Specials:
Snow Hunter, *Dear America: Standing in the Light* (also known as *Standing in the Light,* and *Dear America: Standing in the Light—The Captive Story of Catharine Carey Logan, Delaware Valley, Pennsylvania, 1763*), HBO, 1999.

Television Appearances; Episodic:
Jerry Wakowski, "The Prom," *C.B.C.'s Magic Hour,* CBC, 1990.
John Spencer, "What's Up Doc," *Side Effects,* CBC, 1994.
Young Pete Hogan, "A Match Made in Heaven," *Twice in a Lifetime,* CTV and PAX, 1999.
Adam Lyons, *Queer as Folk* (also known as *Q.A.F.* and *Queer as Folk U.S.A.*), Showtime, 2001.
Wild Card, Lifetime, 2003.
Playmakers, ESPN, 2003.
Robert Newell, "Sea of Love," *1–800–MISSING* (also known as *Missing* and *Porte disparu*), Lifetime, 2004.

Journalism student, "The Miracle Worker," *The Eleventh Hour,* CTV, 2005.
Keys, "Through the Looking Glass," *Kevin Hill,* UPN, 2005.
Jim Hartfield, "The Strip Club Murder," *Til Death Do Us Part* (also known as *Love You to Death*), Court TV, 2007.

NICOLS, Bruno
    See HARTH, C. Ernst

NOLASCO, Amaury 1970–

PERSONAL

Birthname Amaury Nolasco Garrido; born December 24, 1970, in Puerto Rico. *Education:* Studied biology at University of Puerto Rico.

Addresses: *Agent*—William Morris Agency, 1325 Avenue of the Americas, New York, NY 10019. *Manager*—Untitled Entertainment, 1801 Century Park East, Suite 700, Los Angeles, CA 90067.

Career: Actor.

CREDITS

Film Appearances:
Waiter, *Fall,* MGM, 1997.
Victor, *Brother,* Sony, 2000.
Hector Arturo, *Final Breakdown* (also known as *Truth Be Told* and *Turnaround*), 2002.
Orange Julius, *2 Fast 2 Furious,* Universal, 2003.
G–man, *The Librarians* (also known as *Strike Force*), Lions Gate Films Home Entertainment, 2003.
Minadeo, *Mr. 3000,* Buena Vista, 2004.
Carlos, *The Benchwarmers,* Sony, 2006.
ACWO Jorge "Fig" Figueroa, *Transformers* (also known as *Transformers: The IMAX Experience*), Paramount, 2007.
Detective Cosmos Santos, *Street Kings,* Fox Searchlight, 2008.
Jack Lupino, *Max Payne,* Twentieth Century–Fox, 2008.
Palmer, *Armored,* Screen Gems, 2009.

Television Appearances; Series:
Fernando Sucre, *Prison Break,* Fox, 2005—.

Television Appearances; Movies:
Cypriano, *The Dukes of Hazzard: Hazzard in Hollywood*, CBS, 2000.

Television Appearances; Episodic:
Shadow's accomplice number one, *New York Undercover*, Fox, 1997.
Ivory Ortega, "The Stories You Don't Hear About," *Arli$$*, HBO, 1999.
Pedro Mendoza, "Take Me Out to the Ballgame," *Early Edition*, CBS, 1999.
Flaco Rosario, "Bad Boys & Why We Love Them," *The Huntress*, USA Network, 2000.
Waiter, *That 80's Show*, Fox, 2001.
Hector Delgado, "Slaves of Las Vegas," *CSI: Crime Scene Investigation* (also known as *C.S.I., CSI: Las Vegas* and *Les Experts*), CBS, 2001.
Ricky, "Dead Again," *ER*, NBC, 2002.
Young Manny, "Long Time No See," *George Lopez*, ABC, 2002.
Adrian, "Love TKO," *Eve*, UPN, 2004.

Ruben DeRosa, "The Closer," *CSI: NY*, CBS, 2005.
"'Transformers': Their War. Our World," *HBO First Look*, HBO, 2007.
Last Call with Carson Daly, NBC, 2007.
Jimmy Kimmel Live!, ABC, 2008.

Television Appearances; Specials:
The 2006 Teen Choice Awards, Fox, 2006.
Presenter, *2006 Alma Awards*, ABC, 2006.
2007 NCLR Alma Awards, ABC, 2007.

RECORDINGS

Videos:
2 Fast 2 Furious: Driving School, Universal, 2003.
Inside '2 Fast 2 Furious', Universal, 2003.
Fernando Sucre, *Making of "Prison Break,"* 2006.
Our World, 2007.
Yes We Can, 2008.

O–R

ODOM, Leslie, Jr. 1981–

PERSONAL

Born August 6, 1981, in Queens, NY. *Education:* Carnegie Mellon University, B.F.A. (with honors), drama; studied dance with Philadanco's Training Company; studied voice at Freedom Theatre; studied drama at Capa.

Addresses: *Agent*—Bauman, Redanty and Shaul, 5757 Wilshire Blvd., Suite 473, Los Angeles, CA 90036. *Manager*—Joan Sittenfield Management, 8350 Santa Monica Blvd., Suite 108, West Hollywood, CA 90069.

Career: Actor. Eleone Dance Theatre, former member of company; Kariamu and Company, former member of company.

Awards, Honors: Princess Grace Award for Excellence in the Arts, 2002–03; Grace LaVine Theatre Award, for achievement in acting.

CREDITS

Television Appearances; Series:
Joseph Kayle, *CSI: Miami,* CBS, 2003–2006.
Malik Christo, *Vanished,* Fox, 2006.
Freddy, *Big Day,* ABC, 2006–2007.

Television Appearances; Pilots:
Freddy, *Big Day,* ABC, 2006.

Also appeared as Marcus, *Supreme Courtships.*

Television Appearances; Episodic:
Lamont, "Almost Touched by an Angel," *The Big House,* ABC, 2004.
Lamont, "A Friend in Need," *The Big House,* ABC, 2004.
Sergeant Adams, "The Crossing," *Threshold,* CBS, 2006.
Quentin Walsh, "Bridesmaids Revisited," *Gilmore Girls,* The WB, 2006.
Jordan Carter, "Prodigal Son," *Close to Home,* CBS, 2006.
Mr. Pratt, "Good People," *The Bill Engvall Show,* TBS, 2007.
Mr. Pratt, "Feel Free to Say No," *The Bill Engvall Show,* TBS, 2007.
P. J. Walling, "There's No 'I' in Team," *Grey's Anatomy,* ABC, 2008.

Stage Appearances:
(Broadway debut) Paul, *Rent,* 1998.

Also appeared in shepherd boy, *Black Nativity,* Freedom Theatre; Luis, *West Side Story,* West Virginia Public Theatre, Morgantown, WV; Victor, *Smokey Joe's Cafe,* West Virginia Public Theatre; member of ensemble, *Jersey Boys,* La Jolla Theatre, La Jolla, CA; Danny and member of ensemble, *Applause,* Reprise Theatre, Los Angeles; Rodrigo, *Venice,* Kirk Douglas Theatre, Los Angeles; Agwe, *Once on This Island,* Reprise Theatre; Marion, *Letters from 'Nam,* Pittsburgh CLO, Pittsburgh, PA; Shaun, *CAMP: The Movie;* member of chorus, *The Adventures of Tom Sawyer,* Nederlander Theatre, New York City; Seaweed, *Hairspray;* in *Being Alive,* Westport Playhouse, Westport, CT.

ORUCHE, Phina 1972–
(Phina Cruche, Phina)

PERSONAL

Born August 31, 1972, in Liverpool, England; married first husband, August, 2007; children: one son. *Education:* Studied acting at the Actors Studio.

Addresses: *Agent*—Silver, Massetti, and Szatmary, 8730 West Sunset Blvd., Suite 440, West Hollywood, CA 90069.

Career: Actress. Also worked as a model. Qualified Hatha yoga instructor.

Member: The Actors Studio.

CREDITS

Film Appearances:
Model, *Sabrina*, Paramount, 1995.
Leslie James, *How Stella Got Her Groove Back*, Twentieth Century–Fox, 1998.
(As Phina Cruche) Lowanda, *Out in Fifty*, Avalanche Home Entertainment, 1999.
Citizens of Perpetual Indulgence, 1999.
Amanda, *The Sky Is Falling*, Showcase Entertainment, 2000.
Female super model, *Punks*, Urbanworld Films, 2000.
Cym, *The Forsaken* (also known as *The Forsaken: Desert Vampires, Desert Vampires,* and *Vampires of the Desert*), Screen Gems, 2001.
Scouse's girl, *Who's Kyle?* (short), Vanguard Cinema, 2004.
Emily, *Happily Ever Afters*, Buena Vista International, 2009.

Television Appearances; Series:
I'm a Celebrity, Get Me Out of Here! (also known as *I'm a Celebrity*), ITV, 2006.
Liberty Baker, *Footballers' Wives*, ITV, Trio, and BBC America, 2006.
Panelist, *The Wright Stuff*, Channel 5, 2007–2008.

Television Appearances; Movies:
British stewardess, *If Looks Could Kill* (also known as *If Looks Could Kill: From the Files of "America's Most Wanted"* and *If Looks Could Kill: The John Hawkins Story*), Fox, 1996.
Sexy woman, *High Freakquency* (also known as *24/7 Radio*), Black Entertainment Television, 1998.
Isabella, *Blade Squad*, Fox, 1998.

Television Appearances; Specials:
An Audience with "Coronation Street," ITV, 2006.
Screen Nation Television and Film Awards 2006, 2006.

Television Appearances; Episodic:
(As Phina) Ashley, "No Smoking," *Saved by the Bell: The New Class*, NBC, 1995.
Beautiful woman, "Tales from the Dark Side or, Ty Takes the Redeye," *Homeboys in Outer Space*, UPN, 1997.

Victoria, "In Concert," *Players*, NBC, 1997.
Daysha Lang, *Nash Bridges*, CBS, 1997.
Ellen Martin, "Rain of Terror," *Diagnosis Murder*, CBS, 1998.
Olivia, "The Freshman," *Buffy the Vampire Slayer* (also known as *BtVS, Buffy,* and *Buffy, the Vampire Slayer: The Series*), The WB, 1999.
Olivia, "Hush," *Buffy the Vampire Slayer* (also known as *BtVS, Buffy,* and *Buffy, the Vampire Slayer: The Series*), The WB, 1999.
Olivia, "Restless," *Buffy the Vampire Slayer* (also known as *BtVS, Buffy,* and *Buffy, the Vampire Slayer: The Series*), The WB, 2000.
Mercy, "Val Point Blank," *V.I.P.* (also known as *V.I.P.— Die Bodyguards*), syndicated, 2000.
Adult Virginia, "Subject: Fearsum," *Freakylinks*, Fox, 2000.
Doctor, "The Inner Sense: Parts 1 & 2," *The Pretender*, NBC, 2000.
Asia, "Sleight–of–Hand," *Diagnosis Murder*, CBS, 2000.
Jada, "Lucky Charmed," *Charmed*, The WB, 2003.
Mia, "Cliff Mantegna," *Nip/Tuck*, FX Channel, 2003.
Female guard, "Crossed Out," *She Spies*, syndicated, 2003.
Heather Lees, "403," *The Bill*, ITV1, 2006.
Heather Lees, "405," *The Bill*, ITV1, 2006.
This Morning (also known as *This Morning with Richard and Judy*), ITV, 2006.
Herself and Lauryn Hill, "2006 Celebrity 4," *Stars in Their Eyes,* ITV, 2006.
Female chieftain, "The Outsiders," *The Unit,* CBS, 2007.
Little Miss Jocelyn, BBC3, 2008.

WRITINGS

Nonfiction:
Wrote weekly column for the *Liverpool Echo;* wrote column for *Aspire* magazine.

OTHER SOURCES

Electronic:
Phina Oruche Website, http://www.phinarouche.com, January 15, 2009.

OZAKI, Eijiro

PERSONAL

Born in Japan. *Education:* Attended University of Nebraska as an exchange student; trained with Yoko Narahashi and Frank Corsaro.

Addresses: *Agent*—Hervey/Grimes Talent Agency, 10561 Missouri Ave., Suite 2, Los Angeles, CA 90025.

Career: Actor and voice performer. Appeared in several Japanese films and television programs, beginning in the 1990s; appeared in commercials. Also works as interpreter and stunt performer.

CREDITS

Film Appearances:
Kunihilo, *Gaijin—Ama–me como sou* (also known as *Gaijin—Love Me as I Am*), Scena Filmes, 2005.
Lieutenant Okubo, *Letters from Iwo Jima,* Warner Bros., 2006.

Television Appearances; Episodic:
Young Kaito Nakamura, "Chapter Ten: Truth & Consequences," *Heroes,* NBC, 2007.
Maitre d', "The Commitments," *The Game,* CW Network, 2008.
Himself, *Heroes Report,* Super! Drama TV, 2008.

Television Appearances; Other:
Agri (series), NHK, 1997.
Uesugi yozan (special), NHK, 1998.
Kunio Takakura, *Haru to Natsu* (miniseries), NHK, 2005.

Stage Appearances:
Jim, *Rebel without a Cause,* Model Language Studio, Japan, 1994.
Shuriken, Shavian Theatre Company, New Zealand, 1995.
The Winds of God, Judith Anderson Theatre, New York City, then American Place Theatre, New York City, 1999.

Also appeared in Japanese productions of *Dog Day Afternoon,* Theatre V Akasaka; *Fast Forward,* Sparks Third Stage; *Hello X'mas,* Theatre Apple; and *Way of the Sword,* Shinsengumi Festival Theatre.

Major Tours:
The Winds of God, Japanese cities, 1999.

RECORDINGS

Video Games:
Voice of Yoto, *Chronicles of Riddick: Assault on Dark Athena,* Atari, 2009.

OTHER SOURCES

Electronic:
Eijiro Ozaki Official Site, http://www.eijiroozaki.com, December 11, 2008.

PAVAROTTI, Luciano 1935–2007

PERSONAL

Born October 12, 1935, in Modena, Italy; died of pancreatic cancer, September 6, 2007, in Modena, Italy. Opera singer. Blessed with a voice that had a rare range, bell-like clarity, and pristine beauty, Pavarotti is often hailed as the greatest operatic tenor of all time. With his outsized frame and a charismatic personality to match, Pavarotti brought an appreciation of opera to millions of people.

Born in the small town of Modena, Italy, Pavarotti began singing in the church choir at the age of five, imitating his father, a baker and amateur tenor who often sang in the chorus at a Modena opera house. Pavarotti decided at nineteen to become a professional opera singer and began studying seriously with Arrigo Pola. In 1961 Pavarotti won the Concorso Internazionale prize, which included a role in a forthcoming opera; hence, Pavarotti made his professional debut as Rodolfo in Puccini's classic story of impoverished artists, *La Boheme,* a part that became Pavarotti's hallmark role. Pavarotti made his international debut as Rodolfo in 1963, stepping in for Italian opera great and mentor Giuseppe di Stefano in a televised performance of *La Boheme* at London's Royal Opera House.

Pavarotti made his American debut in 1965 at the Miami Opera opposite soprano Joan Sutherland in Donizetti's *Lucia di Lammermoor;* Sutherland and Pavarotti formed a vocal partnership that endured over the decades. Pavarotti performed for the first time at the New York Metropolitan Opera in 1968; in was to become his "home," a venue in which Pavarotti performed more than 375 times during his career. In 1972 Pavarotti returned to the Met to perform a mystical feat: he was able to hit nine consecutive high c notes with full voice as Tonio in Donizetti's *Daughter of the Regiment,* earning Pavarotti the nickname "king of the high c's." This impressive performance brought Pavarotti even greater recognition outside of the opera world and led to an appearance with Johnny Carson on *The Tonight Show.*

By the early 1980s Pavarotti had become a household name with numerous successful concerts, operas, and recordings. In 1990 Pavarotti teamed with fellow tenors Palcido Domingo and Jose Carreras in a performance at the World Cup in Italy. The enormous success of this performance led to concerts and a tour headlined as the *Three Tenors;* the *Three Tenors* became a phenomenon, selling millions of recordings and reaching an even wider audience. In the early 1990s Pavarotti founded and starred in *Pavarotti & Friends,* an annual charity concert featuring Pavarotti singing with current superstars as a way to raise money for many United Nations charities. Pavarotti's popularity skyrocketed, and in 1993 his performance at New York's Central Park was attended by more than 500,000 fans, while millions more watched on television. In 2004 Pavarotti sang in his last opera, as the painter Cavaradossi in Pucini's *Tosca* at the New York Metropolitan Opera. Pavarotti started a 40-city farewell tour in 2005, but his last public appearance was a performance at the opening of the Winter Olympics in Turin, Italy, in 2006. In July 2006 Pavarotti had emergency surgery for pancreatic cancer. Pavarotti was still teaching students for several hours a day until only a few weeks before his death.

PERIODICALS

New York Times, September 6, 2007.
Variety, September 10, 2007.

PHINA
    See ORUCHE, Phina

POLLACK, Sydney 1934–2008

PERSONAL

Birth name, Sydney Irwin Pollack; born July 1, 1934, in Lafayette, IN; died of cancer, May 26, 2008, in Pacific Palisades, CA. Director, producer, and actor. A meticulous craftsman, Pollack achieved acclaim with many of the most memorable and successful mainstream movies starring some of the biggest Hollywood names of the 1970s and 1980s. Born to first-generation Russian-American parents, Pollack developed a love of theater in high school and, upon graduation in 1952, decided to forgo college and move from Indiana to New York to study acting at the Neighborhood Playhouse School of the Theatre with Sanford Meisner.

Pollack began his professional acting career by appearing on Broadway in the 1950s but turned to directing by the 1960s. He directed episodes of television series such as *The Fugitive* and *Ben Casey,* winning an Emmy for an episode of *Bob Hope Presents the Chrysler Theater.* In 1962 Pollack made his film acting debut alongside a little-known actor named Robert Redford in *War Hunt;* the pair formed a friendship that would endure both professionally and personally for more than forty years. Pollack's big-screen movie directing

debut came in 1965 with *The Slender Thread,* starring Sidney Poitier and Anne Bancroft. His first Academy Award nomination as best director came in 1969 with *They Shoot Horses, Don't They?,* a Depression-era drama about marathon dancers starring Jane Fonda. Pollack's next Academy Award nomination for best director came in 1982 with *Tootsie,* a gender-bending comedy in which Pollack also acted alongside Dustin Hoffman. *Tootsie* earned ten Academy Award nominations and was picked in a subsequent American Film Institute Poll as the second funniest comedy film ever made. Pollack cast his friend Redford in 1966 in *This Property is Condemned* opposite Natalie Wood. Pollack and Redford collaborated on six more films together, including *The Way We Were* with Barbra Streisand, *Jeremiah Johnson, Three Days of the Condor* with Faye Dunaway, *The Electric Horseman* with Jane Fonda, and *Havana* with Lena Olin. The Pollack-Redford pairing also produced the enormously successful 1985 picture *Out of Africa,* starring Redford and Meryl Streep, which garnered eleven Academy Award nomination and seven wins, including two top prizes for Pollack, best film and best director.

In the latter part of his career, Pollack became a prolific producer, partnering with director Anthony Minghella to form Mirage Enterprises, a film production company that backed top movies such as *Sliding Doors* in 1998, *Random Hearts* and *The Talented Mr. Ripley* in 1999, *The Quiet American* in 2002, and *Cold Mountain* in 2003. In 2007 Pollack produced and acted in the dramatic legal thriller *Michael Clayton,* starring George Clooney. *Michael Clayton* earned seven Academy Award nominations, including best picture and best actor for Clooney. Pollack's last screen appearance was in *Made of Honor,* playing the father of leading-man Patrick Dempsey's love-stricken character.

PERIODICALS

Newsweek, June 9, 2008.
Variety, June 9, 2008.
New York Times, May 27, 2008.

POOLE, Aaron

PERSONAL

Career: Actor.

Awards, Honors: Award of Excellence, best actor, Alliance of Canadian Cinema, Television, and Radio Artists (ACTRA), 2008, for *This Beautiful City.*

CREDITS

Film Appearances:
Beagle—flat critter, *Strike!* (also known as *The Hairy Bird, All I Wanna Do, College femminile,* and *Les filles font la loi*), Alliance Atlantis Motion Picture Group, 1998.

Michael Lawson, *Slice,* 2000.

Smitty Jacobson, *The Circle* (also known as *Fraternity* and *La fraternite*), Screen Media Films, 2001.

Z–100 judge, *The Safety of Objects,* IFC Films, 2001.

Sean, *White Light* (short), Bloomsday Pictures, 2005.

Duncan, *The House,* Aquila Media, 2006.

Ryan Bladder, *Killing Zelda Sparks,* Shoreline Entertainment, 2007.

Adoration, Sony Pictures Classics, 2008.

Norm (short), 2008.

Big Dave, *Gangster Exchange,* 2009.

Film Work:
Producer, *This Beautiful City,* Seville Pictures, 2007.

Television Appearances; Miniseries:
Private Nash, *ZOS: Zone of Separation,* TMN, 2008.

Television Appearances; Movies:
White kid number one, *Blind Faith,* Showtime, 1998.

The assistant director, *Bojangles,* Showtime, 2001.

Bobby, *The Defectors* (also known as *Crime School*), 2001.

Chris Morris, *Touch on Top of the World,* Arts and Entertainment, 2006.

Television Appearances; Pilots:
Eightball, "Pilot: Part 2," *Doc,* PAX, 2001.

Television Appearances; Episodic:
(Uncredited) Bystander, "D.P.O.," *The X–Files,* Fox, 1995.

Ritchie Patterson, "Fallen Angel," *Twice in a Lifetime,* CTV and PAX, 2000.

Vic, "Lost Contact," *Relic Hunter* (also known as *Relic Hunter—Die Schatzjagerin* and *Sydney Fox l'aventuriere*), syndicated, 2000.

Peter Morton, "The Breed," *Mutant X,* syndicated, 2003.

Grant Wheeler, "Chemistry," *Strange Days at Blake Holsey High,* The Discovery Channel, 2003.

Grant Wheeler, "Technology," *Strange Days at Blake Holsey High,* The Discovery Channel, 2003.

Allan Gold, *This Is Wonderland,* CBC, 2004.

Jason Gamby, *This Is Wonderland,* CBC, 2006.

Danny Anderson, "Good Doctor," *72 Hours: True Crime,* CBC, 2006.

Also appeared as Grant Wheeler, "Echolocation," *Strange Days at Blake Holsey High,* The Discovery Channel.

RANCIC, Giuliana 1975–
(Giuliana DePandi)

PERSONAL

Born August 17, 1975, in Naples, Italy; daughter of Edoardo DePandi (a master tailor and business owner); married Bill Rancic (a business executive), September 1, 2007. *Education:* University of Maryland, B.A.; American University, M.A.

Addresses: *Agent*—Creative Artists Agency, 2000 Avenue of the Stars, Los Angeles, CA 90067; (voice work and commercials) Alix Gucovsky, Special Artists Agency, 9465 Wilshire Blvd., Suite 470, Beverly Hills, CA 90212. *Manager*—Pam Kohl, 3 Arts Entertainment, 9460 Wilshire Blvd., 7th Floor, Beverly Hills, CA 90212.

Career: Actress, producer, news anchor, and writer. Often credited as Giuliana Rancic after 2007. Worked in the mail room of a talent agency.

CREDITS

Television Appearances; Series:
Host, *E! News Daily* (also known as *E! News Live* and *E! News Live Weekend*), E! Entertainment Television, between 2002 and 2006.

Television Appearances; Specials:
Host, *Nicole Richie: Her Simple Life,* E! Entertainment Television, 2004.

Correspondent, *American Idol: Live from the Red Carpet,* E! Entertainment Television, 2004.

Host, *E!'s Live Countdown to the Golden Globes,* E! Entertainment Television, 2004.

Host, *E!'s Live Countdown to the Academy Awards,* E! Entertainment Television, 2004, 2007.

Host, *Live from the Red Carpet: The ... Emmy Awards,* E! Entertainment Television, 2004, 2006, 2007, 2008.

CMT: The Greatest—Sexiest Southern Men, Country Music Television, 2006.

Host, *Live from the Red Carpet: The ... Screen Actors Guild Awards,* E! Entertainment Television, 2006, 2007, 2008.

Host, *Live from the Red Carpet: The ... Academy Awards,* E! Entertainment Television, 2006, 2007, 2008.

Host, *E!'s Live Countdown to the Grammys,* E! Entertainment Television, 2007.

Backstage: Hollywood Fashion, Style Network, 2007.

Host, *Live from the Red Carpet: The 2007 Golden Globe Awards,* E! Entertainment Television, 2007.

Host, *E!'s Live Countdown to the SAG Awards,* E! Entertainment Television, 2007.

Host, *Live from the Red Carpet: The ... Grammy Awards,* E! Entertainment Television, 2007, 2008.

(In archive footage) *Renee Zellweger: The E! True Hollywood Story,* E! Entertainment Television, 2008.

Television Appearances; Episodic:

Interviewer, "Monster's Ball," *E! Behind the Scenes,* E! Entertainment Television, 2001.

(Uncredited) "The Brad Gluckman Special," *The Jamie Kennedy Experiment,* The WB, 2003.

Pyramid (also known as *The $100,000 Pyramid*), syndicated, 2004.

(Uncredited) *The Young and the Restless* (also known as *Y&R*), CBS, 2004.

"Tournament 6, Game 6," *Celebrity Blackjack,* Game Show Network, 2004.

Journalist, "Claude Wants to Know," *Less than Perfect,* ABC, 2004.

Tammy Townsend, "Rock the Vote," *One on One,* UPN, 2004.

Presenter, "Derailed," *E! Behind the Scenes,* E! Entertainment Television, 2005.

Weekends at the DL, Comedy Central, 2005.

Scarborough Country, MSNBC, 2006.

Jimmy Kimmel Live!, ABC, 2007.

The View, ABC, 2007.

(In archive footage) *The Daily Show,* Comedy Central, 2007.

E! News (also known as *E!*), E! Entertainment Television, 2007.

Entertainment anchor, "Dirty, Slutty Whores," *Dirt,* FX Network, 2008.

The Chelsea Handler Show, E! Entertainment Television, 2008.

Television Appearances; Movies:

Florida reporter, *Spring Break Lawyer* (also known as *I'm a Spring Break Lawyer*), MTV, 2001.

Television Executive Producer:

Nicole Richie: Her Simple Life (special), E! Entertainment Television, 2004.

Celebrity Rap Superstar (series), MTV, 2007.

Film Appearances:

Massage therapist, *Malibu's Most Wanted,* Warner Bros., 2003.

Herself, *Paparazzi,* Twentieth Century–Fox, 2004.

Entertainment reporter, *4: Rise of the Silver Surfer* (also known as *Fantastic Four: Rise of the Silver Surfer*), Twentieth Century–Fox, 2007.

WRITINGS

Print Materials:

Think Like a Guy: How to Get a Guy by Thinking Like One, St. Martin's Griffin, 2006.

Contributor to periodicals, including *Detour.*

RASUK, Victor 1984–

PERSONAL

Born January 15, 1984, in New York, NY.

Addresses: *Agent*—The Gersh Agency, 232 North Canon Dr., Beverly Hills, CA 90210. *Publicist*—WKT Public Relations, 335 North Maple Dr., Suite 351, Beverly Hills, CA 90210.

Career: Actor.

Awards, Honors: Independent Spirit Award nomination, best debut performance, 2004, for *Raising Victor Vargas;* Teen Choice Award nomination, choice movie breakout performance—male, 2005, for *Lords of Dogtown.*

CREDITS

Film Appearances:

(Uncredited) Kid from neighborhood, *Flawless,* Metro–Goldwyn–Mayer, 1999.

Victor Vargas, *Raising Victor Vargas* (also known as *Long Way Home* and *Raising Victor Vargas*), Samuel Goldwyn Films, 2002.

Roc, *Rock Steady,* 2002.

Fritz, *Haven,* Freestyle Releasing, 2004.

Tony Alva, *Lords of Dogtown* (also known as *American Knights* and *Dogtown Boys*), Sony, 2005.

Himself, *The Making of "Lords of Dogtown"* (documentary short), Sony Pictures Home Entertainment, 2005.

Himself, *Dogged on Dogtown* (documentary short), Sony Pictures Home Entertainment, 2005.

Frank Cortez, *I'm Reed Fish,* Screen Media Films, 2006.

Bo Douglas, *Bonneville,* SenArt Films, 2006.

Emil (short), 2006.

Fritz, *Haven,* Yari Film Group, 2006.

Simon Colon, *Adrift in Manhattan,* Screen Media Films, 2007.

Patrick Chibas, *Spinning Into Butter,* Screen Media Films, 2007.

Javi, *Feel the Noise,* Sony, 2007.
Private Rico Rodriguez, *Stop–Loss,* Paramount, 2008.
Rogelio Acevedo, *Che: Part One* (also known as *Che—l'ere partie—L'Argentin* and *Che, el Argentino*), IFC Films, 2008.
Manny, *Life Is Hot in Cracktown,* 2008.
Greg, *The War Boys,* 2009.

Television Appearances; Series:
Dr. Ryan Sanchez, *ER,* NBC, 2008.
Cam, *How to Make It in America,* HBO, 2008.

Television Appearances; Movies:
Victor, *Five Feet High and Rising,* Sundance Channel, 2000.

Television Appearances; Pilots:
Cam, *How to Make It in America,* HBO, 2008.

Television Appearances; Specials:
The 2004 IFP/West Independent Spirit Awards, Independent Film Channel and Bravo, 2004.

Television Appearances; Episodic:
Leon Ardilles, "Choice," *Law & Order: Special Victims Unit* (also known as *Law & Order: SVU* and *Special Victims Unit*), NBC, 2003.
Luis Ramirez, "Boys Will Be Boys," *Law & Order: Trial by Jury,* NBC, 2005.

OTHER SOURCES

Periodicals:
Interview, April, 2003, p. 62.

RATLIFF, Elden Ryan
    See HENSON, Elden

RAYMONT, Daniel 1969–

PERSONAL

Born July 28, 1969, in New York, NY. *Education:* Colby College, B.A., 1991.

Addresses: *Agent*—Don Buchwald and Associates, 10 East 44th St., New York, NY 10017; (commercials) Paradigm, 360 Park Ave. S., 16th Floor, New York, NY 10010. *Manager*—Lillian LaSalle, Sweet 180, 141 West 28th St., Suite 300, New York, NY 10001.

Career: Actor. Appeared in numerous commercials, including Visa check card, Heineken beer, Burger King restaurants, Campbell's soup, United Parcel Service, and other products and services.

Member: American Federation of Television and Radio Artists, Screen Actors Guild.

CREDITS

Film Appearances:
Soldier, *Alien: Resurrection* (also known as *Alien 4*), Twentieth Century–Fox, 1997.
Donnie, *Falling Sky,* DEJ Productions, 1998.
Clown, *Special* (short film), Chanticleer Films, 2003.
Brian, *Sticky Fingers* (short film), 2003.
British man, *View from the Top,* Miramax, 2003.
Makeup artist, *Freaky Friday,* Buena Vista, 2003.
Bob, *The Entrepreneurs* (also known as *Just One Look* and *The $cheme*), Artisan Entertainment, 2003.
Warmup comedian, *Carolina* (also known as *Carolina—Auf der suche nach Mr. Perfect*), Miramax, 2004.
Warren, *Recycling Flo* (short film), Chiaroscuro Productions, 2004.
Buddha, *Roadie* (short film), Seventy–One Productions, 2004.
Gee, *The F Word,* DitlevFilms, 2005.
Commercial guy, *Watching the Detectives,* Peace Arch, 2007.
Ray Wyatt, *BuzzKill,* Buzz Kill, 2008.
Markus, *The Good Heart,* Zik Zak Kvikmyndir, 2008.
Colorist, *Bride Wars,* Fox 2000, 2009.
Dr. Kenneth Noonan, *Harvest,* Ibid Filmworks, 2009.

Appeared as Steve, *College Road Trip,* Walt Disney; in title role, *My Name Is Nigel Cook,* Working Pictures; and as Wyndell Stames, *Twist of Fate,* Milagro Films.

Television Appearances; Series:
Miles Bergamont III, a recurring role, *Home James,* VH1, between 2005 and 2007.
Wing and director, *The Naked Brothers Band,* Nickelodeon, 2007–2008.

Television Appearances; Episodic:
Cousin Guido, "All's Well that Ends Well," *Crossroads Cafe,* PBS, 1996.
Doorman, "The Aretha Theory," *Felicity,* The WB, 2000.
Motel receptionist, "Hello Hollywood," *L.A. 7* (also known as *S Club 7 in L.A.*), Fox Family Channel, 2000.

Motel receptionist, "Goodbye Hollywood," *L.A. 7* (also known as *S Club 7 in L.A.*), Fox Family Channel, 2000.

David, *The Young and the Restless* (also known as *Y&R*), CBS, 2001.

Javier, "House Arrest," *The Orlando Jones Show,* FX Network, 2003.

David Sellers, "All that Glitters," *Dragnet* (also known as *L.A. Dragnet*), ABC, 2003.

Calvin, "Operation: Deliver the Case," *The Knights of Prosperity,* ABC, 2007.

Schmulie/Hassid, *Head Case,* Starz!, 2007.

Ken, *Lipstick Jungle,* NBC, 2008.

Television Appearances; Other:
Officer, *The Pentagon Wars* (movie), HBO, 1998.
Max Filshie, *New Amsterdam* (pilot), Fox, 2008.

Appeared as Lazlo in *The Big Picture Show,* and as a librarian in *Angeles.*

Stage Appearances:
Appeared in the solo show *The Store,* Peoples Improv Theatre, New York City; appeared in title role, *Coriolanus,* Gascon Theatre, Los Angeles, and *Dreamcatcher,* Boston Center for the Arts, Boston, MA; as magistrate, *Lysistrata,* Wilshire Ebell Theatre, Los Angeles; and as Andy, *Sex,* Zephyr Theatre, Los Angeles; also performed in the sketch comedies *Finger Chicken Bush,* Second City, Los Angeles, *Hot Tamales Live,* Comedy Store, Los Angeles, *Let Freedom Bling Bling,* Second City, Los Angeles, and *Stovetop Happy,* Second City.

RECORDINGS

Videos:
Hairdresser, *The Extreme Adventures of Super Dave,* Metro–Goldwyn–Mayer, 2000.
(English version) Voice of Ikkyu, *Read or Die* (animated), Manga Video, 2001.

REID, Noah 1987–
(Noah Reed)

PERSONAL

Born May 1987, in Toronto, Ontario, Canada.

Career: Actor and voice artist.

CREDITS

Film Appearances:
Boy, *In Love and War,* New Line Cinema, 1996.

Voice of Tommy, *Pippi Longstocking* (animated), Lyeegacy Releasing, 1997.

Voice of Franklin Turtle, *Franklin and the Green Knight: The Movie* (animated), 2000.

Voice of Franklin Turtle, *Franklin's Magic Christmas* (animated), 2001.

Voice of Screwy, *Rolie Polie Olie: The Great Defender of Fun* (animated; also known as *William Joyce's "Rolie Polie Olie: The Great Defender of Fun"*), Walt Disney Home Video, 2002.

Television Appearances; Series:
Voice of Franklin Turtle, *Franklin* (animated), CBS, 1997–2004.

(As Noah Reed) Voice of Tommy, *Pippi Longstocking* (animated), HBO, 1998.

Voice of Scrul Droptail, *Mattimeo: A Tale of Redwall* (also known as *Brian Jacques' "Mattimeo: A Tale of Redwall*), Teletoon and PBS, 2000.

Keyla, *Martin the Warrior: A Tale of Redwall* (animated), Teletoon and PBS, 2001.

Elmore "Tater" Brochet, *The Strange Legacy of Cameron Cruz,* Nickelodeon, 2002.

Marshall Wheeler, *Strange Days at Blake Hosley High* (also known as *Black Hole High*), The Discovery Channel, 2002–2006.

Voice of Gunther Breech, *Jane and the Dragon* (animated), YTV, 2006.

Television Appearances; Movies:
Darrell Fox, *Terry,* CTV, 2005.

Television Appearances; Episodic:
Kyle, "Treason," *La Femme Nikita* (also known as *Nikita*), USA Network, 1997.

Young Perseus, "Perseus: The Search for Medusa," *Mythic Warriors: Guardians of the Legend,* CBS, 1998.

Mark, "Things That Go Bump in the Night," *In a Heartbeat,* The Disney Channel, 2000.

Mark, "Cinderella Syndrome," *In a Heartbeat,* The Disney Channel, 2000.

Mark, "The Boy's No Good," *In a Heartbeat,* The Disney Channel, 2000.

Ritchie Stein, "Who Do You Know?," *Soul Food,* Showtime, 2001.

Todd, "As the Whirly Turns," *Naturally, Sadie* (also known as *The Complete Freaks of Nature*), The Disney Channel, 2007.

RICHMOND, Tequan 1992–

PERSONAL

Given name is pronounced "Tuh–kwon;" born October 30, 1992, in Burlington, NC; son of Temple Poteat (an actress). *Avocational Interests:* Sports, music, amusement parks.

Addresses: *Agent*—Nancy Chaidez, Nancy Chaidez and Associates, 1555 Vine St., Suite 223, Hollywood, CA 90028.

Career: Actor. Toon Disney Channel, host of programs for young people. Appeared in commercials for Spalding basketballs, Verizon Wireless, Nintendo DS game system, Brand Jordan, and other products, as well as in print advertisements.

CREDITS

Television Appearances; Series:
Drew Rock, *Everybody Hates Chris,* UPN, 2005–2006, then CW Network, 2006–2008.

Television Appearances; Pilots:
Andre Lee, *The Law and Mr. Lee,* CBS, 2003.
Drew Rock, *Everybody Hates Chris,* UPN, 2005.

Television Appearances; Episodic:
Boy, "Chaos Theory," *ER,* NBC, 2002.
Tramelle Willis–Tombs, "Lucky Strike," *CSI: Crime Scene Investigation* (also known as *C.S.I.,* *CSI: Las Vegas,* and *Les experts*), CBS, 2003.
Tyson, *Mad TV,* Fox, 2003.
R. J. Holden in 1999, "The Plan," *Cold Case,* CBS, 2004.
Young "Game", "The Game Featuring 50 Cent: Hate It or Love It," *Access Granted,* Black Entertainment Television, 2005.
Lionel, "Bang," *The Shield,* FX Network, 2005.
Lionel, "A Thousand Deaths," *The Shield,* FX Network, 2005.
Shay Williams, "Clinical Risk," *Strong Medicine,* Lifetime, 2005.
Levi Bishop, "Checkmate," *Numb3rs* (also known as *Num3ers*), CBS, 2008.

Television Appearances; Awards Presentations:
The 31st Annual People's Choice Awards, CBS, 2005.
The … NAACP Image Awards, Fox, 2005, 2006, 2007, 2008.
The 7th Annual Family Television Awards, The WB, 2005.
The 20th Annual Soul Train Music Awards, syndicated, 2006.

Film Appearances:
Ray Charles, Jr. at age nine or ten, *Ray,* Universal, 2004.
Basketball principal player, *The Celestine Prophecy,* RAM Entertainment, 2006.

RECORDINGS

Videos:
Presenter, *15th Annual Inner City Destiny Awards,* Tri Destined Studios, 2006.

Appeared in the music video "Hate It or Love It" by 50 Cent.

OTHER SOURCES

Periodicals:
Jet, October 10, 2005, pp. 56, 60–64.
Word Up, June, 2006, p. 71.

RILEY, Jack 1935–
(Jack B. Riley)

PERSONAL

Original name, John Riley; born December 30, 1935, in Cleveland, OH; son of John A. and Agnes C. (maiden name, Corrigan) Riley; married Ginger Lawrence, January 3, 1970; children: Jamie, Brian. *Education:* John Carroll University, B.S., English, 1961.

Addresses: *Agent*—House of Representatives, 1434 6th St., Suite 1, Santa Monica, CA 90401; Cunningham, Escott, Slevin and Doherty, 10635 Santa Monica Blvd., #130, Los Angeles, CA 90025.

Career: Actor and writer. Sherwood Oaks College, instructor of comedy acting; "Rolling Along of 1960," Department of the Army Traveling Show, member, 1960; Blore and Richman, Los Angeles, CA, copywriter, 1966–84; voice–over actor for television and radio commercials, including CompUSA computer stores, Brodia.com website, Mitsubishi, Country Crock food products, and Three–Day Blinds home furnishings. *Military service:* U.S. Army, 1958–61.

Member: Screen Actors Guild, Actors' Equity Association, Writers Guild of America, Academy of Motion Picture Arts and Sciences, American Federation of Television and Radio Artists, Academy of Television Arts and Sciences.

CREDITS

Film Appearances:
(Uncredited) Waiter, *Days of Wine and Roses,* Warner Bros., 1962.
Doctor, *Catch–22,* Paramount, 1970.

The Todd Killings (also known as *A Dangerous Friend* and *Skipper*), National General, 1971.

Riley Quinn, *McCabe and Mrs. Miller,* Warner Bros., 1971.

Piano player, *The Long Goodbye,* United Artists, 1973.

Second bartender, *California Split* (also known as *Jackpot!*), Columbia, 1974.

Jackson, *Bank Shot,* United Artists, 1974.

Executive, *Silent Movie,* United Artists, 1976.

Projectionist, *The World's Greatest Lover,* Twentieth Century–Fox, 1977.

The desk clerk, *High Anxiety,* Twentieth Century–Fox, 1977.

Agriculture official, *Attack of the Killer Tomatoes!,* Four Square, 1978.

Messenger, *Butch and Sundance—The Early Years,* Twentieth Century–Fox, 1979.

Stoned soldier, *History of the World, Part I* (also known as *Mel Brooks' "History of the World: Part 1"*), Twentieth Century–Fox, 1981.

Bob Barnes, *Frances,* Universal, 1982.

Dobish, *To Be or Not to Be,* Twentieth Century–Fox, 1983.

Agent Ormond, *Finders Keepers,* Warner Bros., 1984.

Dr. Ziegler, *Night Patrol,* New World, 1984.

Television journalist, *Spaceballs* (also known as *Space Balls*), Metro–Goldwyn–Mayer/United Artists, 1987.

Homeowner, *Gleaming the Cube* (also known as *A Brother's Justice* and *Skate or Die*), Twentieth Century–Fox, 1988.

Herb (the auditor), *Rented Lips,* Cineworld, 1988.

Wado, *C.H.U.D. II: Bud the C.H.U.D,* Vestron, 1989.

Coroner, *Payback* (also known as *Revenge*), 1990.

Himself, *The Player,* Fine Line, 1992.

Bandleader, *A Dangerous Woman,* Gramercy, 1993.

Alaric, *Theodore Rex* (also known as *T. Rex*), New Line Cinema, 1995.

Lawyer of Amber Waves ex–husband, *Boogie Nights,* New Line Cinema, 1997.

Mr. Leach, *Venus Envy,* 1997.

Voice of Stu Pickles, *A Rugrats Vacation* (animated), Paramount, 1997.

Voice of Stu Pickles, *The Rugrats Movie* (animated), Paramount, 1998.

Condom boss, *Chairman of the Board,* Trimark Pictures, 1998.

Voice of Stu Pickles, *Rugrats in Paris: The Movie* (animated; also known as *Rugrats in Paris–Der Film* and *Rugrats in Paris: The Movie–Rugrats II*), Paramount, 2000.

Voice of Golfer number one, *Recess: School's Out* (animated), Buena Vista, 2001.

Voice of Stu Pickles, *Rugrats Go Wild* (animated), Paramount, 2003.

Gym instructor, *Burl's* (short), 2003.

James Brewster, *Room 6,* Anchor Bay Entertainment, 2006.

Television Appearances; Series:

Cohost, *Baxter and Riley,* WERE (Cleveland, OH), 1961–65.

Wally Frick, *Occasional Wife,* NBC, 1966–67.

Regular, *Rowan & Martin's Laugh–In,* 1968–70.

Elliott Carlin, *The Bob Newhart Show,* CBS, 1972–78.

Keep on Truckin', ABC, 1975.

Ed Sweetzer, *Joe and Valerie,* NBC, 1978–79.

The Tim Conway Show, CBS, 1980.

Mr. Worthington, *All Night Radio,* 1982.

Leon Buchanan, *Roxie,* CBS, 1987.

Voice of Stu Pickles, *Rugrats* (animated), Nickelodeon, 1991–2002.

Various characters, *The Tonight Show with Jay Leno,* NBC, 1992–99.

Chappy, *Son of the Beach,* FX Channel, 2000–2002.

Voice of Stu Pickles, *All Grown Up* (animated; also known as *Rugrats All Grown Up*), Nickelodeon, 2003.

Television Appearances; Miniseries:

Herb Gallup, *The Rules of Marriage,* CBS, 1982.

Television Appearances; Movies:

Mitzi, 1968.

Director, *Columbo: Candidate for Crime,* 1973.

Owen, *Marriage Is Alive and Well,* NBC, 1980.

Alex, *Love in the Present Tense,* 1982.

Ralph, *When Your Lover Leaves,* NBC, 1983.

Marvin, *Lots of Luck,* The Disney Channel, 1985.

Freeman, *Brothers–in–Law,* ABC, 1985.

Scientist, *The History of White People in America* (also known as *The History of White People in America; Volume I*), HBO, 1985.

Scientist, *The History of White People in America: Volume II,* HBO, 1986.

Martin Mull in Portrait of a White Marriage (also known as *Portrait of a White Marriage* and *Scenes from a White Marriage*), Cinemax, 1988.

Alex, *McBride: The Doctor Is Out ... Really Out,* Hallmark Channel, 2005.

Elder, *Avenging Angel,* Hallmark Channel, 2007.

Television Appearances; Specials:

Wolf Man/Warren the Werewolf, *The Halloween That Almost Wasn't* (also known as *The Night Dracula Saved the World*), ABC, 1979.

Mr. White, "First the Egg," *ABC Afterschool Specials,* ABC, 1985.

This Is Your Life, NBC, 1987.

"Martin Mull Live! From North Ridgeville," *HBO Comedy Hour,* HBO, 1987.

Himself and Elliott Carlin, *The Bob Newhart 19th Anniversary Special* (also known as *The Bob Newhart 20th 19th Anniversary Special*), CBS, 1991.

Voice of Stu Pickles, *A Rugrats Passover* (animated), Nickelodeon, 1995.

Voice of Stu, *A Rugrats Chanukkah* (animated), Nickelodeon, 1996.

Voice of Stuart "Stu" Pickles, *The Rugrats: All Growed Up* (animated), Nickelodeon, 2001.

Announcer, *100 Years of Hope and Humor,* NBC, 2003.

TV Land Landmarks: Breaking the Mold, TV Land, 2004.

The 3rd Annual TV Land Awards (also known as *TV Land Awards: A Celebration of Classic TV*), TV Land, 2005.

Presenter, *The 12th Annual Screen Actors Guild Awards,* TNT, 2006.

Television Appearances; Pilots:

Murphy, the friend, *Bumpers,* NBC, 1977.

Evan Murray, Lil's neighbor, *Mother and Me, M.D.,* NBC, 1979.

Mr. Worthington, *All Night Radio,* HBO, 1982.

Tom Mimelman, *Washingtoon,* Showtime, 1985.

Television Appearances; Episodic:

Larry, "Gomer, the Beautiful Dreamer," *Gomer Pyle, U.S.M.C.,* 1967.

Larry, "The Great Talent Hunt," *Gomer Pyle, U.S.M.C.,* 1967.

(As Jack B. Riley) Leo, "Ah Love, Could You and I Conspire?," *The Flying Nun,* 1967.

Frank, "Abdullah," *I Dream of Jeannie,* NBC, 1968.

Captain, "Operation Hannibal," *Hogan's Heroes,* 1969.

Guard, "At Last–Schultz Knows Something," *Hogan's Heroes,* 1969.

S.S. Man, "The Big Record, *Hogan's Heroes,* 1970.

Mr. Jeffrey, "Whatever Happened to Happy Endings?," *Bracken's World,* 1970.

Danny, "Love and the Good Samaritan," *Love, American Style,* 1970.

Gunslinger, "The Magic Act," *The Red Skelton Show* (also known as *The Red Skelton Hour*), 1970.

Gunslinger, "Freddie's Desperate Hour," *The Red Skelton Show* (also known as *The Red Skelton Hour*), 1970.

Gunslinger, "The Private Detective," *The Red Skelton Show* (also known as *The Red Skelton Hour*), 1970.

Corporal Wrzesinkski, "See Here, Private Partridge," *The Partridge Family,* 1970.

Eldon Colfax, "Didn't You Used to Be ... Wait ... Don't Tell Me," *The Mary Tyler Moore Show* (also known as *Mary Tyler Moore*), CBS, 1971.

Captain Kaplan, "Chief Surgeon Who?" *M*A*S*H,* CBS, 1972.

Barry Barlow, "Rhoda Morgenstern: Minneapolis to New York," *The Mary Tyler Moore Show* (also known as *Mary Tyler Moore*), CBS, 1972.

Mel, "Breaking Up Is Hard to Do," *Getting Together,* 1972.

Programmer, "Catch Me If You Can," *Cannon,* 1973.

Royal, "The Gunman," *Kung Fu,* 1974.

Officer O'Reilly, "The Deadly Dares," *Happy Days,* ABC, 1974.

Joe, "Anatomy of Two Rapes," *Police Woman,* 1974.

Braddock, "Can I Save My Children?," *The ABC Afternoon Playbreak* (also known as *ABC Matinee Today*), ABC, 1974.

Eddie Stern, "Silent Kill," *Harry O,* 1975.

Barney Hamilton, "The Madonna Legacy, *Harry O,* 1975.

Frederick Clooney, "Fear of Flying," *Barney Miller* (also known as *The Life and Times of Captain Barney Miller*), ABC, 1976.

Richard Atkins, "A Call to Arms," *Alice,* 1976.

Tattletales, 1976.

Adrian Lyman, "There's One in Every Port," *The Rockford Files* (also known as *Jim Rockford, Private Investigator*), 1977.

Miles Monroe, "Goodbye Dolly," *Diff'rent Strokes,* NBC, 1978.

Robert Lovell, "The Counterfeiter," *Barney Miller,* 1979.

Charles Sutton, "The New Landlord," *Diff'rent Strokes,* NBC, 1979.

Mr. Crocker, "The Girls School," *Diff'rent Strokes,* NBC, 1979.

Harold J. Crocker, *The Facts of Life,* NBC, 1979.

Joe Roth, "Bradfordgate," *Eight Is Enough,* 1980.

Bank robber, "Who's Afraid of the Big Bad Wolf?" *Too Close for Comfort* (also known as *The Ted Knight Show*), 1980.

Norman Culp, "'Tis the Season to Be Murdered," *Hart to Hart,* ABC, 1980.

The Love Boat, ABC, 1980.

"Night in the Harem/Druids," *Fantasy Island,* ABC, 1981.

Dr. Robert P Medlow, "Ashes to Ashes and None Too Soon," *Simon & Simon,* 1982.

Earl, "Have Gun, Will Unravel," *Family Ties,* 1982.

Mr. Gonagin, "Travel Agent," *One Day at a Time,* CBS, 1983.

Mr. Gonagin, "The Nearness of You," *One Day at a Time,* CBS, 1984.

Sexton/Deacon, "The Boy Who Left Home to Find Out About the Shivers," *Faerie Tale Theatre* (also known as *Shelley Duvall's "Faerie Tale Theatre"*), 1984.

Agent, "Only the Good Die Young/The Light of Another Day/Honey Beats the Odds," *The Love Boat,* ABC, 1984.

Emil Dutton, "Wonder Drugs," *Night Court,* NBC, 1984.

Deep Throat, "The Candidates," *Domestic Life,* 1984.

Warren Wilson, "The Blizzard," *Night Court,* NBC, 1984.

Phil, "Gone with the Wind," *Down to Earth,* 1984.

Pete, "Blue Collar Drummond," *Diff'rent Strokes,* NBC, 1985.

Elliot Carlin, "Close Encounters," *St. Elsewhere,* NBC, 1985.

Mr. Snodgrass, "All the Principal's Men," *Silver Spoons,* 1985.

Dr. Flick, "Dan's Operation: Parts 1 & 2," *Night Court,* NBC, 1986.

Mr. Carlin, "Going out of My Head Over You," *ALF,* 1987.

Professor Kleeman, "Grading Papers," *Charles in Charge,* 1988.

Director, "Brandon's Commercial," *Punky Brewster,* 1988.

Patient, "I Married Dick," *Newhart,* 1988.

Mr. Ledbetter, "The Case of the Deceptive Data," *Mathnet,* 1988.

Herb, "Confidence Game," *Throb,* 1988.

Mr. Ledbetter, *Square One TV,* 1988.

Ray Ragalito, "Th–Th–Th–That's All Folks," *A Fine Romance* (also known as *Ticket to Ride*), 1989.

"Death Do Us Part," *Hard Time on Planet Earth,* 1989.

Beepo, "Clip Show: Parts 1 & 2," *Night Court,* NBC, 1989.

Dave, "It's My Art, and I'll Die If I Want To," *My Two Dads,* 1990.

Voice of Tyrone, "Count Lasanga/U.S. Acres: Mystery Guest/Rodent Rampage," *Garfield and Friends,* 1990.

Jim Wimberly, "To Sleep, No More," *Night Court,* NBC, 1991.

Babes, Fox, 1991.

Evening Shade, CBS, 1992.

Mr. Graves, "How to Succeed in Business without Really Trying," *Hangin' with Mr. Cooper,* ABC, 1992.

Jack Cort, *Civil Wars,* ABC, 1992.

Wayne, "The Way the Ball Bounces," *Family Matters,* NBC, 1993.

Bob, *The Boys Are Back,* CBS, 1994.

Wendell, "Business Sucks: Part 1," *Married ... with Children* (also known as *Married with Children*), Fox, 1994.

Guy, "You Can't Always Get What You Want," *Dave's World,* CBS, 1994.

Bob, "Searching for Sarah Hansen," *The Boys Are Back,* CBS, 1994.

Howie, "The Hit Parade," *Hudson Street,* ABC, 1995.

(Uncredited) Airline passenger, "The One Where Rachel Finds Out," *Friends,* NBC, 1995.

Oliver O. Olson, "Just Short of the Goal," *Coach,* ABC, 1996.

Mr. Jones, "What the Zoning Inspector Saw," *The Drew Carey Show,* ABC, 1996.

Rider, "The Muffin Tops," *Seinfeld,* NBC, 1997.

Himself, "The Cameo Episode," *George and Leo,* CBS, 1997.

"Del Nino," *Baywatch,* 1997.

Mr. O'Reilly, "Driving," *The Secret World of Alex Mack* (also known as *Alex Mack*), Nickelodeon, 1997.

Leo, "Sandcastles," *Touched by an Angel,* CBS, 1997.

Puff Puff the bunny, "A New Leaf: Parts 1 & 2," *Mike Hammer, Private Eye,* CBS, 1998.

Chaplain, *Working,* NBC, 1998.

Harry Tatham, "Timbo," *Oh Grow Up,* ABC, 1999.

"Tim Conway: Just Clowning Around," *Biography,* Arts and Entertainment, 1999.

"Bob Newhart: The Last Sane Man" *Biography,* Arts and Entertainment, 2001.

Piney, "Lie, Cheat & Deal," *Lucky,* FX Channel, 2003.

Old Man Shinsky, "Rip This Joint," *That '70s Show,* Fox, 2004.

Mr. Shipley, "High School Reunion," *Yes, Dear,* CBS, 2005.

Also appeared as guest in *Body Language;* "The Jacket," *Too Something* (also known as *New York Daze*); as voice of Feldman Battery 5 and crowd member 5, "Hole–in–One," *Rugrats* (animated), Nickelodeon.

Stage Appearances:
Small Craft Warnings, West coast production, 1975.
12 Angry Men, Los Angeles, 1985.
Zeitgeist, 1990.
House of Blue Leaves, Cleveland Playhouse, Cleveland, OH, 1993.
The Odd Couple, Beck Center, Cleveland, OH, 1999.

Major Tours:
House of Blue Leaves, Eastern European cities, 1993.

RECORDINGS

Video Games:
Voice of Stu Pickles, *Rugrats Go Wild!,* 2003.

WRITINGS

Television Specials:
The Many Sides of Don Rickles, 1970.

Television Episodes:
The Mort Sahl Show, 1967.
The Don Rickles Show, ABC, 1968.
The Tim Conway Show, CBS, 1980.

RILEY, Michael

PERSONAL

Born in London, Ontario, Canada. *Education:* Graduated from the National Theatre School (Montreal, Quebec, Canada), 1984.

Addresses: *Agent*—Gary Goddard Agency, 10 Saint Mary St., Suite 305, Toronto, Ontario M4Y 1P9 Canada; Global Artists Agency, 6235 Hollywood Blvd., Suite

508, Los Angeles, CA 90028. *Manager*—Thruline Entertainment, 9250 Wilshire Blvd., Suite 100, Beverly Hills, CA 90212.

Career: Actor.

Awards, Honors: Genie Award nomination, best performance by an actor in a supporting role, Academy of Canadian Cinema and Television, 1991, for *Diplomatic Immunity;* Gemini Award nomination, best performance by an actor in a leading role in a dramatic program or miniseries, Academy of Canadian Cinema and Television, 1993, for *To Catch a Killer;* Gemini Award, best performance by an actor in a leading role in a dramatic program or miniseries, 1996, for *Adrienne Clarkson Presents: The Lust of His Eyes;* Gemini Award nomination, best performance by an actor in a guest role—dramatic series, 1996, for "Hawk and a Handsaw," *Due South;* Gemini Award, best actor in a dramatic program or miniseries, 1996, for *Helsinki Roccamatios;* Gemini Award nomination, best performance by an actor in a featured supporting role in a dramatic program or miniseries, 1999, for *Win, Again!;* Genie Award nomination, best performance by an actor in a supporting role, 1999, for *Pale Saints;* Gemini Awards, best performance by an actor in a continuing leading dramatic role, 1999, 2000, both for *Power Play;* Gemini Award nomination, best performance by an actor in a guest role in a dramatic series, 2002, for *The Associates;* Gemini Award, best performance by an actor in a leading role in a dramatic program or miniseries, 2003, for *The Interrogation of Michael Crowe;* Gemini Award nomination, best performance by an actor in a continuing leading dramatic role, 2004, Gemini Award, best performance by an actor in a continuing leading dramatic role, 2005, both for *This Is Wonderland;* four Dora Mavor Moore Award nominations, best actor, Toronto Alliance for the Performing Arts.

CREDITS

Film Appearances:
Horton, *No Man's Land,* Orion, 1987.
Tucker: The Man and His Dream, 1988.
Renzo Parachi, *Perfectly Normal,* Four Seasons Entertainment, 1990.
Les Overtone, *Diplomatic Immunity,* 1991.
Clive Walton, *The Making of ... And God Spoke* (also known as *... And God Spoke*), Live Entertainment, 1993.
Matthew Linden, *Mustard Bath* (also known as *Bain de moutarde*), 1993.
Alex, *Because Why* (also known as *Pourquoi pas*), 1993.
Campbell, *French Kiss* (also known as *Paris Match*), Twentieth Century–Fox, 1995.
Rick Neufeld, *Heck's Way Home,* Hallmark Home Entertainment, 1996.

Roy Timmons, *The Prince,* 1996.
Card player number three, *Hard Men,* Twentieth Century–Fox, 1997.
British officer, *Amistad,* DreamWorks Distribution, 1997.
Dody, *Pale Saints,* Norstar Entertainment, 1997.
Chip, *The Grace of God,* 1997.
Father Ed, *Heart of the Sun,* 1998.
Derek, *Mile Zero,* Wellspring Media, 2001.
Sam, *Punch,* THINKFilm, 2002.
Carl, *Black Swan* (also known as *Murder in Hopeville*), Lions Gate Films, 2002.
The man, *Sugar,* TLA Releasing, 2004.
Jax, *Cube Zero,* Lions Gate Films, 2004.
Carl, *Normal,* Porchlight Home Entertainment, 2007.
Dr. Edgar O. Laird, *What You're Ready For* (short), 2007.

Film Work:
Associate producer, *Black Swan* (also known as *Murder in Hopeville*), Lions Gate Films, 2002.

Television Appearances; Series:
Brett Parker, *Power Play,* CTV and UPN, 1998–2000.
Title role, *Ace Lightening,* 2002.
Elliot Sacks, *This Is Wonderland,* 2004–2006.
Being Erica, 2008.

Television Appearances; Miniseries:
Chris Blaine, *Chasing Rainbows,* CBC, 1988.
Lieutenant Joseph "Joe/Polock" Kozenczak, *To Catch a Killer,* CTV, 1992.
Hamilton K. Fisker, *The Way We Live Now,* BBC, 2001, PBS, 2002.
Harry Stein, *St. Urbain's Horseman,* 2007.
Rick Erwin, *Race to Mars* (also known as *A la conquete de Mars*), 2007.

Television Appearances; Movies:
Rick Morrell, *Many Happy Returns,* CBS, 1986.
The Private Capital, CBC, 1989.
Paul Devereaux, *Lifeline to Victory,* 1993.
Boss, *Race to Freedom: The Underground Railroad,* CTV, 1994.
Dr. Nick Galler, *The Possession of Michael D.* (also known as *Legacy of Evil*), Fox, 1995.
Rick Neufeld, *Heck's Way Home* (also known as *Un drole de cabot*), Showtime, 1996.
Adam Shuster, *Crimes of Passion: Voice from the Grave* (also known as *From the Files of "Unsolved Mysteries": Voice from the Grave, Unsolved Mysteries: Voices from the Grave,* and *Voice from the Grave*), NBC, 1996.
Russell Cameron, *Butterbox Babies* (also known as *Les nourrissons de la misere*), Arts and Entertainment, 1996.

Ray, *Every 9 Seconds* (also known as *A Call for Help*), NBC, 1997.
Win, Again!, 1999.
Dennis Winslow, *Dogmatic,* ABC, 1999.
Greg, *Ice* (also known as *Eis–wenn die welt erfriert*), ABC, 2000.
Jack Turpin, *The Last Debate,* Showtime, 2000.
Rod Dunbar, *100 Days in the Jungle,* 2002.
Stephen Crowe, *The Interrogation of Michael Crowe* (also known as *L'interrogatoire de Michael Crowe* and *Un coupable a tout prix*), Court TV, 2002.
Rod Dunbar, *100 Days in the Jungle,* 2002.
Douglas Conte, Kennedy biographer, *America's Prince: The John F. Kennedy Jr. Story,* TBS, 2003.
Peter, *Homeless to Harvard: The Liz Murray Story,* Lifetime, 2003.
Ty Kellington, *The Perfect Husband* (also known as *Her Perfect Spouse* and *Le mari ideal*), 2004.
Kurt, *Saving Emily,* Lifetime, 2004.
Richard "Rick" Lieberman, *Supervolcano* (also known as *Supervulkan*), BBC and The Discovery Channel, 2005.
Mike Bartholomy, *The Tenth Circle,* Lifetime, 2008.

Television Appearances; Specials:
Johann Strauss Jr., *Strauss: The King of 3/4 Time,* HBO, 1995.
The 1996 Gemini Awards, 1996.

Television Appearances; Pilots:
Gary, *Fast Food,* ABC, 1985.

Television Appearances; Episodic:
Gary, "Fast Food," *Comedy Factory,* 1985.
Medical student, "Kayo on Call," *Kay O'Brien,* CBS, 1986.
Adam Ruskin, "Fit Punishment," *Street Legal,* 1993.
Adam Ruskin, "What's Love Got to Do With It," *Street Legal,* 1993.
Walter, "Hawk and a Handsaw," *Due South* (also known as *Direction: Sud*), CBC, 1995.
Michael, "Chelsea Gets an Opinion," *Style and Substance,* CBS, 1998.
Gerard, "Better Luck Next Time," *The Outer Limits* (also known as *The New Outer Limits*), Showtime and Sci–Fi Channel, 1999.
Jon Tarkman, "Decompression," *The Outer Limits* (also known as *The New Outer Limits*), Showtime and Sci–Fi Channel, 2000.
Gary Singer, "Mea Culpa," *The Associates,* 2002.
Steven McCormick, "Lady Heather's Box," *CSI: Crime Scene Investigation* (also known as *CSI: Las Vegas, C.S.I.,* and *Les Experts*), CBS, 2003.
Steven Dawson, "Off the Grid," *1–800–MISSING* (also known as *Missing* and *Porte disparu*), Lifetime, 2005.
Doctor Burrit Greyson, "Bad Medicine," *Murdoch Mysteries,* 2008.

Also appeared as Robert Fraser, "Sangraal," *Veritas: The Quest.*

Stage Appearances:
You Can't Take It with You, 1988.

ROBINSON, Jane

PERSONAL

Daughter of Cliff (a rugby coach) and Mary Evans; married; children: three. *Education:* Attended Adelphi House and Manchester Regional School of Art.

Addresses: *Contact*—Costume Designers Guild, 13949 Ventura Blvd., Suite 309, Sherman Oaks, CA 91423.

Career: Costume designer and producer. Previously worked in fashion.

Member: Costume Designers Guild, Association of Cinematography, Television, and Allied Technicians.

Awards, Honors: Television Award (with Jill Silverside), best design, British Academy of Film and Television Arts, 1975, for *Jennie: Lady Randolph Churchill;* Emmy Award (with Silverside), best costume design for a single episode of a drama, comedy, or limited series, 1976, for "Recovery," *Jennie: Lady Randolph Churchill;* Emmy Award nomination, best costume design for a single episode of a regular or limited series, 1982, for "Home and Abroad," *Brideshead Revisited;* Television Award, best costume designer, British Academy of Film and Television Arts, 1982, for *Brideshead Revisited;* Emmy Award, best costume design for a single episode of a miniseries or a special, 1987, for Part 1 of *Anastasia: The Mystery of Anna;* Academy Award nomination, best costume design, 1988, and *Evening Standard* Award, both for *A Handful of Dust;* Emmy Award, best costume design for a single episode of a miniseries or a special, 1988, for Part 2 of *Poor Little Rich Girl: The Barbara Hutton Story;* Emmy Award nomination, best costume design for a miniseries or special, 1993, for *Mrs. 'arris Goes to Paris;* ACE Award, for *Separate Tables.*

CREDITS

Film Costume Designer:
(With Luster Bayless and Edna Taylor; for Lee Remick) *Telefon,* Metro–Goldwyn–Mayer/United Artists, 1977.

(For Lee Remick) *The Medusa Touch* (also known as *La grande menace*), Warner Bros., 1978.

Moonlighting (also known as *Schwarzarbeit*), Universal, 1982.

(With Jean Muir) *Betrayal,* Twentieth Century–Fox, 1983.

Sahara, Metro–Goldwyn–Mayer/United Artists/Cannon, 1984.

1919, British Film Institute, 1984.

Secret Places, Twentieth Century–Fox, 1985.

Dreamchild, Universal, 1985.

A Handful of Dust, New Line Cinema, 1988.

Scandal, Miramax, 1989.

Memphis Belle, Warner Bros., 1990.

Rambling Rose, Seven Arts, 1991.

The Public Eye, Universal, 1992.

Indian Summer (also known as *L'ete indien*), Buena Vista, 1993.

Angie, Caravan Pictures/Hollywood Pictures, 1994.

Blue Sky, Orion, 1994.

Speechless, Metro–Goldwyn–Mayer, 1994.

Haunted, October Films, 1995.

Larger Than Life (also known as *Large As Life* and *Nickel and Dime*), Metro–Goldwyn–Mayer/United Artists, 1996.

Out to Sea, Twentieth Century–Fox, 1997.

Picture Perfect, Twentieth Century–Fox, 1997.

Ordinary Decent Criminal (also known as *Ein Ganz gewoehnlicher dieb*), Miramax, 2000.

Breathtaking, IAC Films, 2000.

The Keeper: The Legend of Omar Khayyam, Guide Company Films, 2005.

From Time to Time, Delanic Films, 2009.

Television Costume Designer; Series:
Philip Marlowe, Private Eye, 1984.

Television Costume Designer; Miniseries:
(With Jill Silverside) *Jennie: Lady Randolph Churchill,* PBS, 1974.

Brideshead Revisited, PBS, 1981.

Costumes for Deborah Kerr and Jenny Seagrove, *A Woman of Substance,* syndicated, 1984.

Anastasia: The Mystery of Anna (also known as *Anastasia: The Story of Anna*), NBC, 1986.

Poor Little Rich Girl: The Barbara Hutton Story (also known as *The Barbara Hutton Story*), NBC, 1987.

Beryl Markham: Shadow on the Sun (also known as *The Beryl Markham Story* and *Shadow on the Sun: The Beryl Markham Story*), CBS, 1988.

Liz: The Elizabeth Taylor Story (also known as *Destiny*), NBC, 1995.

Attila (also known as *Attila the Hun*), USA Network, 2001.

Spartacus, USA Network, 2004.

Television Costume Designer; Movies:
Caesar and Cleopatra, NBC, 1976.

Cat on a Hot Tin Roof (also known as *Laurence Olivier Presents: "Cat on a Hot Tin Roof"*), NBC, 1976.

Daphne Laureola (also known as *Laurence Olivier Presents: "Daphne Laureola"*), 1978.

Philip Marlowe—Private Eye, HBO, 1983.

Agatha Christie's "Murder with Mirrors" (also known as *Murder with Mirrors*), CBS, 1985.

Agatha Christie's "Thirteen at Dinner" (also known as *Thirteen at Dinner*), CBS, 1985.

Behind Enemy Lines (also known as *92 Grosvenor Street*), NBC, 1985.

Nazi Hunter: The Beate Klarsfeld Story (also known as *The Beate Klarsfeld Story*), ABC, 1986.

Cold Sassy Tree, TNT, 1989.

Murder by Moonlight (also known as *Dark of the Moon* and *Murder on the Moon*), CBS, 1989.

Mrs. 'arris Goes to Paris (also known as *Mrs. Harris Goes to Paris*), CBS, 1992.

Hope, TNT, 1997.

The Cater Street Hangman (also known as *The Inspector Pitt Mysteries*), Arts and Entertainment, 1998.

The Virginian, TNT, 2000.

Murder on the Orient Express (also known as *Agatha Christie's "Murder on the Orient Express"*), CBS, 2001.

Celebration, 2006.

Television Associate Producer; Movies:
Liz: The Elizabeth Taylor Story, NBC, 1995.

Television Costume Designer; Specials:
Women and Men: Stories of Seduction, HBO, 1990.

Television Costume Designer; Episodic:
"The Landlady," *Tales of the Unexpected* (also known as *Roald Dahl's "Tales of the Unexpected"*), 1979.

"Rocket to the Moon," *American Playhouse,* PBS, 1986.

"Strange Interlude," *American Playhouse,* PBS, 1988.

"Suspicion," *American Playhouse,* PBS, 1988.

"The Heat of the Day," *Masterpiece Theatre,* PBS, 1990.

"The Best of Friends," *Masterpiece Theatre,* PBS, 1992.

Egypt, 2005.

Also designed costumes for *Magpie; The Benny Hill Show.*

Television Appearances; Specials:
The Human Language (documentary), PBS, 1995.

"Attila": The Making of an Epic Miniseries, USA Network, 2001.

Stage Costume Designer:
The Ring of Stones, Charter Players, Lowry Theatre, 2000.

OTHER SOURCES

Periodicals:
Manchester Evening News, November 22, 2000.

ROSS, Franc 1954–
(Franc A. Ross)

PERSONAL

Full name, Franc Albert Ross; born April 6, 1954, in San Diego, CA; married Deborah L. Rinner, September 7, 1973 (divorced, December 29, 1980); married Christy Barrett, October 15, 2004.

Career: Actor.

CREDITS

Film Appearances:
(As Franc A. Ross) Centurion, *Quest of the Delta Knights,* Hemdale Home Video, 1993.
Tobias, *Amityville: Dollhouse* (also known as *Amityville Dollhouse: Evil Never Dies*), Republic Pictures, 1996.
Trucker, *A Fare to Remember,* 1998.
Crackhead, *Special,* Magnet Releasing, 2006.
Generator repairman, *The Perfect Sleep,* 2008.
Hack, *Uncross the Stars,* 2008.

Television Appearances; Series:
Duck, *Days of Our Lives* (also known as *Days* and *DOOL*), NBC, 2007.

Television Appearances; Movies:
A Whisper Kills (also known as *Whisperkill*), ABC, 1988.
Project manager, *Stolen: One Husband* (also known as *I Want Him Back!*), CBS, 1990.
Fred, *The Reading Room,* Hallmark Channel, 2005.
Cleon Winters, *Desolation Canyon,* Hallmark Channel, 2006.
Sheriff, *A Gunfighter's Pledge,* Hallmark Channel, 2008.

Television Appearances; Episodic:
Biker, "Uneasy Rider," *Misery Loves Company,* Fox, 1995.
Zero, "Against the Wall," *Malibu Shores,* NBC, 1996.
"Dean's Office," *The Guilt,* 1996.
Rauschling, "Her Houseboy Coco," *Mad About You,* NBC, 1997.
Billy T, "The Other Slide of Darkness," *Sliders,* Fox, 1997.
Mathias, "Primal Scream," *Profiler,* NBC, 1997.
Pirate captain, *You Wish,* ABC, 1997.
"Red Sonja," *Conan* (also known as *Conan the Adventurer* and *Conan, der abenteurer*), syndicated, 1998.
Pirate captain, "All in the Family Room," *You Wish,* 1998.
Nauhgton, "Vanishing Act," *ER,* NBC, 1998.
Bush pilot, *The Young and the Restless* (also known as *Y&R*), CBS, 1999.
Sonny Saunders, "The Midterms," *The West Wing,* NBC, 2000.
Jack, "Just Harried," *Charmed,* The WB, 2001.
Bartender, "Drew and the Motorcycle," *The Drew Carey Show,* ABC, 2001.
Man number two, "Glengarry Glen Dick," *3rd Rock from the Sun* (also known as *3rd Rock* and *Life As We Know It*), NBC, 2001.
Luther, "Den of Thieves," *The Invisible Man* (also known as *I–Man*), Sci–Fi Channel, 2001.
Frank Z, "Heebee Geebee's," *Dead Last,* The WB, 2001.
Razor, "Bargaining: Parts 1 & 2," *Buffy the Vampire Slayer* (also known as *BtVS, Buffy,* and *Buffy, the Vampire Slayer: The Series*), UPN, 2001.
Wade, "Two Clarks in a Bar," *NYPD Blue,* ABC, 2001.
Jesse Johnson, "It's the Most Wonderful Time of the Year," *Six Feet Under,* HBO, 2002.
Monty Reynolds, "Trash," *Firefly* (also known as *Firefly: The Series*), Fox, 2003.
Samuel Byler, "Rumspringa," *Judging Amy,* CBS, 2003.
Bill Crawford in 2005, "Blank Generation," *Cold Case,* CBS, 2005.
Wayne Osborne, "Sniper Zero," *Numb3rs* (also known as *Num3ers*), CBS, 2005.
Grizzled human, "In the Mirror, Darkly: Part 1," *Enterprise* (also known as *Star Trek: Enterprise*), UPN, 2005.
Pawn shop owner, "Motivational Worker," *Malcolm in the Middle,* Fox, 2005.
Clinic doctor, "Mr. Monk and the Class Reunion," *Monk,* USA Network, 2006.
Louis the bank guard, "Amateur Night," *Deadwood,* HBO, 2006.
Louis, "The Catbird Seat," *Deadwood,* HBO, 2006.
Louis, "Tell Him Something Pretty," *Deadwood,* HBO, 2006.
Victor, "A.K.A. the Plant," *Weeds,* Showtime, 2006.
Danny Pine, "Villains," *Heroes,* NBC, 2008.
Danny Pine, "Chapter Thirteen 'Dual,'" *Heroes,* NBC, 2008.

Also appeared as doctor, "Fathers and Sins," *Midnight Caller,* NBC.

ROSSI, Theo

PERSONAL

Born June 4, Staten Island, NY. *Education:* Studied acting at The Lee Strasberg Theatre Institute, New York City.

Addresses: *Agent*—Greene and Associates, 190 N. Canon Dr., Suite 200, Beverly Hills, CA 90210.

Career: Actor. Appeared in television commercials for McDonalds restaurants, Nissan automobiles, and Budweiser.

CREDITS

Television Appearances; Episodic:
Brandon Webber, "Chapter Twenty–Nine," *Boston Public,* Fox, 2001.
Brandon Webber, "Chapter Thirty," *Boston Public,* Fox, 2002.
Senior, "Humilithon," *Malcolm in the Middle,* Fox, 2002.
Pete Amici, "Chatty Chatty Bang Bang," *NYPD Blue,* ABC, 2004.
Private First Class Joe Vasquez, "Coming Home," *Medical Investigation,* NBC, 2004.
Bobby Santos, "So Long, Farewell," *American Dreams* (also known as *Our Generation*), NBC, 2004.
Eric Fitzgerald, "Rub a Tub Tub," *Blind Justice,* ABC, 2005.
Norris Clayton, "Weapons of Class Destruction," *Veronica Mars,* UPN and CW, 2005.
Corey Williams, "Odds or Evens," *Without a Trace* (also known as *W.A.T*), CBS, 2006.
Sergeant Buccelli, "One of Them," *Lost,* ABC, 2006.
Vinny Momo, "Sex, Lies and Vinny Momo," *Heist,* NBC, 2006.
Vinny Momo, "Strife," *Heist,* NBC, 2006.
Nick Arno, "The Woman in the Sand," *Bones,* Fox, 2006.
Randy Payton, "Rogue River," *Jericho,* CBS, 2006.
Danny Vargas, "Here Comes the Judge," *Shark,* CBS, 2007.
Stan Giamatti, "Crash Into Me: Part 1 & 2," *Grey's Anatomy,* ABC, 2007.
Juan Carlos 'Juice' Ortiz, a recurring role, *Sons of Anarchy,* 2008.

Television Appearances; Movies:
The Mook, *Big Shot: Confessions of a Campus Bookie,* FX Channel, 2002.
Anthony, *The Challenge,* ABC, 2003.

Desantis, *Code Breakers,* ESPN, 2005.
Greg Berlin, *House of the Dead 2* (also known as *House of the Dead 2: All Guts, No Glory* and *House of the Dead II: Dead Aim*), Sci–Fi Channel, 2005.
Antonio Ruiz, *Jane Doe: Yes, I Remember It Well,* Hallmark Channel, 2006.

Television Appearances; Pilots:
Nurses (also known as *Philadelphia General*), Fox, 2007.

Film Appearances:
Montilli, *The Myersons,* 2001.
Teddy, *Buds for Life,* Maverick Entertainment, 2004.
Antonio, *Cloverfield* (also known as *1–18–08* and *Monstrous*), Paramount, 2008.
Spaz, *The Informers,* Senator Entertainment, 2008.
Carlos, *Kill Theory,* Lionsgate, 2009.
Tino Hull, *Red Sands,* Sony Pictures Home Entertainment, 2009.
Fencewalker, 2009.

ROTH, Matt 1964–

PERSONAL

Born September 15, 1964. Married Laurie Metcalf (an actress), 1993; children: (stepdaughter) Zoe, Will, Mae.

Addresses: *Agent*—Bauman, Redanty and Shaul Agency, 5757 Wilshire Blvd., Suite 473, Los Angeles, CA 90036. *Manager*—Joan Sittenfield Management, 8350 Santa Monica Blvd., Suite 108, West Hollywood, CA 90069.

Career: Actor.

Awards, Honors: Olly Award nomination, best actor in a comedy, 1989, for *Noises Off.*

CREDITS

Television Appearances; Series:
Clark Munsinger, *The Antagonists,* CBS, 1991.
Russell Evans, *Blue Skies,* ABC, 1994.
Dr. Rick Buckley, *Crisis Center,* NBC, 1997.

Television Appearances; Episodic:
Paul Brubecker, "Lonely Hearts," *Melrose Place,* Fox, 1992.
Fisher, a recurring role, *Roseanne,* ABC, 1992–1993.

Dan Waters, "Heart of the Matter," *Cupid,* ABC, 1998.

Ted, "The Dog That Rocks the Cradle," *Frasier,* NBC, 1999.

Michael, "About a Girl," *According to Jim,* ABC, 2003.

Michael, "What Have I Done to Deserve This?," *Grey's Anatomy,* ABC, 2006.

Mike Belweather, "Undercurrents," *Numb3rs* (also known as *Num3ers*), CBS, 2006.

Art Shepherd, a recurring role, *Desperate Housewives,* ABC, 2006.

Big Shots, ABC, 2007.

Dave Gilbert, "Shattered," *Crossing Jordan,* NBC, 2007.

Sam Cooper, "Fallen Idols," *CSI: Crime Scene Investigation* (also known as *CSI: Las Vegas, C.S.I.,* and *Les Experts*), CBS, 2007.

Greg, "Tucked, Taped and Gorgeous," *Two and a Half Men,* 2007.

Derek Benjamin, "Slam (aka Slambook)," *Ghost Whisperer,* CBS, 2008.

Television Appearances; Movies:

Michael Stuart, *Goodnight Sweet Wife: A Murder in Boston* (also known as *The Charles Stuart Story*), CBS, 1990.

Film Appearances:

Officer Crowe, *Blink,* Encore, 1994.

Todd, *'Til There Was You,* Paramount, 1994.

Male advertising executive, *Chicago Cab* (also known as "Hellcab"), Castle Hill, 1998.

Client, *Where's Marlowe?,* Paramount, 1998.

Bank worker number one, *Pups,* Allied, 1999.

Greg, *View from the Top,* Miramax, 2003.

Josh, *Forever,* 2007.

Stage Appearances:

Appeared as Phil, *On the Mountain,* South Coast Repertory, Costa Mesa, CA; Purdy, *Purple Heart* Steppenwolf Theatre, Chicago, IL; Homer, *The Dazzle,* South Coast Repertory; Peter Sloan, *Light Up the Sky,* Pasadena, CA; Gene, *Pot Mom,* Steppenwolf Theatre; Jim, *Us and Them,* Hudson Theatre, New York City; Cristoforu, *The Public Eye,* Interplay; Ted, *Private Ear,* Interplay; Demetrius, *A Midsummer Night's Dream,* Steppenwolf Theatre, Chicago, IL; Garry Lejuenne, *Noise's Off,* Pegasus Players, Chicago, IL; Egor Timoveyeyevich, *The Suicide,* BDI Theatre Company; *Wifeswappers,* Third Stage; *Oklahoma,* Third Stage; *Zombie Attack,* Third Stage.

ROWLAND, Kelly 1981–

PERSONAL

Full name, Kelendria Trene (some sources cite Kelandria or Terene) Rowland; born February 11, 1981, in Atlanta, GA; daughter of Doris Garrison (some sources cite Doris Lovett). *Education:* Attended high school in Houston, TX.

Addresses: *Agent*—International Creative Management, 10250 Constellation Way, 9th Floor, Los Angeles, CA 90067.

Career: Actress, singer, and recording artist. Girls Tyme, former member of singing group; Destiny's Child, singer and recording artist, 1992–2005; solo artist, 2005—. Appeared in commercials for McDonald's restaurants and WalMart discount chain; Music Television Network, AIDS awareness ambassador for the program Staying Alive, 2008; also appeared in commercials for other charitable causes. Knowles–Rowland Center for Youth, Houston, TX, cofounder; Survivor Foundation, cofounder (with other members of Destiny's Child).

Awards, Honors: Awards for Destiny's Child include American Music Awards, favorite rhythm and blues group, 2001, 2002, 2005; Black Entertainment Television award, best female group, 2001; Image Award, outstanding duo or group, National Association for the Advancement of Colored People, 2001, 2005, 2006; Teen Choice Award, choice pop group, 2001; Black Reel Award nomination, best song, 2001, for *Charlie's Angels;* MTV Video Music Award, best rhythm and blues video, 2000, and two Grammy Awards, National Academy of Recording Arts and Sciences, 2001, for the song "Say My Name;" Sammy Davis, Jr. Award, entertainer of the year, Soul Train Awards, 2001; MTV Video Music Award, best rhythm and blues video, 2001, and Grammy Award, best rhythm and blues performance, 2002, for the song "Survivor;" American Music Award, favorite pop album, 2002, for *Survivor;* Brit Award, best international group, 2002; World Music Awards, world's best–selling group, 2002, world's best–selling pop group, 2002, 2006, world's best–selling rhythm and blues group, 2002, 2006, and best–selling female group of all time, 2006; Ebel Award, 2003; Artist Achievement Award, *Billboard* Music Awards, 2004; American Music Award, favorite rhythm and blues album, 2005, for *Destiny Fulfilled;* Black Entertainment Television Award, best vocal group, 2005; American Music Award, favorite rhythm and blues band, duo or group, 2005; American Music Award, best rhythm and blues album, 2005, for *Destiny Fulfilled;* received star on Hollywood Walk of Fame, 2006; also received Soul Train Lady of Soul Awards; record sales certifications from Recording Industry Association of America include platinum record for *Destiny's Child,* and multi–platinum records for *Survivor* and *The Writing's on the Wall.* Solo awards include Grammy Award, best rap/sung collaboration, Grammy Award nomination, best rap performance by a duo or group, Capital FM Award, London's favorite international single, Dutch TMF Awards, best international rhythm and blues song and best international video, and *Billboard* Award, hot rap track of the year, all (with Nelly) 2003, for "Dilemma;" Recording Industry Association of America certifications include gold record certification for *Simply Deep,*

CREDITS

Television Appearances; Specials:
Christmas in Rockefeller Center, NBC, 2000, and (with Destiny's Child) 2001.
(With Destiny's Child) *Walt Disney World Summer Jam Concert* (also known as *Summer Jam*), ABC, 2000.
VH1 Divas 2000: A Tribute to Diana Ross (also known as *VH1 Divas 2000*), VH1, 2000.
Gale King Interviews … On the Road with Destiny's Child, Oxygen Network, 2001.
(With Destiny's Child) *MTV Icon: Janet Jackson,* MTV, 2001.
(With Destiny's Child) *Joan Rivers: The E! True Hollywood Story,* E! Entertainment Television, 2001.
Destiny's Child Live, MTV, 2001.
This Is Destiny's Child, Fox, 2001.
(With Destiny's Child) *The Concert for New York City,* VH1, 2001.
(With Destiny's Child) *Michael Jackson: 30th Anniversary Celebration,* CBS, 2001.
Intimate Portrait: Destiny's Child, Lifetime, 2001.
(With Destiny's Child) *Nobel Peace Prize Concert,* USA Network and Trio, 2001.
(With Destiny's Child) *Pop Goes Christmas,* BBC, 2001.
(With Destiny's Child) *The Record of the Year,* ITV, 2001, 2004.
The Victoria's Secret Fashion Show, CBS, 2002.
Lighting Up Fifth, 2003.
The … Annual Sears Soul Train Christmas Starfest, UPN, 2003, The WB, 2004.
Maxim Hot 100, NBC, 2003.
Jingle Ball Rock, Fox, 2003.
E! Entertainer of the Year 2003, E! Entertainment Television, 2003.
Urban Soul: The Making of Modern R&B, BBC, 2004.
Motown 45, ABC, 2004.
(With Destiny's Child) *Live 8,* multiple networks, 2005.
An All–Star Salute to Patti LaBelle: Live from Atlantis, UPN, 2005.
The Story of Beyonce, E! Entertainment Television, 2006.
100 Greatest Songs of the 90's, VH1, 2007.
The British Soap Awards 2008: The Party, ITV, 2008.
T4 on the Beach 2008, Channel 4, 2008.

Television Appearances; Awards Presentations:
(With Destiny's Child) *The 1999 Malibu MOBO Awards,* 1999.
2000 Blockbuster Entertainment Awards, Fox, 2000.
The 2000 Billboard Music Awards, Fox, 2000, 2005.
(With Destiny's Child) *The Teen Choice Awards 2001,* Fox, 2001.

Presenter or performer, *The … Annual Grammy Awards,* CBS, 2001 (with Destiny's Child), 2003, 2006.
BET Awards, Black Entertainment Television, 2001, 2005, 2007.
The … Annual American Music Awards), ABC, 2002, 2005.
MTV Video Music Awards, MTV, 2003.
2003 Trumpet Awards, TBS, 2003.
The … Soul Train Music Awards, The WB, 2004, syndicated, 2006.
ESPY Awards, ESPN, 2005.
(With Destiny's Child) Presenter, *The 2005 World Music Awards,* ABC, 2005.
Presenter, *The British Soap Awards,* ITV, 2008.
Presenter, *2008 Brit Awards,* BBC America, 2008.

Television Appearances; Episodic:
Herself, "Backstage Pass," *The Famous Jett Jackson,* The Disney Channel, 2000.
Carly, "Smells like Free Spirit," *The Hughleys,* UPN, 2002.
Carly, "You've Got Male," *The Hughleys,* UPN, 2002.
Carly, "It's a Girl: Part 2," *The Hughleys,* UPN, 2003.
Martha Reeves, "City on Fire," *American Dreams* (also known as *Our Generation*), NBC, 2003.
Martha Reeves, "Life's Illusions," *American Dreams* (also known as *Our Generation*), NBC, 2003.
Cleo, "Twas the Fight before Christmas," *Eve,* UPN, 2003.
Tammy Hamilton, "Oh, Hell Yes: The Seminar," *Girlfriends,* UPN, 2006.
Tammy Hamilton, "I'll Be There for You … but Not Right Now," *Girlfriends,* UPN, 2006.
Tammy Hamilton, "I Don't Wanna Be a Player No More," *Girlfriends,* UPN, 2006.

Television Talk Show/Variety Show Appearances; Episodic:
(With Destiny's Child) "A Date with Destiny," *Smart Guy,* The WB, 1998.
(With Destiny's Child) "Ghost Town," *Pacific Blue,* USA Network, 1999.
(With Destiny's Child) *The Martin Short Show,* syndicated, 1999.
"Destiny's Child: Independent Women, Part 1," *Making the Video,* MTV, 2000.
(With Destiny's Child) *T4,* Channel 4, 2001.
Revealed with Jules Asner, E! Entertainment Television, 2001.
Wetten, dass …?, 2001, and (with Destiny's Child), 2004.
Sen kvaell med Luuk, 2001.
(Uncredited) Musical guest, *Saturday Night Live* (also known as *SNL*), NBC, 2001, 2002, 2004.
"Destiny's Child: Parts 1 & 2," *Taff,* 2002.
Judge, *Star Search,* CBS, 2003.
The Tonight Show with Jay Leno, NBC, 2003.

The Late Late Show with Craig Kilborn (also known as *The Late Late Show*), CBS, 2003.

The Sharon Osbourne Show (also known as *Sharon*), syndicated, 2003.

Cribs (also known as *MTV Cribs*), MTV, 2003.

The Michael Essany Show, E! Entertainment Television, 2003.

The Saturday Show, BBC, 2003.

CD:UK, ITV, 2003.

Boogie (also known as *Boogie Aarhus, Bookie Listen, Boogie loerdag,* and *Boogie Update*), 2003.

Stjerne for en aften (also known as *Stjerne for en aften—Den sidste mission*), 2003.

Tinseltown TV, International Channel, 2003.

(With Destiny's Child; in archive footage) *Celebrities Uncensored,* E! Entertainment Television, 2003.

Top of the Pops (also known as *All New Top of the Pops* and *TOTP*), BBC, 2002, 2003, (with Destiny's Child) 2004.

"Kentucky Derby," *10 Things Every Guy Should Experience,* Spike, 2004.

(With Destiny's Child) *20/20* (also known as *ABC News 20/20*), ABC, 2004.

(With Destiny's Child) *GMTV,* ITV, 2004.

(With Destiny's Child) *Ant & Dec's Saturday Night Takeaway,* ITV, 2004.

(With Destiny's Child) *The National Lottery: Wright around the World,* BBC, 2004.

The View, ABC, 2004, 2006, 2007.

The Oprah Winfrey Show (also known as *Oprah*), syndicated, 2004 (with Destiny's Child), and 2005.

(With Destiny's Child) *Top of the Pops Saturday,* BBC, 2005.

"Destiny's Child II: Encore!," *Diary,* MTV, 2005.

(With Destiny's Child) *106 & Park Top 10 Live,* Black Entertainment Television, 2005.

Jimmy Kimmel Live!, ABC, 2005 (with Destiny's Child), and 2007.

"Secrets of Music Superstars," *The Tyra Banks Show,* UPN, 2006.

Chancers, Channel 4, 2006.

(With Destiny's Child; in archive footage) "Holiday Crap," *Video on Trial,* MuchMusic, 2006.

Access Granted, Black Entertainment Television, 2007.

Punk'd, MTV, 2007.

Loose Women, ITV, 2007, 2008.

This Morning (also known as *This Morning with Richard and Judy*), ITV, 2008.

TRL Italy (also known as *Total Request Live* and *TRL Italia*), MTV, 2008.

Good News Week, 2008.

Never Mind the Buzzcocks, BBC, 2008.

(In archive footage) *The O'Reilly Factor,* Fox News Channel, 2008.

Television Appearances; Miniseries:

(With Destiny's Child) *100 Greatest Dance Songs of Rock & Roll,* VH1, 2000.

I Love the '80s, VH1, 2002.

I Love the '70s, VH1, 2003.

Clash of the Choirs, NBC, 2007.

Television Appearances; Other:

Herself, *Liza and David* (pilot), VH1, 2002.

Judge, *Born to Diva* (series), VH1, 2003.

Film Appearances:

Second girl, *Beverly Hood,* 1999, York Entertainment, 2002.

Kia Waterson, *Freddy vs. Jason* (also known as *FvJ*), New Line Cinema, 2003.

Jhnelle, *The Seat Filler,* DEJ Productions, 2004.

Bling: A Planet Rock (documentary), Image Entertainment, 2007.

The Beyonce Experience (concert film), Bigger Picture, 2007.

Asterix aux jeux olympiques (also known as *Asterix at the Olympic Games, Asterix alle olimpiadi, Asterix bei den Olympischen Spielen,* and *Asterix en los juegos olimpicos*), Pathe, 2008.

Film Work; Song Performer:

"Train on a Track," *Maid in Manhattan* (also known as *Made in New York*), Columbia, 2002.

"Im Beginning to See the Light," *Mona Lisa Smile,* Columbia, 2003.

"This Is How I Feel," *Hitch,* Columbia, 2005.

"Love Again," *Tyler Perry's "Meet the Browns,"* Lionsgate, 2008.

Also contributor of previously released songs to soundtracks of other films, including *Charlie's Angels,* 2000.

RECORDINGS

Albums with Destiny's Child:

Destiny's Child, Columbia, 1998.

The Writing's on the Wall, Columbia, 1999.

Survivor, Columbia, 2001.

8 Days of Christmas, Columbia, 2001.

This Is the Remix, 2002.

Destiny Fulfilled, Columbia, 2004.

Live in Atlanta, 2007.

Mathew Knowles and Music World Present, Vol. 1: Love Destiny, Sony, 2008.

Several unauthorized albums have also been released by third parties. Singles include "Killing Time" and "No, No, No," both Columbia, 1997; "Bills Bills Bills," "Bug–a–Boo," "Get on the Bus," and "Say My Name," 1999; "Independent Woman" and "Jumpin' Jumpin'," 2000; "Bootylicious," "Emotion," and "Survivor," 2001; "Lost My Breath," 2004; and "Soldier," 2005.

Solo Albums:
Simply Deep, Columbia, 2002.
Ms. Kelly, 2007, expanded all–digital version released
     as *Ms. Kelly: Diva Deluxe,* 2008.

Singles include "Stole," 2002, "Can't Nobody" and "Train on a Track," 2003, and "Work;" also recorded "Dilemma" with Nelly, 2002.:

Videos:
Destiny's Child: Say My Name Multimedia Single
     (video game), 2000.
The Platinum's on the Wall, 2001.
Survivor, Pt. 1, Sony, 2001.
This Is the Remix, Sony, 2002.
Destiny's Child World Tour, 2003.
(With Destiny's Child) *SingStar Party* (video game),
     2004.
Before, During, and "After the Sunset," New Line Home
     Video, 2005.
Destiny's Child: Live in Atlanta, Sony BMG Music
     Entertainment, 2006.
Destiny's Child: A Family Affair, Channel 4 Television
     Corp., 2006.
World Tour, 2007.

Music videos include "Say My Name" with Destiny's Child, 2000; "Bootylicious" and "Survivor" with Destiny's Child, 2001; "Izzo (H.O.V.A.)" with Jay–Z, 2001; "Substitute Love" with Estelle, 2008; "Dilemma" with Nelly; "Get Me Bodied" with Beyonce; and "Here We Go" by Trina.

OTHER SOURCES

Books:
Contemporary Musicians, Volume 64, Gale, 2009.
Newsmakers, Issue 3, Gale, 2001.
Rowland, Kelly, James Patrick Herman, and other
     members of Destiny's Child, *Soul Survivors,*
     HarperCollins, 2002.

Periodicals:
Black Men, April, 2001, pp. 28–29, 86.
Current Biography, August, 2001, pp. 27–31.
Daily Mail (London), January 4, 2008, p. 70.
Jet, July 2, 2007, p. 60.
Teen People, March, 2001, pp. 204–210.
USA Today, February 13, 2006, p. 2D.

Electronic:
Kelly Rowland Official Site, http://www.kellyrowland.
     com, December 24, 2008.

Other:
Intimate Portrait: Destiny's Child (television special),
     Lifetime, 2001.

S

SADOWSKI, Jonathan 1979–

PERSONAL

Born November 23, 1979, in Chicago, IL. *Education:* University of Illinois, B.F.A., theater.

Addresses: *Agent*—Agency for the Performing Arts, 405 South Beverly Dr., Beverly Hills, CA 90212; William Morris Agency, One William Morris Pl., Beverly Hills, CA 90212. *Manager*—Benderspink, 110 South Fairfax Ave., Suite 350, Los Angeles, CA 90036; Essential Talent Management, 6565 Sunset Blvd., Suite 415, Los Angeles, CA 90028.

Career: Actor. Previously worked as the Griddle Cafe (a diner), West Hollywood, CA.

CREDITS

Film Appearances:
Paul, *She's the Man,* DreamWorks, 2006.
Trey, *Live Free or Die Hard* (also known as *Die Hard 4.0* and *Die Hard 4: Live Free or Die Hard*), Twentieth Century–Fox, 2007.
Wade, *Friday the 13th,* Warner Bros., 2009.
Blake, *The Goods: The Don Ready Story,* Paramount Vantage, 2009.
Doug, *Spring Breakdown,* Warner Bros., 2009.

Television Appearances; Series:
ET on MTV, MTV, 2000.
Jefferson, *American Dreams* (also known as *Our Generation*), NBC, 2004.
Gary, *Miss/Guided,* ABC, 2007–2008.

Television Appearances; Movies:
Olufssen Machachi, *Squeegees,* 2008.

Television Appearances; Pilots:
(Uncredited) Roland, *The Loop,* Fox, 2006.

Television Appearances; Episodic:
Lieutenant Nortski, *Navy NCIS: Naval Criminal Investigative Service* (also known as *NCIS* and *NCIS: Naval Criminal Investigative Service*), CBS, 2003.
Bruce Kelso, "The Box," *The Division* (also known as *Heart of the City*), Lifetime, 2004.
Oleg Karponov, "Unscheduled Arrivals," *LAX,* NBC, 2004.
Adam, "The Fantasy," *The Wedding Bells,* Fox, 2007.
Brett's assistant, "The Prince's Bride," *Entourage,* HBO, 2007.
Dr. Mason/Number Ten, "The Right Stuff," *House M.D.* (also known as *House*), Fox, 2007.
Laszlo Mahnovski, "Chuck Versus the Sandworm," *Chuck,* NBC, 2007.
Sayles, "Gnothi Seauton," *Terminator: The Sarah Connor Chronicles,* Fox, 2008.
Sayles, "Dungeons & Dragons," *Terminator: The Sarah Connor Chronicles,* 2008.
Sayles, "Vick's Chip," *Terminator: The Sarah Connor Chronicles,* 2008.

SANDOR, Anna

PERSONAL

Born in Hungary; immigrated to United States, 1989; daughter of Paul and Agnes (maiden name, Laszlo) Sandor; married William Gough; children: Rachel. *Education:* University of Windsor, B.A., 1971. Additional interests: music, reading, ballet.

Addresses: *Agent*—The Sarnoff Company, 10 Universal City Plaza, 20th Floor, Universal City, CA 91608.

Career: Writer.

Member: Academy of Television Arts and Sciences, Crime Writers of Canada, Writers' Guild of Canada, Writers' Guild of America.

Awards, Honors: Gemini Award nomination, best writing in a dramatic program, Academy of Canadian Cinema and Television, 1987, for *The Marriage Bed;* Emmy Award nomination, outstanding individual achievement in writing, 1992, Humanitas Prize, ninety–minute category, Writers Guild of America Award nomination, adapted long form, 1993, for *Miss Rose White;* Gemini Award nomination (with William Gough), best writing in a dramatic program, 1994, for *Family of Strangers;* Margaret Collier Award, Gemini Awards, 1996; Daytime Emmy Award nomination, outstanding writing in a children's special, Humanitas Prize, children's live–action category, Writers Guild of America Award, children's script, 2002, for *My Louisiana Sky;* Humanitas Prize nomination, children's live–action category, 2006, for *Felicity: An American Girl Adventure;* Humanitas Prize, children's live–action category, 2007, for *Molly: An American Girl on the Home Front.*

WRITINGS

Screenplays:
Charlie Grant's War, 1984.
Martha, Ruth & Edie, 1988.

Television Series:
King of Kensington, CBS, 1976–80.
Hangin' In, syndicated, 1981.
Seeing Things, syndicated, 1981.
Tarzan, syndicated, 1991.

Television Movies:
Charlie Grant's War, CBC, 1984.
The Marriage Bed, CBC, 1986.
Mama's Going to Buy You a Mockingbird, CBC, 1987.
Two Men, 1988.
Tarzan in Manhattan, CBS, 1989.
Stolen: One Husband (also known as *I Want Him Back!*), CBS, 1990.
Miss Rose White, NBC, 1992.
A Family of Strangers, CBS, 1993.
For the Love of My Child: The Anissa Ayala Story, NBC, 1993.
Amelia Earhart: The Final Flight, TNT, 1994.
A Gift of Love: The Daniel Huffman Story, Showtime, 1999.
My Louisiana Sky, Showtime, 2001.
Tiger Cruise, The Disney Channel, 2004.
Felicity: An American Girl Adventure, The WB, 2005.

Molly: An American Girl on the Home Front, The Disney Channel, 2006.
Mom, Dad and Her (also known as *Me, Mom, Dad and Her*), Lifetime, 2008.
Accidental Friendship, 2008.
A Kiss at Midnight, Hallmark Channel, 2008.

Television Episodic:
"The Running Man," *For the Record,* CBS, 1981.
"The Dying Swan," *Danger Bay,* CBC and The Disney Channel, 1987.
"Love Game," *Danger Bay,* CBC and The Disney Channel, 1987.

SAXON, Rolf 1955–

PERSONAL

Born in 1955, in Alexandria, VA; children: Reuben. *Education:* Graduated from the Guildhall School of Music and Drama; studied acting with the American Conservatory Theatre.

Career: Actor. Appeared in television commercials for Diet Coke and Stride; performed with the California Shakespeare Festival.

Awards, Honors: *Manchester Evening News* Theatre Award, best actor in a leading role, 2005, for *The Price.*

CREDITS

Film Appearances:
Dick, *Little Lord Fauntleroy,* 1980.
(Uncredited) Second speedboat man, *Curse of the Pink Panther,* Metro–Goldwyn–Mayer/United Artists, 1983.
Rowland, *The Lords of Discipline,* Paramount, 1983.
Patrolman, *Nineteen Eighty–Four,* Atlantic, 1984.
French guard, *The Tripods,* 1984.
Peter, *Invitation to the Wedding,* 1985.
Kentucky, *A Time of Destiny,* Columbia, 1988.
First American sailor, *Joyriders,* 1989.
Yuhudi, *Wild West,* Samuel Goldwyn Company, 1992.
C.I.A. Analyst William Donloe, *Mission: Impossible* (also known as *Mission Impossible*), Paramount, 1996.
Philip Jones, *Tomorrow Never Dies* (also known as *TND*), United Artists, 1997.
Lieutenant Briggs, *Saving Private Ryan,* Paramount, 1998.
Director, *Entrapment* (also known as *Verlockende Falle*), Twentieth Century–Fox, 1999.

Alden Wheaton, *Honest,* Winchester Films, 2000.

Herbie Clayton, *Obedience* (short), 2000.

Hollywood producer, *Einstein* (also known as *The Furnace*), Fortissimo Film Sales, 2000.

Narrator, *Teletubbies: Christmas in the Snow,* Warner Bros., 2000.

Television Appearances; Series:

French guard, *The Tripods,* BBC, 1984.

Jerome Summers, *Pulaski* (also known as *Pulaski: The TV Detective*), 1987.

Hudson J. Talbot III, *Capital City,* 1989–90.

Sam Levinson, *Love Hurts,* 1994.

Narrator, *Teletubbies,* BBC and PBS, 1997.

Television Appearances; Miniseries:

Coldfelt, *The First Olympics: Athens 1896* (also known as *Dream One* and *The First Modern Olympics*), NBC, 1984.

Hollywood director, *Lace II,* ABC, 1985.

American in bar, *Tender Is the Night,* BBC, 1985.

Television Appearances; Movies:

Dick, *Little Lord Fauntleroy,* CBS, 1980.

Robert E. Wright, *The Dirty Dozen: The Next Mission,* NBC, 1985.

Robert Elwell, *Afterwards,* 1985.

Frank, *Tailspin: Behind the Korean Airliner Tragedy* (also known as *Coded Hostile*), HBO, 1989.

Professor Ronald Dworkin, *The Trials of Oz,* BBC, 1991.

Plaskett, *Hostages,* HBO, 1993.

Fisk, *Night Watch* (also known as *Alistair MacLean's "Night Watch," Detonator II: Night Watch,* and *Detonator 2: Night Watch*), USA Network, 1995.

Captain Marks, *The Affair,* HBO, 1995.

(Uncredited) Carl Dolby, *London Suite* (also known as *Neil Simon's "London Suite"*), NBC, 1996.

Hiram Otis, *The Canterville Ghost,* ABC, 1997.

Flunkie number one, *RKO 281* (also known as *RKO 281: The Battle Over Citizen Kane*), HBO, 1999.

Television Appearances; Specials:

Soldier, *Displaced Person* (also known as *D.P.*), PBS, 1985.

Television Appearances; Episodic:

"The Limehouse Connection," *Q.E.D.,* CBS, 1982.

Chemist, "Shall I Be Mother?," *Play for Today,* 1983.

Mike Klobucki, "Digging Up the Future," *Chessgame,* 1983.

Black guard, "The English Channel: July, 2089 AD," *The Tripods,* 1984.

Luke Hennessey, "One Reborn Every Minute," *Boon,* ITV, 1989.

Rodney Kauffman, "Women's Troubles," *Birds of a Feather,* 1989.

Charlie Bodine, "Can't Keep a Dead Man Down: Parts 1 & 2," *She–Wolf of London* (also known as *Love & Curses*), syndicated, 1990.

Dr. Ames, "The Adventure of the Egyptian Tomb," *Poirot* (also known as *Agatha Christie: Poirot* and *Agatha Christie's "Poirot"*), ITV and Arts and Entertainment, 1993.

Verro Walker, "Predator and Prey," *Space Precinct,* syndicated, 1995.

Mr. Roach, "The Rameses Connection: Part 2," *The Tomorrow People,* 1995.

Tom Reid, *Crown Prosecutor,* 1995.

Murray, "Brief Encounter," *Goodnight Sweetheart,* BBC, 1999.

Jerry Corvitz, "Protesting Hippies," *Hippies,* BBC, 1999.

Art Spellman, "The List," *Ultimate Force,* 2003.

Sam Johnson, "Kodevavn: Kerkes—Del 15," *Ornen: En krimi–odysse* (also known as *Ornen* and *The Eagle*), 2005.

Sam Johnson, "Kodevavn: Kerkes—Del 16," *Ornen: En krimi–odysse* (also known as *Ornen* and *The Eagle*), 2005.

Stage Appearances:

Laughter on the 23rd Floor, Library Theatre, Manchester, England, 1995.

Dionysos, *The Frogs,* Barbican Centre, London, 1998.

The Seven Year Itch, Queen's Theatre, London, 2000.

Dinner with Friends, Steppenwolf Theatre Company, Hampstead Theatre, London, 2001.

Polixenes, *The Winter's Tale,* Royal Shakespeare Company, London, 2002.

Simonides, *Pericles; Prince of Tyre,* Royal Shakespeare Company, 2002.

Billy Flynn, *Chicago,* West End Production, London, 2003.

Stephen Marx, *Three on a Couch,* King's Head Theatre, London, 2004.

Victor Franz, *The Price,* Library Theatre, Manchester, England, c. 2005.

Gerardo, *The Death and the Maiden,* New Wolsey Theatre, London, 2005.

Title role, *Jerry Springer: The Opera,* British production, 2006.

Hello Dolly, Theatre Royal, London, 2006.

Major Tours:

Title role, *Jerry Springer: The Opera,* U.K. cities, 2006.

Radio Appearances:

Reader, *Stanley William Galeras Struggle for Survival,* BBC Radio 4, 2001.

RECORDINGS

Video Games:

Voice of George Stobbart, *Broken Sword: The Shadow of the Templars* (also known as *Broken Sword: Circle of Blood*), 1996.

Voice of George Stobbart, *Broken Sword II: The Smoking Mirror,* 1997.
Voice of George Stobbart, *Broken Sword: The Sleeping Dragon,* THQ, 2003.
Voice of George Stobbart, *Broken Sword: The Angel of Death* (also known as *Secrets of the Ark: A Broken Sword Game*), The Adventure Company, 2006.

Albums:

Appeared as narrator, *Teletubbies: The Album,* Kid Rhino.

SCOTT, Willard 1934–

PERSONAL

Full name, Willard Herman Scott, Jr.; born March 7, 1934, in Alexandria, VA; son of Willard Herman (an insurance sales representative) and Thelma Matti (a telephone operator; maiden name, Phillips) Scott; married Mary Ellen Dwyer, August 7, 1959 (died October 28, 2002); children: Mary Phillips, Sally W. *Education:* American University, B.A., 1955. *Religion:* Episcopalian.

Addresses: *Office*—c/o NBC News, 30 Rockefeller Plaza, New York, NY 10112. *Agent*—William Morris Agency, 1 William Morris Pl., Beverly Hills, CA 90212.

Career: Broadcast journalist, weather forecaster, television host, and author. NBC News, Washington, DC, page, beginning 1950; WINX–Radio, Washington, DC, weekend disc jockey, 1950; WOL–Radio, member of Joy Boys broadcast team, 1950–53; WRC–AM Radio, Washington, DC, member of Joy Boys broadcast team, c. 1953–72; WWDC–Radio, Washington, DC, member of Joy Boys broadcast team, 1972–74; NBC News, New York City, weather reporter and program host, 1980—. WRC–TV, Washington, DC, weather reporter, beginning 1968. Epcot Center, appeared in the theme park attraction *Ellen's Energy Adventure,* 1996; performed as Santa Claus at White House functions; appeared in commercials, including appearance as the first Ronald McDonald (originally Donald McDonald) for McDonald's restaurants, 1963, announcer for Smucker's products, and participant in occasional "infomercials." Active as a fund–raiser and volunteer for several charitable organizations.

Awards, Honors: Named Washingtonian of the year, *Washingtonian* Magazine, 1979; humanitarian in residence, National Society of Fund Raisers, 1985; Private Sector Award for Public Service, President Ronald Reagan, 1985; Great American Award, Bards of

Bohemia in New Orleans, 1990; named distinguished Virginian, Virginia Association of Broadcasters, 1990; Daytime Emmy Awards (with others), outstanding special class program, 1997, 1998, both for *The Macy's Thanksgiving Day Parade;* inducted into Newspaper Carrier Hall of Fame, Newspaper Association of America, 2001.

CREDITS

Television Appearances; Series:
Substitute weather reporter and regular contributor, *Today* (also known as *NBC News Today* and *The Today Show*), NBC, 1980—.
Peter Poole, a recurring role, *Valerie* (also known as *The Hogan Family* and *Valerie's Family*), NBC, 1987–89.
Host, *The New Original Amateur Hour,* The Family Channel, 1991.
Host, *Willard Scott's Home and Garden Almanac,* Home and Garden Television, 1994.

Also appeared as Bozo in the syndicated series *Bozo the Clown,* and as a weather reporter on the series *Early Today,* NBC.

Television Appearances; Specials:
Christmas in Washington, NBC, 1985.
Host, *Today at Night, Volume II,* NBC, 1986.
Today at 35, NBC, 1987.
Cohost, *Macy's Thanksgiving Day Parade,* NBC, annually, 1987–97.
Walt Disney World 4th of July Spectacular, syndicated, 1988.
Presidential Inauguration, NBC, 1989.
Host, *The 1990 Clio Awards: The Best TV Commercials in the World,* NBC, 1990.
2 Years ... Later, NBC, 1990.
Host, *The Pillsbury Bake–off,* CBS, 1990, 1992.
Today at 40, NBC, 1992.
Hats Off to Minnie Pearl: America Honors Minnie Pearl, The Nashville Network, 1992.
Great Chefs, Great Bar–B–Q: A Great Chefs Special, PBS, 1992.
Host, *An American Celebration,* The Nashville Network, 1992.
Host, *Kentucky Derby Festival Parade,* The Nashville Network, 1992, 1996.
Today at Night, NBC, 1994.
Host, *Tax Break '94,* PBS, 1994.
Host, *Tax Break '95,* PBS, 1995.
Host, *Christmas across America* (also known as *HGTV's "Christmas across America"*), Home and Garden Television, 1998, 1999, 2000.
Host, *Generation H: National History Day,* History Channel, 2001.

NBC 75th Anniversary Special (also known as *NBC 75th Anniversary Celebration*), NBC, 2002.
The Weather Channel's Twentieth Anniversary Special, The Weather Channel, 2002.
I Love the Holidays, VH1, 2005.

Television Appearances; Episodic:

Hee Haw, syndicated, 1983.
The New Hollywood Squares, syndicated, 1987.
Himself, "Wind," *Bill Nye, the Science Guy* (also known as *Disney Presents "Bill Nye, the Science Guy"*), PBS, 1994.
Himself, "100," *Sisters,* NBC, 1995.
Late Night with Conan O'Brien, NBC, 1998.
(In archive footage) *The O'Reilly Factor,* Fox News Channel, 2008.

Television Producer; Series:

Willard Scott's Home and Garden Almanac, Home and Garden Television, 1994.

Film Appearances:

Himself, *Roommates,* Buena Vista, 1995.
Himself, *Holy Man,* Buena Vista, 1998.

Stage Appearances:

Narrator, *The Night before Christmas,* Boston Symphony Orchestra, Symphony Hall, Boston, MA, 1989.

Appeared at other concert venues, including Carnegie Hall, Palace Theatre, and Grand Ole Opry.

WRITINGS

Books:

Willard Scott's "The Joy of Living," Coward, 1982.
Willard Scott's Down Home Stories, Bobbs–Merrill, 1984.
Willard Scott's All–American Cookbook, Macmillan, 1986.
(With Daniel Paisner) *America Is My Neighborhood,* Simon & Schuster, 1987.
(With Robert Shosteck) *Robert Shosteck's Weekenders Guide to the Four Seasons,* revised edition, edited by Susan C. Dore, Pelican, 1988.
Not Guilty: Detective Stories from the Strand (recorded album), narrated by Edward Raleigh, DH Audio, 1995.
(With Bill Crider) *Murder under Blue Skies* (mystery novel), Dutton, 1998.
(With Crider) *Murder in the Mist: A Stanley Waters Mystery* (novel), Dutton, 1999.
(With Shosteck) *Weekend Getaways around Washington, D.C.: Including Virginia, Maryland, Delaware,* Pennsylvania, New Jersey, West Virginia, and North Carolina, 9th edition, edited by Victoria J. Heland, Pelican, 2000.
(Interviewer and compiler) *The Older the Fiddle, the Better the Tune: The Joys of Reaching a Certain Age,* Hyperion, 2003.
(Interviewer and compiler) *If I Knew It Was Going to Be This Much Fun, I Would Have Become a Grandparent First,* Hyperion, 2004.

Author of introduction to *The Thanksgiving Book: An Illustrated Treasury of Lore, Tales, Poems, Prayers, and the Best in Holiday Feasting,* edited by Jerome Agel and Melinda Corey, Smithmark Publishing, 1995; contributor to other books, including *The Christmas Tree at Rockefeller Center,* by Carla Torcilieri Dagostino, Lickle Publishing, 1997.

ADAPTATIONS

Some of Scott's books have been adapted as audio books, including *The Older the Fiddle, the Better the Tune.* Some of his "Joy Boys" radio broadcasts of the 1960s were collected by American University and released as an audio recording in 2001.

OTHER SOURCES

Periodicals:

Chicago Tribune, June 17, 2003.
Prevention, September, 2001, p. 134.
TV Guide, March 23, 2001, pp. 65–66.

SCOWLEY, Stacey

PERSONAL

Addresses: *Agent*—The McCabe Group, 8285 Sunset Blvd., Los Angeles, CA 90046. *Manager*—The Hofflund Company, 9465 Wilshire Blvd., Suite 420, Beverly Hills, CA 90212.

Career: Actress. Appeared in television commercials, including Kia automobiles, Progressive auto insurance, Sony Vaio laptops, Hanes clothing, Allstate Insurance, Applebee's restaurants, Budweiser, Chevy automobiles, Chili's restaurants, Doritos snack foods, Home Depot home stores, Miller Lite beer, Taco Bell restaurants, and Toyota automobiles; appeared in promos for FX Channel; appeared in public service announcements "Think Before You Speak."

CREDITS

Film Appearances:
Mary Stewart, *The Brotherhood 2: Young Warlocks* (also known as *Young Warlocks*), Regent Entertainment, 2001.
Stacey, *Hell Asylum,* Shadow Entertainment, 2002.
Maura, *For Mature Audiences Only* (short), 2002.
Lisa, *Loveless in Los Angeles,* Slamdance on the Road, 2007.
Stacey, *Asian Arrow IV: Back from Sheboygan* (short), 48 Hour Project, 2007.
Pierced eyebrow girl, *Walk Hard: The Dewey Cox Story* (also known as *Walk Hard* and *Walk Hard: American Cox, the Unbearably Long, Self–Indulgent Director's Cut*), Sony, 2007.
Waitress, *Eagle Eye* (also known as *Eagle Eye—AuBer Kontrolle* and *"Eagle Eye": The IMAX Experience*), DreamWorks, 2008.

Also appeared in *Caught Left–Handed; Nice Day for No Rain; Love and Laundry.*

Television Appearances; Series:
Voice of Hope, *Family Guy* (animated; also known as *Padre de familia*), Fox, 2005–2006.

Television Appearances; Specials:
Bonnie, *Comedy Central Thanxgiveaway: Home Fires,* Comedy Central, 2001.

Television Appearances; Pilots:
Sarah, *Lucky,* FX Channel, 2003.

Television Appearances; Episodic:
Young woman, "Conversations with Dead People," *Buffy the Vampire Slayer* (also known as *BtVS, Buffy,* and *Buffy, the Vampire Slayer: The Series*), UPN, 2002.
Young woman, "Sleeper," *Buffy the Vampire Slayer* (also known as *BtVS, Buffy,* and *Buffy, the Vampire Slayer: The Series*), UPN, 2002.
Sorority girl number two, "Endgame," *Alias,* ABC, 2003.
Laurie, "Mr. Monk and the T.V. Star," *Monk,* USA Network, 2004.
Coffee girl, "The Tire Guy," *Come to Papa,* NBC, 2004.
Martha in 1943, "Factory Girls," *Cold Case,* CBS, 2004.
Patty, "The Slump," *My Boys,* TBS, 2006.
Blonde wife, "Gala Gallardo," *Nip/Tuck,* FX Channel, 2006.
Bride, "Gray Hour," *Dollhouse,* Fox, 2009.

Also appeared in *Party of Five,* Fox.

Stage Appearances:
Appeared in *Good Vibrations,* Court Theatre and Attic Theatre; *The Interrogation,* Coast Playhouse, Los Angeles; *Lovers and Other Strangers,* Sanford Meisner Center, Los Angeles; *Born Yesterday,* Sanford Meisner Center; *Hurly Burly,* Sanford Meisner Center.

RECORDINGS

Music Videos:
Appeared in videos for the Foo Fighters, Tricky, and Boyz and Girls United.

OTHER SOURCES

Electronic:
Stacey Scowley Website, http://www.scowley.com, January 15, 2009.

SEMEL, David

PERSONAL

Addresses: *Agent*—Endeavor, 9601 Wilshire Blvd., 3rd Floor, Beverly Hills, CA 90210. *Manager*—3 Arts Entertainment, 9460 Wilshire Blvd., 7th Floor, Beverly Hills, CA 90212.

Career: Director, producer, and editor.

Awards, Honors: Emmy Award nomination (with others), outstanding drama series, 2006, for *House, M.D.;* Emmy Award nomination, outstanding directing for a drama series, 2007, for *Heroes.*

CREDITS

Television Work; Series:
Associate producer, *Open House,* Fox, 1989.
Associate producer, *Beverly Hills, 90210,* Fox, 1992–95.
Producer, *Dawson's Creek,* The WB, 1998–99.
Co–executive producer, *American Dreams* (also known as *Our Generation*), NBC, 2002–2004.
Executive producer, *American Dreams* (also known as *Our Generation*), NBC, 2004–2005.
Co–executive producer, *House M.D.* (also known as *House*), Fox, 2005–2006.
Executive producer, *House M.D.* (also known as *House*), Fox, 2006–2007.
Executive producer, *Heroes,* NBC, 2006.
Executive producer, *Life,* NBC, 2007—.
Executive producer, *The Cleaner,* Arts and Entertainment, 2008—.

Executive producer, *My Own Worst Enemy*, NBC, 2008.
Executive producer, *My Own Worst Enemy: Conspiracy Theory*, 2008.

Television Assistant Editor; Movies:
Can You Feel Me Dancing?, NBC, 1986.
As Is, Showtime, 1986.
A Fight for Jenny, NBC, 1986.
On Fire, ABC, 1987.

Television Work; Pilots:
Director, *Windfall*, NBC, 2006.
Executive producer and director, "Pilot: Merit Badge," *Life*, NBC, 2007.
Executive producer and director, *The Cleaner*, Arts and Entertainment, 2008.

Television Work; Specials:
Associate producer, *90210: Behind the Scenes*, Fox, 1993.

Television Director; Episodic:
"Divas," *Beverly Hills, 90210*, Fox, 1994.
"Rave On," *Beverly Hills, 90210*, Fox, 1994.
"Rock of Ages" (also known as "The Voodoo That You Do So Well"), *Beverly Hills, 90210*, Fox, 1994.
"Unreal World," *Beverly Hills, 90210*, Fox, 1995.
"Speechless," *Beverly Hills, 90210*, Fox, 1995.
"Breast Side Up," *Beverly Hills, 90210*, Fox, 1995.
"Valentine's Day," *Party of Five*, Fox, 1996.
"The Competitive Edge," *Malibu Shores*, NBC, 1996.
"Hotline," *Malibu Shores*, CBS, 1996.
"Saturday," *7th Heaven* (also known as *7th Heaven: Beginnings* and *Seventh Heaven*), The WB, 1996.
"Flirting with Disaster," *Beverly Hills, 90210*, Fox, 1996.
"Disappearing Act," *Beverly Hills, 90210*, Fox, 1996.
"Judgment Day," *Beverly Hills, 90210*, Fox, 1996.
"Happy's Valentine," *7th Heaven* (also known as *7th Heaven: Beginnings* and *Seventh Heaven*), The WB, 1997.
"See You in September," *7th Heaven* (also known as *7th Heaven: Beginnings* and *Seventh Heaven*), The WB, 1997.
"The Lung and the Restless," *Chicago Hope*, CBS, 1997.
"Welcome to the Neighborhood," *Pacific Palisades*, Fox, 1997.
"The Other Woman," *Pacific Palisades*, Fox, 1997.
"Past & Present Danger," *Pacific Palisades*, Fox, 1997.
"Sweet Revenge," *Pacific Palisades*, Fox, 1997.
"Never Kill a Boy on the First Date," *Buffy the Vampire Slayer* (also known as *Buffy* and *Buffy the Vampire Slayer: The Series*), The WB, 1997.
"What's My Line?: Part 2," *Buffy the Vampire Slayer* (also known as *Buffy* and *Buffy the Vampire Slayer: The Series*), The WB, 1997.
"My Funny Valentine," *Beverly Hills, 90210*, Fox, 1997.

"Forgive and Forget," *Beverly Hills, 90210*, Fox, 1997.
"Go Fish," *Buffy the Vampire Slayer* (also known as *Buffy* and *Buffy the Vampire Slayer: The Series*), The WB, 1998.
"Lover's Walk," *Buffy the Vampire Slayer* (also known as *Buffy* and *Buffy the Vampire Slayer: The Series*), The WB, 1998.
"I Can't Get No Satisfaction," *The Love Boat: The Next Wave*, UPN, 1998.
"Double Date" (also known as "Modern Romance"), *Dawson's Creek*, The WB, 1998.
"Decisions" (also known as "Breaking Away"), *Dawson's Creek*, The WB, 1998.
"The Kiss," *Dawson's Creek*, The WB, 1998.
"Alternate Lifestyles," *Dawson's Creek*, The WB, 1998.
"Full Moon Rising," *Dawson's Creek*, The WB, 1998.
"The All–Nighter," *Dawson's Creek*, The WB, 1998.
"Monsters," *Roswell*, The WB, 1999.
"Missing," *Roswell*, The WB, 1999.
"His Leading Lady," *Dawson's Creek*, The WB, 1999.
"Be Careful What You Wish For," *Dawson's Creek*, The WB, 1999.
"Rest in Peace," *Dawson's Creek*, The WB, 1999.
"Expecting," *Angel* (also known as *Angel: The Series*), The WB, 2000.
"Are You Now or Have You Ever Been," *Angel* (also known as *Angel: The Series*), The WB, 2000.
"Sexual Healing," *Roswell*, The WB, 2000.
"Shaken, Not Stirred," *Judging Amy*, CBS, 2000.
"Bad Hair Week," *That's Life*, ABC, 2000.
"Chapter Eight," *Boston Public*, Fox, 2000.
"Chapter Twenty–Eight," *Boston Public*, Fox, 2001.
Going to California, Showtime, 2001.
"Inter Arma Silent Leges," *The Practice*, ABC, 2001.
"Playing with Matches," *Ally McBeal*, Fox, 2002.
American Dreams (also known as *Our Generation*), NBC, 2002–2005.
"Hour One," *Revelations*, 2005.
"The Mistake," *House M.D.* (also known as *House*), Fox, 2005.
"Need to Know," *House M.D.* (also known as *House*), Fox, 2006.
"Sex Kills," *House M.D.* (also known as *House*), Fox, 2006.
"Chapter One 'Genesis,'" *Heroes*, NBC, 2006.
"The Wrap Party," *Studio 60 on the Sunset Strip* (also known as *Studio 60*), NBC, 2006.
"What You Wish For," *Six Degrees*, ABC, 2006.
"Breakdown," *My Own Worst Enemy*, NBC, 2008.
"The Night Train to Moscow," *My Own Worst Enemy*, NBC, 2008.

Television Assistant Editor; Episodic:
"Under the Gun," *Sledge Hammer!* (also known as *Sledge Hammer: The Early Years*), 1986.

Film Director:
"The Campfire" and "The Locket," in *Campfire Tales*, New Line Cinema, 1997.

Lone Star State of Mind (also known as *Road to Hell* and *Cowboys and Idiots*), Screen Gems, 2002.

SERDENA, Gene

PERSONAL

Career: Set decorator.

Awards, Honors: Emmy Award (with others), outstanding individual achievement in art direction for a series, 1992, for *Northern Exposure*.

CREDITS

Film Set Decorator:
Sorority House Massacre, Concorde Pictures, 1986.
House II: The Second Story, 1987.
Rush Week, Alpine Releasing Corp., 1989.
Martians Go Home, Taurus Entertainment, 1990.
Brain Dead (also known as *Paranoia*), 1990.
Ted and Venus, Double Helix Films, 1991.
Passed Away, Buena Vista, 1992.
The Cemetery Club (also known as *Looking for a Live One*), Buena Vista, 1993.
Tombstone, Buena Vista, 1993.
Mad Love, Buena Vista, 1995.
Steal Big, Steal Little, Twentieth Century–Fox, 1995.
Chain Reaction, Twentieth Century–Fox, 1996.
2 Days in the Valley, Metro–Goldwyn–Mayer, 1996.
U.S. Marshals, Warner Bros., 1998.
Being John Malkovich, USA Films, 1999.
Three Kings, Warner Bros., 1999.
Scream 3, Miramax, 2000.
The Animal, Sony Pictures Entertainment, 2001.
Human Nature, Fine Line, 2001.
Adaptation., Columbia, 2002.
Laurel Canyon, Sony Pictures Classics, 2002.
Auto Focus, Kuleshov Productions, Inc., 2002.
Holes, Columbia, 2003.
House of Sand and Fog, DreamWorks, 2003.
Dodgeball: A True Underdog Story (also known as *Dodgeball* and *Voll auf die nusse*), Twentieth Century Fox, 2004.
I Heart Huckabees (also known as *I Love Huckabees*), Fox Searchlight Pictures, 2004.
Lords of Dogtown (also known as *American Knights* and *Dogtown Boys*), Sony, 2005.
Infamous, Warner Independent Pictures, 2006.
The Guardian, Buena Vista, 2006.
Twilight, Summit Entertainment, 2008.
Extract, Miramax, 2009.
All About Steve, Twentieth Century–Fox, 2009.

Film Work; Other:
Set dresser, *Soul Man* (also known as *The Imposter*), New World Pictures, 1986.
Set dresser, *Cherry 2000,* 1987.
Leadman, *Russkies,* New Century/Vista Film Company, 1987.
Additional set decorator, *Tapeheads,* Avenue Pictures Productions, 1988.
Leadman, *I'm Gonna Git You Sucka* (also known as *I'm Gonna Git You, Sucka*), Metro–Goldwyn–Mayer, 1988.
Swing gang, *Heart of Dixie,* Orion, 1989.
Leadman, *Cameron's Closet,* 1989.

Television Set Decorator; Series:
Northern Exposure, CBS, 1992.

Television Set Decorator; Miniseries:
People Like Us, NBC, 1990.

Television Set Decorator; Movies:
Murder 101, USA Network, 1991.
Sweet Poison, USA Network, 1991.

SHERIDAN, Taylor
(Tayler Sheridan)

PERSONAL

Career: Actor.

CREDITS

Television Appearances; Episodic:
Vernon, "War Zone," *Walker, Texas Ranger* (also known as *Walker*), 1995.
Corporal Winters, "A Matter of Conscience," *Dr. Quinn, Medicine Woman,* 1997.
Counter guy, "Haunted," *Party of Five,* Fox, 1999.
Connor, "The Time They Decided to Go For It," *Time of Your Life,* 2001.
Tucker, "Positive," *Strong Medicine,* Lifetime, 2002.
Tim Dohanic, "Back in the Ring," *The Guardian,* CBS, 2003.
(As Tayler Sheridan) Shooter, "Brothers in Arms," *10–8: Officers on Duty* (also known as *10–8* and *10–8: Police Patrol*), ABC, 2003.
Jareb, "Chosen Realm," *Enterprise* (also known as *Star Trek: Enterprise*), UPN, 2004.
Tim Lewis, "Old Yeller," *NYPD Blue,* ABC, 2004.
Joel Banks, "Supply & Demand," *CSI: NY,* CBS, 2005.

Evan Peters, "Secrets & Files," *CSI: Crime Scene Investigation* (also known as *CSI: Las Vegas, C.S.I.,* and *Les Experts*), CBS, 2005.

Danny Boyd, a recurring role, *Veronica Mars,* UPN, 2005–2007.

Deputy Chief David Hale, a recurring role, *Sons of Anarchy,* FX Channel, 2008.

Television Appearances; Movies:

Chris, *Her Costly Affair* (also known as *Consensual Relations*), NBC, 1996.

Film Appearances:

Tug/Douglas, *White Rush,* 2003.
George, *Stage Kiss,* 2006.

SHORT, Trevor

PERSONAL

Addresses: *Office*—Nu Image/Millennium Films, 6423 Wilshire Blvd., Los Angeles, CA 90048; First Look Studios, 2000 Avenue of the Stars, Suite 410, Los Angeles, CA 90067.

Career: Producer and studio executive. Nu Image (production company), Los Angeles, CA, cofounder, partner, and chief financial officer, c. 1991—; Millennium Films, cofounder, c. 1997—; First Look Studios, Los Angeles, CA, chairman.

CREDITS

Film Executive Producer:

Woman of Desire, Trimark Pictures, 1993.
Point of Impact (also known as *In Too Deep* and *Spanish Rose*), Trimark Pictures, 1993.
Terminator Woman (also known as *Eliminator Woman*), 1993.
Private Lessons: Another Story (also known as *X–tra Private Lessons*), Nu Image, 1994.
Lunarcop (also known as *Solar Force*), Astrocop Productions, 1994.
Freefall, October Films, 1994.
Cyborg Cop II (also known as *Cyborg Soldier*), Trimark Pictures, 1994.
Wild Side (also known as *All the Way*), Evergreen Video, 1995.
Project Shadowchaser III (also known as *Project Shadowchaser 3000*), New Line Cinema, 1995.
Never Say Die, Nu Image, 1995.
The Immortals, Hallmark Home Entertainment, 1995.

Human Timebomb (also known as *Live Wire: Human Time Bomb*), New Line Cinema, 1995.
Hard Justice, New Line Cinema, 1995.
Deadly Outbreak (also known as *Deadly Takeover*), Live Entertainment, 1995.
Cyborg Cop III (also known as *Terminal Impact*), New Line Cinema, 1995.
Warhead, Vidmark Entertainment, 1996.
Orion's Key (also known as *Alien Chaser, Shadowchaser: The Gates of Time,* and *Project Shadowchaser 4*), Unapix Films, 1996.
Judge and Jury (also known as *From Beyond the Grave*), A–pix Entertainment, 1996.
American Perfekt, American Perfekt Productions, 1997.
Top of the World (also known as *Cold Cash* and *Showdown*), Warner Bros., 1997.
Merchant of Death (also known as *Mission of Death*), Artisan Entertainment, 1997.
Macarena, Dow Knut Productions, 1998.
Shadrach, Columbia, 1998.
Outside Ozona, TriStar, 1998.
On the Border, Wavemount, 1998.
Lima: Breaking the Silence, 1998.
Some Girl (also known as *Girl Talk* and *Men*), 1998.
Armstrong, 1998.
October 22, 1998.
Bridge of Dragons, Martien Holdings, 1999.
Guinevere, Miramax, 1999.
The Alternate (also known as *Agent of Death*), Replacement Productions, 1999.
Operation Delta Force 4: Deep Fault, 1999.
Beat, Background Productions/Beat/Martien Holdings/Millennium Pictures/Pendragon Film/Pfilmco/Walking Pictures, 2000.
For the Cause (also known as *Final Encounter*), Dimension Films, 2000.
Beat, 2000.
The Alternate (also known as *Agent of Death*), 2000.
Cold Heart, Diary Productions/Nu Image, 2001.
Disaster (also known as *Cult of Fury* and *Sudden Damage*), 2001.
Nobody's Baby, 2001.
City of Fear, 2001.
Spiders II: Breeding Ground (also known as *Spiders 2*), 2001.
Replicant, Artisan Entertainment, 2001.
Ticker (also known as *The Other Side of the Law*), Artisan Entertainment, 2001.
Prozac Nation, Miramax, 2001.
The Grey Zone, Lionsgate, 2001.
Edges of the Lord (also known as *Boze skrawki*), Miramax, 2001.
Diary of a Sex Addict, Addict Productions, 2001.
Octopus II (also known as *Octopus 2: River of Fear*), Martien Holdings, 2001.
Death Train, Nu Image, 2001.
Crocodile 2: Death Roll (also known as *Crocodile 2: Death Swamp*), Martien Holdings, 2001.
U.S. Seals II (also known as *U.S. Seals II: The Ultimate Force*), Artisan Entertainment, 2001.

The Order (also known as *Jihad Warriors*), Sony, 2001.

Undisputed (also known as *Undisputed—Sieg ohne Ruhm*), Miramax, 2002.

Air Strike, Nu Image Films, 2002.

Derailed (also known as *Terror Train*), 2002.

Shark Attack 3: Megalodon (also known as *Shark Attack III: Megalodon*), Nu Image Films, 2002.

Frogmen Operation Stormbringer (also known as *U.S. Seals 3: Frogmen* and *U.S. Seals: Dead or Alive*), Artisan Entertainment, 2002.

Submarines, Lions Gate Films Home Entertainment, 2003.

Marines, Lions Gate Films Home Entertainment, 2003.

Highwayman (also known as *Pourchasse*), New Line Cinema, 2003.

Death Train, Twentieth Century–Fox Home Entertainment, 2003.

In Hell (also known as *The S.H.U.* and *The Savage*), DEJ Productions, 2003.

Special Forces, Nu Image Films, 2003.

Out for a Kill, Nu Image/Millennium Films, 2003.

Air Marshal, Lions Gate Films Home Entertainment, 2003.

Shark Zone, Twentieth Century–Fox Home Entertainment, 2003.

Belly of the Beast, Nu Image/Millennium Films, 2003.

Target of Opportunity, First Look International, 2004.

Shadow of Fear, Millennium Films, 2004.

Takedown, Dimension Films, 2004.

Unstoppable (also known as *9 Lives*), Columbia TriStar Home Entertainment, 2004.

Control, Lions Gate Films, 2004.

Raging Sharks, Nu Image Films, 2005.

Submerged, Sony Pictures Home Entertainment, 2005.

Mozart and the Whale, Millennium Films, 2005.

Today You Die, Sony Pictures Home Entertainment, 2005.

Edison (also known as *Edison Force*), Sony Pictures Home Entertainment, 2005.

The Mechanik (also known as *The Russian Specialist*), Sony Pictures Home Entertainment, 2005.

The Cutter, Sony Pictures Home Entertainment, 2005.

16 Blocks, Warner Bros., 2006.

End Game, Metro–Goldwyn–Mayer, 2006.

Undisputed II: Last Man Standing (also known as *Undisputed 2*), New Line Home Video, 2006.

Mercenary for Justice (also known as *Mercenary*), Twentieth Century–Fox Home Entertainment, 2006.

Journey to the End of the Night (also known as *12 Horas ate o Amanhecer*), First Look International, 2006.

Lonely Hearts (also known as *Lonely Hearts Killers*), Samuel Goldwyn Films, 2006.

Relative Strangers, First Look International, 2006.

The Black Dahlia (also known as *Black Dahlia* and *Die schwarze dahlie*), Universal, 2006.

Loverboy, ThinkFilm, 2006.

The Wicker Man, Warner Bros., 2006.

The Contract, First Look International, 2006.

Wicked Little Things, Freestyle Releasing, 2006.

Home of the Brave, Metro–Goldwyn–Mayer, 2006.

King of California, First Look International, 2007.

88 Minutes (also known as *88* and *88: 88 Minutes*), Sony, 2007.

The Death and Life of Bobby Z (also known as *Bobby Z* and *Kill Bobby Z—Ein Deal um leben und tod*), 2007.

When Nietzsche Wept, First Look International, 2007.

Cleaner, Screen Gems, 2007.

Blonde Ambition, First Look Pictures, 2007.

Mad Money, Overture Films, 2008.

Rambo (also known as *John Rambo*, *Rambo 4*, and *Rambo 4: John Rambo*), Lionsgate, 2008.

Hero Wanted, Sony, 2008.

Day of the Dead (also known as *Day of the Dead: The Need to Feed*), Nu Image/Millennium Films, 2008.

My Mom's New Boyfriend (also known as *Lauschangriff—My Mom's New Boyfriend* and *My Spy*), Sony Pictures Home Entertainment, 2008.

Righteous Kill, Overture Films, 2008.

The Prince & Me 3: A Royal Honeymoon, 2008.

Thick as Thieves, Millennium Films, 2008.

Direct Contact, Sony Pictures Home Entertainment, 2008.

War, Inc., First Look Pictures, 2008.

The Code, First Look Holdings, 2008.

Lies & Illusions, Nu Image Films, 2009.

Streets of Blood, Millennium Films, 2009.

Solitary Man, 2009.

Ninja, Nu Image Films, 2009.

Leaves of Grass, 2009.

Labor Pains, 2009.

Fake Identity, 2009.

Command Performance, Sony Pictures Home Entertainment, 2009.

Bad Lieutenant: Port of Call New Orleans, 2009.

Film Coproducer:

F.T.W. (also known as *Last Ride*), Ivar Productions/Nu Image/RedRuby Productions, 1994.

Until Death, Sony Pictures Home Entertainment, 2007.

Film Producer:

Blood of the Innocent (also known as *Beyond Forgiveness*, *Aniol smierci*, and *AK–47: The Death Machine*), Republic Pictures, 1994.

No Code of Conduct, Dimension Films, 1998.

Major Movie Star (also known as *Private Valentine: Blonde & Dangerous*), Warner Bros., 2008.

Film Associate Producer:

Search and Destroy (also known as *The Four Rules*), October Films, 1995.

Film Co–Executive Producer:

How to Kill Your Neighbor's Dog, Artistic License, 2000.

Blind Horizon, Lions Gate Films, 2003.

Television Executive Producer; Movies:
Blood Run (also known as *Outside the Law*), 1994.
Angle of Death, Showtime, 1994.
Project Shadowchaser II (also known as *Armed and Deadly, Night Scenes: Project Shadowchaser II,* and *Night Siege*), HBO, 1994.
Man with a Gun, HBO, 1995.
The Last Days of Frankie the Fly (also known as *Frankie the Fly*), HBO, 1996.
Miami Hustle (also known as *Hello, She Lied*), Showtime, 1996.
Plato's Run, HBO, 1996.
Danger Zone, HBO, 1996.
Operation Delta Force (also known as *Great Soldiers*), HBO, 1997.
The Maker, HBO, 1997.
Dog Watch (also known as *Dogwatch*), HBO, 1997.
Operation Delta Force II: Mayday, HBO, 1998.
No Code of Conduct, USA Network, 1998.
On the Border, 1998.
Scar City (also known as *S.C.A.R.* and *Scarred City*), HBO, 1998.
Traitor's Heart, Cinemax, 1999.
Break Up (also known as *The Break Up*), Cinemax, 1999.
The Big Brass Ring, Showtime, 1999.
Sweepers, USA Network, 1999.
Shark Attack, HBO, 1999.
Operation Delta Force III: Clear Target (also known as *Clear Target*), Cinemax, 1999.
Looking for Lola, Showtime, 1999.
Cold Harvest, Cinemax, 1999.
Armstrong, HBO, 1999.
Bridge of Dragons, HBO, 1999.
The 4th Floor, HBO, 2000.
Spiders, USA Network, 2000.
Forever Lulu (also known as *Along for the Ride*), Starz!, 2000.
Crocodile, USA Network, 2000.
Shark Attack 2 (also known as *Shark Attack II* and *Shark II*), USA Network, 2000.
Octopus, USA Network, 2000.
Run for the Money (also known as *Hard Cash*), USA Network, 2002.
Try Seventeen (also known as *All I Want*), Starz!, 2003.
Alien Hunter, Sci–Fi Channel, 2003.
Den of Lions, Starz!, 2003.
Alien Lockdown (also known as *PredatorMan*), Sci–Fi Channel, 2004.
Skeleton Man, Sci–Fi Channel, 2005.
The Snake King (also known as *Snakeman*), Sci–Fi Channel, 2005.
Hammerhead: Shark Frenzy (also known as *Hammerhead* and *SharkMan*), Sci–Fi Channel, 2005.
Mansquito (also known as *Mosquitoman*), Sci–Fi Channel, 2005.
Larva, Sci–Fi Channel, 2005.
The Black Hole, Sci–Fi Channel, 2006.
Gryphon (also known as *Attack of the Gryphon: II*), Sci–Fi Channel, 2007.

Showdown at Area 51, Sci–Fi Channel, 2007.
Mega Snake, Sci–Fi Channel, 2007.
Ghouls, 2008.
Flu Bird Horror (also known as *Flu Birds*), 2008.

Television Story Editor; Movies:
Operation Delta Force (also known as *Great Soldiers*), HBO, 1997.

WRITINGS

Television Movie Stories:
Operation Delta Force (also known as *Great Soldiers*), 1997.

SIMMONS, Jean 1929–
(Jean Simmonds)

PERSONAL

Full name, Jean Merilyn Simmons; born January 31, 1929, in London, England; naturalized U.S. citizen, 1956; daughter of Charles and Winifred Ada (maiden name, Loveland) Simmons; married Stewart Granger (an actor), December 20, 1950 (divorced, 1960); married Richard Brooks (a director and writer), November 1, 1960 (died, 1992); children: (first marriage) Tracy; (second marriage) Kate. *Education:* Attended the Aida Foster School of Dancing.

Addresses: *Agent*—Burnett Granger Associates, Ltd., 3 Clifford St., London W1S 2LF United Kingdom; Mitchell K. Stubbs and Associates, 8675 West Washington Blvd., Suite 203, Culver City, CA 90232.

Career: Actress.

Awards, Honors: Volpi Cup, best actress, Venice Festival, and Academy Award nomination, best supporting actress, 1948, both for *Hamlet;* Bambi Award, 1950; voted one of the ten most popular performers in a *Motion Picture Herald–Fame* poll, 1950–51; National Board of Review Award, best actress, 1953, for *Young Bess, The Actress,* and *The Robe;* Golden Globe Award, best motion picture actress—musical/comedy, 1956, Film Award nomination, best foreign actress, British Academy of Film and Television Arts, 1957, both for *Guys and Dolls;* Special Golden Globe Award, most versatile actress, 1958; Golden Laurel Award nomination, top female dramatic performance, Producers Guild of America, Golden Globe Award nomination, best motion picture actress—drama, 1959, both for

Home before Dark; Golden Laurel Award nomination, top female star, 1959; Golden Laurel Award nomination, top female comedy performance, 1961, for *The Grass Is Greener;* Golden Laurel Award nomination, top female star, 1961; Film Award nomination, best foreign actress, British Academy of Film and Television Arts, Golden Laurel Award nomination, female dramatic performance, Golden Globe Award nomination, best motion picture actress—drama, 1961, all for *Elmer Gentry;* Academy Award nomination, best actress, 1969, Golden Globe Award nomination, best motion picture actress—drama, 1970, both for *The Happy Ending;* Emmy Award, outstanding supporting actress in a limited series or special, 1983, Golden Globe Award nomination, best performance by an actress in a supporting role in a series, miniseries or motion picture made for television, 1984, both for *The Thorn Birds;* Cannes International Film Festival homage, 1988; Emmy Award nomination, outstanding guest actress in a drama series, 1989, for *Murder, She Wrote;* Outstanding Film Achievement Award (Italy), 1989; Commander de L'Ordre des Arts des Lettres (France), 1990; Officer of the Order of the British Empire, 2003; received acting awards from Belgium, Ireland, Italy, and Switzerland.

CREDITS

Film Appearances:

(As Jean Simmonds) Sally Cooper, *Mr. Emmanuel,* Eagle–Lion, 1944.

Eva Watkins, *Meet Sexton Blake,* Anglo–American, 1944.

Molly Dodd, *Kiss the Bride Goodbye,* Butchers, 1944.

Heidi, *Give Us the Moon,* General Films, 1944.

(Uncredited) *Sports Day* (also known as *The Colonel's Cup*), 1944.

Singer, *Johnny in the Clouds* (also known as *The Way to the Stars*), United Artists, 1945.

Harpist and handmaiden, *Caesar and Cleopatra,* Eagle–Lion, 1945.

Lady Jane Broderick, *Hungry Hill,* General Films, 1946.

Kanchi, *Black Narcissus,* General Films, 1946.

Estella as a child, *Great Expectations,* Universal, 1946.

Joy Blake, *The Woman in the Hall,* Eagle–Lion/General Films, 1947.

Caroline Ruthyn, *The Inheritance* (also known as *Uncle Silas*), General Films, 1947.

Ophelia, daughter of Polonius, *Hamlet,* Universal, 1948.

Evalyn Wallace, *Adam and Evalyn* (also known as *Adam and Evelyne*), Two Cities, 1948.

Emmeline Foster, *The Blue Lagoon,* Universal, 1949.

Eve "Evie" Bishop, "Sanitorium," *Trio,* Paramount, 1950.

Vicky Barton, *So Long at the Fair,* Rank, 1950.

Judith Moray, *Cage of Gold,* Ealing, 1950.

Sophie Malraux, *The Clouded Yellow,* General Films, 1950.

Lavinia, *Androcles and the Lion* (also known as *Bernard Shaw's "Androcles and the Lion"*), RKO, 1953.

Diane Tremayne, *Angel Face,* RKO, 1953.

Queen Elizabeth I (title role), *Young Bess,* Metro–Goldwyn–Mayer, 1953.

Diana, *The Robe,* Twentieth Century–Fox, 1953.

Carolyn Parker, *Affair with a Stranger,* RKO, 1953.

Ruth Gordon Jones, *The Actress,* Metro–Goldwyn–Mayer, 1953.

Corby Lane, *She Couldn't Say No* (also known as *Beautiful but Dangerous* and *She Had to Say Yes*), RKO, 1954.

Cally Canham, *A Bullet Is Waiting,* Columbia, 1954.

Meryt (also known as Merit), *The Egyptian,* Twentieth Century–Fox, 1954.

Desiree Clary (title role), *Desiree,* Twentieth Century–Fox, 1954.

(Uncredited) Diana, *Demetrius and the Gladiators,* Twentieth Century–Fox, 1954.

Lily Watkins, *Footsteps in the Fog,* Columbia, 1955.

Sarah Brown, *Guys and Dolls,* Metro–Goldwyn–Mayer, 1955.

Title role, *Hilda Crane,* Twentieth Century–Fox, 1956.

Anne Leeds, *This Could Be the Night,* Metro–Goldwyn–Mayer, 1957.

Barbara Leslie Forbes, *Until They Sail,* Metro–Goldwyn–Mayer, 1957.

Charlotte Brown, *Home Before Dark,* Warner Bros., 1958.

Julie Maragon, *The Big Country,* United Artists, 1958.

Elizabeth Rambeau, *This Earth Is Mine* (also known as *This Land Is Mine*), Universal, 1959.

Varinia, *Spartacus* (also known as *Spartacus: Rebel Against Rome*), Universal, 1960.

Hattie Durant, *The Grass Is Greener,* Universal, 1960.

Sister Sharon Falconer, *Elmer Gantry,* United Artists, 1960.

Mary Follet, *All the Way Home,* Paramount, 1963.

Susan Lampton, *Life at the Top,* Columbia, 1965.

The blonde, *Mister Buddwing* (also known as *Woman without a Face*), Metro–Goldwyn–Mayer, 1966.

Nancy Downes, *Divorce, American Style,* Columbia, 1967.

Molly Lang, *Rough Night in Jericho,* Universal, 1967.

Mary Wilson, *The Happy Ending,* Universal, 1969.

Woman, *Say Hello to Yesterday,* Cinerama, 1971.

Estelle Benbow, *Mr. Sycamore,* Film Ventures, 1975.

Dominique Ballard (title role), *Dominique* (also known as *Avenging Spirit* and *Dominique Is Dead*), Subotsky, 1978.

Maxine de la Hunt, *Yellow Pages* (also known as *Going Undercover*), Miramax, 1988.

Aunt Mary, *The Dawning,* LIVE Home Video, 1988.

The Old Jest, 1988.

Em, *How to Make an American Quilt* (also known as *An American Quilt*), Universal, 1995.

Margaret Drummond, *Paradise Road* (also known as *Beyond the Wire, Captives, The Road to Paradise,* and *A Voice Cries Out*), Fox Searchlight Pictures, 1997.

Voice of council member number two, *Final Fantasy: The Spirits Within* (also known as *Fainaru fantaji*), Sony Pictures Entertainment, 2001.

Herself, *Jean Simmons: Rose of England* (documentary), National Museum of Photography, Film & Television, 2004.

(English version) Voice of Grandma Sophie, *Hauru no ugoku shiro* (animated; also known as *Howl's Moving Castle*), Buena Vista, 2004.

Voice of Shepway, *Thru the Moebius Strip* (animated), Fantastic Films International, 2005.

Hannah, *Shadows in the Sun*, 2008.

Television Appearances; Series:

Elizabeth Collins Stoddard and Naomi Collins, *Dark Shadows* (also known as *Dark Shadows Revival*), NBC, 1991.

Host and narrator (with Richard Kiley), *Mysteries of the Bible* (also known as *Ancient Mysteries*), Arts and Entertainment, 1993.

Irene Larson, *Angel Falls*, CBS, 1993.

Hostess, "Who wrote the Bible?" *Ancient Mysteries* (also known as *Ancient Mysteries: New Investigations of the Unsolved*), 1996.

Narrator, *Mysteries of the Bible*, 1996.

Narrator, *Mysteries of the Bible III*, 1998.

Television Appearances; Miniseries:

Aaronia Haldorn, *The Dain Curse* (also known as *Dashiell Hammett's "The Dain Curse"*), CBS, 1978.

Gretchen Jordache Burke, *Beggarman, Thief*, NBC, 1979.

Helen Lawson, *Jacqueline Susann's "Valley of the Dolls"* (also known as *Valley of the Dolls*), CBS, 1981.

Fiona "Fee" Cleary, *The Thorn Birds*, ABC, 1983.

Clarissa Main, *North and South*, ABC, 1985.

Clarissa Main, *North and South: Book II* (also known as *Love and War*), ABC, 1986.

Miss Havisham, *Great Expectations*, The Disney Channel, 1989.

Peach Prindible Bailey, *People Like Us*, NBC, 1990.

Elizabeth Collins Stoddard, *Dark Shadows*, NBC, 1991.

Television Appearances; Movies:

Jane Kingsley, *Golden Gate*, ABC, 1981.

Margaret Lawrence, *A Small Killing*, CBS, 1981.

Molly Hammond, *Midas Valley*, ABC, 1985.

Laura Kilgallen, *Perry Mason: The Case of the Lost Love* (also known as *The Case of the Lost Love*), NBC, 1987.

Lucy Brady, "Inherit the Wind," *AT&T Presents*, NBC, 1988.

Narrator, *A Friendship in Vienna* (also known as *The Devil in Vienna*), The Disney Channel, 1988.

Connie Harrison, *The Laker Girls*, CBS, 1990.

Carrie–Louise Serrocold, *They Do It with Mirrors* (also known as *Miss Marple: They Do It with Mirrors*), Arts and Entertainment, 1991.

Sarah Keyes, *One More Mountain* (also known as *One More Mountain: An American Epic*), ABC, 1994.

Katherine Palmer, *Daisies in December*, Showtime, 1995.

Katherine Stratten, *Her Own Rules* (also known as *Barbara Taylor Bradford's "Her Own Rules"*), CBS, 1998.

Countess Lucinda Rhives, *Winter Solstice* (also known as *Rosamunde Pilcher—Wintersonne* and *Wintersonne*), 2003.

Television Appearances; Specials:

The 30th Annual Academy Awards, NBC, 1958.

Presenter, *The 31st Annual Academy Awards*, NBC, 1959.

The 33rd Annual Academy Awards, ABC, 1961.

Presenter, *The 37th Annual Academy Awards*, ABC, 1965.

Sarah Churchill, "Soldier in Love" (also known as "George Schaefer's Showcase Theatre: Soldier in Love"), *Hallmark Hall of Fame*, NBC, 1967.

Fraulein Rottenmeier, *Heidi* (also known as *Heidi kehrt heim*), NBC, 1968.

Decisions, Decisions, NBC, 1972.

Constance Payne, *The Easter Promise*, CBS, 1975.

Etta Marsh, "December Flower," *Great Performances*, PBS, 1987.

Older Elinor, "Sensibility and Sense," *American Playhouse*, PBS, 1990.

The 19th Annual American Film Institute Life Achievement Award: A Salute to Kirk Douglas (also known as *An AFI Salute to Kirk Douglas*), CBS, 1991.

Alien Voices: A Halloween Trilogy, Sci–Fi Channel, 1998.

Spencer Tracy: Triumph and Turmoil, Arts and Entertainment, 1999.

Story teller, *Cleopatra's World: Alexandria Revealed*, 1999.

Narrator, *On Cukor* (documentary; also known as *American Masters: On Cukor*), PBS, 2000.

Host, *Scarlet Women of the Bible*, History Channel, 2001.

Host, *Lost Years of Jesus*, History Channel, 2001.

Host, *Heaven and Hell*, History Channel, 2001.

The 100 Greatest Family Films, Channel 4, 2005.

Television Appearances; Pilots:

Enid Travis, *The Home Front*, CBS, 1980.

Television Appearances; Episodic:

Person to Person, CBS, 1955.

Mystery guest, *What's My Line?*, CBS, 1955.

Toast of the Town (also known as *The Ed Sullivan Show*), 1955, 1957.

Suzy, "Crazier Than Cotton," *Bob Hope Presents the Chrysler Theater* (also known as *The Chrysler Theater*), NBC, 1966.

Ruth Bannister, "The Lady Is My Wife," *Bob Hope Presents the Chrysler Theater* (also known as *The Chrysler Theater*), NBC, 1967.

Princess, "The Princess," *The Odd Couple*, ABC, 1972.

"Celebrity Roast: Truman Capote," *The Dean Martin Show* (also known as *The Dean Martin Comedy Hour*), NBC, 1974.

Terri O'Brien, "The Cop on the Cover," *Hawaii Five–O* (also known as *McGarrett*), CBS, 1977.

Milly Toland, "Deceptions," *Hotel* (also known as *Arthur Hailey's "Hotel"*), ABC, 1983.

Jessica Daniels, "Hearts and Minds," *Hotel* (also known as *Arthur Hailey's "Hotel"*), ABC, 1985.

Margaret Lowen, "Pen Pal," *Alfred Hitchcock Presents,* USA Network, 1988.

Eudora McVeigh, "Mirror, Mirror, on the Wall: Parts 1 & 2," *Murder, She Wrote,* CBS, 1989.

Reflections on the Silver Screen with Professor Richard Brown, AMC, 1990.

Admiral Nora Satie, "The Drumhead," *Star Trek: The Next Generation* (also known as *Star Trek: TNG*), syndicated, 1991.

Cordelia, "Ches and the Grand Lady," *In the Heat of the Night,* 1994.

"Deborah Kerr: Getting to Know Her," *Biography,* Arts and Entertainment, 2000.

Narrator, "On Cukor," *American Masters,* 2000.

Stage Appearances:

Power of Darkness, England, 1949.

Big Fish, Little Fish, United States, 1964.

Desiree, *A Little Night Music,* London, 1974.

Major Tours:

A Little Night Music, U.S. cities, 1964.

WRITINGS

Books:

Jean Simmons "Blue Lagoon Diary," World Film Publications, 1949.

OTHER SOURCES

Books:

International Dictionary of Films and Filmmakers, Volume 3: *Actors and Actresses,* St. James Press, 1996.

Periodicals:

Films in Review, February, 1972.

SIMMONS, Johnny 1986–

PERSONAL

Full name, Johnny James Simmons; born November 28, 1986, in Montgomery, AL; raised in Dallas, TX.

Addresses: *Agent*—Brent Morley, Endeavor, 9601 Wilshire Blvd., 3rd Floor, Beverly Hills, CA 90210. *Manager*—Mimi DiTrani, Schiff Co., 9465 Wilshire Blvd., Suite 480, Beverly Hills, CA 90212.

Career: Actor.

CREDITS

Film Appearances:

Jules Walters, *My Ambition* (short film), k2 Productions, 2006.

Dylan Baxter, *Evan Almighty,* Universal, 2007.

Paul, *Boogeyman 2,* Columbia, 2007.

Actor, *Trucker,* Plu, Pictures/Hanson Allen Films, 2008.

Young Denny Colt, *The Spirit* (also known as *Will Eisner's "The Spirit"*), Lionsgate, 2008.

Dave, *Hotel for Dogs,* Paramount, 2009.

Ryan, *The Greatest,* Kimmel International, 2009.

Chip Dove, *Jennifer's Body,* Fox Atomic, 2009.

Television Appearances; Episodic:

Matt McCrary, "Killer Chat," *Numb3rs* (also known as *Num3ers*), CBS, 2006.

"The Ark, the Animals, and 'Evan Almighty'," *HBO First Look,* HBO, 2007.

"Evan Allmaechtig," *Das Grosse RTL Special sum Film,* RTL, 2007.

RECORDINGS

Videos:

Evan Almighty: Training the Animals, Universal Studios Home Entertainment, 2007.

Evan Almighty: Animals on Set Two by Two, Universal Studios Home Entertainment, 2007.

SIMONEAU, Yves 1955–

PERSONAL

Born October 28, 1955, in Quebec City, Quebec, Canada; children: two.

Addresses: *Agent*—Endeavor, 9601 Wilshire Blvd., Third Floor, Beverly Hills, CA 90210.

Career: Director, producer, writer, and editor. Directed music videos; directed and edited commercials. Worked as a camera operator for newscasts. Also worked at Radio–Canada.

Member: Directors Guild of America, Directors Guild of Canada.

Awards, Honors: Golden Berlin Bear, Berlin International Film Festival, 1987, for *Les fous de Bassan;* Genie Award nominations, best achievement in direction and (with Pierre Curzi) best original screenplay, both Academy of Canadian Cinema and Television, 1987, for *Pouvoir intime;* Silver Medal, FIPA (Festival International de Programmes Audiovisuels), and Emmy Award nomination (with others), outstanding miniseries, 1992, both for *Cruel Doubt;* CableACE Award nomination, c. 1997, for *Dead Man's Walk;* Online Television Academy Award, and Gemini Award nomination, best direction in a dramatic program or miniseries, Academy of Canadian Cinema and Television, 2001, both for *Nuremberg;* 7 d'Or, professionals vote: best director— fiction, 7 d'Or Night, Tele 7 Jours, 2003, for *Napoleon;* Emmy Award nomination (with others), outstanding miniseries, 2005, for *The 4400;* Gemeaux Award, meilleur biographie ou portrait (best biography or portrait), Academy of Canadian Cinema and Television, 2007, for *Marie–Antoinette;* Gemeaux Award, meilleur documentaire: culture (best documentary: culture), 2007, for *Marie–Antoinette sur fond vert;* Emmy Award (with others), outstanding made for television movie, and Emmy Award nomination, outstanding directing for a miniseries, movie, or a dramatic special, both 2007, and Directors Guild of America Award (with others), outstanding directorial achievement in movies for television/miniseries, 2008, all for *Bury My Heart at Wounded Knee.*

CREDITS

Film Director:
Les celebrations, Les Productions le Loup Blanc, 1979.
Les yeux rouges (also known as *Red Eyes, The Red Eyes or Accidental Truths,* and *Les yeux rouges ou les verites accidentelles*), Les Productions le Loup Blanc, 1982.
Pourquoi l'etrange Monsieur Zolock s'interessait—il a la bande dessinee? (documentary; also known as *Zolock*), SDA Productions, 1983.
Pouvoir intime (also known as *Blind Trust* and *Intimate Power*), Cinema Group, 1986.
Les fous de bassan (also known as *In the Shadow of the Wind*), Acteurs Auteurs Associes, 1987.

Dans le ventre du dragon (also known as *In the Belly of the Dragon*), Les Films Lenox, 1989.
Perfectly Normal, Skyhost/Ontario Film Development Corporation, 1990.
Mother's Boys, Dimension Films, 1994.
Free Money, Filmline International, 1998.
Ignition, Lionsgate/CLT–UFA International, 2001.
Void Moon, Millennium Films/Nu Image Films, 2009.

Film Editor:
Les celebrations, Les Productions le Loup Blanc, 1979.

Television Executive Producer; Series:
Crusoe (also known as *Robinson Crusoe*), NBC, beginning 2008.

Television Consulting Producer; Series:
Night Visions (also known as *Night Terrors* and *Nightvisions*), Fox, 2001, various episodes of the series formed the television movie *Shadow Realm,* Sci–Fi Channel, c. 2002.

Television Director; Miniseries:
Cruel Doubt, NBC, 1992.
Dead Man's Walk (also known as *Larry McMurtry's "Dead Man's Walk"*), ABC, 1996.
Intensity (also known as *Dean Koontz's "Intensity"*), Fox, 1997.
Nuremberg, TNT, 2000.
Napoleon, Arts and Entertainment, 2002.

Television Director; Movies:
Memphis, TNT, 1991.
Till Death Us Do Part (also known as *Married for Murder*), NBC, 1992.
Amelia Earhart: The Final Flight (also known as *Amelia Earhart*), TNT, 1994.
36 Hours to Die, TNT, 1999.
44 Minutes: The North Hollywood Shoot–Out, FX Network, 2003.
(With Francis Leclerc) *Marie–Antoinette* (also known as *Marie–Antoinette, la veritable histoire*), Tele–Quebec, 2006, France 2, 2007.
Bury My Heart at Wounded Knee, HBO, 2007.
Ruffian, ABC, 2007.

Television Co–Executive Producer; Movies:
Bury My Heart at Wounded Knee, HBO, 2007.

Television Coproducer; Movies:
44 Minutes: The North Hollywood Shoot–Out, FX Network, 2003.

Television Consulting Producer; Movies:
Shadow Realm (consists of "Patterns," "The Maze," "Harmony," and "Voices," all episodes of the television series *Night Visions*), Sci–Fi Channel, c. 2002.

Television Director; Specials:
(With Francis Leclerc) *Marie–Antoinette sur fond vert* (also known as *Marie Antoinette—Green Background*), Tele–Quebec, 2006.

Television Director; Episodic:
"The Passenger List," *Night Visions* (also known as *Night Terrors* and *Nightvisions*), Fox, 2001.
"Rest Stop," *Night Visions* (also known as *Night Terrors* and *Nightvisions*), Fox, 2001.
"Rum and Gunpowder" (also known as "Hour 1—Rum and Gunpowder" and "Hour 2—Rum and Gunpowder"), *Crusoe* (also known as *Robinson Crusoe*), NBC, 2008.

Television Director; Pilots:
The 4400 (also known as *4400* and *Los 4400*), USA Network and Sky One, 2004.
Cult, The WB, c. 2006.
America, Lifetime, 2009.

Director of *Titan Runner.*

Television Producer; Pilots:
The 4400 (also known as *4400* and *Los 4400*), USA Network and Sky One, 2004.

RECORDINGS

Music Videos:
Michel Rivard, "Le prive," 1989.

WRITINGS

Screenplays:
Les celebrations, Les Productions le Loup Blanc, 1979.
Les yeux rouges (also known as *Red Eyes, The Red Eyes or Accidental Truths,* and *Les yeux rouges ou les verites accidentelles*), Les Productions le Loup Blanc, 1982.
(With Pierre Curzi) *Pouvoir intime* (also known as *Blind Trust* and *Intimate Power*), Cinema Group, 1986.
Les fous de bassan (also known as *In the Shadow of the Wind*), Acteurs Auteurs Associes, 1987.
Dans le ventre du dragon (also known as *In the Belly of the Dragon*), Les Films Lenox, 1989.

SIMPSON, Joe 1958–

PERSONAL

Full name, Joe Truett Simpson; born February 17, 1958, in San Antonio, TX; son of Curtis T. and Joyce Alice (maiden name, Adams) Simpson; married Tina Drew, August 19, 1978; children: Jessica (a singer and actress), Ashlee (a singer and actress).

Addresses: *Office*—Papa Joe Film and Television, 14804 Greenleaf St., Sherman Oaks, CA 91403.

Career: Producer, personal manager, and writer. Papa Joe Film and Television, Sherman Oaks, CA, chair, chief executive officer, and producer; Papa Joe Records, owner; personal manager for his daughters and other celebrities, including Ryan Cabrera and Calvin Goldspink. Formerly worked as a Baptist youth pastor in Richardson, TX.

CREDITS

Television Executive Producer; Series:
Co–executive producer, *Newlyweds: Nick & Jessica,* MTV, 2003–2005.
The Ashlee Simpson Show, MTV, 2004.
(And creator) *Filthy Rich: Cattle Drive,* E! Entertainment Television, 2005.
Co–executive producer, *Score,* MTV, 2005.
Women's Murder Club (also known as *wmc*), ABC, 2007–2008.

Television Executive Producer; Specials:
Co–executive producer, *Happy Birthday Jessica, Love Nick,* MTV, 2004.
The Nick & Jessica Variety Hour, ABC, 2004.
Nick & Jessica's Family Christmas, ABC, 2004.
Nick & Jessica's Tour of Duty, ABC, 2005.

Television Producer:
Newlyweds: Nick & Jessica (series), MTV, 2002–2004.
Jessica (pilot), ABC, 2004.

Television Appearances; Series:
Newlyweds: Nick & Jessica, MTV, multiple appearances, 2003–2005.

Television Appearances; Episodic:
"Jessica Simpson: Where You Are," *Making the Video,* MTV, 2000.
Himself, "Down to the Wire: Part 1," *The Apprentice* (also known as *The Apprentice 2, The Apprentice Los Angeles, The Apprentice USA,* and *Celebrity Apprentice*), NBC, 2004.
"Ashlee Rocks Ryan's World," *The Ashlee Simpson Show,* MTV, 2004.
"The Show Must Go On," *The Ashlee Simpson Show,* MTV, 2005.
Jimmy Kimmel Live!, ABC, 2005.

Punk'd, MTV, 2005.
Larry King Live, Cable News Network, 2005.

Television Appearances; Specials:
The Teen Choice Awards 2004, Fox, 2004.
Jessica, Ashlee, and the Simpson Family: The E! True Hollywood Story, E! Entertainment Television, 2005.
MTV Video Music Awards 2005, MTV, 2005.

Film Producer:
Executive producer, *Undiscovered* (also known as *Newcomer—Tausche ruhm gegen leibe*), Lions Gate Films, 2005.
Employee of the Month, Lions Gate Films, 2006.
Blonde Ambition, First Look International, 2007.
Major Movie Star (also known as *Private Valentine: Blonde & Dangerous*), Papa Joe Films, 2008.

WRITINGS

Television Series:
Filthy Rich: Cattle Drive, E! Entertainment Television, 2005.

OTHER SOURCES

Periodicals:
Boston Globe, January 11, 2005, p. E5.

Electronic:
CNN Online, http://www.cnn.com, February 10, 2006.
Fox News Online, http://www.foxnews.com, September 25, 2007.

SIPOS, Shaun 1981–

PERSONAL

Born October 31, 1981, in Victoria, British Columbia, Canada.

Addresses: *Agent*—Innovative Artists Talent and Literary Agency, 1505 10th St., Santa Monica, CA 90401.

Career: Actor.

Awards, Honors: Family Television Award, Alliance for Family Entertainment, 2004.

CREDITS

Television Appearances; Series:
Nick Gibson, *Maybe It's Me,* The WB, 2001.
Jack Savage, *Complete Savages,* ABC, 2004–2005.
Trevor Boyd, a recurring role, *Shark,* CBS, 2007.

Television Appearances; Movies:
Skylar Eckerman, *Comeback Season,* Lifetime, 2006.

Television Appearances; Pilots:
Nick Gibson, *Maybe It's Me,* The WB, 2001.
Jack Savage, *Complete Savages,* ABC, 2004.

Television Appearances; Awards Presentations:
The 6th Annual Family Television Awards, The WB, 2004.
The 31st Annual People's Choice Awards, CBS, 2005.

Television Appearances; Episodic:
Teen guy, "The Wall," *Special Unit 2* (also known as *SU2*), UPN, 2001.
Travis, "Rush," *Smallville* (also known as *Smallville Beginnings* and *Smallville: Superman the Early Years*), The WB, 2003.
Julian, "Date Night," *Black Sash,* The WB, 2003.
Julian, "Prime Suspect," *Black Sash,* The WB, 2003.
Hellys/Gabe Hammond, "Urban Hellraisers," *CSI: Miami,* CBS, 2005.
Nick, "Crisis of Conscience," *ER,* NBC, 2007.

Film Appearances:
Ethan Rawlings, *The Skulls III,* Universal Studios Home Video, 2003.
Frankie, *Final Destination 2,* New Line Cinema, 2003.
Brandon, *SuperBabies: Baby Geniuses 2,* Triumph Films, 2004.
Michael, *The Grudge 2,* Columbia, 2006.
Kyle, *Lost Boys: The Tribe,* Warner Home Video, 2008.
Giovanni, *Lost Dream,* Reel Energy Entertainment, 2008.
Stoic, 2009.
Wade, *Curve of Earth,* Curve of Earth, 2009.
Evan, *Rampage,* Brightlight Pictures, 2009.

SKIFF, Maggie 1974–

PERSONAL

Born June 21, 1974, in Bronx, NY. *Education:* Graduated from Bryn Mawr College, 1996; Tisch School of the Arts, M.A., fine arts.

Addresses: *Agent*—Abrams Artists Agency, 9200 Sunset Blvd., Suite 1130, Los Angeles, CA 90069. *Manager*—James Suskin Management, 253 W. 72nd St., Suite 1014, New York, NY 10023.

Career: Actress.

Awards, Honors: Barrymore Award, outstanding supporting actress, Theatre Alliance of Great Philadelphia, 1998, for *Ghosts;* Screen Actors Guild Award nomination (with others), outstanding performance by an ensemble in a drama series, 2008, for *Mad Men.*

CREDITS

Television Appearances; Series:
Rachel Menken, *Mad Men,* AMC, 2007—.
Tara Knowles, *Sons of Anarchy,* FX Channel, 2008.

Television Appearances; Episodic:
Cindy, "Obsession," *Third Watch,* NBC, 2004.
Young woman at Alcoholics Anonymous, "Twat," *Rescue Me* (also known as *Rescue Me: FDNY*), FX Channel, 2005.
Emily McCooper, "Gone," *Law & Order: Special Victims Unit* (also known as *Law & Order: SVU* and *Special Victims Unit*), NBC, 2006.
Lisa Ketchum, "The God Spot," *3 lbs.,* CBS, 2006.
Ruthie Sales, "The Heart of the Matter," *Grey's Anatomy,* ABC, 2007.
Rachel Ben Natan, "Duke Collins," *Nip/Tuck,* FX Channel, 2007.
Attorney Mahaffey, "Executioner," *Law & Order,* NBC, 2008.
Rachel Ben Natan, "August Walden," *Nip/Tuck,* FX Channel, 2008.
Rachel Ben Natan, "Rachel Ben Natan," *Nip/Tuck,* FX Channel, 2008.

Television Appearances; Movies:
Suze Kowalski, *Philadelphia Diary,* PBS, 2000.

Film Appearances:
Attorney number one, *Michael Clayton,* Warner Bros., 2007.
Girlfriend, *Then She Found Me,* THINKFilm, 2007.
Teresa Stowe, *Push,* Summit, 2009.
Rabbi Zimmerman, *Leaves of Grass,* 2009.

Stage Appearances:
Thomasina, *Arcadia,* Wilma Theatre, Philadelphia, PA, 1997.
Olleanna, Walnut Street Theatre, Philadelphia, PA, 1997.

Aunt Dan & Lemon, Interact Theatre Company, Philadelphia, PA, 1998.
Ghosts, Lantern Theatre Company, Philadelphia, PA, 1998.
Matron and Julia, *Mean white, on the Other Side of Mount Vesuvius,* Adobe Theatre Company, New York City, 1999.
Lulu, *The Ruby Sunrise,* Joseph Papp Public Theatre, New York City, 2005.
Catherine, *Frank's Home,* Playwrights Horizons Theatre, New York City, 2007.

RECORDINGS

Videos:
Rachel Menken, *Scoring 'Mad Men',* Lions Gate Films Home Entertainment, 2008.
Herself/Rachel Menken, *Establishing Mad Men,* Lions Gate Films Home Entertainment, 2008.

SMIGEL, Robert 1960–
(Robert Smigal, Triumph the Insult Comic Dog, Triumph the Insult Dog)

PERSONAL

Born February 7, 1960, in New York, NY; father, a dentist; married Michelle Saks; children: Daniel. *Education:* New York University, degree in communications; also attended Cornell University; studied improvisation at Second City, Chicago, IL.

Addresses: *Agent*—Creative Artists Agency, 2000 Avenue of the Stars, Los Angeles, CA 90067.

Career: Writer, producer, and actor. All You Can Eat (improvisational troupe), Chicago, IL, member, mid–1980s.

Awards, Honors: Emmy Award nominations (with others), outstanding writing in a variety or music program, 1987, 1989, 1990, 1991, 1992, 1993, 2001, 2003, 2008, Emmy Awards (with others), outstanding writing in a variety or music program, 2002, Television Award nominations (with others), best comedy/variety (including talk) series, Writers Guild of America, 2002, 2003, 2007, all for *Saturday Night Live;* First Prize (with J. D. Sedelmaier), World Animation Festival, 1997; Emmy Award nominations (with others), outstanding writing for a variety or music program, 1997, 2000, 2002, Television Award nominations (with others), best comedy/variety (including talk) series, Writers Guild of America, 1999, 2004, Television Awards (with others), best comedy/variety (including talk) series, Writers Guild of America, 2002, 2003, 2005, 2006, all for *Late Night with Conan O'Brien*; Ernie Kovacs Award, Dallas Video Festival, 1998; Television Award (with others), best comedy/variety—music, awards, tributes—specials any length, Writers Guild of America, 2001, for *Saturday Night Live: 25th Anniversary*.

CREDITS

Film Appearances:
Concert nerd, *Wayne's World 2*, Paramount, 1993.
Mr. Oblaski, *Billy Madison*, 1995.
IRS agent, *Happy Gilmore*, Universal, 1996.
Mail room guy with glasses, *Tomorrow Night*, 1998.
Andre, *The Wedding Singer*, New Line Cinema, 1998.
(Uncredited) Voice of the captain, *Titey*, 1998.
Voice, *Hete Roy* (animated short), 2000.
Voice of Mr. Beefy, *Little Nicky*, New Line Cinema, 2000.
Himself, *Adam Sandler Goes to Hell*, New Line Home Video, 2000.
Walter the dentist, *Punch–Drunk Love*, Sony, 2002.
(As Triumph the Insult Comic Dog) Triumph the Insult Comic Dog, *"Late Night with Conan O'Brien": The Best of Triumph the Insult Comic Dog* (also known as *The Best of Triumph the Insult Comic Dog*), 2004.
Various voices, *"Saturday Night Live": The Best of Saturday TV Funhouse*, Universal Studios Home Entertainment, 2006.
Himself, *In Search of Puppy Love* (documentary; also known as *In Search of Puppy Love: Giving Hope to the 104 Million Singles in America*), 2007.
Mailman, *I Now Pronounce You Chuck & Larry*, Universal, 2007.
Yosi, *You Don't Mess with the Zohan*, Sony, 2008.

Film Work:
Producer, *Hete Roy* (animated short), 2000.
Producer, *"Late Night with Conan O'Brien": The Best of Triumph the Insult Comic Dog* (also known as *The Best of Triumph the Insult Comic Dog*), 2004.
Producer and director, *"Saturday Night Live": The Best of Saturday TV Funhouse*, Universal Studios Home Entertainment, 2006.
Producer, *You Don't Mess with the Zohan*, Sony, 2008.

Television Appearances; Series:
Himself and various voices, *Saturday Night Live* (also known as *NBC's Saturday Night*, *SNL*, and *Saturday Night*), NBC, 1985—.
Voices of various characters, *Late Night with Conan O'Brien*, NBC, 1993—.
Various characters, *The Dana Carvey Show* (also known as *The Mug Root Beer Dana Carvey Show* and *The Taco Bell Dana Carvey Show*), ABC, 1996.

Voices of Fogey, Xabu, Triumph, Rocky, and others, *TV Funhouse*, Comedy Central, 2000–2001.
(As Triumph the Insult Comic Dog) *Last Comic Standing: The Search for the Funniest Person in America*, NBC, 2004–2005.

Television Appearances; Movies:
Triumph the Insult Comic Dog, *It's a Very Merry Christmas Movie*, NBC, 2002.

Television Appearances; Specials:
The Brainwave, *Superman 50th Anniversary*, 1988.
A Comedy Salute to Michael Jordan, NBC, 1991.
Superfan, Carl Wollarski, *"Saturday Night Live": The Best of Chris Farley*, NBC, 1998.
(Uncredited) Voice of Triumph, President Clinton, and others, *"Late Night with Conan O'Brien": 5th Anniversary Special*, NBC, 1998.
"Saturday Night Live": 25th Anniversary Primetime Special, NBC, 1999.
Voice of the Triumph the Insult Comic Dog, *Comedy Central Presents: The N.Y. Friars Club Roast of Rob Reiner*, Comedy Central, 2000.
Triumph the Insult Comic Dog, *MTV Video Music Awards 2001*, MTV, 2001.
"Saturday Night Live": TV Tales, 2002.
TV's Most Censored Moments, 2002.
Triumph the Insult Comic Dog, *MTV Video Music Awards 2002* (also known as *VMAs 2002*), MTV, 2002.
(As Triumph the Insult Dog) Triumph the Insult Comic Dog, *It's a Very Merry Muppet Christmas Movie*, 2002.
Triumph the Insult Comic Dog, *"Late Night with Conan O'Brien" 10th Anniversary Special*, NBC, 2003.
Himself and Triumph the Insult Comic Dog, *Heroes of Jewish Comedy*, 2003.
Triumph the Insult Comic Dog, *Comedy Central Presents: The Commies* (also known as *The Commies*), Comedy Central, 2003.
(As Triumph the Insult Comic Dog) Triumph the Insult Comic Dog, *The Osborne Family Christmas Special*, MTV, 2003.
(As Triumph the Insult Comic Dog) *The 2003 Billboard Music Awards*, Fox, 2003.
(As Triumph the Insult Comic Dog) *I Love the '80s Strikes Back*, Fox, 2003.
101 Most Unforgettable SNL Moments, 2004.
(As Triumph the Insult Comic Dog) *How's Your News? On the Campaign Trail*, Trio, 2004.
"Saturday Night Live" in the '80s: Lost & Found, NBC, 2005.
Voice of Triumph the Insult Comic Dog, *Eninem's "Making the Ass,"* 2005.
(As Triumph the Insult Comic Dog) *Earth to America!*, TBS, 2005.
(As Triumph the Insult Comic Dog) Triumph the Insult Comic Dog, *Night of Too Many Stars: An Over-*

booked Event for Autism Education, Comedy Central, 2006.

(As Triumph the Insult Comic Dog) *Comic Relief 2006,* HBO and TBS, 2006.

Himself and Carl Wollarski, *"Saturday Night Live" in the '90s: Pop Culture Nation,* NBC, 2007.

Voice of Palpatine Parody, *Robot Chicken: Star Wars* (animated), Comedy Central, 2007.

Television Appearances; Episodic:

Pearce Dummy, "Pearce on Conan," *LateLine,* NBC, 1999.

(As Triumph the Insult Comic Dog) *Hollywood Squares* (also known as *H2* and *H2: Hollywood Squares*), syndicated, 2002.

Face Time, 2002.

Voice of John Tierney, *Crank Yankers,* Comedy Central and MTV2, 2003.

Voice of Samir, *Crank Yankers,* Comedy Central and MTV2, 2003.

Voice of Triumph the Insult Comic Dog, "Dreams," *Space Ghost Coast to Coast* (animated; also known as *SGC2C*), Cartoon Network, 2004.

Triumph the Insult Comic Dog, *Howard Stern,* 2004, 2005.

Triumph the Insult Comic Dog, *The O'Reilly Factor,* 2004.

Voice of Lawyer, *Crank Yankers,* Comedy Central and MTV2, 2007.

Celebrity judge, *The Gong Show with Dave Attell,* 2008.

(As Robert Smigal) Triumph the Insult Comic Dog, "NRA vs. PETA," *Root of All Evil* (also known as *Lewis Black's "Root of All Evil"*), Comedy Central, 2008.

Television Work; Series:

Coproducer, *Saturday Night Live* (also known as *NBC's Saturday Night, SNL,* and *Saturday Night*), NBC, 1990–92.

Executive producer, *The Dana Carvey Show* (also known as *The Mug Root Beer Dana Carvey Show* and *The Taco Bell Dana Carvey Show*), ABC, 1996.

Producer, *Saturday Night Live* (also known as *NBC's Saturday Night, SNL,* and *Saturday Night*), NBC, 1997–2006.

Executive producer and director, *TV Funhouse,* Comedy Central, 2000.

Television Work; Specials:

Producer, *"Saturday Night Live": The Best of Chris Farley,* NBC, 1998.

Cartoonist, *"Saturday Night Live": 25th Anniversary Primetime Special,* NBC, 1999.

Executive producer, *Night of Too Many Stars,* NBC, 2003.

Executive producer, *Night of Too Many Stars: An Overbooked Event for Autism Education,* Comedy Central, 2006, 2008.

Television Work; Pilots:

Producer, *Lookwell,* NBC, 1991.

Executive producer, *Match Game,* TBS, 2008.

Television Work; Episodic:

Director, "TV Funhouse" segment, *Saturday Night Live* (also known as *NBC's Saturday Night, SNL,* and *Saturday Night*), NBC, 1996–2004.

Consultant, "Fareed Zakaria," *The Colbert Report,* Comedy Central, 2005.

Consultant, "Nina Totenberg," *The Colbert Report,* Comedy Central, 2006.

Consultant, "Paul Begala," *The Colbert Report,* Comedy Central, 2006.

RECORDINGS

Albums:

(As Triumph the Insult Comic Dog) *Come Poop With Me,* Warner Bros., 2003.

Music Videos:

Appeared in Eminem's "Ass Like That."

WRITINGS

Screenplays:

Titey, 1998.

Hete Roy (animated short), 2000.

"Saturday Night Live": The Best of Saturday TV Funhouse, Universal Studios Home Entertainment, 2006.

You Don't Mess with the Zohan, Sony, 2008.

Television Writing; Specials:

Superman 50th Anniversary (also known as *Superman 50th Anniversary: A Conversation of the Man of Steel*), CBS, 1988.

The 40th Annual Primetime Emmy Awards, Fox, 1988.

"Saturday Night Live": 15th Anniversary, NBC, 1989.

(Special material) *A Comedy Salute to Michael Jordan,* NBC, 1991.

"Saturday Night Live": All the Best for Mother's Day, NBC, 1992.

The 2nd Annual "Saturday Night Live" Mother's Day Special, NBC, 1993.

"Saturday Night Live": The Best of Chris Farley (also known as *"Saturday Night Live" Remembers Chris Farley*), NBC, 1998.

"Saturday Night Live": The Best of Phil Hartman, NBC, 1998.

(Uncredited) *"Saturday Night Live": The Best of Jon Lovitz,* NBC, 1998.

"Saturday Night Live": 25th Anniversary, NBC, 1999.

"Saturday Night Live": Mothers' Day Special, NBC, 2001.

"Saturday Night Live" Primetime Extra II, NBC, 2001.

(Additional material) *"Late Night with Conan O'Brien"*: 10th Anniversary Special, NBC, 2003.

Night of Too Many Stars, 2003.

Night of Too Many Stars: An Overbooked Concert for Autism Education, Comedy Central, 2008.

Television Pilots:

Lookwell, NBC, 1991.

Television Episodes:

Saturday Night Live (also known as *NBC's Saturday Night, SNL,* and *Saturday Night*), NBC, 1985—.

Late Night with Conan O'Brien, NBC, 1993–2000.

The Dana Carvey Show (also known as *The Mug Root Beer Dana Carvey Show* and *The Taco Bell Dana Carvey Show*), ABC, 1996.

TV Funhouse, Comedy Central, 2000–2001.

(Special material) *Last Comic Standing: The Search for the Funniest Person in America,* NBC, 2007–2008.

Books:

(With Conan O'Brien, Andy Richter, and Louis C. K.) *If They Mated,* Hyperion, 1995.

(With Adam McKay) *X–Presidents,* Villard Books, 2000.

OTHER SOURCES

Books:

Newsmakers, Issue 3, Gale Group, 2001.

Periodicals:

People Weekly, May 19, 1997, p. 19.

Time, December 4, 2000, p. 174.

SMITH, Amber 1972–

PERSONAL

Born March 2, 1972, in Tampa, FL; father, a professional football player; mother, a model.

Addresses: *Publicist*—Jerry Shandrew Public Relations, 1050 South Stanley Ave., Los Angeles, CA 90019.

Career: Actress. Previously worked as a model; Michelob Ultra Amber Lite, spokesperson, 2006.

CREDITS

Film Appearances:

Debbie, *Faithful,* Savoy Pictures, 1996.

Bridgette, *The Funeral,* October Films, 1996.

Felicia on video, *The Mirror Has Two Faces,* TriStar, 1996.

Paula, *Lowball,* Cinequanon Home Video, 1997.

Cathy, *Sleeping Together,* Trident Releasing, 1997.

Julie, *Private Parts* (also known as *Howard Stern's "Private Parts"*), Paramount, 1997.

Susan Lefferts, *L.A. Confidential,* Warner Bros., 1997.

Amber, *How to Be a Player* (also known as *Def Jam's "How to Be a Player"*), Gramercy, 1997.

Christy Kane, *American Beauty,* DreamWorks, 1999.

Vanessa Rio, *Deception* (also known as *Other Peoples Secrets, Star Struck,* and *Starstruck*), Lions Gate Films, 2000.

Alex, *The Midnight Hour* (also known as *In the Midnight Hour* and *Tell Me No Lies*), Artisan Entertainment, 2000.

Beautiful canyon girl, *Dirk and Betty,* 2000.

Tell Me No Lies, 2000.

Charlie, *Reasonable Doubt* (also known as *Crime Scene* and *The Baptist*), 2001.

Gorgeous redhead, *Tomcats,* Sony, 2001.

Professor Garr, *How High,* Universal, 2001.

Jennifer, *New Suit,* Trillion Entertainment, 2002.

Lady in white, *Dead End,* Lionsgate, 2003.

Enemies of Laughter, Outrider Pictures, 2003.

Television Appearances; Series:

Angelica, *Sin City Diaries,* Cinemax, 2007.

Celebrity Rehab with Dr. Drew (also known as *Celebrity Rehab 2 with Dr. Drew*), VH1, 2008.

Match Mistress, E! Entertainment Television, 2008.

Television Appearances; Movies:

Inferno (also known as *Inferno!*), 1992.

Sheila, *Mars,* HBO, 1997.

Elise Talbot, *Laws of Deception,* Cinemax, 1997.

Broad at casino, *The Rat Pack,* HBO, 1998.

Television Appearances; Specials:

Herself (L.A. Temptation number two), *Lingerie Bowl,* 2006.

Television Appearances; Pilots:

Celebrity Rehab Presents Sober House (also known as *Sober House*), VH1, 2009.

Television Appearances; Episodic:

The model, "Runaway," *Red Shoe Diaries* (also known as *Zalman King's "Red Shoe Diaries"*), Showtime, 1993.

"As She Wishes," *Red Shoe Diaries* (also known as *Zalman King's "Red Shoe Diaries"*), Showtime, 1995.

Rachel, "Gigolo Guy," *Head Over Heels,* UPN, 1997.

Maria the gym lady, "The One with the Ballroom Dancing," *Friends,* NBC, 1997.

Herself, "Sweet Charity," *Just Shoot Me!,* NBC, 1997.

Howard Stern, E! Entertainment Television, 1997, 1998, 2001.

Davina, "Beats Working at a Hot Dog Stand," *V.I.P.* (also known as *V.I.P.—Die Bodyguards*), syndicated, 1998.

Diane Verne, "Cruz Control," *Pacific Blue,* USA Network, 1998.

Virginia, "Noir: Parts 1 & 2," *Silk Stalkings,* USA Network, 1999.

RECORDINGS

Videos:
Appeared in *Amber Smith Raw.*

SMITH, Jamie Renee 1987–

PERSONAL

Born April 10, 1987, in New York, NY. *Education:* Studied acting at Center Stage, Los Angeles, CA. *Avocational Interests:* Gymnastics, rollerblading, roller skating, skiing, ice skating, dancing, and singing.

Addresses: *Agent*—Hervey–Grimes Talent, 10561 Missouri Ave., Suite 2, Los Angeles, CA 90025.

Career: Actress.

Awards, Honors: Young Artist Award, best performance in a feature film: young actress age ten or under, 1998, for *Dante's Peak;* Young Artist Award, best performance in a television movie or pilot—leading young actress, 2000, for *My Last Love;* Young Artist Award nomination, best performance in a feature film—leading young actress, 2001, for *MVP: Most Valuable Primate;* Young Artist Award, best performance in a television drama series—guest starring young actress, 2002, for *ER.*

CREDITS

Film Appearances:
Molly Kang, *Midnight Man* (also known as *Blood for Blood*), 1994.

Natasha, *Ringer,* Precious Films, 1996.

Mary Margaret, *Magic in the Mirror: Fowl Play,* 1996.

Mary Margaret, *Magic in the Mirror,* Paramount Home Video, 1996.

Margaret Rhodes, *Children of the Corn IV: The Gathering* (also known as *Deadly Harvest*), Dimension Films, 1996.

Lauren Wando, *Dante's Peak,* MCA/Universal, 1997.

Elizabeth Robinson, *The New Swiss Family Robinson,* Gross Receipts, Inc., 1998.

Tara Westover, *MVP: Most Valuable Primate,* Keystone Family Pictures, 2000.

Herself and Tara Westover, *The Chimp's a Champ: The Making of a Star Hockey Player* (documentary short), Warner Home Video, 2001.

Television Appearances; Series:
Blair Cody, *Ask Harriet,* Fox, 1998.

Television Appearances; Movies:
Brandy Gardner, *Someone She Knows,* The WB, 1994.

Jennifer, *Roseanne: An Authorized Biography,* Fox, 1994.

Alicia, *Blood Run* (also known as *Outside the Law*), 1994.

Young Katherine, *Toothless,* ABC, 1997.

Ellen Bloom, *Rhapsody in Bloom,* Starz!, 1998.

Carson, *My Last Love* (also known as *To Live For*), ABC, 1999.

Amy, *Up, Up, and Away!,* The Disney Channel, 2000.

Television Appearances; Episodic:
Abby Lasky, "Teacher's Pet," *Saved by the Bell: The College Years,* NBC, 1993.

Monica Gresham, "Shades of Gray," *Dark Skies,* NBC, 1997.

Monica Gresham, "Burn, Baby, Burn," *Dark Skies,* NBC, 1997.

Young Nadine Fine, "Fran's Roots," *The Nanny,* CBS, 1997.

Rebecca, "Send Me an Angel," *VR.5* (also known as *VR*), Fox, 1997.

Young Fran, "The Wedding," *The Nanny,* CBS, 1998.

Young Fran, "The Hanukkah Story," *The Nanny,* CBS, 1998.

"The Children's Hour," *Cupid,* ABC, 1999.

"It's a Man's World," *Any Day Now,* Lifetime, 1999.

Emily Perrault, "Survival of the Fittest," *ER,* NBC, 2001.

Lorna, "Baby Come Back," *Grounded for Life,* 2003.

Paula, "Malcolm Visits College," *Malcolm in the Middle,* Fox, 2004.

Abby Coleman, "One Hit Wonder," *Shark,* CBS, 2008.

Karen, "The Perfect Pieces in the Purple Pond," *Bones,* Fox, 2008.

SOLO, Ksenia 1987–

PERSONAL

Born October, 1987, in Latvia.

Career: Actress.

Awards, Honors: Gemini Awards, best performance in a children's or youth program or series, Academy of Canadian Cinema and Television, 2005, 2006, both for *Renegadepress.com.*

CREDITS

Film Appearances:
Hannah, *A Man of Substance* (short), 2001.
Micheline, *The Republic of Love,* Seville Pictures, 2003.
Emma, *The Factory,* Warner Bros., 2009.

Television Appearances; Series:
Zoey Jones, *Renegadepress.com,* Associated Press Television News, 2004–2008.

Television Appearances; Movies:
Abby Lynn Anders, *My Louisiana Sky,* Showtime, 2001.
Girl, *What Girls Learn,* Showtime, 2001.
Lucinda, *Sins of the Father,* FX Channel, 2002.
Kristyn Posey, *Defending Our Kids: The Julie Posey Story,* Lifetime, 2003.
Amy Stein, *Mayday,* CBS, 2005.
Erin Benson, *Love Thy Neighbor,* Lifetime, 2006.

Television Appearances; Episodic:
Kathy Simmons, "Take No Prisoners," *Earth: Finale Conflict* (also known as *EFC, Gene Roddenberry's "Earth: Final Conflict," Invasion planete Terre,* and *Mission Erde: Sie sind unter uns*), syndicated, 2000.
Natalie, "Village of the Lost," *Adventure Inc.* (also known as *Aventure et associes*), syndicated, 2002.
Megan Hahn, "Judgement Day," *1–800–MISSING* (also known as *Missing* and *Porte Disparu*), Lifetime, 2004.
Angela Howard, "All Bets Off: Part 1," *Kojak,* USA Network, 2005.
Lena, "Cargo," *Cold Case,* CBS, 2007.
Bonnie Morrow, "Fated to Pretend," *Moonlight,* CBS, 2008.

SOUL, David 1943–

PERSONAL

Original name, David Richard Solberg; born August 28, 1943, in Chicago, IL; naturalized British citizen, 2004; son of Richard Solberg (a Lutheran minister, educator, and diplomatic consultant); mother, a singer; married Miriam "Lynn" Russeth, c. 1964 (divorced, 1965); married Karen Carlson (an actress, producer, director, and writer), June 22, 1968 (divorced, 1977); married Patty Sherman (some sources cite name as Patty Kathman), October 12, 1980 (divorced, 1986); married Julia Nickson (an actress), December, 1987 (divorced, 1993); partner of Alexa Hamilton (an actress and singer), beginning c. 1994; children: (first marriage) one son; (second marriage) one son; (third marriage) three sons; (with Hamilton) China Alexandra. *Education:* Attended Augustana College, Sioux Falls, SD, University of the Americas, University of Mexico City, and University of Minnesota—Twin Cities; studied acting with Uta Hagen and Irene Dailey. *Avocational Interests:* Skiing, tennis, soccer spectator (especially Arsenal Football Club in England).

Addresses: *Agent*—(voice work) Lip Service Casting Ltd., 4 Kingly St., Soho, London W1B 5PE, England.

Career: Actor, producer, director, singer, musician, and writer. Performed as a folksinger and toured as opening act for bands, including the Byrds, Jay and the Americans, and the Lovin' Spoonful; toured the United States, Europe, Japan, and South America as a singer and musician, including a British tour, 1999. Previously worked as a grocery boy. Activist for social causes; appears in occasional commercials.

Member: Screen Actors Guild, American Federation of Television and Radio Artists.

Awards, Honors: TV Land Award nominations (with Paul Michael Glaser), favorite crime–stopper duo, 2004, and most uninsurable driver, 2005, both for *Starsky and Hutch.*

CREDITS

Television Appearances; Series:
Joshua Bolt, *Here Come The Brides,* ABC, 1968–69.
Detective Ken "Hutch" Hutchinson, *Starsky and Hutch,* ABC, 1975–79.
Richard "Rick" Blaine, *Casablanca,* NBC, 1983.
Roy Champion, *The Yellow Rose,* NBC, 1983–84.
John Wesley "Westy" Grayson, a recurring role, *Unsub* (also known as *Unknown Subject*), NBC, 1989.

Television Appearances; Miniseries:
Ben Mears, *Salem's Lot* (also known as *Blood Thirst, Salem's Lot: The Miniseries,* and *Salem's Lot: The Movie*), CBS, 1979.
Caleb Staunton, *The Manions of America,* ABC, 1981.
Lieutenant Colonel Jake Caffey, *World War III,* NBC, 1982.

A Parade of Witnesses, 1983.
Alex Wolff, *The Key to Rebecca* (also known as *Ken Follett's "The Key to Rebecca"*), Operation Prime Time, 1985.
Lieutenant Ryker, *The Secret of the Sahara* (also known as *Das Geheimnis der Sahara, El secreto del Sahara,* and *Il segreto del Sahara*), RAI, 1987.
Zoltan Kouros, *Sandra princesse rebelle,* 1995.
Walter, *Les filles du Lido,* 1995.

Television Appearances; Movies:
Captain Roy Bishop, *The Disappearance of Flight 412,* NBC, 1974.
Lyle York, *Little Ladies of the Night* (also known as *Diamond Alley*), ABC, 1977.
Jesse Swan, *Swan Song,* ABC, 1980.
Cal Morrisey, *Rage!,* NBC, 1980.
Jake Seaton, *Homeward Bound,* CBS, 1980.
William Parrish, *Through Naked Eyes,* ABC, 1984.
Captain Kevin Harris, *The Fifth Missile* (also known as *Operation Fire*), NBC, 1986.
Harry Petros, *Harry's Hong Kong* (also known as *China Hand*), ABC, 1987.
Michael "Mike" Lee Platt, *In the Line of the Duty: The F.B.I. Murders* (also known as *The F.B.I. Murders*), NBC, 1988.
Down and Under, 1988.
Peter Armetage, *Prime Target,* NBC, 1989.
Owen Malloy/John McGuire, *The Bride in Black,* ABC, 1990.
Alden Ernst, *So Proudly We Hail,* CBS, 1990.
Terry Anderson, *Cry in the Wild: The Taking of Peggy Ann,* NBC, 1991.
Truman York, *Perry Mason: The Case of the Fatal Framing* (also known as *Perry Mason: The Case of the Posthumous Painter*), NBC, 1992.
Sam Haney, *Grave Secrets: The Legacy of Hilltop Drive* (also known as *Grave Secrets*), CBS, 1992.
Quill, *Vents contraires* (also known as *Crosswinds*), 1995.
Roger Carey, *Terror in the Mall* (also known as *Dark Rain* and *The Mall–Flutkatastrophe im shopping-center*), Fox, 1998.

Television Appearances; Specials:
Host, *The David Soul and Friends Special,* ABC, 1977.
Mac Davis: I Believe in Christmas, NBC, 1977.
The Captain and Tennille in Hawaii, ABC, 1978.
Happy Birthday, Bob (also known as *Bob Hope Special: Happy Birthday, Bob!*), NBC, 1978.
A Country Christmas, CBS, 1979.
Fifteenth Annual Circus of the Stars, CBS, 1990.
Ken "Hutch" Hutchinson (in archive footage), *Derrick contre Superman,* 1992.
Host, *Ira Gershwin: A Centenary Celebration—Who Could Ask for Anything More?,* Arts and Entertainment, 1997.
An All Star Party for Aaron Spelling, ABC, 1998.

Narrator, *Curses of Ancient Egypt,* 2002.
God Save the Queen: The Soundtrack to the Summer of '77, 2002.
EastEnders: Christmas Party, BBC, 2003.
Ken "Hutch" Hutchinson (in archive footage), *Total Cops,* BBC, 2003.
Title role, *Jerry Springer: The Opera,* BBC, 2005.
X Rated: Top 20 Most Controversial TV Moments, E4, 2005.
Forty Years of Fuck, BBC, 2005.
Kings of 70s Romance, BBC, 2007.

Television Appearances; Pilots:
Joshua Bolt, *Here Come the Brides,* ABC, 1968.
Curt Lowens, *Intertect,* ABC, 1973.
Jeff, *Movin' On,* NBC, 1974.
Ken "Hutch" Hutchinson, *Starsky and Hutch,* ABC, 1975.

Television Appearances; Episodic:
(Television debut) The hooded "mystery" singer ("the covered man"), *Merv Griffin Show,* syndicated, 1966.
Orderly, "My Master the Weakling," *I Dream of Jeannie,* NBC, 1967.
Makora, "The Apple," *Star Trek* (also known as *Star Trek: The Original Series* and *Star Trek: TOS*), NBC, 1967.
Dennis Blake, "The Firing Line: Part 1," *Flipper,* 1967.
John Marshall, "The Age of Independence," *The Young Rebels,* 1970.
Lawrence Merrill III, "The Manufactured Man," *Dan August,* CBS, 1971.
Member of "The Predators", "Lesson in Terror," *Ironside* (also known as *The Raymond Burr Show*), NBC, 1971.
Pete, "Eulogy for a Wide Receiver," *Owen Marshall: Counselor at Law,* ABC, 1971.
Szabo Djorak, "Gloria Poses in the Nude," *All in the Family,* 1971.
Clifford Wade, "The Runner," *The F.B.I.,* ABC, 1972.
Inspector James "Jim" Martin, "Hall of Mirrors," *The Streets of San Francisco,* ABC, 1972.
Doug, "Love Child," *Owen Marshall: Counselor at Law,* ABC, 1972.
"The Phantom of Herald Square," *Ghost Story* (also known as *Circle of Fear*), NBC, 1973.
Sean, "Death of a Stone Seahorse," *Cannon,* CBS, 1973.
Udo Giesen, "Lady in Red," *Cannon,* CBS, 1974.
Jerry, "Guilt by Association," *McMillan & Wife* (also known as *McMillan*), NBC, 1974.
Walter, "Kiss and Kill," *Medical Center,* CBS, 1974.
Johnny Dane, "A Test of Courage," *The Rookies,* 1974.
Ike Hockett, "Brides and Grooms," *Gunsmoke* (also known as *Gun Law* and *Marshal Dillon*), 1975.
"The Hottest Guy in Town," *Partners in Crime* (also known as *50/50*), 1984.
Dr. Newhouse, "Blast from the Past," *Crime Story,* 1987.

"Renaissance," *The Hitchhiker* (also known as *Deadly Nightmares* and *Le voyageur*), HBO, 1988.

Nelson Boardman, "How Long Has This Thing Been Going On?" *Jake and the Fatman*, 1988.

Michael Dennison, "Don't Sell Yourself Short," *Alfred Hitchcock Presents*, USA Network, 1989.

The Hawk, "Gathering Clouds: Parts 1 & 2," *The Young Riders*, ABC, 1990.

Wes McSorley, "A Killing in Vegas," *Murder, She Wrote*, CBS, 1991.

Dashiell Jaimeson, "All through the Night," *Jake and the Fatman*, 1992.

Jordan Barnett, "Threshold of Fear," *Murder, She Wrote*, CBS, 1993.

Que apostamos?, 1993.

Brian Landis, "Sitting Ducks," *High Tide*, 1994.

Jerome Keaton, "Danse avec la mort," *Le juge est une femme* (also known as *The Judge Was a Woman*, *Alice Nevers: Le juge est une femme*, and *Florence Larrieu, le juge est une femme*), 1994.

Clement the Hermit, "Vanishing Act," *The New Adventures of Robin Hood* (also known as *Les nouvelles aventures de Robin des Bois*), TNT and syndicated, 1998.

Himself, *Never Mind the Buzzcocks*, BBC, 2000.

Professor Alan Fletcher, "Going Gently," *Holby City* (also known as *Holby*), BBC, 2001.

Voice, "The Wrong Empire," *A History of Britain*, History Channel, 2001.

Breakfast, BBC, 2001, 2006.

Professor Alan Fletcher, "Change of Heart," *Holby City* (also known as *Holby*), BBC, 2002.

Himself, "Tallest Man," *Little Britain*, BBC America, 2003.

Detective Gus D'Amato, "A Game of Soldiers," *Dalziel and Pascoe*, BBC, 2004.

Andrew Pennington, "Death on the Nile," *Agatha Christie: Poirot* (also known as *Agatha Christie's Poirot* and *Poirot*), Arts and Entertainment, 2004.

Johnny Vegas: 18 Stone of Idiot, Channel 4, 2005.

Maestro, 2008.

Television Guest Appearances; Episodic:

Get It Together, ABC, 1970.

Top of the Pops (also known as *TOTP*), BBC, 1977.

Aplauso, 1978.

Friday Night, Saturday Morning, BBC, 1982.

Sabado noche, 1988.

"70s Super Cops," *Light Lunch*, Channel 4, 1997.

Kelly, UTV, 2003.

Top Gear (also known as *Top Gear Xtra*), BBC, 2003.

V Graham Norton, Channel 4, 2003.

Richard & Judy, Channel 4, 2004.

GMTV, ITV, 2004.

This Morning (also known as *This Morning with Richard and Judy*), ITV, 2004.

Loose Women, ITV, 2004.

The Late Late Show, CBS, 2004, 2006.

Today with Des and Mel, ITV, 2004, 2006.

The Heaven and Earth Show (also known as *The Heaven and Earth Show with Gloria Hunniford*), BBC, 2005.

The Daily Politics, BBC, 2005.

Tubridy Tonight, RTE, 2006.

The Alan Titchmarsh Show, ITV, 2008.

Also guest on *Harry Hill* show, Channel 4.

Television Director; Episodic:

"Survival," *Starsky and Hutch*, ABC, 1977.

"Manchild on the Streets," *Starsky and Hutch*, ABC, 1977.

"Huggy Can't Go Home," *Starsky and Hutch*, ABC, 1979.

"No Exit," *Miami Vice*, NBC, 1984.

"Case X," *Hunter*, 1985.

"Blast from the Past," *Crime Story*, 1987.

"Moulin Rouge," *Crime Story*, 1988.

"Warriors," *China Beach*, 1990.

"Blessings," *In the Heat of the Night*, 1990.

Television Work; Other:

Producer, *Swan Song* (movie), ABC, 1980.

Producer and director, *Fighting Ministers* (special), 1986.

Film Appearances:

The Secret Sharer, 1967.

Swede, *Johnny Got His Gun* (also known as *Dalton Trumbo's "Johnny Got His Gun"*), Marketing and Distribution Company, 1971.

Officer John Davis, *Magnum Force*, Warner Bros., 1973.

Pritt, *Dog Pound Shuffle* (also known as *Spot*), Bloom, 1975.

Duke Turnbeau, *The Stick–up* (also known as *Mud*), Trident, 1977.

Oldham, *The Hanoi Hilton*, Cannon, 1987.

Jefferson Cope, *Appointment with Death*, Cannon, 1988.

Dr. Frieberg, *In the Cold of the Night*, Republic, 1991.

Martin Henkle, *Tides of War* (also known as *Cancellate Washington*), Arrow Releasing, 1994.

Henrich Mueller, *Pentathlon*, Live Home Video, 1995.

Harvey, *Tabloid*, 2001.

(Uncredited) Himself (in archive footage), *Dickie Roberts: Former Child Star*, Paramount, 2003.

The original Hutch, *Starsky & Hutch*, Warner Bros., 2004.

Eric Bridges, *Puritan*, 2005.

Appeared in the short film *Old Dog*; appeared in the documentary films *He's Starsky, I'm Hutch, Starsky and Hutch Stories*, and *Top Ten TV Cops*.

Film Work:
Song performer, "Don't Give Up on Us," *The Hitcher,* Rogue Pictures, 2007.

Stage Appearances:
The Glass Menagerie, Actor's Alley, 1975.
Waiting for Godot, Actor's Alley, 1975.
Narrator, *Blood Brothers,* Phoenix Theatre, London, 1996–97.
The Dead Monkey, London, 1997.
Chandler Tate, *Comic Potential,* Lyric Theatre, London, 1999–2000.
Fool for Love, Edinburgh Festival, Edinburgh, Scotland, 2000.
Title role, *Jerry Springer: The Opera,* Cambridge Theatre, London, 2004–2005.
Mack Sennett, *Mack and Mabel* (musical), Criterion Theatre, London, 2006.

Appeared in *Baal, Sergeant Musgrave's Dance,* and *Viet Rock* (one–act plays), all New York City; also appeared in productions with the Firehouse Theatre, Minneapolis, MN, c. 1965, and with Cafe La Mama, New York City, c. 1966.

Major Tours:
Narrator, *Blood Brothers,* Australian and New Zealand cities, 1994.
The Aspern Papers, British cities, 1996.
Death Trap, British cities, 2000.
Mack Sennett, *Mack and Mabel* (musical), British cities, 2006.

Toured British cities in productions of *Catch Me if You Can* and *Speed the Plow.*

Stage Work:
Coproducer, *The Dead Monkey,* London, 1997.
Director, *Fool for Love,* Edinburgh Festival, Edinburgh, Scotland, 2000.

Radio Appearances:
Performed in radio broadcasts of *A Chorus Line; Firefly Summer;* and *I Have No Mouth, and I Must Scream.*

RECORDINGS

Albums:
David Soul, Private Stock Records, 1976.
Playing to an Audience of One, Private Stock Records, 1977.
Band of Friends, Energy Records, 1980.
Best Days of My Life, Energy Records, 1982.

Blood Brothers—Australian Cast, Stetson Records, 1994.
Leave a Light On, 1997.

Also recorded the album *Looking Back.* Singles include "Amoureux sans bagages/Catch Me I'm Falling," AB Production, 1985, "C'est le seul homme/Dream with Me," Epsilon Records, 1988, and "Smoke with Fire," Wotre Music, 1995, all with Claire Severac; "Don't Give Up on Us, Baby"; "Going In with My Eyes Open;" and "Silver Lady."

Videos:
Starsky & Hutch: A Last Look, Warner Bros., 2004.

Appeared in the music videos "Foolin' Around" and "Thrill Me."

WRITINGS

Screenplays:
Cowriter, *Tides of War,* Arrow Releasing, 1994.

OTHER SOURCES

Electronic:
David Soul Official Site, http://www.davidsoul.com, January 7, 2009.

SPEARS, Britney 1981–

PERSONAL

Full name, Britney Jean Spears; born December 2, 1981, in Kentwood, LA; daughter of Jamie (a building contractor and personal manager) and Lynne (an elementary schoolteacher) Spears. Sister of Jamie Lynn Spears (an actress and singer); married Jason Allen Alexander, January 2, 2004 (marriage annulled, 2004); married Kevin Federline (a dancer and entertainer), September 18, 2004 (divorced, 2007); children: (second marriage) Sean Preston, Jayden James. *Education:* Attended school in McComb, MS; trained at Professional Performing Arts School, New York City, and Off–Broadway Dance Academy. *Religion:* Baptist.

Addresses: *Agent*—Jason Trawick, William Morris Agency, 1 William Morris Pl., Beverly Hills, CA 90212. *Contact*—Gina Orr, Jive Records, 138 West 25th St., New York, NY 10001.

Career: Singer, actress, and producer. Performer in concerts around the world, including a tour with the Backstreet Boys, 1998; performance clips featured in numerous film and television broadcasts; Britney Spears Productions, founder, 2002. Appeared in commercials for Pepsi soft drinks, National Milk Promotion Board, Tommy jeans, Target stores, McDonald's restaurants, and other products. Britney Spears Foundation, founder, 2000. Founder of the short–lived New York City restaurant NYLA, 2002; creator of fragrances called "Curious," 2004, and "Fantasy," 2005; once worked at a novelty shop.

Awards, Honors: MTV Europe Music Awards, best female artist, best pop act, best breakthrough act, and best song, all 1999, and two Grammy Award nominations, National Academy of Recording Arts and Sciences, 2000, all for " ... Baby One More Time"; *Billboard* Music Award, 2000; American Music Award, favorite new pop–rock artist, 2000; Teen Choice Award nominations, choice actress in a drama or action adventure movie and choice film chemistry (with Anson Mount), and MTV Movie Award nominations, best dressed and breakthrough female performance, all 2002, for *Crossroads*; received star on Hollywood Walk of Fame, 2003; *Billboard* Music Award, dance single of the year, 2004; Teen Choice Award nomination, choice female television personality, 2005; Grammy Award, best dance recording, 2005, for "Toxic"; BMI Cable Awards, BMI Film and Television Awards, 2005 (with Michael Corcoran), and 2008 (with Scott Bennett), for *Zoey 101;* MTV Video Music Awards, best female video, best pop video, and video of the year, 2008, all for "Piece of Me"; several gold and platinum record certifications, Recording Industry Association of America.

CREDITS

Television Appearances; Series:
Mouseketeer, *The Mickey Mouse Club* (also known as *The All New Mickey Mouse Club, Club MMC,* and *MMC*), The Disney Channel, 1993–94.
Host, *Mission: Makeover,* MTV, 1998.

Television Appearances; Miniseries:
200 Greatest Pop Culture Icons, VH1, 2003.
Britney and Kevin: Chaotic, UPN, 2005.

Television Appearances; Specials:
MMC in Concert, 1993.
Britney Spears and Joey McIntyre in Concert, The Disney Channel, 1999.
Walt Disney World Summer Jam Concert, ABC, 1999.
The 1999 Miss Teen USA Pageant, CBS, 1999.
The 15th Annual Walt Disney World Happy Easter Parade, ABC, 1999.
Teen People's 21 Hottest Stars under 21, ABC, 1999.

L'Oreal Summer Music Mania, UPN, 1999.
Christmas in Rockefeller Center, NBC, 1999.
Big Holiday Help–a–thon, Nickelodeon, 1999.
Arthur Ashe Kids' Day, CBS, 1999.
Britney Live, MTV, 2000.
Britney Spears: There's No Place like Home, Fox, 2000.
Britney in Hawaii (also known as *Britney in Hawaii: Live and More!),* Fox, 2000.
All Access: Backstage with Britney (also known as *MTV's All Access: Backstage with Britney*), MTV, 2000.
Greatest Rock & Roll Moments: 2000, VH1, 2000.
Grammy Countdown, syndicated, 2000.
100 Greatest Pop Songs, MTV, 2000.
Smash Hits 2000, 2000.
The Fake ID Club, MTV, 2000.
Teen People's 25 Hottest Stars under 25, ABC, 2000.
Host, *TRL Superstars,* MTV, 2000.
Music Mania 2000, Fox, 2000.
Britney Spears Live from Las Vegas, HBO, 2001.
Total Britney Live, 2001.
Half–time performer, *Super Bowl XXXV,* CBS, 2001.
Making the Super Bowl Half–time Special, MTV, 2001.
MTV Icon: Janet Jackson, MTV, 2001.
Michael Jackson: 30th Anniversary Celebration, CBS, 2001.
Being Mick, ABC, 2001.
Everybody Talk about ... Pop Music!, MTV, 2001.
There's Only One Madonna, BBC, 2001.
Billboard's Rock 'n' Roll New Year's Eve, Fox, 2001.
Britney Laid Bare, 2002.
Lights, Camera, Magic, 2002.
Voice of Donner, *Robbie the Reindeer: Legend of the Lost Tribe* (animated), CBS, 2002.
Voice of Donner, *Robbie the Reindeer in Hooves of Fire* (animated), CBS, 2002.
NBC All–Star Read to Achieve Celebration, NBC, 2002.
Host, *MTV's Mardi Gras 2002,* MTV, 2002.
Elvis Lives, NBC, 2002.
Bubblegum Babylon, VH1, 2002.
Summer Music Mania, Fox, 2002, 2004.
(In archive footage) *American Bandstand's 50th Anniversary Celebration,* ABC, 2002.
(In archive footage) *Cleavage,* Arts and Entertainment, 2002.
Britney Spears: In the Zone (also known as *In the Zone*), ABC, 2003.
Britney: In the Zone & Out All Night, MTV, 2003.
50 Sexiest Video Moments, VH1, 2003.
Weird Al Presents: Al TV, VH1, 2003.
VH1's 200 Greatest Pop Culture Icons, VH1, 2003.
The Wade Robson Project Audition Special, MTV, 2003.
The Osbourne Family Christmas Special, MTV, 2003.
MTV Bash (also known as *MTV Bash: Carson Daly*), MTV, 2003.
2003 NFL Kickoff Concert, 2003.
Fromage 2003, MuchMusic, 2003.

Junior Eurovision Song Contest (also known as *Europaeisk junior mgp 2003, Junior mgp 2003, Junior ESC 2003,* and *Junior Eurovision Song Contest 2003*), 2003.

(In archive footage) *101 Most Shocking Moments in Entertainment,* E! Entertainment, 2003.

(Uncredited; in archive footage) *Saturday Night Live: The Best of Chris Kattan,* NBC, 2003.

Britney Spears: Live in Miami (also known as *Britney Spears: Live from Miami*), Showtime, 2004.

Britney Spears: E! Entertainment Special, E! Entertainment Television, 2004.

VH1 Divas, VH1, 2004.

Maxim Hot 100, VH1, 2004.

(In archive footage) *20 Most Awesomely Bad Songs of 2004,* 2004.

(In archive footage) *101 Biggest Celebrity Oops,* E! Entertainment Television, 2004.

(Uncredited) Dawn Paslowsky (in archive footage), *Saturday Night Live: The Best of Cheri Oteri,* NBC, 2004.

(In archive footage) *101 Most Unforgettable SNL Moments,* NBC, 2004.

(In archive footage) *Retrosexual: The 80's,* VH1, 2004.

(In archive footage) *The Ultimate Hollywood Blonde,* E! Entertainment Television, 2004.

(In archive footage) *The Most Shocking Celebrity Moments of 2004,* Channel 5, 2005.

(In archive footage) *Britney's Redneck Roots,* Channel 4, 2005.

(Uncredited; in archive footage) *Stars on Trial,* MuchMusic, 2005.

InStyle Celebrity Weddings, ABC, 2005.

All That 10th Anniversary Reunion Special, Nickelodeon, 2005.

(In archive footage) *Britney and Kevin: The E! True Hollywood Story,* E! Entertainment Television, 2005.

40 Dumbest Celeb Quotes ... Ever, 2006.

(In archive footage) *Premios Principales 2006,* 2006.

(In archive footage) *Overrated in '06,* MuchMusic, 2006.

(In archive footage) *100 Greatest Teen Stars,* 2006.

Forbes 20 Richest Women in Entertainment, E! Entertainment Television, 2007.

Out of Control: 10 Celebrity Rehabs Exposed, E! Entertainment Television, 2007.

(Uncredited; in archive footage) *Saturday Night Live in the '90s: Pop Culture Nation,* NBC, 2007.

(In archive footage) *50 Most Shocking Celebrity Scandals,* E! Entertainment Television, 2007.

(In archive footage) *Britney: Off the Rails,* Channel 4, 2007.

(In archive footage) *Mickey Mouse Club: The E! True Hollywood Story,* E! Entertainment Television, 2007.

Britney: For the Record, MTV, 2008.

E! News Special: Britney—Under Siege, E! Entertainment Television, 2008.

Britney Speared by the Paps, Sky One, 2008.

Shooting Britney, Channel 4, 2008.

Saturday Night's Main Event, NBC, 2008.

(In archive footage) *Generation duo,* TF1, 2008.

(In archive footage) *Britney Spears—Price of Fame: The E! True Hollywood Story,* E! Entertainment Television, 2008.

(In archive footage) *Almost Famous II,* BBC, 2009.

Television Appearances; Awards Presentations:

TV Hits Awards, 1999.

Nickelodeon's Annual Kids' Choice Awards, Nickelodeon, 1999, 2003.

The World Music Awards, ABC, 1999, 2000, 2001.

The Teen Choice Awards, Fox, 1999, 2000, 2001, 2002, 2003, 2006.

The Annual American Music Awards, ABC, 1999, 2000, (cohost) 2001, 2002, 2003, 2006.

The MTV Video Music Awards, MTV, 1999, 2000, 2001, 2002, 2003, 2006, 2007, 2008.

The 1999 MTV Europe Music Awards, MTV, 1999, (in archive footage) 2003, 2004, 2008.

The Billboard Music Awards, Fox, 1999, 2000, 2001, 2004.

The MTV Movie Awards, MTV, 2000, 2001.

The Annual Grammy Awards, CBS, 2000, 2002, 2004.

The 2000 Radio Music Awards, ABC, 2000.

2000 MuchMusic Video Music Awards, MuchMusic, 2000.

2nd Annual MTV Video Music Awards Latin America, MTV, 2003.

The 2nd Annual TRL Awards, MTV, 2004.

VH1 Big in '06 Awards, VH1, 2006.

Television Appearances; Episodic:

Star Search, 1992.

Behind the Music, VH1, 1997.

Making the Video, MTV, multiple appearances, beginning 1999.

Top of the Pops (also known as *All New Top of the Pops, Top of the Pops 2,* and *TOTP*), BBC, 1999, 2002, 2004.

Herself, "Aww, Here It Goes to Hollywood: Part 2," *Kenan & Kel,* Nickelodeon, 1999.

Herself, "No Place like Home," *Sabrina, the Teenage Witch* (also known as *Sabrina* and *Sabrina Goes to College*), CBS, 1999.

Herself, "Ghost Dance," *The Famous Jett Jackson,* The Disney Channel, 1999.

Mundo VIP, 1999.

Nyhetsmorgon, 1999.

Voice, "The Mansion Family," *The Simpsons* (animated), Fox, 2000.

First Listen, MTV, 2000.

Diary, MTV, 2000.

Total Access 24/7, Fox Family Channel, 2000, 2001.

The House of Hits, 2000.

Dale's All Stars, BBC1, 2000.

Russell Gilbert Live, Nine Network, 2000.

El rayo, 2000.

TRL Italy (also known as *Total Request Live* and *TRL Italia*), MTV, 2000.

"Pop Princesses," *Top Ten,* Channel 4, 2001.

(In archive footage) "The Merchants of Cool," *Frontline,* PBS, 2001.

(In archive footage) "Pure Pop," *Walk On By: The Story of Popular Song,* ABC, 2001.

"Nick Takes Over Music," *The Nick Cannon Show,* Nickelodeon, 2002.

The Saturday Show, BBC, 2002.

"Britney Spears Special," *The Frank Skinner Show,* BBC, 2002.

The Oprah Winfrey Show (also known as *Oprah*), syndicated, 2002.

"Niemandistperfekt," *Boulevard Bio,* 2002.

Access Hollywood, syndicated, 2002, 2006.

Fame, Set, and Match, BBC, 2002.

CD:UK, ITV, 2002, 2004, 2006.

Otro rollo con: Adal Ramones (also known as *Otro rollo*), 2002.

Leute heute, 2002.

60 Minutes, CBS, 2003.

Punk'd, MTV, 2003.

Total Request Live (also known as *Total Request with Carson Daly, TRL,* and *TRL Weekend*), MTV, 2003.

Extra (also known as *Extra: The Entertainment Magazine*), syndicated, 2003.

Boogie, [Denmark], 2003.

Popworld, 2003.

Top of the Pops Saturday, BBC, 2003, 2004.

(In archive footage) *Celebrities Uncensored,* E! Entertainment Television, multiple appearances, beginning 2003.

(In archive footage) *SexTV,* 2003, 2004, 2005.

"New Kids on the Block: Part 3," *Fashion in Focus,* NYC, 2004.

Tinseltown TV, International Channel, 2004.

4Pop, 2004.

"Britney," *Can You Pull ...?,* Channel 4, 2004.

(In archive footage) "Blonde Ambition," *Real Access,* NBC, 2004.

Best Week Ever (also known as *Best Week Ever with Paul F. Tompkins*), VH1, 2005.

(In archive footage) "Moments of Madness," *20 to 1,* Nine Network, 2005.

(In archive footage) *Corazon de ...,* 2005, 2007.

(In archive footage) *Video on Trial,* 2005, 2006.

Amber–Louise, "Buy, Buy Baby," *Will & Grace,* NBC, 2006.

Inside Edition, syndicated, 2006.

Taff, Pro 7, 2006, 2007.

(In archive footage) *Exclusiv—Das Star–Magazin,* 2006.

Video on Trial (also known as *V.O.T.*), MuchMusic, 2007.

"Welcome to Sunset Tan," *Sunset Tan,* E! Entertainment Television, 2007.

"About the VMAs," *What Perez Sez,* VH1, 2007.

Entertainment Tonight (also known as *Entertainment This Week, E.T., ET Weekend,* and *This Week in Entertainment*), syndicated, multiple appearances, beginning 2007.

(In archive footage) "Welcome to Camp Shawnee," *The Simple Life,* E! Entertainment Television, 2007.

(In archive footage) *The Soup,* 2007.

(In archive footage) *Red Eye,* 2007.

(Uncredited; in archive footage) *Kruegers Woche,* 2007.

(In archive footage) *TMZ on TV,* 2007.

(In archive footage) "Life–Changing Moments," *20 to 1,* Nine Network, 2007.

(In archive footage) "Scandals & Sensations," *20 to 1,* Nine Network, 2007.

(In archive footage) *Quelli che ... il calcio,* 2007, 2008.

Abby, "Ten Sessions," *How I Met Your Mother,* CBS, 2008.

Abby, "Everything Must Go," *How I Met Your Mother,* CBS, 2008.

Showbiz Tonight, Cable News Network, 2008.

"Saving Britney Spears," *First Cut,* Channel 4, 2008.

(In archive footage) *The O'Reilly Factor,* 2008.

(In archive footage) "Child Stars: Where Are They Now?," *20 to 1,* Nine Network, 2008.

Television Guest Appearances; Episodic:

The Priory, Channel 4, 1999.

All That, Nickelodeon, multiple appearances, between 1999 and 2002.

The Rosie O'Donnell Show, syndicated, multiple appearances, between 1999 and 2002.

Wetten, dass ...?, 2002.

Saturday Night Live (also known as *NBC's "Saturday Night," Saturday Night,* and *SNL*), NBC, multiple appearances, beginning 2000.

Late Night with Conan O'Brien, NBC, 2000.

KPTM News at 9 PM, 2000.

The Tonight Show with Jay Leno, NBC, 2001, 2003.

(In archive footage) *Revealed with Jules Asner,* 2002.

Live with Regis and Kelly, syndicated, 2003.

Jimmy Kimmel Live!, ABC, 2003.

V Graham Norton, Channel 4, 2003.

On–Air with Ryan Seacrest, syndicated, 2004.

GMTV, IT, 2004.

Late Show with David Letterman (also known as *The Late Show* and *Letterman*), CBS, 2005, 2006.

Ellen: The Ellen DeGeneres Show, syndicated, 2005, 2008.

Dateline NBC, NBC, 2006.

Good Morning America, ABC, 2006.

The Tyra Banks Show, CW Network, 2006.

Larry King Live, Cable News Network, 2007.

"Rove: L.A.," *Rove Live,* Ten Network, 2007.

Star Academy, TF1, 2008.

Special guest, *The X Factor,* ITV, 2008.

Television Executive Producer; Specials:

Britney Spears Live from Las Vegas, HBO, 2001.

Britney Spears: In the Zone, ABC, 2003.

(And creator) *Britney Spears: Live in Miami,* Showtime, 2004.

Television Executive Producer; Other:
(Uncredited) *Brave New Girl* (movie), ABC Family Channel, 2004.
Britney and Kevin: Chaotic (miniseries), UPN, 2005.

Television Work; Movies:
Song performer, *Quints,* The Disney Channel, 2000.
Song performer, "Brave New Girl," *Brave New Girl,* ABC Family Channel, 2004.
Song performer, "Follow Me," *Zoey 101: Spring Break–up,* Nickelodeon, 2006.
Song performer, "Follow Me," *Zoey 101: The Curse of P.C.A.,* Nickelodeon, 2007.

Television Work; Series:
Song performer, "Follow Me," *Zoey 101,* Nickelodeon, 2004.

Film Appearances:
Flight attendant, *Longshot* (also known as *Jack of All Trades* and *Longshot: The Movie*), 2000.
Lucy Wagner, *Crossroads,* Paramount, 2002.
Herself, *Austin Powers in Goldmember,* New Line Cinema, 2002.
Herself, *Pauly Shore Is Dead,* CKrush Entertainment, 2003.
(In archive footage) *Super Size Me* (documentary), Samuel Goldwyn Films, 2004.
(In archive footage) *Fahrenheit 9/11,* Columbia TriStar Home Entertainment, 2004.
(In archive footage) *Religulous* (documentary), Lionsgate, 2008.

Film Work:
Song performer, *On the Line,* 2001.

Stage Appearances:
Understudy for the role of Tina Denmark, *Ruthless,* off–Broadway production, 1991.

RECORDINGS

Albums:
... Baby One More Time, Jive, 1999.
Star Profile, Master Tone, 1999.
Oops! ... I Did It Again, Jive, 2000.
In Conversation, Baktabak, 2000.
The Interview, Poptalk, 2000.
In the Spotlight with Britney Spears, Matrix Music Marketing, 2000.
Interview, Griffin Music, 2000.
Maximum Britney, Griffin Music, 2000.

Absolutely Britney Spears, Master Tone, 2000.
Britney, Jive, 2001.
In the Zone, Jive, 2003.
Greatest Hits: My Prerogative, Jive, 2004.
Britney Spears in the Mix, Jive, 2006.
Blackout, Jive, 2007.
Circus, Jive, 2008.

Singles include "I'm Not a Girl, Not Yet a Woman," 2002; "Toxic," Jive, 2004; "Gimme More," Jive, 2007; "Everytime;" "Me Against the Music;" and "Overprotected."

Video Appearances:
Time Out with Britney Spears, Jive/Zomba Video, 1999.
Britney Spears: "Star Baby" Scrapbook, 1999.
(And executive producer) *'N Sync & Britney Spears: Your #1 Video Requests ... and More!,* McDonald's, 2000.
Britney Spears Live and More! (also known as *Britney Spears in Hawaii: Live and More!*), 2001.
Britney: The Videos, 2001.
Crossroads: 40 Days with Britney, Paramount, 2002.
Stages: Three Days in Mexico—Britney Spears, NVU Productions, 2002.
Britney's Dance Beat (video game), THQ Interactive, 2002.
Pepsi More Music: The DCD Volume 1, 2003.
Divine Intervention: A Serendipitous Film about Britney Spears, Alexander Video, 2003.
(In archive footage) *Sex at 24 Frames per Second,* Image Entertainment, 2003.
Britney Spears: In the Zone, BMG Distribution, 2004.
Freestyle (with Brian Friedman), Lions Gate Films, 2004.
Britney Spears: Greatest Hits—My Prerogative, BMG Distribution, 2004.
(Uncredited) Krugellam, Queen of Perillians (in archive footage), *Saturday Night Live: The Best of Tracy Morgan,* Lions Gate Films Home Entertainment, 2004.
(In archive footage) *Fahrenhype 9/11,* Trinity Home Entertainment, 2004.
Celebrity News Reels Presents: Best of Paris (also known as *Best of Paris*), Star Rush Media, 2005.
(Uncredited; in archive footage) *Saturday Night Live: The Best of Jimmy Fallon,* 2005.
Singer, *SingStar Pop* (video game), Sony Computer Entertainment America, 2007.
(In archive footage) *The Price of Pleasure: Pornography, Sexuality & Relationships,* Media Education Foundation, 2008.

Music videos include " ... Baby One More Time," Jive, 1998; "Sometimes," Jive, 1999; "Oops! ... I Did It Again," Jive, 2000; "Born to Make You Happy," 2000; "From the Bottom of My Broken Heart," Jive, 2000; "Time Out with Britney Spears," 2000; "Don't Let Me Be the Last to Know," 2001; "Stronger," Jive, 2001; and "I'm a Slave 4 U," Jive, 2001; "I'm Not a Girl, Not Yet a Woman," 2002; "Overprotected," 2002; "I Love Rock n Roll," 2003; "Toxic," 2004; "Piece of Me," 2008; "Do Something;" "Everytime;" "Lucky," "Me Against the Music;" "My Prerogative;" "Outrageous;" "Someday (I Will Understand);" "(You Drive Me) Crazy;" and other singles.

WRITINGS

Books:

(With mother, Lynne Spears) *Britney Spears: Heart to Heart* (autobiography), Three Rivers Press, 2000.
(With Lynne Spears) *A Mother's Gift* (novel), Delacorte, 2001.

Film Music:

Composer, *Crossroads,* Paramount, 2002.

Songwriter:

"Let Me Be," *On the Line* (film), 2001.
"Follow Me," *Zoey 101* (television series), Nickelodeon, 2004.
"Brave New Girl," *Brave New Girl* (television movie), ABC Family Channel, 2004.

Other songwriting credits include "Intimidated."

ADAPTATIONS

The television movie *Brave New Girl,* broadcast by ABC Family Channel in 2004, was reportedly based on the novel *A Mother's Gift,* by Spears and her mother.

OTHER SOURCES

Books:

Contemporary Musicians, Volume 28, Gale, 2000.
Newsmakers 2000, Issue 3, Gale, 2000.
Spears, Britney, and Lynn Spears, *Britney Spears: Heart to Heart,* Three Rivers Press, 2000.

Periodicals:

Entertainment Weekly, November 9, 2001, pp. 28–34.
Evening Standard Hot Tickets, March 29, 2002, pp. 2, 3.
Heat, February 2, 2002, pp. 14–15; February 9, 2002, p. 43.
Newsweek, March 1, 1999.
Now, January 23, 2002, pp. 8–9.
Paris Match, July 27, 2000, pp. 84–87.

People Weekly, February 15, 1999, pp. 71–72; February 14, 2000.
Premiere, October, 2001, pp. 38–41.
Rolling Stone, April 15, 1999.
Sky, June, 1999, pp. 40–43, 45.
Teen People, June, 1999, p. 56; October, 1999, pp. 174–178; June, 2000, pp. 92, 136–140; summer, 2000, p. 83; August, 2000, pp. 144–146; January, 2001, pp. 114–116; May, 2001, p. 104; March, 2002, pp. 92, 96, 98.
Time, March 1, 1999, p. 71.
TV Guide, November 17, 2001, pp. 26–30.
USA Weekend, February 18, 2000.
Us Weekly, April 1, 2002, pp. 30–33.

SPEEDMAN, Scott 1975–

PERSONAL

Original name, Robert Scott Speedman; born September 1, 1975, in London, England; immigrated to Toronto, Ontario, Canada, c. 1979; son of Roy (a department store buyer) and Mary (an elementary school teacher) Speedman. *Education:* Attended University of Toronto, 1994–96; studied acting at Neighborhood Playhouse. *Avocational Interests:* Swimming.

Addresses: *Agent*—Endeavor, 9701 Wilshire Blvd., 3rd floor, Beverly Hills, CA 90210. *Manager*—Frank Frattaroli, D/F Management, 8609 East Washington Blvd., Suite 8607, Culver City, CA 90232. *Publicist*—Baker Winokur Ryder, 5700 Wilshire Blvd., Suite 550, Los Angeles, CA 90036.

Career: Actor. Appeared in print ads for Gap clothing, 2003.

Awards, Honors: Teen Choice Award nominations, best breakout performance on television, 1999, and choice television actor, 2000, and 2002, all for *Felicity;* Golden Wave, best actor, Bordeaux International Festival of Women in Cinema, 2003, for *My Life Without Me;* Cinescape Genre Face of the Future Award, male category, Academy of Science Fiction, Fantasy, and Horror Films, 2004, for *Underworld;* Teen Choice Award nomination, choice actor in a horror or thriller movie, 2008, for *The Strangers.*

CREDITS

Film Appearances:

Can I Get A Witness? (short film; also known as *Urban Myth*), 1996.
Scott, *Kitchen Party,* Myriad Pictures, 1997.

Jason, *Ursa Major,* 1997.

Billy, *Duets,* Buena Vista, 2000.

Bobby Keough, *Dark Blue,* Metro–Goldwyn–Mayer, 2002.

Don, *My Life Without Me* (also known as *Ma vie sans moi* and *Mi vida sin mi*), Columbia, 2003.

Michael Corvin, *Underworld,* Screen Gems, 2003.

Tom, *The 24th Day,* Screen Media Films, 2004.

Agent Kyle Steele, *xXx: State of the Union* (also known as *Cold Circle & Intersection, xXx: The Next Level,* and *xXx 2: The Next Level*), Columbia, 2005.

Michael, *Underworld: Evolution,* Screen Gems, 2006.

Dexter, *Weirdsville,* Magnolia Pictures, 2007.

Carl Uffner, *Anamorph,* First Take, 2008.

Tom, *Adoration,* Sony Pictures Classics, 2008.

James Hoyt, *The Strangers,* Universal, 2008.

Ransom Pride, *The Last Rites of Random Pride,* Horse Thief Pictures/Nomadic Pictures, 2009.

Television Appearances; Series:

Ned Nickerson, *Nancy Drew* (also known as *Alice et les Hardy Boys*), syndicated, 1995–96.

Benjamin "Ben" Covington, *Felicity,* The WB, 1998–2002.

Television Appearances; Movies:

Rookie, *Net Worth,* CBC, 1995.

One of Dan Jansen's friends, *A Brother's Promise: The Dan Jansen Story,* CBS, 1996.

Spanky Riggs, *Giant Mine,* 1996.

Officer Stevie Cardy, *Dead Silence* (also known as *Silence de mort*), HBO, 1997.

Steve Talbert, *What Happened to Bobby Earl?* (also known as *Murder in a College Town*), CBS, 1997.

Greg, *Every 9 Seconds* (also known as *A Call for Help*), NBC, 1997.

Patric, "Marie Taquet," *Rescuers: Stories of Courage; Two Couples,* Showtime, 1997.

Television Appearances; Episodic:

Cam Nillson, "Goodbye Mr. Caine," *Kung Fu: The Legend Continues,* syndicated, 1995.

Officer Madison, "Say Cheese and Die," *Goosebumps* (also known as *Ultimate Goosebumps*), Fox, 1996.

(Uncredited) Ben Covington (in archive footage), "None of the Above," *Dawson's Creek,* The WB, 1999.

Total Request Live (also known as *Total Request with Carson Daly, TRL,* and *TRL Weekend*), MTV, 2003, 2006.

Queer Edge with Jack E. Jett & Sandra Bernhard (also known as *Queer Edge* and *Queer Edge with Jack E. Jett*), 2006.

Guest, *Canada A.M.* (also known as *Canada A.M. Weekend*), CTV, 2007.

eTalk Daily (also known as *eTalk*), CTV, 2007.

Today (also known as *NBC News Today* and *The Today Show*), NBC, 2008.

Television Appearances; Other:

Benjamin "Ben" Covington, *Felicity* (pilot), The WB, 1998.

Underworld: Evolution—Inside the Action (special), MTV, 2006.

Stage Appearances:

Zoo Story, 1999.

OTHER SOURCES

Periodicals:

Maclean's, February 1, 1999, p. 64.

STONE, Lee
See CRANSTON, Bryan

STROH, KayCee 1984–

PERSONAL

Born May 29, 1984, in Salt Lake City, UT; mother, a secretary at a dance studio.

Career: Actress. Model for the Internet retail site Torrid; guest performer at half–time show for Utah Jazz basketball games; guest editor of *Tiger Beat* magazine. Worked as a dance teacher in Salt Lake City, UT. Advocate for Make a Wish Foundation, Starlight Starbright Children's Foundation, and United Cerebral Palsy.

Member: American Federation of Television and Radio Artists, Screen Actors Guild.

CREDITS

Television Appearances; Movies:

Martha Cox, *High School Musical,* The Disney Channel, 2006.

Martha Cox, *High School Musical 2* (also known as *High School Musical 2: Extended Edition*), The Disney Channel, 2007.

Television Appearances; Specials:

High School Musical 2 Dance–along, The Disney Channel, 2007.

The Teen Choice Awards 2007, Fox, 2007.

2007 American Music Awards, ABC, 2007.

Television Appearances; Episodic:

"The 'Grammy' Goes to Camp: You're a Star & Kids Are Helping Kids," *In the Mix* (also known as *In the Cutz*), Urban America, 2006.

Leslie, "Volley Dad," *The Suite Life of Zack and Cody* (also known as *TSL*), The Disney Channel, 2006.

Dancing with the Stars, ABC, 2006, 2007.

High School Musical: Get in the Picture (reality show), ABC, 2008.

Leslie, "Benchwarmers," *The Suite Life of Zack and Cody* (also known as *TSL*), The Disney Channel, 2008.

Film Appearances:

Martha Cox, *High School Musical 3: Senior Year* (also known as *H.S.M. 3*), Buena Vista, 2008.

RECORDINGS

Videos:

Dancer, *Ammon & King Lamoni,* Lightstone, 2004.

HSM2: Rehearsal Cam, Walt Disney Studios Home Entertainment, 2007.

HSM2: On Location, Walt Disney Studios Home Entertainment, 2008.

OTHER SOURCES

Electronic:

KayCee Stroh Official Site, http://www.kayceestroh.com, November 18, 2008.

SUROVY, Nicolas 1944–

(Nicholas Surovy, Nicolas Survoy)

PERSONAL

Born June 30, 1944, in New York, NY; son of Walter (an actor and manager) and Rise (an opera singer; maiden name, Stevens) Surovy; married Marguerite; children: Marisa. *Education:* Attended Northwestern University; studied acting with Sanford Meisner; studied acting at the Juilliard School of Drama, New York City, and at the Neighborhood Playhouse.

Addresses: *Agent*—Susan Smith and Associates, 121 West San Vicente Blvd., Beverly Hills, CA 90211.

Career: Actor. *Military service:* U.S. Army, sergeant, 1968–69; awarded Bronze Star, Air Medal with three clusters.

Awards, Honors: *Theatre World* Award, 1965, for *Helen.*

CREDITS

Stage Appearances:

(Off–Broadway debut) Telemecus, *Helen,* Bowery Lane Theatre, New York City, 1964.

Mick, *The Caretaker,* Buffalo Studio Arena, Buffalo, NY, 1971.

Mercutio, *Romeo and Juliet,* Buffalo Studio Arena, 1971.

Roger, *The Balcony,* Juilliard Theatre Center, New York City, 1972.

Hercules, *Alcestis,* Juilliard Theatre Center, 1972.

Man, *Sisters of Mercy,* Theatre De Lys, New York City, 1973.

(Broadway debut) Bassanio, *The Merchant,* 1977.

Captain Neville St. Claire, *Crucifer of Blood,* Helen Hayes Theatre, New York City, 1978–79.

Uncle Harry/Martin, *Cloud Nine,* Lucille Lortel Theatre, then Theatre de Lys, both New York City, 1981.

Tony Kirby, *You Can't Take It with You,* Plymouth Theatre, New York City, 1983.

Reverend T. Lawrence Shannon, *The Night of the Iguana,* Circle in the Square, New York City, 1988.

Terence O'Keefe, *Breaking Legs,* Promenade Theatre, New York City, 1991–92.

Also appeared as Joe, *The Time of Your Life,* New York City production; Mike Fink, *The Robber Bridegroom,* New York City production; Cousins, *Major Barbara,* New York City production; Peter, *The Kitchen,* Acting Company production; Canterbury, *Edward II,* Acting Company production; Fedotik, *The Three Sisters,* Acting Company production; Marlowe, *She Stoops to Conquer,* Acting Company production; Tom, *The Glass Menagerie,* Acting Company production; title role, *Henry IV,* Acting Company production; Benedick, *Much Ado about Nothing,* Goodman Theatre, Chicago, IL; title role, *Don Juan,* Goodman Theatre, Chicago, IL; Buckingham, *Richard III,* Goodman Theatre; title role, *Hamlet,* California Shakespeare Festival; man, *Sisters of Mercy,* Shaw Festival, Canada; Seymour, *Billy Budd,* Loretto–Hilton Repertory Theatre, St. Louis, MO; Steve, *Domestic Issues,* Yale Repertory Theatre, New Haven, CT.

Film Appearances:

(As Nicolas Surovy) *For Pete's Sake!,* World Wide, 1966.

(As Nicolas Surovy) Larry, *Make a Face,* Sperling, 1971.

Aleck Olsen, Mammoth player, *Bang the Drum Slowly,* Paramount, 1973.

Julian, *The Act* (also known as *Bless 'Em All*), Film Ventures International, 1982.

The Initiation, New World, 1984.

John, *Forever Young,* Warner Bros., 1992.

Mac Lawton, *Breaking Free* (also known as *A Leap of Faith*), Disney, 1995.

Ronald Anderson, *The Undercover Kid,* Leucadia Film Company, 1996.

Jim, Tom's father, *All Over the Guy,* Lionsgate, 2001.

Also appeared in *Nina.*

Television Appearances; Series:

Fred Turner, *A World Apart,* ABC, 1970–71.

Orson Burns, *Ryan's Hope,* ABC, 1981.

Mike Roy, *All My Children,* ABC, 1983–84, 1988, 1998.

Peter Cross, *Bridges to Cross,* CBS, 1986.

P. J. Brakenhouse, *Paradise* (also known as *Guns of Paradise*), 1988–89.

Dylan Elliot, *Wolf,* CBS, 1989–90.

Mayor Boone Penbroke, *Key West,* Fox, 1993.

Television Appearances; Miniseries:

George Bennett, *Mayflower: The Pilgrims' Adventure,* CBS, 1979.

Colonel Thomas Conway, *George Washington,* CBS, 1984.

Serge Markov, *Anastasia: The Mystery of Anna,* NBC, 1986.

Marcus Hiller, *Telling Secrets* (also known as *Contract for Murder*), ABC, 1993.

Television Appearances; Movies:

Davy, *This Savage Land,* 1969.

(As Nicholas Surovy) Joe, *The Time of Your Life,* 1976.

Martin Elson, *Franken* (also known as *Dr. Franken* and *Doctor Franken*), NBC, 1980.

Tony Kirby, *You Can't Take It with You,* Showtime, 1984.

Patrick Evan Stark, *Stark,* CBS, 1985.

Half Nelson, 1985.

Patrick Evan Stark, *Stark: Mirror Image* (also known as *Stark II*), CBS, 1986.

David Mason, *Steal the Sky,* HBO, 1988.

Conway, *Laura Lansing Slept Here,* NBC, 1988.

Jesse Wilder, *Coopersmith,* CBS, 1992.

Robert Denk, *12:01,* Fox, 1993.

Steve Kinsberg, *Crowfeet,* CBS, 1995.

Hans, *The Man Who Captured Eichmann,* TNT, 1996.

Dr. Jimmy Goldrich, *Two Voices* (also known as *Two Small Voices*), Lifetime, 1997.

Harold Rhodes, *When Danger Follows You Home,* USA Network, 1997.

Mr. Spelman, *The Big Time,* TNT, 2002.

Television Appearances; Pilots:

Lawyer Dylan Elliott, *Wolf,* CBS, 1989.

David, *Just Life,* ABC, 1990.

Mayor Penbrooke, *Key West,* 1993.

Also appeared as James, *Century Hill.*

Television Appearances; Episodic:

Billy Joe Gaines, "Judgment in Heaven," *The Big Valley,* ABC, 1965.

Bronc, "A Picture of a Lady," *Death Valley Days* (also known as *Call of the West, The Pioneers, Trails West,* and *Western Star Theater*), syndicated, 1965.

Vinnie Stamp, "This Stage of Fools," *Branded,* 1966.

Tick Gleason, "The Case of the Twice Told Twist," *Perry Mason,* CBS, 1966.

Greg, "Little Boy Lost," *The Twilight Zone* (also known as *The New Twilight Zone*), CBS, 1985.

Sonny Foxx, "Simon without Simon: Parts 1 & 2," *Simon & Simon,* 1985.

Peter Cross, "Memories of Molly," *Bridges to Cross,* CBS, 1986.

Brian Thomas, "Ode to Angela," *Who's the Boss?,* 1989.

Warren Smyth, "Outward Bound," *L.A. Law,* NBC, 1990.

Roger Price, "Dad and Buried," *Over My Dead Body,* 1990.

David Alcott, "Misconceptions," *Law & Order,* NBC, 1991.

Ben Judson, "Night of the Coyote," *Murder, She Wrote,* CBS, 1992.

James Allen Howard, "The Conspiracy," *Matlock,* 1993.

Paul Redding, *South of Sunset,* CBS, 1993.

Roy Hondo, "Hard Rock," *The Adventures of Brisco County Jr.* (also known as *Brisco County Jr.*), Fox, 1994.

Arthur Dennison, "A Model for Murder," *One West Waikiki,* CBS, 1994.

Dr. William Crichton, "Something in the Air," *SeaQuest DSV* (also known as *SeaQuest 2032*), NBC, 1995.

Pe'Nar, Makull, "Time and Again," *Star Trek: Voyager* (also known as *Voyager*), UPN, 1995.

Paul Westlake, "Pulp Addiction," *Silk Stalkings,* USA Network, 1995.

Peter Goodwin, "The Passion of Our Youth," *Sisters,* NBC, 1995.

James Ryerson, "School for Murder," *Murder She Wrote,* CBS, 1995.

Leo Vardian, "Murder among Friends," *Murder She Wrote,* CBS, 1996.

Dan Morrison, "Chapter Nine," *Murder One,* 1996.

"The Catamount," *The Lazarus Man,* 1996.

Stanley Robman, "Marathon," *Nowhere Man,* 1996.

Lieutenant Mark Fox, "Undercover," *Pacific Blue,* 1996.

Ben Proctor, "The Black Box," *The Visitor,* Fox, 1997.

Luther Gannon (codename Curator), "Shadow Play," *Seven Days* (also known as *7 Days* and *Seven Days: The Series*), UPN, 1998.

Ivan Ford, "Trifecta," *Martial Law,* CBS, 1999.

Dr. Daniel Waterston, "All Things," *The X Files,* Fox, 2000.

Hunt Acey, "Redefinition," *Angel* (also known as *Angel: The Series*), The WB, 2001.

Major General Onichimoski, "To Walk on Wings," *JAG* (also known as *JAG: Judge Advocate General*), CBS, 2001.

Richard Baldwin, "Vanished: Parts 1 & 2," *The Practice,* ABC, 2001.

Mr. Lamero, "The Extinction of the Dinosaurs," *Judging Amy,* CBS, 2002.

Mr. Blout, "The Good, the Bad, and the Lawyers," *The Education of Max Bickford,* CBS, 2002.

Arthur Grambill, "Acts of Mercy," *Crossing Jordan,* NBC, 2002.

Mr. Callender, "Deterioration," *Strong Medicine,* Lifetime, 2002.

Christopher Meeker, "For Whom the Whistle Blows," *Dragnet* (also known as *L.A. Dragnet*), ABC, 2003.

Marshall Campbell, "Rich Girl Poor Girl," *The Division* (also known as *Heart of the City*), NBC, 2003.

(As Nicolas Survoy) Captain Massie, "Here Was a Man," *Deadwood,* HBO, 2004.

Captain Massie, "The Trial of Jack McCall," *Deadwood,* HBO, 2004 Massie, "Bullock Returns to the Camp," *Deadwood,* HBO, 2004.

Also appeared in *Ben Casey,* ABC; *Branded,* NBC; *Blue Light,* ABC; *Bob Hope Presents The Chrysler Theatre,* NBC; *The Road West,* NBC; as Steve, *Nurse,* ABC; Billy Simmons, *The Renegades,* ABC; Rudy Lavasso, *One Life to Live,* ABC.

SWANN, Gabriel
See MACHT, Gabriel

SWIT, Loretta 1937–

PERSONAL

Born November 4, 1937, in Passaic, NJ; married Dennis Holahan (an actor), December 21, 1983 (divorced, 1995 [some sources cite 1992]). *Education:* Studied at the American Academy of Dramatic Arts; studied acting at the Gene Frankel Repertoire Theatre, New York City. *Avocational Interests:* Making jewelry, painting, needlepoint.

Addresses: *Agent*—Artists Group, Ltd., 10100 Santa Monica Blvd., Los Angeles, CA 90067–4003.

Career: Actress. Appeared in advertisements. Active in events related to the television series *M*A*S*H.* Jewelry designer and painter; has sold her lines of SwitArts watercolor artwork and SwitHearts Jewelry to raise funds for various animal organizations; sold art and jewelry at shows and through her web page. Spokesperson for the charity Airline Ambassadors; board member for Actors and Others for Animals; also affiliated with other animal rights organizations.

Member: Actors' Equity Association, Screen Actors Guild, American Federation of Television and Radio Artists.

Awards, Honors: Emmy Award nomination, best supporting actress in comedy, 1974, Golden Globe Award nomination, best supporting actress—television, 1974, Emmy Award nominations, outstanding continuing performance by a supporting actress in a comedy series, 1975, 1976, 1977, 1978, and 1979, Emmy awards, outstanding supporting actress in a comedy or variety or music series, 1980 and 1982, Golden Globe Award nominations, best performance by an actress in a television series—musical/comedy, 1980 and 1982, Emmy Award nominations, outstanding supporting actress in a comedy or variety or music series, 1981 and 1983, People's Choice Award (with Linda Evans), favorite female television performer, 1983, Golden Globe Award nomination, best performance by an actress in a supporting role in a series, miniseries, or motion picture made for television, 1983, Silver Satellite Award, American Women in Radio and Television, Genie Award, television performance, Academy of Canadian Cinema and Television, and additional People's Choice awards, all for *M*A*S*H;* received a star on the Hollywood Walk of Fame, 1989; Sarah Siddons Award, Sarah Siddons Society (Chicago, IL), 1991–92, for *Shirley Valentine;* Jean Golden Halo Award; Woman of the Year, Animal Protection Institute; Woman of the Year, International Fund for Animal Welfare; other awards and honors, including recognition from the American Humane Society and awards for her artwork.

CREDITS

Television Appearances; Series:
Major Margaret "Hot Lips" Houlihan, *M*A*S*H* (also known as *MASH*), CBS, 1972–83.

Semiregular panelist, *The Match Game* (also known as *Match Game 73, Match Game 74, Match Game 75, Match Game 76, Match Game 77, Match Game 78,* and *Match Game 79*), CBS, 1973–79.

Cora Lynne, *The Big Battalions,* Channel 4 (England), 1992.

Host, *Those Incredible Animals,* The Discovery Channel, 1992–97.

Television Appearances; Miniseries:
Herself, *The 100 Most Memorable TV Moments,* TV Land, 2004.

Herself, *The 100 Most Unexpected TV Moments,* TV Land, 2005.

Television Appearances; Movies:

Ginny Lomax, *Sam Cade* (edited from "Homecoming" and other episodes of *Cade's County*), 1972.

Linda Bush, *Shirts/Skins*, ABC, 1973.

Daisy, *The Last Day*, NBC, 1975.

Chris LeBlanc, *The Hostage Heart*, CBS, 1977.

B. J., *Friendships, Secrets and Lies* (also known as *The Walls Came Tumbling Down*), NBC, 1979.

Emily, *Valentine*, ABC, 1979.

Sandy McLaren, *Mirror, Mirror*, NBC, 1979.

Caroline Baker, *The Kid from Nowhere*, NBC, 1982.

Laura Bentells, *Games Mother Never Taught You*, CBS, 1982.

Jane Simon, *First Affair*, CBS, 1983.

Marysia Walenka, *The Execution*, NBC, 1985.

Deo Fisher, *Dreams of Gold: The Mel Fisher Story* (also known as *The Mel Fisher Story*), CBS, 1986.

Miss Morton, "14 Going on 30" (also known as "Fassst Forward" and "Fourteen Going on Thirty"), *The Disney Sunday Movie* (also known as *Disneyland, Disneylandia, Disney's Wonderful World, The Magical World of Disney, Walt Disney, Walt Disney Presents, Walt Disney's Wonderful World of Color,* and *The Wonderful World of Disney*), ABC, 1988.

Connie Stewart, *Hell Hath No Fury*, NBC, 1991.

Detective Patricia Staley, *A Killer among Friends* (also known as *Friends to the End*), CBS, 1992.

Television Appearances; Specials:

Major Margaret "Hot Lips" Houlihan, *Rickles* (also known as *The Don Rickles Show*), CBS, 1975.

Sydney, *It's a Bird, It's a Plane, It's Superman* (musical; also known as *Superman the Musical*), ABC, 1975.

CBS team member, *Battle of the Network Stars*, ABC, 1976.

Ted Knight Musical Comedy Variety Special Special, CBS, 1976.

CBS team member, *Battle of the Network Stars II* (also known as *Battle of the Network Stars*), ABC, 1977.

CBS team contestant, *Battle of the Network Stars III* (also known as *Battle of the Network Stars*), ABC, 1977.

Ringmaster, *Circus of the Stars #4*, CBS, 1979.

Herself, *The Bob Hope Christmas Show and All–Star Comedy Special* (also known as *The Bob Hope Christmas Special*), NBC, 1980.

Herself, *CBS All American Thanksgiving Day Parade*, CBS, 1980.

Perry Como's Bahama Holiday, ABC, 1980.

Herself and Major Margaret "Hot Lips" Houlihan, *Making M*A*S*H* (documentary), PBS, 1981.

Texaco Star Theater: Opening Night (also known as *Texaco Salute to Broadway*), NBC, 1982.

Grace Bradley, *The Best Christmas Pageant Ever*, ABC, 1983.

Host, *Animals Are the Funniest People*, NBC, 1983.

Team two member, *The Real Trivial Pursuit*, ABC, 1985.

Host, *Saving the Wildlife*, PBS, 1986.

Narrator, "The Mysterious Black–Footed Ferret," *National Audubon Society Specials* (also known as *World of Audubon Specials*), TBS and PBS, 1986, released on video as *Audubon Video: The Mysterious Black–Footed Ferret.*

Host, "On the Edge of Extinction: Panthers and Cheetahs," *National Audubon Society Specials* (also known as *World of Audubon Specials*), TBS and PBS, c. 1986, released on video as *Audubon Video: On the Edge of Extinction: Panthers and Cheetahs.*

Host and narrator, *A Christmas Calendar*, PBS, 1987.

Herself, *Happy 100th Birthday, Hollywood!* (also known as *Happy Birthday, Hollywood!*), ABC, 1987.

Host, *The Korean War: The Untold Story* (documentary; also known as *Korea: Remembering the Forgotten War*), syndicated, 1988.

Host, *United We Stand*, syndicated, 1988.

Wanda Karpinsky, "My Dad Can't Be Crazy … Can He?" (also known as "My Dad Can't Be Crazy (Can He)?" and "Ricky's Dad Is Crazy"), *ABC Afterschool Specials*, ABC, 1989.

A Matter of Principle, WCVB (ABC affiliate), 1990.

Herself, *Memories of M*A*S*H* (also known as *Memories of MASH*), CBS, 1991.

Herself, *Bob Hope's "America: Red, White and Beautiful—The Swimsuit Edition"* (also known as *Bob Hope's "America: Red, White and Beautiful"*), NBC, 1992.

(In archive footage) Herself performing "Silver Bells," *Bob Hope's "Bag Full of Christmas Memories"* (also known as *Hope for the Holidays* and *Hope for the Holidays—The Best of Bob Hope*), 1993, and special edition released.

Herself, "The Love Boat and M*A*S*H," *The Truth behind the Sitcom Scandals* (also known as *Truth behind the Sitcom Scandals 3* and *TV Guide's "Truth behind the Sitcom Scandals 3"*), Fox, 2000.

Herself, "M*A*S*H": 30th Anniversary Reunion, Fox, 2002.

Herself, *CBS at 75* (also known as *CBS at 75: A Primetime Celebration*), CBS, 2003.

(Uncredited) Herself, *Comic Relief 2006*, HBO and TBS, 2006.

Television Appearances; Awards Presentations:

Herself, *The 15th Annual TV Week Logie Awards*, Nine Network (Australia), 1973.

Presenter, *Your Choice for the Film Awards*, 1984.

Presenter, *The British Comedy Awards*, Independent Television (England), 2001.

Performer in Gray Anatomy sketch, *The Fourth Annual TV Land Awards* (also known as *The Fourth Annual TV Land Awards: A Celebration of Classic TV* and *TV Land Awards 2006*), TV Land, 2006.

Television Appearances; Episodic:

Anna Stockton Schroeder, "A Thousand Pardons—You're Dead!," *Hawaii Five–O* (also known as *McGarrett*), CBS, 1969.

Belle Clark, "The Pack Rat," *Gunsmoke* (also known as *Gun Law* and *Marshal Dillon*), CBS, 1970.

Donna, "Snow Train: Parts 1 & 2," *Gunsmoke* (also known as *Gun Law* and *Marshal Dillon*), CBS, 1970.

Dorothy Harker, "Only One Death to a Customer," *Mannix*, CBS, 1970.

Jill Packard, "Figures in a Landscape," *Mannix*, CBS, 1970.

Midge Larson, "Homecoming," *Mission: Impossible*, CBS, 1970.

Wanda Russell, "Three Dead Cows at Makapuu: Parts 1 & 2," *Hawaii Five-O* (also known as *McGarrett*), CBS, 1970.

Ginny Lomax, "Homecoming," *Cade's County*, CBS, 1971.

Rosalyn, "The Convicts," *The Bold Ones: The New Doctors* (also known as *The Bold Ones* and *The New Doctors*), NBC, 1971.

Betty, "Bait Once, Bait Twice," *Hawaii Five-O* (also known as *McGarrett*), CBS, 1972.

Doris, "Love and the Hairy Excuse/Love and Lady Luck/Love and the Pick-Up Fantasy," *Love, American Style*, ABC, 1972.

Ellen Sue Greely, "A Visit to Upright," *Bonanza* (also known as *Ponderosa*), NBC, 1972.

Guest panelist, *The Hollywood Squares*, NBC and syndicated, multiple appearances, including multiple episodes in 1972, multiple episodes in 1973, multiple episodes in 1974, multiple episodes in 1975, 1976, 1978.

Mary Beth Scoggins, "Love and the Big Top/Love and the Locksmith/Love and the Odd Couples/Love and the Unwedding," *Love, American Style*, ABC, 1973.

Sally Pearson, "Ollinger's Last Case," *Ironside* (also known as *The Raymond Burr Show*), NBC, 1973.

Herself, *The Burns and Schreiber Comedy Hour*, ABC, 1973.

Herself, *The Tonight Show Starring Johnny Carson* (also known as *The Best of Carson*), NBC, 1973.

Ella Knox, "By Reason of Madness," *Petrocelli*, NBC, 1974.

Herself, *Celebrity Sweepstakes*, CBS, 1974.

Herself, *The Merv Griffin Show*, syndicated, 1974.

Herself, *The Mike Douglas Show*, syndicated, 1974.

Herself, *Dinah!* (also known as *Dinah* and *Dinah and Friends*), syndicated, 1974, multiple episodes in 1975, 1976.

Herself, *Celebrity Bowling*, syndicated, multiple episodes in 1975.

Herself, *Tony Orlando and Dawn* (also known as *The Tony Orlando and Dawn Rainbow Hour*), CBS, 1975.

Maxine, "Good Neighbor Maxine," *Good Heavens*, ABC, 1976.

Herself, *Donny and Marie* (also known as *The Osmond Family Show*), ABC, 1976.

Herself, *Liar's Club*, syndicated, 1976.

Herself, *The Captain and Tennille*, ABC, 1976, 1977.

Terry Mason Larsen, "Ex Plus Y/Golden Agers/Graham and Kelly" (some sources cite episode name as "Ex Plus Y/Graham and Kelly/Goldenagers"), *The Love Boat*, ABC, 1977.

Miss Mishancov, "Accidental Cruise/The Song Is Ended/A Time for Everything/Anoushka," *The Love Boat*, ABC, 1978.

Herself, *The $20,000 Pyramid*, ABC, multiple episodes in 1978, 1979.

Alice Phillips, "Hail to the Chief," *Supertrain*, NBC, 1979.

Herself, *Password Plus* (also known as *Password* and *Password All-Stars*), NBC, multiple episodes in 1979, 1980.

Guest host, *The Big Show*, NBC, 1980.

Herself, *The Muppet Show*, syndicated, 1980.

Herself, *The Phil Donahue Show* (also known as *Donahue*), syndicated, 1981.

Kathy Ross, "My Mother, My Chaperone/The Present/The Death and Life of Sir Alfred Demerest/Welcome Aboard: Parts 1 & 2," *The Love Boat*, ABC, 1984.

Sister Gabrielle, "Miracle at Moreaux," *WonderWorks*, PBS, 1985.

Herself, "Between the Lines—Summer, 1972," *Our World*, ABC, 1987.

Herself, *Aspel & Company*, Independent Television (England), 1987.

Voice of Dr. Marcia Cates, "Mad as a Hatter," *Batman: The Animated Series* (animated; also known as *Batman* and *The Adventures of Batman and Robin*), Fox, 1992.

Kim Mitchell, "Portrait of Death," *Murder, She Wrote*, CBS, 1994.

Evelyn Turner, "Who Killed the Sweet Smell of Success?," *Burke's Law*, CBS, 1995.

Herself, "Alan Alda: More Than Mr. Nice Guy," *Biography* (also known as *A&E Biography: Alan Alda*), Arts and Entertainment, 1997.

Voice of the judge, "Lawnmower Chicken/Cow Love Piles/I.M. Weasel: Law of Gravity," *Cow and Chicken* (animated), Cartoon Network, 1997.

Maggie Dennings, "Drill for Death," *Diagnosis Murder*, CBS, 1998.

Narrator, "Mae West," *Intimate Portrait* (also known as *Intimate Portrait: Mae West*), Lifetime, 1999.

Herself, *Hollywood Squares* (also known as *H2* and *H2: Hollywood Squares*), syndicated, 1999, 2004.

Herself, "M*A*S*H: Comedy under Fire," *History vs. Hollywood* (also known as *History: Through the Lens*), History Channel, 2001.

Herself, *So Graham Norton*, Channel 4 (England), 2001.

Herself, "M*A*S*H," *TV Tales* (also known as *M*A*S*H: TV Tales*), E! Entertainment Television, 2002.

Herself, *Pyramid* (also known as *The $100,000 Pyramid*), syndicated, 2004.

Herself (referee), *Battle of the Network Reality Stars*, Bravo, 2005.

(In archive footage) Major Margaret "Hot Lips" Houlihan, *La imagen de tu vida,* Television Espanola (TVE, Spain), 2006.

Appeared in other programs, including *The Bobby Vinton Show,* syndicated; *The Doctors,* CBS; *Dolly,* syndicated; and *The Mac Davis Show,* NBC.

Television Appearances; Pilots:
Major Margaret "Hot Lips" Houlihan, *M*A*S*H* (also known as *MASH*), CBS, 1972.
(Uncredited) Nurse, *Fireball Forward,* ABC, 1972.
Samantha Young, *The Love Tapes* (also known as *They're Playing Our Tape*), ABC, 1980.
Detective Christine Cagney, *Cagney & Lacey,* CBS, 1981.
Samantha Flynn (title role), *Sam,* ABC, 1985.

Television Creative Consultant; Series:
Those Incredible Animals, The Discovery Channel, 1992–97.

Television Director; Episodic:
Directed episodes of *M*A*S*H* (also known as *MASH*), CBS.

Film Appearances:
Hilary McBride, *Stand Up and Be Counted,* Columbia, 1972.
Woman with a glass eye, *Deadhead Miles,* Paramount, 1972.
Meyers's wife, *Freebie and the Bean,* Warner Bros., 1974.
Alice Stewart, *Race with the Devil,* Twentieth Century–Fox, 1975.
(Uncredited) Herself, *The Lion Roars Again* (short documentary), Metro–Goldwyn–Mayer, 1975.
Polly Reed, *S.O.B.,* Paramount, 1981.
B. D. Tucker, *Beer* (also known as *The Selling of America*), Orion, 1985.
President Barbara Adams, *Whoops Apocalypse,* ITC Entertainment Group, 1986, Metro–Goldwyn–Mayer, 1988.
Shirley, *Forest Warrior* (also known as *Lords of Tanglewood*), Nu Image Films, 1996.
Mrs. Jones, *Beach Movie* (also known as *Boardheads* and *Board Heads*), MPCA Pictures, 1998.

Stage Appearances:
Agnes Gooch, *Mame* (musical), Caesar's Palace, Las Vegas, NV, 1968.
Doris, *Same Time, Next Year,* Brooks Atkinson Theatre, New York City, beginning c. 1975.
Angela Prysock and Princess Puffer, *The Mystery of Edwin Drood* (musical), New York Shakespeare Festival, Imperial Theatre, New York City, 1985–87.

Title role (Mame Dennis), *Mame* (musical), Westbury Music Fair, Westbury, NY, 1996.
Betty, *A Passionate Woman,* Coconut Grove Playhouse, Miami, FL, 2000.
The Vagina Monologues, Westside Theatre (Downstairs), New York City, and Arts Theatre, London, both 2001, also produced in Chicago, IL.

Appeared in other productions, including an appearance as Melissa Gardner, *Love Letters;* as one of the Pigeon sisters, *The Odd Couple,* Los Angeles production; and a performance in *The Apple Tree* (also known as *The Apple Tree with Loretta Swit*), Forestburgh Playhouse, Forestburgh, NY.

Major Tours:
Any Wednesday, U.S. cities, 1967.
Title role, *Shirley Valentine* (solo show), various productions, U.S. and Canadian cities, c. 1989, c. 1991, 1995, 1996, 1997.
Same Time, Next Year, U.S. and Canadian cities, 1993.
Song of Singapore (musical), U.S. cities, 1996.
The Vagina Monologues, U.S. and Canadian cities, 2002.
Title role (Mame Dennis), *Mame* (musical), U.S. cities, 2003.

Appeared as one of the Pigeon sisters, *The Odd Couple,* Florida cities.

Radio Appearances; Episodic:
Herself, *Woman's Hour,* BBC Radio Four, 2001.

RECORDINGS

Videos:
Herself, *Muppet Video: The Kermit and Piggy Story,* 1985.
(In archive footage) Herself, *Muppet Video: Rock Music with the Muppets,* 1985.

Appeared in informative videos.

Video Games:
Herself, *TV Land Presents "Blast from the Past,"* 2001.

Albums; with Others:
Various artists, *25th Anniversary Show Stopping Performances* (compilation of songs from stage productions), DRG, 2001.

WRITINGS

Nonfiction:
A Needlepoint Scrapbook, Main Street Books, 1986.

Writings for Children:
Some sources state that Swit wrote and illustrated a book for children.

OTHER SOURCES

Electronic:
SwitHearts, http://www.swithearts.com, January 3, 2009.

SZWARC, Jeannot 1939–
　　(Jean Szwarc)

PERSONAL

Born November 21, 1939 (some sources cite 1937), in Paris, France; married Cara de Menaul (a film production coordinator); children: one son. *Education:* Earned a master's degree in political science.

Addresses: *Manager*—Don Klein Management Group, 8840 Wilshire Blvd., Suite 207, Beverly Hills, CA 90211.

Career: Director, producer, and writer. Universal, temporary worker, 1967; NBC, contract worker, c. 1967. Worked as a production assistant and a second unit director in Paris.

Member: Directors Guild of America.

Awards, Honors: Fantafestival Award, best film, and Critics Award, Avoriaz Fantastic Film Festival, both 1981, for *Somewhere in Time.*

CREDITS

Television Producer; Series:
Associate producer, *Ironside* (also known as *The Raymond Burr Show*), NBC, 1967–69.
Ironside (also known as *The Raymond Burr Show*), NBC, 1969.

Some sources cite work as an associate producer for *Bob Hope Presents the Chrysler Theater* (also known as *The Chrysler Theater* and *Universal Star Time*), NBC.

Television Director; Miniseries:
(With Vittorio Sindoni) *Prigioniera di una vendetta* (also known as *Maximum Exposure*), 1990.

Television Director; Movies:
Night of Terror, ABC, 1972.
The Weekend Nun (also known as *Matter of the Heart*), ABC, 1972.
Columbo: Lovely but Lethal (also known as "Lovely but Lethal," *Columbo*), NBC, 1973.
The Devil's Daughter, ABC, 1973.
A Summer without Boys, ABC, 1973.
You'll Never See Me Again, ABC, 1973.
The Murders in the Rue Morgue (also known as *Le tueur de la Rue Morgue*), CBS, 1986.
Grand Larceny, multiple channels, c. 1987.
Passez une bonne nuit (also known as *Have a Nice Night*), 1990.
Mountain of Diamonds (also known as *Burning Shore, Lady Diamond, Gluehender Himmel, La montagna dei diamenti,* and *La montagne de diamants*), 1991.
Laura, 1995.
The Rockford Files: A Blessing in Disguise, CBS, 1995.
Schrecklicher Verdacht, 1995.
The Rockford Files: If the Frame Fits ... (also known as *The Rockford Files: Suitable for Framing*), CBS, 1996.

Television Director; Specials:
"Lisa, Bright and Dark," *Hallmark Hall of Fame,* NBC, 1973.
"The Small Miracle," *Hallmark Hall of Fame,* NBC, 1973.
"Something Wonderful Happens Every Spring," *Hallmark Hall of Fame,* NBC, 1975.
Supergirl: The Making of the Movie, ABC, 1985.

Television Director; Episodic:
"The Macabre Mr. Micawber," *Ironside* (also known as *The Raymond Burr Show*), NBC, 1968.
"The Beautiful People," *It Takes A Thief,* ABC, 1969.
"The Great Chess Gambit," *It Takes A Thief,* ABC, 1969.
"A Matter of Love and Death," *Ironside* (also known as *The Raymond Burr Show*), NBC, 1969.
"Who'll Bid Two Million Dollars?," *It Takes A Thief,* ABC, 1969.
"Aura to a New Tomorrow," *Marcus Welby, M.D.* (also known as *Robert Young, Family Doctor*), ABC, 1970.
"Call Me Ellen," *Paris 7000,* ABC, 1970.
"Experiment at New Life," *The Men from Shiloh* (also known as *The Virginian*), NBC, 1970.
"The People against Doctor Chapman," *The Bold Ones: The Lawyers* (also known as *The Bold Ones* and *The Lawyers*), NBC, 1970.
"The Shiloh Years," *The Virginian* (also known as *The Men from Shiloh*), NBC, 1970.
(Often credited as Jean Szwarc) *Night Gallery* (also known as *Rod Serling's "Night Gallery"*), NBC, multiple episodes, 1970–73.
"A Company of Victims," *Sarge,* NBC, 1971.

283

"Exit from Wickenburg," *Alias Smith and Jones,* ABC, 1971.

"Karen," *Matt Lincoln,* ABC, 1971.

"Wednesday's Child," *Longstreet,* ABC, 1971.

"Is It So Soon That I Am Done For—I Wonder What I Was Begun For?," *Marcus Welby, M.D.* (also known as *Robert Young, Family Doctor*), ABC, 1972.

"The Case of the Furious Father," *The New Adventures of Perry Mason,* CBS, 1973.

"The Oberon Contract," *Toma,* ABC, 1973.

Kojak, CBS, multiple episodes, 1973–77.

"Population Zero," *The Six Million Dollar Man* (also known as *Cyborg, De Man van zes miljoen, Der sechs Millionen Dollar Mann, El hombre de los seis millones de dolares, Kuuden miljoonan dollarin mies, L'homme qui valait 3 milliards,* and *L'uomo da sei milioni di dollari*), ABC, 1974.

"The Street," *Toma,* ABC, 1974.

"Two into 5.56 Won't Go," *The Rockford Files* (also known as *Jim Rockford, Jim Rockford, Private Investigator,* and *Rockford*), NBC, 1975.

Baretta, ABC, multiple episodes in 1975.

"New Georgia on My Mind," *Baa Baa Black Sheep* (also known as *Black Sheep Squadron*), NBC, 1976.

"So Help Me God," *The Rockford Files* (also known as *Jim Rockford, Jim Rockford, Private Investigator,* and *Rockford*), NBC, 1976.

"It's Hard but It's Fair," *Baretta,* ABC, 1977.

"New Life, Old Dragons," *The Rockford Files* (also known as *Jim Rockford, Jim Rockford, Private Investigator,* and *Rockford*), NBC, 1977.

Director of "The Last Defender of Camelot" segment, "A Day in Beaumont/The Last Defender of Camelot," *The Twilight Zone* (also known as *The New Twilight Zone*), CBS, 1986.

Director of "Red Snow" segment, "Need to Know/Red Snow," *The Twilight Zone* (also known as *The New Twilight Zone*), CBS, 1986.

JAG (also known as *JAG: Judge Advocate General*), CBS, multiple episodes, 1998–2004.

"There's Something about Olga," *Seven Days* (also known as *7 Days* and *Seven Days: The Series*), UPN, 1999.

The Practice, ABC, multiple episodes, 1999–2004.

"Don't Go Changin'," *Providence,* NBC, 2000.

"Girls' Night Out," *Ally McBeal,* Fox, 2000.

"Turning Thirty," *Ally McBeal,* Fox, 2000.

"Blown Away," *Philly,* ABC, 2001.

"Hats Off to Larry," *Ally McBeal,* Fox, 2001.

"Chapter Thirty–Three," *Boston Public,* Fox, 2002.

"Chapter Fifty," *Boston Public,* Fox, 2002.

"A Kick in the Head," *Ally McBeal,* Fox, 2002.

"Woman," *Ally McBeal,* Fox, 2002.

"Dead Woman Walking," *CSI: Miami* (also known as *CSI Miami*), CBS, 2003.

Smallville (also known as *Smallville Beginnings* and *Smallville: Superman the Early Years*), The WB, 2003–2006, The CW, beginning 2006.

"Loose Lips," *Boston Legal* (also known as *Fleet Street, The Practice: Fleet Street,* and *The Untitled Practice*), ABC, 2004.

"Bones of Contention," *Numb3rs* (also known as *Numbers* and *Num3ers*), CBS, 2005.

Without a Trace (also known as *Vanished* and *W.A.T.*), CBS, multiple episodes, 2005–2007.

"Forever Blue," *Cold Case* (also known as *Anexihniastes ypothesis, Caso abierto, Cold case—affaires classees, Cold Case—Kein Opfer ist je vergessen, Doegloett aktak, Kalla spaar, Todistettavasti syyllinen,* and *Victims du passe*), CBS, 2006.

"Word Salad Days," *Boston Legal* (also known as *Fleet Street, The Practice: Fleet Street,* and *The Untitled Practice*), ABC, 2006.

"Distractions" (also known as "Chapter Fourteen 'Distractions'"), *Heroes,* NBC, 2007.

"Family 8108," *Cold Case* (also known as *Anexihniastes ypothesis, Caso abierto, Cold case—affaires classees, Cold Case—Kein Opfer ist je vergessen, Doegloett aktak, Kalla spaar, Todistettavasti syyllinen,* and *Victims du passe*), CBS, 2007.

"The Line" (also known as "Chapter Six 'The Line'"), *Heroes,* NBC, 2007.

"Spaceman in a Crater," *Bones* (also known as *Brennan, Bones—Die Knochenjaegerin, Dr. Csont,* and *Kondid*), Fox, 2007.

"Andy in C Minor," *Cold Case* (also known as *Anexihniastes ypothesis, Caso abierto, Cold case—affaires classees, Cold Case—Kein Opfer ist je vergessen, Doegloett aktak, Kalla spaar, Todistettavasti syyllinen,* and *Victims du passe*), CBS, 2008.

"Eris Quod Sum" (also known as "Chapter Seven 'Eris Quod Sum'"), *Heroes,* NBC, 2008.

"I Will, I'm Will," *Raising the Bar,* TNT, 2008.

"Our Father" (also known as "Chapter Twelve 'Our Father'"), *Heroes,* NBC, 2008.

"The Perfect Pieces in the Purple Pond," *Bones* (also known as *Brennan, Bones—Die Knochenjaegerin, Dr. Csont,* and *Kondid*), Fox, 2008.

"The Verdict in the Story," *Bones* (also known as *Brennan, Bones—Die Knochenjaegerin, Dr. Csont,* and *Kondid*), Fox, 2008.

Directed other programs, including *girls club,* Fox; and *The Man and the City,* ABC.

Television Work; Other; Episodic:
Production assistant, "Code Name: Heraclitus," *Bob Hope Presents the Chrysler Theater* (also known as *The Chrysler Theater* and *Universal Star Time*), NBC, 1967.

Television Director; Pilots:
Crime Club, CBS, 1975.

Hazard's People, CBS, 1976.

Code Name: Diamond Head, NBC, 1977.

(With Melville Shavelson) *True Life Stories,* ABC, 1981.

Television Appearances; Specials:

Himself, *Supergirl: The Making of the Movie,* ABC, 1985.

Himself, *Art of Darkness: A Night Gallery Retrospective,* 2002.

Television Appearances; Episodic:

Himself, "Film 78 Episode 6," *Film '78* (also known as *Film 1978, Film of the Year,* and *The Film Programme*), BBC, 1978.

Himself, "Film 79 Episode 18," *Film '79* (also known as *Film 1979, Film of the Year,* and *The Film Programme*), BBC, 1979.

Himself, "Action!," *Heroes: Unmasked,* BBC, 2008.

Himself, "A Bug's Life," *Heroes: Unmasked,* BBC, 2008.

Himself, "On a Heroic Scale," *Heroes: Unmasked,* 2008.

Himself, "Shock of the Old," *Heroes Unmasked,* BBC, 2008.

Film Director:

Extreme Close–Up (also known as *Sex through a Window*), National General Pictures, 1973.

Bug (also known as *Hesphaestus Plague*), Paramount, 1975.

Jaws 2 (also known as *Jaws II*), Universal, 1978.

Somewhere in Time, Universal, 1980.

Enigma, Embassy Pictures, 1982.

Supergirl (also known as *Supergirl: The Movie*), TriStar, 1984, director's cut also released.

Director of clips from *Bug* and *Jaws 2, Terror in the Aisles,* Universal, 1984.

Santa Claus: The Movie (also known as *Santa Claus*), TriStar, 1985.

Honor Bound (also known as *Red End*), 1988.

La vengeance d'une blonde (also known as *Revenge of a Blonde*), [France], 1994.

Hercule et Sherlock (also known as *Mutts*), 1996.

Les soeurs soleil, 1997.

Documentary Film Appearances:

(Uncredited) Himself, *Life and Legend of Bruce Lee* (also known as *Bruce Lee: Man and Legend*), Golden Harvest Company, 1973.

Himself, *Spine Tingler! The William Castle Story,* 2007.

RECORDINGS

Videos:

Himself, *Back to "Somewhere in Time,"* Universal Studios Home Video, 2000.

(Uncredited) Himself, *John Williams: The Music of "Jaws 2,"* Universal Pictures Home Video, 2001.

Himself, *The Making of "Jaws 2,"* Universal Pictures Home Video, 2001.

Himself, *You Will Believe: The Cinematic Saga of Superman,* Warner Home Video, 2006.

Himself, *Supergirl: The Last Daughter of Krypton,* 2008.

Contributed commentary for DVD releases.

WRITINGS

Teleplays; Movies:

Passez une bonne nuit (also known as *Have a Nice Night*), 1990.

Teleplays; Episodic:

(Story) "Light at the End of the Journey," *Ironside* (also known as *The Raymond Burr Show*), NBC, 1967.

"A Matter of Love and Death," *Ironside* (also known as *The Raymond Burr Show*), NBC, 1969.

"The Old Who Came in from the Spy," *It Takes a Thief,* ABC, 1969.

T

TATUM, Channing 1980–

PERSONAL

Full name, Channing Matthew Tatum; born April 26, 1980, in Cullman, AL. *Education:* Studied acting at Deena Levy Theatre Studio; attended Glenville State College. *Avocational Interests:* Sports, including football, Kung Fu, and Gor–Chor Kung Fu.

Addresses: *Agent*—Innovative Artists, 1505 Tenth St., Santa Monica, CA 90401; United Talent Agency, 9560 Wilshire Blvd., Suite 500, Beverly Hills, CA 90212. *Manager*—Management 360, 9111 Wilshire Blvd., Beverly Hills, CA 90210. *Publicist*—WKT Public Relations, 335 North Maple Dr., Suite 351, Beverly Hills, CA 90210.

Career: Actor. Appeared in fashion show for *Men's Health* magazine, Miami, FL, 2000; worked as a model for Abercrombie & Fitch, Nautica, the Gap, Aeropostale, and Emporio Armani clothing lines; appeared in television commercials, including Budweiser products, Pepsi soft drinks, Mountain Dew soft drinks, and American Eagle clothing stores. Also worked as a construction worker, mortgage broker, a cologne salesman at Dillard's, and at a puppy/kitty nursery.

Awards, Honors: Teen Choice Award, movies—choice breakout (male), Teen Choice Award nomination (with Amanda Bynes), movies—choice liplock, 2006, for *She's the Man;* Special Jury Prize (with others), dramatic, Sundance Film Festival, Breakthrough Award nomination, Gotham Awards, Gijon International Film Festival Award (with others), best actor, 2006, Independent Spirit Award nomination, best supporting male, Independent Features Project, 2007, all for *A Guide to Recognizing Your Saints;* Teen Choice Award (with Jenna Dewan), choice movie—dance, Teen Choice Award nomination, choice movie actor—drama, 2007, both for *Step Up;* Teen Choice Award, choice movie actor—drama, 2008, for *Stop–Loss.*

CREDITS

Film Appearances:
Jason Lyle, *Coach Carter,* Paramount, 2005.
Rowdy Sparks, *Supercross* (also known as *Supercross: The Movie*), Twentieth Century–Fox, 2005.
(Uncredited) Boy in church scene, *War of the Worlds,* Paramount, 2005.
Nick, *Havoc,* New Line Home Video, 2005.
Duke, *She's the Man,* DreamWorks, 2006.
Tyler Gage, *Step Up,* Buena Vista, 2006.
Young Antonio, *A Guide to Recognizing Your Saints,* First Look Pictures, 2006.
Johnson, *Battle in Seattle,* Redwood Palms Pictures, 2007.
Greg, *The Trap* (short), 2007.
Tyler Gage, *Step Up 2: The Streets,* Buena Vista, 2008.
Sergeant Steve Shriver, *Stop–Loss,* Paramount Pictures, 2008.
Himself, *The Making of "Stop–Loss"* (short), Paramount Home Entertainment, 2008.
Sean Arthur, *Fighting,* Universal, 2009.
Pretty Boy Floyd, *Public Enemies,* Universal, 2009.
Duke, *G.I. Joe: Rise of the Cobra* (also known as *G.I. Joe*), Paramount, 2009.
John Tyree, *Dear John,* Screen Gems, 2009.

Television Appearances; Specials:
Host, *"Step Up" BET Music Special,* Black Entertainment Television, 2006.
Host, *On the Set:"Step Up,"* Black Entertainment Television, 2006.
The Teen Choice Awards 2008, Fox, 2008.

Television Appearances; Episodic:
Bob Davenport, "Pro Per," *CSI: Miami,* CBS, 2004.

"Top 4: The Finale," *So You Think You Can Dance,* Fox, 2006.
The Early Show, CBS, 2006.
TRL Italy (also known as *TRL Italia* and *Total Request Live (Italy),* MTV, 2006.
Entertainment Tonight (also known as *E.T.*), syndicated, 2008.
Cartaz Cultural, 2008.

RECORDINGS

Music Videos:
Ciara's "Get Up," 2006.
Sean Paul featuring Keyshia Cole's "Give It Up to Me," 2006.

Also appeared in Ricky Martin's "She Bangs"; Twista's "Hope."

OTHER SOURCES

Periodicals:
Entertainment Weekly, September 1, 2006, p. 25.
Newsweek, August 14, 2006, p. 10.
USA Today, August 15, 2006, p. 3D.

Electronic:
Channing Tatum Website, http://www.channingtatumunwrapped.com, January 15, 2009.

THOMAS, Richard 1951–
   (Richard E. Thomas, Richard Earl Thomas)

PERSONAL

Born June 13, 1951, in New York, NY; son of Richard S. (a ballet dancer and instructor and owner of a ballet school) and Barbara (a ballet dancer and instructor and owner of a ballet school; maiden name, Fallis) Thomas; married Alma Gonzales (a teacher and welfare worker), February 14, 1975 (divorced, 1993); married Georgiana Bischoff, November 20, 1994; children: (first marriage) Barbara Ayala, Gwyneth Gonzales, and Pilar Alma (triplets), Richard Francisco; (second marriage) Montana James, (stepchildren) Brooke, Kendra. *Education:* Attended Columbia University. *Religion:* Christian.

Addresses: *Agent*—Steve Tellez, Creative Artists Agency, 2000 Avenue of the Stars, Los Angeles, CA 90067; (voice work) Marcia Hurwitz, Innovative Artists Talent and Literary Agency, 1505 10th St., Santa Monica, CA 90401. *Manager*—Brookside Artists Management, 250 West 57th St., Suite 2303, New York, NY 10019.

Career: Actor, director, and producer. Melpomene Productions, owner. Voice for commercials, including work for Mercedes–Benz, 2007; appeared in commercials for Minute Maid fruit juice with his triplet daughters. Also poet and author; lecturer at colleges and universities. Better Hearing Institute, national chair, 1987—.

Awards, Honors: Emmy Award, 1973, Emmy Award nomination, 1974, and Golden Globe Award nomination, 1974, 1975, all best actor in a drama series, for *The Waltons;* Lucille Lortel Award nomination, and Outer Critics Circle Award nomination, both outstanding lead actor, 2004, for *The Stendahl Syndrome;* Friends of Robert Frost Award; honorary D.Arts, University of South Carolina.

CREDITS

Television Appearances; Series:
Ben Schultz, Jr., *The Edge of Night,* CBS, 1961.
Richard, *From These Roots,* NBC, 1961.
Assistant, *1, 2, 3, Go!,* NBC, 1961–62.
Chris Austen, *A Flame in the Wind,* ABC, 1964–65, renamed *A Time for Us,* ABC, 1965–66.
Thomas Christopher "Tom"/"Tommy" Hughes, *As the World Turns,* CBS, 1966–67.
John "John Boy" Walton, Jr., *The Waltons,* CBS, 1972–78.
David Robinson, *The Adventures of Swiss Family Robinson,* PAX, 1998.
Hamilton Whitney III, *Just Cause,* PAX, 2002–2003.

Television Appearances; Movies:
Title role, "Oliver Twist," *The DuPont Show of the Month,* 1959.
Sixteen (also known as *Like a Crow on a June Bug),* 1972.
The Thanksgiving Story, 1973.
Private Henry Fleming, *The Red Badge of Courage,* NBC, 1974.
Cadet James Pelosi, *The Silence,* NBC, 1975.
Michael Carboni, *Getting Married,* CBS, 1978.
Andrew Madison, *No Other Love,* CBS, 1979.
Paul Baumer, *All Quiet on the Western Front,* CBS, 1979.
David Benjamin, *To Find My Son,* CBS, 1980.
Lieutenant Sandy Mueller, *Berlin Tunnel 21,* CBS, 1981.
William "Bill" Richmond, *Johnny Belinda,* CBS, 1982.
Will Mossop, *Hobson's Choice,* CBS, 1983.
Title role, *Living Proof: The Hank Williams, Jr., Story,* NBC, 1983.
Henry Durrie, *The Master of Ballantrae,* CBS, 1984.

Marty Campbell, *Final Jeopardy,* NBC, 1985.

Greg Madison, *Go Toward the Light* (also known as *Go to the Light*), CBS, 1988.

Andy Colby's Incredible Adventure (also known as *Andy Colby's Incredible Video Adventure, Andy Colby's Incredibly Awesome Adventure,* and *Andy and the Airwave Rangers*), 1988.

Colin Diver, *Common Ground,* CBS, 1990.

Lieutenant Steven Scott, *Mission of the Shark* (also known as *Mission of the Shark: The Saga of the U.S.S. Indianapolis*), CBS, 1991.

James O'Hanlan, *Yes, Virginia, There Is a Santa Claus,* ABC, 1991.

Gary Brown, *Crash Landing: The Rescue of Flight 232* (also known as *A Thousand Heroes*), ABC, 1992.

Richard Farley, *I Can Make You Love Me: The Stalking of Laura Black* (also known as *I Love You to Death, The Laura Black Story,* and *Stalking Laura*), CBS, 1993.

John–Boy Walton, *A Walton Thanksgiving Reunion,* CBS, 1993.

Don Weber, *Precious Victims,* CBS, 1993.

Paul Cowley, *Linda* (also known as *Lust for Murder*), USA Network, 1993.

David Young, *To Save the Children,* CBS, 1994.

Richard Lyon, *Death in Small Doses,* ABC, 1995.

John–Boy Walton, *A Walton Wedding* (also known as *John–Boy's Wedding*), CBS, 1995.

Richard Evans, *The Christmas Box,* CBS, 1995.

Tim Willows, *Down, Out & Dangerous,* USA Network, 1995.

Gordon Holly, *What Love Sees,* CBS, 1996.

Richard Evans, *Timepiece,* CBS, 1996.

John–Boy Walton, *A Walton Easter,* CBS, 1997.

Hugh "Bud" Keenan, *A Thousand Men and a Baby* (also known as *Narrow Escape*), CBS, 1997.

Herb Dellenbach, *Flood: A River's Rampage,* The Family Channel, 1997.

Victor Dewlap, *Big and Hairy,* Showtime, 1998.

Host, *It's a Miracle,* PAX, 1999–2003.

Charles Ingalls, *Beyond the Prairie: The True Story of Laura Ingalls Wilder,* CBS, 2000.

Jack Murphy, *In the Name of the People,* CBS, 2000.

Jerry McNeil, *The Christmas Secret* (also known as *Flight of the Reindeer*), 2000.

Dr. Neal Kassell, *The Miracle of the Cards* (also known as *Le miracle des cartes*), PAX, 2001.

Charles Ingalls, *Beyond the Prairie, Part 2: The True Story of Laura Ingalls Wilder* (also known as *Beyond the Prairie II: The True Story of Laura Ingalls Wilder Continues*), CBS, 2001.

Rod Morgan, *Anna's Dream,* PAX, 2002.

Richard Eason, *Annie's Point,* Hallmark Channel, 2005.

Bob, *Wild Hearts,* Hallmark Channel, 2006.

Television Appearances; Miniseries:

Cohost, *CBS: On the Air,* CBS, 1978.

Jim Warner, *Roots: The Next Generations,* ABC, 1979.

Reverend Bobby Joe Stuckey, *Glory! Glory!* (also known as *Sister Ruth*), HBO, 1989.

Bill "Stuttering Bill" Denbrough, "It" (also known as "Stephen King's 'It',"), *ABC Novel for Television,* ABC, 1990.

Jerry Thayer, *The Invaders,* Fox, 1995.

Narrator, *West Virginia,* 1996.

TV Land Moguls, TV Land, 2004.

Television Appearances; Specials:

(As Richard Earl Thomas) Joey, "A Christmas Tree," *Hallmark Hall of Fame* (also known as *Hallmark Television Playhouse*), NBC, 1959.

(As Richard E. Thomas) Ivor, "A Doll's House," *Hallmark Hall of Fame* (also known as *Hallmark Television Playhouse*), NBC, 1959.

The boy, "Give Us Barabbas!," *Hallmark Hall of Fame* (also known as *Hallmark Television Playhouse*), NBC, 1961.

The Bobby Van and Elaine Joyce Show, CBS, 1973.

Host, "H.M.S. Pinafore," *The CBS Festival of Lively Arts for Young People,* CBS, 1973.

Mac Davis Christmas Special … When I Grow Up, HBO, 1976.

Miss Teenage America Pageant, NBC, 1977.

"San Francisco Ballet: Romeo and Juliet," *Great Performances: Dance in America* (also known as *Dance in America*), PBS, 1978.

Paul Bratter, *Barefoot in the Park,* HBO, 1982.

Host, *Christmas at Kennedy Center with Leontyne Price* (also known as *Kennedy Center Tonight: Christmas at Kennedy Center with Leontyne Price*), 1982.

Kenneth Talley, Jr., *Fifth of July,* Showtime, 1982.

Pavarotti and Friends, ABC, 1982.

Broadway Plays Washington: Kennedy Center Tonight, PBS, 1982.

The American Film Institute Salute to Lillian Gish, CBS, 1984.

The Night of 100 Stars II, ABC, 1985.

Host, *Un ballo in maschera* (also known as *A Masked Ball*), PBS, 1987.

Jonathan Smith, *The Blessings of Liberty,* ABC, 1987.

Host and narrator, *Scenes from La Boheme: A Pavarotti Celebration,* PBS, 1988.

Host, *A Grand Night: The Performing Arts Salute Public Television,* PBS, 1988.

Cal Porter, "Andre's Mother," *American Playhouse,* PBS, 1990.

The Los Angeles Music Center's 25th Anniversary Celebration (also known as *The Music Center 25th Anniversary*), PBS, 1990.

The All–Star Salute to Our Troops, CBS, 1991.

The National Memorial Day Concert 1992, PBS, 1992.

Voice of John Hay, *Lincoln,* ABC, 1992.

CBS: The First 50 Years, CBS, 1998.

Cincinnati Pops Holiday: A Family Thanksgiving, PBS, 1999.

Narrator, *Humans: Who Are We?,* Discovery Channel, 2000.

The 70s: The Decade that Changed Television, ABC, 2000.

CBS at 75, CBS, 2003.

John Ritter Remembered, VH1, 2003.

Tennessee Williams, *Sweet Tornado: Margo Jones and the American Theater,* 2006.

Television Appearances; Pilots:

John–Boy Walton, *The Homecoming: A Christmas Story* (pilot for *The Waltons*), CBS, 1971.

Hamilton Whitney III, *Just Cause,* PAX, 2002.

Television Appearances; Episodic:

Jeremy Keeler, "The Croaker," *Way Out,* CBS, 1961.

Conradin, "Srendhi Vashtar," *Great Ghost Tales,* NBC, 1961.

Johnny Remington, "The Boy Between," *The Defenders,* 1961.

Martin Anderson, "The Last Voyage," *Seaway,* 1965.

Alan, "Fallen, Fallen Is Babylon," *Bracken's World,* 1969.

Dennis Alan Graham, "Echo of a Baby's Laugh," *Marcus Welby, M.D.* (also known as *Robert Young, Family Doctor*), ABC, 1969.

Toby Tavormina, "Runaway," *Medical Center,* CBS, 1970.

Billy, "The Weary Willies," *Bonanza* (also known as *Ponderosa*), 1970.

"All the Golden Dandelions Are Gone," *Marcus Welby, M.D.* (also known as *Robert Young, Family Doctor*), ABC, 1970.

Ian Evans, "The Sins of the Fathers," *Night Gallery* (also known as *Rod Serling's "Night Gallery"*), NBC, 1971.

"Game of Terror," *The F.B.I.,* ABC, 1971.

Match Game 73, 1973.

The Tonight Show Starring Johnny Carson, 1973, 1975.

The Sonny and Cher Show, 1976.

The Mike Douglas Show, 1977.

Our World, ABC, 1986.

Dr. Trask, "Mute Witness to Murder," *Tales from the Crypt* (also known as *HBO's "Tales from the Crypt"*), HBO, 1990.

Dr. Stephen Ledbetter, "The New Breed," *The Outer Limits* (also known as *The New Outer Limits*), Showtime and syndicated, 1995.

Dr. Stephen Ledbetter (in archive footage), "The Voice of Reason," *The Outer Limits* (also known as *The New Outer Limits*), Showtime and syndicated, 1995.

Himself, "L.A. Times," *Dave's World,* CBS, 1996.

The Rosie O'Donnell Show, syndicated, 1997.

Joe Greene, "The Road Home: Part 1," *Touched by an Angel,* CBS, 1997.

Joe Greene, "Vengeance Is Mine: Part 1," *Touched by an Angel,* CBS, 1998.

Joe Greene, "The Road Home: Part 2," *Promised Land* (also known as *Home of the Brave*), CBS, 1997.

Joe Greene, "Two for the Road," *Promised Land* (also known as *Home of the Brave*), CBS, 1998.

Joe Greene, "A Hand Up Is Not a Hand Out: Parts 1 & 2," *Promised Land* (also known as *Home of the Brave*), CBS, 1998.

Host, *It's a Miracle,* PAX, 1999.

Walter Arens, "Committed," *The Practice,* ABC, 1999.

Daniel Varney, "Scourge," *Law & Order: Special Victims Unit* (also known as *Law & Order: SVU* and *Special Victims Unit*), NBC, 2001.

"The Waltons," *After They Were Famous,* 2002.

Dr. Brezak, "Sweet Child of Mine," *Century City,* CBS, 2004.

The Tony Danza Show, syndicated, 2005.

Howard Cottrell, "Autopsy Room Four," *Nightmares and Dreamscapes: From the Stories of Stephen King,* TNT, 2006.

According to some sources, also appeared as guest bowler, *Celebrity Bowling;* and in an episode of *Love, American Style,* ABC.

Television Appearances; Awards Presentations:

The 35th Annual Tony Awards, 1981.

Presenter, *The 43rd Annual Tony Awards,* CBS, 1989.

Host, *Family Guide to Quality Children's Television: The 1989 Ollie Awards,* PBS, 1989.

Presenter, *The 60th Annual Tony Awards,* 2006.

Television Work; Series:

Director, *The Waltons,* CBS, multiple episodes, between 1975 and 1977.

Television Work; Movies:

Executive producer, *Living Proof: The Hank Williams, Jr. Story,* NBC, 1983.

Co–executive producer, *Summer of Fear* (also known as *Father's Day* and *Simon Says*), CBS, 1996.

Coproducer, *What Love Sees,* CBS, 1996.

Co–executive producer, *For All Time,* CBS, 2000.

Stage Appearances:

(Stage debut) Singer, *Damn Yankees,* Sacandaga Garden Theatre, Sacandaga Park, NY, 1957.

(Broadway debut) John Roosevelt, *Sunrise at Campobello,* Cort Theatre, New York City, 1958–59.

John Henry, *The Member of the Wedding,* Equity Library Theatre, New York City, 1959.

Gordon Evans (as a child), *Strange Interlude,* Hudson Theatre, then Martin Beck Theatre, both New York City, 1963.

Edward, Prince of Wales, *King Richard III,* American Shakespeare Festival, Stratford, CT, 1964.

Eric, *The Playroom,* Brooks Atkinson Theatre, New York City, 1965–66.

Richard, Duke of York, *King Richard III,* New York Shakespeare Festival, Delacorte Theatre, Public Theatre, New York City, 1966.

Roger, *Everything in the Garden,* Plymouth Theatre, New York City, 1967–68.

Saint Joan, Center Theatre Group, Ahmanson Theatre, Los Angeles, 1974.

Merton of the Movies, Center Theatre Group, Ahmanson Theatre, 1977.

Hamlet, Hartford Stage Company, Hartford, CT, 1978.

Kenneth Talley, Jr., *Fifth of July,* New Apollo Theatre, New York City, 1980–82.

Treplev, *The Seagull,* Circle Repertory Company, American Place Theatre, New York City, 1983.

Title role, *The Count of Monte Cristo,* Eisenhower Theatre, John F. Kennedy Center for the Performing Arts, Washington, DC, 1985.

The Night of 100 Stars II, Radio City Music Hall, New York City, 1985.

Title role, *Citizen Tom Paine,* Eisenhower Theatre, John F. Kennedy Center for the Performing Arts, 1986.

Hildy Johnson, *The Front Page,* Vivian Beaumont Theatre, Lincoln Center, New York City, 1986–87.

Andrew Makepeace Ladd III, *Love Letters,* Promenade Theatre, New York City, 1989, then Edison Theatre, New York City, 1989, then Canon Theatre, Los Angeles, 1990.

Adam, *Square One,* Second Stage Theatre Company, McGinn–Cazale Theatre, New York City, 1990.

Stephen, *The Lisbon Traviata,* Center Theatre Group, Mark Taper Forum, 1990.

Danton's Death, Alley Theatre, Houston, TX, 1992.

Richard II, 1993.

Richard III, 1994.

Brother Julian, *Tiny Alice,* Hartford Stage Company, 1998, then Second Stage Theatre Company, 2000–2001.

Angelo, *Measure for Measure,* Ahmanson Theatre, 1999.

Puck, *A Midsummer Night's Dream,* Ahmanson Theatre, 1999.

Yvan, *ART,* Wyndham Theatre, London, 2000, 2001.

A Distant Country Called Youth, 2002.

Conductor, *The Stendahl Syndrome,* Primary Stages Theatre, New York City, 2004.

Gunter Guillaume, *Democracy,* Brooks Atkinson Theatre, 2004–2005.

Jeffrey Lapin, *A Naked Girl on the Appian Way,* Roundabout Theatre Company, American Airlines Theatre, New York City, 2005.

Touchstone, *As You Like It,* New York Shakespeare Festival, Delacorte Theatre, Public Theatre, 2005.

Twelve Angry Men, Dallas, TX, 2006, 2007.

Also appeared in *Arms and the Man,* Pasadena Playhouse, Pasadena, CA; as John Henry, *Member of the Wedding,* New York Shakespeare Festival, then American Shakespeare Festival; in title role, *Peer Gynt,* Hartford Stage Company, Hartford, CT; and in *Streamers,* Los Angeles.

Major Tours:

Ken Harrison, *Whose Life Is It Anyway?,* U.S. cities, 1980.

Stage Director:

Director of *The Red Badge of Courage,* John F. Kennedy Center for the Performing Arts, Washington, DC.

Film Appearances:

Charley, *Winning,* Universal, 1969.

Peter, *Last Summer,* Allied Artists, 1969.

Joshua Arnold, *Red Sky at Morning,* Universal, 1971.

Billy Roy, *The Todd Killings* (also known as *A Dangerous Friend* and *Skipper*), National General, 1971.

Harley MacIntosh, *Cactus in the Snow* (also known as *You Can't Have Everything*), General Film, 1972.

Kenny, *You'll Like My Mother,* Universal, 1972.

Narrator, *Sisters of the Space Age* (also known as *Freres de l'ere spatiale*), 1974.

Jimmy J., *9/30/55* (also known as *September 30, 1955* and *24 Hours of the Rebel*), Universal, 1977.

Shad, *Battle beyond the Stars,* New World, 1980.

Narrator, *Riding the Rails,* Artistic License, 1997.

Ted Hunter, *The Million Dollar Kid* (also known as *Fortune Hunters*), A–Pix Entertainment, 1999.

Walter Gaskell, *Wonder Boys* (also known as *Die Wonder Boys*), Paramount, 2000.

Bloodhounds, Inc., 2000.

Narrator, *Sacred Stage: The Mariinsky Theater,* First Run Features, 2005.

Broadway: The Next Generation, Second Act Productions, 2009.

Broadway: Beyond the Golden Age (also known as *B.G.A.2* and *Broadway: The Golden Age Two*), Second Act Productions, 2009.

Film Work:

Producer, *Camping with Camus,* 2000.

RECORDINGS

Videos:

Voice of Mark, *The Easter Story* (animated; also known as *Greatest Adventure Stories from the Bible: The Easter Story*), Hanna–Barbera Productions, 1989.

BloodHounds, Inc. #1: The Ghost of KRZY, (also known as *Bloodhounds, Inc.*), 2000.

Robert Hunter, *BloodHounds, Inc. # 3: Phantom of the Haunted Church,* (also known as *Bloodhounds, Inc.*), Marcia Silen Films, 2000.

Robert Hunter, *BloodHounds, Inc. # 5: Fangs for the Memories,* (also known as *Bloodhounds, Inc.*), Marcia Silen Films, 2000.

Member of jury for touring production, *Beyond a Reasonable Doubt: Making "12 Angry Men,"* Twentieth Century–Fox Home Entertainment, 2008.

Audio Books; Narrator:
Accept This Gift, Audio Renaissance, 1988.
A Gift of Healing, Audio Renaissance, 1989.
The Haymeadow, Bantam Audio, 1992.
The Homecoming, by Earl Hamner, Audio Renaissance, 1995.
Spencer's Mountain, by Earl Hamner, Audio Renaissance, 1995.

WRITINGS

Poems by Richard Thomas, Avon, 1974.
In the Moment (poetry), Avon, 1979.
(Compiler) *It's a Miracle: Real–Life Inspirational Stories Based on the PAX TV Series It's a Miracle,* Delta, 2002.

Also author of *Glass.*

TOLES–BEY, John
(John Toles Bey)

PERSONAL

Addresses: *Agent*—Larry O. Williams, Williams Talent Agency, Sunset Gower Studios, 1438 North Gower St., Building 35, Box 43, Hollywood, CA 90028.

Career: Actor and writer. Kuumba Workshop, member of repertory company, 1974.

Member: Independent Features Project Award, 1985, for *Honky Tonk Bud.*

CREDITS

Film Appearances:
Honky Tonk Bud (short film), 1985.
Navarro, *Weeds,* De Laurentiis Entertainment Group, 1987.
Monroe Bouchet, *Midnight Run,* Universal, 1988.
Joe Kane, *La grieta* (also known as *Endless Descent* and *The Rift*), Live Video, 1990.

Anthony Lawrence, *Cadence* (also known as *Count a Lonely Cadence* and *Stockade*), New Line Cinema, 1991.
King, *Out for Justice,* Warner Bros., 1991.
Jodie, *A Rage in Harlem,* Miramax, 1991.
Titus, *Leap of Faith,* Paramount, 1992.
Goose, *Trespass* (also known as *Looters*), Universal, 1992.
Marcus Jackson, *Payback,* 1994.
Jay Liebowitz, *Love Is a Gun,* Trimark Pictures, 1994.
Hospital guard, *Angie,* Buena Vista, 1994.
Plane gunner, *Waterworld,* Universal, 1995.
William, *Wet* (also known as *Feucht*), 1995.
Trooper at roadblock, *Nature of the Beast* (also known as *Bad Company* and *The Hatchet Man*), 1995.
Bobby, *Extreme Measures,* Columbia, 1996.
The Best Revenge, Panorama Entertainment, 1996.
Vallie, *Hoodlum,* Metro–Goldwyn–Mayer/United Artists, 1997.
Charley, *A Kid in Aladdin's Palace,* 1997.
Lee, *Sour Grapes,* Sony Pictures Entertainment, 1998.
Tommy Zimmer, *Evasive Action,* Hallmark Entertainment, 1998.
George, *Facade* (also known as *Death Valley*), Cinequanon Pictures International, Inc., 1999.
Mr. Pizzacoli, *Dude, Where's My Car?,* Twentieth Century–Fox, 2000.
(As John Toles Bey) *100 Kilos,* Virtuosos Worldwide Entertainment, 2001.
Russell, *K–PAX* (also known as *K–PAX—Alles ist moeglich*), Universal, 2001.
Otis, *Bottoms Up,* Sony Pictures Home Entertainment, 2006.

Television Appearances; Movies:
Arquette, *Shoot First: A Cop's Vengeance* (also known as *Vigilante Cop*), NBC, 1991.
Detective Steve Totten, *Steel Justice,* NBC, 1992.
Stoney Wiley, *Always Outnumbered* (also known as *Always Outnumbered, Always Outgunned*), HBO, 1998.
John Roxborough, *Joe and Max* (also known as *Joe and Max—Rivalen im Ring*), Starz!, 2002.

Television Appearances; Episodic:
Policeman asking for password, "Over My Dead Bodyguard," *Sledge Hammer!* (also known as *Sledge Hammer: The Early Years*), ABC, 1986.
"Promised Land," *Tour of Duty,* CBS, 1989.
Mike Saunders, "The Prisoner: Parts 1 & 2," *Matlock,* NBC, 1989.
Bernie Kilgus, "When Push Comes to Shove," *Knots Landing,* CBS, 1989.
Bernie Kilgus, "Oh, Brother," *Knots Landing,* CBS, 1990.
Billy Swayne, "Too Much, Too Late," *Miami Vice,* NBC, 1990.
Father Michael, "Out of Control," *The Flash,* CBS, 1990.
Father Michael, "Beat the Clock," *The Flash,* CBS, 1991.

Cab driver, "Safe Sex," *Red Shoe Diaries,* Showtime, 1992.

Brother Shabazz, "Credit Card Blues," *Martin,* Fox, 1993.

Cab driver (in archive footage), "Safe Sex" segment, *Red Shoe Diaries* (selected episodes from television series; also known as *Red Shoe Diaries 2: Double Dare*), 1993.

Bernard, "From Who the Skell Rolls," *NYPD Blue,* ABC, 1994.

Pearlie, "Momma's Baby, Maybe Martin," *Martin,* Fox, 1994.

"Resurrection/Niles and Bob/Harry Stenz," *The Watcher,* UPN, 1995.

John Speranza, "The List," *The X-Files,* Fox, 1995.

Sonny Hayes, "Vegas Heist," *Seven Days* (also known as *Seven Days: The Series*), UPN, 1999.

Terrell Biggs, "These Shoots Are Made for Joaquin," *NYPD Blue,* ABC, 2000.

Sonny Hayes, "The Cuban Missile," *Seven Days* (also known as *Seven Days: The Series*), UPN, 2000.

Tweedy, "Don't Fence Me In," *The District,* CBS, 2001.

Freddie Bell, "Loving Sons," *Philly,* ABC, 2001.

Moses, "No One's Girl," *Karen Sisco,* ABC, 2004.

Joe Boony, "Meet Market," *CSI: Crime Scene Investigation* (also known as *C.S.I., CSI: Las Vegas,* and *Les experts*), CBS, 2007.

WRITINGS

Screenplays:

Honky Tonk Bud (short film), 1985.
A Rage in Harlem, Miramax, 1991.

ADAPTATIONS

Toles–Bey's appearance as a cab driver in the "Safe Sex" episode of the television series *Red Shoe Diaries* was selected for inclusion in the compilation film *Red Shoe Diaries 2: Double Dare* in 1993. His appearance as William in the short film *Wet* was included in the film *Tales of Erotica* (also known as *Erotic Tales*) released by Trimark Pictures in 1996.

TOY, Camden 1957–

PERSONAL

Born in 1957, in Pittsburgh, PA; son of Malcolm Toy (an employee in the makeup department of Paramount).

Career: Actor and editor.

CREDITS

Film Appearances:
Mailman, *Faith,* American Film Institute, 1997.
Dr. Fred, *My Chorus* (short), 2000.
Television announcer, *Backgammon,* Vanguard Cinema, 2001.
Janitor, *The Works,* Showcase Entertainment, 2004.
Gabby, *Irascible* (short), 2004.
Fresh Dead/Dead Raoul, *All Souls Days: Dia de los muertos* (also known as *Dia de los muertos*), Anchor Bay Entertainment, 2005.
Dogsbody, *Outta Sync,* 2006.
The judge, *The Black Door* (short), Elevate Films, 2006.
Cemetery watchman, *Sin–Jin Smyth,* Sunn Classic Pictures, 2007.
Farmer, *Trickery Mimicry,* 2008.
Krampus, *Krampus,* 2008.
Henry, *Immortally Yours* (also known as *Kiss of the Vampire*), MTI Home Video, 2009.
Manager, *Bare Knuckles,* 2009.
Himself, *One for the Fire: "Night of the Living Dead" 40th Anniversary Documentary* (documentary), 2009.
Creepy guy, *Legend of the Mountain Witch,* 2009.

Film Work:
Additional editor, *Betaville,* PorchLight Entertainment, 2001.
Editor, *Deeper Mark* (short), 2002.
Additional editor, *Lightning Bug,* Anchor Bay Entertainment, 2004.
Post–production supervisor and editor, *Zen Noir,* Magic Lamp Releasing, 2004.
Producer and editor, *Irascible* (short), 2004.
Additional editor, *USA the Movie,* Mantic Eye, 2005.
Editor, *Over Breakfast* (short), 2005.

Television Appearances; Specials:
Himself, *Twisted History: Vampires,* The Discovery Channel, 2005.

Television Appearances; Episodic:
Ubervamp and others, *Buffy the Vampire Slayer* (also known as *BtVS, Buffy,* and *Buffy, the Vampire Slayer: The Series*), The WB then UPN, 1999–2003.
Prince of Lies, "Why We Fight," *Angel* (also known as *Angel: The Series*), The WB, 2004.
Baba, "First Sight," "11 Cut to 10 & 10 Directors Complete," *On the Lot,* Fox, 2007.

TRACHTENBERG, Michelle 1985–
(Michelle C. Trachtenberg)

PERSONAL

Full name, Michelle Christine Trachtenberg; born October 11, 1985, in New York, NY; daughter of

Michael (an engineer) and Lana (an actress, puppeteer, and manager) Trachtenberg. *Education:* Attended high school in Sherman Oaks, CA. *Avocational Interests:* Writing (including poetry), reading, making jewelry, playing tennis, swimming, ice skating.

Addresses: *Agent*—Creative Artists Agency, 2000 Avenue of the Stars, Los Angeles, CA 90067. *Manager*—Framework Entertainment, 9057 Nemo St., Suite C, West Hollywood, CA 90069. *Publicist*—WKT Public Relations, 335 North Maple Dr., Suite 351, Beverly Hills, CA 90210.

Career: Actress. Appeared in more than 100 commercials, including Wisk laundry detergent, Panasonic electronic products, Kraft foods, Kleenex, and Hoover; Williamstown Theatre Festival, MA, apprentice, 2005. RAD Kids (anti–drug organization), ambassador; volunteer with Care America and other organizations, including DARE, Starlight Children's Foundation, and Youth of America. Sometimes credited as Michelle C. Trachtenberg.

Awards, Honors: Young Artist Award, best performance in a feature film—leading young actress, 1997, for *Harriet the Spy;* Young Artist Award, best performance in a television comedy series—supporting young actress, 1998, for *Meego;* Young Artist Award nomination, best performance in a feature film—supporting young actress, YoungStar Award nomination, best young actress/performance in a motion picture comedy, 2000, both for *Inspector Gadget;* Young Artist Award, best performance in a television drama series—supporting young actress, Teen Choice Award nomination, television—choice sidekick, 2001, Saturn Award nomination, best supporting actress, Academy of Science Fiction, Fantasy and Horror Films, 2001, 2002, 2003, all for *Buffy the Vampire Slayer;* Young Artist Award nomination, best performance in a television comedy series—guest starring young actress, 2002, for *Mad TV;* Young Artist Award nomination, best performance in a television comedy series—leading young actress, 2002, Daytime Emmy Award nomination, outstanding performer in a children's series, 2004, both for *Truth or Scare;* Special Jury Prize, breakthrough performer award, Sarasota Film Festival, 2007, for *Beautiful Ohio.*

CREDITS

Film Appearances:

(Uncredited) Lena, *Melissa* (also known as *Secret Sins*), 1995.

Harriet M. Welsch, *Harriet the Spy,* Paramount, 1996.

Gloria, *Richie Rich's Christmas Wish* (also known as *Richie Rich: A Christmas Story*), Warner Bros. Home Video, 1998.

Penny, John's niece, *Inspector Gadget,* Buena Vista/Walt Disney, 1999.

Julie, *Can't Be Heaven,* Unapix/World International Network, 1999.

Jenny, *EuroTrip,* DreamWorks, 2004.

Herself, *"Buffy": Season 6 Overview* (documentary short), Fox Box, 2004.

Herself, *"Eurotrip": Nude Beach Exposed* (documentary short), DreamWorks Home Entertainment, 2004.

Herself, *"Eurotrip": The Making of "Eurotrip"* (documentary short), DreamWorks Home Entertainment, 2004.

Herself, *"Buffy": Season 7 Overview* (documentary short), Fox Box, 2004.

Casey Carlyle, *Ice Princess* (also known as *Une princesse sur la glace*), Buena Vista, 2005.

Wendy Peterson, *Mysterious Skin,* TLA Entertainment Group, 2005.

Sandra, *Beautiful Ohio,* 2006.

Melissa, *Black Christmas* (also known as *Black X–Mas* and *Noel noir*), Metro–Goldwyn–Mayer, 2006.

Indie chick, *Kickin' It Old School,* Yari Film Group, 2007.

Herself, *May All Your Christmases Be Black* (documentary short), Dimension Home Video, 2007.

Voice of Tika, *Dragonlace: Dragons of Autumn Twilight* (also known as *A Dungeons & Dragons Adventure Tale*), Paramount Home Video, 2008.

Suzanne, *Against the Current,* 2009.

Kitchelle Storms, *Young Americans,* Universal, 2009.

Maggie O'Donnell, *17 Again,* Warner Bros., 2009.

Television Appearances; Series:

Lily Benton Montgomery, *All My Children,* ABC, 1993–96.

Elsie Soaperstein, *Clarissa Explains It All* (also known as *Clarissa*), Nickelodeon, 1993–96.

Nona Mecklenberg, *The Adventures of Pete & Pete* (also known as *Pete & Pete*), Nickelodeon, 1994–96.

Maggie Parker, *Meego,* CBS, 1997.

Panelist, *Figure It Out* (also known as *Figure It Out: Family Style* and *Figure It Out: Wild Style*), Nickelodeon, 1997–99.

Dawn Summers (The Key), *Buffy the Vampire Slayer* (also known as *Buffy* and *Buffy the Vampire Slayer: The Series*), The WB, 2000–2001, UPN, 2001–2003.

Host and narrator, *Truth or Scare,* 2001.

Celeste, *Six Feet Under,* HBO, 2004.

Georgina Sparks, *Gossip Girl,* The CW, 2008.

Television Appearances; Miniseries:

The Enforcers, 2001.

Television Appearances; Movies:

Noelle Murphy, *A Holiday for Love* (also known as *Christmas in My Hometown*), CBS, 1996.

Kelly McClain, *A Father's Choice,* CBS, 2000.

Carrie Beal, *The Dive from Clausen's Pier*, Lifetime, 2005.

Kylie Shines, *The Circuit*, ABC Family, 2008.

Television Appearances; Specials:

The 2001 Teen Choice Awards, Fox, 2001.

Lifestory: Rosie O'Donnell, Nickelodeon, 2001.

Buffy's Back, E! Entertainment Television, 2001.

Presenter, *The Teen Choice Awards 2002*, Fox, 2002.

A Merry Mickey Celebration, ABC, 2003.

Best Year Ever, VH1, 2004.

The 20th IFP Independent Spirit Awards, 2005.

Hilary Duff Revealed: The E! True Hollywood Story, E! Entertainment Television, 2006.

What Have You Done?: The Remaking of "Black Christmas," 2006.

Also appeared as presenter, *Nickelodeon Kids' Choice Awards*, Nickelodeon.

Television Appearances; Episodic:

(Uncredited) Dinah Driscoll, "God Bless the Child," *Law & Order*, NBC, 1991.

First prankster, "All You Can Eaty," *Space Cases*, Nickelodeon, 1996.

Angela, "Solitaire," *Dave's World*, CBS, 1996.

The Rosie O'Donnell Show, 1996, 2001.

Herself, "Blue's Birthday," *Blue's Clues*, Nickelodeon, 1998.

Katie, "Maestro's First Crush," *Guys Like Us*, UPN, 1998.

Voice of herself, "Math Curse," *Reading Rainbow*, PBS, 1998.

Mad TV, Fox, 2000, 2001.

HypaSpace (also known as *HypaSpace Daily* and *HypaSpace Weekly*), Space, 2002.

"Buffy the Vampire Slayer: Television with a Bite," *Biography*, Arts and Entertainment, 2003.

The Sharon Osbourne Show (also known as *Sharon*), syndicated, 2004.

Beat Seekers (also known as *MTV Hits*), MTV, 2004.

On–Air with Ryan Seacrest, syndicated, 2004.

The Late Late Show with Craig Kilborn (also known as *The Late Late Show*), CBS, 2004.

"50 Worst Songs, Britney's New Video and More," *Best Week Ever* (also known as *Best Week Ever with Paul F. Tompkins*), 2004.

The View, ABC, 2005.

Total Request Live (also known as *TRL, TRL Weekend*, and *Total Request with Carson Daly*), MTV, 2005.

Jimmy Kimmel Live!, ABC, 2005.

"Child Stars II: Growing Up in Hollywood," *Biography*, Arts and Entertainment, 2005.

Melinda Bardach, "Safe," *House M.D.* (also known as *House*), Fox, 2006.

Lisa Willow Tyler, "Weeping Willow," *Law & Order: Criminal Intent* (also known as *Law & Order: CI*), NBC, 2006.

Punk'd, MTV, 2006.

Late Night with Conan O'Brien, NBC, 2006.

"Michelle Trachtenberg," *Fuse Celebrity Playlist*, Fuse, 2006.

Voice of Dina Lohan, "Celebrity Rocket," *Robot Chicken* (animated), Comedy Central, 2006.

Voice of cleaning woman, woman, and mugging victim, "Dragon Nuts," *Robot Chicken* (animated), Comedy Central, 2006.

Voice of woman and wife, "Tapping a Hero," *Robot Chicken* (animated), Comedy Central, 2007.

"Chicks That Kick," *Space Top 10 Countdown*, Space, 2007.

Entertainment Tonight (also known as *E.T.*), syndicated, 2008.

Also appeared *Saturday Night Live*, NBC.

Stage Appearances:

Spalding Gray: Stores Left to Tell, Minetta Lane Theatre, New York City, 2007.

RECORDINGS

Albums:

Dorothy, *The Children's Museum of Los Angeles' "The Wonderful Wizard of Oz—A Centennial Celebration,"* 2000.

Music Videos:

Trapt's "Echo," 2003.

Ringside's "Tired of Being Sorry," 2005.

Also appeared in Fall Out Boy's "This Ain't a Scene, It's an Arms Race."

OTHER SOURCES

Periodicals:

Buffy the Vampire Slayer, spring, 2001, pp. 24–31.

Daily Variety, May 12, 1999.

SFX, January, 2002, pp. 46–47.

TRAVOLTA, Margaret

PERSONAL

Daughter of Helen Travolta; sister of John Travolta (an actor).

Addresses: *Agent*—The Gage Group, 14724 Ventura Blvd., Suite 505, Sherman Oaks, CA 91403.

Career: Actress.

CREDITS

Film Appearances:

Sandra Harris, *Losing Isaiah*, Paramount, 1995.
Admitting nurse, *While You Were Sleeping*, Buena Vista, 1995.
Anita Fermi, *Chain Reaction*, Twentieth Century–Fox, 1996.
First reporter, *Michael*, New Line Cinema, 1996.
Autism expert nurse, *Mercury Rising*, MCA/Universal, 1998.
Rob's mom, *High Fidelity*, Buena Vista/Touchstone Pictures, 2000.
Nurse, *Lucky Numbers* (also known as *Le bon numero*), Studio Canal, 2000.
Economist, *Traffic* (also known as *Traffic—Die Macht des kartells*), USA Films, 2000.
Hostage, *Swordfish*, Warner Bros., 2001.
Vera Whitner, *Pumpkin*, Metro–Goldwyn–Mayer, 2002.
Ms. Davenport, *Catch Me If You Can*, DreamWorks, 2002.
Judge, *National Security*, Sony, 2003.
Nurse number one, *Basic*, Sony, 2003.
Debi Wyrthen, *Hangman's Curse* (also known as *The Veritas Project: Hangman's Curse*), Twentieth Century–Fox, 2003.
Marge, *Be Cool*, Metro–Goldwyn–Mayer, 2005.
Aunt Nina, *Guilt* (short), 2005.
Nurse Reynolds, *Solace* (short), 2006.
Mineola female dispatcher, *Lonely Hearts* (also known as *Lonely Heart Killers*), Samuel Goldwyn Films, 2006.
Academy counselor, *Accepted*, Universal, 2006.
Narrator, *In the Tall Grass* (documentary), 2006.
Dana, *Wild Hogs* (also known as *Blackberry*), Buena Vista, 2007.
Bank's secretary, *Ocean's Thirteen* (also known as *13*), Warner Bros., 2007.
Voice of radio therapist, *Enchanted*, Buena Vista, 2007.
Gale, *Sex and Breakfast* (also known as *Sex & Breakfast*), Bandman Productions, 2007.

Television Appearances; Movies:

Dr. Kohanek, *In the Company of Darkness*, CBS, 1993.

Television Appearances; Specials:

John Travolta: The Inside Story, 2004.

Television Appearances; Episodic:

"People Don't Talk to Cops, People Lie to Cops," *Missing Persons*, 1993.
Congressman's wife, "Meat Market," *Cupid*, ABC, 1998.

High school principal, "Teen Angels," *Early Edition*, CBS, 1998.
Claire Strummond, "Friends and Strangers," *Turks*, CBS, 1999.
Ms. Bishop, "Daddy Dearest," *The Drew Carey Show*, ABC, 2002.
Sheila's mom, *Strong Medicine*, Lifetime, 2002.
Dr. Helen Boyd, "Keeping Abreast," *NYPD Blue*, ABC, 2003.
Dr. Helen Boyd, "It's to Die For," *NYPD Blue*, ABC, 2003.
Secretary, "Hardcore," *The Handler*, CBS, 2003.
American Dreams, NBC, 2004.
Secretary, "From Here to Paternity," *ER*, NBC, 2007.

TREBEK, Alex 1940–

PERSONAL

Various sources cite original name as George Alexander Trebek, Giorgi Suka–Alex Trebek, or Georgi Suri–Alex Trebek; born July 22, 1940, in Sudbury, Ontario, Canada; immigrated to the United States, 1973; became a naturalized U.S. citizen, 1998; son of George Edward and Lucille (maiden name, Lagace) Trebek; married Elaine Callei, 1974 (divorced, 1981); married Jean Currivan (in real estate), April 30, 1990; children: (second marriage) Emily, Matthew. *Education:* University of Ottawa, bachelor of philosophy, 1961; some sources cite another degree in philosophy; attended the Malvern Collegiate Institute. *Religion:* Roman Catholic. *Avocational Interests:* Ice skating, hockey, golf, tennis, traveling, collecting and drinking wine.

Addresses: *Agent*—International Creative Management, 10250 Constellation Way, Ninth Floor, Los Angeles, CA 90067.

Career: Game show host and actor. Canadian Broadcasting Company (CBC), Toronto, Ontario, Canada, staff announcer, newscaster, and reporter for television and radio broadcasts, 1961–73; appeared in advertisements and infomercials. Has appeared as a host of the theme part attraction Ellen's Energy Adventure as part of the Universe of Energy pavilion, EPCOT Center, Orlando, FL. National Geography Bee (U.S. and Canada), host; also served as the host of awards presentations. Creston Farms (a thoroughbred breeding and training facility), Creston, CA, owner; Creston Vineyards, Creston, CA, owner. National Geographic Society Education Foundation, board member; National Advisory Council for the Literary Volunteers of America, board member; active in World Vision charitable organizations as a spokesperson; also participated in tours with the United Service Organizations (USO) and affiliated with the United

Negro College Fund. Affiliated with *Jeopardy!* merchandise. Some sources state that Trebek worked as a garbage collector in Cincinnati, OH.

Member: Screen Actors Guild, American Federation of Television and Radio Artists, Alliance of Canadian Cinema, Television and Radio Artists (formerly known as the Association of Canadian Television and Radio Artists).

Awards, Honors: Gemini Award nomination, best performance by an host, interviewer, or anchor, Academy of Canadian Cinema and Television, 1987, for *The 1987 National Hockey League Awards;* Daytime Emmy Award, outstanding game show host, 1989, 1990, 2003, 2006, and 2008, and Daytime Emmy Award nominations, outstanding game show host, 1999, 2000, 2001, 2002, 2004, 2005, and 2007, all for *Jeopardy!;* Daytime Emmy Award nomination, outstanding game show host, 1990, for *Classic Concentration;* ran with the Olympic torch, 1996; Bob Hope Entertainment Award, 1998, for his work with the USO; received a star on the Hollywood Walk of Fame, 1999; named to Canada's Walk of Fame, 2006; Trebek's handprints and footprints are in front of Hollywood Hills Ampitheater at Disney's Hollywood Studios, Walt Disney World; other awards and honors include induction into broadcasting hall of fames.

CREDITS

Television Appearances; Series:
Host, *Music Hop*, CBC, 1963–64.
Cohost, *Vacation Time*, [Canada], 1964.
Quizmaster, *Reach for the Top*, CBC, 1966–73.
Host, *Strategy*, CBC, 1969.
Host, *Jackpot!*, [Canada], beginning 1970.
Host, *Pick and Choose*, CBC, 1971.
Host, *Outside/Inside*, CBC, 1972.
Announcer, *T.G.I.F.*, CBLT (Toronto, Ontario, Canada), beginning 1973.
Host, *The Wizard of Odds*, NBC, 1973–74.
Host, *Stars on Ice*, CTV (Canada), 1974–77 (some sources cite 1976–80).
Host, *High Rollers* (also known as *The New High Rollers*), NBC, 1974–80.
Host, *Double Dare*, CBS, 1976–77.
Host, *The $128,000 Question*, syndicated, 1977–78.
Host, *Pitfall*, syndicated, 1981–82.
Host, *Battlestars*, NBC, 1981–83.
Host, *Jeopardy!*, syndicated, 1984—.
Cohost, *VTV—Value Television* (also known as *Value Television* and *ValueTelevision*), syndicated, beginning 1987.
Host, *Classic Concentration*, NBC, 1987–94.
Host, *Super Jeopardy!*, ABC, 1990.
Host, *To Tell the Truth*, NBC, 1991.

Television Appearances; Specials:
Himself, *What's Alan Watching?*, CBS, 1989.
Host and commentator, *The 100th Tournament of Roses Parade*, NBC, 1989.
Performer, *Circus of the Stars #14* (also known as *The 14th Annual Circus of the Stars*), CBS, 1989.
Best Catches, CBS, 1989.
A Day to Care for the Children, syndicated, 1989.
Himself, *The Earth Day Special* (also known as *Time Warner Presents "The Earth Day Special"*), ABC, 1990.
The Sports Comedy Network, CBS, 1990.
Himself, *WrestleMania VII*, pay–per–view, 1991.
Host, *The American Memory Test*, CBS, 1991.
Host, *A Salute to America's Pets*, ABC, 1991.
Host and narrator, *Heart of Courage* (also known as *Courage au coeur*), The Discovery Channel, c. 1993.
Moderator, *National Geography Bee* (also known as *The National Geography Bee*), PBS, 1993, 1994, 1995.
Host, *The Pillsbury Bake–Off*, CBS, 1994, 1996.
Hollywood Hockey Cup, Comedy Central, 1996.
Himself, *Ragtime: The American Premiere*, UPN, 1997.
I Am Your Child, ABC, 1997.
Plugged In: A Parents' Guide to TV, Family Channel, 1997.
Himself, *Live from the Hollywood Bowl*, 1997, 1999.
Host, *The 67th Annual Hollywood Christmas Parade*, UPN, 1998.
Host, *Watch & Make Money with Alex Trebek* (also known as *Watch and Make Money: A User's Guide to CNBC*), CNBC, 1998.
Host, *The National Geography Bee* (also known as *National Geography Bee*), PBS, 1999.
Host, *The 68th Annual Hollywood Christmas Parade*, UPN and syndicated, 1999.
Narrator, *Countdown 100: Greatest Achievements of the 20th Century*, The Learning Channel, 1999.
Himself, *Blacklight Dreams: The 25 Years of the Famous People Players*, 2000.
TV Guide's Greatest Moments 2004, ABC, 2004.
Himself, *Behind the Clues: 10 Years with Blue* (also known as *Behind the Blue*), Nickelodeon, 2006.

Television Appearances; Awards Presentations:
The 1987 National Hockey League Awards, 1987.
The 17th Annual Daytime Emmy Awards, ABC, 1990.
Presenter, *The 19th Annual Daytime Emmy Awards*, NBC, 1992.
Presenter, *The 21st Annual People's Choice Awards*, CBS, 1995.
Presenter, *The 27th Annual Daytime Emmy Awards*, ABC, 2000.
Presenter, *The 31st Annual Daytime Emmy Awards*, NBC, 2004.
An Evening of Stars 25th Anniversary: Tribute to Lou Rawls, NBC, 2004.

The 32nd Annual Daytime Emmy Awards, CBS, 2005.
The 33rd Annual Daytime Emmy Awards, 2006.

Television Appearances; Episodic:

Himself, *Dinah!* (also known as *Dinah* and *Dinah and Friends*), syndicated, 1973.

Guest panelist, *The Hollywood Squares,* NBC and syndicated, multiple episodes in 1974, 1975, 1976, and 1977.

Himself, *The Alan Hamel Show,* CTV (Canada), 1977.

Himself, *Tattletales,* syndicated, 1977.

Arthur Martin, "The Games Girls Play," *Vega$* (also known as *High Roller* and *Vegas*), ABC, 1978.

Himself, "Mama on *Jeopardy!,*" *Mama's Family,* syndicated, 1987.

Himself, "What Is ... Cliff Clavin?," *Cheers,* NBC, 1990.

Himself, *A Conversation with Dinah,* The Nashville Network (TNN), 1990.

Guest, *Late Night with David Letterman,* NBC, 1990.

Himself, "Questions and Answers," *The Golden Girls* (also known as *Golden Girls, Miami Nice, Bnot Zahav, Cuori senza eta, Las chicas de oro, Les craquantes, Los anos dorados, Oereglanyok, Pantertanter,* and *Tyttoekullat*), NBC, 1992.

Himself, "Hank's Wedding," *The Larry Sanders Show,* HBO, 1993.

Voice of Alan Quebec, "Game Show Didi," *Rugrats* (animated; also known as *Adventures in Diapers, Aventuras en panales, Ipanat, Las diabluras de Tommy, Les razmoket,* and *Rollinger*), Nickelodeon, 1993.

(In archive footage) Himself, "Hank's Divorce," *The Larry Sanders Show,* HBO, 1994.

Himself, *Late Show with David Letterman* (also known as *The Late Show, Late Show Backstage,* and *Letterman*), CBS, 1994, 1995, 1998.

Himself, "Double Jeopardy," *Beverly Hills 90210,* Fox, 1995.

Himself, "Franny and the Professor," *The Nanny,* CBS, 1995.

Himself, "A Kiss Is Just a Kiss," *Blossom,* NBC, 1995.

Himself, "Who's Not on First," *Blossom,* NBC, 1995.

Voice of himself, "Ellen's Improvement," *Ellen* (also known as *These Friends of Mine*), ABC, 1995.

"Bear with Me," *Dave's World,* CBS, 1995.

Man in black, "Jose Chung's 'From Outer Space,'" *The X-Files,* Fox, 1996.

Voice of himself, "The Abstinence," *Seinfeld* (also known as *The Seinfeld Chronicles* and *Stand-Up*), NBC, 1996.

Voice of game show host, "Shows and Tells," *The Magic School Bus* (animated; also known as *Scholastic's "The Magic School Bus"*), PBS, 1996.

Himself, *Before They Were Stars,* ABC, c. 1996.

Himself, "Back to School," *The Weird Al Show,* CBS, 1997.

Himself, "It's a Mad, Mad, Mad, Mad Eric," *Ned and Stacey,* Fox, 1997.

Himself, "Sex, Lies, and Commercials," *Ned and Stacey,* Fox, 1997.

Voice of himself, "Miracle on Evergreen Terrace," *The Simpsons* (animated), Fox, 1997.

(Uncredited) Himself, *This Hour Has 22 Minutes,* CBC, 1997.

Guest host, *Wheel of Fortune,* syndicated, 1997.

Himself, "Group Soup," *The Charlie Horse Music Pizza,* PBS, 1998.

Himself, "Swept Away," *Baywatch* (also known as *Baywatch Hawaii* and *Baywatch Hawai'i*), syndicated, 1998.

Himself, *The Tom Green Show,* c. 1998.

Voice of himself, "The Dirty Little Secret," *Mad about You* (also known as *Loved by You*), NBC, 1999.

Narrator, "Betty White," *Intimate Portrait* (also known as *Intimate Portrait: Betty White*), Lifetime, 2000.

Voice of Alex Lebek, "Arthur and the Big Riddle/Double Dare," *Arthur* (animated), PBS, 2000.

Voice of himself, "Unhappy Campers/The Search for Pepper Ann Pearson," *Pepper Ann* (animated; also known as *Disney's "Pepper Ann"*), ABC, 2000.

Voice of himself, "The Finale," *Pepper Ann* (animated; also known as *Disney's "Pepper Ann"*), ABC, 2000.

Himself, "A Quiet Evening at Home," *Ladies Man,* CBS, 2001.

Himself, "The 31-Inch-High Club," *Ladies Man,* CBS, 2001.

Himself, *The View,* ABC, 2001.

Himself (audience member), "Elwood City Turns 100!," *Arthur* (animated), PBS, 2002.

(Uncredited) Voice of himself, "Family Guy Viewer Mail #1," *Family Guy* (animated; also known as *Padre de familia* and *Padre del familia*), Fox, 2002.

(Uncredited) Himself, *Saturday Night Live* (also known as *NBC's "Saturday Night," Saturday Night, Saturday Night Live '80, SNL,* and *SNL 25*), NBC, 2002.

Himself, *This Hour Has 22 Minutes,* CBC, 2002.

Himself, *The Wayne Brady Show,* syndicated, 2003.

Voice of himself, "Whose Pants Are Smarter?," *Married to the Kellys* (also known as *Back to Kansas*), ABC, 2004.

Himself, *The Late Late Show with Craig Kilborn* (also known as *The Late Late Show*), CBS, 2004.

Himself and commentator, *101 Most Unforgettable SNL Moments* (also known as *E's "101"* and *101 Most ...*), E! Entertainment Television, multiple episodes in 2004.

Himself (audience member), "Top 7 Perform," *American Idol* (also known as *American Idol: The Search for a Superstar, American Idol 2, American Idol 3,* and *American Idol 4*), Fox, 2005.

Himself, "Tournament 6, Game 4," *Celebrity Poker Showdown,* Bravo, 2005.

Himself (audience member), "Who's out of the Top 7," *American Idol* (also known as *American Idol: The Search for a Superstar, American Idol 2, American Idol 3,* and *American Idol 4*), Fox, 2005.

(Uncredited; in archive footage) Himself, *The Late Late Show with Craig Ferguson* (also known as *The Late Late Show*), CBS, 2005.

Himself, *Live with Regis & Kelly,* syndicated, 2005, 2006.

Himself, *Ellen: The Ellen DeGeneres Show* (also known as *Ellen* and *The Ellen DeGeneres Show*), syndicated, 2005, 2008.

Voice of himself, "I Take Thee, Quagmire," *Family Guy* (animated; also known as *Padre de familia* and *Padre del familia*), Fox, 2006.

Himself, *Late Night with Conan O'Brien,* NBC, 2006, 2007.

Himself, *Entertainment Tonight* (also known as *Entertainment This Week, E.T., ET Weekend,* and *This Week in Entertainment*), syndicated, 2007.

Himself, *The Hour* (also known as *CBC News: The Hour*), CBC, 2008.

Himself, *Jimmy Kimmel Live!* (also known as *The Jimmy Kimmel Project*), ABC, 2008.

Appeared as Alec the Trojan, "Is There a Problem?," *Nick's Got a Problem;* as himself, *ALF,* NBC; and as a guest panelist, *Front Page Challenge* (also known as *FPC*), CBC; provided the voice of himself, "CatDog Meets Alex Trebek," *CatDog* (animated), Nickelodeon; appeared as himself in "No Cinco, Seis!," an unaired episode of *Ladies Man,* CBS; some sources cite an appearance as a substitute host, *Wheel of Fortune,* NBC.

Television Appearances; Pilots:
Cohost and announcer, *Barris & Company,* CBC, 1968.

Appeared as a panelist in various pilots for *To Tell the Truth,* NBC; appeared as the host in the unaired second pilot of *Starcade.*

Television Producer; Series:
Jeopardy!, syndicated, 1984–87.

Film Appearances:
Himself, *Dying Young* (also known as *The Choice of Love*), Twentieth Century–Fox, 1991.

Himself, *White Men Can't Jump,* Twentieth Century–Fox, 1992.

Himself, *Short Cuts,* Fine Line Features, 1993.

Agency tape recorder voice, *Spy Hard* (also known as *Live and Let Spy*), Buena Vista, 1996.

(Uncredited) Himself, *Jane Austen's "Mafia!"* (also known as *Mafia!*), Buena Vista, 1998.

Himself, *The Male Swagger,* 1999.

(Uncredited) *Jeopardy!* host, *Random Hearts,* Columbia, 1999.

Himself, *Charlie's Angels* (also known as *Charlie's Angels: The Movie* and *3 Engel fuer Charlie*), Columbia, 2000.

Himself, *Finding Forrester,* Columbia, 2000.

Himself, *Little Manhattan,* Twentieth Century–Fox, 2005.

Himself, *The Bucket List,* Warner Bros., 2007.

RECORDINGS

Videos:
(In archive footage) Himself, *Lord Stanley's Cup: Hockey's Ultimate Prize,* 2000.

Himself, *Reflections on "The X–Files,"* Twentieth Century–Fox Home Entertainment, 2004.

Video Games:
Host, *Jeopardy!,* Hasbro Interactive, 1998.

Host, *Jeopardy! DVD Game,* 2007.

OTHER SOURCES

Periodicals:
Parade, August 25, 2002, p. 8.

TRIUMPH THE INSULT COMIC DOG
   See SMIGEL, Robert

TRUMAN, Tim

PERSONAL

Born in La Mesa, CA; one son. *Education:* University of Southern California, degree (honors), musical composition. *Avocational Interests:* Traveling, visiting cultural centers, attending museums.

Addresses: *Agent*—Soundtrack Music Associates, 2229 Cloverfield Blvd., Santa Monica, CA 90405.

Career: Composer. Global Sanity Studio Complex, owner and operator; Tim Truman Music and the World Music Group, owner; composed, arranged, and produced for recording artists, including Nancy Wilson,

Patti Austin, Peter Cetera, Michael Jackson, Donna Summer, Mark Nelson, Kenny Rogers, Don Johnson, Ali Woodson, and Wildside.

Awards, Honors: Emmy Award nomination, outstanding individual achievement in main title theme music, 1996, for *Central Park West;* ASCAP Awards, top television series, American Society of Composers and Authors, 1996, 1997, both for *Melrose Place;* ASCAP Award, top TV series, 1999, for *Charmed;* Golden Hugo Award, best score, for *Techno–Shock;* Emmy Award, outstanding youth special, for *Baby Wild.*

CREDITS

Television Work; Movies:
Music conductor, orchestrator, and score mixer, *Bet Your Life,* NBC, 2004.

Television Work; Specials:
Worked as producer, *Baby Wild.*

WRITINGS

Film Scores:
Final Cut, 1988.
Kid (also known as *Back for Revenge*), Intercontinental, 1991.
South Central, Warner Bros., 1992.
Mikey, 1992.
Good Luck (also known as *Gimps, Guys Like Us,* and *The Ox and the Eye*), Moki Mac River Expedition, 1997.
Retroactive, Orion, 1997.
Executive Power, Naegele–Derrick Productions, 1997.
Boogie Boy, Sterling Home Entertainment, 1997.
Angel's Dance (also known as *Ein hoffnungsvoller nachwuchskiller*), Promark Entertainment Group, 1999.
The 10th Kingdom: The Making of an Epic, 2000.
Ca$h, 2008.

Also scored *Captain EO; Inferno.*

Television Scores; Series:
Fan Club, syndicated, 1987.
Miami Vice, NBC, 1988–90.
The Round Table, NBC, 1992.
Melrose Place, Fox, 1992–96.
Models Inc., Fox, 1994.
The Marshal, ABC, 1995.
Central Park West (also known as *C.P.W.*), CBS, 1995.

Charmed, The WB, 1998–99.
Jeremiah, 2002–2004.

Television Main Themes; Series:
It's a Great Life, syndicated, 1985.
Coming of Age, NBC, 1988.
Melrose Place, Fox, 1992–97.
Central Park West (also known as *C.P.W.*), CBS, 1995.
The Marshal, ABC, 1995.
Sunset Beach, NBC, 1997.
Pacific Palisades, Fox, 1997.
Charmed, The WB, 1998–2000.
Providence, NBC, 1999–2000.
Jeremiah, 2002–2004.

Also wrote theme for *Bullet Hearts,* Fox; *Buffalo Bill.*

Television Special Musical Material; Miniseries:
Fresno, 1986.

Television Scores; Movies:
L.A. Takedown (also known as *L.A. Crimewave* and *Made in L.A.*), NBC, 1989.
Double Your Pleasure (also known as *The Reluctant Agent*), NBC, 1989.
Deadly Game, USA Network, 1991.
Dead Silence (also known as *Crash*), Fox, 1991.
In the Company of Darkness, CBS, 1993.
Knight Rider 2010, UPN, 1994.
Sketch Artist II: Hands That See (also known as *A Feel for Murder* and *Sketch Artist II*), Showtime, 1995.
The Price of Love, Fox, 1995.
Marshal Law, Showtime, 1996.
Kiss and Tell, ABC, 1997.
Retroactive, HBO, 1997.
Bet Your Life, NBC, 2004.

Also scored *Fresno.*

Television Scores; Pilots:
Microcops, CBS, 1989.

Also scored *The Round Table,* NBC; *Ruth Harper,* CBS; *Get a Life,* Fox; *Flipside.*

Television Title Theme; Pilots:
Melrose Place, Fox, 1992.

Television Scores; Specials:
The Extreme Edge, ABC, 1992.
America Behind Closed Doors, ABC, 1992.

Also scored *The Criminal Mind; When All Else Fails,* NBC; *Inside the Jury Room,* ABC; *The Making of "The Invisible Man,"* HBO; *Classic Mel Gibson: The Making of "Hamlet,"* HBO; *1996 Olympic Campaign,* NBC; *NBC 70th Anniversary Special,* NBC; *1999 Olympic Campaign,* NBC; *2000 Olympic Campaign,* NBC.

Television Themes; Specials:
The Extreme Edge, ABC, 1992.
Love Thy Neighbor: The Baddest and the Best of "Melrose Place," Fox, 1995.

Television Scores; Episodic:
"The First Commandment," *Stargate SG–1* (also known as *La porte des etoiles*), Showtime and syndicated, 1997.

Also wrote scores for *Buffalo Bull; Duck Factory; Newhart; The Popcorn Kid; South Central; Bullet Hearts,* Fox; *Fame; It's a Great Life.*

Television Additional Music; Episodic:
Newhart, CBS, 1982.
That's Amore, syndicated, 1992.

Stage Scores:
Scored *Good Luck,* East West.

OTHER SOURCES

Electronic:
Tim Truman Website, http://www.timtruman.com, January 14, 2009.

TULLOCH, Bitsie 1981–

PERSONAL

Birth name Elizabeth, born January 19, 1981, in New York, NY. *Education:* Attended Harvard University.

Addresses: *Agent*—William Morris Agency, 1325 Avenue of the Americas, New York, NY 10019. *Manager*—Archetype, 1608 Argyle Ave., Los Angeles, CA 90028. *Publicist*—PMK/HBH Public Relations, 161 Avenue of the Americas, 10th Floor, New York, NY 10013.

Career: Actress. Appeared in television commercials for Diet Coke, 2007.

CREDITS

Television Appearances; Series:
Current TV, 2007.
Dylan Krieger, *Quarterlife,* NBC, 2008.
Alexandra Hubbard, *Tyranny,* 2008.

Television Appearances; Episodic:
Susan, "Third Day Story," *The West Wing,* NBC, 2004.
Tara Kozlowski, "The War at Home," *Cold Case,* CBS, 2006.
Last Call with Carson Daly, NBC, 2007.
The Sauce, Fuse, 2008.
CW 11 Morning News, CW, 2008.
Today (also known as *NBC News Today* and *The Today Show*), NBC, 2008.
The View, ABC, 2008.
Celeste, "The Mortal Cure," *Moonlight,* 2008.
Whitney, "Joy to the World," *House M.D.* (also known as *House*), Fox, 2008.

Television Appearances; Pilots:
April, *Wahingtonienne,* HBO, 2009.

Television Appearances; Specials:
Bitsy, *R2–D2: Beneath the Dome,* 2001.

Film Appearances:
Marcy, *Life Is Short,* 2006.
Angel, *Sent,* 2006.
Molly, *Two Doors* (also known as *Ring Tone*), The Coca–Cola Company, 2007.
Nadine, *Lakeview Terrace,* Sony, 2008.
Corrine, *Uncross the Stars,* 2008.
Trudy, *Riding the Pine,* 2009.

Stage Appearances:
Sally, *Quarterlife,* Pico Playhouse, Los Angeles, CA, 2006.

V

VAN ARK, Joan 1943–
(Joan Van Arc, Joan van Ark)

PERSONAL

Born June 16, 1943, in New York, NY; raised in Boulder, CO; daughter of Carroll (in advertising and public relations) and Dorothy Jean (a writer; maiden name, Hemenway) Van Ark; sister of Carol Kuykendall (a writer); married John Marshall (various sources cite original last name as Marsilio or Marsillo; a journalist), February 1, 1966; children: Vanessa Jean Marshall (an actress, voice artist, director, and comedienne). *Education:* Graduated from Yale University. *Religion:* Presbyterian. *Avocational Interests:* Running (including marathons).

Addresses: *Agent*—The Chasin Agency, 8899 Beverly Blvd., Suite 716, Los Angeles, CA 90048; Danis Panaro Nist, 9201 West Olympic Blvd., Beverly Hills, CA 90212 (voice work). *Manager*—Sterling/Winters Company, 10900 Wilshire Blvd., Suite 1550, Los Angeles, CA 90024.

Career: Actress, voice artist, and director. Appeared in and provided voice work for advertisements; served as a spokesperson for Estee Lauder cosmetics; made a number of public service announcements. Anne Douglas Center of the Los Angeles Mission, Los Angeles, member of the celebrity action council; Barbara Davis Center for Childhood Diabetes, Denver, CO, member of the advisory council; participated in the Revlon Run/Walk for Women, Los Angeles; advocate for the Humane Society.

Member: Screen Actors Guild, American Federation of Television and Radio Artists, Actors' Equity Association, Directors Guild of America (member of the Women's Steering Committee), San Fernando Valley Track Club.

Awards, Honors: *Theatre World* Award and Antoinette Perry Award nomination, best featured actress in a play, both 1971, for *The School for Wives;* Los Angeles Drama Critics Award, featured performance, 1973, for *As You Like It; Theatre World* Award, c. 1974, for *The Rules of the Game;* Daytime Emmy Award nomination (with others), outstanding special class program, 1985, *The CBS Tournament of Roses Parade; Soap Opera Digest* awards, outstanding actress in a leading role on a primetime serial, 1986, and outstanding actress in a leading role: primetime, 1989, and *Soap Opera Digest* Award nominations, outstanding actress in a leading role: primetime, 1988, and outstanding lead actress: primetime, 1991, all for *Knots Landing;* New York Festivals Award nomination, best young adult programming, 1995, and Humanitas Award nomination, Human Family Educational and Cultural Institute, both for "Boys Will Be Boys," *ABC Afterschool Specials;* Dutch American Heritage Award, Dutch American Heritage Foundation, 1996; received a local Emmy Award nomination for directing a documentary about homelessness and domestic violence.

CREDITS

Television Appearances; Series:
Nurse Paula, *Peyton Place,* ABC, 1968.
Janine Whitney, *Days of Our Lives* (also known as *Cruise of Deception: Days of Our Lives, Days, DOOL, Tropical Temptation, Tropical Temptation: Days of Our Lives, Des jours et des vies, Horton-sagaen, I gode og onde dager, Los dias de nuestras vidas, Meres agapis, Paeivien viemaeae, Vaara baesta aar, Zeit der Sehnsucht,* and *Zile din viata noastra*), NBC, 1970.
Nurse Ann "Annie" Carlisle, *Temperatures Rising* (also known as *The New Temperatures Rising Show*), ABC, 1972–73.
Dee Dee Baldwin, *We've Got Each Other,* CBS, 1977–78.
Voice of Manta in "Manta and Moray, Monarchs of the Deep" segment, *Tarzan and the Super 7* (animated), CBS, 1978–80.

Valene Joan Clements Ewing, *Dallas* (also known as *Oil*), CBS, 1978–81.

Voice of Jessica Drew/Spider–Woman (title role), *Spider–Woman* (animated), ABC, 1979–80.

Valene Joan Clements Ewing Gibson Waleska, *Knots Landing,* CBS, 1979–93.

Voice of Moray in "Manta and Moray, Monarchs of the Deep" segment, *Batman and the Super 7* (animated), NBC, 1980–81.

Voice, *Heathcliff and Dingbat* (animated; also known as *Dingbat and the Creeps* and *The Heathcliff and Dingbat Show*), ABC, 1980–81.

Voices of Amelia and others, *Santo Bugito* (animated), CBS, 1995–96.

Gloria Fisher Abbott, *The Young and the Restless* (also known as *Y&R, The Innocent Years, Atithasa niata, Les feux de l'amour, Schatten der Leidenschaft,* and *Tunteita ja tuoksuja*), CBS, 2004–2005.

Television Appearances; Miniseries:

Jane Robson, *Testimony of Two Men,* syndicated, 1977.

Valene Joan Clements Ewing Gibson Waleska, *Knots Landing: Back to the Cul–de–Sac,* CBS, 1997.

Herself, *I Love the '80s Strikes Back,* VH1, 2003.

Television Appearances; Movies:

Frankie Banks, *The Last Dinosaur* (also known as *Kyokutei tankensen Pora–Bora*), ABC, 1977.

Marie Rivers, *Red Flag: The Ultimate Game,* CBS, 1981.

Brenda Allen, *Shakedown on the Sunset Strip,* CBS, 1988.

Claire Thomas, *My First Love,* ABC, 1988.

Julia Alberts, *Menu for Murder* (also known as *Murder at the P.T.A. Luncheon*), CBS, 1990.

Martha Mendham, *Always Remember I Love You* (also known as *To Cast a Shadow*), CBS, 1990.

Leslie Renner, *Terror on Track 9* (also known as *Janek: The Grand Central Murders*), CBS, 1992.

Cinnie Merritt, *In the Shadows, Someone's Watching* (also known as *Someone's Watching* and *With Harmful Intent*), NBC, 1993.

Mrs. Drew, *Tainted Blood,* USA Network, 1993.

Nora McGill, *Moment of Truth: A Mother's Deception* (also known as *Moment of Truth: Cult Rescue*), NBC, 1994.

Julianne "Julie" Kaiser, *When the Dark Man Calls,* USA Network, 1995.

Vice president Elizabeth Lane, *Loyal Opposition: Terror in the White House,* Family Channel, 1998.

Mayor McAnders, *Tornado Warning,* PAX TV, 2002.

Television Appearances; Specials:

Voice of Roxanne, "Cyrano" (animated), *ABC Afterschool Specials,* ABC, 1974.

Silia Gala, "The Rules of the Game," *Theatre in America,* PBS, 1975.

Herself (CBS team contestant), *Battle of the Network Stars VIII,* ABC, 1980.

Herself (CBS team contestant), *Battle of the Network Stars IX,* ABC, 1980.

Celebrity Challenge of the Sexes, CBS, 1980.

Ladies and Gentlemen ... Bob Newhart, CBS, 1980.

Herself (CBS team contestant), *Battle of the Network Stars XII,* ABC, 1982.

Herself (CBS team contestant), *Battle of the Network Stars XIII,* ABC, 1982.

Herself (CBS team contestant), *Battle of the Network Stars XV,* ABC, 1983.

Host, *The 1984 Miss Universe Pageant,* CBS, 1984, 1985.

Host, *The 1984 Miss USA Pageant,* CBS, 1984, 1985.

Host, *The CBS Tournament of Roses Parade,* CBS, 1984, 1985, 1986, 1989, 1992.

Host, *Battle of the Network Stars XVIII,* ABC, 1985.

Herself, *Bob Hope's "Comedy Salute to the Soaps"* (also known as *Comedy Salute to the Soaps*), NBC, 1985.

Herself, *Joan Rivers and Friends Salute Heidi Abromowitz,* Showtime, 1985.

Herself, *Night of 100 Stars II* (also known as *Night of One Hundred Stars*), ABC, 1985.

Dom DeLuise and Friends, Part 4, ABC, 1986.

Fit for a Lifetime, Lifetime, 1986.

Herself, *Happy 100th Birthday, Hollywood!* (also known as *Happy Birthday, Hollywood!*), ABC, 1987.

Host, *Women of Seoul,* Lifetime, 1988.

The Hollywood Christmas Parade, syndicated, 1988.

Host, *The CBS All–American Thanksgiving Day Parade,* CBS, 1989.

Anchor, *The CBS All–American Thanksgiving Day Parade,* CBS, 1990.

Ringmaster, *The 15th Annual Circus of the Stars* (also known as *Circus of the Stars #15*), CBS, 1990.

Bob Hope's "1990 Christmas Show from Bermuda" (also known as *Bob Hope's "Christmas Special from Bermuda"*), NBC, 1990.

Night of 100 Stars III (also known as *Night of One Hundred Stars*), NBC, 1990.

The 61st Annual Hollywood Christmas Parade, syndicated, 1992.

(In archive footage) Herself, *Bob Hope's "Bag Full of Christmas Memories"* (also known as *Hope for the Holidays* and *Hope for the Holidays—The Best of Bob Hope*), 1993, special edition released.

Herself, *The Knots Landing Block Party,* CBS, 1993.

Judge, *The Miss America Pageant,* NBC, 1993.

Susan Cooper, "Boys Will Be Boys," *ABC Afterschool Specials,* ABC, 1994.

More True Stories from Touched by an Angel, CBS, 1999.

Herself, *The 42nd Annual L.A. County Arts Commission Holiday Celebration,* 2001.

Herself, *CBS at 75* (also known as *CBS at 75: A Primetime Celebration*), CBS, 2003.

(Uncredited; in archive footage) Valene Joan Clements Ewing, *Dallas Reunion: Return to Southfork*, CBS, 2004.

Valene Joan Clements Ewing Gibson Waleska, *Knots Landing Reunion: Together Again*, CBS, 2005.

Television Appearances; Awards Presentations:
The 37th Annual Prime Time Emmy Awards, ABC, 1985.

The Stuntman Awards, syndicated, 1986.

Presenter, *The 13th Annual People's Choice Awards*, CBS, 1987.

Host, *The Ninth Annual Emmy Awards for Sports*, syndicated, 1988.

The 14th Annual People's Choice Awards, CBS, 1988.

All–Star Tribute to Kareem Abdul–Jabbar, NBC, 1989.

The 47th Annual Golden Globe Awards, TBS, 1990.

Presenter, *The 18th Annual Daytime Emmy Awards*, CBS, 1991.

Presenter, *The 49th Annual Tony Awards*, CBS, 1995.

Presenter, *The 13th Annual Genesis Awards*, Animal Planet, 1999.

Presenter, *The 14th Annual Genesis Awards*, Animal Planet, 2000.

The TV Lands Awards (also known as *The TV Land Awards: A Celebration of Classic TV*), TV Land, 2003.

Television Appearances; Episodic:
Angie Cameron, "The Vendetta," *The F.B.I.*, ABC, 1966.

Donna Hayward, "Cry Hard, Cry Fast: Parts 1 & 2," *Run for Your Life*, NBC, 1967.

April Showers, "Twinkle, Twinkle, Little Starlet," *The Mod Squad*, ABC, 1968.

Lynne Thackeray, "A Fashion for Dying," *The Felony Squad*, ABC, 1968.

Annie Laurie Adams, "Sweet Annie Laurie," *Bonanza* (also known as *Ponderosa*), NBC, 1969.

Eleanor O'Keefe, "The Maze," *The F.B.I.*, ABC, 1969.

Laurie, "The Man Who Killed Jim Sonnett," *The Guns of Will Sonnett*, ABC, 1969.

Sara Jean Stryker, "Stryker," *Gunsmoke* (also known as *Gun Law* and *Marshal Dillon*), CBS, 1969.

Betty Jane, "Love and the Fighting Couple/Love and the Pick–Up/Love and the Proposal," *Love, American Style*, ABC, 1970.

Cynthia "Cindy" Scott, "The Condemned," *The F.B.I.*, ABC, 1970.

Freda Cowan, "The Double Wall," *Hawaii Five–O* (also known as *McGarrett*), CBS, 1970.

Katherine, "Nick," *Matt Lincoln*, ABC, 1970.

"A Deadly Game of Love," *The Silent Force*, ABC, 1970.

"The Union Forever," *Dan August*, ABC, 1970.

Deborah Walters, "Edge of Violence," *Medical Center*, CBS, 1971.

Evelyn Baker, "Close Up," *Bold Ones: The Doctors* (also known as *Bold Ones* and *The Doctors*), NBC, 1971.

Francine Dexter, "Country Blues," *Cannon*, CBS, 1971.

Julie Rhodes, "The Deadly Gift," *The F.B.I.*, ABC, 1971.

Alice, "Love and the Know–It–All/Love and the Perfect Wife/Love and the Sensuous Twin/Love and the Triple Threat," *Love, American Style*, ABC, 1972.

(As Joan van Ark) Sandra Blanco, "The Ring with the Red Velvet Ropes," *Night Gallery* (also known as *Rod Serling's "Night Gallery"*), NBC, 1972.

Trudy, "A Night to Dismember," *The Odd Couple*, ABC, 1972.

"The Break–Up," *The F.B.I.*, ABC, 1972.

Jennifer Crane, "The Girl in the Polka Dot Dress," *Mannix*, CBS, 1973.

Lieutenant Erica Johnson, "Radar's Report," *M*A*S*H* (also known as *MASH*), CBS, 1973.

Anna, "The Man Who Couldn't Forget," *Cannon*, CBS, 1974.

(As Joan Van Arc) Barbara Kelbaker and Florence Baker, "Find Me If You Can," *The Rockford Files* (also known as *Jim Rockford, Jim Rockford, Private Investigator*, and *Rockford*), NBC, 1974.

Caroline, "Trial of Terror," *Ironside* (also known as *The Raymond Burr Show*), NBC, 1974.

Chris, "Adults Only," *Medical Center*, CBS, 1974.

Cynthia, "Burst of Flame," *Firehouse*, ABC, 1974.

Nona, "Duel in the Desert," *Cannon*, CBS, 1974.

Samantha, "A Zircon in the Rough," *The Girl with Something Extra*, NBC, 1974.

Sheila Barner, "The Challenge," *Barnaby Jones*, CBS, 1974.

Victoria, "The Deadly Brothers," *Manhunter*, CBS, 1974.

"The Seven Million Dollar Man," *The Six Million Dollar Man* (also known as *Cyborg, De Man van zes miljoen, Der sechs Millionen Dollar Mann, El hombre de los seis millones de dolares, Kuuden miljoonan dollarin mies, L'homme qui valait 3 milliards*, and *L'uomo da sei milioni di dollari*), ABC, 1974.

Eileen, "Too Late for Tomorrow," *Medical Center*, CBS, 1975.

Eleanor, "Guns for a Queen," *Barbary Coast*, ABC, 1975.

Marian Gerard, "Rhoda Meets the Ex–Wife," *Rhoda*, CBS, 1975.

Peggy Fowler, "Woman in White," *Medical Story*, NBC, 1975.

Susan Alexander, "Resurrection in Black and White," *The Rockford Files* (also known as *Jim Rockford, Jim Rockford, Private Investigator*, and *Rockford*), NBC, 1975.

Voice of Cora Munro, "The Last of the Mohicans" (animated), *Famous Classic Tales*, CBS, 1975.

Chris, "The Night Visitor," *Petrocelli*, NBC, 1976.

Valerie Sheffield, "The Bionic Boy: Parts 1 & 2," *The Six Million Dollar Man* (also known as *Cyborg, The Six Million Dollar Man: The Bionic Boy, De Man van zes miljoen, Der sechs Millionen Dollar Mann, El hombre de los seis millones de dolares, Kuuden miljoonan dollarin mies, L'homme qui valait 3 milliards*, and *L'uomo da sei milioni di dollari*), ABC, 1976.

"Girl on a String," *Joe Forrester,* NBC, 1976.

Christina Marks, "There's One in Every Port," *The Rockford Files* (also known as *Jim Rockford, Jim Rockford, Private Investigator,* and *Rockford*), NBC, 1977.

Detective Josephine Long, "Lady in the Squadroom," *Kojak,* CBS, 1977.

Georgie, "Have You Heard about Vanessa?," *McMillan* (also known as *McMillan and Wife*), NBC, 1977.

Herself, *The Alan Hamel Show,* CTV (Canada), 1977, 1978.

Bert Phillips, "Gone but Not Forgotten," *Quincy, M.E.* (also known as *Quincy*), NBC, 1978.

Cassandra Loren, "Time Bomb," *Wonder Woman* (also known as *The New Adventures of Wonder Woman* and *The New Original Wonder Woman*), CBS, 1978.

Princess Libido, "All the Emperor's Quasi–Norms: Parts 1 & 2," *Quark,* NBC, 1978.

Having Babies (also known as *Julie Farr, M.D.*), ABC, 1978.

Dr. Haven Grant, "Death Mountain," *Vega$* (also known as *High Roller* and *Vegas*), ABC, 1979.

Kris Hailey, "Cindy/Play by Play/What's a Brother For?," *The Love Boat,* ABC, 1979.

Mary Sue Huggins, "She Stole His Heart/Return of the Captain's Brother/Swag and Mag," *The Love Boat,* ABC, 1980.

Voice of Captain Cordon, "Treasure of the Moks," *Thundarr the Barbarian* (animated), ABC, 1980.

Ms. Chandler, "The Incredible Hunk/Isaac, the Marriage Counselor/Jewels & Jim," *The Love Boat,* ABC, 1981.

Voices of Cinda and Crystal, "Prophecy of Peril," *Thundarr the Barbarian* (animated), ABC, 1981.

"And One to Grow On/Seems Like Old Times/I'll Never Forget What's Her Name," *The Love Boat,* ABC, 1984.

(Uncredited; in archive footage) Valene Joan Clements Ewing Gibson Waleska, "Comings and Goings," *Dallas* (also known as *Oil*), CBS, 1989.

Herself, *The Pat Sajak Show,* CBS, 1989.

Valene Joan Clements Ewing Gibson Waleska, "Conundrum: Part 1," *Dallas* (also known as *Oil*), CBS, 1991.

Herself, *Marilu,* syndicated, 1994.

Jewel Pemberton, "Breaking Up Is Hard to Do: Part 1," *The Fresh Prince of Bel–Air,* NBC, 1995.

Herself, "Women in Film," *Women of the House,* CBS, 1995.

Kim Carpenter, "Til We Meet Again," *Touched by an Angel,* CBS, 1995.

Gretchen Wainwright, "The Morning After," *The Client* (also known as *John Grisham's "The Client"*), CBS, 1996.

Herself, "Mother's Day," *Cybill,* CBS, 1997.

Voice of Queen Esther, "Friendship"/"Loyalty," *Adventures from the Book of Virtues* (animated; also known as *The Book of Virtues*), PBS, 1997.

Herself, "Hollywood," *Tracey Takes On ...,* HBO, 1998.

Margo Lange (some sources cite role as Margo Lane), "One False Mole and You're Dead," *The Nanny,* CBS, 1998.

Herself, "Michele Lee," *Intimate Portrait* (also known as *Intimate Portrait: Michele Lee*), Lifetime, 1999.

Herself, "Ava Gardner," *Intimate Portrait* (also known as *Intimate Portrait: Ava Gardner*), Lifetime, 2000.

Camila Bianco, "Mama Mia," *Twice in a Lifetime,* CTV (Canada) and PAX TV, 2001.

Ima Cummings, "Light My Firebush," *Son of the Beach* (also known as *Babewatch, Hijo de la playa, Rantojen kunkku,* and *Strandloven*), FX Network, 2001.

Herself, "Classic TV Stars" (also known as "Classic TV Faves Edition #2"), *Weakest Link* (also known as *The Weakest Link* and *The Weakest Link USA*), NBC, 2001.

Narrator, "Lisa Hartman Black," *Intimate Portrait* (also known as *Intimate Portrait: Lisa Hartman Black*), Lifetime, 2001.

Guest, *Hollywood Squares* (also known as *H2* and *H2: Hollywood Squares*), syndicated, multiple episodes in 2001.

Guest, *The Test,* FX Network, 2001.

Herself, "Joan Van Ark," *Intimate Portrait* (also known as *Intimate Portrait: Joan Van Ark*), Lifetime, 2002.

Herself, "Linda Gray," *Intimate Portrait* (also known as *Intimate Portrait: Linda Gray*), Lifetime, 2002.

Herself, "Michelle Phillips," *Intimate Portrait* (also known as *Intimate Portrait: Michelle Phillips*), Lifetime, 2003.

Herself, *Open Mike with Mike Bullard* (also known as *The Mike Bullard Show* and *Open Mike*), CanWest Global Television, 2003.

Herself, *Soap Talk,* SOAPnet, 2003.

Herself, "Alec Baldwin," *Biography* (also known as *A&E Biography: Alec Baldwin*), Arts and Entertainment, 2004.

Voices of Wanda, woman, and third Mandy, "Whatever Happen to Billy Whatsisname?/Just the Two of Pus," *Grim & Evil* (animated; also known as *The Grim Adventures of Billy & Mandy*), Cartoon Network, 2004.

Herself, *Pyramid* (also known as *The $100,000 Pyramid*), syndicated, 2004.

Herself, *TV Land Moguls,* TV Land, 2004.

Herself, "Breakout and Disappearing Star," *TV Land Confidential* (also known as *TV Land Confidential: The Untold Stories*), TV Land, 2005.

Herself, "Holiday Moments," *TV Land's "Top Ten"* (also known as *TV Land Top Ten*), TV Land, 2005.

Herself, "Top 10 TV Spinoffs," *TV Land's "Top Ten"* (also known as *TV Land Top Ten*), TV Land, 2006.

Annette Wainwright, "Lulu Grandiron," *Nip/Tuck,* FX Network, 2008.

Herself, *Today* (also known as *NBC News Today* and *The Today Show*), NBC, 2008.

Appeared in other programs, including an appearance in *Access Hollywood,* syndicated; and as a guest, *Battlestars,* NBC.

Television Appearances; Pilots:
Alicia Dodd, *The Judge and Jake Wyler,* NBC, 1972.

Captain Newman, M.D., ABC, 1972.

Nina, *Big Rose: Double Trouble* (also known as *Big Rose* and *Double Trouble*), CBS, 1974.

Shirley, *Shell Game,* CBS, 1975.

Valene Joan Clements Ewing, *Knots Landing,* CBS, 1979.

Novelist, *Glitter,* ABC, 1984.

Television Additional Voices; Animated Series:
Thundarr the Barbarian, ABC, 1980–82, NBC, 1983–84.

Television Executive Producer; Movies:
In the Shadows, Someone's Watching (also known as *Someone's Watching* and *With Harmful Intent*), NBC, 1993.

Television Director; Specials:
"Boys Will Be Boys," *ABC Afterschool Specials,* ABC, 1994.

Director of a documentary about homelessness and domestic violence for the Directors Guild of America.

Television Director; Episodic:
"Letting Go," *Knots Landing,* CBS, 1992.

"Hints and Evasions," *Knots Landing,* CBS, 1993.

Stage Appearances:
The Miser, Tyrone Guthrie Theater, Minneapolis, MN, c. 1960.

Death of a Salesman, Tyrone Guthrie Theater, MN, 1963.

Corie Bratter, *Barefoot in the Park,* Biltmore Theatre, New York City, 1966–67, also in a London production, c. 1960.

Chemin de Fer, New Theatre for Now, Los Angeles, 1969.

Agnes, *The School for Wives,* Lyceum Theatre, New York City, 1971.

In a Fine Castle, New Theatre for Now, 1971.

Roxane, *Cyrano de Bergerac,* Center Theatre Group, Ahmanson Theatre, Music Center, Los Angeles, 1973.

As You Like It, Los Angeles production, c. 1973.

Silia Gala, *The Rules of the Game,* New Phoenix Repertory Company, Helen Hayes Theatre, New York City, 1974.

Ring round the Moon, Center Theatre Group, Ahmanson Theatre, Los Angeles, 1975.

Herself, *Night of 100 Stars II* (also known as *Night of One Hundred Stars*), Radio City Music Hall, New York City, 1985.

Maxine Faulk, *The Night of the Iguana,* Williamstown Theatre Festival, Main Stage, Williamstown, MA, 1987.

Jocasta, *The Legend of Oedipus,* Williamstown Theatre Festival, Main Stage, 1988.

Melissa Gardner, *Love Letters,* Promenade Theatre, New York City, 1989.

Night of 100 Stars III (also known as *Night of One Hundred Stars*), Radio City Music Hall, 1990.

Desiree Armfeldt, *A Little Night Music* (musical), Williamstown Theatre Festival, Main Stage, 1994.

Woman B, *Three Tall Women,* Promenade Theatre, 1995.

Stardust (also known as *Squall* and *Star Dust*), Tiffany Theater, Hollywood, CA, 1997.

The Exonerated, The Culture Project, Bleecker Street Theatre, New York City, c. 2000.

Marguerite Gautier, *Camino Real,* Shakespeare Theatre Company, The Landsburgh Theatre, Washington, DC, 2000.

The Vagina Monologues, Canon Theatre, Beverly Hills, CA, and Denver Center for the Performing Arts, Stage Theatre, Denver, CO, both 2001.

Blackout, McCadden Place Theatre, Hollywood, CA, 2003.

Mrs. Fenway, *Escape,* produced as part of *Five by Tenn* (collection of one–act plays by Tennessee Williams), John F. Kennedy Center for the Performing Arts, Washington, DC, 2004.

Harriet, *Private Fittings,* La Jolla Playhouse, Sheila and Hughes Potiker Theatre, La Jolla, CA, 2005.

Helena, *A Lovely Sunday for Creve Coeur,* Hartford Stage, Hartford, CT, 2006.

You'll Never Be Young Again, Los Angeles production, c. 2007.

Appeared as Lady Macbeth, *Macbeth,* Grove Shakespeare Festival; appeared in *Heartbreak House,* Los Angeles production; appeared in productions at other venues, including Arena Stage, Washington, DC.

Major Tours:
Corie Bratter, *Barefoot in the Park,* U.S. cities, 1965.

Film Appearances:
Karen Crockett, *Frogs,* American International Pictures, 1972.

Nancy Donovan, *Held for Ransom,* Cutting Edge Entertainment, 2000.

Voice of secretary, *It's the Pied Piper, Charlie Brown* (animated), Paramount, 2000.

Deborah Michaels, *UP, Michigan!,* 2nd Busiest Bean Entertainment, 2001.

Dr. Klein and others, *Net Games* (also known as *Net G@mes*), 2003.

The Hemingway Diamond, *Diamond Zero* (also known as *IceMaker*), Xenon Pictures, 2005.

Megan Phillips, *Channels,* Vanguard Cinema, 2008.

RECORDINGS

Music Videos:
Los Angeles Dodgers, "Baseball Boogie," 1986.

OTHER SOURCES

Periodicals:
People Weekly, February 11, 1980.

Electronic:
Joan Van Ark, http://www.joanvanark.com, November 25, 2008.

VAN DEN BLINK, Kieren 1972–

PERSONAL

Born March 11, 1972, in Princeton, NJ. *Education:* Graduated from Barnard College.

Career: Actress.

CREDITS

Television Appearances; Series:
Isabelle Lorenz, *Tyranny,* 2008.

Television Appearances; Episodic:
Erica Clemens, *Without a Trace* (also known as *W.A.T*), CBS, 2004.
Nikki, "Vector," *Numb3rs* (also known as *Num3ers*), CBS, 2005.
Voice of Rogue, "Hindsight: Part 1 & 2," *Wolverine and the X–Men,* 2008.
Voice of Rogue, "Time Bomb," *Wolverine and the X–Men,* 2008.
Voice of Rogue, "Past Discretions," *Wolverine and the X–Men,* 2008.

Television Appearances; Movies:
Young Rachel, *Point Last Seen,* CBS, 1998.

Film Appearances:
Alicia, *Drown Soda,* 1997.
Girl on television, *Anywhere But Here,* Twentieth Century–Fox, 1999.
Jamie, *The Four of Us,* 2001.
Amanda, *Fancy,* 2005.

Stage Appearances:
Anne Frank, Margot Frank and Miep Gies, *The Diary of Anne Frank,* Music Box Theatre, Chicago, IL, 1997–98.

VAN PATTEN, Dick 1928–
(John Acerno, John Irwin, Dickie Van Patten, Richard Van Patten)

PERSONAL

Full name, Richard Vincent Van Patten; born December 9, 1928, in Kew Gardens neighborhood of Queens County, NY; son of Richard Byron (an interior decorator) and Josephine Rose (in advertising; maiden name, Acerno) Van Patten; brother of Joyce Van Patten (an actress) and Tim Van Patten (an actor and director); married Patricia Poole (a dancer and actress), April 25, 1954; children: Nels (an actor), James (an actor), Vincent (an actor). *Education:* Attended public schools in Richmond Hills, NY. *Religion:* Roman Catholic.

Addresses: *Manager*—Budd Burton Moss, Burton Moss Management, 10533 Strathmore Dr., Los Angeles, CA 90024.

Career: Actor. Also worked as stage manager for theatrical productions. Natural Balance (pet food company), founder and commercial spokesperson, c. 1990—; commercial spokesperson for Zaken Corp., 2008; appeared in other commercials.

Member: Screen Actors Guild, Actors' Equity Association, American Federation of Television and Radio Artists.

Awards, Honors: Donaldson Award, *Billboard* readers' poll, 1941, for *The Lady Who Came to Stay;* named honorary mayor of Sherman Oaks, CA, 2001; received star on Hollywood Walk of Fame.

CREDITS

Television Appearances; Series:
Nels Hansen, *Mama* (also known as *I Remember Mama*), CBS, 1949–57.
Larry Renfrew, *Young Dr. Malone,* NBC, 1961–63.
Sergeant Nelson Higgenbottom, *The Partners,* NBC, 1971–72.
Friar Tuck, *When Things Were Rotten,* ABC, 1975.
Tom Bradford, *Eight Is Enough,* ABC, 1977–81.
Floyd Graham, *WIOU,* CBS, 1990–91.

Television Appearances; Movies:
Edward, *The Crooked Hearts,* ABC, 1972.
Alvin Andrews, *With This Ring,* ABC, 1978.
Herb Thurston, *Diary of a Teenage Hitchhiker* (also known as *Diary of a Hitchhiker*), ABC, 1979.

Tom Reed, *High Powder,* 1982.

Martin Grenville, *The Midnight Hour* (also known as *In the Midnight Hour*), ABC, 1985.

Principal, *Combat High* (also known as *Combat Academy*), NBC, 1986.

Tom Bradford, *Eight Is Enough: A Family Reunion,* NBC, 1987.

Rick Schuler, *Wedding Day Blues* (also known as *Going to the Chapel* and *Wedding Day*), NBC, 1988.

Principal Loomis, *14 Going on 30,* ABC, 1988.

Tom Bradford, *An Eight Is Enough Wedding,* NBC, 1989.

The commodore, *Jake Spanner, Private Eye* (also known as *Hoodwinked* and *The Old Dick*), USA Network, 1989.

Roy, *The Odd Couple: Together Again,* CBS, 1993.

Levi Downs, *Another Pretty Face,* PAX, 2002.

Santa Claus, *The Santa Trap,* PAX, 2002.

Jamie Denton, *The Sure Hand of God* (also known as *Sinners Need Company*), Lifetime, 2004.

Television Appearances; Miniseries:

Y2K: A World in Crisis, NBC, 1999.

Television Appearances; Specials:

Raymond, *A Memory of Two Mondays,* PBS, 1971.

Ernie, Madge, and Artie, ABC, 1974.

Mr. Humphries, *Ladies of the Corridor,* 1975.

Mr. Mason, *Ace,* ABC, 1976.

Celebrity Challenge of the Sexes 2, 1977.

Disco Fever: "Saturday Night Fever" Premiere Party, 1977.

Contestant, *All–Star Family Feud,* ABC, 1977.

ABC Presents Tomorrow's Stars, ABC, 1978.

Mickey's 50, 1978.

That Second Thing on ABC, ABC, 1978.

Rich Little's Washington Follies, ABC, 1978.

Pat Boone and Family, ABC, 1978.

ABC team captain, *Battle of the Network Stars VI,* ABC, 1979.

ABC team captain, *Battle of the Network Stars VII,* ABC, 1979.

Thanksgiving Special, 1980.

Take One Starring Jonathan Winters, NBC, 1981.

Host, *Whatever Became of ...?,* ABC, 1981.

Host, *State Fair USA,* syndicated, 1981.

I Love Liberty, ABC, 1982.

Andy Williams' Early New England Christmas, CBS, 1982.

Host, *The Fairest of Them All,* 1983.

Mayor, "The Hoboken Chicken Mystery" (also known as "The Hoboken Chicken Emergency"), *Wonder-Works,* PBS, 1984.

Macy's Thanksgiving Day Parade, NBC, 1986.

Howard Bevans, "Picnic," *Broadway on Showtime,* Showtime, 1986.

Lifetime Salutes Mom, Lifetime, 1987.

Jay Leno's Family Comedy Hour (also known as *Family Comedy Hour*), NBC, 1987.

George Crandall and Santa Clause, *A Mouse, a Mystery and Me,* NBC, 1987.

Jackie Gleason: The Great One (also known as *How Sweet It Is: A Wake for Jackie Gleason*), CBS, 1988.

1989 Johnnie Walker National Comedy Search, Comedy Central, 1989.

The Television Academy Hall of Fame, Fox, 1990.

Fifteenth Annual Circus of the Stars, CBS, 1990.

Host, *The Innocent of Hollywood,* syndicated, 1990.

Host, *The Comedy Concert Hour,* The Nashville Network, 1990.

NY TV: By the People Who Made It—Parts 1 & 2, PBS, 1998.

Eight Is Enough: The E! True Hollywood Story, E! Entertainment Television, 2000.

Narrator, *Gilligan's Island: The E! True Hollywood Story,* E! Entertainment Television, 2000.

"Dick Van Patten: The Sure Bet," *Biography,* Arts and Entertainment, 2001.

Playboy: Inside the Playboy Mansion, Arts and Entertainment, 2002.

TVography: Lee Majors—Hollywood's Bionic Hero, Arts and Entertainment, 2002.

Comedic Genius: The Work of Bernard Slade, 2003.

"Don Adams: Would You Believe?," *Biography,* Arts and Entertainment, 2004.

Television Appearances; Pilots:

Walter Granscog, *Arnie,* 1970.

Sergeant Nelson Higgenbottom, *Confessions of a Top Crime Buster,* 1971.

Earl Enright, *Hec Ramsey* (also known as *The Century Turns*), NBC, 1972.

Waldon, *S.W.A.T.,* ABC, 1975.

Mr. Unger, *Grandpa Max,* CBS, 1975.

Dr. Adam O'Neil, *The Love Boat,* ABC, 1976.

Chaplain, *Charo and the Sergeant,* ABC, 1976.

Palmer, *The Bionic Boy* (also known as *The Six Million Dollar Man: The Bionic Boy*), 1976.

King Alfred, *Fit for a King,* NBC, 1982.

Floyd Graham, *WIOU,* CBS, 1990.

Television Appearances; Episodic:

Story Hour, DuMont Network, 1936.

The Colgate Comedy Hour (also known as *Colgate Summer Comedy Hour, Colgate Variety Hour,* and *Michael Todd Revue*), NBC, 1950.

Paul, "The Broken Frame," *Mike Hammer* (also known as *Mickey Spillane's "Mike Hammer"*), 1958.

Matt Reston, "Incident of the Power and the Plow," *Rawhide,* 1959.

"Men in White," *The Du Pont Show of the Month,* CBS, 1960.

The Nurses, ABC, 1965.

The Face Is Familiar, 1966.

Market clerk, "My Master the Chili King," *I Dream of Jeannie,* NBC, 1970.

Bertrum Bannister, "Fail Safe," *The Governor & J. J.,* 1970.

Mr. Morse, "Rattle of a Single Girl," *That Girl,* 1970.

Jack, "Love and the Particular Girl," *Love, American Style,* ABC, 1971.

April's father, "Young Love," *The Doris Day Show,* 1971.

"Anniversary Gift," *The Doris Day Show,* 1972.

David, "The Dr. Rudolph Affair," *The Don Rickles Show,* 1972.

Earl Gifford, "Time to Kill," *Banyon,* 1972.

Johnny Collins, "45 Minutes from Home," *The Streets of San Francisco,* ABC, 1972.

Mr. Covington, "The Harry Award," *The New Dick Van Dyke Show,* CBS, 1972.

Hamlin, "The Great Sanford Siege," *Sanford and Son,* 1972.

Dr. Whittaker, "Awakening," *Medical Center,* 1972.

Man with hand stuck in sink, "Women," *Emergency!* (also known as *Emergency One* and *Emergencia*), 1972.

Wollner, "Howie Comes Home to Roost," *The Paul Lynde Show,* 1972.

"Love and the Tycoon," *Love, American Style,* ABC, 1972.

George, "Love and the Parent's Sake," *Love, American Style,* ABC, 1973.

Max Mathias, "Dennis Takes a Life," *The New Dick Van Dyke Show,* CBS, 1973.

Max Mathias, "One of the Boys," *The New Dick Van Dyke Show,* CBS, 1973.

(As John Irwin) Max Mathias, "The Young Surgeons," *The New Dick Van Dyke Show,* CBS, 1973.

Max Mathias, "He Who Steals My Friends," *The New Dick Van Dyke Show,* CBS, 1973.

Dr. Willis, "Back Talk," *The Paul Lynde Show,* 1973.

George Abel, "Murder for Murder," *Cannon,* CBS, 1973.

Fullmer, "Life Robbery (also known as Tribute to a Veteran)," *The Rookies,* 1973.

Henry, "No Hearts, No Flowers," *McMillan & Wife* (also known as *McMillan*), NBC, 1973.

John, "The Piano Teacher," *Thicker than Water,* 1973.

Commissioner Hoyt, "Katey at the Bat," *Adam's Rib,* 1973.

Jerry, "Roommates on a Rain Day," *Insight,* 1973.

Alfred Brindle, "They Have Been, They Are, They Will Be … " (also known as "UFO"), *The Night Stalker* (also known as *Kolchak: The Night Stalker*), ABC, 1974.

Harry Curtis, "Alcohol," *Adam–12,* 1974.

Donald Morgan, "Rocket to Oblivion," *Banacek,* NBC, 1974.

"The Informer," *Chopper One,* 1974.

Morgan, "The New Broom," *The Girl with Something Extra,* 1974.

Melvin Pearson, "Odd Man Loses," *Barnaby Jones,* 1974.

A. J. Horn, "The Rent Increase," *The Hot L Baltimore,* 1975.

Harry Green, "The E.S.P. Spy," *The Six Million Dollar Man,* ABC, 1975.

Phil Hunsberger, "Fonzie the Salesman," *Happy Days,* ABC, 1975.

Man at hotel, "Street Girl," *Medical Center,* 1975.

Jack Wood, "Beauty on Parade," *Wonder Woman* (also known as *The New Adventures of Wonder Woman* and *The New Original Wonder Woman*), ABC, 1976.

Merle Overton, "Deadly Reunion," *Barnaby Jones,* 1976.

"Clown of Death," *The Streets of San Francisco,* ABC, 1976.

Thurman Barber, "The Thrill Killers: Parts 1 & 2," *The Streets of San Francisco,* ABC, 1976.

Billy Geeter, "The Adventure of the Eccentric Engineer," *Ellery Queen* (also known as *The Adventures of Ellery Queen*), 1976.

Carter Merkle, "Grateful," *Emergency!* (also known as *Emergency One* and *Emergencia*), 1976.

Gordon Coleman, "Walter's Crisis: Part 1," *Maude,* 1976.

Mr. Claxton, "The Burger Queen," *What's Happening!!,* 1976.

Myron C. Dobbs, "Case: O Come All Ye Wastrels," *The Tony Randall Show,* 1976.

Patrick Malloy, "Chautauqua, Chautauqua, Chautauqua," *Gibbsville,* 1977.

Frank, "Ginny's Child," *One Day at a Time,* 1977.

Assistant Principal Marvin Conners, "The Graduation: Parts 1 & 2," *Happy Days,* ABC, 1977.

Dinah! (also known as *Dinah! & Friends*), 1977.

The Hollywood Squares, 1978.

"Eight Is Enough vs. Family," *Family Feud* (game show; also known as *The Best of Family Feud* and *Family Fortune*), ABC, 1978.

The Tonight Show Starring Johnny Carson, NBC, 1978, 1981.

Congressman John Whiteout, "The Congressman Was Indiscreet/Isaac's History Lesson/The Winner Takes Love," *The Love Boat,* ABC, 1978.

Himself, "Roller Disco: Part 2," *CHiPs* (also known as *CHiPs Patrol*), NBC, 1979.

Charlie Dillinger, "The Mallory Quest/Two Hours/The Offer/Julie the Vamp: Parts 1 & 2," *The Love Boat,* ABC, 1980.

(Uncredited) Himself, "The Great 5K Star Race and Boulder Wrap Party," *CHiPs* (also known as *CHiPs Patrol*), NBC, 1980.

Howard Ethan, "His Girls Friday/A Wife for Wilfred/The Girl Who Stood Still," *The Love Boat,* ABC, 1982.

The Great Stellini, "The Professor Has Class/When the Magic Disappears/We the Jury," *The Love Boat,* ABC, 1983.

Arthur, "Don't Rock the Boat," *Too Close for Comfort* (also known as *The Ted Knight Show*), 1983.

"The Day Everything Went Wrong," *Insight,* 1983.

Herbert Pitts, "Charades," *Hotel* (also known as *Arthur Hailey's "Hotel"*), 1983.

Just Men!, NBC, 1983.

"Dom DeLuise," *This Is Your Life,* syndicated, 1983.

Alan Nettles, "Undying Love," *Finder of Lost Loves,* 1984.

George Hayes, "How Do I Love Thee?/No More Alimony/Authoress! Authoress!" *The Love Boat,* ABC, 1984.

"Sleeper," *Masquerade,* 1984.

"Cold Target," *Mike Hammer* (also known as *Mickey Spillane's "Mike Hammer"* and *The New Mike Hammer*), 1984.

"Murder Is a Two Stroke Penalty," *Crazy Like a Fox,* 1985.

Frasier Pratt, "Second Offense" (also known as "Missing Pieces"), *Hotel* (also known as *Arthur Hailey's "Hotel"*), 1985.

District attorney Fred Whittaker, "Murder in the Electric Cathedral," *Murder, She Wrote,* CBS, 1985.

True Confessions, syndicated, 1986.

Frank Stickle, "Ex Marks the Spot," *The Facts of Life,* 1987.

Phil Johnson, "Dear Diary," *Rags to Riches,* 1987.

The New Hollywood Squares, syndicated, 1987.

Nick Simpson, "Fortunate Son," *Growing Pains,* 1989.

Taylor Michaels, "Heartbreak Hotel," *The Golden Palace,* CBS, 1993.

Monty Emerson, "Murder at the Telethon," *Diagnosis Murder,* CBS, 1993.

Sam/Henry Krebbs, "Guys & Dolls," *Baywatch,* syndicated, 1994.

Orphanage worker and Santa, "Season's Greedings," *Lois and Clark: The New Adventures of Superman* (also known as *Lois and Clark* and *The New Adventures of Superman*), ABC, 1994.

Dr. Paul Hampton, "Who Killed Skippy's Master?" *Burke's Law,* CBS, 1994.

Jerry, "In the Name of God," *Touched by an Angel,* CBS, 1995.

Jack, "Break a Leg," *Maybe This Time,* ABC, 1995.

Himself, "Nice Work If You Can Get It," *Cybill,* CBS, 1995.

Jacob, "You Can Go Home Again," *Boy Meets World,* ABC, 1996.

Thief, "Al Gets Robbed," *The Weird Al Show,* CBS, 1997.

Himself, "Because I Said So," *The Weird Al Show,* CBS, 1997.

The Rosie O'Donnell Show, syndicated, 1997.

Sid Glacken, "How Long Has This Been Going On?," *Love Boat: The Next Wave,* UPN, 1998.

Eb, "Lady of the Lake," *Touched by an Angel,* CBS, 1998.

Voice of Tom Bradford, "Brian: Portrait of a Dog," *Family Guy* (animated; also known as *Padre de familia*), Fox, 1999.

Hollywood Squares (also known as *H2* and *H2: Hollywood Squares*), syndicated, 1999, 2001.

Himself, "Training Camp," *The Man Show,* Comedy Central, 2000.

Himself, "Phone Sex," *The Man Show,* Comedy Central, 2001.

"Bruce Jenner," *ESPN SportsCentury,* ESPN, 2001.

"Jimmy Asks Women 'What Do You Weigh?'," *The Man Show,* Comedy Central, 2003.

"Camp Kournikova," *The Man Show,* Comedy Central, 2003.

Himself, "It's a Wonderful Job," *Life with Bonnie,* ABC, 2003.

James Rodgers, Sr., "Two Weddings, an Engagement, and a Funeral," *7th Heaven* (also known as *Seventh Heaven* and *7th Heaven: Beginnings*), The WB, 2004.

"Dick Van Patten," *Living in TV Land,* TV Land, 2004.

"Greatest TV Romances," *TV Land's Top Ten,* TV Land, 2005.

Cal Cullen, "Spring Breakout," *Arrested Development,* Fox, 2005.

Cal Cullen, "Righteous Brothers," *Arrested Development,* Fox, 2005.

The John Kerwin Show, 2005.

"Writing, Rehearsing & Recording," *TV Land Confidential* (also known as *TV Land Confidential: The Untold Stories*), TV Land, 2005.

Jimmy Kimmel Live!, ABC, 2005, 2006.

Murph, "Sweet Lady," *That '70s Show,* Fox, 2006.

In the Mix (also known as *In the Cutz*), Urban America, 2006.

Entertainment Tonight (also known as *Entertainment This Week, E.T., ET Weekend,* and *This Week in Entertainment*), syndicated, 2006, 2008.

"Movies," *TV Land Confidential* (also known as *TV Land Confidential: The Untold Stories*), TV Land, 2007.

"Finales," *TV Land Confidential* (also known as *TV Land Confidential: The Untold Stories*), TV Land, 2007.

Jury member, *Jury Duty,* 2007.

Dr. Eddie Hackmeyer, "Fetus Don't Fail Me Now," *The Sarah Silverman Program,* Comedy Central, 2008.

The O'Reilly Factor, Fox News Channel, 2008.

Guest panelist, *Battlestars;* also appeared in episodes of *Diamonds; Hearts Are Wild; Kraft Television Theatre; Silent Service;* and *The Verdict Is Yours.*

Television Appearances; Awards Presentations:

Presenter, *The 32nd Annual Tony Awards,* 1978.

The 2nd Annual Family Television Awards, CBS, 2000.

Film Appearances:

Jimmy Dugan, *Reg'lar Fellers,* Producers Releasing, 1941.

Lieutenant Edgar Palmer, *Psychomania* (also known as *Black Autumn* and *Violent Midnight*), Victoria/Emerson, 1964.

(As Richard Van Patten) Bert, *Charly* (also known as *The Two Worlds of Charly Gordon*), Cinerama Releasing, 1968.

The Dude, *Zachariah,* Cinerama Releasing, 1971.

Warren, *Making It,* Twentieth Century–Fox, 1971.

Hotel manager, *Joe Kidd,* Universal, 1972.

Harry, *Dirty Little Billy,* Columbia, 1972.

Scoutmaster Adleman, *Beware! The Blob* (also known as *Beware of the Blob, Son of Blob,* and *Son of the Blob*), Video Gems, 1972.

Mr. Carruthers, *Snowball Express,* Buena Vista, 1972.

Banker, *Westworld,* Metro–Goldwyn–Mayer, 1973.

First usher, *Soylent Green,* Metro–Goldwyn–Mayer, 1973.

Ira Hershaw, *Superdad,* Buena Vista, 1974.

Harry, *The Strongest Man in the World,* Buena Vista, 1975.

The gambler, *Treasure of Matecumbe,* Buena Vista, 1976.

Raymond, *The Shaggy D.A.,* Buena Vista, 1976.

Cal Wilson, *Gus,* Buena Vista, 1976.

Harold Jennings, *Freaky Friday,* Buena Vista, 1976.

Dr. Wentworth, *High Anxiety,* Twentieth Century–Fox, 1977.

Voice of King Goodwin, *Nutcracker Fantasy* (animated), Sanrio, 1979.

King Roland, Ruler of Druidia, *Spaceballs,* Metro–Goldwyn–Mayer/United Artists, 1987.

Greg the glue man, *The New Adventures of Pippi Long-stocking* (also known as *Pippi Laengstrump–starkast I vaerlden*), Columbia, 1988.

Detective Wendell Larch, *Final Embrace,* New Horizon Home Video, 1992.

Max, *Body Trouble* (also known as *Joker's Wild*), Triboro Entertainment Group, 1992.

The abbot, *Robin Hood: Men in Tights* (also known as *Sacre Robin des bois*), Twentieth Century–Fox, 1993.

Principal, *A Dangerous Place* (also known as *No Surrender*), PM Home Video, 1995.

General Wainswright, *Demolition High,* Cabin Fever Entertainment, 1996.

Dr. Rodino, *Love Is All There Is,* Samuel Goldwyn Company, 1996.

Game show host, *For Goodness Sake II,* 1996.

Army general, *Demolition University,* 1997.

Parole officer, *Evasive Action,* Hallmark Entertainment, 1998.

Preacher, *Angel on Abbey Street,* 1999.

Captain Stacey, *Big Brother Trouble,* Mainline Releasing, 2000.

Mr. Rye, *The Price of Air,* Artistic License, 2000.

Frank Rubin, *Quiet Kill* (also known as *Nightmare Boulevard*), 2001, I.Q. Entertainment, 2004.

Irv Barnett, *Groom Lake* (also known as *The Visitor*), Full Moon Entertainment, 2002.

Himself, *Dickie Roberts: Former Child Star* (also known as *Dickie Roberts: (Former) Child Star*), Paramount, 2003.

Alan Merkel, *Freezerburn,* Brookturn, 2005.

Narrator, *The Christmas Conspiracy* (animated short film), Jenkev Productions, 2008.

Mister Rye, *Los Angeles,* Westlake Entertainment Group, 2008.

Jack Benson, *Opposite Day,* Identity Studios, 2009.

Himself, *The Making of a Film,* Under Dog Distribution, 2009.

Hollywood Moments (documentary), Film Pharm, 2009.

According to Dom (documentary), Film Pharm, 2009.

Stage Appearances:

(Stage debut) The child, *Tapestry in Gray,* Shubert Theatre, New York City, 1935.

Henry Wadsworth Benson, *Home Sweet Home,* Greenwich Guild Theatre, Greenwich, CT, 1936.

(As Dickie Van Patten) Isaac, *The Eternal Road* (musical), Manhattan Opera House, New York City, 1937.

Theodore, *Good–bye Again,* Theatre at Pine Brook Country Club, Nichols, CT, 1937.

Boy in tree, *On Borrowed Time,* Longacre Theatre, New York City, 1938.

(As Dickie Van Patten) Nine, *Run Sheep, Run,* Windsor Theatre, New York City, 1938.

(As Dickie Van Patten) Karl Gunther at age nine, *The American Way,* Center Theatre, New York City, 1939.

(As Dickie Van Patten) Pete Brown, *The Woman Brown,* Wharf Theatre, Provincetown, NJ, then Biltmore Theatre, New York City, 1939.

Tommy, *Ah! Wilderness,* Wharf Theatre, 1939, then Maplewood Theatre, NJ, 1940.

Jessie, *Our Girls,* Starlight Theatre, Pawling, NY, 1940.

Moses, *Something about a Soldier,* Bucks County Playhouse, New Hope, PA, 1940.

Toby, *Carriage Trade,* Stamford Playhouse, Stamford, CT, 1940.

(As Dickie Van Patten) Roger, *The Lady Who Came to Stay,* Maxine Elliott's Theatre, New York City, 1941.

(As Dickie Van Patten) Timothy Kincaid, *The Land Is Bright,* Music Box Theatre, New York City, 1941–42.

Bodo, *The Watch on the Rhine,* Majestic Theatre, Boston, MA, 1942.

"Short Pants" Houlihan, *Evening Rise,* Woodstock Playhouse, Woodstock, NY, 1942.

(As Dickie Van Patten) Telegraph boy, *The Skin of Our Teeth,* Plymouth Theatre, New York City, 1942–43.

(As Dickie Van Patten) Elwood, *The Snark Was a Boojum,* Forty–Eighth Street Theatre, New York City, 1943.

Dexter Franklin, *Kiss and Tell,* Biltmore Theatre, 1943.

(As Dickie Van Patten) Felix, *Decision,* Belasco Theatre, then Ambassador Theatre, both New York City, 1944.

(As Dickie Van Patten) Sergeant Walter Burrows, *Too Hot for Maneuvers,* Broadhurst Theatre, New York City, 1945.

(As Dickie Van Patten) Ernie Sheffield, *The Wind Is Ninety,* Booth Theatre, New York City, 1945.

Michael Brown, *O Mistress Mine,* Empire Theatre, New York City, 1946–47.

Ensign Pulver, *Mister Roberts,* Alvin Theatre, New York City, 1948, then Quarterdeck Theatre, Atlantic City, NJ, 1951.

Toto, *Cry of the Peacock,* Locust Theatre, Philadelphia, PA, 1950.

Nels, *Here's Mama,* Ogunquit Playhouse, Ogunquit, ME, then Cape Playhouse, Dennis, MA, 1952.

Michael Barnes, *The Male Animal,* Music Box Theatre, then Jamaica Theatre, New York City, 1952.

Charles Reader, *The Tender Trap,* Pocono Playhouse (now Bucks County Playhouse), New Hope, PA, 1955.

Grant Cobbler, *Oh Men! Oh Women!,* Pocono Playhouse, 1955.

Happy, *Death of a Salesman,* Long Beach Playhouse, New York City, 1955.

Francis X. Dignan, *King of Hearts,* Avondale Playhouse, Indianapolis, IN, 1956.

Ruby Pulaski, *Have I Got a Girl for You!,* Music Box Theatre, 1963.

A Very Rich Woman, Belasco Theatre, 1965.

Mr. Hollender, *Don't Drink the Water,* Coconut Grove Playhouse, Miami, FL, 1968.

Hal, *Lovers and Other Strangers,* Brooks Atkinson Theatre, New York City, 1968.

The Honorable Newton Prince, *But, Seriously …,* Henry Miller's Theatre, New York City, 1969.

Marion Cheever, *Next, Adaptation,* Greenwich Mews Theatre, New York City, 1969.

Charlie, *Thieves,* Broadhurst Theatre, 1974, then Longacre Theatre, New York City, 1974–75.

Cap'n Andy, *Showboat,* Auditorium Theatre, Chicago, IL, 1996.

Scandals, Virginia Theatre, New York City, 1999.

Al Lewis, *The Sunshine Boys,* Falcon Theatre, Burbank, CA, 2002.

Major Tours:

O Mistress Mine, U.S. cities, 1948.

George Macauley, *Will Success Spoil Rock Hunter?,* U.S. cities, 1957.

Ensign Beau Gillian, *Golden Fleecing,* U.S. cities, 1960.

Henry Greene, *Strictly Dishonorable,* U.S. and Canadian cities, 1964–65.

Cap'n Andy, *Showboat,* U.S. cities, 1996.

The Sunshine Boys, 2001.

Radio Appearances:

Mark Brown, *Young Widder Brown,* NBC, 1941.

Dexter Franklin, *Kiss and Tell,* 1947.

Wayne, *State Fair,* 1950.

Ben Banks, *Father of the Bride,* 1951.

Nat Kahn, *Good Housekeeping,* 1951.

Also appeared as Ray, *David Harum;* Wilfred, *Duffy's Tavern;* Nick Kane, *Elmer the Great;* Toby Smith, *Henry Aldrich;* Cadet Osborne, *The Major and the Minor;* in *The March of Time;* as Teddy Thompson, *Miss Hatty;* Michael Brown, *O Mistress Mine;* Hartzell, *One Foot in Heaven;* Jimmy Dugan, *Reg'lar Fellers;* Teddy, *Right to Happiness;* Roger, *Theatre;* and Chic, *Wednesday's Child.*

RECORDINGS

Videos:

(As John Acerno) Title role, *The Secret Dream Models of Oliver Nibble,* Something Weird Video, 1967.

Couples Do It Debbie's Way, 1988.

Narrator, *Single Parenting,* 1989.

Radon Free, 1989.

Dirty Tennis, 1989.

Narrator, *Blended Families: Yours, Mine, Ours,* 1991.

(Uncredited; in archive footage) *The "Weird Al" Yankovic Video Library: His Greatest Hits,* BMG Music, 1992.

(In archive footage) *"Weird Al" Yankovic: The Videos,* 1996.

Himself, *Buckle Up,* 1998.

Spaceballs: The Documentary, Metro–Goldwyn–Mayer, 2002.

(Uncredited; in archive footage) *"Weird Al" Yankovic: The Ultimate Video Collection,* Volcano Entertainment Group, 2003.

Himself, *Christmas in Tinseltown,* New Line Home Video, 2004.

Appeared in music videos, including "Bedrock Anthem" and "Smells like Nirvana" by "Weird Al" Yankovic.

WRITINGS

Nonfiction:

(With Peter Berk) *Launching Your Child in Show Biz: A Complete Step–by–Step Guide,* General Publishing Group, 1997.

Totally Terrific TV Trivia, 2007.

OTHER SOURCES

Other:

"Dick Van Patten: The Sure Bet" (television special), *Biography,* Arts and Entertainment, 2001.

VAN SUSTEREN, Greta 1954–

PERSONAL

Born June 11, 1954, in Appleton, WI; married John P. Coale (a lawyer). *Education:* University of Wisconsin, bachelor's degree with distinction, economics; Georgetown Law Center, J.D., 1979, master of law, 1982.

Career: Television news host. Began career as a trial attorney; Georgetown Law Center, adjunct professor, 1984–99; Cable News Network (CNN), legal analyst and television show host, 1991–2002; joined Fox News, 2002.

Awards, Honors: Sandra Day O'Connor Medal of Honor, Seton Hall University, 2001; Presidential Award for excellence in journalism, American Bar Association, c. 2001; National Headliners Award, 2002; honorary J.D., Stetson Law School.

CREDITS

Television Appearances; Series:
Cohost, *Burden of Proof,* Cable News Network, 1995–2002.
On the Record w/Greta Van Susteren, Fox News, 2002—.
The O'Reilly Factor, Fox News, multiple appearances, 2005—.
Crime Scene, 2006.

Also appeared as host, *The Point with Greta Van Susteren,* Cable News Network.

Television Appearances; Specials:
Presenter, *The Fifth Annual Trumpet Awards,* TBS, 1997.
Correspondent, *How Safe Is Your Food?,* Cable News Network, 1997.
Host, *Burden of Proof: Clinton, Congress, and the Constitution,* Cable News Network, 1998.
Intimate Portrait: Sharon Osbourne, Lifetime, 2002.
Judge, *Miss America Pageant,* ABC, 2003.

Television Appearances; Pilots:
Herself, *Damages,* FX Channel, 2007.

Television Appearances; Episodic:
Herself, "Lawsuit," *Space Ghost Coast to Coast* (also known as *SGC2C*), Cartoon Network, 1998.
Herself, "What Goes Up …," *The Osbournes* (also known as *The Curse of the Osbournes*), MTV, 2002.
The Tonight Show with Jay Leno, NBC, 2002, 2005.
Legal analyst, "Why O. J. Simpson Won," *American Justice,* 2004.
(Uncredited) *Late Night with Conan O'Brien,* NBC, 2004.
At Large with Geraldo Rivera (also known as *Geraldo at Large*), syndicated, 2005.
The Big Story, Fox News, 2005.
Hannity & Colmes, Fox News, 2005.
The View, ABC, 2005, 2007.

Herself, "We Are Not Animals," *Damages,* FX Channel, 2007.
Voice of herself, *America's Pulse,* 2008.
Entertainment Tonight (also known as *E.T.*), syndicated, 2008.
Just In with Laura Ingraham, 2008.

WRITINGS

Nonfiction:
Cowrote *My Turn at the Bully Pulpit: Straight Talk About the Things That Drive Me Nuts.*

VINCENT, E. Duke
(Duke Vincent, Duke E. Vincent)

PERSONAL

Some sources cite original name as Duke Ventigmilia; raised in New York and New Jersey; mother, an organ player at silent movie theatres; married Pamela Gail Hensley (an actress). *Avocational Interests:* Flying, golfing, fly fishing.

Addresses: *Office*—Spelling Television, Inc., 5700 Wilshire Blvd., Fifth Floor, Los Angeles, CA 90036–3659.

Career: Producer, writer, and executive. Spelling Television, Inc., Los Angeles, producer, executive producer, and vice chairperson. Owner of a restaurant and cocktail lounge in New Jersey. National Museum of Naval Aviation, Pensacola Naval Air Station (NAS), Pensacola, FL, trustee. Also known as Duke E. Vincent. *Military service:* Served as an aviator in the U.S. Navy, c. 1954–63; flew with the Blue Angels (U.S. Naval Flight Demonstration Squadron), 1960–61.

Member: Writers Guild of America, West.

Awards, Honors: Emmy Award nomination (with others), outstanding drama series, 1982, for *Dynasty;* Emmy Award (with others), outstanding drama/comedy special, 1989, for *Day One;* Emmy Award, outstanding made for television movie, 1994, and CableACE Award nomination, movie or miniseries, 1995, both with others, for *And the Band Played On.*

CREDITS

Television Work; Series:
Pilot, *The Blue Angels,* syndicated, 1960.
Producer, *Man in Space* (documentary series), c. 1960.

Producer and story consultant, *Gomer Pyle, U.S.M.C.,* CBS, 1964–69.

Producer, *Arnie,* CBS, 1970–72.

Producer, *The Little People* (also known as *The Brian Keith Show*), NBC, 1972–74.

Producer, *Temperatures Rising* (also known as *The New Temperatures Rising Show*), ABC, 1972–74.

Executive producer, *The San Pedro Beach Bums,* ABC, 1977.

Supervising producer, *Vega$* (also known as *High Roller* and *Vegas*), ABC, 1978–81.

Supervising producer, *Friends,* ABC, 1979.

Supervising producer, *B.A.D. Cats,* ABC, 1980.

Supervising producer, *Aloha Paradise,* ABC, 1981.

Supervising producer, *Strike Force,* ABC, 1981–82.

Producer and executive supervising producer, *Dynasty,* ABC, 1981–89.

Supervising producer, *Matt Houston,* ABC, 1982–85.

Executive producer and supervising producer, *At Ease,* ABC, 1983.

Supervising producer, *Hotel* (also known as *Arthur Hailey's "Hotel"*), ABC, 1983–88.

Supervising producer, *Glitter,* ABC, 1984, 1985.

Supervising producer, *Finder of Lost Loves,* ABC, 1984–85.

Executive supervising producer, *Hollywood Beat,* ABC, 1985.

Supervising producer, *MacGruder and Loud,* ABC, 1985.

Executive producer and supervising producer, *The Colbys* (also known as *Dynasty II: The Colbys*), ABC, 1985–87.

Executive supervising producer, *Life with Lucy,* ABC, 1986.

Supervising producer, *Free Spirit,* ABC, 1989–90.

Executive producer, *Hearts Are Wild,* CBS, 1992.

Executive producer, *The Round Table,* NBC, 1992.

Executive producer, *2000 Malibu Road,* CBS, 1992.

Producer, *The Heights,* Fox, 1992.

Executive producer, *Melrose Place,* Fox, 1992–99.

Executive producer, *Heaven Help Us,* syndicated, 1994.

Executive producer, *Winnetka Road,* NBC, 1994.

Executive producer, *Burke's Law,* CBS, 1994–95.

Executive producer, *Madman of the People,* NBC, 1994–95.

Executive producer, *Models Inc.,* Fox, 1994–95.

Executive producer, *Robin's Hoods* (also known as *Robins Club, A toca de Robin, Les anges gardiens,* and *Mis cinco delincuentes*), syndicated, 1994–95.

Executive producer, *University Hospital,* syndicated, 1995.

Executive producer, *Beverly Hills 90210,* Fox, 1995–99.

Executive producer, *Kindred: The Embraced,* Fox, 1996.

Executive producer, *Malibu Shores,* CBS, 1996.

Executive producer, *Savannah,* The WB, 1996–97.

Executive producer, *7th Heaven* (also known as *Seventh Heaven* and *7th Heaven: Beginnings*), The WB, 1996–2006, The CW, 2006–2007.

Executive producer, *Pacific Palisades,* Fox, 1997.

Executive producer, *Sunset Beach,* NBC, 1997–99.

Executive producer, *Buddy Faro,* CBS, 1998.

Executive producer, *The Love Boat: The Next Wave,* UPN, 1998–99.

Executive producer, *Any Day Now,* Lifetime, 1998–2002.

Executive producer, *Charmed,* The WB, 1998–2006.

Executive producer, *Rescue 77,* The WB, 1999.

Executive producer, *Safe Harbor,* The WB, 1999.

Executive producer, *Titans,* NBC, 2000.

Executive producer, *All Souls,* UPN, 2001.

Executive producer, *Deep Cover,* c. 2002.

Executive producer, *Kingpin,* NBC, 2003.

Executive producer, *Queens Supreme,* CBS, 2003.

Executive producer, *10–8: Officers on Duty* (also known as *10–8* and *10–8: Police Patrol*), ABC, 2003–2004.

Executive producer, *Clubhouse* (also known as *Homerun!*), CBS, 2004.

Executive producer, *Summerland* (also known as *Immediate Family* and *Summerland Beach*), The WB, 2004–2005.

Executive producer, *Wanted,* TNT, 2005.

Television Work; Miniseries:

Supervising producer, *The French Atlantic Affair,* ABC, 1979.

Supervising producer, *Hollywood Wives,* ABC, 1985.

Supervising producer, *Crossings,* ABC, 1986.

Executive supervising producer, *Dynasty: The Reunion,* ABC, 1991.

Executive producer, *Grass Roots,* NBC, 1992.

Executive producer, *James A. Michener's "Texas"* (also known as *Texas*), ABC, 1995.

Supervising producer, *A Season in Purgatory,* CBS, 1996.

Television Work; Movies:

Executive producer, *Panache,* ABC, 1976.

Supervising producer, *Kate Bliss and the Ticker Tape Kid,* ABC, 1978.

Supervising producer, *Love's Savage Fury,* ABC, 1979.

Supervising producer, *Murder Can Hurt You* (also known as *Murder Can Hurt You!* and *Nojack & Co*), ABC, 1980.

Supervising producer, *The Best Little Girl in the World,* ABC, 1981.

Supervising producer, *Sizzle* (also known as *Golden Club*), ABC, 1981.

Supervising producer, *Don't Go to Sleep,* ABC, 1982.

Supervising producer, *The Wild Women of Chastity Gulch,* ABC, 1982.

Supervising producer, *Making of a Male Model,* ABC, 1983.

Supervising producer, *Dark Mirror,* ABC, 1984.

Supervising producer, *Dark Mansions,* ABC, 1986.

Supervising producer, *Cracked Up,* ABC, 1987.

Supervising producer, *The Three Kings,* ABC, 1987.

Executive producer, *Day One* (also known as *Hiroshima*), CBS, 1989.

Executive producer, *Rich Men, Single Women,* ABC, 1990.

Executive producer, *Jailbirds,* CBS, 1991.

Executive producer, *Back to the Streets of San Francisco,* NBC, 1992.

Executive producer, *Sexual Advances,* ABC, 1992.

Executive producer, *Terror on Track 9* (also known as *Janek: The Grand Central Murders*), CBS, 1992.

Executive producer, *And the Band Played On,* HBO, 1993.

Executive producer, *Sidney Sheldon's "A Stranger in the Mirror"* (also known as *A Stranger in the Mirror*), ABC, 1993.

Executive producer, *Jane's House,* CBS, 1994.

Executive producer, *Love on the Run,* NBC, 1994.

Executive producer, *After Jimmy,* CBS, 1996.

Executive producer, *Satan's School for Girls* (also known as *Satan School*), ABC, 2000.

Producer of *The Imposter.* Worked on other television projects.

Television Work; Specials:

Executive producer, *The Best Moments of 90210,* Fox, 1996.

Executive producer, *Beverly Hills 90210: 10–Year High School Reunion,* Fox, 2003.

Television Work; Pilots:

Coproducer, *Day by Day,* ABC, 1973.

Coproducer, *Patsy,* NBC, 1973.

Executive producer, *Salt and Pepe,* CBS, 1975.

(As Duke Vincent) Producer, *The San Pedro Bums* (also known as *The San Pedro Beach Bums*), ABC, 1977.

Supervising producer, *Eddie and Herbert,* CBS, 1977.

Producer, *Vega$* (also known as *High Roller* and *Vegas*), ABC, 1978.

Producer, *Wild and Wooly,* ABC, 1978.

Producer, *The Power Within* (also known as *Power Man*), ABC, 1979.

Producer, *Casino,* ABC, 1980.

Supervising producer, *Waikiki* (also known as *Waikiki Mission*), ABC, 1980.

Supervising producer, *Hotel* (also known as *Arthur Hailey's "Hotel"*), ABC, 1982.

Supervising producer, *Massarati and the Brain,* ABC, 1982.

Supervising producer, *Scared Silly,* ABC, 1982.

Supervising producer, *Shooting Stars,* ABC, 1983.

Supervising producer, *Venice Medical,* ABC, 1983.

Supervising producer, *Velvet,* ABC, 1984.

Supervising producer and executive producer, *Glitter,* ABC, 1984.

Supervising producer, *International Airport,* ABC, 1985.

Supervising producer, *Mr. & Mrs. Ryan,* ABC, 1986.

Executive supervising producer, *Harry's Hong Kong,* ABC, 1987.

Producer and executive supervising producer, *The Hope Division* (also known as *Hope Division* and *Shades of Blue*), ABC, 1987.

Executive producer, *Heartbeat* (also known as *HeartBeat*), ABC, 1988.

Executive producer, *The Loner,* ABC, 1988.

Executive producer, *Just Life,* ABC, 1990.

Executive producer, *Partners,* ABC, 1993.

Producer, *Green Dolphin Beat* (also known as *Green Dolphin Street*), Fox, 1994.

Executive producer, *Crosstown Traffic* (also known as *Cross Town Traffic*), 1995.

Executive producer, *"The Embraced," Kindred: The Embraced,* Fox, c. 1996.

Executive producer, *Bullet Hearts,* Fox, 1996.

Executive producer, *Malibu Shores,* CBS, 1996.

Executive producer, *Pier 66,* ABC, 1996.

Executive producer, *7th Heaven* (also known as *Seventh Heaven* and *7th Heaven: Beginnings*), The WB, 1996.

Executive producer, *"Welcome to the Neighborhood," Pacific Palisades,* Fox, 1997.

Executive producer, *"Something Wicca This Way Comes," Charmed,* The WB, 1998.

Executive producer, *Buddy Faro,* CBS, 1998.

Executive producer, *Glory, Glory,* CBS, 1998.

Executive producer, *Odd Jobs,* NBC, 1998.

Executive producer, *Forbidden Island,* UPN, 1999.

Executive producer, *Rescue 77,* The WB, 1999.

Executive producer, *Titans,* NBC, 2000.

Executive producer, *All Souls,* UPN, 2001.

Executive producer, *Deep,* The WB, 2001.

Executive producer, *Home of the Brave* (also known as *Brats*), The WB, 2002.

Executive producer, *Deep Cover,* c. 2002.

Executive producer, *Hotel,* UPN, 2003.

Executive producer, *The Law and Mr. Lee* (also known as *The Henry Lee Project, Junkyard Dog,* and *The Law and Henry Lee*), CBS, 2003.

Executive producer, *Queens Supreme,* CBS, 2003.

Executive producer, *Clubhouse* (also known as *Homerun!*), CBS, 2004.

Executive producer, *Silver Lake,* UPN, 2004.

Executive producer, *Summerland* (also known as *Immediate Family* and *Summerland Beach*), The WB, 2004.

Executive producer, *Bounty Hunters* (also known as *The Bounty Hunters*), CBS, 2005.

Executive producer, *Crazy,* UPN, 2005.

Executive producer, *Hitched,* Fox, 2005.

Executive producer, *Wanted,* TNT, 2005.

Executive producer, *Split Decision,* The CW, 2006.

Executive producer, *Mermaid,* The WB, 2007.

Executive producer, *Saving Grace* (also known as *Grace*), TNT, 2007.

Executive producer for the pilots *Austin,* CBS; *Conflict of Interest,* UPN; *Dark Matters,* CBS; *Fat Friends,* Fox; *Ghost Walker,* The WB; *The Green Ray,* CBS; *Hot Springs,* UPN; *Kincaid,* The WB; *Malpractice,* UPN; *The Second Assistant,* UPN; *State,* The WB; *The Tribe,* The WB; and *Wolf Pack,* CBS. Also worked on other pilots.

Television Appearances; Specials:
Himself, *The Women of Charmed,* 2000.

Television Appearances; Episodic:
Police officer, "First Down and 200 Miles to Go," *Good Morning, World,* CBS, 1968.

Himself, "The Mod Squad," *The E! True Hollywood Story* (also known as *Beverly Hills 90210: The E! True Hollywood Story* and *THS*), E! Entertainment Television, 2000.

Himself, "Beverly Hills 90210," *The E! True Hollywood Story* (also known as *Beverly Hills 90210: The E! True Hollywood Story* and *THS*), E! Entertainment Television, 2001.

Himself, "Alyssa Milano," *Intimate Portrait* (also known as *Intimate Portrait: Alyssa Milano*), Lifetime, 2003.

Himself, *Larry King Live,* Cable News Network, 2005.

Film Appearances:
(Uncredited) Vincent, *Off and Running* (also known as *Moon over Miami*), 1991.

WRITINGS

Teleplays; Movies:
Panache, ABC, 1976.

Wrote *The Imposter.*

Teleplays; Episodic:
The Dick Van Dyke Show, CBS, episodes c. 1960.

(With others) *Man in Space* (documentary series), c. 1960.

Head writer, *Gomer Pyle, U.S.M.C.,* CBS, 1964–69.

Good Morning, World, CBS, multiple episodes, 1967–68.

"The Friend," *The Doris Day Show,* CBS, 1968.

"The Date," *The Doris Day Show,* CBS, 1969.

Head writer, *The Jim Nabors Hour,* CBS, 1969–71.

(As Duke Vincent) "A Classic Case," *Temperatures Rising* (also known as *The New Temperatures Rising Show*), ABC, 1973.

Teleplays; Pilots:
Salt and Pepe, CBS, 1975.

Look Out, World, NBC, 1977.

The San Pedro Bums (also known as *The San Pedro Beach Bums*), ABC, 1977.

Novels:
Mafia Summer, Bloomsbury USA, 2005.

Black Widow, Bloomsbury USA, 2007.

W

WACHS, Caitlin 1989–

PERSONAL

Full name, Caitlin Elizabeth Wachs; born March 15, 1989, in Eugene, OR (some sources cite Los Angeles, CA); daughter of Allan and Patrice Wachs. *Avocational Interests:* Swimming, bicycling, dancing, singing, traveling.

Addresses: *Agent*—International Creative Management, 10250 Constellation Way, 9th Floor, Los Angeles, CA 90067. *Publicist*—Jeff Raymond, Rogers and Cowan Public Relations, Pacific Design Center, 7th Floor, 8687 Melrose Ave., Los Angeles, CA 90069.

Career: Actress. Appeared in more than fifty television commercials, including work for Mattel toys, Dial soap, McDonald's restaurants, and Gap Kids clothing line; also worked as a model.

Awards, Honors: Young Artist Award nomination, best supporting young actress age ten or under in a television comedy or drama, 1997, YoungStar Award nomination, best young actress in a television drama series, *Hollywood Reporter,* 1998, and Young Artist Award nomination, best supporting young actress in a television drama series, 1998, 1999, all for *Profiler;* Young Artist Award nomination, best guest starring young actress in a television comedy series, 1999, for *To Have & to Hold;* Young Artist Award nomination, best guest starting young actress in a television drama series, for *The Pretender;* Young Artist Award (with others), best young ensemble in a feature film or television movie, 2000, for *Shiloh 2: Shiloh Season;* Young Artist Award nomination, best supporting young actress in a television movie comedy, 2001, for *Phantom of the Megaplex;* Young Artist Award nomination, best supporting young actress in a feature film, and Young Artist Award (with others), best ensemble in a feature film, both 2001, for *My Dog Skip;* Young Artist Award nomination (with others), best ensemble in a television series, 2003, for *Family Affair;* DVD Premiere Award nomination, best actress, DVD Exclusive Awards, 2003, for *Air Bud: Seventh Inning Fetch;* DVDX Award nomination, best supporting actress in a DVD premiere movie, DVD Exclusive Awards, 2003, for *Inspector Gadget 2;* Young Artist Award nomination, best supporting young actress in a television drama series, 2006, for *Commander in Chief.*

CREDITS

Film Appearances:
Dara Lynn Preston, *Shiloh 2: Shiloh Season* (also known as *Shiloh 2: A Dog's Tale* and *Shiloh 2: Shiloh Season*), Warner Bros., 1999.

Rivers Applewhite, *My Dog Skip,* Warner Bros., 2000.

Rachel, *The Next Best Thing,* Paramount, 2000.

Kathy O'Donnell, *Thirteen Days,* New Line Cinema, 2000.

Andrea Framm, *Air Bud: World Pup* (also known as *Air Bud 3* and *Tobby III: Le chien etoile*), Miramax Home Entertainment, 2000.

Andrea Framm, *Air Bud: Seventh Inning Fetch* (also known as *Tobby, le frappeur etoile*), Miramax Home Entertainment, 2001.

Vivi Abbott as a child, *Divine Secrets of the Ya–Ya Sisterhood,* Warner Bros., 2002.

Penny, *Inspector Gadget 2* (also known as *IG2*), Buena Vista, 2003.

Katie Carmichael, *Kids in America,* Slowhand Cinema Releasing, 2005.

Anne, *Endless Bummer,* Lighthouse Entertainment/Vans Warped Tour, 2008.

Mary Worth, *The Legend of Bloody Mary,* Grindstone Entertainment Group, 2008.

Jill, *Privileged,* Glass House Productions, 2009.

Alyssa, *Way of the Dolphin,* Quantum Releasing, 2009.

Television Appearances; Series:
Chloe Waters, *Profiler*, NBC, 1996–98.
Anna McGrail, *To Have & To Hold*, CBS, 1998.
Sigourney "Sissy" Davis, *Family Affair*, The WB, 2002–2003.
Chloe Shackleton, *Cracking Up*, Fox, 2004–2006.
Rebecca Calloway, *Commander in Chief*, ABC, 2005–2006.

Television Appearances; Movies:
Molly, *Shattered Mind* (also known as *The Terror Inside*), NBC, 1996.
Amy, *Race against Time: The Search for Sarah*, CBS, 1996.
Karen Riley, *Phantom of the Megaplex*, The Disney Channel, 2000.

Television Appearances; Pilots:
Anna McGrail, *To Have & To Hold*, CBS, 1998.
Sigourney "Sissy" Davis, *Family Affair*, The WB, 2002.
Chloe Shackleton, *Cracking Up*, Fox, 2004.
Rebecca Calloway, *Commander in Chief*, ABC, 2005.

Television Appearances; Specials:
National Memorial Day Concert, PBS, 2008.

Television Appearances; Episodic:
Penny Jillette, "Save the Last Trance for Me," *The Fresh Prince of Bel–Air*, NBC, 1995.
Bridgit Forrester, *The Bold and the Beautiful* (also known as *Belleza y poder*), CBS, 1995.
Annie Anderson, "Home," *Early Edition*, CBS, 1997.
Faith Parker, "At the Hour of Our Death," *The Pretender*, NBC, 1999.
Young Brooke, "Slumber Party Massacre," *Popular*, The WB, 1999.
Grace Frame, "The Wee Hours," *Judging Amy*, CBS, 2000.
Chloe, "Play Dead, Clown," *Shasta McNasty* (also known as *Shasta*), UPN, 2000.
Herself, "Malibu Charity Bash," *I Married a Princess*, Lifetime, 2005.
Angelique Burcell, "Pro–Life," *Masters of Horror*, Showtime, 2006.
Cat Crosby, "Love Triangle," *Shark*, CBS, 2006.

Stage Appearances:
Appeared in *Carbondale Dreams*, Sanford Meisner Center Theatre, Los Angeles.

RECORDINGS

Videos:
Disney Sing–Along–Songs: Beach Party at Walt Disney World, Walt Disney, 1995.

Behind the Scenes of "Inspector Gadget 2" (also known as *The Making of "Inspector Gadget 2"*), Buena Vista Home Video, 2003.

Appeared in music videos by Gladys Knight and Santana.

WALKER, Kelly

PERSONAL

Born in Brisbane, Australia; daughter of Ross and Kathryn.

Career: Actress. Appeared in commercials.

Awards, Honors: In The Bin Festival Award, best actress, In The Bin Short Film Awards, 2004, for *Now*.

CREDITS

Film Appearances:
Brittany Dantel, *The List*, Milknose Films, 2004.
Shawna DeCert, *Signed in Blood*, Milknose Films, 2006.
Stephanie, *The Gift A.D.*, Samson Entertainment, 2006.
Mary, *Man Alive*, Milknose Films, 2007.
Analyst number two, *Boogeyman 2* (video), Sony Pictures Home Entertainment, 2007.
Chloe, *Deserted: The Ultimate Special Deluxe Director's Version of the Platinum Limited Edition Collection of the Online Micro–Series* (video), Skelligs Productions, 2007.
Zoe Twill, *Slight of Life*, Angerman Distribution, 2008.
Impact Point, Sony, 2008.

Television Appearances; Episodic:
Maura, "Carrie Kelly," *Diary of an Affair*, Style, 2004.

Also appeared as girl number one, in "Everybody Hates Varsity Jackets," *Everybody Hates Chris*, UPN.

Television Appearances; Miniseries:
Cheerleader, *Mr. Robinson's Driving School*, 2007.

Stage Appearances:
Appeared as lead in *In Truth*, AAA Showcase; *The Mikado*, Somerville House; lead role, *Hotel Chicago*.

WALSH, M. Emmet 1935–
(Emmet Walsh)

PERSONAL

Full name, Michael Emmet Walsh; born March 22, 1935, in Ogdensburg, NY; son of Harry Maurice, Sr. (a customs agent) and Agnes Kathrine (maiden name, Sullivan) Walsh. *Education:* Thomas S. Clarkson Memorial College of Technology (now Clarkson University), bachelor's degree in business administration, 1958; trained for the stage at the American Academy of Dramatic Arts, 1959–61.

Addresses: *Agent*—Don Buchwald & Associates, 6500 Wilshire Blvd., Suite 2200, Los Angeles, CA 90048; Metropolitan Talent Agency, 4526 Wilshire Blvd., Los Angeles, CA 90010; *Manager*—SLJ Management, 8265 West Sunset Blvd., Suite 203, West Hollywood, CA 90046.

Career: Actor. University of Kentucky, Lexington, KY, artist–in–residence, 1966; University of Tulsa, Tulsa, OK, artist–in–residence, 1983.

Member: Actors' Equity Association, Screen Actors Guild, American Federation of Radio and Television Artists, Academy of Motion Picture Arts and Sciences, Academy of Television Arts and Sciences, Players Club.

Awards, Honors: Independent Spirit Award, best actor, Independent Feature Project/West, 1986, for *Blood Simple.;* Best Ensemble Cast Award (with others), Method Festival, 2007, for *Man in the Chair.*

CREDITS

Film Appearances:
Group W sergeant, *Alice's Restaurant,* United Artists, 1969.
(Uncredited) *Midnight Cowboy,* United Artists, 1969.
Stiletto, Avco–Embassy Pictures, 1969.
Crab man and tutu man, *End of the Road,* Allied Artists, 1970.
Shotgun guard, *Little Big Man,* National General, 1970.
Warden Brodski, *The Traveling Executioner,* Metro–Goldwyn–Mayer, 1970.
Loving, Columbia, 1970.
Art, *Cold Turkey,* United Artists, 1971.
First sanitation man, *They Might Be Giants,* Universal, 1971.
General Winthrop's aide, *Escape from the Planet of the Apes,* Twentieth Century–Fox, 1971.

Arresting officer, *What's Up, Doc?,* Warner Bros., 1972.
Mr. Wendell, *Get to Know Your Rabbit,* Warner Bros., 1972.
Barber, *Kid Blue,* Twentieth Century–Fox, 1973.
Gallagher, *Serpico,* Paramount, 1973.
Las Vegas gambler, *The Gambler,* Paramount, 1974.
Door man, *The Prisoner of Second Avenue,* Warner Bros., 1975.
Harold, *At Long Last Love,* Twentieth Century–Fox, 1975.
Bus driver, *Mikey and Nicky,* Paramount, 1976.
"Father" Logan, *Nickelodeon,* Columbia, 1976.
Husband in trailer automobile, *Bound for Glory,* United Artists, 1976.
Dickie Dunn, *Slap Shot,* Universal, 1977.
Dr. Williams, *Airport '77* (also known as *Airport 1977* and *Airport 77*), Universal, 1977.
Earl Frank, *Straight Time,* Warner Bros., 1978.
Madman, *The Jerk,* Universal, 1979.
Wally Cantrell, *The Fish That Saved Pittsburgh,* United Artists, 1979.
Albert "Vinnie" Giordino, *Raise the Titanic,* Associated Film Distributors, 1980.
C. P. Woodward, *Brubaker,* Twentieth Century–Fox, 1980.
Coach Salan, *Ordinary People,* Paramount, 1980.
Arthur, *Back Roads* (also known as *Love with a Sinner*), Warner Bros., 1981.
Speaker at the Liberal Club, *Reds,* Paramount, 1981.
Captain Bryant, *Blade Runner,* Warner Bros., 1982, director's cut and final cut also released.
Fritz, *The Escape Artist,* Warner Bros., 1982.
Mack, *Cannery Row* (also known as *John Steinbeck's "Cannery Row"*), Metro–Goldwyn–Mayer/United Artists, 1982.
Sergeant Sanger, *Fast–Walking,* Pickman Films, 1982.
Walt Yarborough, *Silkwood,* Twentieth Century–Fox, 1983.
Burns, *The Pope of Greenwich Village* (also known as *Village Dreams*), Metro–Goldwyn–Mayer/United Artists, 1984.
Colonel Crouse, *Raw Courage* (also known as *Courage*), New World Pictures, 1984.
Dr. Dolan, *Fletch,* Universal, 1984.
Mr. Clark, *Grandview, U.S.A.,* Warner Bros., 1984.
Private detective Visser, *Blood Simple.* (also known as *Blood Simple* and *Blood Simple: The Thriller*), Circle Films, 1984, director's cut also released.
Simon Reynolds, *Scandalous,* Orion, 1984.
Tuck, *Missing in Action,* Cannon, 1984.
Charlie, *The Best of Times,* Universal, 1986.
Coach Turnbull, *Back to School,* Orion, 1986.
Harv, *Critters,* New Line Cinema, 1986.
Walt Coes, *Wildcats* (also known as *First and Goal*), Warner Bros., 1986.
Captain Haun, *No Man's Land,* Orion, 1987.
George Henderson, Sr., *Harry and the Hendersons* (also known as *Bigfoot* and *Bigfoot and the Hendersons*), Universal, 1987.

Machine shop worker, *Raising Arizona,* Twentieth Century–Fox, 1987.

Chief Dibner, *Sunset* (also known as *Catalina*), TriStar, 1988.

Governor, *The Milagro Beanfield War,* Universal, 1988.

Richard Dirks, *Clean and Sober,* Warner Bros., 1988.

Colin Detweiler, *War Party* (also known as *War Game*), TriStar, 1989.

Dewey Ferguson, *Red Scorpion* (also known as *Red Exterminator*), Shapiro Glickenhaus Entertainment, 1989.

Johnny Phatmun, *Catch Me If You Can* (also known as *Heart Power*), Management Company Entertainment Group, 1989.

Wedge (truck driving evangelist), *Thunderground* (also known as *Boxcar Blues*), Shapiro Glickenhaus Entertainment, 1989.

Miller, *The Mighty Quinn* (also known as *Big Bad Man, Finding Maubee,* and *Jamaica Cop*), Metro–Goldwyn–Mayer, 1990.

Morris, *Chattahoochee,* Hemdale Releasing, 1990.

Sergeant Dominick Benti, *Narrow Margin,* TriStar, 1990.

Mort Bisby, *Sundown: The Vampire in Retreat* (also known as *Sundown*), Vestron Pictures, 1991.

Bert Gibson, *White Sands,* Warner Bros., 1992.

Sam (some sources cite John) Kane, *Killer Image* (also known as *Muerte dans l'objectif*), Groundstar Entertainment, 1992.

Calvin Murks, *The Music of Chance,* IRS Releasing, 1993.

Fire chief, *Wilder Napalm,* TriStar, 1993.

Pete Petosa, *Equinox* (also known as *Isimeria*), IRS Releasing, 1993.

Sheriff Bob, *Bitter Harvest,* Prism Entertainment, 1993.

Earl, *Relative Fear* (also known as *The Child*), 1994.

Hal, *The Glass Shield* (also known as *The Johnny Johnson Trial*), 1994.

T. R. Polk, *Camp Nowhere,* Buena Vista, 1994.

(Uncredited) *Cops and Robbersons,* TriStar, 1994.

Dorsett, *Panther,* Gramercy Pictures, 1995.

Martin, *Criminal Hearts* (also known as *High Desert Run*), Libra Home Entertainment, 1995.

Sergeant Miller Hoskins, *Dead Badge,* 1995.

Wilcox, *Free Willy 2: The Adventure Home* (also known as *Free Willy 2*), Warner Bros., 1995.

Apothecary, *Romeo + Juliet* (also known as *Romeo and Juliet* and *William Shakespeare's "Romeo + Juliet"*), Twentieth Century–Fox, 1996.

(Uncredited) Dr. Willard Tyrell "W. T." Bass (psychologist), *A Time to Kill,* Warner Bros., 1996.

Raymond Garrison, *Portraits of a Killer* (also known as *Portraits of Innocence*), Live Entertainment, 1996.

Sheriff Foley, *The Killing Jar,* Curb Entertainment, 1996.

Dino, *Albino Alligator,* 1996, Miramax, 1997.

Joe O'Neal, *My Best Friend's Wedding,* TriStar, 1997.

Sam, *Retroactive,* Orion Pictures Entertainment, 1997.

Dean, *Me and Will,* Bedford Entertainment, 1998.

Freemont, *Chairman of the Board,* Trimark Pictures, 1998.

Lester Ivar, *Twilight* (also known as *The Magic Hour*), Paramount, 1998.

Marshal Phillips, *Nightmare in Big Sky Country* (also known as *Strangers in a Small Town*), ABC Pictures Corporation, 1998.

Ralph Worth, *Erasable You,* Dorian Films, 1998.

Coleman, *Wild Wild West,* Warner Bros., 1999.

Commissioner Menlo Boyce, *Jack of Hearts,* 1999.

(Uncredited) Marvin, *Random Hearts,* Columbia, 1999.

Voice of Earl Stutz, *The Iron Giant* (animated), Warner Bros., 1999.

Baggage, Cinewave Productions/Terence Michael Productions, 1999.

Coach Cook, *Eyeball Eddie,* Pupil Productions, 2000.

Judge Pike, *Poor White Trash,* Hollywood Independents/Xenon Entertainment Group, 2000.

Stu O'Malley, *Christmas in the Clouds,* Random Ventures/Stockbridge Munsee Band of Mohican Indians, 2000.

George, *Snow Dogs,* Buena Vista, 2002.

Walt Scheel, *Christmas with the Kranks* (also known as *John Grisham's "Skipping Christmas"* and *Skipping the Holidays*), Columbia, 2004.

Woodzie, *Racing Stripes,* Warner Bros., 2005.

Lew Popper, *Big Stan,* Metro–Goldwyn–Mayer, 2007.

Mickey Hopkins, *Man in the Chair,* Outsider Pictures, 2007.

Chuck Ireland, *Chasing 3000,* Pretty Dangerous Films/Velocity Pictures, 2008.

Hoyt, *Sherman's Way,* Starry Night Entertainment, 2008.

Kroger, *Your Name Here,* MEB Entertainment/Raz Entertainment, 2008.

Lance McKyle, *Roney's Point,* Birds–Eye Media, 2008.

Muggs, *Greener Mountains,* Allumination Filmworks, 2008.

Neil, *Haunted Echoes* (also known as *Darkness Visible*), Mainline Releasing, 2008.

Mr. Beudreaux, *The Assignment,* New Movie Group, 2009.

Samuel, *Don McKay,* 2009.

Youth in Revolt, Lions Gate Films, 2009.

Television Appearances; Series:

Gabe McCutcheon, *Nichols* (also known as *James Garner as Nichols*), NBC, 1971–72.

Alex Lambert (some sources say Lembeck), *The Sandy Duncan Show,* CBS, 1972.

Police chief Demsey, *Amy Prentiss,* NBC, 1974–75.

Captain Mike Gorcey, *Dear Detective,* CBS, 1979.

Ned Platt, *Unsub* (also known as *Unknown Subject* and *UNSUB*), NBC, 1989.

Henry Allen, *The Flash,* CBS, c. 1990–91.

Coach, *Dogs,* ABC, 1997–98.

Voice of Mack, *Big Guy and Rusty the Boy Robot* (animated), Fox and Family Channel, 1999–2001.

Randall Evans, *The Mind of the Married Man* (also known as *My Dirty Little Mind*), HBO, 2001–2002.

Television Appearances; Miniseries:
Harry, *The French Atlantic Affair,* ABC, 1979.
Sheriff Horace Quinn, *John Steinbeck's "East of Eden"* (also known as *East of Eden*), ABC, 1981.
Detective Sam Davies, *The Deliberate Stranger,* NBC, 1986.
Vern Humphrey, *Murder Ordained* (also known as *Broken Commandments* and *Kansas Gothic*), CBS, 1987.
Hardy, *Brotherhood of the Rose,* NBC, 1989.
Voice, *The Civil War* (documentary; also known as *The American Civil War*), PBS, 1990.
Voice, *Baseball* (documentary; also known as *The History of Baseball*), PBS, 1994.
Voice, *The Way West* (documentary), broadcast as part of *The American Experience,* PBS, 1995.
Voice, *The West* (documentary), PBS, 1996.

Television Appearances; Movies:
The Law, NBC, 1974.
Panic on Page One, ABC, 1974.
Mr. Peterson, *Sarah T.—Portrait of a Teenage Alcoholic,* NBC, 1975.
Irvine, *The Invasion of Johnson County* (also known as *Brahmin*), NBC, 1976.
Sheriff Sweeney, *Red Alert,* CBS, 1977.
McCartney, *A Question of Guilt,* CBS, 1978.
Whitley, *Superdome,* ABC, 1978.
DeFranco, *No Other Love,* CBS, 1979.
Legion commander, *The Gift,* CBS, 1979.
Mrs. R's Daughter, NBC, 1979.
Harold Patton, *High Noon, Part II: The Return of Will Kane* (also known as *High Noon, Part II* and *The Return of Will Kane*), CBS, 1980.
Sheldon Lewis, *City in Fear,* ABC, 1980.
General Presser, "Hero in the Family," *The Disney Sunday Movie* (also known as *Disneyland, Disneylandia, Disney's Wonderful World, The Magical World of Disney, Walt Disney, Walt Disney Presents, Walt Disney's Wonderful World of Color,* and *The Wonderful World of Disney*), ABC, 1986.
Mayor, *The Right of the People,* ABC, 1986.
Detective Mulligan, *Broken Vows* (also known as *Hennessey* and *Where the Dark Streets Go*), CBS, 1987.
Don Nichols, *The Abduction of Kari Swenson* (also known as *Innocent Prey* and *Open Season*), NBC, 1987.
Clyde Wilson, *Love and Lies* (also known as *The Kim Paris Story* and *True Betrayal*), ABC, 1990.
Harry, *Fourth Story* (also known as *Basic Deception* and *Deadly Identity*), Showtime, 1991.
Mayor Thornbush, *Four Eyes and Six–Guns,* TNT, 1992.
Mose, *Wild Card* (also known as *Preacher*), USA Network, 1992.
Garcia and Gesundheim, *The Naked Truth,* Cinemax, 1993.
Sadler, *Probable Cause* (also known as *Sleepless*), Showtime, 1994.

Morris, *From the Mixed–Up Files of Mrs. Basil E. Frankweiler,* ABC, 1995.
Rudolph Thorndyke, *Madness of Method,* 1996.
Sheriff, *The Lottery,* NBC, 1996.
Sam, *Retroactive,* HBO, 1997.
Junior assistant dispatch trainee Stanley Snyder, *Men in White* (also known as *National Lampoon's "Men in White"*), Fox Family Channel, 1998.
Lloyd, *Monster!,* UPN, 1999.

Television Appearances; Specials:
Joe Lempke, "The Woman Who Willed a Miracle," *ABC Afterschool Specials,* ABC, 1983.
Rocco, "The Adventures of Con Sawyer and Hucklemary Finn," *ABC Weekend Specials,* ABC, 1985.
Earl Crockett, *Rich Hall's "Vanishing America"* (also known as *Vanishing America*), Showtime, 1986.
Sarge, "Resting Place," *Hallmark Hall of Fame,* CBS, 1986.
Himself, *On the Edge of Blade Runner,* Channel 4 (England), 2000.
Himself, *AFI's 100 Years, 100 Thrills: America's Most Heart–Pounding Movies,* CBS, 2001.

Television Appearances; Episodic:
"Who's Got the Bundle?," *N.Y.P.D.,* ABC, 1969.
Cliff, "To Buy or Not to Buy?," *Arnie,* CBS, 1970.
Billy, "The Saga of Cousin Oscar," *All in the Family* (also known as *Justice for All* and *Those Were the Days*), CBS, 1971.
Gus Anderson, "Courting Time," *Julia,* NBC, 1971.
Lionel Atkins, "Another Day, Another Scholar," *The Jimmy Stewart Show,* NBC, 1971.
(As Emmet Walsh) Mattheson, "Warbonnet," *Bonanza* (also known as *Ponderosa*), NBC, 1971.
Telegraph clerk, "Dear Fran …," *Ironside* (also known as *The Raymond Burr Show*), NBC, 1971.
Arthur Kingston, "Janie's Kitchen," *The Don Rickles Show,* CBS, 1972.
Officer Ames, "Buried Alive," *McMillan & Wife* (also known as *McMillan*), NBC, 1974.
David Fletcher, "The Venture," *The Waltons,* CBS, 1975.
Edgar Burch, "Counter Gambit," *The Rockford Files* (also known as *Jim Rockford, Jim Rockford, Private Investigator,* and *Rockford*), NBC, 1975.
Potter, "The Secret of Terry Lake," *Baretta,* ABC, 1975.
"Accounts Receivable," *Kate McShane,* CBS, 1975.
Lloyd Herman Eckworth, "Vendetta (a.k.a. The Monster)," *Starsky and Hutch,* ABC, 1976.
McDade, "Dead Man Out," *Baretta,* ABC, 1976.
"Afternoon Waltz," *Gibbsville,* NBC, 1976.
The Nancy Walker Show, ABC, 1976.
Freddie, "The Action," *Starsky and Hutch,* ABC, 1978.
Callahan, "Chicago," *Little House on the Prairie* (also known as *Little House: A New Beginning*), NBC, 1981.
Detective Underhill, "Ghostwriter," *The Hitchhiker* (also known as *Deadly Nightmares* and *Le voyageur*), HBO, 1985.

Peter, "Dealer's Choice," *The Twilight Zone* (also known as *Twilight Zone* and *The Twilight Zone: The Original Series*), CBS, 1985.

Grandpa Norman, "Magic Saturday," *Amazing Stories* (also known as *Steven Spielberg's "Amazing Stories"*), NBC, 1986.

Jonas, "Collection Completed," *Tales from the Crypt* (also known as *HBO's "Tales from the Crypt"*), HBO, 1987.

Arlen Thomas, "Aloha, Io–wahu," *The Jackie Thomas Show,* ABC, 1993.

Colonel Patterson, "The Colonel," *Home Improvement* (also known as *Hammer Time* and *Tool Time*), ABC, 1994.

Colonel Patterson, "'Twas the Night before Chaos," *Home Improvement* (also known as *Hammer Time* and *Tool Time*), ABC, 1994.

(In archive footage) Kane, *Joe Bob's Drive–In Theater,* The Movie Channel, 1994.

Sanford Valle, "The Refuge," *The Outer Limits* (also known as *The New Outer Limits*), Showtime, Sci–Fi Channel, and syndicated, 1996.

Santa, "Christmas," *Early Edition,* CBS, 1996.

Voice of Buck Strickland, "The Company Man," *King of the Hill* (animated), Fox, 1997.

Jimmy Duff, "Sports," *Tracey Takes On ...,* HBO, 1998.

Jimmy Duff, "The Best of 'Tracey Takes On ...,' Season 3," *Tracey Takes On ...,* HBO, 1998.

Arthur Dales, "The Unnatural," *The X–Files,* Fox, 1999.

Voice of first gemsbok, "Rain Dance," *The Wild Thornberrys* (animated; also known as *The Thornberrys*), Nickelodeon, 1999.

Aubrey Lang, "The Book of Danny," *Cover Me: Based on the True Life of an FBI Family* (also known as *Cover Me* and *FBI Family*), USA Network, 2000.

Dr. Joe Kroft, "Roll out the Barrel," *NYPD Blue,* ABC, 2000.

Dr. Matthews, "A Routine Case," *Gideon's Crossing,* ABC, 2000.

Mayor Kendricks, "Home Is Where the Ducks Are," *Ed* (also known as *Stuckeyville*), NBC, 2000.

Gus, "Reunion," *Night Visions,* Fox, 2001.

Richard "Rich" Koechner, "Bully for Martin," *Frasier* (also known as *Dr. Frasier Crane*), NBC, 2001.

Voice of Jeb, "A Scooby–Doo Christmas," *What's New, Scooby–Doo?* (animated), The WB, 2002, released on video as *Merry Scary Holiday* (also known as *Volume 4: Merry Scary Holiday*).

Cubby, "New Kid in School," *Charlie Lawrence,* CBS, 2003.

Ezra Pence, "Big Coal," *The Guardian* (also known as *El guardia, The Guardian—Retter mit Herz, Le protecteur, O allos mou eaftos, Ochita bengoshi Nick Fallin, Ochita bengoshi Nick Fallin 2,* and *Oikeuden puolesta*), CBS, 2003.

Himself, "Racing Stripes," *Only in LA,* 2005.

Also appeared in other programs, including *AfterMash* (also known as *AfterMASH* and *AfterM*A*S*H*), CBS; *The Cop and the Kid,* NBC; *The Doctors,* NBC; *Joe and Sons,* CBS; *Love of Life,* CBS; *Mary Hartman, Mary Hartman,* syndicated; *Men at Law* (also known as *The Storefront Lawyers*), CBS; *The Mississippi,* CBS; *Prudential's "On Stage"; The Texas Wheelers,* ABC; and *The Tony Randall Show,* ABC and CBS.

Television Appearances; Pilots:

Jack Hoover, "P–I–L–O–T," *The Bob Newhart Show,* CBS, 1972.

Mr. Wallace, *Doctor Dan,* CBS, 1974.

Lieutenant Jack Doyle, *Crime Club,* CBS, 1975.

Captain Mike Gorcey, *Dear Detective,* CBS, 1979.

Moran, *Skag,* NBC, 1980.

Mr. Graebner, *Hellinger's Law,* CBS, 1981.

Officer Joe Kirby, *Night Partners,* CBS, 1983.

Warden MacDonald, *The Outlaws,* ABC, 1983.

Samuel Lynn, *You Are the Jury,* NBC, 1984.

Bear Werner, *The City,* ABC, 1986.

Ned Platt, *Unsub* (also known as *Unknown Subject* and *UNSUB*), NBC, 1989.

Henry Allen, *The Flash,* CBS, 1990.

Charles Blankenship, *Silverfox* (also known as *Double Old 7* and *Our Man James*), ABC, 1991.

Mr. Walgrave, *The Nerd,* NBC, 1996.

Randall Evans, *The Mind of the Married Man* (also known as *My Dirty Little Mind*), HBO, 2001.

Wally Westland, *Tracey Ullman in the Trailer Tales,* HBO, 2003.

Appeared as Jack Hoover in the original pilot for *The Bob Newhart Show,* CBS.

Stage Appearances:

Shepards of the Shelf, Blackfriars Theatre, New York City, 1961.

Citizen of Boston, *My Kinsman Major Molineux,* and American sailor, *Benito Cereno,* both produced as part of *The Old Glory* (double–bill), American Place Theatre, New York City, 1964.

The Outside Man, American Place Theatre, 1964.

Bill Leap, *The Death of the Well–Loved Boy,* St. Mark's Playhouse, New York City, 1967.

Three from Column A, Theatre 73, New York City, 1968.

Ringo, *Does a Tiger Wear a Necktie?,* Belasco Theatre, New York City, 1969.

George Sikowski, *That Championship Season,* Booth Theatre, New York City, 1973.

Are You Now or Have You Ever Been?, Ford's Theatre, Washington, DC, then Los Angeles, both 1975.

Dodge, *Buried Child,* National Theatre, Lyttelton Theatre, London, 2004.

Appeared in productions at other venues, including the College Theatre, American Academy of Dramatic Arts, 1954–61; Bucks County Playhouse, New Hope, PA, 1962; Brattleboro Summer Theatre, Brattleboro, VT,

1963; Caravan Theatre, Dorset, CT, 1964; Theatre of the Living Arts, Philadelphia, PA, 1965; Studio Arena Theatre, Buffalo, NY, 1966; Long Wharf Theatre, New Haven, CT, 1967; Berkshire Theatre Festival, Stockbridge, MA, 1967–70; Vermont Summer Theatre Festival, Johnson, VT, 1974; and the Santa Barbara Theatre Festival, Santa Barbara, CA, 1985.

Stage Work:

Production assistant, *The Beauty Part,* Music Box Theatre, New York City, 1962.

RECORDINGS

Videos:

(In archive footage) Bryant, *Blade Runner: Deleted and Alternate Scenes,* Warner Home Video, 2007.

Himself, *Dangerous Days: Making Blade Runner* (also known as *Dangerous Days*), Warner Home Video, 2007.

OTHER SOURCES

Periodicals:

Shock Cinema, issue 22, 2003, pp. 8–11.

WALTER, Tracey 1942(?)–
(Tracy Walter, Tracey Walters)

PERSONAL

Born November 25, 1942 (some sources cite 1947), in Jersey City, NJ; father, a truck driver. *Education:* Attended high school in Jersey City, NJ; studied acting with David Le Grant.

Addresses: *Agent*—Stone Manners Talent and Literary, 6500 Wilshire Blvd., Suite 550, Los Angeles, CA 90048; Kazarian, Spencer & Associates (KSA), 11969 Ventura Blvd., Third Floor, Studio City, CA 91604; Cunningham–Escott–Slevin–Doherty (CESD) Talent Agency, 10635 Santa Monica Blvd., Suite 130, Los Angeles, CA 90025.

Career: Actor. Totem Pole Playhouse, Fayetteville, PA, apprentice; appeared in advertisements. Appeared on the back cover of the Aerosmith album *A Little South of Sanity,* Geffen, 1998. Worked in a auto parts store in Jersey City, NJ.

Awards, Honors: Saturn Award, best supporting actor, Academy of Science Fiction, Fantasy & Horror Films, 1985, for *Repo Man;* Method Fest Award (with others), best ensemble cast, 2007, for *Man in the Chair.*

CREDITS

Film Appearances:

Ginger's brother, *Ginger,* Joseph Brenner Associates, 1971.

(As Tracy Walter) Delivery person, *Badge 373,* Paramount, 1973.

(Uncredited) Street urchin, *Serpico,* Paramount, 1973.

Actor in Rob's television show, *Annie Hall* (also known as *Anhedonia, It Had to Be Jew,* and *A Roller Coaster Named Desire*), United Artists, 1977.

Coogan, *Goin' South,* Paramount, 1978.

Union member, *Blue Collar,* Universal, 1978.

Male teller, *Hardcore* (also known as *The Hardcore Life*), Columbia, 1979.

(Uncredited) Mr. Beedy, *The Octagon* (also known as *The Man without Mercy*), 1980.

Psychiatric patient, *The Fifth Floor,* Film Ventures International, 1980.

Rocco Mason, *The Hunter,* Paramount, 1980.

Space, *Getting Wasted* (also known as *Soft Explosion*), Diversified Film Distribution, 1980.

Arnold, *Raggedy Man,* Universal, 1981.

Police officer, *The Hand,* Warner Bros., 1981.

Pooch, *Honkytonk Man,* Warner Bros., 1982.

Carl Dorsett, *Timerider: The Adventures of Lyle Swann* (also known as *Timerider*), 1982, Jensen Farley Pictures, 1983.

First alley mugger, *Rumble Fish,* MCA/Universal, 1983.

Groom, *The Horse Dealer's Daughter,* 1983.

Malak, *Conan the Destroyer,* Universal, 1984.

Miller, *Repo Man,* Universal, 1984.

The country squire, *Something Wild,* Orion, 1985.

Patch, *At Close Range,* Orion, 1986.

Calvin Bollard, *Malone,* Orion, 1987.

Diner counter man, *Midnight Run,* Universal, 1988.

Don Dickson, *Mortuary Academy,* RCA–Columbia/Taurus Entertainment, 1988.

Mr. Chicken Lickin', *Married to the Mob,* Orion, 1988.

Lieutenant Frank Meyers, *Out of the Dark,* Asso Film, 1988, New Line Cinema, 1989.

Dusty, *The Cowboy and the Frenchman* (short film), Erato Films/Figaro Films/Socpress, broadcast on the television program *Les francais vu par ...* (also known as *The French as Seen by ...*), [France], c. 1988, included in *The Short Films of David Lynch,* 2002.

Bob the goon, *Batman,* Warner Bros., 1989.

Homeless person, *Under the Boardwalk,* New World Pictures, 1989.

Tommy Dearly, *Homer & Eddie,* Skouras Pictures, 1989.

Beever Smith, *Young Guns II* (also known as *Hell Bent for Leather* and *Young Guns II: Blaze of Glory*), Twentieth Century–Fox, 1990.

Exterminator, *Pacific Heights,* Twentieth Century–Fox, 1990.

(Scenes deleted) Traveller, *Wild at Heart* (also known as *David Lynch's "Wild at Heart"* and *Sailor & Lula*), Samuel Goldwyn Company, 1990.

Tyrone Otley, *The Two Jakes,* Paramount, 1990.

Cookie, *City Slickers,* Columbia, 1991.

Hotel desk clerk, *Delusion,* IRS Releasing, 1991.

Lamar, *The Silence of the Lambs,* Orion, 1991.

Cecil, *Liquid Dreams,* Northern Arts Entertainment, 1992.

Elton, *Guncrazy,* First Look Pictures Releasing, 1992.

Bloodhound Bob, *Amos & Andrew,* Columbia, 1993.

Elton Spoole, *Public Enemy #2,* Imagination Productions, 1993.

Librarian, *Philadelphia* (also known as *At Risk* and *People Like Us*), TriStar, 1993.

Wild Card, *Cyborg 2* (also known as *Cyborg 2: Glass Shadow* and *Glass Shadow*), Trimark Pictures, 1993.

(Uncredited) Janitor with information, *Junior,* Universal, 1994.

Television repairperson, *Mona Must Die* (also known as *Ein Fast perfektes Verhaeltnis*), Carolco Pictures/ Mona Must Die Productions, 1994.

Pappy, *Destiny Turns on the Radio* (also known as *Johnny Destiny* and *Mister Destiny*), Savoy Pictures, 1995.

Paul McCarthy, *Fist of the North Star* (also known as *Hokuto no Ken*), Overseas FilmGroup, 1995.

Angel number 85, *Teddy & Philomina,* 1996.

(Uncredited) Area 51 laboratory technician, *Independence Day* (also known as *ID4*), Twentieth Century–Fox, 1996.

Bill, *Matilda* (also known as *Roald Dahl's "Matilda"*), TriStar, 1996.

Hedgehog, *Drive* (also known as *Fugue*), Road to Ruin, 1996.

Joe Bennett, *Entertaining Angels: The Dorothy Day Story* (also known as *Entertaining Angels*), Paulist Pictures, 1996.

The vagrant, *The Size of Watermelons,* Norstar Entertainment, 1996.

Wee St. Francis, *Larger Than Life,* United Artists, 1996.

Amanda, Sony Pictures Entertainment, 1996.

(Uncredited) Clerk in bookstore, *Kiss the Girls,* Paramount, 1997.

Jim, *Playing God* (also known as *Playing Hero*), Buena Vista, 1997.

Leon, *Wild America* (also known as *Born to Be Wild*), Warner Bros., 1997.

Medical inmate, *Desperate Measures,* TriStar, 1998.

Security guard, *Mighty Joe Young* (also known as *Mighty Joe*), Buena Vista, 1998.

Slave catcher, *Beloved,* Buena Vista, 1998.

Jake, *Facade* (also known as *Death Valley*), Cinequanon Pictures International, 1999.

National Enquirer editor, *Man on the Moon* (also known as *Der Mondmann*), MCA/Universal, 1999.

Charles Embry, *Erin Brockovich,* MCA/Universal, 2000.

Clarence, *Drowning Mona,* Destination Films, 2000.

Zeke, *Blast,* Zeta Entertainment, 2000.

Bartender, *The Man from Elysian Fields,* Samuel Goldwyn Films, 2001.

Leon Gates, *Face Value,* Testimony Productions, 2001.

Mortician, *Jack the Dog,* 2001.

Professor Wood, *How High,* MCA/Universal, 2001.

Ben Franks, *Death to Smoochy* (also known as *Toetet Smoochy*), Warner Bros., 2002.

Mr. Siegel, *Imposter,* Miramax/Dimension Films, 2002.

Randy Myers, *Ted Bundy* (also known as *Bundy, Serial Killer: The True Story of Ted Bundy,* and *The Ted Bundy Story*), First Look International, 2002.

Desk clerk, *Masked and Anonymous,* Sony Pictures Classics, 2003.

Nicky, *One Last Ride,* Eclectic Entertainment, 2003.

Pharmacy customer, *Duplex* (also known as *Our House* and *Der Appartement–Schreck*), Miramax, 2003.

Night clerk, *The Manchurian Candidate,* Paramount, 2004.

Draft board doctor, *Berkeley,* Rivercoast Films, 2005.

Toupee salesperson, *Relative Strangers,* First Look International, 2006.

Mr. Klein, *Man in the Chair,* Outsider Pictures, 2007.

Mr. Whicks, *Wasting Away,* K5, 2007.

One–Way, *The Death and Life of Bobby Z* (also known as *Bobby Z* and *Kill Bobby Z—Ein Deal um Leben und Tod*), Millennium Films, 2007.

Simon Ahrens, *Nobel Son,* Freestyle Releasing, 2007.

Ancient trucker, *Trailer Park of Terror,* Summit Entertainment, 2008.

Clem, *Just Add Water* (also known as *One Part Sugar*), 2008.

Freddy, *Cat Dragged In* (short film), Shorts International, 2008.

Police officer, *The Perfect Game,* Lionsgate, 2008.

Roy White, *Dark Reel,* Barnholtz Entertainment, 2008.

Janitor, *Midnight Son,* c. 2008.

John Johnson, *Pickin' & Grinnin',* 2009.

Television Appearances; Series:

Frog Rothchild, Jr., *Best of the West,* ABC, 1981–82.

Blinky Watts, *On the Air,* ABC, 1992.

Angel, *Nash Bridges* (also known as *Nash*), CBS, 1996–2001.

Sheriff Walter Chechekevitch, *Reno 911!,* Comedy Central, 2003–2006.

Television Appearances; Miniseries:

Francis Bartley, *Ride with the Wind,* ABC, 1994.

Jim Ragg, *Buffalo Girls,* CBS, 1995.

Television Appearances; Movies:

Coley Turner, *Mad Bull* (also known as *The Aggressor*), CBS, 1977.

Harlan Tyler, *High Noon, Part II: The Return of Will Kane* (also known as *High Noon, Part II* and *The Return of Will Kane*), CBS, 1980.

Kenny, *Bill: On His Own* (also known as *Bill on His Own*), CBS, 1982.

Sam, *Timestalkers* (also known as *Time Stalkers*), CBS, 1987.

Henry, *Not of This World* (also known as *Shock Killer* and *Space Killers*), CBS, 1991.

Leo Mirita, *The Companion*, USA Network, 1994.

Oliver Tracy, *In the Line of Duty: Kidnapped* (also known as *Kidnapped: In the Line of Duty*), NBC, 1995.

(Uncredited) Ezra Hersch, *The Devil's Child*, ABC, 1997.

Sean Ferguson, *Tell Me No Secrets*, ABC, 1997.

(Uncredited) *The Inheritance* (also known as *Louisa May Alcott's "The Inheritance"*), CBS, 1997.

Attorney, *Manhood*, Showtime, 2003.

Morley Todd, *Monster Makers*, The Hallmark Channel, 2003.

Doc, *The Trail to Hope Rose*, The Hallmark Channel, 2004.

Lou, *Family Plan*, The Hallmark Channel, 2005.

Television Appearances; Specials:

Elton Spoole, *Public Enemy Number 2*, Showtime, 1991.

Leonard Eels, *Basic Values: Sex, Shock & Censorship in the 90s* (also known as *Sex, Shock & Censorship in the 90s*), Showtime, 1993.

Homeless man, *Jazz Night*, Lifetime, 1999.

Abominable snowman, *The Year without a Santa Claus*, NBC, 2006.

Television Appearances; Episodic:

(Credited as Tracey Walters) Leo, "Dandruff," *Starsky and Hutch*, ABC, 1978.

Jimmy Potter, "Mixed Blessings," *Vega$* (also known as *High Roller* and *Vegas*), ABC, 1979.

Second Don Pesola, "The Contest Nobody Could Win," *WKRP in Cincinnati*, CBS, 1979.

Clint Mason, "An Angel's Trail," *Charlie's Angels* (also known as *The Alley Cats*), ABC, 1980.

Alvin Essary, "Take This Job and Love It: Part 2," *Filthy Rich*, CBS, 1982.

Lucky, "Gold Fever," *Seven Brides for Seven Brothers*, CBS, 1982.

Sammy, "Shooter," *Hill Street Blues*, NBC, 1982.

Skip, "The Silent Partner," *The Fall Guy*, ABC, 1982.

Alvin Essary, "The Country Club," *Filthy Rich*, CBS, 1983.

Boone, "The Gang's All Here," *Cagney & Lacey*, CBS, 1983.

Panhandler, "A Grand Gesture," *Taxi*, ABC, 1983.

Willie Laporter, "Here's Adventure, Here's Romance," *Hill Street Blues*, NBC, 1983.

Archie O'Hare, "Pen Pals," *Hunter*, NBC, 1984.

Ezra, "Mummy, Daddy," *Amazing Stories* (also known as *Steven Spielberg's "Amazing Stories"*), NBC, 1985.

Alvin, "Wildfire," *Airwolf* (also known as *Blackwolf, Lonewolf, Supercopter,* and *Lobo del aire*), CBS, 1986.

Blaze, "The Wedding Ring," *Amazing Stories* (also known as *Steven Spielberg's "Amazing Stories"*), NBC, 1986.

Minister, "I Do, I Don't," *Designing Women*, CBS, 1986.

Arnie Steckler, "Cool Hand Dave: Parts 1 & 2," *Moonlighting*, ABC, 1987.

Gravel Gus, "Night Train," *ALF*, NBC, 1987.

Kayron, "The Last Outpost," *Star Trek: The Next Generation* (also known as *The Next Generation* and *Star Trek: TNG*), syndicated, 1987.

Malcolm, "Seams from a Marriage," *Designing Women*, CBS, 1987.

Mr. Woshinsky, "The Gospel Truth," *The Bronx Zoo*, NBC, 1988.

Mr. Woshinsky, "Ties That Bind," *The Bronx Zoo*, NBC, 1988.

Mr. Woshinsky, "Truancy Blues," *The Bronx Zoo*, NBC, 1988.

Dusty, *The Cowboy and the Frenchman* (short film), Erato Films/Figaro Films/Socpress, broadcast on the television program *Les francais vu par ...* (also known as *The French as Seen by ...*), [France], c. 1988, included in *The Short Films of David Lynch*, 2002.

Eugene Moss (a gravedigger), "Lucky Stiff," *Freddy's Nightmares* (also known as *Freddy's Nightmares: A Nightmare on Elm Street: The Series, Freddy, le cauchemar de vos nuits, Freddyn painajaiset, Las pesadillas de Freddy,* and *Les cauchemars de Freddy*), syndicated, 1989.

(Uncredited; in archive footage) Kayron, "Shades of Gray," *Star Trek: The Next Generation* (also known as *The Next Generation* and *Star Trek: TNG*), syndicated, 1989.

Tom Mulden, "The Takeover," *Alien Nation* (also known as *Spacecop L.A., Alien nacion,* and *Alien nation—ciudadanos del espacio*), Fox, 1989.

Eugene Moss (a gravedigger), "Easy Come, Easy Go," *Freddy's Nightmares* (also known as *Freddy's Nightmares: A Nightmare on Elm Street: The Series, Freddy, le cauchemar de vos nuits, Freddyn painajaiset, Las pesadillas de Freddy,* and *Les cauchemars de Freddy*), syndicated, 1990.

(As Tracy Walter) Ride operator, "Terror on the Hell Loop 2000," *Get a Life*, Fox, 1990.

"Desert Run," *Nasty Boys*, NBC, 1990.

Boris, "Bride of the Wolfman," *She–Wolf of London* (also known as *Love & Curses*), syndicated, 1991.

"Hostile Takeover," *Monsters*, syndicated, 1991.

Berik, "Rascals," *Star Trek: The Next Generation* (also known as *The Next Generation* and *Star Trek: TNG*), syndicated, 1992.

Tucker, "Two Jerks and a Jill," *Wings*, NBC, 1992.

Clerk, "Christmas," *The Mommies* (also known as *Mommies*), NBC, 1993.

Phil Swill, "Mail Order Brides," *The Adventures of Brisco County, Jr.* (also known as *Brisco Country, Jr.*), Fox, 1993.

Phil Swill, "No Man's Land," *The Adventures of Brisco County, Jr.* (also known as *Brisco Country, Jr.*), Fox, 1993.

"Dino Might (Gomora)," *Ultraman: The Ultimate Hero* (also known as *Ultraman Powered* and *Urutoraman pawado*), c. 1993.

Ed, "Love, Mancini Style," *Melrose Place,* Fox, 1994.

Packy, "George Gets Some Money," *The George Carlin Show,* Fox, 1994.

Rosten, "Whistle Stop," *L.A. Law,* NBC, 1994.

(In archive footage) Librarian, "Quadriplegia, Nymphomania, and HIV–Positive Night," *Joe Bob's Drive–In Theater,* The Movie Channel, 1995.

Drugstore man, "Endless Bummer," *L.A. Doctors* (also known as *L.A. Docs, Kliniken, Kohtaloni Los Angeles,* and *Medicos de Los Angeles*), CBS, 1998.

Knapsack and homeless man, "Repentance," *Brimstone,* Fox, 1998.

McCain, "Get Me Cody Swift," *Buddy Faro,* CBS, 1998.

Dwayne, "Reelin' in the Years," *Boomtown,* NBC, 2002.

Tom Johnson, "Forgive Me, Father," *The Division* (also known as *Heart of the City*), Lifetime, 2002.

Voice of Mophir, "Eclipsed: Parts 1 & 2," *Justice League* (animated; also known as *JL, JLA, Justice League of America,* and *Justice League Unlimited*), Cartoon Network, 2003.

Voice of Puppet King, "Switched," *Teen Titans* (animated), Cartoon Network, 2003.

Manager, "Rat Saw God," *Veronica Mars,* UPN, 2005.

Bum, "Bums: Making a Mess All over the City," *It's Always Sunny in Philadelphia* (also known as *It's Always Sunny ...*), FX Network, 2007.

Ike Stratman, "Elephant's Memory," *Criminal Minds* (also known as *Quantico, Criminal Minds—FBI tutjijat, Esprits criminels, Gyilkos elmek, Kurjuse kannul,* and *Mentes criminales*), CBS, 2008.

The Professor, "Mr. Monk and the Miracle," *Monk,* USA Network, 2008.

Appeared as Mr. Malloy in *Empty Nest* (also known as *Harry's Nest*), NBC; and as Tommy Bass, *Michael Hayes,* CBS.

Television Appearances; Pilots:
Frog Rothchild, Jr., *Best of the West,* ABC, 1981.

Laird Sussman, *Camp California,* ABC, 1989.

William Jones, *Raines,* NBC, 2007.

Stage Appearances:
Freddy (modern statuary), *American Gothics,* Roundabout Theatre Company, Roundabout Stage I, New York City, 1972.

The Time Trial, New York Shakespeare Festival, New York City, c. 1975.

Soldier, *Rebel Woman,* New York Shakespeare Festival, Joseph Papp Public Theater, Estelle R. Newman Theater, New York City, 1976.

Appeared in other productions, including *Jesse and the Bandit Queen,* New York Shakespeare Festival.

RECORDINGS

Videos:
Dusty in *The Cowboy and the Frenchman* (short film), included in *The Short Films of David Lynch,* 2002.

Himself, *Batman: The Motion Picture Anthology 1989–1997—Beyond Batman from Jack to the Joker* (short), Warner Home Video, 2005.

Himself, *Batman: The Villains* (short), Warner Home Video, 2005.

Himself, *Shadows of the Bat: The Cinematic Saga of the Dark Knight—The Legend Reborn* (short), Warner Home Video, 2005.

Video Games:
Voice of Popocorn, *50 Cent: Bulletproof,* Vivendi Universal Games, 2005.

Music Videos:
ZZ Top, "Sleeping Bag," 1985.

OTHER SOURCES

Electronic:
Tracey Walter Online, http://www.traceywalter.com, November 26, 2008.

WARD, Vincent
(Vincent M. Ward)

PERSONAL

Education: Attended South Suburban College, South Holland, IL, 1993.

Addresses: *Agent*—Hervey/Grimes Talent Agency, 10561 Missouri Ave., Suite 2, Los Angeles, CA 90025. *Manager*—Joy Stevenson, 22838 Epsilon St., Woodland Hills, CA 91364.

Career: Actor. Appeared as a construction worker in a commercial for Diet Pepsi soft drinks; appeared in print ads for AT&T and Country Crock margarine; also performer for other commercials, music videos, radio programs, and industrial films. Formerly worked as a shoe salesman and security guard.

Member: Screen Actors Guild, American Federation of Television and Radio Artists.

CREDITS

Film Appearances:
(As Vincent M. Ward) Second Uzi–carrying guard, *Ocean's Eleven* (also known as *11* and *O11*), Warner Bros., 2001.
(As Vincent M. Ward) Big man, *Bringing Down the House,* Buena Vista, 2003.
Mr. Redd Dog, *Confessions of a Thug,* Polychrome Pictures, 2005.
Bouncer, *Lonely in Los Angeles* (short film), MoHo Productions, 2006.
Huge musclebound guy, *18 Fingers of Death!,* Screen Media Films, 2006.
Mike V, *All Lies on Me,* Visionary Entertainment, 2007.
First young man, *Three Can Play That Game,* Sony Pictures, 2007.
Jet Lewis, *Cordially Invited,* Equalaris Productions, 2007.
(As Vincent M. Ward) CIA agent, *Get Smart's Bruce and Lloyd Out of Control,* Warner Bros., 2008.
Bishop Ussian Brown, *Who Killed Bishop Brown,* Upliftworks Entertainment, 2008.
Cedric, *Robbin' in da Hood,* InaVision, 2008.

Also appeared in the films *Revealed* and *So Cold.*

Television Appearances; Episodic:
Security guard, "The Wedding," *Girlfriends,* UPN, 2003.
Guard, *The Bold and the Beautiful* (also known as *Belleza y poder*), CBS, 2003.
(As Vincent M. Ward) Space, "Viva Las Vegas," *CSI: Crime Scene Investigation* (also known as *C.S.I.,* *CSI: Las Vegas,* and *Les experts*), CBS, 2004.
Blings right–hand man, "Malpractice Makes Perfect," *Head Cases,* Fox, 2005.
(As Vincent M. Ward) Guard, "Everybody Hates Malvo," *Everybody Hates Chris,* CW Network, 2006.
FBI agent, "Everybody Hates Chain Snatching," *Everybody Hates Chris,* CW Network, 2007.
(As Vincent M. Ward) Marshall Abrams, "Chain Reaction," *CSI: Miami,* CBS, 2007.
Black bus driver, "Everybody Hates Tattaglia," *Everybody Hates Chris,* CW Network, 2008.
Parking officer, "Sex Be Not Proud," *Big Shots,* ABC, 2008.
(As Vincent M. Ward) Butchie's bodyguard, "Not for Attribution," *The Wire,* HBO, 2008.
Guard, "Yorkshire Terrier Sucked into the Internet," *Unhitched,* Fox, 2008.
Police officer, "The Accidental Occidental Conception," *The Middleman,* ABC Family Channel, 2008.
Police officer, "The Manicoid Teleportation Conundrum," *The Middleman,* ABC Family Channel, 2008.
Bo, *The Starter Wife,* USA Network, 2008.

Also appeared in episodes of *Desperate Housewives,* ABC, *Knight Rider, Robbery Homicide,* and *Viva Laughlin.*

Television Appearances; Other:
Host of *Son of Kaos Talk Show.*

Stage Appearances:
Appeared as Roland, *The Bachelorette Party;* Sticks, *The Gift;* David, *If You Really Love Me;* Floyd Burns/Satan, *Lord There's a Stranger in My House;* Rico, *My Brother's Keeper;* Tony "The Tiger" Lee, *Riff Raff;* Calving Savage James, *Savage World;* Laurence, *A Sugga Daddy Ain't Always Sweet;* and Max, *Through the Storm;* also appeared in *Baldwin Hills* and *Baldwin Hills II, Believe Me When I Say I Love You, Love Games, Leave the 99, Man that Finds a Wife, Sweet Inspirations, What Is the World Coming To?, Will You Be Ready,* and *You Better Check Yourself.*

WILLIAMS, Brian 1959–

PERSONAL

Full name, Brian Douglas Williams; born May 5, 1959, in Elmira, NY; son of Gordon and Dorothy (an amateur actress) Williams; married Jane Stoddard (a television talk show producer), June 7, 1986; children: Allison, Douglas. *Education:* Attended Brookdale Community College, Lincroft, NJ, George Washington University, and Catholic University of America. *Religion:* Roman Catholic. *Avocational Interests:* Stock car races, presidential history.

Addresses: *Office*—c/o NBC News, 30 Rockefeller Plaza, New York, NY 10112.

Career: Broadcast journalist, correspondent, news anchor, and writer. KOAM–TV, Pittsburg, KS, reporter, 1980–81; WTTG–TV, Washington, DC, general assignment reporter, 1981–88, and host of the local talk show *Panorama,* 1985; WCAU–TV, Philadelphia, PA, correspondent and anchor, c. 1985–87; WCBS–TV, New York City, correspondent and anchor, c. 1987–93; NBC News, New York City, correspondent, 1993—, chief White House correspondent, beginning 1994. Worked as a White House intern during the Jimmy Carter administration; National Association of Broadcasters, assistant administrator of political action committee; Congressional Medal of Honor Foundation, member of board of directors. Lecturer at Columbia University and elsewhere. Multiple Myeloma Research Foundation, honorary board member. Worked as a volunteer firefighter in New Jersey.

Member: Council on Foreign Relations, Sigma Delta Chi.

Awards, Honors: Named father of the year, National Father's Day Committee, 1996; named man of the year, *Gentleman's Quarterly,* 2001; George Foster Peabody Broadcasting Award, Henry W. Grady School of Journalism and Mass Communications, University of Georgia, 2005; president's medal, Tulane University, 2006; received at least five Emmy Awards, four Edward R. Murrow Awards, Radio and Television News Directors Association, and Alfred I. duPont–Columbia University Award; honorary doctorates from several institutions, including Elmira College, 1998, Providence College, 2002, Villanova University, 2003, Catholic University of America, 2004, Bates College, 2005, and Ohio State University, 2008.

CREDITS

Television Appearances; Series:
Anchor, *NBC Nightly News* (also known as *NBC Nightly News with Brian Williams*), Saturday edition, NBC, 1993–99.
Anchor, *The News with Brian Williams* (also known as *The News* and *The News on CNBC*), MSNBC, 1996–2002, then CNBC, 2002–2004.
Anchor, *MSNBC Live* (also known as *MSNBC Dayside* and *MSNBC Right Now*), MSNBC, 1996–2003.
Anchor, *NBC Nightly News,* weekday edition, 2004—.

Also appeared as a correspondent for *Dateline NBC,* NBC.

Television Appearances; Specials:
Correspondent, *To Your Health,* NBC, 1994.
Anchor, *The People vs. O. J. Simpson,* NBC, 1994.
Correspondent, *Decision '96: The Republican National Convention,* NBC, 1996.
Correspondent, *Decision '96: The Democratic National Convention,* NBC, 1996.
Correspondent, *Decision '96 Election Night,* NBC, 1996.
Host, *The American Presidency: Real to Reel,* MSNBC, 1999.
Host, *NASCAR behind the Scenes,* NBC, 1999.
Moderator, *Shades of Progress, Shadows of Hate,* MSNBC, 2000.
Night of Too Many Stars, NBC, 2003.
Macy's 4th of July Fireworks Spectacular, NBC, 2004.
Anchor, *Katrina's Fury: A Dateline Special,* NBC, 2004.
In His Own Words: Brian Williams on Hurricane Katrina, Sundance Channel, 2005.
A Concert for Hurricane Relief, NBC, 2005.
Tsunami Aid: A Concert of Hope, multiple networks, 2005.
Katrina: The Long Road Back, NBC, 2006.

Generation Boom, TV Land, 2006.
Night of Too Many Stars: An Overbooked Event for Autism Education, Comedy Central, 2006.
That's the Way It Is: Celebrating Cronkite at 90, CBS, 2007.
Dale, Country Music Television, 2007.
Stand Up to Cancer, multiple networks, 2008.
Voice of Rock Granite, *Little Spirit: Christmas in New York* (animated), NBC, 2008.

Television Appearances; Movies:
(Uncredited) Himself (in archive footage), *Sometimes in April,* HBO, 2005.

Television Appearances; Awards Presentations:
Presenter, *The 19th Annual CableACE Awards,* TNT, 1997.
Presenter, *25th Annual News and Documentary Emmy Awards,* Discovery Times Channel, 2004.

Television Guest Appearances; Episodic:
Late Show with David Letterman (also known as *The Late Show* and *Letterman*), CBS, multiple appearances, beginning 1996.
The Tonight Show with Jay Leno, NBC, 1997, 2008.
Late Night with Conan O'Brien, NBC, multiple appearances, beginning 1998.
The Rosie O'Donnell Show, syndicated, 2001.
"Dale Earnhardt," *ESPN SportsCentury,* ESPN, 2001.
The Daily Show (also known as *A Daily Show with Jon Stewart, The Daily Show with Jon Stewart Global Edition,* and *Jon Stewart*), Comedy Central, multiple appearances, beginning 2003.
(Uncredited) *Saturday Night Live* (also known as *SNL*), NBC, 2004, 2006, 2007.
Hardball with Chris Matthews, CNBC, 2004, 2006, 2007.
Ellen: The Ellen DeGeneres Show, syndicated, 2005.
Larry King Live, Cable News Network, 2005, 2008.
The Colbert Report, Comedy Central, 2007.
Jimmy Kimmel Live!, ABC, 2007.
"The Bookaneers," *Sesame Street* (also known as *The New Sesame Street, Open Sesame,* and *Sesame Street Unpaved*), PBS, 2007.
Good Morning America, ABC, 2008.
Entertainment Tonight (also known as *Entertainment This Week, E.T., ET Weekend,* and *This Week in Entertainment*), syndicated, 2008.
Real Time with Bill Maher (also known as *Real Time with Bill Maher: Electile Dysfunction '08*), HBO, 2008.
(In archive footage) "Robbing Hollywood's A–List/Soaking the Rich at Auction," *American Greed,* CNBC, 2008.
(In archive footage) *The O'Reilly Factor,* Fox News Channel, multiple episodes, 2008.

Television Managing Editor; Series:

NBC Nightly News (also known as *NBC Nightly News with Brian Williams*), Saturday edition, NBC, 1993–99.

The News with Brian Williams (also known as *The News* and *The News on CNBC*), MSNBC, 1996–2002, then CNBC, 2002–2004.

NBC Nightly News (also known as *NBC Nightly News with Brian Williams*), weekday edition, 2004–2008.

Film Appearances:

(Uncredited) Himself (in archive footage), *The 11th Hour,* Warner Independent Pictures, 2007.

WRITINGS

Television Specials:

Host, *The American Presidency: Real to Reel,* MSNBC, 1999.

Print Journalism:

Contributor to periodicals, including *Los Angeles Times, New York Times, Time,* and *TV Guide.*

OTHER SOURCES

Periodicals:

AARP, January, 2005, p. 46; November, 2008, pp. 38–41, 79.

American Journalism Review, January–February, 1997, p. 40.

Chicago Tribune, June 3, 2002.

Good Housekeeping, April, 2008, p. 60.

New York Times, October 27, 2002.

People Weekly, April 29, 1996, p. 101; December 29, 1997, p. 126.

TV Guide, May 18, 2002, p. 45; September 5, 2004, pp. 59–63; September 25, 2005, p. 14; December 19, 2005, p. 31.

USA Today, November 10, 2004, p. 1D.

Vanity Fair, January, 1999, pp. 90–95, 132–133.

Variety, June 30, 2003, p. 18.

Washington Post, July 15, 2002, pp. C1, C4.

Electronic:

MSNBC Online, http://www.msnbc.msn.com, December 5, 2008.

WILLIAMS, Michelle 1980–

PERSONAL

Full name, Michelle Ingrid Williams; born September 9, 1980, in Kalispell, MT; daughter of Larry (a commodities trader) and Carla (a homemaker) Williams; children: (with actor Heath Ledger) Matilda Rose. *Education:* Briefly attended a Christian high school in Rancho Santa Fe, CA, then was home–schooled. *Avocational Interests:* Reading, watching boxing matches, collecting rare books.

Addresses: *Agent*—Hylda Queally, Creative Artists Agency, 2000 Avenue of the Stars, Los Angeles, CA 90067. *Publicist*—Mara Buxbaum, I/D Public Relations, 8409 Santa Monica Blvd., West Hollywood, CA 90069.

Career: Actress. Appeared in community theatre productions as a child in San Diego, CA; also appeared in commercials.

Awards, Honors: Young Artist Award nomination, best young actress costarring in a motion picture, 1995, for *Lassie;* Young Star Award nominations, best young actress in a television drama series, 1998 and 1999, both for *Dawson's Creek;* Young Artist Award nomination, best supporting young actress in a feature film, 1999, for *Halloween H20: 20 Years Later;* Young Artist Award nomination, best leading young actress in a feature film, 2000, for *Dick;* Lucy Award (with others), Women in Films, 2000; Screen Actors Guild Award nomination and Phoenix Film Critics Society Award nomination, both best ensemble cast (with others), 2004, for *The Station Agent;* Gotham Award nomination (with others), best ensemble cast, 2005, Phoenix Film Critics Society Award and Washington DC Area Film Critics Association Award nomination, both best supporting actress, 2005, Golden Globe Award nomination, best supporting actress in a film, 2006, Academy Award nomination, Film Award nomination, British Academy of Film and Television Arts, Screen Actors Guild Award nomination, Independent Spirit Award nomination, Independent Features Project West, Chicago Film Critics Association Award nomination, Critics Choice Award, Broadcast Film Critics Association, and Online Film Critics Society Award nomination, all best supporting actress, 2006, and Screen Actors Guild Award nomination (with others), outstanding cast in a motion picture, 2006, all for *Brokeback Mountain;* Independent Spirit Award nomination, best actress, 2007, for *Land of Plenty;* Independent Spirit Award nomination, best actress, 2008, for *Wendy and Lucy;* Robert Altman Award (with others), Independent Spirit Awards, 2009, for *Synecdoche, New York.*

CREDITS

Film Appearances:

April Porter, *Lassie,* Paramount, 1994.

Young "Sil," *Species,* Metro–Goldwyn–Mayer, 1995.

Annie, *Timemaster,* Shapiro/Glickenhaus Entertainment, 1995.

Pammy, *A Thousand Acres,* Buena Vista, 1997.

Molly Cartwell, *Halloween H2O: 20 Years Later* (also known as *Halloween: H2O* and *Halloween: H2O (20 Years Later)*), Dimension Films, 1998.

Arlene Lorenzo, *Dick* (also known as *Dick, les coulisses de la presidence*), Columbia/TriStar, 1999.

Kimberly, *But I'm a Cheerleader* (also known as *Dress to Kill*), Lions Gate Films, 2000.

Ruby, *Prozac Nation*, Miramax, 2001.

Holly, *Me Without You* (also known as *Meine beste freundin*), Samuel Goldwyn Films, 2001.

Halley, *Perfume*, Lions Gate Films, 2002.

Emily, *The Station Agent*, Miramax, 2003.

Anna Watson, *A Hole in One*, Beech Hill Films, 2004.

Julie Pollard, *The United States of Leland*, Paramount, 2004.

Penny Travis, *Imaginary Heroes*, Columbia, 2004.

Lana, *Land of Plenty*, IFC Films, 2004.

Cecil Mills, *The Baxter*, IFC Films, 2005.

Alma Beers Del Mar, *Brokeback Mountain*, Focus Features, 2005.

Betty, *The Hawk Is Dying*, Strand Releasing, 2006.

Samantha, *The Hottest State*, ThinkFilm, 2006.

Coco Rivington, *I'm Not There*, Weinstein Company, 2007.

Young mother, *Incendiary*, Optimum Releasing, 2008.

S, *Deception*, Twentieth Century–Fox, 2008.

Wendy, *Wendy and Lucy*, Oscilloscope Pictures, 2008.

Claire Keen, *Synecdoche, New York*, Columbia, 2008.

Allison Gould, *Mammoth* (also known as *Mammut*), Svensk Filmindustri, 2009.

Television Appearances; Series:

Jennifer "Jen" Lindley, *Dawson's Creek*, The WB, 1998–2003.

Television Appearances; Movies:

Donna Winston, *My Son Is Innocent*, ABC, 1996.

Maya Tashjian, *Killing Mr. Griffin*, NBC, 1997.

Linda, "1972" segment, *If These Walls Could Talk 2*, HBO, 2000.

Television Appearances; Pilots:

Trish Caines, *Raising Caines*, NBC, 1995.

Jennifer "Jen" Lindley, *Dawson's Creek*, The WB, 1998.

Television Appearances; Episodic:

Bridget Bowers, "Race against Time: Part 1," *Baywatch*, NBC, 1994.

J. J., "Something Wild," *Step by Step*, ABC, 1994.

Jessica Lutz, "Wilson's Girlfriend," *Home Improvement*, ABC, 1995.

The Rosie O'Donnell Show, syndicated, 1998, 1999.

Late Night with Conan O'Brien, 1999.

The Howard Stern Radio Show, 1999.

The Tonight Show with Jay Leno, NBC, 2002, 2006.

Corazon de ..., 2005, 2006.

The Oprah Winfrey Show (also known as *Oprah*), syndicated, 2006.

"Filmen 'Brokeback Mountain'/Nyheter och vaeder," *Nyhetsmorgon*, 2006.

Entertainment Tonight (also known as *Entertainment This Week*, *E.T.*, *ET Weekend*, and *This Week in Entertainment*), syndicated, 2007, 2008.

Cartaz Cultural, 2008.

Television Appearances; Specials:

Dawson's Creek: Behind the Scenes, E! Entertainment Television, 1998.

Seventeen: The Faces for Fall, The WB, 1998.

Teen People's 21 Hottest Stars under 21, ABC, 1999.

Jennifer "Jen" Lindley, *Songs from Dawson's Creek*, 1999.

Intimate Portrait: Jamie Lee Curtis, Lifetime, 2000.

Kids of Dawson's Creek: The E! True Hollywood Story, E! Entertainment Television, 2005.

Logo Movie Special: "Brokeback Mountain," Logo, 2005.

Como conseguir un papel en Hollywood, 2007.

(In archive footage) "Heath Ledger Special," *A Current Affair*, Nine Network, 2008.

(In archive footage) *Heath Ledger: The E! True Hollywood Story*, E! Entertainment Television, 2008.

Television Appearances; Awards Presentations:

Presenter, *The 51st Annual Primetime Emmy Awards*, Fox, 1999.

6th Annual Blockbuster Entertainment Awards, Fox, 2000.

The 11th Annual Critics' Choice Awards, 2006.

12th Annual Screen Actors Guild Awards, TNT, 2006.

2006 Independent Spirit Awards, Independent Film Channel, 2006.

The 78th Annual Academy Awards, ABC, 2006.

Television Director; Episodic:

Directed episodes of *Dawson's Creek*, The WB.

Stage Appearances:

Dottie, *Killer Joe*, Soho Playhouse, New York City, 1999.

Melanie–Jane, *Smelling a Rat*, Samuel Beckett Theatre, New York City, 2002.

Varya, *The Cherry Orchard*, Williamstown Theatre Festival, Williamstown, MA, 2004.

The Sisters Rosensweig (benefit), Virginia Theatre, New York City, 2004.

RECORDINGS

Videos:

Herself and Molly, *Unmasking the Horror*, 1998.

The Making of "Dick," Columbia, 1999.

Appeared in a music video by the Comas.

OTHER SOURCES

Periodicals:

Bikini, September, 1998, pp. 56–61.
Empire, November, 1998, pp. 66–67.
Femme Fatales, November, 1998, pp. 52–53.
FHM, November, 1998, pp. 108–109, 111–112.
George, July, 1999, pp. 40–41.
Girlfriend, March, 2000.
Movieline, September, 1998, pp. 66–67.
Teen, June, 1999, pp. 56, 58.
TV Guide, March 7, 1998, pp. 18–25.
Twist, October, 1998, pp. 44–47.
USA Today, January 20, 1998.

WILLIAMS, Serena 1981–

PERSONAL

Full name, Serena Jameka Williams; born September 26, 1981, in Saginaw, MI; daughter of Richard (a tennis coach and former operator of a private security firm) and Oracene (a nurse) Williams; sister of Venus Williams (a professional tennis player). *Education:* Studied at Art Institute of Florida. *Religion:* Jehovah's Witness.

Addresses: *Agent*—William Morris Agency, 1 William Morris Pl., Beverly Hills, CA 90212. *Publicist*—Ina Treciokas, Ina Treciokas Public Relations, 8332 Beverly Blvd., Suite 201, Los Angeles, CA 90048.

Career: Professional tennis player, actress, and voice performer. Professional tennis player, 1995—. Appeared in commercials for McDonald's restaurants, Double-Mint chewing gum, Vick's NyQuil and DayQuil cold medications, and other products; appeared in print advertisements. Fashion designer, including her Aneres clothing line. Serena Williams Foundation, founder and philanthropist.

Member: Women's Tennis Association.

Awards, Honors: Winner of U.S. Open doubles tennis championship (with sister, Venus Williams), 1999, French Open doubles championship (with Venus), 1999, Olympic doubles tennis gold medal (with Venus), 2000, 2008, U.S. Open tennis singles championship, 1999, 2002, 2008, Wimbledon doubles championship (with Venus), 2000, 2002, Women's Tennis Association singles championship, 2001, Australian Open doubles championship (with Venus), 2001, 2003, French Open singles championship, 2002, Wimbledon singles championship, 2002, 2003, Australian Open singles championship, 2003, 2005, 2007, Bangalore Open singles championship, 2008, and Family Circle Cup singles championship, 2008, among many other tennis awards; named tennis player of the year, *Tennis* (magazine), 1999; named female athlete of the year, Associated Press, 2003; ESPY Awards, female tennis player of the year, 2003, 2004, and female athlete of the year, Entertainment and Sports Network, 2003; four–time winner of Sony Ericsson Open championship, including 2007; named sportswoman of the year, Laureus World Sports Academy; Serena Williams Secondary School was named in her honor in Makueni District, Kenya.

CREDITS

Television Appearances; Miniseries:

Sydney 2000: Games of the XXVII Olympiad, NBC, 2000.
(Uncredited) *Heroes of Black Comedy,* Comedy Central, 2002.
Venus and Serena: For Real, ABC Family Channel, 2005.
Fast Cars and Superstars: The Gillette Young Guns Celebrity Race, ABC, 2007.
Beijing 2008: Games of the XXIX Olympiad, NBC, 2008.

Television Appearances; Specials:

Sports Illustrated's Sportsman of the Year 2000, CBS, 2000.
Raising the Roof: Seven Athletes for the 21st Century, ABC, 2000.
Elvis Lives, NBC, 2002.
On the Record with Bob Costas: A 2002 Special Edition, HBO, 2002.
(In archive footage) *Cleavage,* Arts and Entertainment, 2002.
Sports Illustrated Swimsuit 2003, Spike, 2003.
Glam Slam: WTA Fashion Show, Tennis Channel, 2003.
Model, *Sports Illustrated 40th Anniversary Swimsuit Special: American Beauty,* Spike, 2004.
Presenter, *Fashion Rocks,* Fox, 2004.
Out of Africa: Heroes and Icons, BBC, 2005.
25 Strong: The BET Silver Anniversary Special, Black Entertainment Television, 2005.
The History of Argentine Tennis, Tennis Channel, 2006.
Forbes Celebrity 100: Who Made Bank?, E! Entertainment Television, 2006.
Arthur Ashe Kids' Day, CBS, 2006.
Herself, *Props,* Cartoon Network, 2007.
The Black List: Volume One, HBO, 2008.

Television Appearances; Episodic:

Voice, "Tennis the Menace," *The Simpsons* (animated), Fox, 2001.

Miss Wiggins, "Crouching Mother, Hidden Father," *My Wife and Kids*, ABC, 2002.

Meeka Hayes, "Fly Girl," *Street Time*, Showtime, 2003.

Chloe Spears, "Brotherhood," *Law & Order: Special Victims Unit* (also known as *Law & Order: SVU, SVU,* and *Special Victims Unit*), NBC, 2004.

Jennifer Davis, "Lost and Found," *The Division* (also known as *Heart of the City*), Lifetime, 2004.

Voice of snowplow driver hero, "Higgly Hoedown/ Eubie's Turbo Sled," *Higglytown Heroes* (animated), The Disney Channel, 2005.

Alice Watson, "Two Ships," *ER*, NBC, 2005.

Wanda, "Not So Wonderful News," *All of Us*, UPN, 2005.

Herself, "Spinning Wheels," *The Bernie Mac Show*, Fox, 2006.

Voice of Queen Athena, "Apocalypso," *Loonatics Unleashed* (animated), CW Network, 2007.

Voice of Ming, "The Day of Black Sun: Part 1—The Invasion," *Avatar: The Last Airbender* (animated), Nickelodeon, 2007.

Black Team captain, "Serena Williams," *Nick Cannon Presents: Wild 'n Out*, MTV, 2007.

Television Guest Appearances; Episodic:

Hollywood Squares (also known as *H2* and *H2: Hollywood Squares*), syndicated, 1999.

Late Night with Conan O'Brien, NBC, 1999, 2007.

The Tonight Show with Jay Leno, NBC, 2001, 2003.

The Wayne Brady Show, syndicated, 2003.

"Serena Williams," *Center Court*, Tennis Channel, 2004.

Jimmy Kimmel Live!, ABC, 2004.

Richard & Judy, Channel 4, 2004.

"Steffi Graf," *ESPN SportsCentury*, ESPN, 2004.

The Late Late Show with Craig Kilborn, CBS, 2004.

Live with Regis and Kelly, syndicated, 2004, 2005.

Ellen: The Ellen DeGeneres Show, syndicated, 2004, 2007.

"Miami," *Open Access*, Tennis Channel, 2004.

"Wimbledon '05," *Open Access*, Tennis Channel, 2005.

Charity Jam, Tennis Channel, 2005.

The Oprah Winfrey Show (also known as *Oprah*), syndicated, 2005.

"The Girl with the Worst Photo in History," *America's Next Top Model* (also known as *America's Next Top Model 2, America's Next Top Model with Tyra Banks, ANTM,* and *Top Model*), UPN, 2005.

Punk'd, MTV, 2005.

(In archive footage) "Sex and Sports," *Beyond the Glory*, Fox Sports Channel, 2005.

Friday Night with Jonathan Ross, BBC, 2005, 2007.

Martha, syndicated, 2006.

The Tony Danza Show, syndicated, 2006.

(Uncredited; in archive footage) "It's Your Lucky Day," *The Tyra Banks Show*, UPN, 2006.

Larry King Live, Cable News Network, 2007.

Today (also known as *NBC News Today* and *The Today Show*), NBC, 2008.

Mad TV, Fox, 2008.

Also guest for an episode of *The Game*, CW Network.

Television Appearances; Awards Presentations:

The 2000 Teen Choice Awards, Fox, 2000.

Presenter, *The 2000 MTV Video Music Awards*, MTV, 2000.

Essence Awards (also known as *The 2001 Essence Awards*), Fox, 2001.

Presenter, *ESPY Awards*, ESPN, 2002, 2003, 2004, 2005, 2007.

The 34th Annual NAACP Image Awards, Fox, 2003.

Presenter, *MTV Video Music Awards*, MTV, 2003.

Presenter, *The Teen Choice Awards 2004*, Fox, 2004.

Presenter, *Nickelodeon's 17th Annual Kids' Choice Awards*, Nickelodeon, 2004.

VH1 Big in 04, VH1, 2004.

2005 Trumpet Awards, TBS, 2005.

Presenter, *2005 American Music Awards* (also known as *The 33rd Annual American Music Awards*), ABC, 2005.

Film Appearances:

Herself, *She Got Game* (documentary), Fireworks International, 2003.

Agent Ross, *Hair Show*, Innovation Film Group, 2004.

RECORDINGS

Videos:

Raising Tennis Aces: The Williams Story, Xenon Pictures, 2003.

Before, During, and "After the Sunset," New Line Home Video, 2005.

Appeared in the music video "I Want You" by Common.

OTHER SOURCES

Books:

Contemporary Black Biography, Volume 41, Gale, 2004.

Newsmakers 1999, Issue 4, Gale, 1999.

Notable Black American Women, Book 3, Gale, 2002.

Notable Sports Figures, Gale, 2004.

Periodicals:

Essence, August, 1998, p. 78.

Jet, December 1, 1997, p. 48; February 9, 1998, p. 49; July 20, 1998, p. 51; September 21, 1998, p. 49; March 15, 1999, p. 51; February 12, 2001, p. 51.

Parade, March 16, 2003, p. 26.

Tennis, February, 2000, pp. 28–30.

TV Guide, October 18, 2003, p. 18; July 24, 2005, p. 12.

USA Today, November 14, 1997, p. 3C; September 13, 1999, pp. 3C, 13C.

Vogue, May, 1998, p. 270.

Women's Sports and Fitness, November–December, 1998, p. 102.

Electronic:

Serena Williams Official Site, http://www. serenawilliams.com, December 10, 2008.

Other:

Raising Tennis Aces: The Williams Story (video), Xenon Pictures, 2003.

The Williams Sisters: The E! True Hollywood Story (television special), E! Entertainment Television, 2004.

WOODWARD, Joanne 1930–

PERSONAL

Full name, Joanne Gignilliat Trimmier Woodward; born February 27, 1930, in Thomasville, GA; daughter of Wade (a school administrator, state educator, and publishing executive) and Elinor (maiden name, Trimmier) Woodward; married Paul Newman (an actor, producer, director, writer, and philanthropist), January 29, 1958 (died, September 26, 2008); children: Elinor "Nell" Terese, Melissa "Lissy" Stewart, Claire "Clea" Olivia; stepchildren: Scott (deceased), Susan, Stephanie. *Education:* Studied acting at Louisiana State University, 1947–49; studied acting with Sanford Meisner at the Neighborhood Playhouse Drama School; also studied at the Actors Studio; attended the Directing Workshop for Women, American Film Institute; Sarah Lawrence College, B.A., 1990. *Politics:* Democrat. *Religion:* Episcopalian. *Avocational Interests:* Ballet, horseback riding.

Addresses: *Agent*—International Creative Management, 10250 Constellation Way, Ninth Floor, Los Angeles, CA 90067. *Publicist*—Warren Cowan & Associates, 8899 Beverly Blvd., Suite 919, Los Angeles, CA 90048.

Career: Actress, director, producer, and philanthropist. Dancers (ballet company), New York City, board chairperson and major financial supporter, beginning c. 1975; Westport Country Playhouse, Westport, CT, artistic director, 2000–05 and beginning c. 2008, also a member of the board of trustees. Neighborhood Playhouse, New York City, instructor at performing workshops. Affiliated with the antidrug organization the Scott Newman Foundation; active in philanthropic causes. Affiliated with the organizations Another Mother for Peace and Women for a Meaningful Summit; Environmental Defense Fund, member of the board of trustees and appeared in advertisements for the organization.

Member: Actors' Equity Association, Screen Actors Guild, American Federation of Television and Radio Artists, Actors Studio, Directors Guild of America, Chi Omega.

Awards, Honors: National Board of Review Award, best actress, 1957, for *The Three Faces of Eve* and *No Down Payment;* Academy Award, best actress in a leading role, Golden Globe Award, best motion picture actress—drama, and Film Award nomination, best foreign actress, British Academy of Film and Television Arts, all 1958, for *The Three Faces of Eve;* Golden Laurel Award, top new female personality, Producers Guild of America, 1958; Film Award nomination, best foreign actress, British Academy of Film and Television Arts, 1959, for *No Down Payment;* named Hasty Pudding Woman of the Year, Hasty Pudding Theatricals, Harvard University, 1959; Golden Laurel Award nomination, top female comedy performance, 1959, for *Rally 'round the Flag, Boys!;* Zulueta Prize (Golden Shell), San Sebastian International Film Festival (Spain), best actress, 1960, for *The Fugitive Kind;* received a star on the Hollywood Walk of Fame, 1960; Golden Laurel Award nominations, top female star, 1962, 1966, and 1967; Golden Globe Award, best motion picture actress—musical/comedy, 1964, for *A New Kind of Love;* Golden Laurel Award nomination, top female dramatic performance, 1964, for *The Stripper;* Golden Laurel Award nomination, top female comedy performance, 1967, for *A Big Hand for the Little Lady;* New York Film Critics Circle Award, best actress, 1968, Golden Globe Award, best motion picture actress—drama, Kansas City Film Critics Circle Award, best actress, Academy Award nomination, best actress in a leading role, and Film Award nomination, best actress, British Academy of Film and Television Arts, all 1969, and Golden Laurel Award nomination, best female dramatic performance, both 1970, all for *Rachel, Rachel;* Golden Laurel Award nominations, best female star, 1968, 1970, and 1971; Cannes International Film Festival Award, best actress in a full-length film, and Golden Globe Award nomination, best motion picture actress—drama, both 1973, and Kansas City Film Critics Circle Award, best actress, 1974, for *The Effect of Gamma Rays on Man-in-the-Moon Marigolds;* New York Film Critics Circle Award, best actress, 1973, Golden Globe Award nomination, best motion picture actress—drama, 1974, Academy Award nomination, best actress in a leading role, 1974, Film Award, British Academy of Film and Television Arts Award, and Kansas City Film Critics Circle Award, both best actress, 1975, all for *Summer Wishes, Winter Dreams;* Gala Tribute, Film Society of Lincoln Center, 1975; Golden Apple, star of the year, Hollywood Women's Press Club, 1976; Emmy Award nomination, outstanding lead actress in a drama or comedy special, 1977, and TV Land Award nomination (with Sally Field), blockbuster movie of the week, 2006, both for *Sybil;* Emmy Award, outstanding lead actress in a drama or comedy special,

1978, for "See How She Runs," *General Electric Theater;* Emmy Award nomination, outstanding actress in a limited series or special, 1981, and Golden Globe Award nomination, best performance by an actress in a miniseries or motion picture made for television, 1982, both for *Crisis at Central High;* Emmy Award, outstanding lead actress in a limited series or special, 1985, and Golden Globe Award nomination, best performance by an actress in a miniseries or motion picture made for television, 1986, both for *Do You Remember Love;* Life Achievement Award, Screen Actors Guild, 1986; Independent Spirit Award nomination, best female lead, Independent Feature Project/West, 1988, for *The Glass Menagerie;* Emmy Award (with others), outstanding informational special, and Emmy Award nomination, outstanding performance in informational programming, both 1990, for "Broadway's Dreamers: The Legacy of the Group Theatre," *American Masters;* New York Film Critics Circle Award, best actress, 1990, Kansas City Film Critics Circle Award, best actress, Academy Award nomination, best actress in a leading role, Golden Globe Award nomination, best performance by an actress in a motion picture—drama, and Independent Spirit Award nomination, best female lead, all 1991, all for *Mr. & Mrs. Bridge;* Franklin D. Roosevelt Four Freedoms Award (with Paul Newman), freedom from want category, 1991; Lifetime Achievement Award, Kennedy Center Honors, John F. Kennedy Center for the Performing Arts, 1992; Emmy Award nomination, outstanding lead actress in a miniseries or special, 1993, for "Blind Spot," *Hallmark Hall of Fame;* Emmy Award nomination, outstanding lead actress in a miniseries or special, 1994, Golden Globe Award, best performance by an actress in a miniseries or movie made for television, 1995, and Screen Actors Guild Award, outstanding performance by a female actor in a television movie or miniseries, 1995, all for "Breathing Lessons," *Hallmark Hall of Fame;* Emmy Award nomination, outstanding supporting actress in a miniseries or a movie, 2005, Golden Globe Award nomination, best performance by an actress in a supporting role in a series, miniseries, or motion picture made for television, 2006, and Screen Actors Guild Award nomination, outstanding performance by a female actor in a television movie or miniseries, 2006, all for *Empire Falls;* William J. German Human Relations Award, American Jewish Committee; also the winner or runner–up of a number of beauty contests.

CREDITS

Film Appearances:

Lissy, *Count Three and Pray* (also known as *The Calico Pony*), Columbia, 1955.

Dorothy "Dorie" Kingship, *A Kiss before Dying,* United Artists, 1956.

Eve White/Eve Black/Jane, *The Three Faces of Eve,* Twentieth Century–Fox, 1957.

Leola Boone, *No Down Payment,* Twentieth Century–Fox, 1957.

Clara Varner, *The Long, Hot Summer,* Twentieth Century–Fox, 1958.

Grace Bannerman, *Rally 'round the Flag, Boys!,* Twentieth Century–Fox, 1958.

Quentin Compson and narrator, *The Sound and the Fury,* Twentieth Century–Fox, 1959.

Carol Cutrere, *The Fugitive Kind,* United Artists, 1960.

Mary St. John and Mrs. Alfred Eaton, *From the Terrace,* Twentieth Century–Fox, 1960.

Lillian Corning, *Paris Blues,* United Artists, 1961.

Lila Green (title role), *The Stripper* (also known as *Celebration, A Woman in July, A Woman of July,* and *Woman of Summer*), Twentieth Century–Fox, 1963.

Samantha "Sam" Blake and Mimi, *A New Kind of Love* (also known as *Samantha*), Paramount, 1963.

Molly Thomas, *Signpost to Murder,* Metro–Goldwyn–Mayer, 1964.

Mary Meredith and Ruby, *A Big Hand for the Little Lady* (also known as *Big Deal at Dodge City*), Warner Bros., 1966.

Rhoda Shillitoe, *A Fine Madness,* Warner Bros., 1966.

Rachel Cameron (title role), *Rachel, Rachel* (also known as *A Jest of God*), Warner Bros./Seven Arts, 1968.

Elora Capua, *Winning* (also known as *Indianapolis*), Universal, 1969.

Geraldine, *WUSA* (also known as *Hall of Mirrors*), Paramount, 1970.

Herself (commentator), *King: A Filmed Record … Montgomery to Memphis* (documentary), Maron Films, 1970.

Dr. Mildred Watson, *They Might Be Giants,* Universal, 1971.

Beatrice, *The Effect of Gamma Rays on Man–in–the–Moon Marigolds,* Twentieth Century–Fox, 1972.

Rita Walden, *Summer Wishes, Winter Dreams,* Columbia, 1973.

Iris Devereaux, *The Drowning Pool,* Warner Bros., 1975.

Jessica, *The End,* United Artists, 1978.

Lilly, *Harry & Son* (also known as *Harry and Son*), Orion, 1984.

Herself, *Sanford Meisner: The American Theatre's Best Kept Secret* (documentary), Columbia, 1985.

Herself, *Women—for America, for the World* (short documentary), 1986.

Amanda Wingfield, *The Glass Menagerie,* Cineplex Odeon, 1987.

India Bridge, *Mr. & Mrs. Bridge,* Miramax, 1990.

Narrator, *The Age of Innocence,* Columbia, 1993.

Sarah Beckett, *Philadelphia* (also known as *At Risk* and *People Like Us*), TriStar, 1993.

Narrator and in introduction, *Even If a Hundred Ogres…,* 1996.

Narrator, *My Knees Were Jumping: Remembering the Kindertransports* (documentary), Anthology Film Archives/National Center for Jewish Films, 1998.

(In archive footage) Herself, *James Dean: Forever Young* (documentary), Warner Bros., 2005.

Narrator, *Keepers of Eden* (documentary), 2007.

(In archive footage) *Sebring* (documentary), 2009.

Film Director:
The Hump Back Angel, 1984.

Television Appearances; Series:
Host, *American Masters,* PBS, 1985–90.
Host, *Live at the Met,* PBS, 1986–88.

Television Appearances; Miniseries:
Francine Whiting, *Empire Falls,* HBO, 2005.

Television Appearances; Movies:
Dr. Cornelia Wilbur, *Sybil,* broadcast as part of *The Big Event,* NBC, 1976.
Mildred McCloud, *A Christmas to Remember,* CBS, 1978.
Lady Chatterly's Lover, 1978.
Beverly, *The Shadow Box,* ABC, 1980.
Elizabeth Huckaby, *Crisis at Central High,* CBS, 1981.
Catherine Kennerly, *Passions,* CBS, 1984.
Barbara Wyatt–Hollis, *Do You Remember Love,* CBS, 1985.
Vinnie Miner, *Foreign Affairs,* TNT, 1993.

Television Appearances; Specials:
Herself, *At This Very Moment,* 1962.
Mary Follett, "All the Way Home," *Hallmark Hall of Fame,* NBC, 1971.
Host, *The Wild Places,* NBC, 1974.
Narrator, *The Fragile Mind,* ABC, 1974.
Margaret "Marmee" March, *Little Women,* broadcast as part of *NBC Special Treat,* NBC, 1976.
The John Denver Special, ABC, 1976.
Lola Delaney, "Come Back, Little Sheba," *Laurence Olivier Presents* (also known as *Laurence Olivier Presents: "Come Back, Little Sheba"*), NBC, 1977.
Cohost, *A Salute to American Imagination,* CBS, 1978.
Narrator, *Angel Death* (documentary), syndicated, 1979.
Narrator, *Fred Astaire: Change Partners and Dance,* PBS, 1980.
Narrator, *Fred Astaire: Puttin' on His Top Hat,* PBS, 1980.
Comedy, Cartwheels, Kung Fu and Capers: The Super Spectacle of the Peking Opera, Showtime, 1981.
Candida Morell (title role), "Candida," *Broadway on Showtime* (also known as *Broadway on Showtime: Candida*), Showtime and The Entertainment Channel, 1983.

(In archive footage) Herself, *TV's Funniest Game Show Moments,* ABC, 1984.
Host, *Private Conversations: The Making of the Television Adaptation of "Death of a Salesman" with Dustin Hoffman,* PBS, 1985.
Born America: A March of Dimes Television Event, syndicated, 1986.
Narrator, *A Thousand Cranes,* PBS, 1989.
Congressional representative Nell Harrington, "Blind Spot" (also known as "A Death in the Family"), *Hallmark Hall of Fame,* CBS, 1993.
Voice of Margaret Sanger, *The Roots of Roe,* PBS, 1993.
What Is This Thing Called Love? (also known as *What Is This Thing Called Love? The Barbara Walters Special*), ABC, 1993.
Maggie Moran, "Breathing Lessons" (also known "Maggie, Maggie!"), *Hallmark Hall of Fame,* CBS, 1994.
Herself, "Gore Vidal's Gore Vidal," *A&E Stage,* Arts and Entertainment, 1995.
Herself, *The Rosemary Clooney Golden Anniversary Celebration* (also known as *Demi–Centennial, Golden Anniversary, Rosemary Clooney's Demi–Centennial,* and *Rosemary Clooney's Golden Anniversary*), Arts and Entertainment, 1995.
Host, "A Renaissance Revisited," *Dance in America* (also known as *Dance in America: A Renaissance Revisited*), broadcast as part of *Great Performances,* PBS, 1996.
Herself, *James Dean: A Portrait* (also known as *James Dean*), Disney Channel, 1996.
(In archive footage) Herself, *Cleopatra: The Film That Changed Hollywood,* American Movie Classics, 2001.
Herself, *The John Garfield Story,* TCM, 2003.
Herself, *The Adventures of Errol Flynn,* TCM, 2005.

Television Appearances; Awards Presentations:
Herself, *The 30th Annual Academy Awards,* NBC, 1958.
Presenter, *The 34th Annual Academy Awards,* ABC, 1962.
Presenter, *The 38th Annual Academy Awards,* ABC, 1966.
Presenter, *The 22nd Annual Tony Awards,* NBC, 1968.
Herself, *An All–Star Tribute to Elizabeth Taylor,* ABC, 1977.
(Uncredited) *The 55th Annual Academy Awards,* ABC, 1983.
The Spencer Tracy Legacy: A Tribute by Katharine Hepburn (also known as *The Spencer Tracy Legacy*), PBS, 1986.
(In archive footage) India Bridge, *The 63rd Annual Academy Awards,* ABC, 1991.
The Kennedy Center Honors: A Celebration of the Performing Arts, CBS, 1992, 1997.

Television Appearances; Episodic:
Penny, "Penny," *Robert Montgomery Presents* (also known as *Lucky Strike Theatre, Montgomery's*

Summer Stock, *Robert Montgomery Presents "Your Lucky Strike Theatre,"* and *The Robert Montgomery Summer Theater*), NBC, 1952.

"The Bitter Storm," *Tales of Tomorrow,* ABC, 1952.

"The Kill," *Studio One* (also known as *Studio One, Studio One in Hollywood, Summer Theatre, Westinghouse Studio One,* and *Westinghouse Summer Theatre*), CBS, 1952.

Ann Rutledge, "Mr. Lincoln: Parts 1–5," *Omnibus,* CBS, 1952–53.

Emily, "The Dancers," *Philco Television Playhouse* (also known as *Arena Theatre, The Philco–Goodyear Television Playhouse,* and *Repertory Theatre*), NBC, 1953.

"New Salem," *Omnibus,* CBS, 1953.

"The Young and the Fair," *Goodyear Playhouse* (also known as *Goodyear Television Playhouse*), NBC, 1953.

"A Young Lady of Property," *Philco Television Playhouse* (also known as *Arena Theatre, The Philco–Goodyear Television Playhouse,* and *Repertory Theatre*), NBC, 1953.

Elsie, "Homecoming," *Robert Montgomery Presents* (also known as *Lucky Strike Theatre, Montgomery's Summer Stock, Robert Montgomery Presents "Your Lucky Strike Theatre,"* and *The Robert Montgomery Summer Theater*), NBC, 1954.

Jane Ledbetter, "Segment," *The Ford Television Theater* (also known as *Ford Theater*), NBC, 1954.

Jen Townsend, "Five Star Final," *Lux Video Theatre* (also known as *Summer Video Theatre*), NBC, 1954.

Lisa (some sources cite role as Elsa), "Stir Mugs," *Studio One* (also known as *Studio One, Studio One in Hollywood, Summer Theatre, Westinghouse Studio One,* and *Westinghouse Summer Theatre*), CBS, 1954.

Nancy, "High Man," *The Elgin Hour,* ABC, 1954.

Vicki Hallock, "Interlude," *Four Star Playhouse* (also known as *Best in Mystery, Four Star Theatre, Singer Playhouse,* and *Star Performance*), CBS, 1954.

"Brink of Disaster," *The Armstrong Circle Theater* (also known as *Armstrong Circle Theater* and *Circle Theater*), NBC, 1954.

"In the Line of Duty," *Danger,* CBS, 1954.

"The Oklahoma Land Rush (April 22, 1889)," *You Are There,* CBS, 1954.

"Unequal Contest," *Kraft Television Theatre* (also known as *Kraft Mystery Theatre, Kraft Theatre,* and *Ponds Theatre*), ABC, 1954.

"Welcome Home," *The Web,* CBS, 1954.

Eleanor Apley, "The Late George Apley" (also known as "Back Bay Romance"), *The Twentieth Century–Fox Hour* (also known as *Fox Hour of Stars* and *The 20th Century–Fox Hour*), CBS, 1955.

Jill, "Dark Stranger," *Henry Fonda Presents "The Star and the Story"* (also known as *The Henry Fonda Show* and *The Star and the Story*), syndicated, 1955.

Roxy (some sources cite role as Rocky), "White Gloves," *The U.S. Steel Hour* (also known as *The United States Steel Hour*), CBS, 1955.

Terry Thomas, "Full Circle," *Four Star Playhouse* (also known as *Best in Mystery, Four Star Theatre, Singer Playhouse,* and *Star Performance*), CBS, 1955.

"Cynara," *Kraft Television Theatre* (also known as *Kraft Mystery Theatre, Kraft Theatre,* and *Ponds Theatre*), ABC, 1955.

"Dark Stranger," *Rheingold Theater,* NBC, 1955.

"Death of a Stranger," *Star Tonight,* ABC, 1955.

"Eleven o'Clock Flight," *Kraft Television Theatre* (also known as *Kraft Mystery Theatre, Kraft Theatre,* and *Ponds Theatre*), ABC, 1955.

Ann Benton, "Watch the Sunset," *Four Star Playhouse* (also known as *Best in Mystery, Four Star Theatre, Singer Playhouse,* and *Star Performance*), CBS, 1956.

Ann Rutledge, "Prologue to Glory," *General Electric Theater* (also known as *G.E. Theater* and *G.E. True Theater*), CBS, 1956.

Beth Paine, "Momentum," *Alfred Hitchcock Presents,* CBS, 1956.

Christiana, "A Man's World," *Studio One* (also known as *Studio One, Studio One in Hollywood, Summer Theatre, Westinghouse Studio One,* and *Westinghouse Summer Theatre*), CBS, 1956.

Daisy, "Family Protection," *Studio One* (also known as *Studio One, Studio One in Hollywood, Summer Theatre, Westinghouse Studio One,* and *Westinghouse Summer Theatre*), CBS, 1956.

Katherine, "Savage Portrait," *Climax!* (also known as *Climax* and *Climax Mystery Theater*), CBS, 1956.

Margaret Spencer, "The Girl in Chapter One," *The Alcoa Hour,* NBC, 1956.

"Starfish," *Kraft Television Theatre* (also known as *Kraft Mystery Theatre, Kraft Theatre,* and *Ponds Theatre*), ABC, 1956.

Person to Person, CBS, 1957, 1958.

Louise Darling, "The 80 Yard Run," *Playhouse 90,* CBS, 1958.

Herself, *The Ed Sullivan Show* (also known as *Toast of the Town*), CBS, 1958.

Herself (mystery guest), *What's My Line?,* CBS, 1959.

Herself, *The Mike Douglas Show,* syndicated, 1971.

Herself, *Dinah's Place,* NBC, 1971, 1974.

Midge Gibson, *The Carol Burnett Show* (also known as *Carol Burnett and Friends*), CBS, 1976.

Host, "Georgia O'Keeffe," *American Masters,* PBS, 1977.

Herself, *Dinah!* (also known as *Dinah* and *Dinah and Friends*), syndicated, 1977.

Betty Quinn, "See How She Runs," *General Electric Theater* (also known as *G.E. Theater* and *G.E. True Theater*), CBS, 1978.

Carol Schramm, "The Streets of L.A.," *General Electric Theater* (also known as *G.E. Theater* and *G.E. True Theater*), CBS, 1979.

"Jane Adams," *An American Portrait,* CBS, 1985.

Herself, *Face to Face with Connie Chung,* CBS, 1990.

Herself, "Miracle on 44th Street: A Portrait of the Actors Studio," *American Masters,* PBS, 1991.

Herself, "Paul Newman: Hollywood's Charming Rebel," *Biography* (also known as *A&E Biography: Paul Newman*), Arts and Entertainment, 1995.

(In archive footage) Sarah Beckett, "Quadriplegia, Nymphomania, and HIV–Positive Night," *Joe Bob's Drive–In Theater,* The Movie Channel, 1995.

Herself, "Joan Collins: A Personal Dynasty," *Biography* (also known as *A&E Biography: Joan Collins*), Arts and Entertainment, 1997.

Herself, "Robert Wagner: Hollywood's Prince Charming," *Biography* (also known as *A&E Biography: Robert Wagner*), Arts and Entertainment, 1999.

Herself, "Allison Janney," *Intimate Portrait* (also known as *Intimate Portrait: Allison Janney*), Lifetime, 2001.

Herself and Clara Varner, "The Long, Hot Summer," *Backstory* (also known as *AMC Backstory, AMC Backstory: The Long Hot Summer,* and *Hollywood Backstories*), American Movie Classics, 2001.

Herself, "A Man for All Stages: The Life and Times of Christopher Plummer," *Life and Times,* CBC, 2002.

Anne Martin, "Safe for Democracy," *Freedom: A History for Us,* PBS, 2003.

Reader, "The Education of Gore Vidal," *American Masters,* PBS, 2003.

Herself, *Inside the Actors Studio* (also known as *Inside the Actors Studio: The Craft of Theatre and Film*), Bravo, 2003.

Narrator, "Pale Male," *Nature,* PBS, 2004.

(In archive footage) Herself, "Las Vegas: An Unconventional History: Part 1," *The American Experience,* PBS, 2005.

(In archive footage) Herself, *Entertainment Tonight* (also known as *Entertainment This Week, E.T., ET Weekend,* and *This Week in Entertainment*), syndicated, 2008.

Appeared as herself, "The Films of James Ivory," *The Directors,* Encore.

Television Work; Specials:

Director, "Come along with Me," *American Playhouse,* PBS, 1982.

Coproducer, "Blind Spot" (also known as "A Death in the Family"), *Hallmark Hall of Fame,* CBS, 1993.

Executive producer and artistic director (Westport Country Playhouse), *Our Town,* Showtime, 2003, broadcast on *Masterpiece Theatre* (also known as *ExxonMobil Masterpiece Theatre* and *Mobil Masterpiece Theatre*), PBS, 2003.

Television Production Assistant; Episodic:

"Another Caesar," *Studio One* (also known as *Studio One, Studio One in Hollywood, Summer Theatre, Westinghouse Studio One,* and *Westinghouse Summer Theatre*), CBS, 1953.

"Music and Mrs. Pratt," *Studio One* (also known as *Studio One, Studio One in Hollywood, Summer Theatre, Westinghouse Studio One,* and *Westinghouse Summer Theatre*), CBS, 1953.

Television Work; Other; Episodic:

Director, "Thanksgiving," *Family,* ABC, 1979.

Producer, "Broadway's Dreamers: The Legacy of the Group Theatre," *American Masters* (also known as *American Masters: Broadway's Dreamers: The Legacy of the Group Theatre*), PBS, 1989.

Stage Appearances:

Understudy, *Picnic,* Music Box Theatre, New York City, 1953–54.

Douane, *The Lovers,* Martin Beck Theatre, New York City, 1956.

Mavis, *Baby Want a Kiss,* Little Theatre, New York City, 1964.

Candida Morell (title role), *Candida,* Circle in the Square, New York City, 1981–82.

Arkadina, *The Sea Gull* (also known as *The Seagull*), River Arts Repertory, Woodstock, NY, 1985.

Amanda Wingfield, *The Glass Menagerie,* Williamstown Theatre Festival, Main Stage, Williamstown, MA, 1985, and Long Wharf Theatre, New Haven, CT, 1985–86.

Alexandra del Lago (also known as Princess Kosmonopolis), *Sweet Bird of Youth,* Royal Alexandra Theatre, Toronto, Ontario, Canada, 1988.

Mrs. Alving, *Ghosts,* Bearsville Theater, Woodstock, NY, 1991.

Abby Brewster, *Arsenic and Old Lace,* Long Wharf Theatre, 1994–95.

Judith Bliss, *Hay Fever,* Berkshire Theatre Festival, Stockbridge, MA, 1996.

Melissa Gardner, *Love Letters,* Westport Country Playhouse, Westport, CT, 2000.

Ancestral Voices (reading), Westport Country Playhouse, 2000.

Come Be My Love … Love Spoken Here (benefit reading), Westport Country Playhouse, 2007.

One of the Brewster sisters, *Arsenic and Old Lace* (reading), Westport Country Playhouse, 2008.

A Holiday Garland, Westport Country Playhouse, 2008.

Member of Little Theatre Group, Greenville, SC; appeared in summer stock productions, Chatham, MA.

Stage Director:

The Depot, Westport Country Playhouse, Theatre Artists Workshop, Westport, CT, 1986, John F. Kennedy Center for the Performing Arts, Washington, DC, c. 1980, Interart Theatre, New York City, 1987, Ethel Walker School, Simsbury, CT, 1987, performed as a benefit at the Westport Country Playhouse, 1987.

Golden Boy, Williamstown Theatre Festival, The Extension, Williamstown, MA, 1987.

Golden Boy, Blue Light Theatre Company, 45th Street Theatre, New York City, 1995.

Rocket to the Moon, Williamstown Theatre Festival, The Other Stage, Williamstown, MA, 1996.

La Ronde, Williamstown Theatre Festival, The Other Stage, 1997.

The Big Knife, Williamstown Theatre Festival, The Nikos Stage, Williamstown, MA, 1998.

Waiting for Lefty, Blue Light Theatre Company, Classic Stage Company Theatre, New York City, 1998.

The Constant Wife, Westport Country Playhouse, 2000.

Three Days of Rain, Westport Country Playhouse, 2001.

(With Anne Keefe) *David Copperfield,* Westport Country Playhouse, 2005.

The Member of the Wedding, Westport Country Playhouse, 2005.

Also directed *Velvet Elvis.*

Stage Director; Major Tours:

The Depot, productions at various American venues, including college campuses and military schools, and produced at rallies, c. 1980.

Stage Artistic Director:

Our Town, Westport Country Playhouse, Westport, CT, 2002–2003.

Thurgood (solo show), Westport Country Playhouse, 2008.

Artistic director for various productions of the Westport Country Playhouse.

Stage Producer:

Our Town, Booth Theatre, New York City, 2002–2003.

Thurgood (solo show), Booth Theatre, 2008.

RECORDINGS

Videos:

Herself, *Edward R. Murrow: The Best of "Person to Person,"* 1993.

WRITINGS

Teleplays; Specials:

(With Neal Miller and June Finfer) "Come along with Me" (based on an unfinished work by Shirley Jackson), *American Playhouse,* PBS, 1982.

OTHER SOURCES

Books:

International Dictionary of Films and Filmmakers, Volume 3: *Actors and Actresses,* St. James Press, 1996.

Morella, Joe, and Edward Z. Epstein, *Paul and Joanne: A Biography of Paul Newman and Joanne Woodward,* W. H. Allen, 1989.

Netter, Susan, *Paul Newman and Joanne Woodward,* Piatkus Books, 1989.

The Scribner Encyclopedia of American Lives, Thematic Series: The 1960s, Charles Scribner's Sons, 2003.

Periodicals:

American Theatre, September, 1996, p. 56.

People Weekly, July 21, 1975.

WOPAT, Tom 1951–

PERSONAL

Full name, Thomas S. Wopat; born September 9, 1951, in Lodi, WI; father, a dairy farmer; married Vickie Allen, October 27, 1984 (divorced); married and divorced an additional time; children: Lindsey, Joey, Adam, Taylor, Walker. *Education:* Studied music at the University of Wisconsin. *Avocational Interests:* Fishing, cooking.

Addresses: *Agent*—Innovative Artists, 1505 10th St., Santa Monica, CA 90401 and 235 Park Ave. South, Tenth Floor, New York, NY 10003. *Publicist*—The Brokaw Company, 9255 Sunset Blvd., Suite 804, Los Angeles, CA 90069–3309.

Career: Actor, singer, and director. Singer and guitarist with musical groups, including the North Hollywood All–Stars and the Full Moon Band; performer at various venues; performed with the Los Angeles Philharmonic at the Hollywood Bowl; also performed with the Cincinnati Pops Orchestra. Worked as a roofer.

Member: Actors' Equity Association, Directors Guild of America.

Awards, Honors: Antoinette Perry Award nomination, best actor in a musical, and Drama Desk Award nomination, outstanding actor in a musical, both 1999, for *Annie Get Your Gun;* Drama Desk Award nomination (with others), outstanding ensemble performance, 2005, for *Glengarry Glen Ross;* Antoinette Perry Award nomination, best actor in a musical, and Drama Desk Award nomination, outstanding featured actor in a musical, both 2008, for *A Catered Affair.*

CREDITS

Television Appearances; Series:

Luke Duke, *The Dukes of Hazzard,* CBS, 1979–82, 1983–85.

Voice of Luke Duke, *The Dukes* (animated), CBS, 1983.
Frank Cobb, *Blue Skies,* CBS, 1988.
Performer of theme song, *Empty Nest,* NBC, 1988–95.
Dr. Jed McFadden, *A Peaceable Kingdom,* CBS, 1989.
Jeff Robbins, *Cybill,* CBS, 1995–98.
Host, *Prime Time Country,* The Nashville Network (TNN), beginning 1996.
Hank Pelham, *All My Children* (also known as *All My Children: The Summer of Seduction* and *La force du destin*), ABC, 2001–2002.
Host, *Circle of Honor,* The Outdoor Channel, beginning 2003.

Television Appearances; Movies:
Tom Silver, *Burning Rage,* CBS, 1984.
Pete, *Christmas Comes to Willow Creek,* CBS, 1987.
Bobby Rex, *Just My Imagination* (also known as *The Girl in the Song Title*), NBC, 1992.
Luke Duke, *The Dukes of Hazzard: Reunion!* (also known as *Reunion in Hazzard*), CBS, 1997.
Sam, *Contagious* (also known as *Virus*), USA Network, 1997.
Tom Johnson, *Meteorites!,* USA Network, 1998.
Luke Duke, *The Dukes of Hazzard: Hazzard in Hollywood,* NBC, 2000.
Bill, *The Hive,* Sci–Fi Channel, 2008.
Mr. Phelps, *Taking Chance,* HBO, 2009.

Television Appearances; Specials:
Celebrity Challenge of the Sexes, CBS, 1980.
A Country Christmas, CBS, 1980.
CBS team member, *Battle of the Network Stars XII,* ABC, 1982.
CBS team captain, *Battle of the Network Stars XIV,* ABC, 1983.
Story, Songs and Stars, 1984.
Performer, *American Bandstand's 33 1/3 Celebration,* ABC, 1985.
We the People 200: The Constitutional Gala, CBS, 1987.
Anchor, *All New Circus of the Stars and Side Show* (also known as *Circus of the Stars #16* and *Circus of the Stars XVI*), CBS, 1991.
Segment host, *A '70s Celebration: The Beat Is Back,* NBC, 1993.
Host, *Great American Music: A Salute to Fast Cars,* Family Channel, 1994.
Performer, *Cincinnati Pops Holiday: Erich Kunzel's Halloween Spooktacular,* PBS, 1996.
Himself, *Entertainment Tonight Presents: The Dukes of Hazzard—The Untold Story,* 1999.
America's Millennium, CBS, 1999.
The Life and Times of The Dukes of Hazzard, The Nashville Network (TNN), 1999.
The Great American History Quiz: Heroes and Villains, History Channel, 2000.
Himself, "My Favorite Broadway: The Love Songs," *Great Performances,* PBS, 2001.

Narrator, *The Bear: The Legend of Coach Paul Bryant,* CBS, 2001.
Performer, *Cincinnati Pops Holiday: Fourth of July from the Heartland,* PBS, 2001.
Himself, *Heart–throbs of the 70s* (documentary), Sky, 2001.
National Memorial Day Concert, PBS, 2001.
Himself, *CBS at 75* (also known as *CBS at 75: A Prime-time Celebration*), CBS, 2003.
Himself, *Broadway under the Stars,* CBS, 2004, 2005.
(In archive footage) Luke Duke, "20 Greatest Country Comedy Shows," *The Greatest* (also known as *CMT: The Greatest* and *CMT: The Greatest—20 Greatest Country Comedy Shows*), Country Music Television (CMT), 2006.

Television Appearances; Awards Presentations:
The 39th Annual Tony Awards, CBS, 1985.
The 37th Annual Primetime Emmy Awards, ABC, 1985.
The 40th Annual Tony Awards, CBS, 1986.
The 22nd Annual Academy of Country Music Awards, NBC, 1987.
The 53rd Annual Tony Awards, CBS, 1999.
The Fourth Annual TV Land Awards (also known as *The Fourth Annual TV Land Awards: A Celebration of Classic TV* and *TV Land Awards 2006*), TV Land, 2006.

Television Appearances; Episodic:
David Chilton, "Flying Aces/The Mermaid Returns," *Fantasy Island,* ABC, 1980.
Himself, *The Midnight Special,* NBC, 1981.
Guest, *Password Plus* (also known as *Password* and *Password All–Stars*), NBC, 1982.
Performer, *American Bandstand* (also known as *AB* and *Bandstand*), ABC, 1982.
Cohost and performer, *Solid Gold,* syndicated, 1983.
Himself, *Hee Haw,* syndicated, 1983.
Bill Dawson, "Kendo Killing," *Murder, She Wrote,* CBS, 1996.
Chuck Goodman, "Someone to Watch over Me," *Crisis Center* (also known as *The Center*), NBC, 1997.
Ian, "Jill's Passion," *Home Improvement* (also known as *Hammer Time* and *Tool Time*), ABC, 1997.
Ian, "Taking Jill for Granite," *Home Improvement* (also known as *Hammer Time* and *Tool Time*), ABC, 1998.
Himself, *The Rosie O'Donnell Show,* syndicated, 1999.
Presenter, *Top Ten,* Channel 4 (England), 2000.
Hanley Rand, "Lost Causes," *100 Centre Street* (also known as *101 Centre Street* and *Tribunal central*), Arts and Entertainment, 2001.
Himself, "The Dukes of Hazzard," *The E! True Hollywood Story* (also known as *The Dukes of Hazzard: The E! True Hollywood Story* and *THS*), E! Entertainment Television, 2001.
Himself, "Cybill Shepherd," *Biography* (also known as *A&E Biography: Cybill Shepherd*), Arts and Entertainment, 2004.

Senator Jack Jennings, "Exposed," *Smallville* (also known as *Smallville: Beginnings* and *Smallville: Superman the Early Years*), The WB, 2005.

Himself, "Dukes of Hazzard," *Inside Fame*, Country Music Television (CMT), 2005.

Himself, "Action Heroes," *My First Time*, TV Land, 2006.

Himself, "Special Edition: The Dukes of Hazzard," *CMT Insider*, Country Music Television (CMT), 2006.

Himself, *CMT Insider*, Country Music Television (CMT), another episode in 2006.

Himself, "Locations," *TV Land Confidential* (also known as *TV Land Confidential: The Untold Stories*), TV Land, 2007.

Himself, *The Graham Norton Show*, BBC, 2007.

Himself, *The View*, ABC, 2008.

Appeared as himself in "Dukes of Hazzard v. Angie," "Dukes of Hazzard v. The Waltons," "Heroes v. Villains 2," and "Heroes v. Villains 3," all episodes of *Family Feud* (also known as *All–Star Family Feud, The Family Feud, Family Fortune,* and *The Best of Family Feud*), ABC and syndicated. Appeared as a guest panelist, *Battlestars*, NBC; as a performer, *On Stage* (also known as *TNN On Stage*), The Nashville Network (TNN); and as himself, *The Tom Green Show*, MTV; also appeared in other programs, including *Fantasy*, NBC.

Television Appearances; Pilots:

Luke Duke, "One Armed Bandits," *The Dukes of Hazzard*, CBS, 1979.

Dr. Jed McFadden, *A Peaceable Kingdom*, CBS, 1989.

Jeff Robbins, "Virgin, Mother, Crone," *Cybill*, CBS, 1995.

Rick Kesslar, *Standoff* (also known as *Primary*), Fox, 2006.

Television Director; Episodic:

"The Boar's Nest Bears," *The Dukes of Hazzard*, CBS, 1983.

"Lulu's Gone Away," *The Dukes of Hazzard*, CBS, 1983.

"Happy Birthday, General Lee," *The Dukes of Hazzard*, CBS, 1984.

"Enos and Daisy's Wedding," *The Dukes of Hazzard*, CBS, 1985.

"The Haunting of J. D. Hogg," *The Dukes of Hazzard*, CBS, 1985.

Stage Appearances:

Title role, *The Robber Bridegroom* (musical), Ford's Theatre, Washington, DC, 1977.

Wally, *I Love My Wife* (musical), Ethel Barrymore Theatre, New York City, c. 1977.

Dan, *A Bistro Car on the CNR* (revue), Playhouse Theatre, New York City, 1978.

Oklahoma! (musical), Equity Library Theatre, Master Theatre, New York City, 1978.

Member of the ensemble, *Hey, Look Me Over* (revue), Lincoln Center, Avery Fisher Hall, New York City, 1981.

Billy Bigelow, *Carousel* (musical), John F. Kennedy Center for the Performing Arts, Opera House, Washington, DC, 1986.

Jove/Jupiter/Zeus and Amphytrion, *Olympus on My Mind* (musical), Lamb's Theatre, New York City, 1986–87.

Detective Stone, *City of Angels* (musical), Virginia Theatre, New York City, 1990.

Sky Masterson, *Guys and Dolls* (musical), Martin Beck Theatre, New York City, c. 1992, some sources cite a production at the John F. Kennedy Center for the Performing Arts.

The Rainmaker, Barn Theatre, Augusta, MI, 1993.

Billy Flynn, *Chicago* (musical), Richard Rogers Theatre, New York City, 1996, Ambassador Theatre, New York City, 2004, 2004–2005, 2007, 2008.

South Pacific (musical), Barn Theatre, 1998.

Frank Butler, *Annie Get Your Gun* (musical), Marquis Theatre, New York City, 1999, 2001.

Nick (a fire captain), *The Guys* (staged reading), Flea Theater, New York City, 2002.

Julian Marsh, *42nd Street* (musical), Ford Center for the Performing Arts, New York City, 2002, Pittsburgh CLO, Pittsburgh, PA, 2006.

Jeeter, *The Last of the Boys*, McCarter Theatre, Berlind Theatre, Princeton, NJ, 2004.

James Lingk, *Glengarry Glen Ross*, Royale Theatre, New York City, 2005.

Performer, *Harold Arlen: A Centennial Celebration*, Carnegie Hall, New York City, 2005.

Tom (the father), *A Catered Affair* (musical), Walter Kerr Theatre, New York City, 2008.

Guest artist at the Barn Theatre, 1992–93; cabaret performer at Arci's Place, New York City, 2002. Appeared in other productions, including the rock opera *Jesus Christ Superstar* and the musicals *South Pacific* and *West Side Story*, all produced at the University of Wisconsin.

Major Tours:

Frank Butler, *Annie Get Your Gun*, U.S. cities, 1999, 2001.

Billy Flynn, *Chicago* (musical), U.S. cities, 2004.

Over the Rainbow (concert tour), U.S. cities, 2005.

Film Appearances:

Arlo Brimm, *Bonneville*, SenArt Films, 2006.

Detective Jones, *The Understudy*, 2008.

RECORDINGS

Albums:

A Little Bit Closer, EMI America, 1977.

Tom Wopat, 1977.

Don't Look Back, Capitol, 1991.
Learning to Love, Epic, 1992.
The Still of the Night, Angel Records, 2000.
Tom Wopat Sings Harold Arlen: Dissertation on the State of Bliss, Sin–Drome Records, 2005.

Albums; with Others:
The Dukes of Hazzard (songs recorded by the cast of the television series), 1979.
Annie Get Your Gun 1999 Broadway revival cast recording), Angel Records, 1999.
A Catered Affair (original Broadway cast recording), P.S. Classics, 2008.

Singles:
"A Little Bit Closer," 1987.
"The Rock and Roll of Love," 1987.
"Too Many Honky Tonks (On My Way Home)," Epic, 1991.

Recorded other singles, including "Back to the Well," "Susannah," and "Too Many Honky Tonks (On My Way Home)"/"I've Been There."

Music Videos:
"A Little Bit Closer," 1987.

Some sources cite appearances in other music videos.

Music Video Work:
Directed music videos.

Videos:
Himself, *Bo, Luke & Daisy: Just Good Ole Friends,* Warner Home Video, 2005.
Voice, *The History of Wisconsin Football* (documentary), Warner Home Video, 2007.

Video Games:
Voice of Luke Duke, *The Dukes of Hazzard: Racing for Home,* 1999.
Voice of Luke Duke, *The Dukes of Hazzard: Return of the General Lee,* 2004.

Audiobooks:
Clive Cussler, *Deep Six,* Simon & Schuster Audio, 1991.
Phyllis Reynolds Naylor, *Walker's Crossing,* Listening Library, 2000.
Sandra Brown, *The Crush,* Simon & Schuster Audio, 2002.
James Grippando, *Beyond Suspicion,* HarperAudio, 2002.
Brown, *The Sandra Brown Suspense Collection* (includes *The Crush*), Simon & Schuster Audio, 2003.

Landon Y. Jones, editor, *The Essential Lewis and Clark* (selections), HarperAudio, 2003.
Nicholas Sparks, *The Wedding,* 2003.
Robert Hicks, *The Widow of the South,* Grand Central Publishing, 2005.

WRITINGS

Songs:
Wrote songs, including "Look Up on Your Way Down," "Shadow of a Doubt," and "A Step in the Right Direction."

OTHER SOURCES

Periodicals:
Billboard, January 20, 1996, p. 25.
People Weekly, February 5, 1996, p. 14.

Electronic:
Wopat.com, http://www.tomwopat.com, January 9, 2009.

WRIGHT, Sarah 1983–
(Sarah Mason)

PERSONAL

Full name, Sarah Fay Wright; born September 28, 1983; daughter of Robert (a preacher) and Debbie Wright; married A. J. Mason, 2005 (divorced, 2006). *Education:* Attended high school in Kentucky.

Addresses: *Agent*—Chris Hart, International Creative Management, 10250 Constellation Way, 9th Floor, Los Angeles, CA 90067. *Manager*—Ellen Meyer, Ellen Meyer Management, 8899 Beverly Blvd., Suite 612, Los Angeles, CA 90048.

Career: Actress and singer. Ford Models Los Angeles, worked as a model; Kentucky Ambassadors of Music, member of singing group.

CREDITS

Television Appearances; Series:
(As Sarah Mason) Paige Chase, *Quintuplets,* Fox, 2004–2005.

(Credited as Sarah Mason in 2006) Jane, a recurring role, *7th Heaven* (also known as *Seventh Heaven* and *7th Heaven: Beginnings*), CW Network, 2006–2007.
(As Mason) Lizzy, *The Loop,* Fox, 2007.

Television Appearances; Movies:

David's high school date, *Enchanted,* Showtime, 1998.
(As Sarah Mason) Laura McDonald, *All You've Got* (also known as *Rumble*), MTV, 2006.

Television Appearances; Specials:

The Teen Choice Awards 2004, Fox, 2004.
(As Sarah Mason) Kris) *Up All Night,* CBS, 2007.

Television Appearances; Pilots:

(As Sarah Mason) Paige Chase, *Quintuplets,* Fox, 2004.
(As Mason) Lizzy, *The Loop,* Fox, 2007.

Television Appearances; Episodic:

(As Sarah Mason) Sara Jennings, "Prey," *CSI: Miami,* CBS, 2004.

(As Mason) Vicki, "Secret Boyfriend," *Malcolm in the Middle,* Fox, 2005.
Susie, "Maidenform," *Mad Men,* AMC, 2008.

Film Appearances:

(As Sarah Mason) Jane, *X's & O's,* Seventh Art Releasing, 2008.
(As Mason) Sexy blonde, *Made of Honor* (also known as *Made of Honour*), Columbia, 2008.
(As Mason) Lavender, *Wieners,* Screen Gems, 2008.
(As Mason) Stacey, *Surfer, Dude,* Anchor Bay Entertainment, 2008.
Ashley, *The House Bunny,* Columbia, 2008.
Ashley, *Streak* (short film), Freestyle, 2008.

RECORDINGS

Videos:

Thesis: Work vs. Play, Twentieth Century–Fox Home Entertainment, 2007.

Appeared in the music video "Yes We Can," 2008.

Z

ZANUCK, Lili Fini 1954–
(Lili Zanuck)

PERSONAL

Original name, Lili Fini; born April 2, 1954, in Leominster, MA; married Richard Darryl Zanuck (a film producer and studio executive), September 23, 1978; stepchildren: Virginia, Janet, Harrison (a visual effects coordinator), Dean. *Education:* Attended Northern Virginia Community College.

Addresses: *Office*—Zanuck Co., 9465 Wilshire Blvd., Suite 930, Beverly Hills, CA 90212. *Agent*—Risa Gertner, Creative Artists Agency, 2000 Avenue of the Stars, New York, NY 90067. *Manager*—David Naylor, David Naylor and Associates, 6535 Santa Monica Blvd., Hollywood, CA 90038.

Career: Producer and director. Zanuck–Brown Co. (film production company), Los Angeles, worked in research and development, 1978–89; Zanuck Co., Beverly Hills, CA, cofounder and partner, 1989—. World Bank, Washington, DC, worked as research assistant, 1970–78; Carnation Co., Los Angeles, office manager, 1977–78. California Film Commission, member; Los Angeles Music Center, member of board of directors.

Awards, Honors: ShoWest Award (with husband Richard D. Zanuck and David Brown), producer of the year, National Association of Theatre Owners, 1985, for *Cocoon;* Golden Globe Award, best motion picture musical or comedy, National Board of Review Award, best picture, 1989, Academy Award, best picture, Film Award nomination, best film, British Academy of Film and Television Arts, Golden Laurel Award, motion picture producer of the year, Producers Guild of America, nomination for Wise Owl Award, television and theatrical film fiction category, Retirement Research Foundation, all (with others), 1990, for *Driving Miss Daisy;* Emmy Award nomination (with others), outstanding variety, music or comedy special, 2000, for *The 72nd Annual Academy Awards;* Country Music Association Award, best music video, 2000, for "Breathe."

CREDITS

Film Producer:
(With Richard D. Zanuck and David Brown) *Cocoon,* Twentieth Century–Fox, 1985.
(With Richard D. Zanuck and Brown) *Cocoon: The Return,* Twentieth Century–Fox, 1988.
(With Richard D. Zanuck) *Driving Miss Daisy,* Warner Bros., 1989.
(With Richard D. Zanuck) *Rich in Love,* Metro–Goldwyn–Mayer, 1993.
Clean Slate (also known as *Cool Slate*), Metro–Goldwyn–Mayer/United Artists, 1994.
Dvoynik (also known as *The Double*), 1995.
Wild Bill, Metro–Goldwyn–Mayer/United Artists, 1995.
Mulholland Falls, Metro–Goldwyn–Mayer/United Artists, 1996.
True Crime, Warner Bros., 1999.
Reign of Fire, Buena Vista, 2002.

Film Director:
Rush, Metro–Goldwyn–Mayer/Pathe, 1991.

Television Work; Specials:
Producer, *The 72nd Annual Academy Awards,* ABC, 2000.
Executive producer, *Countdown to Oscar 2000,* ABC, 2000.

Television Executive Producer; Pilots:
"Barrington," *CBS Summer Playhouse,* CBS, 1987.
Dead Lawyers, Sci–Fi Channel, 2004.

Television Director; Episodic:
"Hour Two," *Revelations,* NBC, 2005.
"Hour Three," *Revelations,* NBC, 2005.
"Hour Four," *Revelations,* NBC, 2005.

Television Director; Miniseries:
"We Have Cleared the Tower" segment, *From the Earth to the Moon,* HBO, 1998.

Television Appearances; Specials:
Judge, *The 1988 Miss America Pageant,* NBC, 1988.
The Blockbuster Imperative, Trio, 2003.

Television Appearances; Episodic:
On the Inside, The Learning Channel, c. 1997.
"Behind the Scenes: Making 'From the Earth to the Moon'," *HBO First Look,* HBO, 1998.

Television Appearances; Awards Presentations:
The 62nd Annual Academy Awards, ABC, 1990.
The 75th Annual Academy Awards, ABC, 2003.
(As Lili Zanuck) *The Award Show Awards Show,* Trio, 2003.

Television Appearances; Miniseries:
Hollywood Women, Carlton, 1994.

RECORDINGS

Video Appearances:
Filming "Rush," Metro–Goldwyn–Mayer Home Entertainment, 2002.
Miss Daisy's Journal: From Stage to Screen, Warner Home Video, 2003.
Jessica Tandy: Theatre Legend to Screen Star, Warner Home Video, 2003.
Morality and the Code: A How–to Manual for Hollywood, Warner Home Video, 2006.
Molls and Dolls: The Women of Gangster Films, Warner Home Video, 2006.
Stool Pigeons and Pine Overcoats: The Language of Gangster Films, Warner Home Video, 2006.
Welcome to the Big House, Warner Home Video, 2006.
Gangsters: The Immigrant's Hero, Warner Home Video, 2006.

Video Director:
Director of music videos, including "Island Life" by Michael Franks, 1987; "Tears in Heaven" by Eric Clapton, 1992; "Pilgrim" by Clapton, 1998; "Let's Make Love" by Faith Hill and Tim McGraw, 1999; and "Breathe" by Hill, c. 2000.

OTHER SOURCES

Books:
Newsmakers 1994, Issue 4, Gale, 1994.

Periodicals:
Hollywood Reporter, March 9, 1990.
Interview, January, 1992, p. 77.

ZIMBALIST, Efrem, Jr. 1918–

PERSONAL

Born November 30, 1918, in New York, NY; son of Efrem (a violinist) and Alma (an opera singer; maiden name, Gluck) Zimbalist; married Emily McNair, 1945 (died, 1950); married Loranda Stephanie Spalding, February 2, 1956 (divorced, c. 1961); remarried Spalding, 1972 (died February 5, 2007); children: (first marriage) Nancy, Efrem III; (second marriage) Stephanie (an actress). *Education:* Attended Yale University, 1935–37; studied for the theatre at Neighborhood Playhouse, New York City. *Politics:* Republican. *Religion:* Christian.

Career: Actor, voice artist, and producer. NBC–Radio, New York City, worked as a page; performed with a stock theatre company, Hammonton, NJ, 1954; Trinity Broadcasting Network, voice performer, 2007. Curtis Institute of Music, worked as assistant director and researcher. *Military service:* U.S. Army, served for five years during World War II; served in Europe; became first lieutenant; received Purple Heart.

Member: Actors' Equity Association, Screen Actors Guild, American Federation of Television and Radio Artists.

Awards, Honors: New York Drama Critics Award, outstanding producer, c. 1950, for *The Consul;* Laurel Award nomination, top new male personality, Producers Guild of America, 1958; Golden Globe Award, most promising male newcomer, 1959; Golden Globe Award nomination, best supporting actor, 1959, for *Home before Dark;* Emmy Award nomination, best actor in a dramatic series, 1959, for *77 Sunset Strip;* Golden Globe Award nomination, best supporting actor, 1968, for *Wait until Dark;* Golden Globe Award nomination, best male television star, 1969, for *The F.B.I.;* Emmy Award nomination, outstanding supporting actor in a comedy or drama special, 1978, for *A Family Upside Down;* received star on Hollywood Walk of Fame.

CREDITS

Television Appearances; Series:
Jim Gavin, *Concerning Miss Marlowe,* NBC, 1954–55.

Dandy Jim Buckley, a recurring role, *Maverick,* ABC, 1957–58.

Stuart Bailey, *77 Sunset Strip,* ABC, 1958–64.

Inspector Lewis Erskine, *The F.B.I.,* ABC, 1965–74.

Charles Cabot, a recurring role, *Hotel* (also known as *Arthur Hailey's "Hotel"*), ABC, between 1984 and 1988.

Streets, 1989.

Don Alejandro de la Vega, *Zorro* (also known as *The New Zorro, Zorro: The Legend Continues,* and *Les nouvelles aventures de Zorro*), The Family Channel, 1990.

Voice of King Arthur, *The Legend of Prince Valiant* (animated; also known as *Prince Valiant*), The Family Channel, 1991.

Voice of Alfred Pennyworth, *Batman* (animated; also known as *The Adventures of Batman & Robin* and *Batman: The Animated Series*), Fox, 1992–95.

Voice of Otto Octavius/Dr. Octopus, a recurring role, *Spider–Man* (animated), Fox, between 1995 and 1997.

Voice of Alfred Pennyworth, *The New Batman Adventures* (animated; also known as *Batman: The Animated Series Volume Four*), The WB, 1997–98.

Host, *A Year to Remember,* 1999.

Television Appearances; Movies:

Lewis Erskine, *Cosa Nostra, Arch Enemy of the FBI,* 1967.

Sergeant Harry Hansen, *Who Is the Black Dahlia?,* NBC, 1975.

Mike Long, *A Family Upside Down,* NBC, 1978.

David Martin, *Terror Out of the Sky* (also known as *The Revenge of the Savage Bees*), CBS, 1979.

Victor Wainwright, *The Gathering, Part II,* NBC, 1979.

Bill Reardan, *The Best Place to Be,* NBC, 1979.

Robert Cluso, *Shooting Stars,* ABC, 1983.

Tom Burroughs, *Baby Sister,* ABC, 1983.

Voice of Alfred Pennyworth, *The Batman/Superman Movie* (animated; also known as *Batman/Superman Adventures: World's Finest*), 1998.

Voice of Alfred Pennyworth, *Batman & Mr. Freeze: Subzero* (animated; also known as *Subzero*), The WB, 1998.

The vice chancellor, *Cab to Canada,* CBS, 1998.

Benjamin Hart, *The First Day,* 2001.

Television Appearances; Pilots:

Harry Baxter, *Wild about Harry,* NBC, 1978.

Aristotle Bolt, *Beyond Witch Mountain,* CBS, 1982.

Marty Malone, *Family in Blue,* CBS, 1982.

Host, *You Are the Jury,* NBC, 1984.

Don Alejandro de la Vega, *Zorro—The Legend Begins,* The Family Channel, 1990.

Television Appearances; Miniseries:

Ellis Ikehorn, *Scruples,* CBS, 1980.

Christof Philips, *Trade Winds,* NBC, 1993.

Television Appearances; Specials:

Mr. and Mrs. North, 1946.

A Salute to Television's 25th Anniversary, ABC, 1972.

The Anita Bryant Spectacular, syndicated, 1980.

Colonel Francis Chesney, *Charley's Aunt,* PBS, 1983.

Kennedy Center Honors: A Celebration of the Performing Arts, CBS, 1984.

The 50th Presidential Inaugural Gala, ABC, 1985.

Host, *You Are the Jury,* NBC, 1986.

Gian Carlo Menotti: The Musical Magician, PBS, 1986.

The 38th Annual Primetime Emmy Awards, NBC, 1986.

Host, *Killers at the Box Office,* syndicated, 1989.

Narrator, *Hollywood behind the Badge: A Century of Cinema Cops and Detectives,* AMC, 1999.

Television Appearances; Episodic:

Sean O'Neill, "Stopover at Sublimity," *The U.S. Steel Hour* (also known as *The United States Steel Hour*), CBS, 1956.

"The Long View," *Star Tonight,* 1956.

Stuart Bailey, "Anything for Money," *Conflict,* ABC, 1957.

Stuart Bailey, "Execution Night," *Conflict,* ABC, 1957.

Kerrigan the Great, "The Wizard," *Sugarfoot* (also known as *Tenderfoot*), 1958.

Stu Bailey, "Malihini Holiday," *Hawaiian Eye,* 1959.

Stu Bailey, "Three Tickets to Lani," *Hawaiian Eye,* 1959.

John Conrad, "The Trial of Reno McKee," *The Alaskans,* 1960.

Stu Bailey, "Wed Three Wives," *Hawaiian Eye,* 1960.

Edwin Booth, "The Prince of Darkness," *Bronco,* 1961.

What about Linda? (also known as *March of Dimes, What about Linda*), 1961.

Stu Bailey, "Blackmail in Satin," *Hawaiian Eye,* 1962.

Here's Hollywood, 1962.

John Ferris, "The Sojourner," *Bob Hope Presents the Chrysler Theatre* (also known as *The Chrysler Theatre* and *Universal Star Time*), 1964.

Charles Durwood, "Super–Star," *The Reporter,* 1964.

Stranger, "See the Monkey Dance," *The Alfred Hitchcock Hour,* CBS, 1964.

Jeff McKeever, "The Diehard" (also known as "The Last Order"), *Rawhide,* 1965.

Contestant, "Angie Dickinson vs. Efrem Zimbalist Jr.," *Password* (also known as *Password All–Stars*), 1965.

"The Day God Died," *Insight,* syndicated, 1970.

Charles de Foucauld, "The Hermit," *Insight,* syndicated, 1970.

The Tonight Show Starring Johnny Carson, 1972.

"When You See Arcturus," *Insight,* syndicated, 1974.

God, "Checkmate," *Insight,* syndicated, 1979.

"A Family of Winners," *Insight,* syndicated, 1979.

"The Hit Man," *Insight,* syndicated, 1979.

Mr. Baldwin, "The Butler's Affair/Roarke's Sacrifice," *Fantasy Island,* ABC, 1983.

Daniel Chalmers, "Sting of Steele," *Remington Steele,* 1983.

Daniel Chalmers, "Blue Blooded Steele," *Remington Steele,* 1984.

"Polly's Poker Palace/Shop Ahoy/Double Date/The Hong Kong Affair/Two Tails of a City: Parts 1 & 2," *The Love Boat,* ABC, 1984.

"Murder in the Museum," *Partners in Crime* (also known as *50/50*), 1984.

E. G. Dawson, "Writer's Block," *Cover Up,* 1984.

Emmett Pernell, "The Georgia Street Motors," *Hardcastle and McCormick,* 1984.

Alexander Heath, "Flesh and Blood," *Hotel,* 1984.

Judge Alex Hale, "Mister Wonderful," *Finder of Lost Loves,* 1985.

Daniel Chalmers, "Steele Searching: Part 2," *Remington Steele,* 1985.

Daniel Chalmers, "Steeled with a Kiss: Parts 1 & 2," *Remington Steele,* 1987.

General Havermeyer, "The Last Flight of the Dixie Damsel," *Murder, She Wrote,* CBS, 1988.

Clarence Hyland, "Murder He Wrote," *Hunter,* 1988.

Richard Thompson Grant, "Hannigan's Wake," *Murder, She Wrote,* CBS, 1990.

Robert Robinson, "Operation Mona," *Who's the Boss?,* 1990.

Adam Quatrain, "Sugar & Spice, Malice & Vice," *Murder, She Wrote,* CBS, 1992.

Sam Gallagher, "Who Killed the Legal Eagle?" *Burke's Law,* CBS, 1994.

Theodore Timmons, "Material Fran," *The Nanny,* CBS, 1994.

Voice of Mace Malone, "Revelations," *Gargoyles* (animated), syndicated, 1994.

Vicki!, 1994.

Hal Klosterman and Lester Blodgett, "Forget Selma," *Picket Fences,* CBS, 1995.

Walter Mansfield, "Flowers of Evil," *One West Waikiki,* 1995.

Voice of King Arthur, "Biker Knights of the Round Table: Parts 1 & 2," *Biker Mice from Mars* (animated), 1995.

Voice of Justin Hammer, "The Beast Within," *Iron Man* (animated; also known as *The Marvel Action Hour: Iron Man*), 1995.

Voices of Justin Hammer and Firebrand, "The Armor Wars: Parts 1 & 2," *Iron Man* (animated; also known as *The Marvel Action Hour: Iron Man*), 1995.

Voice of Dr. Denton P. Hookerman, "Zap Attack," *Mighty Ducks* (animated; also known as *Disney's "Mighty Ducks"* and *Mighty Ducks: The Animated Series*), 1996.

Wayland Scott, "Miracles," *The Visitor,* Fox, 1997.

William Edgars, "Conflicts of Interest," *Babylon 5* (also known as *B5*), TNT, 1997.

William Edgars, "Moments of Transition," *Babylon 5* (also known as *B5*), TNT, 1997.

William Edgars, "The Face of the Enemy," *Babylon 5* (also known as *B5*), TNT, 1997.

William Edgars, "The Exercise of Vital Powers," *Babylon 5* (also known as *B5*), TNT, 1997.

Voice of Alfred Pennyworth, "World's Finest: Parts 1–3," *Superman* (animated; also known as *Superman: The Animated Series*), 1997.

Voice of Alfred Pennyworth, "Demon Reborn," *Superman* (animated; also known as *Superman: The Animated Series*), 1999.

Voice of Alfred Pennyworth, "Hard as Nails," *Static Shock* (animated), The WB, 2003.

Voice of Alfred Pennyworth, "Hereafter: Part 1," *Justice League* (animated; also known as *JL* and *Justice League Unlimited*), Cartoon Network, 2003.

Voice of Alfred Pennyworth, "Starcrossed: Parts 2 & 3," *Justice League* (animated; also known as *JL* and *Justice League Unlimited*), Cartoon Network, 2004.

"The 50's," *TV Land Moguls,* TV Land, 2004.

Guest panelist, *The Celebrity Game;* also appeared in episodes of *Goodyear Playhouse,* NBC; *Philco Television Playhouse,* NBC; and *Praise the Lord.*

Film Appearances:

Tony Monetti, *House of Strangers,* Twentieth Century–Fox, 1950.

Colonel Jim Herlihy, *Bombers B–52* (also known as *No Sleep Till Dawn*), Warner Bros., 1957.

Lieutenant Ethan Sears, *Band of Angels,* Warner Bros., 1957.

Lieutenant Blanchard, *The Deep Six,* Warner Bros., 1958.

George Lawrence, *Violent Road* (also known as *Hell's Highway*), Warner Bros., 1958.

Vincent Bryant, *Too Much, Too Soon* (also known as *Too Much, Too Soon: The Daring Story of Diana Barrymore*), Warner Bros., 1958.

Jacob "Jake" Diamond, *Home before Dark,* Warner Bros., 1958.

Stuart Bailey, *Girl on the Run* (also known as *77 Sunset Strip*), Astor, 1958.

Dale Heath, *The Crowded Sky,* Warner Bros., 1960.

Judge Leland Hoffman, *A Fever in the Blood,* Warner Bros., 1961.

Arthur Winner, *By Love Possessed,* United Artists, 1961.

Paul Radford, *The Chapman Report,* Warner Bros., 1962.

Frank Bryant, *The Reward,* Twentieth Century–Fox, 1965.

William Mansfield, *Harlow,* Electronovision, 1965.

Sam Hendrix, *Wait until Dark,* Warner Bros., 1967.

Captain Stacy, *Airport 1975* (also known as *Airport '75*), Universal, 1974.

Wilson, *Hot Shots!,* Twentieth Century–Fox, 1991.

Jacob Anderson, *The Avenging* (also known as *Two Against the Wind*), Imperial Entertainment Corp., 1992.

Voice of Alfred Pennyworth, *Batman: Mask of the Phantasm* (animated; also known as *Batman: Mask of the Phantasm; The Animated Movie* and *Batman:*

The Animated Movie, Batman: The Animated Movie—Mask of the Phantasm, and *Mask of the Phantasm: Batman the Animated Movie),* Warner Bros., 1993.

Narrator, *Jack L. Warren: The Last Mogul* (documentary), 1993.

Marty, *The Street Corner Kids,* 1994.

Marty, *The Street Corner Kids: The Sequel,* 1995.

Voice of Dr. Octopus, *The Amazing Adventures of Spider–Man* (animated short film), Universal, 1999.

Voice of Alfred Pennyworth, *Batman: Mystery of the Batwoman* (animated), Warner Bros., 2003.

Himself, *The Brothers Warner,* Promise Documentary/Warner Sisters Productions, 2008.

Stage Appearances:

(Stage debut) Gil Hartnick, *The Rugged Path,* Playwrights' Company, Plymouth Theatre, New York City, 1945–46.

Duke of Suffolk, *Henry VIII,* American Repertory Theatre Company, International Theatre, New York City, 1946–47.

Secutor, *Androcles and the Lion* (double–bill with *A Pound on Demand),* American Repertory Theatre Company, International Theatre, 1946–47.

Butler and member of ensemble, *What Every Woman Knows,* American Repertory Theatre Company, International Theatre, 1946–47.

Aristides Agramonte, *Yellow Jack,* American Repertory Theatre Company, International Theatre, 1946–47.

Eilert Lovborg, *Hedda Gabler,* American Repertory Theatre Company, Cort Theatre, New York City, 1948.

Maurice Duclos, *Fallen Angels,* Pocono Playhouse (now Bucks County Playhouse), New Hope, PA, 1955–56, then Playhouse Theatre, New York City, 1956.

Narrator, *A Lincoln Portrait,* Academy of Music, Philadelphia, PA, 1961.

Night of the Iguana, Ventura, CA, and Manitoba Theatre Center, Winnipeg, Manitoba, Canada, 2004.

Appeared in summer stock productions at Pocono Playhouse, 1955.

Stage Producer:

The Medium (musical), Ballet Society, Ethel Barrymore Theatre, New York City, 1947–48.

The Telephone (musical), Balley Society, Ethel Barrymore Theatre, 1948–49.

The Consul (opera), Ethel Barrymore Theatre, 1950.

RECORDINGS

Videos:

Prospero, *The Tempest,* Bard Productions, 1983.

Hot Shots: The Making of an Important Movie, 1991.

Stacy (in archive footage), *The Making of "Midway,"* 2001.

Video Games:

Voice of Uncle Wolfgang, *Gabriel Knight: Sins of the Fathers,* Sierra, 1994.

Voice of Dr. Octopus/Dr. Otto Octavius, *Spider–Man,* Activision, 2000.

Voice of Alfred Pennyworth, *Batman: Vengeance,* 2001.

Albums:

Contributor, *We Wish You a Merry Christmas,* Warner Bros., 1959.

WRITINGS

Books:

My Dinner of Herbs (memoir), Limelight Editions, 2003.

OTHER SOURCES

Books:

Zimbalist, Efrem, Jr., *My Dinner of Herbs,* Limelight Editions, 2003.

ZUCKER, Jeff 1965–

PERSONAL

Born April 9, 1965, in Miami, FL; son of Matthew (a cardiologist) and Arline (an English teacher) Zucker; married Caryn; children: Andrew, Elizabeth, two additional. *Education:* Harvard University, B.A., American history, 1986.

Addresses: *Office*—General Electric Company, 1251 Avenue of the Americas, New York, NY 10020; NBC Universal, 30 Rockefeller Plaza, New York, NY 10112.

Career: Producer and television executive. NBC, researcher for 1988 Summer Olympic Games, 1986–88; NBC Entertainment, president, 2000–05; NBC Entertainment, News and Cable Group, 2003–04; NBC Universal Television Group, president, 2004–05; NBC Universal, New York City, chief executive officer, 2005–07, then chairman and chief executive officer, 2007—; General Electric Company, New York City, vice chairman. Began career as a stringer for *Miami Herald.* Member of the board of the Memorial Sloan Kettering Cancer Center, Temple Emanu–El, the Robin Hood Foundation, the American Film Institute, the Paley Center for Media, and the Museum of the Moving Image.

Awards, Honors: Five news Emmy Awards.

CREDITS

Television Work; Series:
Field producer, *Today* (also known as *NBC News Today* and *The Today Show*), NBC, 1989–90.
Supervising producer, *Today* (also known as *NBC News Today* and *The Today Show*), 1990–92.
Executive producer, *Today* (also known as *NBC News Today* and *The Today Show*), 1992–2000.
Executive producer, *NBC Nightly News,* NBC, 1993.
Executive producer, *Now with Tom Brokow and Katie Couric,* NBC, 1993.
Executive in charge of production, *Later Today,* NBC, 1999.
(Uncredited) Network executive, *The Apprentice,* NBC, 2003–2004.
Network executive, *Joey,* NBC, 2004–2005.
Network executive, *Father of the Pride* (animated), NBC, 2004–2005.
Producer, *Today* (also known as *NBC News Today* and *The Today Show*), NBC, 2006.

Television Work; Specials:
Olympic research, *1988 Summer Olympic Games,* NBC, 1988.
Senior producer, *The Lost Youth of Hollywood,* NBC, 1991.
Executive producer, *Brokaw Reports: 58 Days* (also known as *58 Days*), NBC, 1992.
Executive producer, *Inaugural '93,* NBC, 1993.
Executive producer, *Hillary: America's First Lady,* NBC, 1993.
Producer, *The People vs. O. J. Simpson,* NBC, 1994.
Executive producer, *Decision '96: The Republican National Convention,* NBC and PBS, 1996.
Executive producer, *Decision '96: The Democratic National Convention,* NBC and PBS, 1996.

Television Appearances; Specials:
Katie Couric: The E! True Hollywood Story, E! Entertainment Television, 2004.
Kathy Griffin: The E! True Hollywood Story, E! Entertainment Television, 2007.
Remembering Tim Russert, NBC, 2008.

Television Appearances; Episodic:
Audience member, *Inside the Actors Studio* (also known as *Inside the Actors Studio: The Craft of Theatre and Film*), Bravo, 2003.
Tavis Smiley, PBS, 2004.
Himself, "Big Butts," *Fat Actress,* Showtime, 2005.
Himself, "Hold This," *Fat Actress,* Showtime, 2005.
Himself, "I Won't Die with a Little Help from My Friends: Part 1," *My Name Is Earl,* NBC, 2008.

OTHER SOURCES

Books:
Newsmakers 1993, Issue 4, Gale Research, 1993.

Periodicals:
Broadcasting & Cable, January 22, 2001, p. 22; September 8, 2003, p. 45; December 18, 2006, p. 4; February 12, 2007, pp. 5, 12.
Crain's New York Business, August 1, 2005, p. 2.
Esquire, October, 2002, p. 134.
Fortune, May 12, 2003, p. 94.
New York Times, December 3, 1991; January 14, 1993; March 16, 1993; December 16, 2005, p. C4; February 7, 2007, p. C3.
USA Today, February 7, 2007, p. 4B.
Variety, March 12, 2001, p. 1; December 22, 2003, p. 26; January 16, 2006, p. 1; February 12, 2007, p. 22.

Cumulative Index

To provide continuity with *Who's Who in the Theatre*, this index interfiles references to *Who's Who in the Theatre*, 1st–17th Editions, and *Who Was Who in the Theatre* (Gale, 1978) with references to *Contemporary Theatre, Film and Television*, Volumes 1–92.

References in the index are identified as follows:

CTFT and volume number—*Contemporary Theatre, Film and Television*, Volumes 1–92
WWT and edition number—*Who's Who in the Theatre*, 1st–17th Editions
WWasWT—*Who Was Who in the Theatre*

Cumulative Index

Cumulative Index

E

Cumulative Index

Cumulative Index

G

GILLOTT

Cumulative Index

Cumulative Index

Cumulative Index

Cumulative Index

Padhora, Roman
    See .... Podhora, Roman
Pagano, Giulia 1949– CTFT–1
Pagan, Michael J. CTFT–74
Page, Anthony 1935– CTFT–23
    Earlier sketches in CTFT–2, 12; WWT–17
Page, Ashley 1956– CTFT–12
Page, Austin.. WWasWT
Page, Dallas 1956– CTFT–65
Page, Ellen 1987– CTFT–86
Page, Evelyn CTFT–32
Page, Geraldine 1924–1987 .... CTFT–4
    Obituary in CTFT–5
    Earlier sketches in CTFT–1; WWT–17
Page, Harrison... CTFT–46
    Earlier sketch in CTFT–7
Page, Ken 1954– CTFT–83
    Earlier sketch in CTFT–38
Page, Louise 1955– CTFT–37
    Earlier sketch in CTFT–12
Page, Norman ?–1935 .... WWasWT
Page, Philip P. 1889– .... WWasWT
Page, Rita 1906–1954 .... WWasWT
Page, Samuel 1976– CTFT–76
Page, Tilsa 1926– .... WWasWT
Paget, Cecil ?–1955 .... WWasWT
Paget–Bowman, Cicely 1910– WWT–17
Pagett, Nicola 1945– CTFT–5
    Earlier sketch in WWT–17
Paggi, Nicole 1977– CTFT–89
Pagnol, Marcel 1895–1974 .... WWasWT
Paige, Elaine 1952– CTFT–33
    Earlier sketch in CTFT–6
Paige, Janis 1924– CTFT–19
    Earlier sketches in CTFT–2; WWT–17
Paige, Richard
    See .... Koontz, Dean R.
Paige, Tarah 1982– CTFT–88
Painter, Eleanor 1890–1947 .... WWasWT
Pais, Josh 1964(?)– CTFT–75
    Earlier sketch in CTFT–34
Paisley Park
    See .... Prince
Paisner, Dina CTFT–2
Pakledinaz, Martin CTFT–87
    Earlier sketch in CTFT–39
Pakula, Alan 1928– CTFT–13
    Earlier sketches in CTFT–1, 6
Pal, George 1908–1980............................ CTFT–19
Paladini, Ettore 1849–? .... WWasWT
Paladini–Ando, Celestina .... WWasWT
Palance, Jack 1920(?)– CTFT–47
    Earlier sketches in CTFT–5, 12, 23
Palcy, Euzhan 1958– CTFT–39
    Earlier sketch in CTFT–16
Pale, Paul
    See .... Pape, Paul
Palerme, Gina .... WWasWT
Palermo, Brian CTFT–86
Paley, William S. 1901–1990 .... CTFT–5
Palffy, David 1969– CTFT–79
Palfrey, May Lever 1867–1929 .... WWasWT
Palicki, Adrianne 1983– CTFT–83
Palillo, Ron 1949(?)– CTFT–79
Palin, Michael 1943– CTFT–56
    Earlier sketches in CTFT–5, 16, 26
Palladino, Aleksa 1982(?)– CTFT–80
Palladino, Erik 1968– CTFT–68
    Earlier sketch in CTFT–30
Pallana, Kumar 1919– CTFT–80
Pallavera, Franco
    See .... Soldati, Mario

Pallfy, David
    See .... Palffy, David
Palma, Loretta 1946– CTFT–2
Palmer, Barbara 1911– .... WWasWT
Palmer, Betsy 1926– CTFT–89
    Earlier sketches in CTFT–2, 19, 41; WWT–17
Palmer, Charles 1869–1920 .... WWasWT
Palmer, Geoffrey 1927– CTFT–69
    Earlier sketches in CTFT–2, 8, 20, 31
Palmer, Gregg 1927– CTFT–7
Palmer, Gretchen 1961– CTFT–59
Palmer, Joel 1986– CTFT–70
Palmer, John 1885–1944 .... WWasWT
Palmer, Keke 1993– CTFT–88
Palmer, Lilli 1914–1986 .... CTFT–3
    Earlier sketch in WWT–17
Palmer, Minnie 1857–1936 .... WWasWT
Palmer, Patrick J. 1935– CTFT–56
    Earlier sketch in CTFT–26
Palmer, Vera Jane
    See .... Mansfield, Jayne
Palmieri, Joe 1939– CTFT–1
Palminteri, Chazz 1952(?)– CTFT–56
    Earlier sketches in CTFT–16, 26
Palmisano, Conrad E. 1948– CTFT–53
Paltrow, Bruce 1943–2002 .... CTFT–9
    Obituary in CTFT–48
Paltrow, Gwyneth 1972– CTFT–56
    Earlier sketches in CTFT–16, 26
Palzis, Kelly
    See .... Preston, Kelly
Pammy
    See .... Anderson, Pamela
Pan, Hermes 1910(?)–1990 .... CTFT–9
Panabaker, Danielle 1987– CTFT–71
Panabaker, Kay 1990– CTFT–70
Panahi, Jafar 1960– CTFT–35
Panama, Norman 1920(?)– CTFT–22
Panettiere, Hayden 1989– CTFT–48
    Earlier sketch in CTFT–23
Pankin, Stuart 1946– CTFT–53
    Earlier sketches in CTFT–7, 14, 25
Pankow, Joanne CTFT–54
Pankow, John 1957(?)– CTFT–53
    Earlier sketches in CTFT–8, 15, 25
Panou CTFT–62
Panter, Joan 1909– .... WWasWT
Pantoliano, Joe 1951(?)– CTFT–50
    Earlier sketches in CTFT–5, 24
Panzer, William N. CTFT–56
Paolantonio, Bill CTFT–48
Paolillo, Ronald G.
    See .... Palillo, Ron
Paolo, Connor 1990– CTFT–83
Paolone, Catherine CTFT–74
Paonessa, Nick CTFT–80
Papa, Sharon CTFT–48
Papa, Tom CTFT–86
Papaelias, Lucas CTFT–80
Papajohn, Michael 1964– CTFT–86
Papamichael, Phedon 1962– CTFT–59
Papamichael, Phedon, Sr.
    See .... Papmichael, Phedon
Papamichael, Thedon
    See .... Papmichael, Phedon
Papas, Irene 1929(?)– CTFT–40
    Earlier sketches in CTFT–2, 8, 16
Papathanassiou, Vangelis
    See .... Vangelis
Pape, Joan CTFT–1
Pape, Paul 1952– CTFT–69
Papineau, Dany 1974– CTFT–91
Papmichael, Phedon CTFT–27

Papp, Joseph 1921–1991 .... CTFT–12
    Earlier sketches in CTFT–1; WWT–17
Pappas, Irini
    See .... Papas, Irene
Pappenbrook, Bob CTFT–48
Paquin, Anna 1982– CTFT–58
    Earlier sketch in CTFT–27
Paradis, Vanessa 1972– CTFT–77
Paragon, John CTFT–8
Parcaro, Steve
    See .... Porcaro, Steve
Pardo, Don 1918– CTFT–79
Pardo, J. D. 1980– CTFT–89
Parducci, Paul CTFT–79
Pardue, Kip 1976– CTFT–65
Pare, Jessica 1982– CTFT–67
Pare, Michael 1959– CTFT–52
    Earlier sketches in CTFT–5, 25
Parent, Gail 1940– CTFT–62
    Earlier sketch in CTFT–8
Parenteau, John K. F. CTFT–80
Parfitt, Judy 1935– CTFT–85
    Earlier sketches in CTFT–2, 13, 37; WWT–17
Parichy, Dennis CTFT–8
Parikh, Devika CTFT–79
    Earlier sketch in CTFT–45
Parilla, Lana 1977– CTFT–72
Parillaud, Anne 1960– CTFT–69
    Earlier sketch in CTFT–30
Paris, Jerry 1925–1986 .... CTFT–3
Parise, Jeff CTFT–84
Parish, James .... WWasWT
Parisot, Dean CTFT–53
    Earlier sketch in CTFT–25
Parisys, Marcelle....................................... WWasWT
Park, Chul–Soo 1947(?)– CTFT–35
Park, Grace 1980– CTFT–65
Park, Linda 1978– CTFT–79
Park, Nick 1958– CTFT–75
    Earlier sketch in CTFT–33
Park, Nira CTFT–86
Park, Randall CTFT–89
Park, Ray 1974– CTFT–72
Park, Sung Hee
    See .... Whang, Suzanne
Parke, Evan 1968– CTFT–83
Parker, Alan 1944– CTFT–53
    Earlier sketches in CTFT–5, 25
Parker, Andrea 1969– CTFT–56
    Earlier sketch in CTFT–26
Parker, Anthony 1912– .... WWasWT
Parker, Anthony Ray CTFT–79
Parker, Bert
    See .... Ellsion, Harlan
Parker, Cecil 1897–1971 .... WWasWT
Parker, Corey 1965– CTFT–56
    Earlier sketches in CTFT–8, 16, 26
Parker, David... CTFT–81
Parker, Doug.. CTFT–48
Parker, Eleanor 1922– CTFT–5
Parker, Ellen 1949– CTFT–6
Parker, Erica
    See .... Durance, Erica
Parker, F. William CTFT–77
    Earlier sketch in CTFT–35
Parker, Frank 1864–1926......................... WWasWT
Parker, Jameson 1947– CTFT–56
    Earlier sketch in CTFT–6
Parker, John 1875–1952 .... WWasWT
Parker, Joy 1924– .... WWasWT
Parker, Leni CTFT–75
    Earlier sketch in CTFT–34
Parker, Lew 1906–1972 .... WWasWT

0

Cumulative Index

S

Cumulative Index

X